Network Administrators Survival Guide

Anand Deveriya, CCIE No. 10401

Cisco Press
800 East 96th Street
Indianapolis, IN 46240 USA

Network Administrators Survival Guide

Anand Deveriya

Published by:
Cisco Press
800 East 96th Street
Indianapolis, IN 46240 USA

Printed in the United States of America 1 2 3 4 5 6 7 8 9 0

First Printing September 2006

Library of Congress Cataloging-in-Publication Number: 2004111841

ISBN: 1-58705-211-3

Warning and Disclaimer

This book is designed to provide information about Cisco network administration using open source and freeware tools. Every effort has been made to make this book as complete and as accurate as possible, but no warranty or fitness is implied.

The information is provided on an "as is" basis. The authors, Cisco Press, and Cisco Systems, Inc. shall have neither liability nor responsibility to any person or entity with respect to any loss or damages arising from the information contained in this book or from the use of the discs or programs that may accompany it.

The opinions expressed in this book belong to the author and are not necessarily those of Cisco Systems, Inc.

Trademark Acknowledgments

All terms mentioned in this book that are known to be trademarks or service marks have been appropriately capitalized. Cisco Press or Cisco Systems, Inc. cannot attest to the accuracy of this information. Use of a term in this book should not be regarded as affecting the validity of any trademark or service mark.

Corporate and Government Sales

Cisco Press offers excellent discounts on this book when ordered in quantity for bulk purchases or special sales.

For more information please contact: U.S. Corporate and Government Sales 1-800-382-3419 corpsales@pearsontechgroup.com

For sales outside the U.S. please contact: International Sales international@pearsoned.com

Feedback Information

At Cisco Press, our goal is to create in-depth technical books of the highest quality and value. Each book is crafted with care and precision, undergoing rigorous development that involves the unique expertise of members from the professional technical community.

Readers' feedback is a natural continuation of this process. If you have any comments regarding how we could improve the quality of this book, or otherwise alter it to better suit your needs, you can contact us through e-mail at feedback@ciscopress.com. Please make sure to include the book title and ISBN in your message.

We greatly appreciate your assistance.

Publisher	John Wait
Editor-in-Chief	John Kane
Cisco Representative	Anthony Wolfenden
Cisco Press Program Manager	Jeff Brady
Production Manager	Patrick Kanouse
Development Editor	Grant Munroe
Senior Project Editor	San Dee Phillips
Copy Editor	John Edwards
Technical Editors	Mark Gallo William Parkhurst Peter Welcher
Editorial Assistant	Tammi Barnett
Book and Cover Designer	Louisa Adair
Composition	Mark Shirar
Indexer	Tim Wright

Printed in the USA

About the Author

Anand Deveriya, CCIE No. 10401, graduated from the University of Bombay, where he earned his bachelor's degree in electronics engineering. During the dot-com boom, he worked in the heart of Silicon Valley, where he deployed secure, scalable, and redundant networks using Cisco technology and products. Highlights of his accomplishments include the design and deployment of BGP-based redundant network backbones for networks spanning multiple collocation data centers design and configuration of network backbones for e-commerce setup using firewalls and load balancers. Later, he worked as a network communications manager, solving network administration issues at various levels. In his role as a network communications manager, he designed and deployed IPsec-based VPN solutions to replace the existing frame relay based WAN. Currently, he works for NEC Unified Solutions as a senior network engineer with a focus on network security. He has also served as technical editor for the Cisco Press book *CCIE Security Exam Certification Guide*. Anand lives with his wife and children in San Ramon, California.

About the Technical Reviewers

Mark Gallo is a technical manager with America Online, where he leads a group of engineers who are responsible for the design and deployment of the domestic corporate intranet. His network certifications include Cisco CCNP and Cisco CCDP. He has led several engineering groups responsible for designing and implementing enterprise LANs and international IP networks. He has a bachelor of science degree in electrical engineering from the University of Pittsburgh. Mark resides in northern Virginia with his wife, Betsy, and son, Paul.

William R. Parkhurst, Ph.D., CCIE No. 2969, is a design consultant with Cisco Systems, specializing in IP core and mobile wireless networks. Prior to his current position, Bill was on the CCIE team and managed the development of the CCIE Service Provider and Voice tracks. Bill holds a Ph.D. in electrical and computer engineering from Wichita State University and a bachelor's degree in political science from the University of Maryland.

Peter J. Welcher, Ph.D., CCIE No. 1773, CCIP, CCSI No. 94014, earned his doctorate in mathematics from the Massachusetts Institute of Technology (MIT). He started out teaching math at the U.S. Naval Academy. While there, he also bought and maintained UNIX systems, wrote a book on the PERL programming language, and wrote a major computer program in C. This explains his occasional brief lapses into PERL programming. He changed careers in 1993 to teach a wide variety of Cisco courses for Mentor Technologies, formerly Chesapeake Computer Consultants, while also doing network consulting whenever possible. Pete is now doing high-level network consulting with Chesapeake Netcraftsmen, with tasks including network design, security, quality of service (QoS), wireless, and IP telephony, for customers that include several large corporations and government agencies. He has reviewed a number of books for Cisco Press and other publishers, and has authored or managed development of several courses for Cisco and other companies. Pete writes articles for *Enterprise Networking* magazine. He can also sometimes be found presenting his own seminars at East Coast Cisco offices, on topics ranging from campus network design to WLAN security. The articles and seminars can be found at http://www.netcraftsmen.net/welcher.

Dedications

This book is dedicated to Dr. Kailash Sharma, our angel to whom I, my wife, and my son owe everything. I also take this opportunity to pay tribute to my late uncle, Mr. Bankatlal Deveriya, whose selfless attitude and dedication enabled my parents to become self-reliant.

Thanks to my wife, Shweta, without whom I am nothing. Thanks to my son, Ayush, and daughter, Avanti, for providing me with the greatest joy on earth—parenthood. Thanks to my sister, Meera, for her unconditional support throughout all the ups and downs. Thanks to my aunt, Mrs. Kamala Deveriya, for her love and affection.

Thanks to my parents, for overcoming all the hardships in bringing up the family and providing us with a good education.

Special thanks to Snigdha Sharma for all the help when I needed it the most.

Acknowledgments

Without the trust and belief shown by John Kane, this book would have never seen the light of day. His positive attitude and support have helped me to become a better person.

I am grateful to the entire Cisco Press team for their professionalism. Thanks to Christopher "Screenshot" Cleveland, or Chris as we call him, for his guidance and extreme patience while dealing with my mistakes. It is an honor to work with Peter Welcher, William Parkhurst, and Mark Gallo. Their contributions as technical editors have added tremendous value to the book. Special thanks to Grant Munroe, the development editor, who helped and supported me throughout the technical editing process. Last but not least, San Dee Phillips picked up all the loose ends to ensure that the book reached the press well in time.

This Book Is Safari Enabled

Safari BOOKS ONLINE ENABLED

The Safari® Enabled icon on the cover of your favorite technology book means the book is available through Safari Bookshelf. When you buy this book, you get free access to the online edition for 45 days.

Safari Bookshelf is an electronic reference library that lets you easily search thousands of technical books, find code samples, download chapters, and access technical information whenever and wherever you need it.

To gain 45-day Safari Enabled access to this book:

- Go to http://www.ciscopress.com/safarienabled
- Complete the brief registration form
- Enter the coupon code K8GM-NMGH-KZJB-D9IS-AS4I

If you have difficulty registering on Safari Bookshelf or accessing the online edition, please e-mail customer-service@safaribooksonline.com.

Contents at a Glance

Contents

Icons Used in This Book

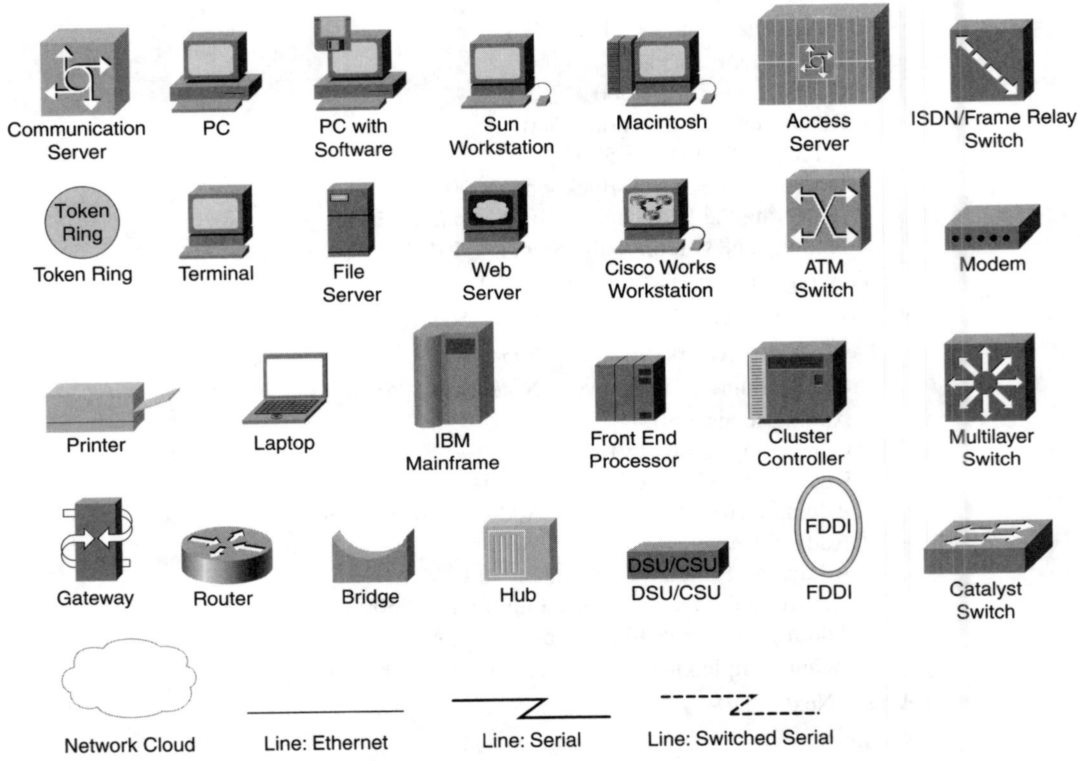

Command Syntax Conventions

The conventions used to present command syntax in this book are the same conventions used in the IOS Command Reference. The Command Reference describes these conventions as follows:

- **Boldface** indicates commands and keywords that are entered literally as shown. In actual configuration examples and output (not general command syntax), boldface indicates commands that are manually input by the user (such as a **show** command).
- *Italics* indicate arguments for which you supply actual values.
- Vertical bars (|) separate alternative, mutually exclusive elements.
- Square brackets [ ] indicate optional elements.
- Braces { } indicate a required choice.
- Braces within brackets [{ }] indicate a required choice within an optional element.

Introduction

Due to the high cost of commercial tools and the crippling post-dot-com economy, I was forced to look for freeware tools to help me administer my network. I spent a lot of time on the Internet searching for the right tool and then even more time trying to configure it to suit my needs. Some tools offer too much information, while others provide too little. Realizing my plight, and that of my fellow Netadmins, I decided to document my experience—and this book was born.

Objectives

The goal of this book is to empower Netadmins to quickly understand and deploy the freeware tools necessary for maintaining a Cisco network. Freeware tools, available from the Internet, spare the Netadmin from the hassles of budgeting, purchasing, and shipping.

I have made every attempt to include both Linux- and MS-Windows–based tools and applications. However, you also find references to some built-in features of MS-Windows. While MS-Windows is not free software, it is prevalent in most networks. The idea is to let Netadmins leverage the existing resource without buying new software.

This book can help you to understand the following:

- Why a tool or technology is relevant to the role of the network administrator
- What are the available tools
- How you can deploy the tools
- How you can configure Cisco devices for the particular tools

Who Should Read This Book

This book is intended to help individuals support a Cisco network, not achieve Cisco certification. The following professionals will find the book useful:

- Network administrators
- Network engineers
- Network consultants
- Network managers
- NOC engineers
- Cisco Network Academy students who want to learn real-world issues and not just attain certification

Networking professionals invest time and money to support their network. This book saves you money by focusing on freeware tools. So why should you administer a network using freeware? Because like every other department, IT departments have an allocated budget, and you want to efficiently use your funds for other important things, such as training, certifications, and new hardware. Additionally, you do not need budgeting approval from the Purchasing or Accounting department or your supervisor.

This book saves you time by choosing the most suitable tools—for each function and for you. Furthermore, the discussion includes configuration and troubleshooting steps for each tool. The book also includes relevant sample configurations for each tool.

How This Book Is Organized

Based on the various functions, the books is divided into the following four parts:

- Basic network administration
- Network management systems
- Security
- Documentation tools

Each chapter focuses on a function and its related tools. Although the chapters follow a logical sequence, you can also read the chapters in any order.

Chapters 1 through 11 cover the following topics:

- **Chapter 1, "Cisco Device Installation"**—This chapter discusses the various methods of accessing and configuring devices, followed by methods for storing the configuration files. The discussion also provides some practical tips on simplifying the tasks of network administration.
- **Chapter 2 "Basic Network Connectivity"**—This chapter discusses the most common tools used to test and monitor network connectivity. The tools discussed are ping, traceroute, whois, nslookup, dig, netstat, and nbtstat.
- **Chapter 3, "Access Control"**—This chapter discusses the AAA technology framework for securing Cisco networks. Based on the protocols used by AAA, this chapter covers Linux- and MS-Windows–based tools for implementing TACACS+ and RADIUS Servers. The configuration of Cisco IOS devices, Catalyst switches, PIX Firewalls, and VPN 3000 concentrators for AAA is also covered.
- **Chapter 4, "Using Syslog"**—This chapter discusses the syslog protocol and its relevance in the Cisco networking world. In addition to Linux- and MS-Windows–based syslog servers, this chapter also covers configuring Cisco IOS devices, Catalyst switches, PIX Firewalls, and VPN 3000 concentrators for syslog.

- **Chapter 5, "Monitoring Network Availability"**—This chapter discusses the need, methods, and tools for network monitoring using Linux- and MS-Windows–based tools.
- **Chapter 6, "Network Performance Monitoring"**—This chapter discusses the tools for monitoring network performance parameters such as throughput, latency, CPU utilization, and memory utilization. Both Linux- and MS-Windows–based tools are covered.
- **Chapter 7, "Network Security Testing"**—This chapter introduces you to the tools and methodologies of network security testing using network scanners, vulnerability scanners, and sniffers.
- **Chapter 8, "Router and Switch Security"**—This chapter discusses tools for hardening Cisco routers and switches against security vulnerabilities and common attacks.
- **Chapter 9, "Intrusion Detection System (IDS)"**—This chapter covers the nuances of deploying intrusion detection systems (IDS) in a Cisco network. The chapter also discusses the use of IDS sensors that are built into Cisco IOS devices and PIX Firewalls.
- **Chapter 10, "Virtual Private Networks (VPN)"**—This chapter introduces the IPSec protocol and its role in providing VPN service. Furthermore, the chapter focuses on the interoperability of Cisco devices with IPSec using preshared keys.
- **Chapter 11, "Documentation Tools: Network Diagrams"**—This chapter covers one of the most fundamental aspects of the networking profession—the network diagram. The discussion covers the need for network diagrams and the tools used to fulfill that need.

PART I

Basic Network Administration

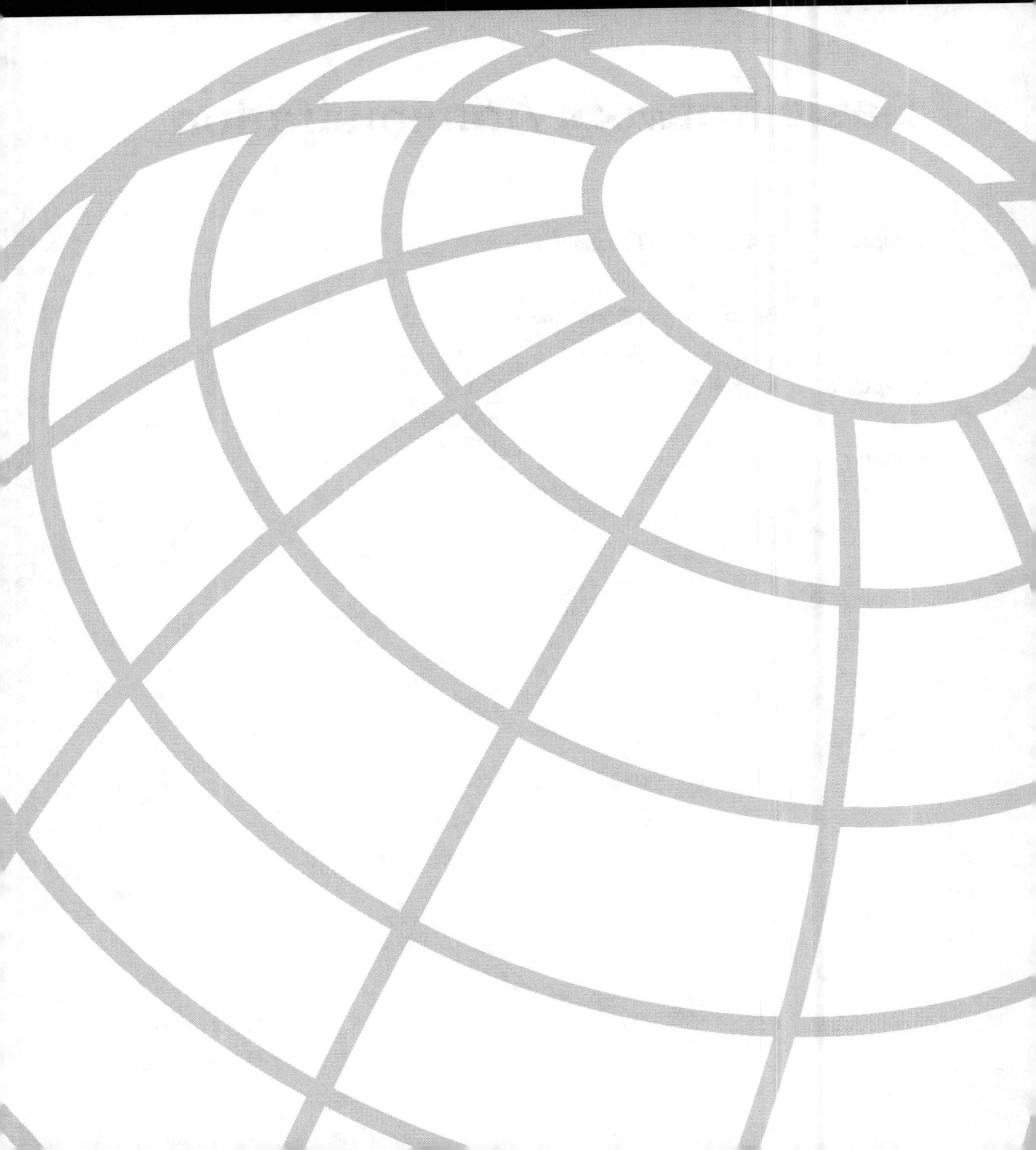

CHAPTER 1

Cisco Device Installation

Introduction

All Cisco networking devices are shipped with a factory default configuration. For the device to function according to your networking needs, this default configuration should be customized. The process of modifying the configuration can be achieved through various means. For administrative purposes, such as backup, security, and disaster recovery, these configurations are often saved in various formats and locations. Netadmins use various tools for accessing, configuring, and managing Cisco devices. This chapter discusses tools for the following items:

- Connecting to Cisco devices for configuration
  - Local connection using a console interface
  - Remote connection using Telnet
- Securing remote connections to Cisco devices using SSH
  - Cisco device configuration for SSH
  - SSH client installation
- Configuring Cisco devices using GUI tools
  - HTTP interface for IOS-based devices
  - PIX Device Manager
  - Security Device Manager
  - Other GUI tools for configuring Cisco devices
- Managing system files
  - File management using a TFTP server
  - Configuring Cisco devices to use TFTP
  - Using an FTP server for file management

Connecting to Cisco Devices for Configuration

The first step in configuring any Cisco device is to physically connect the device and the configuring computer. This connectivity can be accomplished through one of the following mechanisms:

- **Console or auxiliary**—Physical connectivity mechanisms, also classified as out-of-band management interfaces, consist of a console cable that connects the console port on the Cisco device to the COM port on the computer. The console connection method is typically used when the device is physically nearby.
- **Telnet, SSH, File Transfer Protocol (FTP), Trivial File Transfer Protocol (TFTP), or Hypertext Transfer Protocol (HTTP)**—IP-based remote connectivity mechanisms, also classified as in-band management methods, consist of connecting to the Cisco device, from a computer, through the network connection. However, the devices should be configured and connected to the network to allow the computer to communicate with the devices. For remote access to the device, a Telnet (or SSH) connection is typically used.

NOTE **In-band Versus Out-of-band:** Out-of-band signaling involves using control signals to access a path outside the one used by the data signal. For example, console ports use a separate cable from the Cisco device to the configuring computer's serial port. This port does not carry LAN/WAN traffic that flows through the router. In-band signaling uses the same path for data and control signals. For example, when a computer establishes a Telnet session with the router for configuration, the Telnet traffic is part of the LAN/WAN traffic that flows through the router.

Local Connection Using a Console Interface

The console connection consists of the following items:

- A computer terminal.
- A console cable that connects the serial port (also known as the COM port) of the terminal to the Cisco device. This cable is an 8-wire flat ribbon cable.
- A port on the Cisco device, called the *console port,* that the 8-wire console cable connects to. Generally, this port is an RJ-45 port.
- A software application on the computer to control the COM port.

Some older Cisco devices that have a non-RJ-45 port require the use of a connector (also called an adapter or converter). Likewise, newer laptops do not have COM ports. You should use a USB–to–serial port adapter to connect the laptop to the console cable.

At the terminal end, the console cable goes into the serial port adapter (DB9–to–RJ-45 adapter), which in turn connects to the serial port. Figure 1-1 depicts console cable details.

Figure 1-1 *Cisco Console Cable Connection*

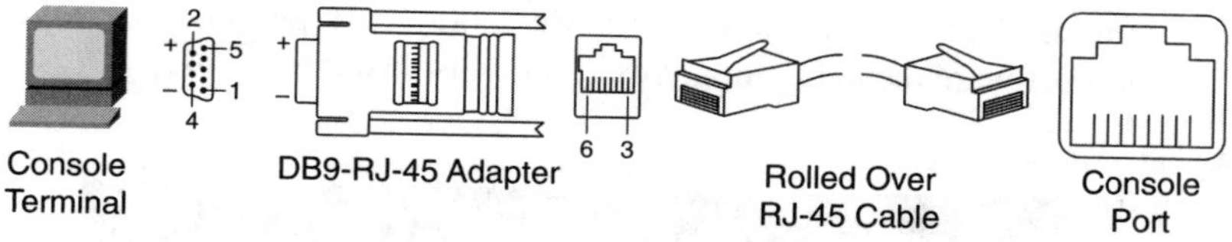

NOTE For more information on cabling for console ports, refer to the article "Cabling Guide for Console and AUX Ports," which you can find at the following URL:

http://www.cisco.com/en/US/products/hw/routers/ps332/products_tech_note09186a0080094ce6.shtml

The connection through the console port, Telnet, or SSH provides a text-based interface called the *command-line interface (CLI)* for configuring the device. This CLI can be used to view device statistics and parameters. To use a PC or laptop computer as a terminal, it should be loaded with terminal emulation software for serial communication. The configuration settings on the software should correspond to those on the Cisco device. Table 1-1 shows the default console settings for most Cisco devices.

Table 1-1 *Cisco Console Settings*

Speed	Parity	Data Bits	Stop Bits	Flow Control
9600	N	8	1	Hardware

To use the COM port on your computer, you need a software application. Such software application tools are also referred to as *terminal emulation software.* Although the choice of the terminal emulation software depends on the operating system and your preference, Table 1-2 lists the more popular terminal emulation software packages.

Table 1-2 *Terminal Emulation Software*

Program	OS	Interface
HyperTerminal	Windows	GUI
HyperTerminal Private Edition (HTPE)	Windows	GUI
TeraTerm	Windows	GUI
PuTTY	Windows	GUI
Minicom	Linux	CLI
Cu	Linux	CLI
GtkTerm	Linux	GUI

Using Windows-Based Console Tools

HyperTerminal, by Hilgraeve Inc.(http://www.hilgraeve.com), as shown in Figure 1-2, comes preinstalled with Windows 95/98/Me/2000/XP. HyperTerminal is the terminal emulation software most commonly used for console connections.

Figure 1-2 *HyperTerminal Software*

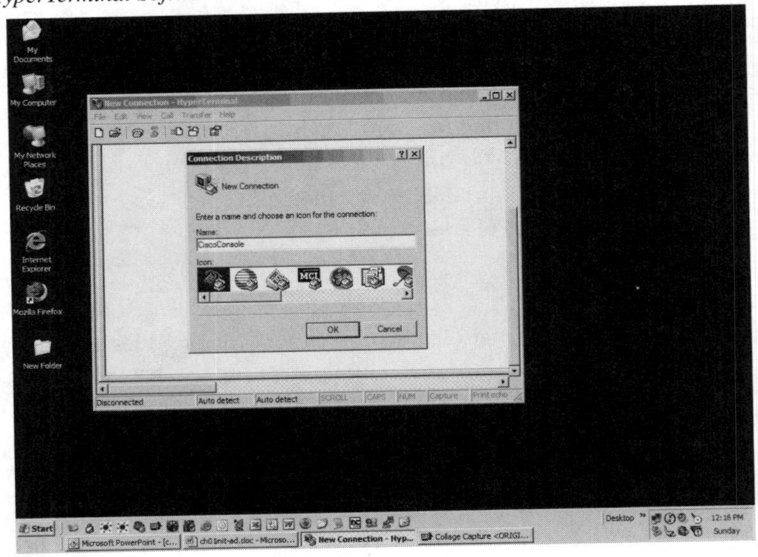

Assume that COM1 of the Windows-based PC is connected to the console port of the device. To configure the PC for a Cisco console connection, follow these steps:

Step 1 Start the HyperTerminal application in Windows.

Step 2 Choose **File > Properties > Configure** and enter the settings shown in Figure 1-3.

Figure 1-3 *HyperTerminal Configuration Settings*

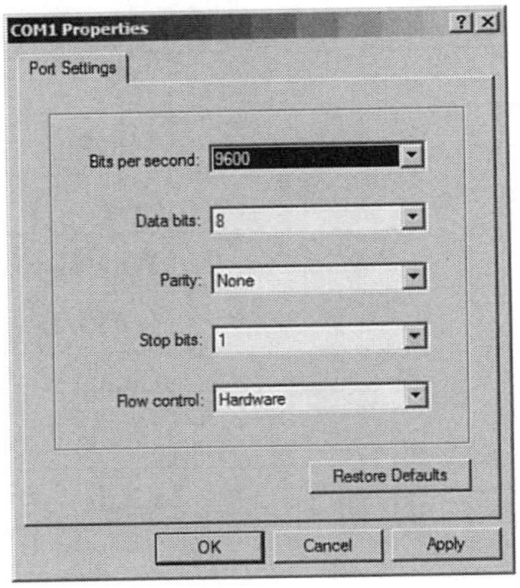

Step 3 Click the **OK** button to save the settings.

Step 4 Press **Enter** to start communication with the device. Figure 1-4 shows the console output from a Cisco router through HyperTerminal.

Figure 1-4 *HyperTerminal Console Session*

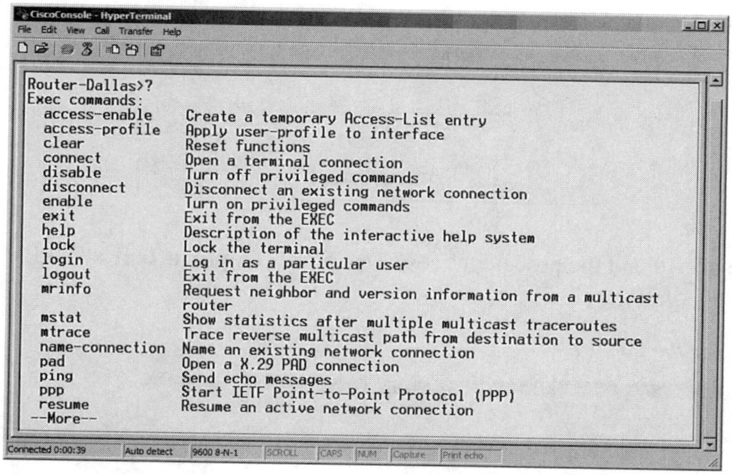

It is common networking practice to document the configuration process or record the output of a command. The copy-and-paste method is a quick and easy way to accomplish this. However, this method can be cumbersome for copying a large quantity of data. HyperTerminal has a built-in feature, called Capture Text, that allows you to save the entire session directly to a text file. The following steps are involved in using Capture Text:

Step 1 To begin capturing the text, choose **Transfer > Capture Text**, as illustrated in Figure 1-5.

Figure 1-5 *Capturing Text Through HyperTerminal*

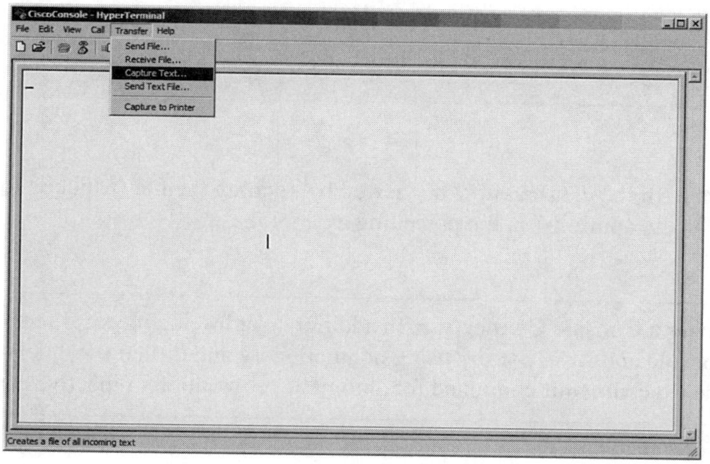

Step 2 A prompt appears, asking for the location of the new file to be saved. Enter the name of the file and click the **Start** button to begin the capture, as shown in Figure 1-6.

Figure 1-6 *Saving Captured Text*

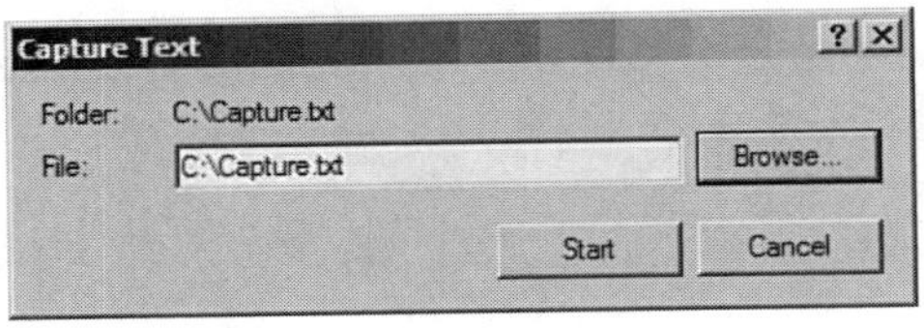

Step 3 To end the process, choose **Transfer > Capture Text > Stop**, as shown in Figure 1-7.

Figure 1-7 *Stopping the Capture*

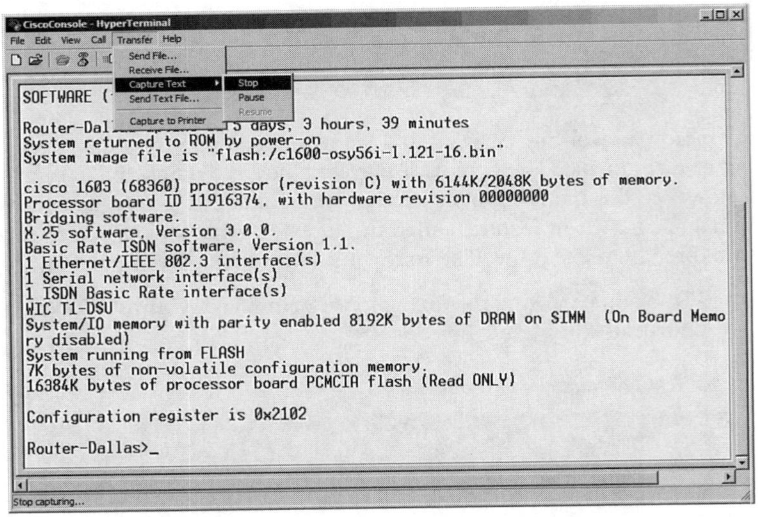

Step 4 All the data can now be viewed by opening the file (which is found at c:\capture.txt in the preceding example).

CAUTION **Securing a Console Connection**: In addition to enforcing physical security, always secure the console and AUX port by using nondictionary and difficult-to-guess passwords. Also, use the **exec-timeout** command for automatic termination of inactive console connections.

Using Linux-Based Console Tools

The Linux community is more inclined to use CLI-based tools. For a new Linux user, the CLI can be challenging. Fortunately, Linux features both CLI- and GUI-based tools for terminal emulation. This section features the following Linux-based terminal emulation tools:

- **Minicom**—A command-line interface (CLI)–based tool that offers customizable macros for task automation
- **cu**—A CLI-based tool that has simplicity and a small footprint, which make it an ideal tool for a network administrator's tool kit
- **GtkTerm**—Offers a graphical user interface (GUI) that allows customizable macros for task automation

Minicom for Console Connections

Minicom is often called HyperTerminal for Linux. Although Minicom is CLI-based, its ease of use and flexibility make it popular open source terminal emulation software. Minicom is included with most Linux distributions; it can also be downloaded from the following website:

http://freshmeat.net/redir/minicom/6437/url_homepage/minicom

The configuration steps for Minicom are as follows:

Step 1 Log in to the Linux computer with root privileges. Open a command-line session and enter **minicom –s** to display the screen shown in Figure 1-8.

Figure 1-8 *Minicom Configuration Screen*

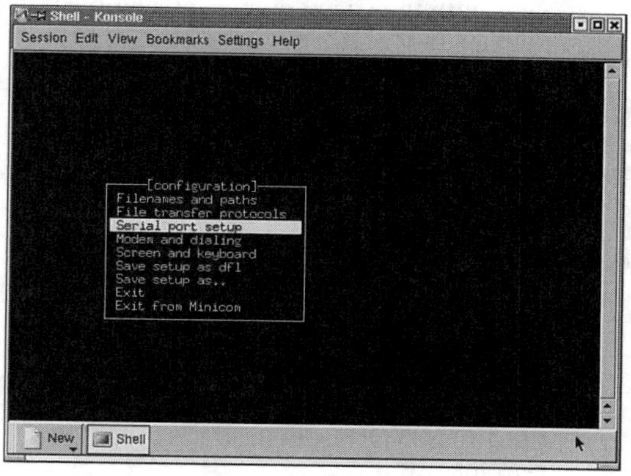

Step 2 Select the **Serial port setup** option and press **A** to change the serial device settings. This example assumes that you would use COM1 to connect the console cable; hence **/dev/ttyS0** is selected. To use COM2,

select **/dev/ttyS1**. Note the uppercase *S*. This example chooses COM1 as the serial port. You should also change the Bps setting to **9600 8N1** (option **E**). Figure 1-9 shows the final settings for the Serial port setup screen.

Figure 1-9 *Minicom Serial Port Setup*

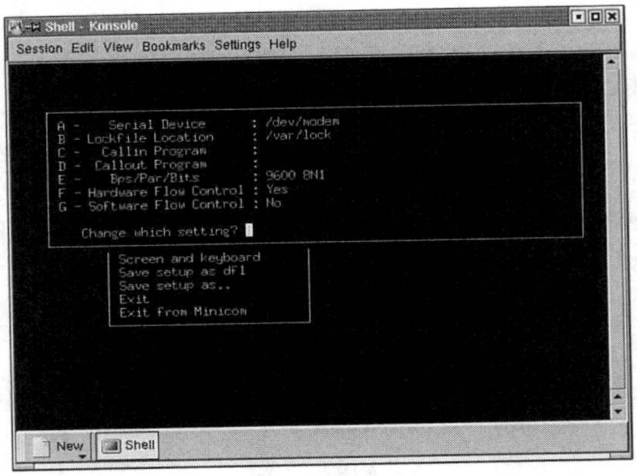

Step 3 Press **Enter** to return to the configuration screen. Select **Save setup as**, and when prompted with **Give name to save this configuration?** enter the name of your choice (such as **ciscoconsole**); then press **Enter**.

Step 4 Exit the program by selecting the **Exit from Minicom** option.

Step 5 Connect the Cisco device to COM1 of the Linux computer using the console cable. Open a command-line session and enter **minicom –o ciscoconsole** at the command line; then press **Enter** twice. This starts the console session with the Cisco device, as demonstrated in Example 1-1.

Example 1-1 *Console Session Through Minicom*

```
Welcome to minicom 2.1

OPTIONS: History Buffer, F-key Macros, Search History Buffer, I18n
Compiled on May 18 2003, 22:13:42.

Press CTRL-A Z for help on special keys

Router>show ?
  backup          Backup status
  cca             CCA information
  cdapi           CDAPI information
  cef             Cisco Express Forwarding
  class-map       Show QoS Class Map
  clock           Display the system clock
  compress        Show compression statistics
  controllers     Interface controller status
  crypto          Encryption module
 --More--
```

To begin capturing data, press **Ctrl-a** and then press **l**. The system prompts you for the destination file. Then press **Enter** to choose the default filename of minicom.cap.

To end the capture, press **Ctrl-a**, **l** again. To exit the program, press **Ctrl-a**, **q**.

NOTE

minicom: cannot open /dev/ttyS0: Permission denied

This error message in Minicom indicates that the user has insufficient permission. While the user is logged in as root, issuing the following command gives the required permission:

```
chmod 666 /dev/ttyS0
```

The same solution applies to a **Permission denied** or **Line in use** error message while using the cu tool, which is discussed in next section.

Using cu for Console Connections

Another serial communication software tool for Linux is cu, which is part of the UUCP (UNIX-to-UNIX Copy Program).

To connect to the Cisco device through the console connection, open a terminal session on the Linux PC and enter the following command:

```
cu -l /dev/ttyS0 -s 9600
```

To exit, enter **~.** (a tilde followed by a period).

Example 1-2 shows the console session using cu on the Linux computer with the console cable connected to COM1.

Example 1-2 *Console Session Through* **cu**

```
anand@linuxbox:~$ cu -l /dev/ttyS0 -s 9600
Connected.

Router>show ip interface brief
Interface              IP-Address      OK? Method Status                Protocol
BRI0                   unassigned      YES NVRAM  administratively down down
BRI0:1                 unassigned      YES unset  administratively down down
BRI0:2                 unassigned      YES unset  administratively down down
Ethernet0              unassigned      YES NVRAM  administratively down down
Serial0                unassigned      YES NVRAM  administratively down down
Router>
Router>~.

Disconnected.
anand@linuxbox:~$
```

Using GtkTerm for Serial Communications

GtkTerm is another Linux-based serial communication software tool that has a GUI similar to HyperTerminal. The steps for using GtkTerm are as follows:

Step 1 To start the software from the command line, enter **gtkterm**.

Step 2 Press **Ctrl-S** to invoke the configuration window, as shown in Figure 1-10. Select the settings shown in Table 1-3. Note that the port setting of **/dev/ttyS0** is chosen assuming that the console is connected to COM1 of the computer.

Figure 1-10 *GtkTerm Configuration Screen*

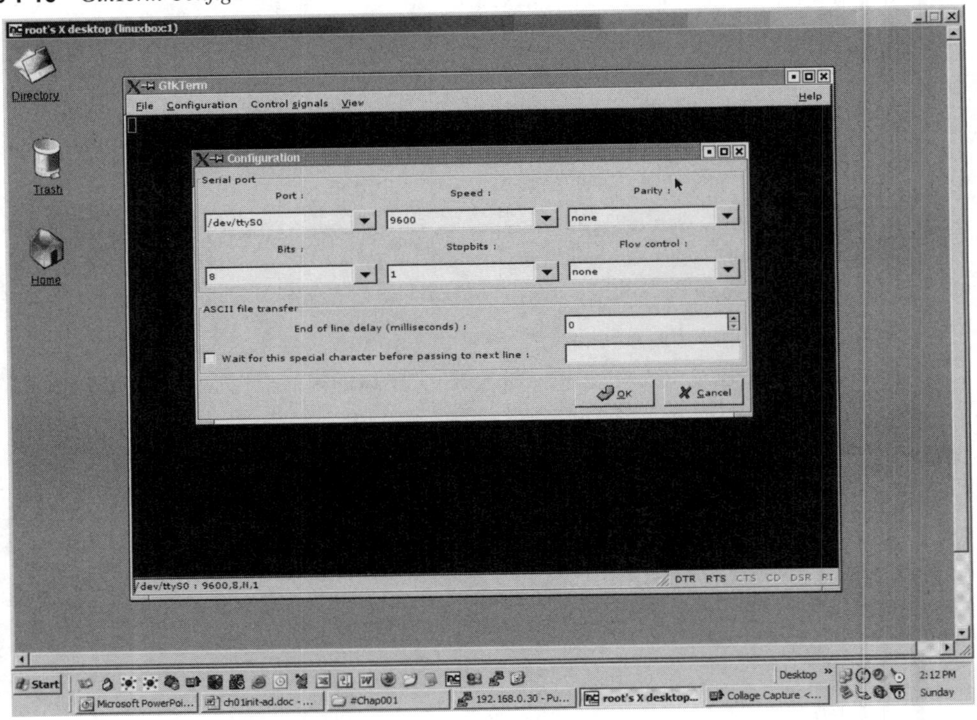

Table 1-3 *GtkTerm Settings*

Port	Speed	Parity	Bits	Stopbits	Flow Control
/dev/ttyS0	9600	None	8	1	None

Step 3 Click the **OK** button to save the configuration and begin the connection.

Step 4 To save the configuration for future use, choose **Configuration > Save Configuration**.

Step 5 In the **Save Configuration** window, enter a name for the configuration and click the **OK** button.

Step 6 To start GtkTerm with the preconfigured setting, use the following CLI command:

```
gtkterm --config configname
```

Remote Connection Using Telnet

Telnet, a TCP-based protocol using port 23, is most commonly used for remote connectivity. While console connection provides a simple way to configure the device, it has one major limitation—the length of the console cable. The Telnet protocol overcomes this limitation with its quick and easy functionality, allowing remote logins to the device for viewing or changing configurations. You can initiate a Telnet session from the MS-Windows, Linux, Cisco CatOS, or IOS command shells. To connect to a remote device through the network, enter the following command at the command prompt:

```
telnet ip-address-of-the-remote-device
```

TIP If a remote host you are trying to Telnet to is unreachable, your Telnet session will hang until the timeout value is reached. To save time, check the network connection to the target before initiating a Telnet connection. You can use the ping utility to do this.

You can also use the host name instead of the IP address to Telnet or ping to the remote host, provided that the host is listed under the DNS.

Most Cisco devices are not Telnet ready with the out-of-the-box default configuration. Each hardware platform has different command and configuration parameters for enabling the built-in Telnet daemon. Refer to the Cisco documentation CD-ROM (also known as the UniverCD) that is shipped with every Cisco product. You can also refer to the Cisco documentation website (http://www.cisco.com/univercd/home/home.htm), which provides information similar to that found on the UniverCD.

TIP Cisco IOS has a built-in Telnet client, too. To connect to a different device from the IOS CLI, enter **telnet *ip-address*** or simply type the IP address without the word **telnet**.

In the scenario shown in Figure 1-11, the network administrator is trying to access a remote router with IP address 192.168.100.1 from her laptop with IP address 10.1.1.26.

Figure 1-11 *Network Administrator Accessing a Remote Router*

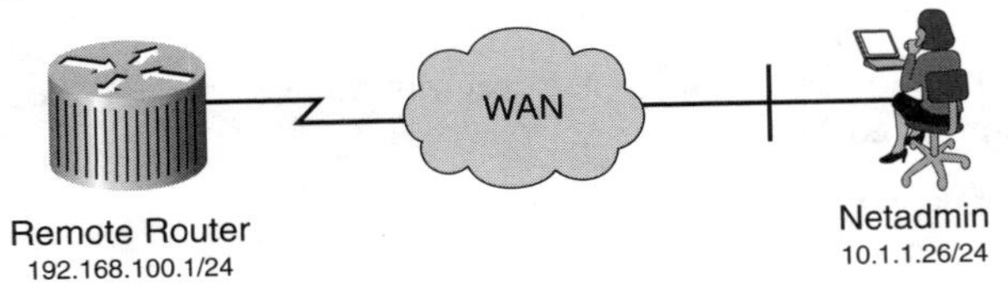

The network administrator opens a command-line session on the Linux laptop and enters **telnet 192.168.100.1** to connect to the remote router with IP address 192.168.100.1.

To end the Telnet session, the network administrator uses the **exit** command.

Example 1-3 shows the output of the Telnet session. Note the output in the fourth line. In this case, pressing **^]** (pressing the **Ctrl** and **]** keys together) can help the user temporarily leave the current session without disconnecting.

Example 1-3 *Telnet Session*

```
netadmin@linuxbox:~$ telnet 192.168.100.1
Trying 192.168.100.1...
Connected to 192.168.100.1.
Escape character is '^]'.
User Access Verification
Password:
Router>exit
Logoff
Connection closed by foreign host.
```

TIP Linux users can log Telnet sessions by using the **tee** command with the pipe options, as follows:

```
telnet host-ip-address 2>&1 | tee text-file
```

For example:

```
telnet 192.168.10.10 2>&1 | tee routerlog.txt
```

MS-Windows users can use the **set logfile** *filename* option within the Telnet utility, as follows:

```
c:\windows\system32>telnet
Welcome to Microsoft Telnet Client
Escape Character is 'CTRL+]'
Microsoft Telnet> set logfile routerlog.txt
Log file : routerlog.txt
Client logging on
Microsoft Telnet> open 192.168.10.10
Connecting To 192.168.10.10...
```

After the Telnet session is over, you can read the text file (routerlog.txt, in this example) using any text editor.

The following software allows you to use a GUI-based Telnet client in MS-Windows:

- HyperTerminal Private Edition (HTPE)
- TeraTerm
- PuTTY

Linux does not offer a good GUI client for Telnet. This section discusses HyperTerminal Private Edition (HTPE). The HTPE (http://www.hilgraeve.com) is a freely available software tool that has more functionality than the one preinstalled with Windows 9X/Me/XP/2000. HTPE features a built-in Telnet client that facilitates remote logins to network devices. This feature simplifies device configuration because the network administrator can access multiple devices through the same window. HTPE also provides the network administrator with advanced tools, such as file capture and macros (as discussed later in this chapter in the "Windows-Based Macro Tools" and "Linux-Based Macro Tools" sections).

To use HTPE to establish a Telnet session, follow these steps:

Step 1 Start the HTPE program, by selecting **Start > Programs > HyperTerminal Private Edition > HyperTerminal Private Edition**.

Step 2 Choose **File > Properties > Connect Using: TCP/IP(Winsock)**.

Step 3 In the **Host address** dialog box, enter the IP address of the remote device and then click the **OK** button to connect, as shown in Figure 1-12.

Figure 1-12 *Telnet Through HyperTerminal*

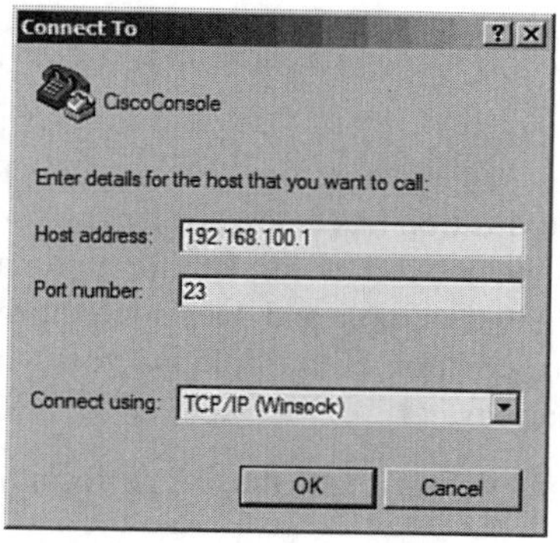

Automating Tasks Using Macros

The routine tasks performed by Netadmins often consist of similar steps and commands. Netadmins can save time by automating such repetitive tasks. Consider a typical case of a network administrator trying to change enable passwords on all the remote routers for security reasons. The steps involved are similar for all the routers, as shown in Example 1-4. In this example, the enable password for the router was changed from **password1** to **longpassword**.

Example 1-4 *Telnet Session*

```
C:\WINNT>telnet 192.168.100.1

User Access Verification

Password:
Router>enable
Password:
Router#config terminal
Enter configuration commands, one per line.  End with CNTL/Z.
Router(config)#enable password longpassword
Router(config)#exit

Router# copy running-config startup-config
Building configuration...
[OK]
Router#exit

Connection to host lost.

C:\WINNT>
```

Except for the first part of the Telnet connection and authentication, the remaining steps (as highlighted) would be the same for all remote routers. These identical configuration steps can be automated using a script or a macro tool.

Windows-Based Macro Tool

HyperTerminal Private Edition has a powerful, easy-to-use scripting feature called macro. This feature can help the network administrator automate repetitive tasks. The process of creating a macro in HTPE is simple and does not require knowledge of a scripting language or syntax. It allows the creation of multiple macros, which can be invoked by pressing different key combinations.

To configure HTPE and define a new macro, perform the following steps:

Step 1 Start the HTPE program, by selecting **Start > Programs > HyperTerminal Private Edition > HyperTerminal Private Edition**.

Step 2 Choose **View > Key Macros**, as shown in Figure 1-13.

Figure 1-13 *HyperTerminal Macro Configuration*

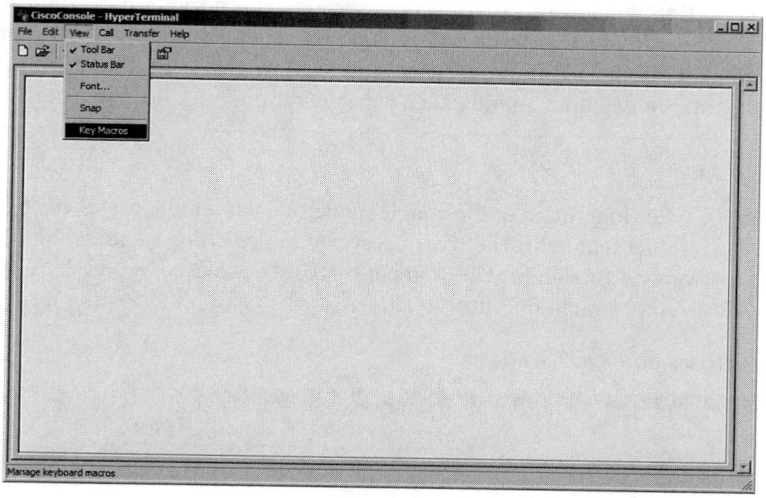

Step 3 In the **Keys** window, click the **New** button to define a new key macro, as shown in Figure 1-14.

Step 4 In the **Key** window, define a key combination that, when pressed, would invoke this macro. Figure 1-14 shows the key combination **Ctrl-Q** (**Ctrl** key and the **Q** key). In the **Action** window, enter all the IOS commands in the desired sequence. Click the **OK** button to save the macro.

Figure 1-14 *HyperTerminal: Defining a New Macro*

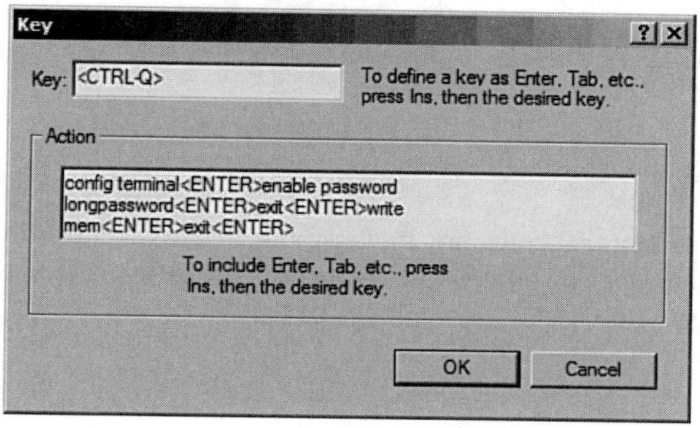

NOTE In the **Action** window of Figure 1-14, notice how each router IOS command is separated by the term **<ENTER>**. To insert keyboard commands such as **Enter** (a carriage return) or special keys such as **Tab**, press **Insert** followed by the desired function key on the keyboard. For example, to indicate a carriage return, press **Insert-Enter**.

Step 5 After logging in to the enable mode of each remote router (using the Telnet feature of HTPE as described in preceding sections), the entire process (highlighted in Example 1-4) can be achieved by pressing **Ctrl-Q**, as demonstrated in Figure 1-15.

Figure 1-15 *HyperTerminal: Using the Macro*

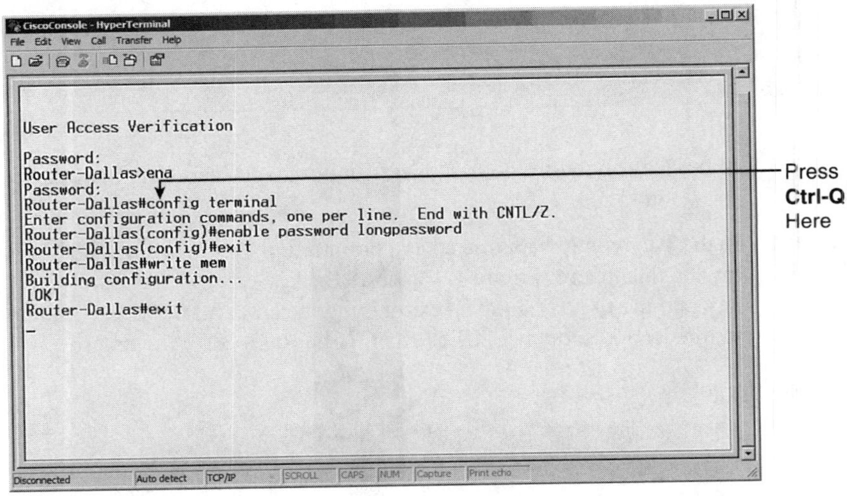

Linux-Based Macro Tools

Linux-based terminal emulation tools provide macro functionality, too. However, the configuration steps for Minicom and GtkTerm are different than those for the Windows operating systems.

Macros in Minicom

Linux-based Minicom also provides macro functionality. However, Minicom is limited to ten macros; these macros are invoked by pressing the function (F1–F10) keys.

To configure a macro, perform the following steps:

Step 1 Start Minicom with root privileges at the command shell by entering **minicom –s** and choosing the **Screen and keyboard** option.

Step 2 Press **M** to edit macros. In the **Macros** window, press **1** to configure the first macro, which can be invoked by pressing **F1**. Likewise, you can press **A** to configure the macro for **F10**, or press **2** through **9** for **F2** through **F9**, respectively. Configure the selected macro by entering the sequence of commands for the desired function key. For example, in Figure 1-16, a password-changing macro is defined for **F1**. Notice how each command is separated by the carriage return, which is represented as **^M** (**Shift-6** followed by **M**).

Figure 1-16 *Minicom: Configuring Macros*

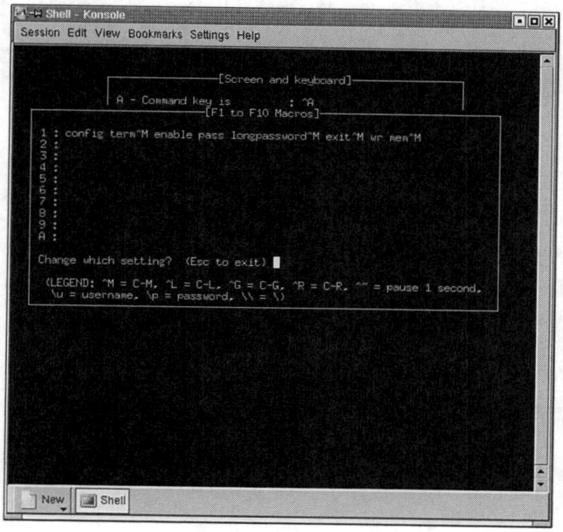

Step 3 Press **Enter** three times to save and exit to the configuration screen. Press **Esc** to exit and return to the router prompt.

Step 4 While in the enable mode of the IOS, invoke this macro by pressing **F1**.

Macros in GtkTerm

GtkTerm also provides easily configurable macros. To create a GtkTerm macro based on Example 1-4, follow these steps:

Step 1 In the GtkTerm window, select **Configuration > Macros**, as shown in Figure 1-17.

Figure 1-17 *GtkTerm: Configuring Macros*

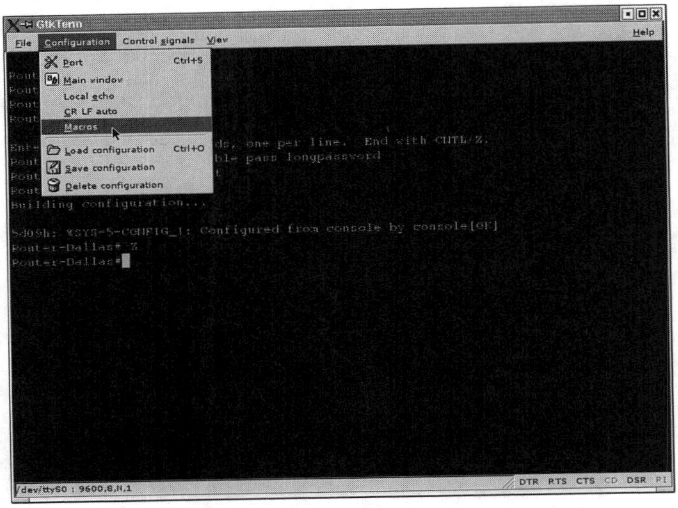

Step 2 In the **Configure Macros** window, click the **Add** button to create a blank macro.

Step 3 Select the new macro and click the **Capture Shortcut** button. Press the preferred key combination to create the shortcut. Figure 1-18 shows **Ctrl-Q** (the Control and the Q key together).

Figure 1-18 *GtkTerm: Adding Commands in Macro*

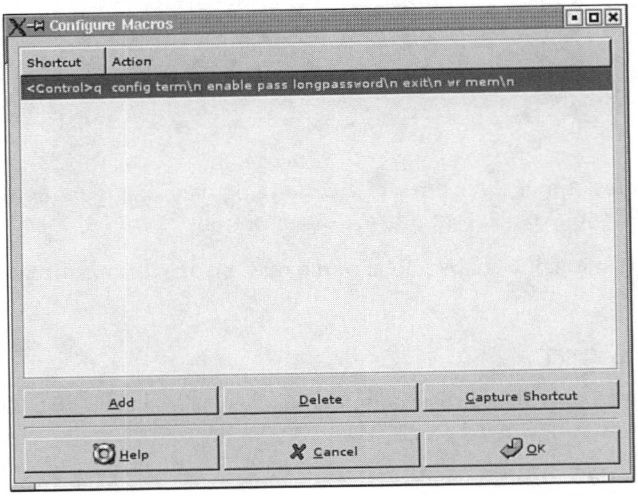

Step 4 Click in the **Action** window and enter the list of commands, with each command separated by **\n** (backslash key followed by n key). GtkTerm uses the **\n** key combination to define a carriage return.

Step 5 Click the **OK** button to save and exit the **Configure Macro** window.

Step 6 To invoke the macro, press **Ctrl-Q**.

WARNING Exercise caution when choosing the shortcut key combination for invoking macros. Both MS-Windows and Linux have predefined shortcut keys such as **Ctrl-V** or **Alt-F2**. Using one of the predefined shortcut keys can create unwanted results or misconfigurations.

Securing Remote Connections to Cisco Devices Using Secure Shell (SSH)

Telnet has been around since the early days of TCP/IP. Hence, it is the most widely used remote connection method; however, Telnet is inherently insecure because the packets are sent in clear text. This results in vulnerability to the capture of usernames and passwords through commonly available packet analyzer (popularly known as sniffer) programs.

NOTE For more information on packet analyzer programs, refer to Chapter 7, "Network Security Testing."

Secure Shell (SSH) was created to overcome this inherent weakness. SSH provides encryption of the session using a cryptographic mechanism, making the session more secure against man-in-the-middle attacks and IP spoofing. SSH uses TCP port 22. Cisco products support only SSH version 1.0, although limited support for version 2.0 was introduced in Cisco IOS Release 12.1(19)E and higher. Beginning with IOS Release 12.3(4)T, the SSH version 2.0 server is supported.

NOTE A Cisco Security Advisory has reported multiple SSH vulnerabilities. Refer to the following SSH Security Advisory page for more information:

http://www.cisco.com/en/US/tech/tk583/tk617/tech_security_advisories_list.html

---

Establishing an SSH connection from a PC to a Cisco device involves the following tasks:

1. Configuring an SSH server on the Cisco device
2. Deploying an SSH client on the PC

Cisco Device Configuration for SSH

Cisco devices offer support for the SSH protocol, but the factory default configuration is not SSH ready. Use the following steps to enable SSH on routers with Cisco IOS Release 12.1 and later:

Step 1 **Host name**—Assign a host name to the device using the **hostname** *name* command in the global configuration mode.

Step 2 **Domain name**—Assign the device to a DNS domain using the **ip domain-name** *name-of-the-domain* command.

Step 3 **SSH key**—Generate an SSH key using the **crypto key generate rsa** command in the global configuration mode. When prompted, specify a minimum modulus size of 1024.

Optionally, fine-tune the SSH parameters using the following command in global configuration mode:

```
ip ssh {[timeout seconds] | [authentication-retries integer]}
```

Step 4 **SSH protocol**—Enable the SSH protocol on the vty lines using the **transport input ssh** command in the line configuration mode.

The router configuration snippets shown in Example 1-5 detail the relevant commands for starting an SSH server on an IOS device.

Example 1-5 *IOS Configuration for SSH*

```
hostname Router-Dallas
username stevepope password cisco123
ip domain-name admin.stevepope.com
!
crypto key generate rsa
ip ssh time-out 60
ip ssh authentication-retries 2
!
line vty 0 4
transport input ssh
```

NOTE Refer to the Tech notes section of the SSH technology page on Cisco.com for more details on specific hardware platforms. You can find this information at the following URL:

http://www.cisco.com/en/US/tech/tk583/tk617/tech_tech_notes_list.html

SSH Client Installation

To connect to a Cisco device using the SSH protocol, an SSH client should be installed on the PC. Table 1-4 lists the popular and widely used SSH clients based on the operating system used.

Table 1-4 *SSH Clients, Listed by Operating System*

Operating System	SSH Client
Windows	PuTTY(http://www.chiark.greenend.org.uk/~sgtatham/putty/)
	SSH Secure Shell (http://www.ssh.com)
	TeraTermPro (http://www.ayera.com)
Linux	SSH client (http://www.openssh.com)

Windows-Based SSH Client: PuTTY

PuTTY is one of the popular SSH clients for Windows 9*X*/Me/2000/XP.

To configure PuTTY, perform the following steps:

Step 1 Download and save the .exe file from the URL listed in Table 1-4.

Step 2 Double-click the saved .exe file to launch the configuration page.

Step 3 In the **Host Name (or IP address)** field, enter the IP address of the target device and select the **SSH** option in the **Protocol** field, as shown in Figure 1-19. PuTTY automatically selects the default port 22 for SSH.

Step 4 Click the **Open** button to start an SSH session on the target device.

Figure 1-19 *PuTTY Configuration*

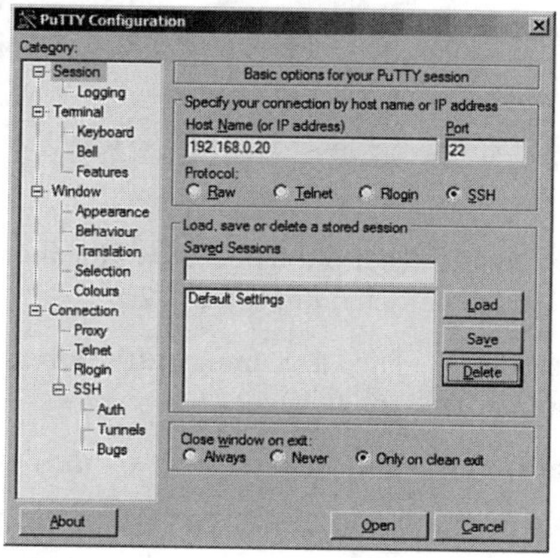

Windows-Based SSH Client: SSH Secure Shell Client

The noncommercial version of SSH Secure Shell Client for Windows is available at http://www.ssh.com. Be sure to read the licensing terms before using the product.

Before using the SSH Secure Shell Client for Windows, you must download the installation files from the website (http://www.ssh.com) and install them in MS-Windows. To configure the SSH Secure Shell Client, perform the following steps:

Step 1 Launch the program by selecting **Start > Program > SSH Secure Shell > Secure Shell Client**.

Step 2 Select **Profiles > Add Profiles** to create a new profile. In the **Add Profile** window, enter the preferred name (for example, Firewall-Dallas) and click the **Add to profile** button.

Step 3 To edit the settings for the new profile, select **Profile > Edit Profiles**. Figure 1-20 shows the settings.

Figure 1-20 *SSH Secure Shell Client: Profile Configuration*

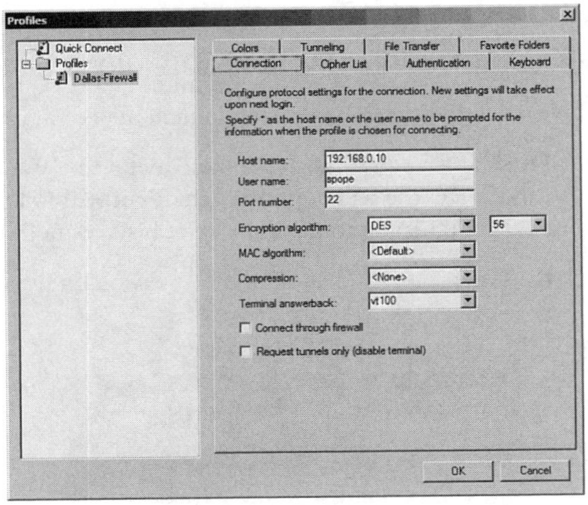

The following is a description of some of the more important fields of the **Connection** tab depicted in Figure 1-20:

— **Host name**—The DNS name or IP address of the target device (for example, 192.168.0.10).

— **User name**—This field depends on the device, as follows:

For IOS-based routers or switches, this is the username defined by the **username** ***name*** **password** [*encryption-type*] ***password*** command or as defined on the AAA server.

For a Cisco PIX Firewall, the default username is **pix** or as defined by the AAA server. Figure 1-20 shows username **spope**.

— **Port number**—The default SSH port number of TCP 22 is automatically entered in this field.

— **Encryption algorithm**—This can be DES or 3DES, depending on the encryption supported by the IOS image of the router, switch, or firewall.

The rest of the fields, including all other tabs, should be left at their the default values.

Step 4 Save the configuration by selecting **File > Save Settings**.

Step 5 To connect, click the **Profile** button and choose the configured profile.

SSH Using the Linux Client

Most of the Linux distributions come prebundled with the command-line SSH client utility. It can also be downloaded freely from http://www.openssh.com or http://www.ssh.com.

To configure the SSH Linux client, open a command shell and enter the following command to connect to a Cisco IOS–based router or switch:

```
ssh -l username -c 3DES ip-address
```

NOTE Replace 3DES with DES if the IOS only supports DES encryption.

For example, to connect to a router as user **stevepope** with IP address 192.168.0.10, you would enter the following code:

```
[user@linuxbox]$ ssh -l -c 3DES stevepope 192.168.0.10
```

To connect to a PIX Firewall with IP address 192.168.0.20, you would enter the following code:

```
[user@linuxbox]$ ssh -l pix -c 3DES 192.168.0.20
```

SSH Using the Cisco IOS Device as an SSH Client

After the IOS-based device is configured for accepting inbound SSH connections, it can also be used as an SSH client to initiate an SSH connection to other Cisco devices.

For example, to connect to a remote router 10.10.10.46 with username **stevepope**, you would enter the following code:

```
Router-Dallas# ssh -l stevepope -c 3des 10.10.10.46
```

Configuring Cisco Devices Using GUI Tools

So far, this chapter has discussed the tools for CLI-based device configurations. Cisco also offers an array of GUI-based configuration tools specific to these devices. Table 1-5 provides a partial list of these GUI tools.

Table 1-5 *Cisco GUI Tools*

Device	Configuration Tool
IOS-based HTTP interface	Web-based configuration of Cisco IOS-based devices
PIX Device Manager	Web-based configuration of Cisco PIX Firewall
Router and Security Device Manager	Web-based configuration tool for IOS devices with security auditing and VPN
Cisco Configmaker	Windows-based configuration tool for Cisco routers and switches
IDS Device Manager	Web-based configuration tool for Cisco IDS Sensor
VPN Device Manager	Web-based configuration tool for Cisco VPN–enabled servers
QoS Device Manager	Web-based configuration tool for QoS features in Cisco IOS

The following sections discuss the first three tools in detail.

NOTE Cisco has recently introduced a PC-based tool called Cisco Network Assistant (CNA) for configuring routers, switches, and access-points. CNA enables users to perform common tasks such as configuration management, inventory reports, password synchronization, and Drag and Drop IOS Upgrade for switches, routers, and access points.

HTTP Interface for IOS-Based Devices

Cisco IOS Releases 11.3 and later include a built-in HTTP server. This creates a browser-based GUI through which most of the Cisco IOS commands can be issued to the router. To use the Cisco web-based GUI, the client computer must have a web browser application and should have network reachability to the router. The tasks involved for using the web-based GUI are as follows:

1. Enable IOS for HTTP.
2. Connect to the router home page.

Enabling IOS for HTTP

The IOS HTTP server on Cisco IOS devices is disabled by default. To use the feature, you must configure an HTTP server on the IOS devices. Table 1-6 shows the IOS commands required to configure the built-in HTTP server.

Table 1-6 *IOS Commands for HTTP server*

Command	Explanation
Router(config)#**ip http server**	Enables the HTTP server (web server) on the system.
Router(config)#**ip http secure-server**	(Optional) Enables a secure HTTP server on the system. Preferred because of the inherent security offered by HTTPS.
Router(config)#**ip http authentication** {**aaa** | **enable** | **local** | **tacacs**}	Specifies how the HTTP server users are authenticated.
Router(config)#**username** *name* [**privilege** *level*]	Assigns a username for HTTP access with a privilege level.
Router(config)#**username** *name* **password** *secret*	Assigns a password to the username.

Example 1-6 shows the relevant router configuration snippet for enabling the HTTP server.

Example 1-6 *Enabling the IOS HTTP Server*

```
username stevepope password cisco123
username stevepope privilege 15
ip http server
ip http authentication local
```

Connecting to the Router Home Page

To connect to the router home page, enter the IP address of the router in the address field of the web browser on the client computer, as illustrated in Figure 1-21. Note that the client computer should have network reachability to the router.

Figure 1-21 *IOS HTTP Home Page*

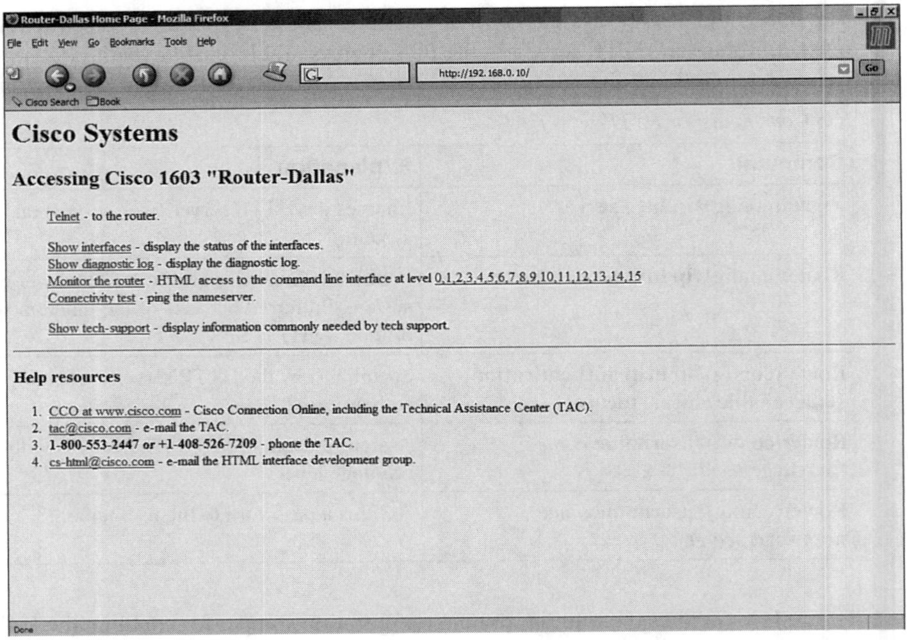

Based on the privilege levels defined for a user, the IOS HTTP-based router home page can be customized for restricted access to particular commands. This feature can effectively provide system administrators at remote offices with easy and limited access to router-monitoring commands. The router home page can also be added as an embedded link inside customized web pages. For more information on customizing the IOS HTTP interface, refer to the Using the Cisco Web Browser User Interface page at Cisco.com:

http://www.cisco.com/en/US/products/sw/iosswrel/ps1831/products_configuration_guide_chapter09186a00800ca66a.html

PIX Device Manager

The Cisco PIX Device Manager (PDM) provides a browser-based graphical tool for simplified configuration, operation, and monitoring of Cisco PIX Firewalls. PDM is built in with Cisco PIX Firewall version 6 and later. For example, PDM version 3.0 comes pre-installed with Cisco PIX Software 6.3.

Follow these steps to use the PDM:

Step 1 Enable PDM access on the Cisco PIX Firewall.

Step 2 Connect to the PDM through your browser.

Enabling PDM Access on the Cisco PIX Firewall

Table 1-7 lists the commands that enable PDM access on the Cisco PIX Firewall.

Table 1-7 *Enabling PDM Access on the Cisco PIX Firewall*

Command	Explanation
http server enable	Enables the internal web server to start the PDM
http ip_address [*netmask*] [*if_name*]	Creates a list of hosts or networks that can access the PDM

The following is a sample configuration for the Cisco PIX Firewall to enable PDM access. This configuration assumes that the client computer accessing the PDM is in the same subnet as the **Inside** interface of the Cisco PIX Firewall and has network reachability to the **Inside interface** of the Cisco PIX Firewall. The code is as follows:

```
pix(config)# http server enable
pix(config)# http 192.168.0.0 255.255.255.0 inside
```

Connecting to the PDM Through the Browser

The URL to connect to the PDM from a client computer is as follows:

https://<*ip address of Inside interface*>

NOTE Please note the *S* in https. The PDM can only be accessed through HTTPS (HTTP over SSL). HTTPS provides a secure connection.

Figure 1-22 shows a Netadmin trying to access the **Inside** interface of the Cisco PIX Firewall from a PC with IP address 192.168.0.109.

Figure 1-22 *Cisco PIX Firewall Access Through the PDM*

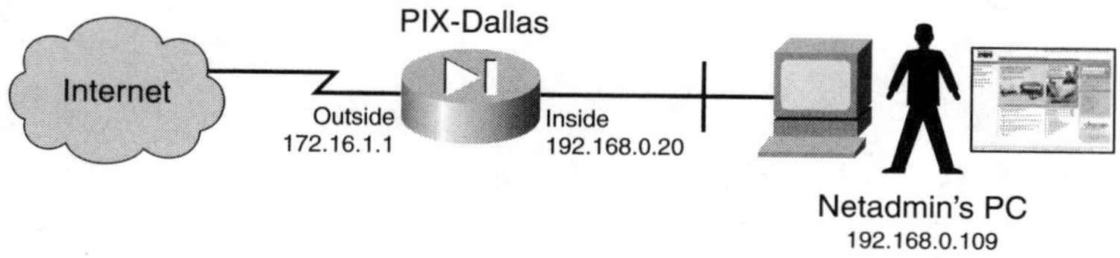

Figure 1-23 shows the PDM window for configuring and monitoring a Cisco PIX Firewall.

Figure 1-23 *PDM Window*

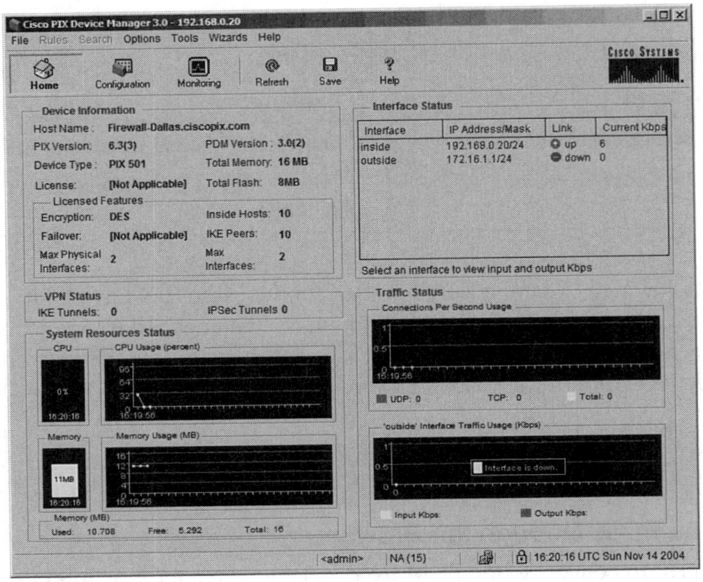

Security Device Manager

The Cisco Router and Security Device Manager (SDM) is a web-based tool for auditing and securing Cisco routers. The SDM, which is similar to the PDM, is discussed in greater detail in Chapter 8, "Router and Switch Security."

NOTE For Cisco IOS–based switches, the PDM and SDM require Java-enabled web browsers. While enabling Java on MS-Windows platforms for Netscape or Internet Explorer is comparatively easy, it can be difficult to install Java on Linux platforms. The Knoppix CD-ROM mentioned in Chapter 7 provides preinstalled Java-enabled web browsers for Linux.

Other GUI Tools for Configuring Cisco Devices

Cisco also offers PC-based and web-based tools for device configuration. These are often specialized tools for a specific task. One tool worth mentioning is the Cisco Configmaker, which can be downloaded from the following URL:

http://www.cisco.com/en/US/products/sw/netmgtsw/ps754/index.html

The Cisco Configmaker is a Windows-based application for older models of routers (800, 1000, 1600, 1700, 2500, 2600, 3600, and 4000 Series), switches, hubs, and other network devices. The Cisco Configmaker enables network administrators to configure various IOS features without an extensive command-line knowledge of Cisco IOS Software. Configmaker is no longer being developed; Cisco is offering the SDM and CNA as a replacement, instead.

Managing System Files

One of the most common tasks faced by Cisco network administrators is file management for various Cisco devices. This includes backing up the system image (for example, the IOS image stored in the flash memory of the router) and configuration files to a centralized location. Almost all Cisco devices offer CLI-based file-management utilities to copy files to TFTP and FTP servers.

File Management Using a TFTP Server

Most Cisco devices allow saving the configuration files or flash images to a backup server using the Trivial File Transfer Protocol (TFTP), which uses UDP port 69 and is a stripped-down version of FTP protocols. TFTP aids in simplified network maintenance by allowing a quick and simple way of copying to a centralized location. In case of a device failure or configuration change resulting in network outage, the administrator can simply restore the configuration or the flash image from the TFTP server. TFTP is also used as the auto-install method for new devices. The auto-install method is designed to automatically configure a router after it connects to a WAN. For auto-install to work properly, a TFTP server must be on the remote side of the router's synchronous serial connection to the WAN.

Figure 1-24 shows a WAN setup with a central TFTP server for storing configuration and flash images.

Figure 1-24 *WAN Setup with TFTP Server*

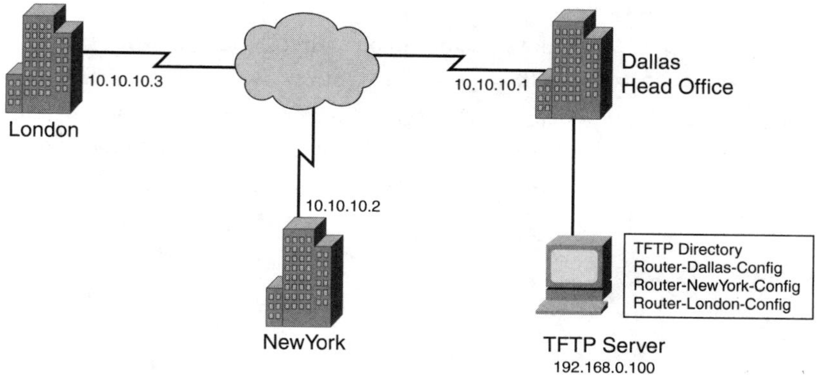

Table 1-8 lists the popular TFTP servers categorized on the basis of operating system.

Table 1-8 *TFTP Servers*

Platform	Product
Windows	Solarwinds TFTP Server, 3COM TFTP Daemon
Linux	Built-in TFTP server with Xinetd
Cisco IOS	Built-in TFTP with limited capability

The sections that follow discuss these details of TFTP-based file management:

- Configuring Windows-based TFTP servers
- Configuring Linux-based TFTP servers
- Configuring Cisco devices to use TFTP

Configuring Windows-Based TFTP Servers

Solarwind's TFTP server is a freeware utility that runs on Windows 9*X*/Me/2000/XP. It can be downloaded from the Solarwinds website (http://www.solarwinds.net) and is easy to run with the default configuration. It provides the following advanced security features:

- Runs the TFTP server in transmit-only mode
- Runs the TFTP server in receive-only mode
- Allows only a range of IP addresses to access the server
- Provides auto-shutoff after a specified time period
- Provides logging capability
- Allows the TFTP root directory to be redirected to a network share for easy maintenance and backup

To configure all these features, choose **File > Configure**. After the server has been configured, it is ready to use. As shown in Figure 1-25, the default root directory is c:\TFTP-Root.

Figure 1-25 *Solarwinds TFTP Server Configuration*

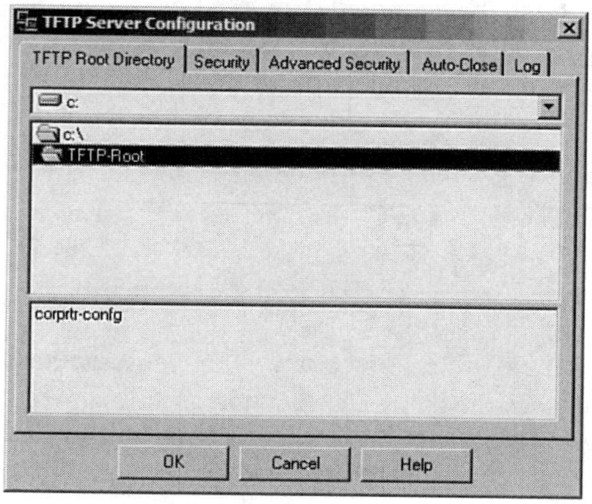

Configuring Linux-Based TFTP Servers

The Linux TFTP server is called TFTP Daemon (tftpd). Tftpd is controlled through the xinetd or inetd daemon. Xinetd is used by Red Hat Linux, whereas inetd is used by Debian Linux. Hence, to restart (or stop) the TFTP server, you need to restart (or stop) the inetd server. The steps involved in deploying a Linux-based TFTP server are as follows:

- Install the TFTP server.
- Edit the /etc/inetd.conf file.
- Create the tftpboot directory.
- Create the configuration files.
- Restart the inetd server.

Following are the details of each step:

Step 1 **Install the TFTP server (tftpd)**—The exact installation procedure depends on the Linux distribution. The command to install tftpd over Debian Linux is **apt-get install tftpd**.

Step 2 **Edit the /etc/inetd.conf file**—You can configure default parameters for tftpd through the /etc/inetd.conf file. One such parameter is the directory location used by tftpd to store the files. While the default location is /boot, you should change it to /tftpboot, as highlighted in Example 1-7. This isolates the system file present in the /boot directory.

Example 1-7 *Editing the /etc/inetd.conf File*

```
root@linuxbox:~# cat /etc/inetd.conf  | grep tftp
tftp          dgram   udp    wait    nobody  /usr/sbin/tcpd  /usr/sbin/
  in.tftpd  /tftpboot
```

Step 3 **Create the tftpboot directory**—You must create a tftpboot directory that matches the name and location specified in the /etc/inetd.conf file. Additionally, change the owner to **nobody** and the file permission to allow read and write permissions for all users. Without the read and write permissions, you cannot use the TFTP server. The tftpboot directory is used by the tftpd server to store all the files that are to be exchanged through TFTP. Example 1-8 shows the commands that are used in creating the directory and changing the permissions.

Example 1-8 *Adding the tftpboot Directory*

```
# create the /tftpboot directory
root@linuxbox:~# mkdir /tftpboot
# change the permission for the /tftpboot directory
root@linuxbox:~# chmod 666 /tftpboot
# change the owner for the /tftpboot directory
root@linuxbox:~# chown nobody /tftpboot
root@linuxbox:~# ls -l / | grep tftpboot
drw-rw-rw-    2 nobody root   4096 Feb 12 18:49 tftpboot
```

Step 4 **Create the configuration files**—The Linux tftp daemon (tftpd) has a built-in security feature that prevents access to files unless they are already created on the tftp server. Hence, before writing to any file, you must create it on the TFTP server. Moreover, the file must have read-and-write permissions. For example, if the configurations of the Cisco router (host name Router-Dallas) are to be saved in this TFTP server, a file named router-dallas-confg should be created. (As shown later in Example 1-11, this is the default filename created by the **copy running-config tftp** command on the router.) Example 1-9 shows the creation of the file in the tftpboot directory.

Example 1-9 *Creating Configuration Files*

```
root@linuxbox:~# cd /tftpboot
# create empty directories
root@linuxbox:/tftpboot# touch router-dallas-config
root@linuxbox:/tftpboot# touch switch-dallas.cfg
root@linuxbox:/tftpboot# touch pix-dallas-config
# change the file permissions
root@linuxbox:/tftpboot# chmod a+wr *
root@linuxbox:/tftpboot# ls -l
-rw-rw-rw-  1 root root 0 Feb 12 19:24 pix-dallas-config
-rw-rw-rw-  1 root root 0 Feb 12 19:24 router-dallas-config
-rw-rw-rw-  1 root root 0 Feb 12 19:24 switch-dallas.cfg
root@linuxbox:/tftpboot#
```

Step 5 **Restart the inetd server**—Because tftpd is controlled by the inetd server, all the changes made in previous steps can only take effect if the inetd server is restarted as follows:

```
root@linuxbox:~# /etc/init.d/inetd restart
Restarting internet superserver: inetd.
```

The TFTP server is ready for use. After the files are written or copied, it is good security practice to remove the read/write permissions. (Use the **chmod a-wr** *filename* command.) Better yet, move the files to a different location. As good Netadmin practice, save the files in a directory named with the creation date of the configuration files. This way, you have a chronological record of all the changes, thus facilitating troubleshooting.

If you get a **Timed out** error message from Cisco devices while uploading through TFTP, check the file and directory permissions. Additionally, ensure that the host firewall on the Linux server is set to allow incoming TFTP.

Configuring Cisco IOS–Based TFTP Servers

Cisco devices running IOS can be configured as TFTP servers for sharing IOS images stored in flash memory. This feature is useful during disaster recovery because the IOS images for similar hardware platforms can be copied quickly and easily. The command to accomplish this, **tftp-server**, should be executed in the global configuration mode of the IOS, as shown in Example 1-10.

Example 1-10 *Router as TFTP Server*

```
Router-Dallas#show flash
PCMCIA flash directory:
File  Length   Name/status
  1   10685392  /c1600-osy56i-l.121-16.bin
[10685456 bytes used, 6091760 available, 16777216 total]
16384K bytes of processor board PCMCIA flash (Read ONLY)
Router-Dallas#conf t
Enter configuration commands, one per line.  End with CNTL/Z.
Router-Dallas(config)#tftp-server flash:c1600-osy56i-l.121-16.bin
Router-Dallas(config)#exit
Router-Dallas#exit
```

Configuring Cisco Devices to Use TFTP

Now that you have configured the TFTP server, you are ready to use it for uploading or downloading files from Cisco devices. While covering each TFTP-related command for each Cisco device is beyond the scope of this book, Table 1-9 lists common commands for saving and restoring configurations on IOS, CatOS, and PIX platforms.

Table 1-9 *IOS, CatOS, and PIX Commands*

Platform	Command	Description
IOS	**copy running-config tftp:**	Copy running configuration to a TFTP server
	copy startup-config tftp:	Copy startup configuration to a TFTP server
	copy tftp running-config	Copy from files stored on a TFTP server to the running configuration
	copy tftp startup-config	Copy from files stored on a TFTP server to the startup configuration
CatOS	**copy config tftp**	Copy configuration to a TFTP server
	copy tftp config	Copy configuration from file stored on a TFTP server to the switch
PIX	**write net** *tftp-ip-address***:***filename*	Copy running configuration to a TFTP server
	config net *tftp-ipaddress***:** *filename*	Copy configuration from a specified file on the TFTP server

The following examples, based on the commands listed in Table 1-9, illustrate several of most common TFTP-related tasks on Cisco devices:

- Example 1-11: Saving IOS configurations
- Example 1-12: Saving CatOS configurations
- Example 1-13: Saving PIX configurations
- Example 1-14: Restoring PIX configurations

Example 1-11 *Saving Cisco IOS Configurations*

```
Router-Dallas#ping 192.168.0.100

Type escape sequence to abort.
Sending 5, 100-byte ICMP Echos to 192.168.0.100, timeout is 2 seconds:
!!!!!
Success rate is 100 percent (5/5), round-trip min/avg/max = 4/4/8 ms
Router-Dallas#copy running-config tftp:
Address or name of remote host []? 192.168.0.100
Destination filename [router-dallas-confg]?
!!
490 bytes copied in 3.360 secs (163 bytes/sec)
Router-Dallas#
```

Example 1-12 *Saving Catalyst Switch Configurations*

```
Console> (enable) copy config tftp:switch-dallas.cfg

IP address or name of remote host [192.168.0.100]? y

Upload configuration to tftp:switch-dallas.cfg (y/n) [n]? y

.........
.........
.........
.
/
Configuration has been copied successfully. (10299 bytes).
Console> (enable)
```

Example 1-13 *Saving PIX Configurations*

```
Pix-Dallas# write net 192.168.0.100:pix-dallas-config
Building configuration...
TFTP write 'pix-dallas-config' at 192.168.0.100 on interface 1
[OK]
Pix-Dallas#
```

Example 1-14 *Restoring PIX Configurations*

```
Pix-Dallas# config term
Pix-Dallas(config)# config  net 192.168.0.100:pix-dallas-config

Cryptochecksum(unchanged): 97814530 04080483 a1197964 d944bf56
Config OK
Pix-Dallas(config)# exit
Pix-Dallas#
```

NOTE The preceding examples are indicative only of the most common tasks using TFTP. Refer to the Cisco product documentation home page at Cisco.com for device-specific information. The URL is as follows:

http://www.cisco.com/univercd/home/home.htm

Using an FTP Server for File Management

As discussed in the previous section, TFTP provides a handy tool for backup and recovery, but it has the following inherent weaknesses:

- Absence of a built-in security mechanism
- 16-MB file size limitation
- Uses User Datagram Protocol (UDP)

To overcome these limitations, the latest versions of IOS now support FTP, which is more secure and reliable. It uses TCP port 21 and allows password protection. FTP is more reliable because it depends on retransmit by TCP, whereas TFTP lacks a retransmit feature because of the underlying UDP. Cisco devices can copy images or configuration files to and from FTP servers. An FTP server should be configured to effectively use this feature. Although FTP is more secure than TFTP, FTP is still prone to eavesdropping of username and password information, which is sent in clear text.

Linux and Windows 2000/NT can both act as robust FTP servers.

This section covers the following topics:

- Configuring Windows-based FTP servers
- Configuring Linux-based FTP servers
- Configuring Cisco devices to use FTP

Configuring Windows-Based FTP Servers

Windows 2000/2003/XP offer a built-in FTP server within the Internet Information Services (IIS) framework. A Windows-based FTP server offers the following advantages:

- Integrated authentication with the domain controller
- Simple to install and administer using the Computer Management Console

The installation consists of installing the IIS server followed by configuring the FTP services under the IIS server. The steps discussed in this section are based on MS-Windows XP. However, the steps are similar to those for MS-Windows 2000 or 2003.

Installing the IIS Server

The steps for installing the IIS server are as follows:

Step 1 Choose **Start**, **Settings**, **Control Panel**, **Add/Remove Programs**, **Add/ Remove Windows Component** to start the Windows Component Wizard.

Step 2 In the **Windows Component Wizard** window, select Internet Information Services (IIS).

Step 3 Click the **Details** button to view the components of the IIS server. Make sure that **Common Files**, **Documentation**, **File Transfer Protocol (FTP) Server**, and **Internet Information Services Snap-In** are selected.

Step 4 Click the **OK** button to return to the Windows Component Wizard.

Step 5 Click the **Next** button, and then click the **Finish** button.

Step 6 Close the **Add/Remove Programs** window.

Configuring FTP Services on the IIS Server

The steps for configuring FTP services on the IIS server are as follows:

Step 1 Open the Computer Management Console by right-clicking the **My Computer** icon and selecting the **Manage** option.

Step 2 Click the plus sign (+) next to **Services and Applications** to expand the menu.

Step 3 Click the plus sign (+) next to **Internet Information Services** to expand the menu.

Step 4 Right-click **Default FTP Site** and then click **Properties**, as shown in Figure 1-26. Some versions of MS-Windows have **Default FTP Site** listed under **FTP Sites**, as shown in Figure 1-26.

Figure 1-26 *Computer Management Console for IIS*

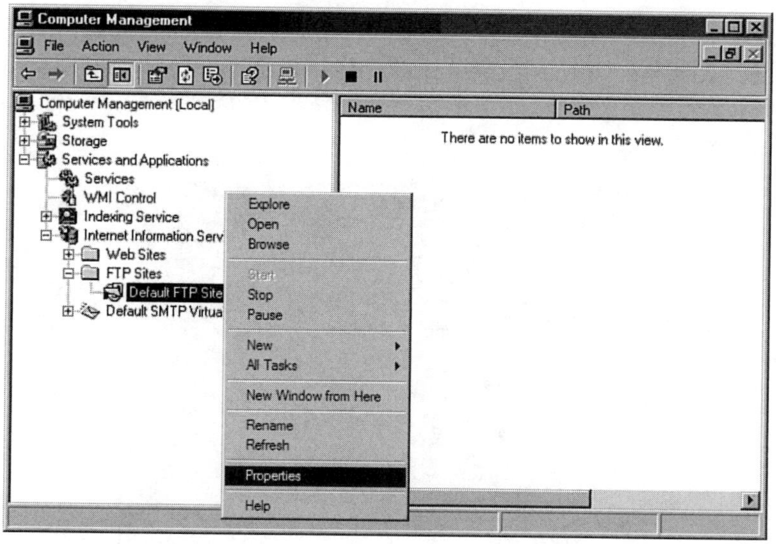

Step 5 In the **Default FTP Site Properties** window that appears, click the **Security Accounts** tab, as shown in Figure 1-27.

Figure 1-27 *FTP Server—Security Accounts*

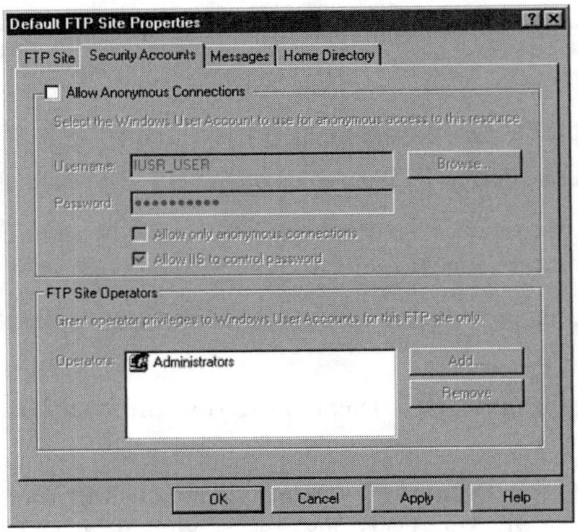

Step 6 Deselect the **Allow Anonymous Connections** check box. This prevents unauthorized users from accessing FTP files.

Step 7 Click the **Home Directory** tab, as shown in Figure 1-28. In the **FTP Site Directory** section, the **Local Path** field defines the location of files for sharing through FTP. The default location is c:\inetpub\ftproot.

Figure 1-28 *FTP Server—Home Directory*

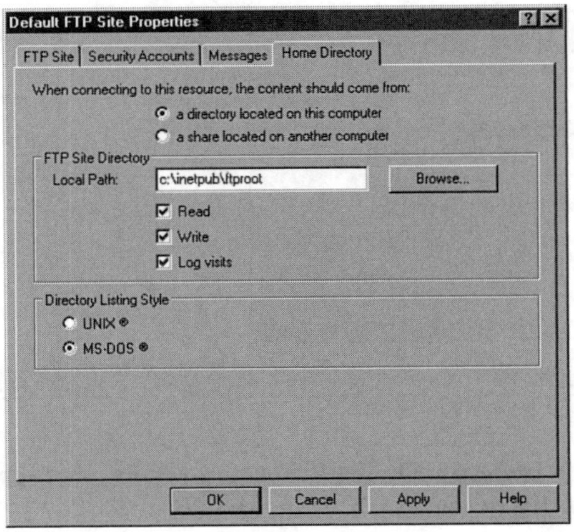

WARNING The default path for the location of files for sharing is c:\inetpub\ftproot. However, users are strongly encouraged to change the default path to a different drive, such as d:\ftproot. Also, this drive should not contain system files such as command.com. This prevents unicode traversal exploits on the FTP server.

Step 8 Select the **Read**, **Write**, **and Log visits** check boxes.

Step 9 Click the **OK** button to save these settings.

The server is now configured to accept incoming FTP read and write requests. In the preceding example, c:\inetpub\ftproot is the location of files that can be published through the FTP server. The username and password are the same as those created on this computer through the **Users and Password** option in the Control Panel.

Configuring Linux-Based FTP Servers

A command-line–based FTP server can be installed in Linux. This places less demand on the hardware because CLI-based applications eliminate the overhead of running a GUI. Although many FTP servers are available, the following are some popular FTP servers for Linux:

- **vsFTP**—Available at http://vsftpd.beasts.org/
- **ProFTP**—Available at http://www.proftpd.org/
- **WUFTP**—Available at http://www.wu-ftpd.org/

The server vsFTP, which stands for Very Secure FTP, is one of the most popular choices because of performance and security. Additionally, ProFTP is feature rich but has been reported to have more security vulnerabilities than vsFTP. Finally, WUFTP, although older than the other two, is not as secure as vsFTP. This section covers setting up vsFTP on a Linux-based FTP server.

The steps involved in deploying a vsFTP server are as follows:

- Install the vsFTP daemon.
- Edit the vsftpd.conf file.
- Create an FTP user.
- Restart the vsFTP server.

Following are the details of each step:

Step 1 **Install the vsFTP daemon**— Whereas the exact installation steps vary for each Linux distribution, for Debian Linux, use **apt-get install vsftpd**.

Step 2 **Edit the vsftpd.conf file**—The /etc/vsftpd.conf file controls the behavior of the vsFTP server. You can also specify the banner message. Following are the contents of the /etc/vsftpd.conf file:

```
# disable anonymous login
anonymous_enable=NO
# enable local user to login
local_enable=YES
write_enable=YES
local_umask=022
dirmessage_enable=YES
xferlog_enable=YES
connect_from_port_20=YES
ftpd_banner=UNAUTHORIZED ACCESS PROHIBITED, PLEASE EXIT NOW
```

Step 3 **Create an FTP user**—You must create a local user on the Linux machine. This username is used to log in to the FTP server. You can use the **useradd** command to create the new user. The following snippet illustrates a new user being created with the username **ftp-user**:

```
[root@localhost root]# /usr/sbin/useradd ftp-user
[root@localhost root]# passwd ftp-user
Changing password for user ftp-user.
New password:
Retype new password:
passwd: all authentication tokens updated successfully.
[root@localhost root]#
```

Step 4 **Restart the vsFTP server**—After editing the default /etc/vsftpd.conf file and creating a new user, you must restart the vsftpd server to allow the new settings to take effect. Use the following command:

```
[root@localhost root]# /etc/init.d/vsftpd restart
```

The files, shared through the FTP server, are located in the user's home directory. In the preceding example, the files uploaded by the user **ftp-user** can be found in the **/home/ftp-user** directory.

Configuring Cisco Devices to Use FTP

Cisco IOS Software also supports FTP for system file maintenance. Table 1-10 describes the IOS commands that perform various file maintenance operations.

Table 1-10 *IOS Commands for File Maintenance Operations*

Command	Explanation
Router# **copy** *flash-filesystem:filename* **ftp**:[[[//[*username* [:*password*]@]*location*]/*directory*]/*filename*]	Copies an image from flash memory to an FTP server
Router# **copy ftp:** [[[//[*username*[:*password*]@]*location*] / *directory*]/*filename*] *flash-filesystem*:[*filename*]	Copies an image from an FTP server to a flash memory file system
Router# **copy system:running-config ftp:**[[[// [*username*[:*password*]@]*location*] /*directory*]/*filename*] or Router# **copy nvram:startup-config ftp:[[[//** [*username*[:*password*]@]*location*] /*directory*]/*filename*]	Copies a configuration file from the router to the FTP server
Router# **copy ftp:**[[[//[*username*[:*password*]@]*location*]/ *directory*]/*filename*] **system:running-config** or Router# **copy ftp:**[[[//[*username*[:*password*]@]*location*] / *directory*]/*filename*] **nvram:startup-config**	Copies a configuration file from an FTP server to the router

Figure 1-29 illustrates a LAN with Router-Dallas and an FTP server.

Figure 1-29 *LAN with FTP Server*

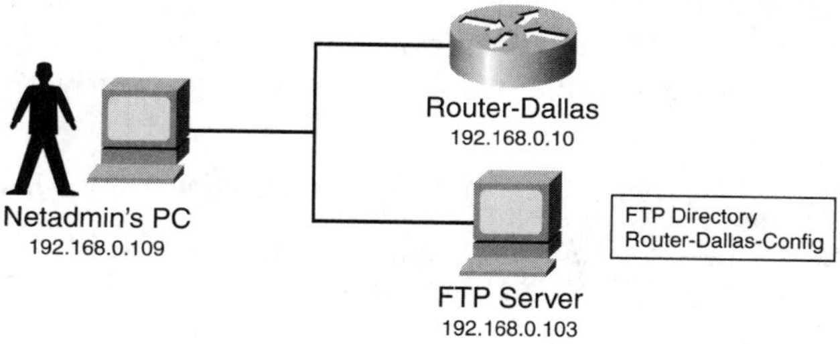

Example 1-14 shows the commands that copy the running configuration of the router (Router-Dallas with IP address 192.168.0.10) to the FTP server (IP address 192.168.0.103). The username is **ftp-user** and the password is **cisco123**.

Example 1-15 *Saving Router Configuration to FTP Server*

```
Router-Dallas#copy running ftp://ftp-user:cisco123@192.168.0.103/router-dallas-
  confg
Address or name of remote host [192.168.0.103]?
Destination filename [router-dallas-confg]?
Writing router-dallas-confg !
569 bytes copied in 3.188 secs (189 bytes/sec)
Router-Dallas#
```

Example 1-15 shows the output of the home directory on the Linux-based FTP server. The configuration file router-dallas-confg was created by ftp-user on August 31 at 20:39.

Example 1-16 *Contents of FTP Server*

```
[ftp-user@localhost ftp-user]$ ls -l
total 4
-rw-r--r--    1 ftp-user ftp-user      569 Aug 31 20:39 router-dallas-confg
```

The output of the ftproot directory on a Windows-based FTP server shows the same information, as depicted in Example 1-16.

Example 1-17 *Contents of Windows FTP Server*

```
C:\Inetpub\ftproot>dir
 Volume in drive C has no label.
 Volume Serial Number is 2C6A-5594

 Directory of C:\Inetpub\ftproot

08/31/2003  08:52p      <DIR>          .
08/31/2003  08:52p      <DIR>          ..
08/31/2003  08:51p                 569 router-dallas-confg
               1 File(s)            569 bytes
               2 Dir(s)   8,495,082,496 bytes free
```

Although better than TFTP, FTP suffers from a major security weakness—FTP transmits passwords in clear text. To overcome this limitation, Cisco IOS Release 12.2 T and higher support Secure Copy Protocol (SCP). The global configuration command to enable SCP is **ip scp server enable**. While Linux provides built-in support for SCP, you can use WinSCP3 (available for download at http://winscp.sourceforge.net) as an SCP client on MS-Windows machines.

The following Cisco.com URL provides more information on the IOS implementation of SCP:

> http://www.cisco.com/en/US/products/sw/iosswrel/ps1839/
> products_feature_guide09186a0080087b18.html#wp1043332

Summary

This chapter introduces the network administrator to the basic tools used for configuring and maintaining Cisco devices. These tools are part of the fundamental steps involved in the process of Cisco network administration. The network administrators should be able to perform the following tasks:

- Use MS-Windows– and Linux-based tools to establish a console connection to Cisco devices
- Use MS-Windows– and Linux-based tools for Telnet and SSH connections to Cisco devices

- Use Java-enabled web browsers to configure Cisco devices
- Deploy MS-Windows and Linux-based TFTP and FTP servers to maintain configuration images and operating system images for Cisco devices

Table 1-11 provides a list of the network administration tools covered in this chapter.

Table 1-11 *List of Tools Used in This Chapter*

Tool	Features	OS	Website/Details
HyperTerminal	Terminal emulation	Windows	Comes pre-installed with Windows OS
HyperTerminal Private Edition (HTPE)	Terminal emulation with Telnet client and ability to run macros	Windows	http://www.hilgraeve.com
Minicom	Terminal emulation with macros	Linux	http://freshmeat.net/redir/minicom/6437/url_homepage/minicom
GtkTerm	GUI-based terminal emulation with macros	Linux	http://www.jls-info.com/julien/linux/
PuTTY	SSH client	Windows	http://www.chiark.greenend.org.uk/~sgtatham/putty/
SSH Secure Shell Client	SSH client	Windows	http://www.ssh.com/
PIX Device Manager (PDM)	GUI based configuration and administration of Cisco PIX firewall	Web-based	http://www.cisco.com
Solarwinds TFTP server	TFTP server	Windows	http://www.solarwinds.net
3COM TFTP server	TFTP server	Windows	http://support.3com.com/software/utilities_for_windows_32_bit.htm
Linux TFTP server	TFTP server	Linux	http://www.rpmfind.net/
vsFTP server	FTP server	Linux	http://vsftpd.beasts.org/
Microsoft FTP server	FTP server	Windows	Part of the Microsoft Windows NT/200*X* server

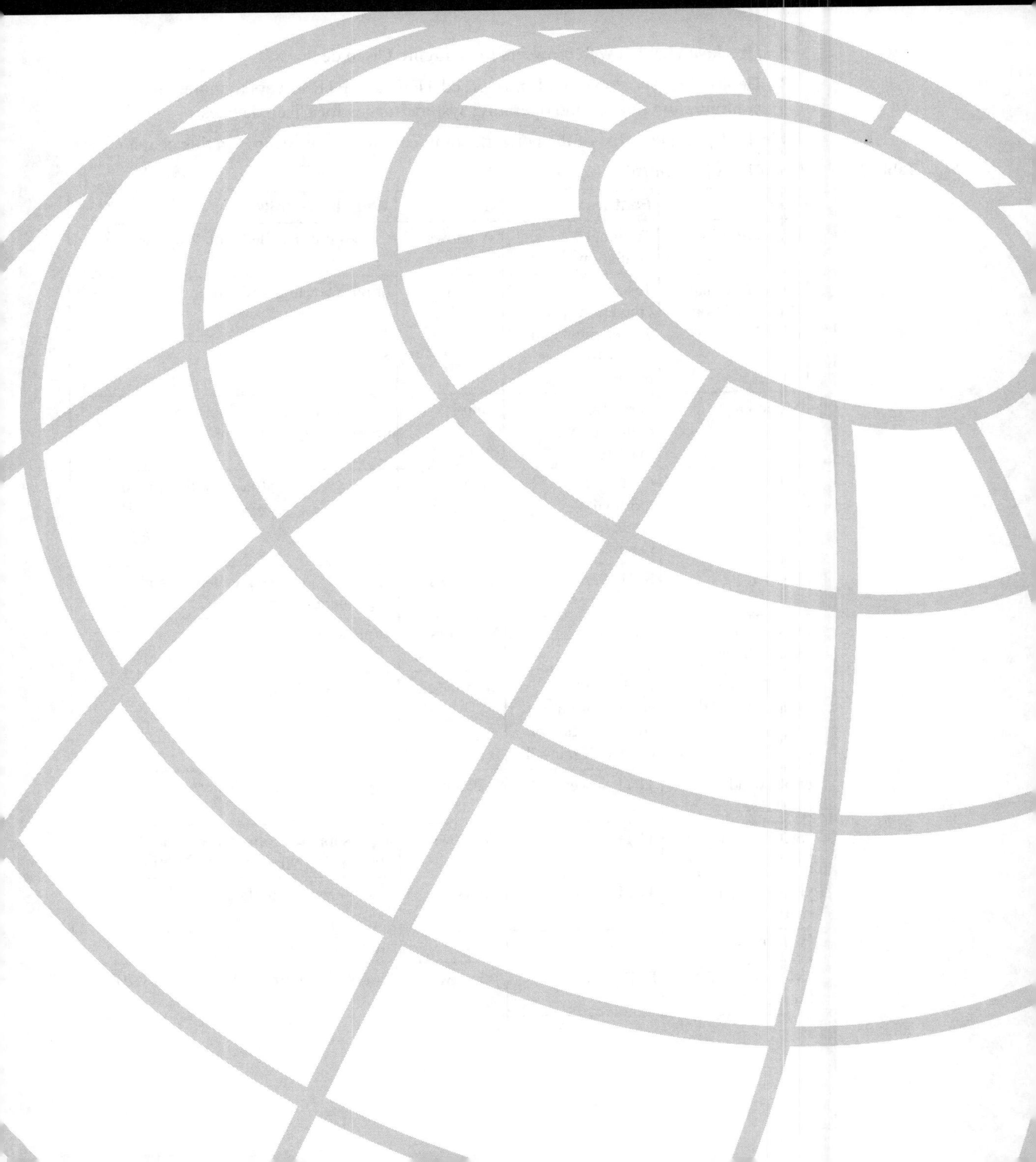

CHAPTER 2

Basic Network Connectivity

Essentially, networking is all about connecting two nodes. A successful network connection is established between any two nodes when data can flow from one node to the other. By monitoring the behavior of this path, network administrators can isolate and diagnose network issues.

This chapter discusses the most common tools used for testing and monitoring network connectivity. All the tools discussed in this chapter are available within the operating system and do not require installation. This chapter is divided into the following two sections:

- Common network connectivity tools
  - ping
  - traceroute
- Miscellaneous network connectivity tools
  - whois
  - nslookup
  - dig
  - netstat
  - nbtstat
  - arp

Netadmins with a beginner's level of experience can find this chapter useful. Networking professionals who are familiar with these tools can skip this chapter if they want to.

Basics of Network Monitoring Tools: ping and traceroute

Basic network tools like ping and traceroute are probably the most commonly used tools by network administrators. These two simple, yet powerful, tools can determine network parameters like connectivity, latency, hop count, round-trip delay, TimeToLive (TTL), and others. Netadmins can, then, use the results from these tools to isolate the root cause of a network issue.

Verifying Network Connectivity Using ping

Ping is arguably the most popular tool used to verify the following parameters:

- Network connectivity between two endpoints
- Round-trip delay in communicating with the host
- Packet loss

These parameters can be applied to diagnose network problems. Ping works by sending an Internet Control Message Protocol (ICMP) Echo Request message and waiting for the ICMP Echo Reply packets. Successful receipt of an Echo Reply message verifies that the connection is working. The round-trip time is calculated as the total time taken to successfully send and receive a packet. The value of round-trip time helps a network administrator to recognize a problem, even though the packets might be getting through.

NOTE According to its author, Mike Muuss, the ping tool is analogous to the sonar system, and hence he named it after the sound made by the sonar system. This is contrary to the popular myth of ping being an acronym of *p*acket *in*ternet *g*roper. The acronym was later coined by Dr. Dave Mills, who had previously done similar work.

Ping is a client-based tool for which no installation is required on the target node. It is preinstalled in most operating systems, and it requires no configuration to use. The following sections discuss the three main environments in which you can use ping:

- MS-Windows–based **ping** command
- Linux-based **ping** command
- IOS-based **ping** command

Using the MS-Windows–Based **ping** Command

You can use ping to verify network connectivity from a Windows machine. The **ping** command is preinstalled in MS-Windows (Windows 95 and higher). The command, which is command-line interface (CLI)–based, can be used through the MS-Windows command prompt. To verify network connectivity from an MS-Windows 95/98/Me/NT/2000/XP–based machine to a target host, follow these steps:

Step 1 Open a command-line session. In most versions of Windows, you do this by choosing **Start > Run**. In the **Run** window, enter **command** and click the **OK** button.

Step 2 In the command-line session, enter the **ping** *hostname-or-IP-address* command and press **Enter**.

Example 2-1 shows the use of a **ping** command in Windows XP. Depending on your version of Windows, the output can be slightly different. However, the functions discussed throughout this chapter are applicable to all versions of Windows.

Example 2-1 *Output of the* **ping** *Command in Windows XP*

```
C:\WINDOWS\system32>ping /?

Usage: ping [-t] [-a] [-n count] [-l size] [-f] [-i TTL] [-v TOS]
            [-r count] [-s count] [[-j host-list] ¦ [-k host-list]]
            [-w timeout] target_name

Options:
    -t             Ping the specified host until stopped.
                   To see statistics and continue - type Control-Break;
                   To stop - type Control-C.
    -a             Resolve addresses to hostnames.
    -n count       Number of echo requests to send.
    -l size        Send buffer size.
    -f             Set Don't Fragment flag in packet.
    -i TTL         Time To Live.
    -v TOS         Type Of Service.
    -r count       Record route for count hops.
    -s count       Timestamp for count hops.
    -j host-list   Loose source route along host-list.
    -k host-list   Strict source route along host-list.
-w timeout     Timeout in milliseconds to wait for each reply.
```

In Example 2-1, the **-t**, **-a**, and **-w** options are available in all versions of Windows. These options are discussed in greater detail in the following sections.

NOTE Before verifying network connectivity to remote machines, it is good practice to verify that the Transmission Control Protocol/Internet Protocol (TCP/IP) stack on the Windows machine works correctly. To verify the IP address of the local Windows machine, open a command prompt and enter **ipconfig**. This command shows the configured IP address for each of the network interfaces, along with their subnet mask and default gateway. Try using the **ipconfig /all** command for detailed information.

For Linux/UNIX–based machines, use the **ifconfig** command.

Verifying Basic Network Connectivity with the **ping** Command

The scenario in Figure 2-1 shows a Windows computer connected to its default gateway through an Ethernet network.

Figure 2-1 *MS-Windows–Based* **ping** *Command*

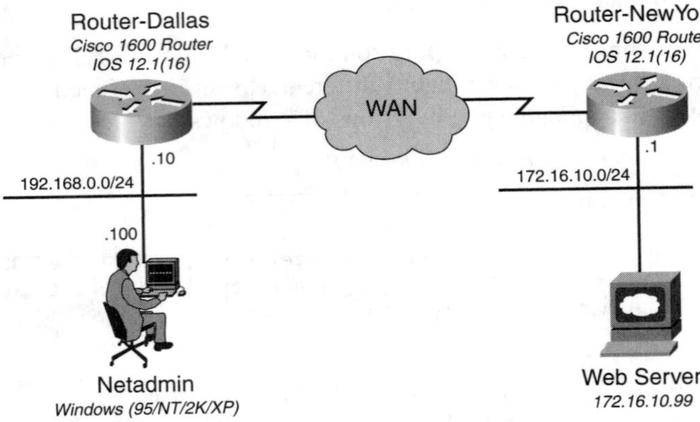

To verify the connectivity between the Windows host and its default gateway, the administrator enters the **ping 192.168.0.10** command on the Windows XP computer.

Example 2-2 shows the output of the ping session.

Example 2-2 *Using the* **ping** *Command to Verify Connectivity*

```
C:\WINDOWS\system32>ping 192.168.0.10
Pinging 192.168.0.10 with 32 bytes of data:
Reply from 192.168.0.10: bytes=32 time=30ms TTL=255
Reply from 192.168.0.10: bytes=32 time=15ms TTL=255
Reply from 192.168.0.10: bytes=32 time=15ms TTL=255
Reply from 192.168.0.10: bytes=32 time=10ms TTL=255

Ping statistics for 192.168.0.10:
    Packets: Sent = 4, Received = 4, Lost = 0 (0% loss),
Approximate round trip times in milli-seconds:
Minimum = 10ms, Maximum = 30ms, Average = 17ms
```

The first line of the **ping** command output shows that the **ping** command is using 32 bytes of data in the payload.

Lines 2–5 of the command output show the details of each packet as follows:

- 192.168.0.10 is the IP address of the target.
- 32 is the size of each transmitted packet.
- The round-trip time is measured in milliseconds (ms).
- The TimeToLive (TTL) field is set to 255.

If the connection is of bad quality or the host is down, the output shows a **Request timed out** message instead of the message shown in Example 2-2.

Lines 6–9 show the summary of the result. Because the 4 packets were sent and received, there is 0 percent loss. Also, the minimum, average, and maximum values of the round-trip time are calculated based on the round-trip time of each packet. Depending on the speed of the link, the round-trip times and TTL values can differ.

TIP Use the **ping** command to determine the round-trip time for a network segment. Round-trip time is important for proper functioning of some real-time applications. For example, Voice over IP (VoIP) has a maximum of 300 ms, whereas Citrix has a maximum of 250 ms for acceptable performance.

Inaccurate Results of the **ping** Command

Ping uses ICMP traffic, whereas most of the user traffic consists of TCP or User Datagram Protocol (UDP). If ICMP traffic is blocked on a network, the web traffic can still pass but ping will fail. Thus, ping can potentially produce inaccurate results. This section discusses inaccurate results because of the following issues:

- Timeout value of the **ping** command
- Maximum transmission unit (MTU) value of the link

Timeout Value of the Windows **ping** *Command*

The default timeout value for the Windows **ping** command is 1000 milliseconds (1 second). If the Echo Reply message fails to reach the sender before the end of 1000 milliseconds, the packet is considered lost. The output of the **ping** command shows the **Request timed out** message (see Example 2-3). This can cause inaccurate results on slower links such as satellite-based connections. You should use the **–w** *milli-seconds* option of the **ping** command to change the default timeout value. For example, using the **ping -w 5000 192.168.0.10** command sets the timeout value to 5000 milliseconds (5 seconds).

Example 2-3 shows the output of the **ping** command. The destination address 172.16.10.99 is a web server, as previously shown in Figure 2-1.

Example 2-3 **Ping** *Command with Increased Timeout*

```
C:\WINDOWS\system32>ping  172.16.10.99
Pinging 172.16.10.99 with 32 bytes of data:

Request timed out.
Request timed out.
Request timed out.
Request timed out.

Ping statistics for 172.16.10.99:
    Packets: Sent = 4, Received = 0, Lost = 4 (100% loss),
```

continues

Example 2-3 **Ping** *Command with Increased Timeout (Continued)*

```
C:\WINDOWS\system32>ping 172.16.10.99 -w 5000

Pinging 172.16.10.99 with 32 bytes of data:

Reply from 172.16.10.99: bytes=32 time=1032ms TTL=103
Reply from 172.16.10.99: bytes=32 time=1055ms TTL=103
Reply from 172.16.10.99: bytes=32 time=1059ms TTL=103
Reply from 172.16.10.99: bytes=32 time=1096ms TTL=103

Ping statistics for 172.16.10.99:
    Packets: Sent = 4, Received = 4, Lost = 0 (0% loss),
Approximate round trip times in milli-seconds:
    Minimum = 1055ms, Maximum = 1032ms, Average = 1010ms
```

Example 2-3 shows that changing the timeout value to 5000 ms by using the **–w 5000** option results in no timeouts.

MTU Value of the Link

The maximum IP datagram size, also known as the MTU, depends on the type of network. On an Ethernet network, the MTU is 1500 bytes. When a host transmits an IP datagram larger than the MTU size, the router fragments the datagram into smaller chunks. The receiving station reassembles the smaller chunks to recover the original IP datagram. If the Don't Fragment (DF) bit in the IP header of the datagram is set, the router cannot fragment the datagram. But at the same time, larger packets cannot be transmitted on links with lower MTU values. Hence, the router drops the bigger packets and sends an ICMP **Destination Unreachable, fragmentation needed and DF set** message to the source. On receiving the ICMP message, the source host lowers the datagram size.

Because of growing security concerns, ICMP traffic is often blocked by firewalls and routers. Netadmins selectively allow ICMP Echo Request and Echo Reply messages (which are legitimate ping traffic) through the firewalls. In such cases, the source host never receives the ICMP Unreachable messages and continues to send the larger packets. The network connection between the source and destination hosts is effectively down, because the intermediate router drops the packets.

When a Netadmin uses ping to troubleshoot MTU-related connectivity issues, the ping traffic always succeeds. This is because Windows uses a default ping packet size of 56 bytes, which is smaller than the typical MTU size of the network. This leads to inaccurate conclusions. Ping packets with the DF bit set and with larger IP datagram sizes produce accurate results. The same applies to MTU tests using Linux- or IOS-based ping. Linux uses a default packet size of 56 bytes, whereas IOS uses 100 bytes.

To elaborate further, consider the network scenario shown in Figure 2-1. The Netadmin is facing connectivity issues to the web server 172.16.10.99. All the users in the 192.168.0.0/24 LAN can access the remote web server but cannot download large files from the server.

The Netadmin pings from the Windows machine (192.168.0.100) to the web server (172.16.10.99) using the **ping 172.16.10.99** command. The results are successful, as shown in Example 2-4. Suspecting the culprit to be MTU size, the Netadmin sends larger ping packets with the DF bit set. As mentioned in Example 2-1, the **-f** option sets the DF bit, and the **-l** *buffer-size* option specifies the data payload size. The **ping -f -l 1500 172.16.10.99** command sets the DF bit and specifies the packet size of 1500 bytes. The output in Example 2-4 shows that the replies were not received. Instead, the output displays the **Request timed out** message. The system might also display the **Packet needs to be fragmented but DF set** message.

On lowering the payload size to 1273 bytes, the replies are still failing. After reducing the payload size to 1272, the replies are received.

The actual MTU of the link is the sum of payload size and the IP header size. Because Windows uses 28 bytes for the IP header of the ping packet, the MTU in this example is 1272 + 28 = 1300 bytes. Hence, the MTU for successful data transfer from the web server is 1300 bytes. The webmaster should reduce the MTU size on the web server to 1300 to solve the issue.

Example 2-4 *Using the* **ping** *Command to Determine MTU Size*

```
# Regular ping succeeds
c:\windows\system32>ping 172.16.10.99

Pinging 172.16.10.99 with 32 bytes of data:

Reply from 172.16.10.99: bytes=32 time=17ms TTL=254
Reply from 172.16.10.99: bytes=32 time=18ms TTL=254
Reply from 172.16.10.99: bytes=32 time=18ms TTL=254
Reply from 172.16.10.99: bytes=32 time=21ms TTL=254

Ping statistics for 172.16.10.99:
    Packets: Sent = 4, Received = 4, Lost = 0 (0% loss),
Approximate round trip times in milli-seconds:
    Minimum = 17ms, Maximum = 21ms, Average = 18ms

# ping packet with DF bit set and payload size 1500 fails
c:\windows\system32>ping -f -l 1500 172.16.10.99

Pinging 172.16.10.99 with 1273 bytes of data:

Request timed out.
Request timed out.
Request timed out.
Request timed out.

Ping statistics for 172.16.10.99:
```

continues

Example 2-4 *Using the* **ping** *Command to Determine MTU Size (Continued)*

```
    Packets: Sent = 4, Received = 0, Lost = 4 (100% loss),

# ping packet with DF bit set and payload size 1273 still  fails
c:\windows\system32>ping -f -l 1273 172.16.10.99

Pinging 172.16.10.99 with 1273 bytes of data:

Request timed out.
Request timed out.
Request timed out.
Request timed out.

Ping statistics for 172.16.10.99:
    Packets: Sent = 4, Received = 0, Lost = 4 (100% loss),

# ping packet with DF bit set and payload size 1272 succeeds
c:\windows\system32>ping -f -l 1272 172.16.10.99

Pinging 172.16.10.99 with 1272 bytes of data:

Reply from 172.16.10.99: bytes=1272 time=25ms TTL=254
Reply from 172.16.10.99: bytes=1272 time=24ms TTL=254
Reply from 172.16.10.99: bytes=1272 time=26ms TTL=254
Reply from 172.16.10.99: bytes=1272 time=23ms TTL=254

Ping statistics for 172.16.10.99:
    Packets: Sent = 4, Received = 4, Lost = 0 (0% loss),
Approximate round trip times in milli-seconds:
Minimum = 23ms, Maximum = 26ms, Average = 24ms
```

NOTE MTU-related issues are common in IP Security (IPSec)–based virtual private networks (VPN). IPSec encapsulates the original IP datagram with an IPSec header, thus making the packet larger. The following two documents, which you can find on Cisco.com, provide more information on the MTU issue:

- IP Fragmentation and MTU Path Discovery with VPN (http://www.cisco.com/en/US/products/hw/routers/ps4081/products_tech_note09186a0080094268.shtml)
- Adjusting IP MTU, TCP MSS, and PMTUD on Windows and Sun Systems (http://www.cisco.com/en/US/tech/tk870/tk472/tk473/technologies_tech_note09186a008011a218.shtml)

Because of misuse of ICMP for network reconnaissance by malicious users, Netadmins often block ICMP on the router or firewalls. The unwanted side effect of this action is blocking the legitimate ping traffic.

The ping process is assigned a lower priority on the routers. If the router CPU utilization is high, the ping process might not respond, although the legitimate traffic is flowing. Additionally, the ICMP traffic is often assigned a lower priority.

Quite often, as a security measure, firewalls block traffic originating from the outside network into the inside (protected) network. In such cases, only the ping initiated from the inside network succeeds. The ping from outside the network fails.

All these factors can also lead to inaccurate and misleading results from the **ping** command.

Using Continuous ping for Extended Monitoring

In a real network, successful receipt of four ping packets does not guarantee a perfect connection. The result merely indicates that the connection was working during the test interval. However, certain network conditions, such as routing or switching reconvergence, can cause a periodic drop in the connection. For example, the drops might only occur once every 5 minutes but cause the user sessions to reset. The administrator might need to run the **ping** command for an extended period of time to detect such conditions. Refer to the output of the **ping /?** command in Example 2-1 for the option available for running the **ping** command for an extended period of time. This option, also shown in Example 2-1, is as follows:

```
Options:
    -t              Ping the specified host until stopped.
                    To see statistics and continue - type Control-Break;
                    To stop - type Control-C.
```

To run a continuous **ping** command, use the **–t** switch.

Press **Ctrl-C** to stop the command as needed and view the summary. Alternately, press **Ctrl-Break** to view the summary without stopping.

Example 2-5 shows the output of an extended **ping** command.

Example 2-5 *Extended* **ping** *Command*

```
C:\WINDOWS\system32>ping -t 192.168.0.10

Pinging 192.168.0.10 with 32 bytes of data:

Reply from 192.168.0.10: bytes=32 time=87ms TTL=255
Reply from 192.168.0.10: bytes=32 time=9ms TTL=255
Reply from 192.168.0.10: bytes=32 time=61ms TTL=255
Reply from 192.168.0.10: bytes=32 time=32ms TTL=255
Reply from 192.168.0.10: bytes=32 time=104ms TTL=255
Reply from 192.168.0.10: bytes=32 time=11ms TTL=255
Reply from 192.168.0.10: bytes=32 time=27ms TTL=255
Reply from 192.168.0.10: bytes=32 time=14ms TTL=255
Request timed out.
Reply from 192.168.0.10: bytes=32 time=11ms TTL=255
Reply from 192.168.0.10: bytes=32 time=11ms TTL=255
Reply from 192.168.0.10: bytes=32 time=16ms TTL=255
```

continues

Example 2-5 *Extended* **ping** *Command (Continued)*

```
Ping statistics for 192.168.0.10:
    Packets: Sent = 12, Received = 11, Lost = 1 (8% loss),
Approximate round trip times in milli-seconds:
    Minimum = 9ms, Maximum = 104ms, Average = 34ms
Control-Break (the user entered CNTRL-Break for summary)
Reply from 192.168.0.10: bytes=32 time=95ms TTL=255
Reply from 192.168.0.10: bytes=32 time=9ms TTL=255
Reply from 192.168.0.10: bytes=32 time=15ms TTL=255

Ping statistics for 192.168.0.10:
    Packets: Sent = 15, Received = 14, Lost = 1 (6% loss),
Approximate round trip times in milli-seconds:
    Minimum = 9ms, Maximum = 104ms, Average = 35ms
Control-C (the user entered CNTRL-C to stop)
^C
```

As shown on line 10 of Example 2-5, the packet loss results in the **Request timed out** message. Also, lines 15–18 show the summary of the results with 1 packet lost [or 8 percent (100 * 1/12)]. The command output continues until the user presses **Ctrl-C,** which is shown in the highlighted text as **^C**.

Using the **ping** Command for Name Resolution

On many occasions, an administrator needs to investigate a network issue to isolate a troublemaker's IP address when the administrator doesn't know the Domain Name System (DNS) name. For example, a host might be infected by a virus, or music files can be illegally shared by a host. The network traffic or syslog can indicate the IP address of the offending host, but not the DNS name.

The DNS name of a device can be resolved by pinging the IP address of the target host in conjunction with the –**a** option, as shown in Example 2-6.

Example 2-6 *Using the* **ping** *Command to Resolve Host Name*

```
C:\WINDOWS\system32>ping -a 192.168.0.10

Pinging Router-Dallas [192.168.0.10] with 32 bytes of data:

Reply from 192.168.0.10: bytes=32 time=9ms TTL=255
Reply from 192.168.0.10: bytes=32 time=149ms TTL=255
Reply from 192.168.0.10: bytes=32 time=6ms TTL=255
Reply from 192.168.0.10: bytes=32 time=123ms TTL=255

Ping statistics for 192.168.0.10:
    Packets: Sent = 4, Received = 4, Lost = 0 (0% loss),
Approximate round trip times in milli-seconds:
    Minimum = 6ms, Maximum = 149ms, Average = 71ms
```

The first line of the output shows the host name of the device 192.168.0.10 as Router-Dallas.

Both the source and destination should be configured with valid DNS information for successful resolution of the host name to the IP address. If you can ping the device by its IP address but not by its host name, the problem is usually a missing or incorrect DNS entry.

NOTE Only the MS-Windows–based **ping** command features the IP address–to–name resolution mechanism. On most other platforms, such as Linux, this feature is not included. Use the **nslookup** command in Windows or **dig** command in Linux to resolve the name of a remote device, given its IP address.

Using the Linux-Based **ping** Command

Almost all Linux distributions (various distributions of GNU/Linux using Linux kernels) come with a **ping** command. The command is similar to its Windows counterpart. To verify network connectivity from a Linux-based machine to a target host, follow these steps:

Step 1 Start a command-line session.

Step 2 Type the command **ping** *hostname-or-IP-address* and then press **Enter**.

NOTE Unlike MS-Windows, commands in Linux are case-sensitive. **PING** is not the same as **ping** in Linux.

Example 2-7 shows the output of the **ping** command in Linux.

Example 2-7 *Output of the* **ping** *Command in Linux*

```
netadmin@linuxbox:/$ ping
usage: ping [-LRdfnqrv] [-c count] [-i wait] [-l preload]
        [-p pattern] [-s packetsize] [-t ttl] [-I interface address] host
```

Although the exact command output can vary according to the Linux distribution and version, Table 2-1 lists some of the options available for Debian Linux 3.0 and higher.

Table 2-1 *Linux* **ping** *Options*

Option	Description
-b	Allows pinging to a broadcast address.
-c *number-of-packets*	Specifies the number of ping packets to be sent.

continues

Table 2-1 *Linux* **ping** *Options (Continued)*

Option	Description
-i *seconds*	Specifies the interval in seconds between sending each ping packet; the default is 1 second.
-I *interface address*	In the case of multiple interface addresses, specifies the source address used by the ping packet.
-M *hint*	Specifies Path MTU discovery; possible values are **do** (set DF bit) and **dont** (do not set DF bit). Useful when used in conjunction with **-s** options for isolating MTU issues.
-q	Suppresses output details and only displays summary.
-s *data-bytes*	Specifies the number of bytes of data; default is 56 bytes. Useful in conjunction with **-M** options in troubleshooting MTU-related issues.
-t *ttl*	Specifies the TTL.
-v	Displays details. Useful for overriding the default ping behavior to suppress output when replies are not being received.
-V	Only displays the version of the **ping** command; additional options are ignored.
-w *seconds*	Specifies the maximum interval in seconds, after which the **ping** command stops.
-W *timeout-seconds*	Specifies the timeout interval for each packet. If the reply is not received within the timeout period, the packet is assumed to be lost.

A Continuous **ping** Command for Basic Connectivity

The scenario in Figure 2-2 shows a Linux-based computer connected to the default gateway through an Ethernet network.

Figure 2-2 *Network Setup for a Linux Computer*

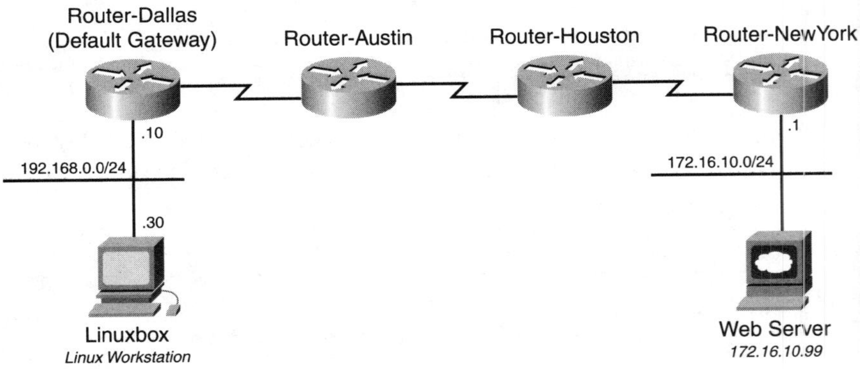

To verify the connectivity between these two machines, the administrator enters the following command on the Linux computer:

```
ping router-dallas
```

Example 2-8 shows the output of the session.

Example 2-8 *Using the* **ping** *Command to Verify Connectivity*

```
netadmin@linuxbox:/$ ping router-dallas
ping router-dallas (192.168.0.10): 56 data bytes
64 bytes from 192.168.0.10: icmp_seq=0 ttl=255 time=2.3 ms
64 bytes from 192.168.0.10: icmp_seq=5 ttl=255 time=2.3 ms
64 bytes from 192.168.0.10: icmp_seq=6 ttl=255 time=2.3 ms

--- router-dallas192.168.0.10 ping statistics ---
7 packets transmitted, 3 packets received, 57% packet loss
round-trip min/avg/max = 2.3/2.3/2.3 ms
```

The first line shows that the IP address of the target Router-Dallas is 192.168.0.10.

The next three lines of the command output show the details of each packet as follows:

- 192.168.0.10 is the IP address of the target.
- The sequence number of each packet is denoted by **icmp_seq**, followed by an integer. The sequence number is useful for quickly identifying missing reply packets. With every instance of the **ping** command, the sequence number starts with 0 and is incremented for each packet.
- The round-trip time of the packets is measured in milliseconds (ms).
- The TimeToLive field is 255.

The output of the **ping** command shows that only the packets with sequence numbers 0, 5, and 6 were received. The packets with sequence numbers 1, 2, 3, and 4 are missing or lost. This is confirmed in the last two lines, which show the summary statistics. Of the 7 packets transmitted, only 3 were received. Also, the minimum, average, and maximum round-trip values are calculated based on the round-trip times of the received packets.

Using Limited ping for Basic Connectivity Testing

Unlike the Windows **ping** command, the default **ping** command in Linux continuously sends packets until it is interrupted by the administrator by pressing **Ctrl-C**. To avoid the default behavior and limit the maximum number of packets sent by **ping** command, you can use the **-c** option.

Example 2-9 shows the **ping** command using the **-c 2** option for sending 2 packets to the target Router-Dallas.

Example 2-9 *Using the* **ping** *Command to Verify Connectivity*

```
netadmin@linuxbox:/$ ping -c 2 router-dallas
PING router-dallas192.168.0.10 (192.168.0.10): 56 data bytes
64 bytes from 192.168.0.10: icmp_seq=0 ttl=255 time=4.4 ms
64 bytes from 192.168.0.10: icmp_seq=1 ttl=255 time=2.2 ms

--- router-dallas192.168.0.10 ping statistics ---
2 packets transmitted, 2 packets received, 0% packet loss
round-trip min/avg/max = 2.2/3.3/4.4 ms
```

Using ping for MTU Testing

As discussed in the Windows-based ping section, ping can also determine the MTU of the network path between two nodes. To determine the MTU using the Linux-based **ping** command, use the **-M** option to set the DF bit and use the **-s** option to specify the data size.

Consider the scenario shown in Figure 2-2. The Netadmin is trying to determine the MTU between the 192.168.0.0/24 LAN and the web server 172.16.10.99. To determine the MTU, the Netadmin uses the **ping -c 4 -M do -s 1273 172.16.10.99** command. The **-c 4** option limits the count to only 4 ping packets. The **-s 1273** option specifies 1273 bytes of data, while the **-M do** option sets the DF bit. As shown in Example 2-10, 0 packets were received. After reducing the data byte size to 1272, the replies are successfully received.

The actual MTU of the link is the sum of the payload size and the IP header size. Because Linux uses 28 bytes for the IP header of the ping packet, the MTU in this example is 1272 + 28 = 1300 bytes. Unlike the Windows **ping** command, which only shows the size of the data payload, the Linux version also shows the actual packet size.

Example 2-10 *MTU Testing Using the Linux* **ping** *Command*

```
netadmin@linuxbox:/$ ping -c 4 -M do -s 1273 172.16.10.99
# Linux ping command also shows the actual size of IP packet
# The data payload is 1273 bytes, the total IP packet is 1301 bytes long
PING 172.16.10.99 (172.16.10.99) 1273(1301) bytes of data.

--- 172.16.10.99 ping statistics ---
4 packets transmitted, 0 received, 100% packet loss, time 3018ms

 netadmin@linuxbox:/$ ping -c 4 -M do -s 1272 172.16.10.99
PING 172.16.10.99 (172.16.10.99) 1272(1300) bytes of data.
1280 bytes from 172.16.10.99: icmp_seq=1 ttl=124 time=32.9 ms
1280 bytes from 172.16.10.99: icmp_seq=2 ttl=124 time=24.5 ms
1280 bytes from 172.16.10.99: icmp_seq=3 ttl=124 time=25.6 ms
1280 bytes from 172.16.10.99: icmp_seq=4 ttl=124 time=29.5 ms

--- 172.16.10.99 ping statistics ---
4 packets transmitted, 4 received, 0% packet loss
rtt min/avg/max = 24.592/28.189/32.940 ms
```

Using the IOS-Based **ping** Command

The IOS **ping** command enables an Netadmin to quickly diagnose network issues from within the IOS shell. As a result, IOS-based **ping** is one of the most commonly used utilities. In addition to IP protocol, the Cisco IOS Software–based **ping** command also supports Apollo, AppleTalk, Clns, Decnet, IP, IPX, Vines, XNS, and so on. Cisco IOS offers the following two modes of the **ping** command:

- User mode
- Privileged mode

User Mode **ping** Command

The user mode **ping** command has the basic feature for users who do not have system privileges. This feature allows the Cisco IOS Software to perform the simple default ping functionality for a number of protocols, including IP, IPX, AppleTalk, and so on.

NOTE Throughout this chapter and the book, the term *IOS-based devices* refers to the Cisco routers and switches that are loaded with Cisco IOS Software. Unless specified otherwise, the features and commands discussed should be available on Cisco IOS Release 12.0 and later.

To verify network connectivity from an IOS-based device to a target host, follow these steps:

Step 1 Start a console or Telnet session to the IOS-based device and log in to the user mode using the username and password, if they are required.

Step 2 Type the **ping** [*protocol*] {*host* | *address*} command and press **Enter**.

Table 2-2 lists the options available with the IOS **ping** command.

Table 2-2 *IOS* **ping** *Options*

Option	Description
protocol	(Optional) Specifies the protocol; possible keywords are **apollo, appletalk**, **clns**, **decnet**, **ip**, **ipx**, **vines**, and **xns**. The default is **IP**.
host	Host name of the target.
address	IP address of the target.

The scenario in Figure 2-3 depicts a regular user trying to verify the connectivity from the IOS device Router-Dallas to a website http://www.testwebsite.com.

The user first initiates a Telnet session from the machine LINUXBOX to Router-Dallas to log in to the user EXEC mode.

From the user EXEC prompt (Router-Dallas>), the user issues a **ping** command from the router to the target host. The host name gets resolved to the IP address through the DNS server 192.168.0.15.

The captured session in Example 2-11 details the steps involved and the output of the IOS **ping** command.

Figure 2-3 *Using the* **ping** *Command from an IOS Device*

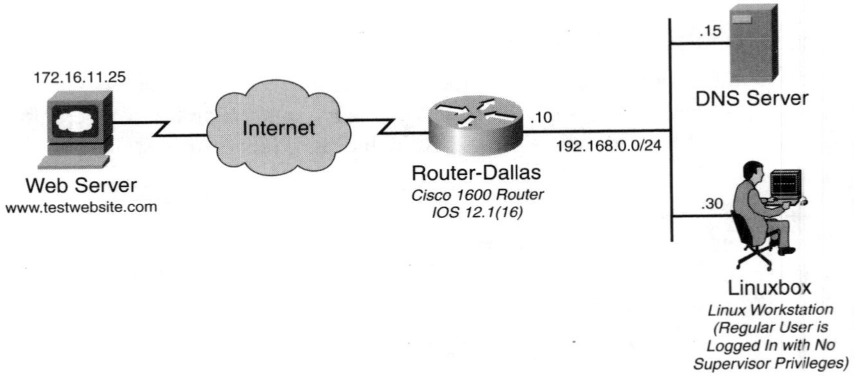

Example 2-11 *IOS* **ping** *Command*

```
spope@linuxbox:/$ telnet 192.168.0.10
Trying 192.168.0.10...
Connected to 192.168.0.10.
Escape character is '^]'.

User Access Verification
Password:

Router-Dallas>ping www.testwebsite.com
Translating "www.testwebsite.com"...domain server (192.168.0.15) [OK]

Type escape sequence to abort.
Sending 5, 100-byte ICMP Echos to 172.16.11.25, timeout is 2 seconds:
!!!!!
Success rate is 100 percent (5/5), round-trip min/avg/max = 16/22/28 ms
```

The last three lines of the output summarize the results of the IOS **ping** command. These lines show that the router sent 5 ICMP Echo packets of 100 bytes each to the IP address (172.16.11.25) of the target host. The timeout value for each packet was set to 2 seconds.

In other words, the packet would be treated as lost if no replies were received within 2 seconds.

In the summary line that shows five exclamation marks, each exclamation mark signifies a successful reply from the target. Depending on the state of the message received, the output can contain other test characters, as shown is Table 2-3. Recall that the output of the Windows/Linux **ping** command shows details of each packet. In contrast, the IOS shows only a single character for the result of the ICMP reply messages.

The last output line summarizes the success rate based on the total packets sent and received. Based on the round-trip times of the received packets, the minimum, average, and maximum round-trip times are also calculated.

Table 2-3 **Ping** *Test Characters*

Character	Description
!	Each exclamation point indicates receipt of a reply.
..	Each period indicates that the network server timed out while waiting for a reply.
U	Indicates a destination unreachable error.
C	Indicates that a congestion experienced packet was received.
I	Indicates that the user interrupted the test.
?	Indicates an unknown packet type.
&	Indicates that the packet lifetime was exceeded.

TIP The output of the **ping** command can be interrupted by pressing **Ctrl-Shift-6** followed by pressing **X**.

Privileged Mode ping Command

As seen in the preceding section, the basic IOS **ping** command is limited in terms of available options. Some of the default parameters used by the **ping** command are as follows:

- Packet count of 5
- Packet size of 100 bytes
- Timeout value of 2 seconds
- Outgoing interface as the source address of the packets

The IOS **ping** command in privileged EXEC mode provides customizable options, as shown in Table 2-4.

Table 2-4 *Enhanced* **ping** *Options*

Field	Description
Protocol [ip]:	Specifies one of the supported protocols; choices are appletalk, clns, ip, novell, apollo, vines, decnet, and xns. Default: ip.
Target IP address:	Prompts for the IP address or host name of the destination node that you plan to **ping**. If you have specified a supported protocol other than IP, enter an appropriate address for that protocol here. Default: none.
Repeat count [5]:	Number of ping packets that are to be sent to the destination address. Useful for pinging with large numbers of packets. Default: **5**.
Datagram size [100]:	Size of the ping packet (in bytes). Useful in diagnosing slower link issues by specifying a larger packet size. Also handy in isolating MTU-related issues when used in conjunction with the DF option. Default: **100**. In contrast, the Windows and Linux counterparts only let you specify the size of the payload.
Timeout in seconds [2]:	Timeout interval (in seconds). The ping is declared successful only if the Echo Reply packet is received before this time interval. Useful in diagnosing slower links. Default: **2**.
Extended commands [n]:	Specifies whether a series of additional commands appears. Default: **no**.
Source address or interface:	The interface or IP address of the router to use as a source address for the probes. The router normally picks the IP address of the outbound interface to use. The interface might also be mentioned, but with the correct syntax, as follows: `Source address or interface: ethernet 0` Useful for diagnosing connectivity issues related to routing misconfiguration on hosts and routers.
Type of service [0]:	Specifies the type of service (ToS). The requested ToS is placed in each probe, but there is no guarantee that all routers can process the ToS. Default: **0**.
Set DF bit in IP header? [no]:	Specifies setting the Don't Fragment (DF) bit on the ping packet. If set to **yes**, the DF option prevents fragmentation when the packet has to go through a segment with a smaller maximum transmission unit (MTU); you receive an error message from the device that wanted to fragment the packet. This is useful for determining the smallest MTU in the path to a destination. Handy in isolating MTU-related issues through VPN tunnels. Default: **no**.

Table 2-4 *Enhanced* **ping** *Options (Continued)*

Field	Description
Validate reply data? [no]:	Specifies whether to validate the reply data. Default: **no**.
Data pattern [0xABCD]	Specifies the data pattern. Different data patterns can troubleshoot line coding such as AMI or B8ZS, framing errors, and clocking problems on serial lines. Default: **0xABCD**.
Loose, Strict, Record, Timestamp, Verbose[none]:	IP header options. This prompt offers the following options: • **Verbose**—Automatically selected along with any other option. • **Record**—Displays the addresses of the hops (up to nine) that the packet goes through. • **Loose**—Allows you to influence the path by specifying the addresses of the hops that you want the packet to go through. • **Strict**—Specifies the hops that you want the packet to go through, but no other hops are allowed to be visited. • **Timestamp**—Measures the round-trip time to particular hosts. The difference between using the Record option of this command and using the **traceroute** command is that the Record option not only informs you of the hops that the Echo Request (ping) went through to get to the destination, but it also informs you of the hops it visited on the return path. With the **traceroute** command, you do not get information about the path that the Echo Reply takes. The **traceroute** command issues prompts for the required fields. Note that the **traceroute** command places the requested options in each probe; however, there is no guarantee that all routers (or end nodes) can process the options. Default: **none**.
Sweep range of sizes [n]:	Allows you to vary the sizes of the Echo packets being sent. This determines the minimum sizes of the MTUs configured on the nodes along the path to the destination address. Performance problems caused by packet fragmentation are thus reduced. Default: **no**.

The steps involved in initiating a privileged EXEC mode **ping** command are as follows:

Step 1 Start a console or Telnet session to the IOS-based device and log in to the privileged EXEC mode using the appropriate username and password. (Privileged EXEC mode can be identified by the pound sign (#) in the prompt. **Router#** indicates privileged EXEC mode, while **Router>** indicates user EXEC mode.)

Step 2 Type the **ping** command and press **Enter**. Follow the prompts and enter suitable information for each field. For an explanation of each field, refer to Table 2-2.

Consider the scenario in Figure 2-4 in which all the users in the subnet 192.168.0.0/24 are not able to connect to server 172.16.11.50.

Figure 2-4 *Ping from IOS Device*

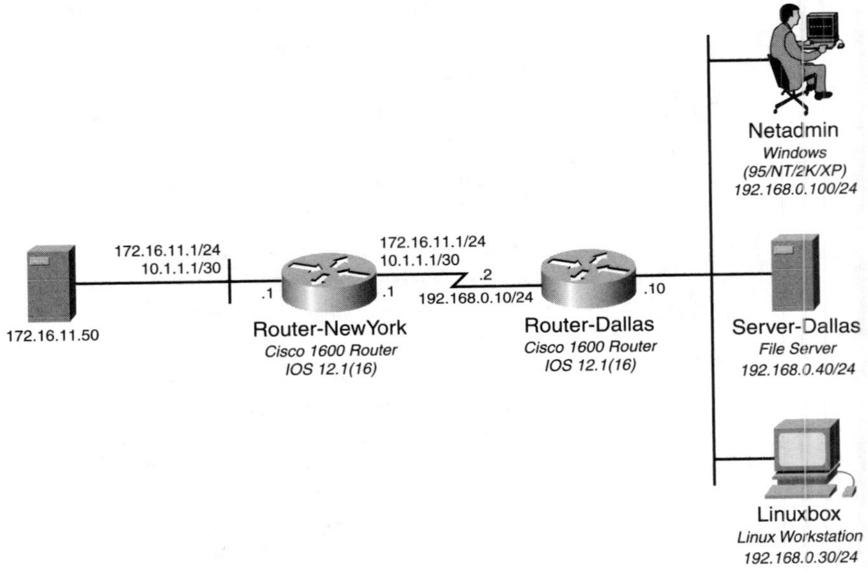

Console (or Telnet) into Router-Dallas for troubleshooting. The steps involved in identifying and solving the network issue are as follows:

Step 1 **Ping to the other end of serial link**—Check the serial link between routers, using the **ping 10.1.1.1** command. As shown in Example 2-12, the ping replies are received successfully, thus eliminating serial line issues.

Step 2 **Ping the remote server**—Check the Ethernet connectivity of the remote server using the **ping 172.16.11.50** command. Again, as shown in Example 2-12, the successful receipt of ping replies eliminates Ethernet connectivity issues between the remote server and the remote router.

Step 3 **Extended ping to the remote server**—Ping the remote server (172.16.11.50) using the source address (192.168.0.10) of the Ethernet interface of Router-Dallas. By default the router will use the source address of the outgoing interface for the ping packet. To specify the use of a source address other than the default, use the extended version of the

ping command, as shown in Example 2-12. The extended ping can verify the connectivity and reveal routing issues between the 172.16.11.0/24 and 192.168.0.0/24 LANs. As shown in the last part of Example 2-12, no packets are being received, indicating connectivity failure between the two LANs. Also note that the extended ping in this example is using 10 packets instead of the default. Using a larger number of packets provides monitoring over a longer period of time.

Failure of the extended ping in Step 3 indicates that Router-NewYork is not aware of the route to the 192.168.0.0/24 LAN. This is confirmed by the output of the **show ip route 192.168.0.0** command on Router-NewYork. After adding the static route for the 192.168.0.0/24 network on Router-NewYork, the extended ping, from the Ethernet interface of Router-Dallas to the remote server, succeeds. The users from the 192.168.0.0/24 LAN can now access the 172.16.11.50 server, and the issue is resolved.

Example 2-12 *Enhanced* **ping** *Session*

```
!Ping to the other end of serial link
Route-dallas#ping 10.1.1.1
Type escape sequence to abort.
Sending 5, 100-byte ICMP Echos to 10.1.1.1, timeout is 2 seconds:
!!!!!
Success rate is 100 percent (5/5), round-trip min/avg/max = 1/2/4 ms
!Ping to the remote server
Route-dallas#ping 172.16.11.50

Type escape sequence to abort.
Sending 5, 100-byte ICMP Echos to 172.16.11.50, timeout is 2 seconds:
!!!!!
Success rate is 100 percent (5/5), round-trip min/avg/max = 4/4/4 ms
! Extended ping to the remote server using the IP address of ethernet interface
! as the source address for the ping packets
Route-dallas#ping
Protocol [ip]:
Target IP address: 172.16.11.50
! Specify 10 packets instead of default 5
Repeat count [5]: 10
Datagram size [100]:
Timeout in seconds [2]:
Extended commands [n]: y
! You can also enter name of the interface "ethernet0"
Source address or interface: 192.168.0.10
Type of service [0]:
Set DF bit in IP header? [no]:
Validate reply data? [no]:
Data pattern [0xABCD]:
Loose, Strict, Record, Timestamp, Verbose[none]:
Sweep range of sizes [n]:
Type escape sequence to abort.
Sending 10, 100-byte ICMP Echos to 172.16.11.50, timeout is 2 seconds:
..........
Success rate is 0 percent (0/10)
```

continues

Example 2-12 *Enhanced* **ping** *Session (Continued)*

```
!Check the route to the 192.168.0.0/24 network on the remote router - Router-newyork
Router-newyork#show ip route 192.168.0.0
% Network not in table
!Add the route for 192.168.0.0/24 network on Router-newyork
Router-newyork#config terminal
Enter configuration commands, one per line.  End with CNTL/Z.
Router-newyork(config)#ip route 192.168.0.0 255.255.255.0 10.1.1.2
Router-newyork(config)#end
!Check the added route on Router-newyork
Router-newyork#show ip route 192.168.0.0
Routing entry for 192.168.0.0/24
  Known via "static", distance 1, metric 0
  Routing Descriptor Blocks:
  * 10.1.1.2
      Route metric is 0, traffic share count is 1
!  Extended ping to check again, this time the replies are received successfully
Router-Dallas# ping
Protocol [ip]:
Target IP address: 172.16.11.50
Repeat count [5]: 10
Datagram size [100]:
Timeout in seconds [2]:
Extended commands [n]: y
Source address or interface: 192.168.0.10
Type of service [0]:
Set DF bit in IP header? [no]:
Validate reply data? [no]:
Data pattern [0xABCD]:
Loose, Strict, Record, Timestamp, Verbose[none]:
Sweep range of sizes [n]:
Type escape sequence to abort.
Sending 10, 1600-byte ICMP Echos to 172.16.11.50, timeout is 2 seconds:
!!!!!!!!!!
Success rate is 100 percent (10/10), round-trip min/avg/max = 8/8/12 ms
```

Continuous ping

As observed in the preceding examples, a continuous ping is handy for network administrators, but the IOS-based ping lacks this feature. A suggested workaround is to use a high value for the **Repeat count** parameter. Example 2-13 shows an IOS ping with a Repeat count of 9999999. (The output in Example 2-13 has been truncated for illustration purposes.)

Example 2-13 *Continuous* **ping** *Session*

```
Router-Dallas#ping
Protocol [ip]:
Target IP address: 192.168.0.1
Repeat count [5]: 9999999
Datagram size [100]:
```

Example 2-13 *Continuous* **ping** *Session (Continued)*

```
Timeout in seconds [2]:
Extended commands [n]:
Sweep range of sizes [n]:
Type escape sequence to abort.
Sending 9999999, 100-byte ICMP Echos to 192.168.0.1, timeout is 2 seconds:
!!!!!!!!!!!!!!!!!!!!!!!!!!!!!!!!!!!!!!!!!!!!!!!!!!!!!!!!!!!!!!!!!!!!!!
!!!!!!!!!!!!!!!!!!!!!!!!!!!!!!!!!!!!!!!!!!!!!!!!!!!!!!!!!!!!!!!!!!!!!!
!!!!!!!!!!!!!!!!!!!!!!!!!!!!!!!!!!!!!!!!!!!!!!!!!!!!!!!!!!!!!!!!!!!!!!
!!!!!!!!!!!!!!!!!!!!!!!!!!!!!!!!!!!!!!!!!!!!!!!!!!!!!!!!!!!!!!!!!!!!!!
!!!!!!!!!!!!!!!!!!!!!!!!!!!!!!!!!!!!!!!!!!!!!!!!!!!!!!!!!!!!!!!!!!!!!!
!!!!!!!!!!!!!!!!!!!!!!!!!!!!!!!!!!!!!!!!!!!!!!!!!!!!!!!!!!!!!!!!!!!!!!
!!!!!!!!!!!!!!!!!!!!!!!!!!!!!!!!!!!!!!!!!!!!!!!!!!!!!!!!!!!!!!!!!!!!!!
!!!!!!!!!!!!!!!!!!!!!!!!!!!!!!!!!!!!!!!!!!!!!!!!!!!!!!!!!!!!!!!!!!!!!!
!!!!!!!!!!!!!!!!!!!!!!!!!!!!!!!!!!!!!!!!!!!!!!!!!!!!!!!!!!!!!!!!!!!!!!
! ------ Truncated output  -----
```

Using ping for MTU Testing

The extended **ping** command in IOS also provides the ability to set the DF bit and use a larger packet size. As discussed in the Windows and Linux ping sections, these features are handy when determining the MTU for a network link.

Example 2-14 shows the capture of an extended **ping** command on Router-Dallas. The first half of the example shows an extended **ping** command using the packet size of 1301 bytes. The command fails because 0 packets are received. The second half of the example uses the packet size of 1300 bytes. The replies are received successfully. Hence, the MTU value for the link between Router-Dallas and the web server 172.16.10.99 is 1300 bytes.

Example 2-14 *IOS Extended* **ping** *Command—MTU Testing*

```
! Extended ping with the IP packet size of 1301 bytes
Router-Dallas# ping
Protocol [ip]:
Target IP address: 172.16.10.99
Repeat count [5]:
Datagram size [100]: 1301
Timeout in seconds [2]:
Extended commands [n]: y
Source address or interface:
Type of service [0]:
Set DF bit in IP header? [no]: yes
Validate reply data? [no]:
Data pattern [0xABCD]:
Loose, Strict, Record, Timestamp, Verbose[none]:
Sweep range of sizes [n]:
Type escape sequence to abort.
Sending 5, 1301-byte ICMP Echos to 172.16.10.99, timeout is 2 seconds:
.....
Success rate is 0 percent (0/5)
! Extended ping with the IP packet size of 1300 bytes
```

continues

Example 2-14 *IOS Extended* **ping** *Command—MTU Testing (Continued)*

```
Router-Dallas# ping
Protocol [ip]:
Target IP address: 172.16.10.99
Repeat count [5]:
Datagram size [100]: 1300
Timeout in seconds [2]:
Extended commands [n]: y
Source address or interface:
Type of service [0]:
Set DF bit in IP header? [no]: yes
Validate reply data? [no]:
Data pattern [0xABCD]:
Loose, Strict, Record, Timestamp, Verbose[none]:
Sweep range of sizes [n]:
Type escape sequence to abort.
Sending 5, 1300-byte ICMP Echos to 172.16.10.99, timeout is 2 seconds:
!!!!!
Success rate is 100 percent (5/5), round-trip min/avg/max = 24/28/32 ms
Router-Dallas#
```

NOTE To enable the IOS device to ping by name, use the **ip name-server** *IP-address-of-DNS-Server* command.

Use the **no ip directed-broadcast** command to prevent the ICMP flooding attack that results when a ping is sent to a network address. The DDoS attacks, such as Smurf, use the directed broadcast of ICMP packets to flood the target network with broadcast replies. Cisco.com provides more information in the article "Characterizing and Tracing Packet Floods Using Cisco Routers." The URL is as follows:

http://www.cisco.com/en/US/tech/tk59/technologies_tech_note09186a0080149ad6.shtml

Other Cisco products, including PIX Firewall, VPN concentrators, CatOS-based Catalyst switches, Content switches, and so on, also provide the **ping** command. However, they do not offer as many options as are provided by IOS.

Other OS-Based Variations of **ping**

Encouraged by the utility and popularity of the ping tool, many variations and clones of the tool were created. Some are commercial versions with a GUI, whereas others were developed by the hacker community for reconnaissance purposes. Several popular ping variations are as follows:

- fping
- hping
- SmokePing

fping

Whereas the ping tool can only test one host at a time, fping can test multiple hosts simultaneously. The hosts can be either specified through the command line or listed in a text file. This is useful for administrators who want to quickly diagnose network connectivity issues. Fping, which is Linux-based, provides a fast response and is suitable for use in scripts. You can download and install fping from http://www.fping.com.

hping

The original ping tool uses ICMP Echo Requests. Hping provides additional capability to use TCP, UDP, ICMP, and RAW-IP for testing remote host connectivity. The ability to use TCP or UDP is useful in verifying connectivity, even if router and firewall ACLs are blocking ICMP traffic. Hping is a command-line–based Linux tool that provides additional features. You can download and install hping from http://www.hping.org/.

SmokePing

SmokePing provides a continuous output of latency, latency distribution, and packet loss in the network. It can provide detailed graphic records of network performance over extended periods of time. You can download and install SmokePing from http://people.ee.ethz.ch/~oetiker/webtools/smokeping/.

Network Troubleshooting Steps Using ping

Even the most seasoned network engineers often do not use the humble **ping** command to its full potential. When contacted with a connectivity issue with a target host, the first reaction is to ping it from the source address. This, of course, fails because the network is down. To quickly isolate network issues, follow these steps:

Step 1 Ping the loopback address, if any, of the source device. A successful reply confirms that the local TCP/IP stack is in good shape. Windows and Linux machines use 127.0.0.1 as the loopback address. If this step fails, the issue is with the local device's operating system or the TCP/IP stack.

Step 2 Ping the external network interface of the source device. This confirms the working of both the physical link and the TCP/IP protocol on that device. If this step fails, the issue is with the network interface or the connecting cable.

Step 3 Ping the default gateway of the source device. This confirms that the basic connectivity and routing works between the source device and the default gateway. If this step fails, the issue is either with the IP configuration of the host or the default gateway or the connectivity between the source host and default gateway.

Step 4 Ping the destination device to confirm network connectivity. If this step fails, the issue is between the default gateway and the target host.

Figure 2-5 depicts the troubleshooting steps using the **ping** command.

Figure 2-5 *Troubleshooting Using the* **ping** *Command*

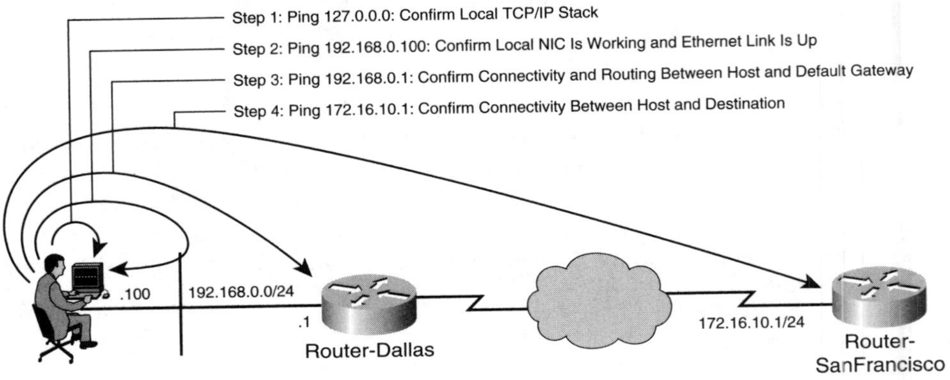
Step 1: Ping 127.0.0.0: Confirm Local TCP/IP Stack
Step 2: Ping 192.168.0.100: Confirm Local NIC Is Working and Ethernet Link Is Up
Step 3: Ping 192.168.0.1: Confirm Connectivity and Routing Between Host and Default Gateway
Step 4: Ping 172.16.10.1: Confirm Connectivity Between Host and Destination
.100
192.168.0.0/24
.1
Router-Dallas
172.16.10.1/24
Router-SanFrancisco

Verifying Network Connectivity Using traceroute

Traceroute, as the name suggests, allows you to trace the route or the path traversed by the data packets from the source to the destination. It also records the latency of each intermediate hop. While ping can only report connectivity to a target host, traceroute helps to pinpoint the node, within that path, that is causing network issues. The tool was written by Van Jacobson in 1988 at the Lawrence Berkeley National Laboratory.

IP packets have a TTL field for preventing routing loops. The TTL field limits the life of the IP packet in terms of hops. The TTL value can be an integer between 0 and 255. On receiving an IP packet, the router decrements the TTL value of the packet by 1. The router then uses the modified IP header for routing the packet. However, if the TTL value of the packet is 0, the router discards the IP packet and sends an ICMP type 11 **Time exceeded** message back to the sender. Traceroute uses this property and sends the first packets with TTL = 1. As soon as the packet reaches the first router, the TTL decrements to 0 and the router sends a **Time exceeded** message back to the source. Traceroute then sends another packet with TTL = 2, causing the second router in the path to send the **Time exceeded** message back. This process is repeated until the destination is reached and all the intermediate hops are recorded.

Traceroute is a client-based tool because no installation is required on the target node. It is preinstalled with most operating systems. This section discusses the most common traceroute implementations used by the network administrator, which are as follows:

- MS-Windows–based **tracert** command
- Linux-based **traceroute** command
- IOS-based **traceroute** command

Using the MS-Windows–Based **tracert** Command

The **tracert** command is preinstalled with versions Windows 95 and higher of MS-Windows in the form of tracert.exe. Tracert determines the path taken to a destination by sending ICMP Echo Request messages to the destination with incrementally increasing TTL field values.

To use the tracert tool to trace the network path from an MS-Windows 95/98/Me/NT/2000/XP–based machine to a target host, follow these steps:

Step 1 Open the command-line session by choosing **Start > Programs > MS-DOS Prompt**.

Step 2 Type the command **tracert** *<hostname-or-ip-address>* and press **Enter**.

The **tracert /?** command on Windows machines provides information on the usage of the **tracert** command. Example 2-15 shows the output of the **tracert /?** command in Windows XP. The output can be slightly different in other versions of Windows. However, the options discussed in this chapter are applicable to all versions of Windows.

Example 2-15 *Output of the* **tracert** *Command*

```
C:\WINDOWS\system32>tracert /?

Usage: tracert [-d] [-h maximum_hops] [-j host-list] [-w timeout] target_name

Options:
    -d                 Do not resolve addresses to hostnames.
    -h maximum_hops    Maximum number of hops to search for target.
    -j host-list       Loose source route along host-list.
    -w timeout         Wait timeout milliseconds for each reply.
```

Using **tracert** for Basic Tracing

The scenario in Figure 2-6 shows an Ethernet network connecting a Windows-based computer to a network with host http://www.testwebsite.com (172.16.17.71).

Figure 2-6 *MS-Windows–Based* **tracert**

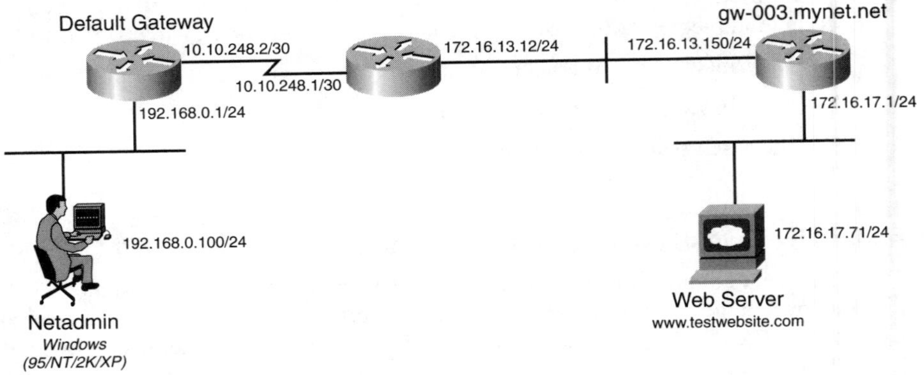

To determine the network path between a Windows machine and the target (http://www.testwebsite.com), the administrator enters the following command on the Windows computer:

```
tracert 172.16.17.71
```

Example 2-16 shows the output of the session.

Example 2-16 *Windows-Based* **traceroute** *- Using* **tracert** *Command*

```
C:\WINDOWS\system32>tracert 172.16.17.71

Tracing route to www.testwebsite.com [172.16.17.71]
over a maximum of 30 hops:

  1     2 ms     2 ms     2 ms  192.168.0.1
  2    15 ms     9 ms    14 ms  10.10.248.1
  3    46 ms    15 ms    15 ms  gw-003.mynet.net [172.16.13.150]
  4   235 ms   256 ms   262 ms  www.testwebsite.com [172.16.17.71]
Trace complete.
```

The first line in Example 2-16 shows the command itself.

The next two lines show that tracert has resolved the DNS name of the target (http://www.testwebsite.com) and is trying to trace the route with a limit set to 30 hops.

The next four lines are the hop-by-hop trace of the path to the destination. Each line has 3-ms entries followed by a host name or IP address. The ms entries are the round-trip time for the three ICMP Echo Request probes sent by the Windows machine. The host name or IP address belongs to the node that replied to these probes.

The round-trip time for each hop is helpful in isolating latency issues. Considering the output in Example 2-16, the first three hops have faster response times. The last hop has an unusually slow round-trip time of 235 ms. This indicates a slower link between the nodes 172.16.13.150 and 172.16.17.71.

Inaccurate Results of the **tracert** Command

Although the round-trip values provide clues to the latency and network issues, the results might not always be accurate.

The routers are sometimes configured to assign higher priority to the data traffic and lower priority to ICMP packets. Some routers do not return **Time exceeded** messages. Many Internet service providers (ISP) block ICMP packets. All these factors can result in high round-trip-time values or even timeouts. This can lead to some confusion regarding network connectivity. Exercise caution before jumping to "network unreachable" conclusions.

Using the Linux-Based **traceroute** Command

Almost all Linux distributions come with the **traceroute** command. The Linux implementation of traceroute uses UDP datagrams to determine the network path. This is in contrast with the Windows **tracert** command, which uses ICMP Echo Requests. Most of the Linux and UNIX implementations of traceroute use UDP port 33434 for sending the first packet. Subsequent packets use incrementing port numbers. Using different ports numbers eliminates false results if one particular port is blocked. Higher port numbers are used to minimize possible conflicts with other services or applications.

Figure 2-7 provides packet-by-packet details for a traceroute session from a Linux host with IP address IP-a to a destination host with IP address IP-e. The two hosts are connected through a network consisting of Routers B, C, and D, with the IP addresses as shown. You should assume that routing between the two hosts is working properly.

Figure 2-7 *Linux traceroute Mechanism*

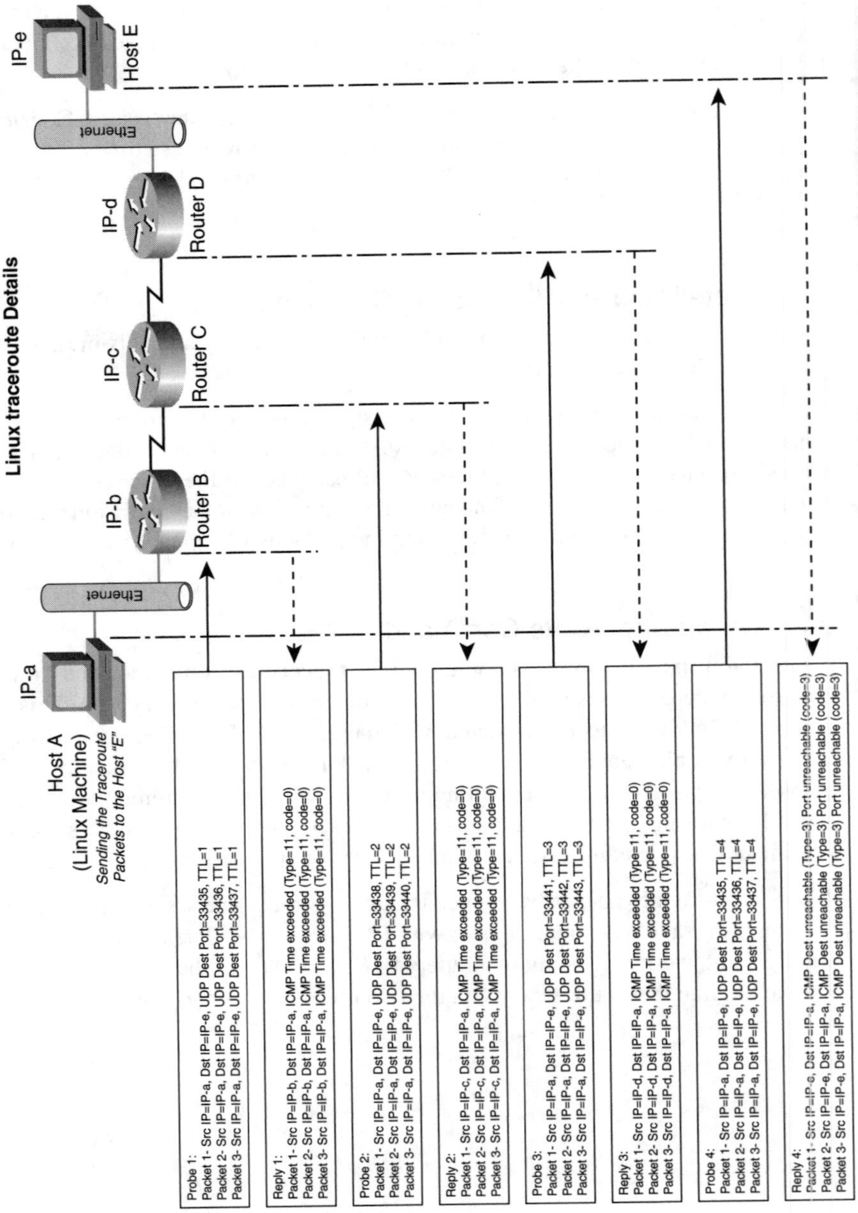

The command **traceroute 2.2.2.2** (assuming that IP-e = 2.2.2.2) is issued on the Linux machine shown in Figure 2-7. As a result, the Linux machine sends three probes to its default gateway. The probe consists of 3 separate UDP packets, each with TTL = 1. Also, note the incrementing destination UDP port number for each packet. The 3 packets reach Router B, which decrements the TTL value by 1, resulting in the new TTL = 0. Router B then sends three replies to the sender (host A) with an ICMP **Time exceeded** message denoted by ICMP type=11, code=0.

The next probe from host A consists of 3 packets, each with TTL = 2. These packets cross Router B, which decrements the new TTL = 1. After reaching Router C, the TTL = 0. This causes Router C to reply to host A with the ICMP **Time exceeded** message.

This process continues for each intermediate hop until the probe packets reach their target host E. Host E also decrements the TTL to 0. However, instead of sending the ICMP **Time exceeded** message, host E sends back the **Destination unreachable, Port unreachable** message.

To trace the network path from a Linux-based machine to a target host, follow these steps:

Step 1 Start a command-line session on the Linux machine.

Step 2 Type the command **traceroute** *hostname-or-IP-address* and press **Enter**.

Table 2-5 lists some of the options offered by the Linux **traceroute** command. Note that the options can vary slightly with each Linux distribution.

Table 2-5 *Linux traceroute Options*

Option	Description
-i *interface*	Specifies a network interface whose source IP address is to be used for outgoing probe packets; useful on a multihomed host.
-f *integer*	Specifies the initial TTL for the first outgoing probe packet; useful for skipping the first few hops, which are generally part of the internal network.
-I	Uses ICMP Echo Requests instead of UDP datagrams.
-m *number-of-hops*	Specifies the maximum number of hops; default is **30**.
-n	Disables the DNS lookup for the host name; useful for faster output.
-p *UDP-port-number*	Specifies the base UDP port number; default is **33434**.
-s *ip-address*	Specifies the source IP address for the probe packets; default is that of the outgoing interface; similar to the **-i** *interface* option.
-w *seconds*	Specifies the timeout period, in seconds, for waiting for a reply; default is **5**.
-z *milliseconds*	Specify the time to wait, in milliseconds, between successive probes; default is **0**. This option is useful when edge routers or firewalls enforce an ICMP rate limit.

To display the network path between a Linux machine running traceroute and the target (http://www.cisco.com), issue the **traceroute www.cisco.com** command on the Linux machine.

Example 2-17 shows the output of the traceroute session.

Example 2-17 *Linux-Based* **traceroute** *Command*

```
spope@linuxbox:~# traceroute www.cisco.com
traceroute to www.cisco.com (198.133.219.25), 30 hops max, 38 byte packets
 1  192.168.0.1 (192.168.0.1)  0.711 ms  0.280 ms  0.654 ms
 2  10.146.248.1 (10.146.248.1)  11.183 ms  7.978 ms  5.343 ms
 3  12.244.97.161 (12.244.97.161)  10.734 ms  8.362 ms  43.133 ms
 4  12.244.67.78 (12.244.67.78)  9.967 ms  9.917 ms  7.017 ms
 5  12.244.67.82 (12.244.67.82)  12.559 ms  11.380 ms  9.722 ms
 6  12.127.32.17 (12.127.32.17)  118.244 ms  *  115.079 ms
 7  tbr2-p013701.sffca.ip.att.net (12.123.13.177)  6.574 ms  16.656 ms  16.359 ms
 8  gbr5-p20.sffca.ip.att.net (12.122.11.90)  16.435 ms  14.334 ms  14.892 ms
 9  gar1-p360.sj2ca.ip.att.net (12.122.2.253)  6.211 ms  10.122 ms  22.096 ms
10  12.127.200.82 (12.127.200.82)  17.115 ms  23.219 ms  15.543 ms
11  sjce-dmzbb-gw1.cisco.com (128.107.239.53)  18.284 ms  24.111 ms  15.808 ms
12  sjck-dmzdc-gw1.cisco.com (128.107.224.69)  15.716 ms  16.968 ms  15.798 ms
13  www.cisco.com (198.133.219.25)  16.133 ms  22.774 ms  15.927 ms
```

Interpreting the Output of traceroute

As shown is the first line of Example 2-17, the host name is resolved to the IP address; the maximum number of hops is set to 30, and the packet size is 38 bytes. The next 13 lines (beginning with line 1) represent the response from each intermediate hop. Each row shows the IP addresses with the round-trip time for the 3 probe packets.

As highlighted, the round-trip times in line 6 have an asterisk (*), indicating a timeout. Also, note the high round-trip-time values of 118.244 ms and 115.079 ms. These times indicate congestion or a slower link between hops 12.244.67.82 and 12.127.32.17.

Some of the lines also show the host name along with the IP address. Traceroute responds faster if the name resolution is suppressed by using the –**n** switch. Example 2-18 shows the output of the **traceroute –n** command. The output shows only the IP addresses with the round-trip time for each hop.

Example 2-18 **Traceroute** *Command with the –***n** *Option*

```
spope@linuxbox:~# traceroute -n www.cisco.com
traceroute to www.cisco.com (198.133.219.25), 30 hops max, 38 byte packets
 1  192.168.0.1  0.585 ms  0.745 ms  0.490 ms
 2  10.146.248.1  19.304 ms  14.632 ms  7.667 ms
 3  12.244.97.161  7.553 ms  13.108 ms  9.600 ms
 4  12.244.67.78  7.218 ms  7.757 ms  11.274 ms
 5  12.244.67.82  8.103 ms  10.044 ms  8.176 ms
 6  12.127.32.17  14.589 ms  15.468 ms  23.110 ms
 7  12.123.13.177  11.225 ms  22.109 ms  15.973 ms
 8  12.122.11.90  11.825 ms  17.520 ms  13.860 ms
```

Example 2-18 **Traceroute** *Command with the* **–n** *Option (Continued)*

```
 9  12.122.2.253  8.550 ms  22.518 ms  14.165 ms
10  12.127.200.82  13.215 ms  19.282 ms  20.061 ms
11  128.107.239.53  10.584 ms  21.665 ms  19.873 ms
12  128.107.224.69  8.385 ms  23.932 ms  18.562 ms
13  198.133.219.25  8.307 ms  24.625 ms  15.269 ms
```

traceroute Fails Even If the Host Is Up

By default, the Linux implementation of **traceroute** sends UDP probe messages. Many devices might not respond to the UDP probe packets causing **traceroute** to produce inconclusive results. Example 2-19 shows output of **traceroute** command with the packets timing out (indicated by the *) after the first probe; however, as verified by the **ping www.testsite.net** command, the target host is not down.

Example 2-19 *Failure of* **traceroute** *command*

```
spope@linuxbox:~$ traceroute www.testsite.net
traceroute to www.testsite.net (208.36.86.73), 30 hops max, 38 byte packets
 1  192.168.0.1 (192.168.0.1)  1.139 ms  0.578 ms  0.716 ms
 2  * * *
 3  * * *
…output truncated for clarity …
29  * * *
30  * * *
spope@linuxbox:~$ ping www.testsite.net
PING www.testsite.net (208.36.86.73): 56 data bytes
64 bytes from 208.36.86.73: icmp_seq=0 ttl=39 time=90.8 ms
64 bytes from 208.36.86.73: icmp_seq=1 ttl=39 time=92.3 ms

--- www.testsite.net ping statistics ---
2 packets transmitted, 2 packets received, 0% packet loss
round-trip min/avg/max = 90.8/91.5/92.3 ms
```

In such cases, you can instruct the **traceroute** command to use ICMP probes. To trace the path to the target host with ICMP probes instead of the default UDP probes, use the **traceroute –I www.testsite.net** command, as shown in Example 2-20. The traceroute succeeds, with replies from all the intermediate hosts.

Example 2-20 **Traceroute** *Command with the* **–I** *Option*

```
spope@linuxbox:~$ traceroute -I www.testsite.net
traceroute to www.testsite.net (208.36.86.73), 30 hops max, 38 byte packets
 1  192.168.0.1 (192.168.0.1)  0.641 ms  0.664 ms  0.669 ms
 2  10.146.248.1 (10.146.248.1)  16.911 ms  7.878 ms  8.369 ms
 3  12.244.97.161 (12.244.97.161)  11.852 ms  11.654 ms  9.779 ms
 4  12.244.67.78 (12.244.67.78)  9.756 ms  9.096 ms  11.050 ms
 5  12.244.67.82 (12.244.67.82)  8.736 ms  10.687 ms  9.545 ms
 6  12.127.33.73 (12.127.33.73)  13.233 ms  13.154 ms  14.174 ms
 7  gbr5-p30.sffca.ip.att.net (12.123.13.158)  14.943 ms  15.044 ms  15.444 ms
 8  tbr2-p013501.sffca.ip.att.net (12.122.11.89)  15.591 ms  33.922 ms  15.357 ms
 9  ggr2-p390.sffca.ip.att.net (12.123.13.194)  19.458 ms  14.896 ms  14.707 ms
10  att-gw.sfo.qwest.net (192.205.32.82)  14.727 ms  15.670 ms  20.539 ms
```

continues

Example 2-20 **Traceroute** *Command with the* **–I** *Option (Continued)*

```
11  svx-core-02.inet.qwest.net (205.171.214.137)  15.686 ms  14.283 ms  16.360 ms
12  svl-core-03.inet.qwest.net (205.171.14.81)  18.843 ms  16.833 ms  16.095 ms
13  svl-core-01.inet.qwest.net (205.171.14.121)  16.340 ms  31.363 ms  15.966 ms
14  iah-core-01.inet.qwest.net (205.171.8.130)  55.004 ms  56.289 ms  56.105 ms
15  * tpa-core-02.inet.qwest.net (205.171.5.105)  79.213 ms  77.061 ms
16  nap-edge-01.inet.qwest.net (205.171.27.174)  96.872 ms  106.207 ms  107.447 ms
17  65.124.216.54 (65.124.216.54)  91.313 ms  88.074 ms  86.725 ms
18  ftl-core1a-v6.valueweb.com (216.219.251.33)  85.303 ms  135.629 ms  312.926ms
19  208-36-86-73.www.testsite.net (208.36.86.73)  84.526 ms  84.339 ms  85.381 ms
```

TIP To avoid using copy and paste to record the output of the **ping** and the **traceroute** command, use the output redirector **>**. The format is **command > filename**. This works for both Linux and Windows operating systems.

For example, the **ping 10.10.10.10 > test1.txt** command redirects the output of the **ping** command to the file test1.txt.

To append the output without erasing the original file, use the following code (note the two redirector signs):

```
command >> filename
```

For example, the **ping 10.10.10.10 >> test1.txt** command redirects the output of the **ping** command to test1.txt without overwriting the existing contents of the file.

Using the IOS-Based **traceroute** Command

While the Linux- and Windows-based **traceroute** command support IP, the IOS-based **traceroute** command supports AppleTalk, Clns, IP, and Vines. Traceroute is supported in Cisco IOS Release 10.0 and higher. Cisco IOS offers the following two modes of the **traceroute** command:

- User mode
- Privileged mode

User Mode **traceroute** *Command*

The user mode **traceroute** command has a basic feature for users who do not have system privileges. This feature allows the Cisco IOS Software to perform the simple default traceroute functionality without knowing privilege-level passwords.

To determine the network path from an IOS-based device to a target host, follow these steps:

Step 1 Start a console or Telnet session to the IOS-based device and log in to the user mode using applicable authentication information.

Step 2 Type the command **traceroute** [*protocol*] *destination* and press **Enter**. Optionally, try using the **traceroute ?** command to find available options. Table 2-6 explains each of the command options.

Table 2-6 *IOS* **traceroute** *Options*

Option	Description
protocol	(Optional) Protocol keyword; one of the following: **apollo**, **appletalk**, **clns**, **ip**, **vines**, **novell**, **decnet**, or **xns**
destination	Host name or IP address of the target

The scenario in Figure 2-8 depicts a regular user trying to determine the network path from the IOS device Router-Dallas to the website http://www.cisco.com.

Figure 2-8 **Traceroute** *from an IOS Device*

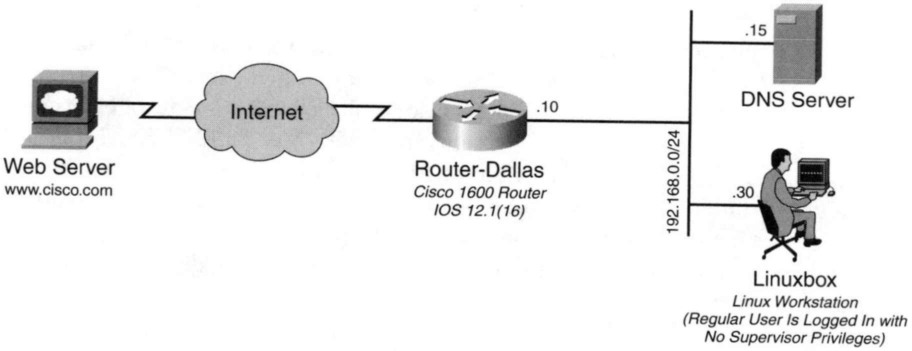

The user first initiates a Telnet session from the machine LINUXBOX to Router-Dallas to log in to the user EXEC mode. From the user EXEC prompt (Router-Dallas>), the user issues the **traceroute www.cisco.com** command. The host name gets resolved to the IP address through the DNS server 192.168.0.15. The captured session in Example 2-21 details the steps involved and the output of the IOS **traceroute** command.

Example 2-21 *IOS* **traceroute** *Command*

```
spope@linuxbox:/$ telnet 192.168.0.10
Trying 192.168.0.10...
Connected to 192.168.0.10.
Escape character is '^]'.

User Access Verification
Password:

Router-Dallas>traceroute www.cisco.com
 Translating "www.cisco.com"...domain server (192.168.0.15) [OK]

 Type escape sequence to abort.
 Tracing the route to www.cisco.com (198.133.219.25)

   1 ge5-3-0d4.RR2.-TX.us.wwt.net (65.106.2.49) 0 msec 4 msec 0 msec
   2 p1-0.IR1.s2-TX.us.wwt.net (65.106.4.186) 4 msec 0 msec 4 msec
   3 206.111.5.26.ptr.us.weo.net (206.11.5.26) 8 msec 4 msec 4 msec
   4 tbr1-p01.dlx.ip.asrpt.net (12.23.16.242) 0 msec 4 msec 4 msec
   5 tbr1-cl2.l2a.ip.spr.net (12.12.10.50) 36 msec 40 msec 40 msec
   6 gar1-p370.sj2ca.ip.swet.net (12.12.2.249) 48 msec 44 msec 44 msec
   7 12.12.200.82 44 msec 48 msec 44 msec
   8 sjck-dm-gw1.cisco.com (128.10.239.9) 44 msec 44 msec 44 msec
   9 www.cisco.com (198.133.219.25) 44 msec 44 msec 44 msec
```

The output is similar to the output of the Linux **traceroute** command. The destination website, http://www.cisco.com, is nine hops away from the host. The output lists each of the hops by the IP address. The output also resolves the DNS name of each hop. However, only the IP address of the seventh hop is listed. The host 12.12.200.82 is most likely not configured with a name server. After the IP address of each hop, the command lists numeric values in milliseconds (msec). These are the round-trip reply times for the probe packets sent to each hop. By default, traceroute sends 3 probe packets to each hop. Hence, each output line shows three values in msec. Instead of an integer, the * character indicates no reply or timeout.

TIP The output of the **traceroute** command can be interrupted by pressing **Ctrl-Shift-6** followed by pressing **X**.

Privileged Mode traceroute Command

As seen in the preceding section, the basic IOS **traceroute** command is not very flexible. It also uses default parameters that the user cannot change. These parameters are as follows:

- Probe count of 3
- UDP port number 33434

- Timeout value of 3 seconds
- Outgoing interface as the source address of the packets

The IOS **traceroute** command in the privileged EXEC mode provides customizable options, as shown is Table 2-7.

Table 2-7 *Enhanced* **traceroute** *Options*

Field	Description
Target IP address	Specifies the IP address of the target host.
Source address	Specifies one of the interface addresses of the router to be used as the source address; by default, the router uses the IP address of the outgoing interface.
Numeric display [n]	The default is to have both a symbolic and a numeric display; however, you can suppress the symbolic display. The default is **no**.
Timeout in seconds [3]	The number of seconds to wait for a response from a probe packet. The default is **3**.
Probe count [3]	The number of probes to be sent at each TTL level. The default is **3**.
Minimum Time to Live [1]	The TTL value for the first probe. The default is **1**, but it can be set to a higher value to suppress the display of known hops.
Maximum Time to Live [30]	The largest TTL value that can be used. The default is **30**. The **traceroute** command terminates when the destination is reached or when this value is reached.
Port Number [33434]	The destination port used by the UDP probe messages. The default is **33434**.
Loose, Strict, Record, Timestamp, Verbose [none]	IP header options. You can specify any combination. The **traceroute** command issues prompts for the required fields. Note that traceroute places the requested options in each probe; however, there is no guarantee that all routers (or end nodes) can process the options. These options are as follows: • **Loose**—Allows you to specify a list of nodes that must be traversed when going to the destination. • **Strict**—Allows you to specify a list of nodes that must be the only nodes traversed when going to the destination. • **Record**—Specifies the number of hops. • **Timestamp**—Specifies the number of time stamps. • **Verbose**—If you select any option, the verbose mode is automatically selected and traceroute prints the contents of the option field in incoming packets. Y.ou can prevent verbose mode by selecting it again, toggling its current setting.

The steps involved in initiating a privileged EXEC mode **traceroute** command are as follows:

Step 1 Start a console or Telnet session to the IOS-based device and log in to the privileged EXEC mode using the appropriate username and password. (Privileged EXEC mode can be identified by the # [pound sign] in the prompt. **Router#** indicates privileged EXEC mode, while **Router>** indicates user EXEC mode.)

Step 2 Type the command **traceroute** and press **Enter**. Follow the prompts and enter suitable information for each field. For an explanation of each field, refer to Table 2-7.

Example 2-22 illustrates the enhanced **traceroute** command with an Ethernet interface (192.168.0.10) as the source address of the traceroute packets. Also, the command sends 2 packets with a default timeout value of 3 seconds. The probe packets are using UDP port 24 instead of the default 33434.

Example 2-22 *Enhanced* **traceroute** *Session*

```
Router-Dallas# traceroute
Protocol [ip]:
Target IP address: www.cisco.com
Source address: 192.168.0.10
Numeric display [n]: n
Timeout in seconds [3]:
! Specify only 2 probe packets to be sent to each hop
Probe count [3]:2
Minimum Time to Live [1]:
Maximum Time to Live [30]:
Port Number [33434]:24
Loose, Strict, Record, Timestamp, Verbose[none]:
Type escape sequence to abort.
Tracing the route to 198.133.219.25

  1 ge5-3-0d4.RAR2.dallas-TX.us.xo.net (65.106.2.49) 8 msec 0 msec
  2 p1-0.IR1.dallas2-TX.us.xo.net (65.106.4.186) 4 msec 4 msec
  3 206.111.5.26.ptr.us.xo.net (206.111.5.26) 4 msec 4 msec
  4 tbr1-p012201.dlstx.ip.att.net (12.123.16.242) 4 msec 4 msec
  5 tbr1-cl2.la2ca.ip.att.net (12.122.10.50) 40 msec 36 msec
  6 gar1-p370.sj2ca.ip.att.net (12.122.2.249) 44 msec 44 msec
  7 12.127.200.82 48 msec 48 msec
  8 sjck-dmzbb-gw1.cisco.com (128.107.239.9) 44 msec 44 msec
  9 www.cisco.com (198.133.219.25) 44 msec 44 msec
```

Note that for each hop, the output only indicates two values in milliseconds. This is the desired behavior because only 2 probe packets per hop are specified in the extended **traceroute** command.

Case Study: Using ping and traceroute to Isolate a BGP Meltdown Emergency

The Netadmin of Super E-commerce Company reported a performance issue with its existing e-commerce network. The company network has a mix of Windows and Linux servers at the data center, which is located in the corporate office. According to the network administrators, only external customers were facing issues while placing online orders. Many of them complained of long response times, and some said they had to log in several times as the session was being reset. The test team (located on the campus) as well as the employees did not experience the same issue.

The fact that the campus users were unaffected leads to the conclusion that the issue is related to the WAN connection. But it could be anything from a defective cable to a routing issue with the ISP.

After reaching the customer's site, the author was provided with the network layout, shown in Figure 2-9.

Figure 2-9 *Logical Network Layout for Super E-commerce Co.*

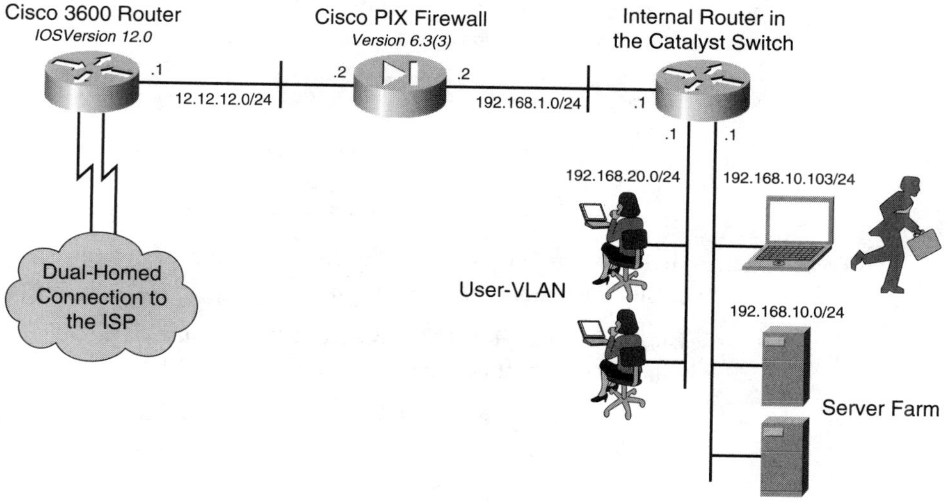

Based on the discussion in this chapter, the author utilized the following step-by-step approach for troubleshooting:

Step 1 Connect the laptop to the server virtual LAN (VLAN) and use the **ipconfig /all** command to determine the IP address, default gateway, and DNS information as follows:

```
Ethernet adapter Local Area Connection:

        Connection-specific DNS Suffix  . : superecommerceinc.com
```

```
        Description . . . . . . . . . . . . : Broadcom 370x  Controller
        Physical Address. . . . . . . . . : 00-0c-66-er-35-A6
        Dhcp Enabled. . . . . . . . . . . : Yes
        Autoconfiguration Enabled . . . . : Yes
        IP Address. . . . . . . . . . . . : 192.168.10.103
        Subnet Mask . . . . . . . . . . . : 255.255.255.0
        Default Gateway . . . . . . . . . : 192.168.10.1
        DHCP Server . . . . . . . . . . . : 192.168.10.8
        DNS Servers . . . . . . . . . . . : 192.168.10.9
        Lease Obtained. . . . . . . . . . : Wednesday, July 20, 2005
11:30:53 PM

        Lease Expires . . . . . . . . . . : Wednesday, July 27, 2005
11:30:53 PM
```

Step 2 After collecting the network information, use the **traceroute** command to identify the routing hops, as follows:

```
c:\windows\system32>tracert www.cisco.com

Tracing route to www.cisco.com [198.133.219.25]
over a maximum of 30 hops:

  1     <1 ms    <1 ms    <1 ms  192.168.10.1
  2     50 ms     9 ms     9 ms  12.12.12.1
  3     29 ms     9 ms     9 ms  12.44.197.161
  4      8 ms     8 ms     9 ms  12.244.67.78
  5     16 ms    16 ms    16 ms  www.cisco.com [198.133.219.25]
```

Step 3 On the Windows-based laptop, open four command-line sessions and tile them to create a concurrent view as shown in Figure 2-10 and as follows:

— Session 1 uses the **ping 192.168.10.103 -t** command. The continuous ping monitors the network interface of the laptop.

— Session 2 uses the **ping 192.168.10.1 –t** command. The continuous ping monitors the default gateway for the Server-Farm VLAN.

— Session 3 uses the **ping 192.168.1.1 –t** command. The continuous ping monitors the inside interface of the firewall.

— Session 4 uses the **ping 12.12.12.1 –t** command. The continuous ping monitors the Ethernet interface of the edge router.

Figure 2-10 *Concurrent View of Multiple Sessions*

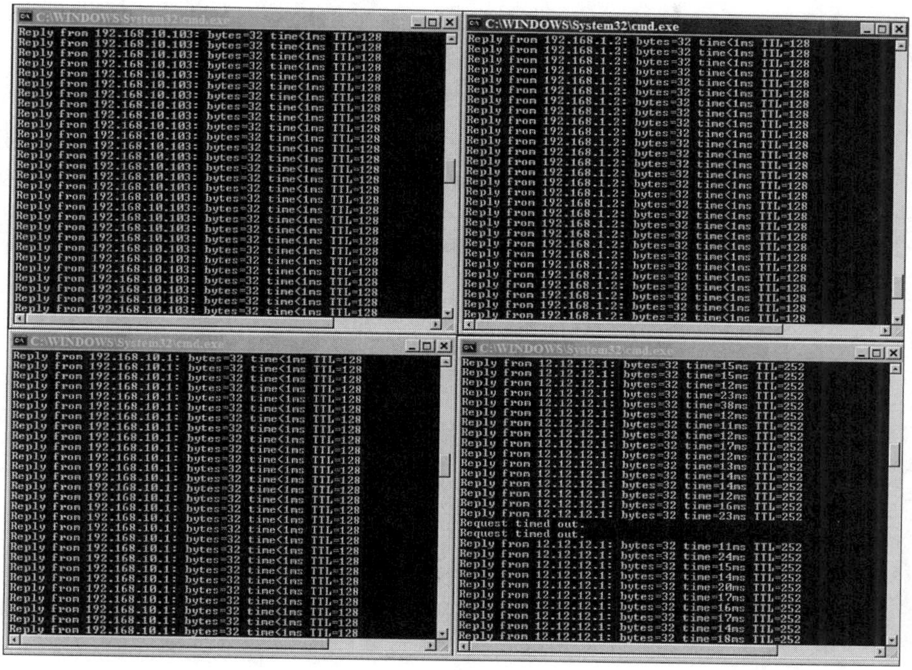

Observation

All sessions have good response times, but after observing over a longer period, a pattern shows up. Session 4 (the one with continuous **ping** to the edge router **12.12.12.1**) times out for a period of approximately 4 seconds at an interval of 30 seconds. Apart from the timeouts on the Ethernet interface of the edge router, all other responses are consistently less than 1 ms.

Conclusions

Based on the observations made in previous section, the conclusions are as follows:

- The internal network, including the firewall, is functioning properly.
- The problem is related to the edge router.
- Because of the periodic recurrence of the timeouts, the problem is probably related to a software issue that occurs every 30 seconds.

Actions

Telnet into the edge router and issue a **show proc cpu** command to verify the CPU load, as follows:

```
edge-router# show proc cpu
  CPU utilization for five seconds: 3%/0%; one minute: 82%; five minutes: 91%
```

The output shows a high load on the CPU. Further investigation reveals that the edge router was incorrectly configured with the **no ip route-cache** command. This stops the fast switching of the packets in the router. At the same time, the edge router is receiving full Border Gateway Protocol (BGP) routes from the ISP every 30 seconds. So, during that interval, the router processes the routes and stops processing the data traffic.

After adding the **ip route-cache** command to the configurations, the router starts fast-switching the data traffic, even during high CPU intervals. The problem was solved.

Once again, the super **ping** command saves the world!

Advanced Network Connectivity Testing Tools

Although a plethora of tools are at the disposal of the Netadmin, most of the commonly available tools are not used to their full potential. Some of these tools are built into the OS. This section discusses the usage of the following built-in tools:

- whois
- nslookup
- netstat
- nbtstat
- arp

Using whois Lookup for Domain Registration Information

The whois tool provides administrative information for an Internet domain name. It is handy for finding the contacts and registration information for a domain name.

The command is natively supported by Linux but is not a part of MS-Windows. While many freeware and commercial versions of whois are available for the MS-Windows version, this section covers those available for the Linux version. To use the command-line version of whois tools, follow these steps:

Step 1 Start a command-line session.

Step 2 Type the command **whois** *domain-name* and press **Enter**.

To investigate details of the domain mydomain.com, type **whois mydomain.com** at the command line, as shown in Example 2-23.

Example 2-23 *Output of the* **whois** *Command*

```
spope@linuxbox# whois mydomain.com

Whois Server Version 1.3

Domain names in the .com and .net domains can now be registered
with many different competing registrars. Go to http://www.internic.net
for detailed information.

   Domain Name: MYDOMAIN.COM
   Registrar: NETWORK SOLUTIONS, INC.
   Whois Server: whois.networksolutions.com
   Referral URL: http://www.networksolutions.com
   Name Server: NS2.NYC.BIGISP.NET
   Name Server: NS1.NYC.BIGISP.NET
   Name Server: NS2.DAL.BIGISP.NET
   Name Server: NS1.DAL.BIGISP.NET
   Status: ACTIVE
   Updated Date: 08-aug-2002
   Creation Date: 28-nov-1995
   Expiration Date: 27-nov-2009


>>> Last update of whois database: Sun, 25 Jul 2004 08:27:47 EDT <<<



Registrant:
SUPER ECOMMERCE Companys L.P. (SUPER ECOMMERCE-DOM)
   300 Anybig Road
   Suite 100
   Dallas, TX 75201
   US

   Domain Name: MYDOMAIN.COM

   Administrative Contact:
      Companny , SUPER ECOMMERCE  (34410541I)              alert1@MYDOMAIN.COM
      SUPER ECOMMERCE Companys.
      300 Anybig Road
      Suite 100
      Dallas, TX 75201
      US
      214-111-111

   Technical Contact:
      Steve, smith  (PS11887)             ssmith@MYDOMAIN.COM
      SUPER ECOMMERCE Companys L.P.
      300 Anybig Road
      Suite 100
```

continues

Example 2-23 *Output of the* **whois** *Command (Continued)*

```
      Dallas, TX 75201
      US
      214-111-111   fax: (214) 111-9999
      (214) 758-6171

   Record expires on 27-Nov-2009.
   Record created on 28-Nov-1995.
   Database last updated on 25-Jul-2004 18:00:42 EDT.

   Domain servers in listed order:

   NS1.DAL.BIGISP.NET            26.152.10.11
   NS2.NYC.BIGISP.NET            29.91.129.5
   NS1.NYC.BIGISP.NET            29.171.129.11
   NS2.DAL.BIGISP.NET            26.52.40.37
```

The output provides administrative and technical contacts as well as the registration details. The command output also provides the expiration date for the record, as highlighted in Example 2-23. The expiration information is helpful when isolating issues related to web or e-mail connectivity. For example if mydomain.com has expired, the DNS query for the domain will fail. As a result, users cannot access the website www.mydomain.com by using the domain name. Consequently, e-mail delivery to mydomain.com also fails.

TIP cygwin enables the use of Linux commands and tools, including whois, in Windows. cygwin is available for download at http://www.cygwin.com/.

Using nslookup to Find DNS Information

Nslookup is a command-line tool that verifies Domain Name System (DNS) information using the local DNS server. The tool queries DNS servers to retrieve various data types associated with an Internet domain. These data types are as follows:

- **MX**—Mail exchanger records
- **A**—IP addresses
- **CNAME**—Canonical names

If you have an IP address, you can get a canonical name back for the address. If you have a canonical name, you can get an IP address. Another useful feature is the ability to get a list of mail servers for the target domain. Nslookup is available in both MS-Windows and Linux versions.

Using the MS-Windows–Based nslookup Tool

Nslookup comes preinstalled with version Windows 95 and higher of MS-Windows as a command-line tool. To query DNS information about the target domain or host, follow these steps:

Step 1 Open a command-line session by choosing **Start > Programs > MS-DOS Prompt**.

Step 2 Type the command **nslookup** and press **Enter**. This starts the tool in interactive mode.

Example 2-24 shows the Windows **nslookup** command output that determines the mail and DNS server for mydomain.com.

Example 2-24 *Output of the MS-Windows* **nslookup** *Command*

```
c:\windows\system32>nslookup
Default Server:  ns2.myisp.com
Address:  26.48.227.68

> set query=all
> mydomain.com
Server:  ns2.myisp.com
Address:  26.48.227.68

Non-authoritative answer:
mydomain.com  nameserver = ns5.mydomain.com
mydomain.com  nameserver = ns4.mydomain.com
mydomain.com  nameserver = ns3.mydomain.com
mydomain.com  MX preference = 10, mail exchanger = mail1.mydomain.com
mydomain.com  MX preference = 20, mail exchanger = mail2.mydomain.com
mydomain.com
        primary name server = ns4.mydomain.com
        responsible mail addr = hostmaster.mydomain.com
        serial  = 2004072000
        refresh = 7200 (2 hours)
        retry   = 600 (10 mins)
        expire  = 2592000 (30 days)
        default TTL = 600 (10 mins)

mydomain.com  nameserver = ns4.mydomain.com
mydomain.com  nameserver = ns3.mydomain.com
ns4.mydomain.com      internet address = 131.91.51.1
ns3.mydomain.com      internet address = 126.18.10.178
>exit
```

The details of the output are as follows:

- The first two lines of the output show the name and IP address of the default DNS server used by the host. This is typically provided to the host by the Dynamic Host Configuration Protocol (DHCP) server or is manually configured in the TCP/IP properties of the network interface card (NIC).
- The **set query=all** command instructs the tool to query all the available information.
- To selectively view only the mail server records, you can use the **set query=MX** command.
- The **exit** command, as shown in the last line, returns you to the command shell.
- The last four lines indicate the details of the DNS servers for mydomain.com.

Using the Linux-Based nslookup /dig Tool

The Linux version of nslookup is similar to its Windows counterpart. To query DNS information about the target domain or host, follow these steps:

Step 1 Start a command-line session.

Step 2 Type the command **nslookup** and press **Enter**.

Example 2-25 shows the **nslookup** command retrieving the available information for mydomain.com.

Example 2-25 *Output of the Linux* **nslookup** *Command*

```
spope@linuxbox# nslookup
Note:  nslookup is deprecated and may be removed from future releases.
Consider using the `dig' or `host' programs instead.  Run nslookup with
the `-sil[ent]' option to prevent this message from appearing.
> set querytype=ANY
> mydomain.com
Server:         26.48.227.68
Address:        26.48.227.68#53

Non-authoritative answer:
mydomain.com  nameserver = ns5.mydomain.com.
mydomain.com  nameserver = ns4.mydomain.com.
mydomain.com  nameserver = ns3.mydomain.com.
mydomain.com  mail exchanger = 10 mail1.mydomain.com.
mydomain.com  mail exchanger = 20 mail2.mydomain.com.
Name:   mydomain.com
Address: 131.91.51.10

Authoritative answers can be found from:
mydomain.com  nameserver = ns4.mydomain.com.
mydomain.com  nameserver = ns3.mydomain.com.
ns4.mydomain.com      internet address = 131.91.51.1
ns3.mydomain.com      internet address = 126.18.10.178
> exit
```

Note the **set querytype=ANY** command, which retrieves the available information. The output is similar to that of its MS-Windows counterpart.

The highlighted text indicates the MX record, whereas the last two lines, before the **exit** command, indicate the DNS servers used by mydomain.com.

The **exit** command, as shown in the last line, returns you to the command shell.

Although nslookup is an integral part of Linux, it has been deprecated. Users are encouraged to use the **dig** command because of its enhanced functionality, flexibility, ease of use, and clarity of output. To query DNS information about the target domain or host using the **dig** command, follow these steps:

Step 1 Start a command-line session.

Step 2 Type the command **dig** *target-domain-name* and press **Enter**.

Although the **dig** command offers various options, the most common format is as follows:

```
dig @dns-server targetdomain query-type
```

Example 2-26 shows the **dig** command retrieving available information for mydomain.com from the DNS server 26.48.27.168.

Example 2-26 *Output of the Linux* **dig** *Command*

```
spope@linuxbox# dig @26.48.27.168 craigslist.org ANY
; <<>> DiG 9.2.4rc2 <<>> @26.48.27.168 mydomain.com ANY
;; global options:  printcmd
;; Got answer:
;; ->>HEADER<<- opcode: QUERY, status: NOERROR, id: 4367
;; flags: qr rd ra; QUERY: 1, ANSWER: 6, AUTHORITY: 3, ADDITIONAL: 5

;; QUESTION SECTION:
;mydomain.com.                IN      ANY

;; ANSWER SECTION:
mydomain.com.         6598    IN      NS      ns5.mydomain.com.
mydomain.com.         6598    IN      NS      ns4.mydomain.com.
mydomain.com.         6598    IN      NS      ns3.mydomain.com.
mydomain.com.         194    IN     SOA     ns4.mydomain.com. hostmaster.mydomain.com.
2004072000 7200 600 2592000 600
mydomain.com.         253     IN      MX      10 mail1.mydomain.com.
mydomain.com.         253     IN      MX      20 mail2.mydomain.com.

;; AUTHORITY SECTION:
mydomain.com.         6598    IN      NS      ns5.mydomain.com.
mydomain.com.         6598    IN      NS      ns4.mydomain.com.
mydomain.com.         6598    IN      NS      ns3.mydomain.com.

;; ADDITIONAL SECTION:
ns5.mydomain.com.     150     IN      A     130.94.251.2
ns4.mydomain.com.     150     IN      A     130.94.251.1
ns3.mydomain.com.     37732     IN      A     216.218.210.178
```

continues

Example 2-26 *Output of the Linux* **dig** *Command (Continued)*

```
anco.mydomain.com.     260     IN     A     123.44.14.26
dsqd.mydomain.com.     260     IN     A     123.44.14.151

;; Query time: 136 msec
;; SERVER: 26.48.27.168#53(26.48.27.168)
;; WHEN: Sun Jul 25 13:14:53 2001
;; MSG SIZE  rcvd: 299
```

When compared to the **nslookup** command, the **dig** command has the following features:

- It is easier to use because all the options can be specified in a single line. This helps when using the command in automated scripts.
- The output is easier to read and decipher because it is better organized in various sections.
- The output is more detailed.

Using netstat for Port and Connection Information

To design, deploy, and troubleshoot a network, network administrators need to determine the traffic flowing through it. This traffic is generated by the end stations. The administrators often require an X-ray tool to directly view the TCP/IP statistics on the servers and workstations.

Netstat (or *net*work *stat*istics) is just the tool to directly show these TCP/IP statistics. It provides the following items:

- The current network session to and from the host
- Protocol statistics, including those for TCP and UDP
- Display of a routing table
- Display of the number of bytes sent, received, or dropped

It is one of the most useful yet underused tools for administrators. A thorough understanding of this tool aids in configuring or troubleshooting the following:

- Access lists on routers and firewalls
- Intrusion detection
- Network protection from viruses, worms, Trojan horses, and so on

Netstat is available for both MS-Windows and Linux. Because of the importance of this tool, the following sections discuss both versions in detail.

Using the MS Windows—Based **netstat** Command

The **netstat** command is preinstalled with all versions of MS-Windows. This section discusses the Windows 2000/XP version of the command. To list the active connections on a Windows computer, follow these steps:

Step 1 Open the command-line session by choosing **Start > Programs > MS-DOS Prompt**.

Step 2 Type the command **netstat** and press **Enter**.

The **netstat /?** command on Windows machines provides information on the usage of the **netstat** command. Example 2-27 shows the output of the **netstat /?** command in Windows XP. The output can be slightly different in other Windows versions. However, the options discussed in this chapter are applicable to all versions of Windows.

Example 2-27 *Output of the Windows* **netstat /?** *Command*

```
c:\windows\system32>netstat /?

Displays protocol statistics and current TCP/IP network connections.

NETSTAT [-a] [-e] [-n] [-o] [-s] [-p proto] [-r] [interval]

  -a            Displays all connections and listening ports.
  -e            Displays Ethernet statistics. This may be combined with the -s
                option.
  -n            Displays addresses and port numbers in numerical form.
  -o            Displays the owning process ID associated with each connection.
  -p proto      Shows connections for the protocol specified by proto; proto
                may be any of: TCP, UDP, TCPv6, or UDPv6.  If used with the -s
                option to display per-protocol statistics, proto may be any of:
                IP, IPv6, ICMP, ICMPv6, TCP, TCPv6, UDP, or UDPv6.
  -r            Displays the routing table.
  -s            Displays per-protocol statistics.  By default, statistics are
                shown for IP, IPv6, ICMP, ICMPv6, TCP, TCPv6, UDP, and UDPv6;
                the -p option may be used to specify a subset of the default.
  interval      Redisplays selected statistics, pausing interval seconds
                between each display.  Press CTRL+C to stop redisplaying
                statistics.  If omitted, netstat will print the current
                configuration information once.
```

The sections that follow discuss the use of various netstat options on an MS-Windows computer for displaying the following items:

- Active connections
- All network connections
- Network statistics
- Routing table

Using the Windows **netstat** Command to Display Active Connections

Use the **netstat** command with no option to display the currently active TCP connections. Example 2-28 shows the output of the **netstat** command.

Example 2-28 *Windows* **netstat** *Command: Active Connections*

```
c:\windows\system32>netstat

Active Connections

  Proto  Local Address          Foreign Address        State
  TCP    WINXPBOX:4343          localhost:4344         ESTABLISHED
  TCP    WINXPBOX:4344          localhost:4343         ESTABLISHED
  TCP    WINXPBOX:3480          www.website1.com:http  TIME_WAIT
  TCP    WINXPBOX:3485          123.38.12.57:http      TIME_WAIT
  TCP    WINXPBOX:3488          www.website2.com:http  TIME_WAIT
  TCP    WINXPBOX:3494          62.14.80.250:http      SYN_SENT
```

This command can provide a quick snapshot of currently active connections. You can also use the *interval* option to view a continuous display that gets refreshed periodically. For example, the **netstat 5** command displays the same output as in Example 2-28, but it is refreshed every 5 seconds until interrupted by the user pressing **Ctrl-C**.

NOTE A large number of connections with the *SYN_RECEIVED* state indicate a half-open TCP connection. This can be an indication of a SYN flood attack.

To get the output in numerical format, use the –**n** option. Numerical format shows only IP addresses and port numbers (for example 192.168.10.10:80, instead of www.website1.com:http).

Using the Windows **netstat** Command to Display All Connections

To view both TCP and UDP connection statistics, use the –**a** options with the **netstat** command. The **-a** option can also display all the ports in the LISTENING state. Netadmins can use this list to verify whether malicious programs are active on the local machine. The output in Example 2-29 displays all active TCP connections and the TCP and UDP ports on which the computer is listening.

Example 2-29 *Windows* **netstat** *Command: All Connections*

```
c:\windows\system32>netstat -ao

Active Connections

  Proto  Local Address          Foreign Address        State           PID
```

Example 2-29 *Windows* **netstat** *Command: All Connections (Continued)*

```
TCP    WINXPBOX:epmap          WINXPBOX:0        LISTENING       1500
TCP    WINXPBOX:microsoft-ds   WINXPBOX:0        LISTENING       4
TCP    WINXPBOX:1025           WINXPBOX:0        LISTENING       1608
TCP    WINXPBOX:1030           WINXPBOX:0        LISTENING       4
TCP    WINXPBOX:3214           WINXPBOX:0        LISTENING       5384
TCP    WINXPBOX:3389           WINXPBOX:0        LISTENING       1608
TCP    WINXPBOX:4344           WINXPBOX:0        LISTENING       2312
TCP    WINXPBOX:58581          WINXPBOX:0        LISTENING       1728
TCP    WINXPBOX:3001           WINXPBOX:0        LISTENING       432
TCP    WINXPBOX:3002           WINXPBOX:0        LISTENING       1608
TCP    WINXPBOX:3003           WINXPBOX:0        LISTENING       1608
TCP    WINXPBOX:4343           WINXPBOX:0        LISTENING       2312
TCP    WINXPBOX:4343           localhost:4344    ESTABLISHED     2312
TCP    WINXPBOX:4344           localhost:4343    ESTABLISHED     2312
TCP    WINXPBOX:netbios-ssn    WINXPBOX:0        LISTENING       4
TCP    WINXPBOX:31337          WINXPBOX:0        LISTENING       1928
UDP    WINXPBOX:microsoft-ds   *:*                               4
UDP    WINXPBOX:3012           *:*                               1792
UDP    WINXPBOX:3147           *:*                               1792
UDP    WINXPBOX:62515          *:*                               476
UDP    WINXPBOX:62517          *:*                               476
UDP    WINXPBOX:62519          *:*                               476
UDP    WINXPBOX:62521          *:*                               476
UDP    WINXPBOX:62523          *:*                               476
UDP    WINXPBOX:62524          *:*                               476
UDP    WINXPBOX:netbios-ns     *:*                               4
UDP    WINXPBOX:netbios-dgm    *:*                               4
```

The output lists various TCP and UDP ports, the local and foreign addresses associated with the ports, and the current state of the ports. While most ports are referred to by the port number, some of the ports are indicated by well-known services associated with the port. For example, the second line of the output shows the port name microsoft-ds instead of the port number 445. Similarly, the command displays the host name instead of the IP address.

While most of the ports appear to be legitimate traffic, note the highlighted line showing TCP 31337 in the LISTENING state. The local host might be running a Trojan server on TCP 31337, because this port is associated with many malicious programs, including Backorifice. The Trojan server provides back-door entry into the host and is a security vulnerability.

Also, note the use of the **-o** option in Example 2-29. This option, available only in Windows XP and 2003, adds another column for process identification (PID). The PID view is useful in identifying a process associated with each of the TCP or UDP ports. Armed with the knowledge of the TCP/UDP port numbers used by a worm or Trojan, administrators can use the **-o** option to determine the PID of the malicious code and disarm it.

Using the Windows **netstat** Command to Display Network Statistics

To view a summary of protocol statistics, use the **-s** option. The output in Example 2-30 shows the protocol summary statistics for IP, ICMP, TCP, and UDP.

Also note the use of the **-e** option to display a summary of the Ethernet network interface.

Example 2-30 *Windows* **netstat** *Command: Network Statistics*

```
c:\windows\system32>netstat -es
Interface Statistics

                           Received            Sent

Bytes                     152762747        25211410
Unicast packets              322126          297809
Non-unicast packets           34543             952
Discards                          0               0
Errors                            0               2
Unknown protocols                 0

IPv4 Statistics

  Packets Received                   = 361884
  Received Header Errors             = 0
  Received Address Errors            = 32389
  Datagrams Forwarded                = 0
  Unknown Protocols Received         = 0
  Received Packets Discarded         = 0
  Received Packets Delivered         = 329497
  Output Requests                    = 304814
  Routing Discards                   = 0
  Discarded Output Packets           = 0
  Output Packet No Route             = 0
  Reassembly Required                = 0
  Reassembly Successful              = 0
  Reassembly Failures                = 0
  Datagrams Successfully Fragmented  = 0
  Datagrams Failing Fragmentation    = 0
  Fragments Created                  = 0

ICMPv4 Statistics

                            Received    Sent
  Messages                  315         321
  Errors                    0           0
  Destination Unreachable   8           17
  Time Exceeded             21          0
  Parameter Problems        0           0
  Source Quenches           0           0
  Redirects                 0           0
  Echos                     27          277
  Echo Replies              259         27
  Timestamps                0           0
```

Example 2-30 *Windows* **netstat** *Command: Network Statistics (Continued)*

```
    Timestamp Replies          0           0
    Address Masks              0           0
    Address Mask Replies       0           0

  TCP Statistics for IPv4

    Active Opens                             = 4129
    Passive Opens                            = 19
    Failed Connection Attempts               = 688
    Reset Connections                        = 362
    Current Connections                      = 3
    Segments Received                        = 187087
    Segments Sent                            = 161377
    Segments Retransmitted                   = 1346

  UDP Statistics for IPv4

    Datagrams Received       = 141829
    No Ports                 = 554
    Receive Errors           = 0
    Datagrams Sent           = 141711
```

The **-es** option is useful in detecting the traffic generated or received by the machine. The interface statistics provide a summary of packets sent and received. A high number of discards, errors, or unknown protocols indicates problems at the Ethernet level caused by cabling, duplex, and autonegotiation issues.

When the **netstat** command is used in conjunction with the **interval** option, network administrators can analyze traffic patterns. For example, the command **netstat -e 5** displays the Ethernet statistics summary and refreshes the output every 5 seconds. High numbers of errors, discards, failed connection attempts, and so on indicate problems that include Ethernet interface malfunction, cabling issues, DOS attacks, and so forth.

Using the Windows **netstat** Command to Display a Routing Table

Although the **route print** command can be used in MS-Windows to display the route table, the same output is available through the **netstat –r** command, as demonstrated in Example 2-31.

Example 2-31 *Windows* **netstat** *Command: Routing Table*

```
c:\windows\system32>netstat -r

Route Table
===========================================================================
Interface List
0x1 ........................... MS TCP Loopback interface
0x2 ...00 0d 56 df 86 a6 ...... Broadcom 570x Gigabit Integrated Controller - Pa
```

continues

Example 2-31 *Windows* **netstat** *Command: Routing Table (Continued)*

```
cket Scheduler Miniport
===========================================================================
===========================================================================
Active Routes:
Network Destination        Netmask          Gateway       Interface  Metric
          0.0.0.0          0.0.0.0      192.168.0.1   192.168.0.103       20
        127.0.0.0        255.0.0.0        127.0.0.1       127.0.0.1       1
      192.168.0.0    255.255.255.0    192.168.0.103   192.168.0.103       20
    192.168.0.103  255.255.255.255        127.0.0.1       127.0.0.1       20
    192.168.0.255  255.255.255.255    192.168.0.103   192.168.0.103       20
        224.0.0.0        240.0.0.0    192.168.0.103   192.168.0.103       20
  255.255.255.255  255.255.255.255    192.168.0.103   192.168.0.103       1
Default Gateway:       192.168.0.1
===========================================================================
Persistent Routes:
  Network Address          Netmask  Gateway Address  Metric
    64.154.80.250  255.255.255.255        127.0.0.1       1
```

This is useful in isolating routing or remote-connection issues faced by the machine, especially when other computers in the same subnet are working properly.

Using the Linux-Based **netstat** Command

The command-line–based **netstat** command is part of a standard Linux installation. To list active connections on a Linux computer, follow these steps:

Step 1 Open the command-line session.

Step 2 Type the command **netstat** and press **Enter**.

Optionally, type **netstat --help** for more information, as shown in Example 2-32.

Example 2-32 *Linux* **netstat** *Command: Help Output*

```
spope@linuxbox# netstat --help
usage: netstat [-veenNcCF] [<Af>] -r         netstat {-V¦--version¦-h¦--help}
       netstat [-vnNcaeol] [<Socket> ...]
       netstat { [-veenNac] -i ¦ [-cnNe] -M ¦ -s }

        -r, --route              display routing table
        -i, --interfaces         display interface table
        -g, --groups             display multicast group memberships
        -s, --statistics         display networking statistics (like SNMP)
        -M, --masquerade         display masqueraded connections

        -v, --verbose            be verbose
        -n, --numeric            don't resolve names
        --numeric-hosts          don't resolve host names
        --numeric-ports          don't resolve port names
        --numeric-users          don't resolve user names
```

Example 2-32 *Linux* **netstat** *Command: Help Output (Continued)*

```
        -N, --symbolic              resolve hardware names
        -e, --extend                display other/more information
        -p, --programs              display PID/Program name for sockets
        -c, --continuous            continuous listing

        -l, --listening             display listening server sockets
        -a, --all, --listening      display all sockets (default: connected)
        -o, --timers                display timers
        -F, --fib                   display Forwarding Information Base (default)
        -C, --cache                 display routing cache instead of FIB

  <Socket>={-t¦--tcp} {-u¦--udp} {-w¦--raw} {-x¦--unix} --ax25 --ipx --netrom
  <AF>=Use '-6¦-4' or '-A <af>' or '--<af>'; default: inet
  List of possible address families (which support routing):
    inet (DARPA Internet) inet6 (IPv6) ax25 (AMPR AX.25)
    netrom (AMPR NET/ROM) ipx (Novell IPX) ddp (Appletalk DDP)
    x25 (CCITT X.25)
```

If you compare the available options for the Windows **netstat** command (Example 2-27) to those of the Linux **netstat** command (Example 2-32), the latter offers far more flexibility.

The sections that follow discuss the use of various **netstat** options on a Linux computer for displaying the following items:

- Active connections
- All network connections
- Ethernet interface statistics
- Network statistics
- Routing table

Using the Linux **netstat** Command to Display Active Connections

Use the **netstat –t** command to display the currently active TCP connections. Example 2-33 shows the output of the **netstat –t** command.

Example 2-33 *Linux* **netstat** *Command: Active TCP Connections*

```
spope@linuxbox#netstat -t
Active Internet connections (w/o servers)
Proto Recv-Q Send-Q Local Address           Foreign Address         State

tcp        0      0 linuxbox:32855          www.myweb.com:www       ESTABLISHED
tcp        0      0 linuxbox:32854          www.myweb.com:www       ESTABLISHED
tcp        0      0 linuxbox:32857          www.myweb.com:www       ESTABLISHED
tcp        0      0 linuxbox:32856          www.myweb.com:www       ESTABLISHED
tcp        0    216 linuxbox:ssh            192.168.0.103:3578      ESTABLISHED
tcp        0      1 linuxbox:32858          64.154.80.250:www       SYN_SENT
tcp        0      0 linuxbox:5902           192.168.0.103:3645      ESTABLISHED
```

This command provides a quick snapshot of currently active TCP connections. You can also use the **–c** option to view a continuous display that gets refreshed periodically until interrupted by the user pressing **Ctrl-C**. The command syntax is as follows:

```
netstat -t -c
```

You can also force the output to use numeric format by using the **-n** option. For example, instead of showing the host name and the service (such as www.myweb.com:www), the command will display the IP address and the port number (such as 192.168.10.11:80). The command syntax is **netstat –tn**. Moreover, the **-n** option is also available in the Windows version of **netstat** command.

Using the Linux **netstat** Command to Display All Connections

The default **netstat** command with no option displays all the active network connections, including the UNIX sockets. To display all the active connections except the UNIX sockets, use the **netstat –atuwp** command. The **-p** option displays the PID/program pair for each listed connection. Example 2-34 shows the output of the **netstat –atuwp** command.

Example 2-34 *Linux* **netstat** *Command: All Connections*

```
spope@linuxbox#netstat -atuwp
Active Internet connections (servers and established)
Proto Recv-Q Send-Q Local Address           Foreign Address         State       PID/
Program name
tcp        0      0 *:5902                  *:*                     LISTEN      4649/Xrealvnc
tcp        0      0 *:x11                   *:*                     LISTEN      4433/XFree86
tcp        0      0 *:x11-2                 *:*                     LISTEN      4649/Xrealvnc
tcp        0      0 *:ssh                   *:*                     LISTEN      882/sshd
tcp        0      0 192.168.0.30:ssh        192.168.0.103:3578      ESTABLISHED3438/0
tcp        0      0 192.168.0.30:5902       192.168.0.103:3645      ESTABLISHED4649/
Xrealvnc
```

As discussed in the section "Using the Windows **netstat** Command to Display All Connections," earlier in this chapter, the PID/program name information is useful in identifying the source of network issues.

Using the Linux **netstat** Command to Display Ethernet Network Statistics

Use the **netstat –i** command to display the statistics of the Ethernet interface, as shown in Example 2-35. A high number of the errors, drops, or overruns indicate cabling or hardware issues. This command, when used in conjunction with the **-c** option (for continuous display), can aid in investigating abnormal data traffic originating from or terminating at the host.

Example 2-35 *Linux* ***netstat*** *Command: Ethernet Statistics*

```
spope@linuxbox# netstat -i
Kernel Interface table
Iface    MTU Met    RX-OK RX-ERR RX-DRP RX-OVR    TX-OK TX-ERR TX-DRP TX-OVR Flg
eth0    1500 0      89886      0      0      0    84992      1      0      0 BMRU
lo     16436 0        190      0      0      0      190      0      0      0 LRU
```

Using the Linux **netstat** Command to Display Network Statistics

Use the **netstat –s** command to get a summary of IP, ICMP, TCP, and UDP, as demonstrated in Example 2-36.

Example 2-36 *Linux* ***netstat*** *Command: Network Statistics*

```
spope@linuxbox# netstat -s
Ip:
    89849 total packets received
    0 forwarded
    0 incoming packets discarded
    70740 incoming packets delivered
    85127 requests sent out
Icmp:
    106 ICMP messages received
    3 input ICMP message failed.
    ICMP input histogram:
        destination unreachable: 17
        timeout in transit: 39
        echo requests: 33
        echo replies: 17
    53 ICMP messages sent
    0 ICMP messages failed
    ICMP output histogram:
        destination unreachable: 20
        echo replies: 33
Tcp:
    154 active connections openings
    12 passive connection openings
    0 failed connection attempts
    16 connection resets received
    2 connections established
    69608 segments received
    84542 segments send out
    4 segments retransmited
    0 bad segments received.
    30 resets sent
Udp:
    453 packets received
    3 packets to unknown port received.
    0 packet receive errors
    463 packets sent
TcpExt:
    27 TCP sockets finished time wait in fast timer
```

continues

Example 2-36 *Linux* **netstat** *Command: Network Statistics (Continued)*

```
    4471 delayed acks sent
    6 delayed acks further delayed because of locked socket
    Quick ack mode was activated 2 times
    953 packets directly queued to recvmsg prequeue.
    646566 of bytes directly received from prequeue
    20998 packet headers predicted
    618 packets header predicted and directly queued to user
    24212 acknowledgments not containing data received
    4642 predicted acknowledgments
    0 TCP data loss events
    2 other TCP timeouts
    23 DSACKs sent for old packets
    16 connections reset due to early user close
root@0[root]#
```

High numbers of errors, timeouts, and so on indicate problems including Ethernet interface malfunctions, cabling issues, DOS attacks, and so on.

Under ICMP input histogram and ICMP output histogram, the Echo Requests counter indicates the number of ping packets received by the host. A rapid increase in Echo Requests indicates that the host is under an ICMP flood attack.

Under TCP, a large number of segments retransmitted indicates packet loss. Also, a rapid increase in resets sent indicates that the host is being subjected to a TCP port scan.

Using the Linux **netstat** Command to Display a Routing Table

Use the **netstat –r** command to display a routing table of the host, as demonstrated in Example 2-37. Note that the **route** command provides an identical output.

Example 2-37 *Linux* **netstat** *Command: Routing Table*

```
spope@linuxbox# netstat -r
Kernel IP routing table
Destination     Gateway         Genmask         Flags   MSS Window  irtt Iface
192.168.0.0     *               255.255.255.0   U         0 0          0 eth0
default         192.168.0.1     0.0.0.0         UG        0 0          0 eth0
```

The routing table information is useful in isolating routing or remote-connection issues faced by the machine, especially when other computers in the same subnet are working properly.

Using the MS-Windows nbtstat Command to Trace MAC Addresses and Network Details

The Windows-based **nbtstat** command is an effective tool to remotely determine the current user on a Windows machine. Even in larger networks, it is comparatively easy to identify the source of a problem by its IP address. To determine the user on a Windows machine with that IP address, use the **nbtstat** command. It also provides the MAC address of the Ethernet interface.

To query the remote Windows computer for the name of the current user, follow these steps:

Step 1 Open the command-line session by choosing **Start > Programs > MS-DOS Prompt**.

Step 2 Type the command **nbtstat –A** *remote-ip-address* and press **Enter**.

Example 2-38 shows the Windows **nbtstat –A 192.168.0.15** command, which determines the current user on the Windows machine with an IP address of 192.168.0.15. As shown in the highlighted text, the current user is SPOPE. Also, the MAC address used by the Ethernet interface of that Windows machine is 00-0E-A6-13-41-62.

Example 2-38 *Output of the Windows* **nbtstat** *Command*

```
c:\windows\system32>nbtstat -A 192.168.0.15

Local Area Connection:
Node IpAddress: [192.168.0.103] Scope Id: []

          NetBIOS Remote Machine Name Table

      Name               Type         Status
   ---------------------------------------------
   WINPC1          <00>  UNIQUE      Registered
   WINPC1          <20>  UNIQUE      Registered
   WORKGROUP       <00>  GROUP       Registered
   WORKGROUP       <1E>  GROUP       Registered
   SPOPE           <03>  UNIQUE      Registered
   WORKGROUP       <1D>  UNIQUE      Registered
   ..__MSBROWSE__.<01>  GROUP       Registered

   MAC Address = 00-0E-A6-13-41-62
```

To determine which computer is connected to a switch port, network administrators typically trace the physical cable. This can get cumbersome in a larger network. The following example shows how to use the **nbtstat** command to do the same task:

Step 1 Use the **show mac-address-table dynamic** command on the Cisco Catalyst switch to view the MAC address of the devices connected to each port. The highlighted text in the following output of the command shows the MAC address learned through port 5/7 of the Catalyst switch:

```
Router# show mac-address-table dynamic

vlan   mac address      type     protocol  qos              ports
-----+---------------+--------+---------+---+------------------------
-------
 200  0010.0d40.37ff  dynamic        ip   --  5/8
  10 0080.1c93.8040   dynamic        ip   --  5/7
```

Step 2 Use the **show arp** command on a Cisco router to obtain the MAC address–to–IP address listing of devices connected to each port. As highlighted in the following output of the **show arp** command, MAC address 0080.1c93.8040 belongs to the IP address 172.20.52.12:

```
Router# show arp
Protocol  Address          Age (min)  Hardware Addr   Type   Interface
Internet  172.20.52.11             4  0090.2156.d800  ARPA   Vlan10
Internet  172.20.52.12            58  0080.1c93.8040  ARPA   Vlan10
```

Step 3 Use the **nbtstat –A** *ip-address* command to determine the user who is logged in to the machine with that IP address. The MAC address included in the output of the **nbtstat** command should verify the results. As highlighted in the following output, SPOPE is the user logged in to machine 172.20.52.115 with the Ethernet MAC address 0080.1c93.8040:

```
c:\windows\system32>nbtstat -A 172.20.52.12

Local Area Connection:
Node IpAddress: [172.20.52.115] Scope Id: []

           NetBIOS Remote Machine Name Table
       Name                  Type         Status
    ---------------------------------------------
    XPDOMAIN11974       <00>  UNIQUE      Registered
    XPDOMAIN            <00>  GROUP       Registered
    XPDOMAIN11974L      <20>  UNIQUE      Registered
    XPDOMAIN            <1E>  GROUP       Registered
    XPDOMAIN11974L      <03>  UNIQUE      Registered
    SPOPE               <03>  UNIQUE      Registered
    XPDOMAIN            <1D>  UNIQUE      Registered
    ..__MSBROWSE__.<01>  GROUP        Registered

    MAC Address = 0080.1c93.8040
```

Alternately, you can use the **nbtstat -A** *ip-address* command first to determine the username and the MAC address. Using the MAC address, you can then identify the user's switch port.

Using the arp Command to Trace Layer 2 Issues

The **arp** command is useful in checking the local arp table of a host. The arp table contains the MAC address (also referred to as the physical address)–to–IP address mappings. Checking the arp table is most useful when dealing with Layer 2 or duplicate IP address issues.

To use the **arp** command on Linux or Windows, follow these steps:

Step 1 Open the command-line session.

Step 2 Type the command **arp** *option* [*parameter*] and press **Enter**.

Table 2-8 lists the most useful options for the **arp** command. These options are applicable to both Windows and Linux versions.

Table 2-8 *Options for the* **arp** *Command*

Option	Description
-a	Displays the current arp entries.
-s *ip-address mac-address*	Manually adds an IP address–to–MAC address mapping.
-d *ip-address*	Deletes a particular entry by the IP address; the Windows version also allows you to use the **-d** option without specifying an IP address to clear all the arp entries.

NOTE Although the MAC address is expressed as a 12-digit hexadecimal number, the exact format is different on each OS platform. The formats for various platforms are as follows:

- **Windows**—NN-NN-NN-NN-NN-NN; example: 00-11-22-33-44-55
- **Linux**—NN:NN:NN:NN:NN:NN; example: 00:11:22:33:44:55
- **Cisco IOS and PIX**—NNNN.NNNN.NNN; example: 0011.2233.4455
- **Cisco CatOS**—NN-NN-NN-NN-NN-NN; example: 00-11-22-33-44-55

The arp tables are populated dynamically and do not require manual intervention. However, the arp table might be corrupt because of false arp entries. In that case, Netadmins can flush the arp table using the **arp -d** command. Netadmins can also use the **arp -s** command to manually override the arp entries. Manually setting the arp entry is useful when dealing with duplicate IP address issues.

The following scenario elaborates the use of the **arp** command to troubleshoot Layer 2 issues.

Scenario: Consider a LAN scenario shown in Figure 2-11, where all the hosts use the Ethernet interface of the router as the default gateway. The IP address of the default gateway is 192.168.10.254.

Figure 2-11 *Using the* **arp** *Command for Troubleshooting*

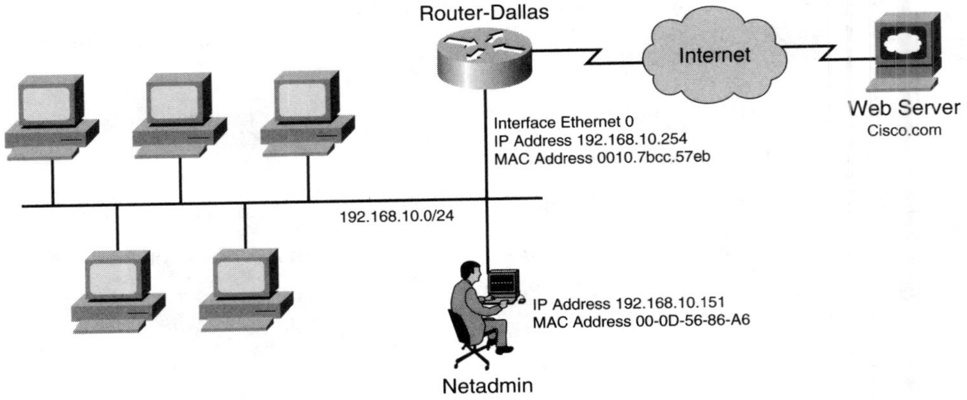

Problem: All the hosts in the 192.168.10.0/24 subnet of the LAN are facing intermittent connectivity issues. The regular applications like web and e-mail are either not working or are extremely slow.

Troubleshooting: Because all the hosts in the LAN are facing the issue, the Netadmin pings the default gateway to verify the connectivity. The ping replies from 192.168.10.254 are successful, but pings to any address beyond the Ethernet interface fails. So the Netadmin tries to Telnet into the router for further investigation. However, the Telnet connection fails, too. The Netadmin then consoles into the router and issues the **show interface ethernet0** command, as shown in Example 2-39.

Example 2-39 *Router* **show interface** *Command*

```
Router-Dallas# show interface ethernet0
Ethernet0 is up, line protocol is up
  Hardware is QUICC Ethernet, address is 0010.7bcc.57eb (bia 0010.7bcc.57eb)
  Internet address is 192.168.10.254/24
  MTU 1500 bytes, BW 10000 Kbit, DLY 1000 usec, rely 255/255, load 1/255
  Encapsulation ARPA, loopback not set, keepalive set (10 sec)
  ARP type: ARPA, ARP Timeout 04:00:00
  Last input 00:00:04, output 00:00:01, output hang never
  Last clearing of "show interface" counters never
  Queueing strategy: fifo
  Output queue 0/40, 0 drops; input queue 0/75, 0 drops
  5 minute input rate 1000 bits/sec, 1 packets/sec
```

Example 2-39 *Router* **show interface** *Command (Continued)*

```
  5 minute output rate 0 bits/sec, 0 packets/sec
     40160541 packets input, 3615923641 bytes, 44 no buffer
     Received 1536632 broadcasts, 0 runts, 6 giants, 51 throttles
     35 input errors, 0 CRC, 29 frame, 0 overrun, 0 ignored, 0 abort
     0 input packets with dribble condition detected
     29464546 packets output, 3879477225 bytes, 0 underruns
     0 output errors, 109366 collisions, 3 interface resets
     0 babbles, 0 late collision, 91503 deferred
     0 lost carrier, 0 no carrier
     0 output buffer failures, 0 output buffers swapped out
```

The output of the **show interface ethernet0** command indicates that the interface and the protocol are up. The output also shows 0010.7bcc.57eb as the MAC address assigned to the Ethernet interface of the router.

The Netadmin then uses the **arp -a** command to check the local arp table on his workstation, as shown in Example 2-40.

Example 2-40 *Checking the Local* **arp** *Table*

```
c:\windows\system32>arp -a

Interface: 192.168.10.151 --- 0x2
  Internet Address      Physical Address      Type
  192.168.10.254        00-d0-c8-af-e2-5e     dynamic
```

The arp table entries indicate that 192.168.10.254 is mapped to MAC address 00-d0-c8-af-e2-5e instead of 00-10-7b-cc-57-eb. The incorrect mapping misdirects all the Internet traffic to the host with the MAC address 00-d0-c8-af-e2-5e.

Following are the possible causes of the incorrect entry in the local host:

- The IP address of the default gateway is also used by another host in the local subnet.
- A local host is running a malicious program to poison the arp table of all the hosts in the subnet.

The Netadmin must identify and reconfigure the offending machine. Meanwhile, to restore the connectivity between the local host and the default gateway, the Netadmin should clear the arp table and then manually map the IP address 192.168.10.254 to the correct MAC address of 00-10-7b-cc-57-eb, as shown in Example 2-41. Although the commands shown in Example 2-41 are on a Windows platform, the syntax should work on Linux as well.

Example 2-41 *Manipulating the* **arp** *Table*

```
# Delete the current arp entry for 192.168.10.254
c:\windows\system32> arp -d 192.168.10.254
# add a static entry for 192.168.10.254
c:\windows\system32> arp -s 192.168.10.254 00-10-7b-cc-57-eb
# Display the arp table
```

continues

Example 2-41 *Manipulating the* **arp** *Table (Continued)*

```
c:\windows\system32> arp -a

Interface: 192.168.10.151 --- 0x2
  Internet Address      Physical Address      Type
  192.168.10.254        00-10-7b-cc-57-eb     static
```

Note that the manually added entry for 192.168.10.254 shows up as static. The arp entries that are automatically learned show up as dynamic in the arp table. After manually mapping the MAC address, the local host is able to communicate with the rest of the network beyond the default gateway.

Summary

The topics covered in this chapter prepare network administrators for verifying basic network connectivity. Administrators should be able to perform the following tasks:

1. Use the **ping** command to verify connectivity between two networked nodes.
2. Use the **traceroute** command to determine the path traversed by the packets flowing between two networked nodes.
3. Use the **whois** command to determine the administrative information of a host or domain in a public network.
4. Use the **dig** or **nslookup** command to determine the DNS and mail server details for a host or Internet domain.
5. Use the **netstat** and **nbtstat** commands to determine TCP/IP sessions and statistics for network end stations.
6. Use the **arp** command to verify Layer 2 information on TCP/IP hosts.

Table 2-9 provides a list of all the tools discussed in this chapter.

Table 2-9 *Tools Discussed in This Chapter*

Tool	Function	Supported OS	Installable Files
ping	Verifies connectivity and round-trip time	Windows, Linux, IOS, CatOS	Preloaded with all supported OSs
fping	Pings multiple hosts simultaneously; faster response	Linux	http://www.fping.com
hping	Adds functionality to ping	Linux	http://www.hping.org/

Table 2-9 *Tools Discussed in This Chapter (Continued)*

Tool	Function	Supported OS	Installable files
SmokePing	Provides prolonged and graphic version of Ping	Linux	http://people.ee.ethz.ch/~oetiker/webtools/smokeping/
traceroute	Traces the data path	Windows, Linux, IOS, CatOS	Preloaded with all supported OSs
whois	Determines administrative and registration information for an Internet domain	Linux	Preloaded with all supported OSs
nslookup	Queries DNS server to determine information about an Internet domain or host	Part of Windows and Linux	Preloaded with all supported OSs
dig	Queries DNS server to determine information about an Internet domain or host; advanced version of nslookup	Linux	Preloaded with all supported OSs
netstat	Determines TCP/IP active sessions and statistics	Windows, Linux	Preloaded with all supported OSs
nbtstat	Determines network information for remote Windows computers	Windows	Preloaded with all supported OSs

CHAPTER 3

Access Control

As discussed in the previous chapter, you can configure a Cisco device through the console port or through remote access, such as Telnet or SSH. However, to prevent unauthorized use, such access to the devices should be controlled. This chapter covers the tools that control and record administrative access to Cisco devices. The three functions of securing access to a Cisco device, controlling user activity, and recording user activity are together known as authentication, authorization, and accounting—or AAA. Terminal Access Controller Access Control System Plus (TACACS+) and Remote Authentication Dial-In User Service (RADIUS) are the two protocols for implementing the AAA technology framework.

Based on the protocols used by AAA, this chapter consists of the following three parts:

- Overview of AAA technology
- Using TACACS+ for AAA
- Using RADIUS for AAA

Overview of AAA Technology

Cisco created the AAA technology framework for configuring three separate features on Cisco devices. According to Cisco, AAA consists of the following components:

- **Authentication**—The process of validating the claimed identity of an end user or a device, such as a host, server, switch, router, and so on
- **Authorization**—The act of granting access rights to a user, groups of users, a system, or a process
- **Accounting**—The methods to establish who or what performed a certain action, such as tracking user connection and logging system users

The AAA architectural framework defines the use of RADIUS and TACACS+ protocols (discussed later in this chapter) for access control. AAA provides flexible, scalable, modular access control of network devices. However, the capability to centrally manage access to all the networking devices is a major advantage of AAA.

To understand the significance of AAA, consider a typical case where a user connects to a network device using the Telnet password, changes configuration, and logs out. There is no record of the time of login, identity of the user, or change in the configuration. By enabling AAA on the device, you can do the following:

- Control who logs in to the device (authentication)
- Control what commands the user can use (authorization)
- Record the changes made by the user (accounting)

A detailed record of user activities, also known as an *audit trail*, helps in troubleshooting or auditing at a later stage. The audit trails are also helpful in investigating cyber-crimes. In many industries, audit trails can be mandatory because of government regulation. For example, the U.S. Health Insurance Portability and Accountability Act (HIPAA) defines a set of security standards for the healthcare industry. Another advantage of AAA in a multi-administrator site is that you can centrally restrict access to devices when a particular user's employment is terminated. Otherwise, without AAA, you need to change the authentication information on each device.

The AAA architecture framework defines the following two components:

- **AAA Client**—A AAA Client is any network device that is being monitored for authentication, authorization, and accounting. The device should be configured to use the AAA feature. It should also have IP connectivity to the AAA Servers. The client communicates with the AAA Server to verify the access rights for a user.
- **AAA Server**—A AAA Server functions as a service running over the Windows or Linux operating system (OS). While the AAA Server is available as application software for various OSs, Windows 2000 and 2003 also feature a built-in AAA Server. The AAA Server responds to the requests made by the AAA Clients. The server uses an internal database to validate the requests made by the AAA Client. Additionally, the database must be populated with the list of all valid AAA Clients. A network can have a single AAA Server for centralized access control. However, deploying multiple AAA Servers provides redundancy.

Figure 3-1 depicts a scenario in which a Cisco router acts as a AAA Client. The netadmin attempts to access the router via telnet or SSH or console. The router queries the AAA Server to validate access control requests.

The AAA framework is flexible because it supports either of the following two protocols:

- RADIUS
- TACACS+

The following sections provide more history, features, and operational details regarding each of these protocols. Readers who are familiar with TACACS+ and RADIUS can skip these sections if they want to.

Figure 3-1 *AAA Scenario*

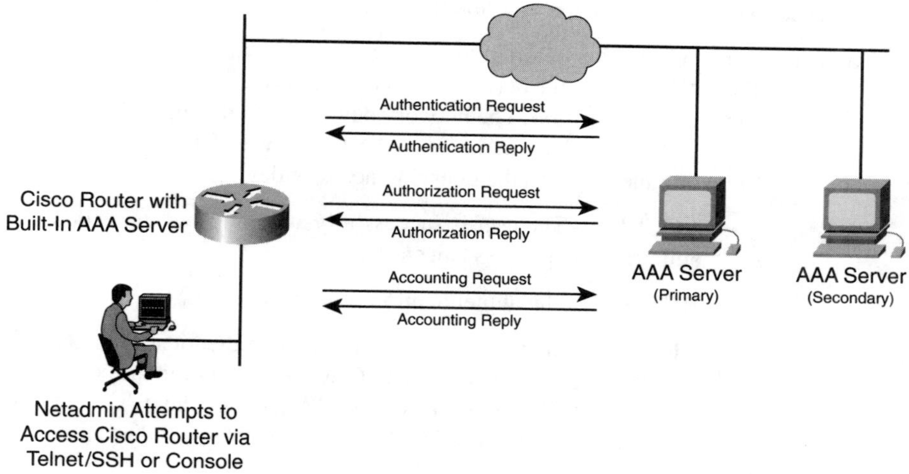

TACACS+

TACACS+ was developed by Cisco and was proposed as an Internet Engineering Task Force (IETF) draft. TACACS+, a set of client/server software and protocols that provides AAA services, offers the following features:

- **Centralized access control**—Provides centralized management of access control services across the network.
- **Modular services**—Provides separate and modular authentication, authorization, and accounting services. These services can use a single database, or each service can have its own database to leverage other services that are available on that server or on the network.
- **Encryption**—All protocol exchanges between the client and a TACACS+ Server are encrypted. Both the client and the server should be configured with the same encryption key.
- **Reliability**—Uses the Transmission Control Protocol (TCP) for a reliable and robust connection between the client and the server. The default TCP port number is 49, although this can be changed.

Although Cisco has submitted TACACS+ to the IETF, it has yet to be approved. This makes it a Cisco-proprietary protocol, with little acceptance outside Cisco.

TACACS+ works within the AAA framework to provide the authentication, authorization, and accounting function. As defined under the AAA framework, TACACS+ consists of two components—the TACACS+ Client and the TACACS+ Server. The TACACS+ Client can be any network device that queries the TACACS+ Server to validate access control requests. The following steps describe the operation of the TACACS+ protocol:

Step 1 When a user tries to log in to a network device that is working as a TACACS+ Client, the network device prompts the user for username and password information. The network device sends this information back to the TACACS+ Server. The TACACS+ Server responds with one of the following messages to the querying network device:

- **ACCEPT**—The user is successfully authenticated. If needed, the authorization process can start.
- **REJECT**—The authentication process failed for the user.
- **ERROR**—An error occurred during the authentication process. The error can be either in the TACACS+ Server or in the connection between the TACACS+ Server and TACACS+ Client. The network device can use another TACACS+ Server.
- **CONTINUE**—The user is prompted for additional information.

Step 2 After completing the authentication process, the user can begin the optional authorization process. The TACACS+ Server is contacted again to authorize the commands run by the user. The TACACS+ Server returns an ACCEPT or REJECT authorization response. The ACCEPT response contains additional attributes that provide the EXEC or NETWORK privileges for that user.

Step 3 The accounting process can only begin after completion of the authentication and authorization processes. Similar to the authorization process, the accounting process is also optional. The TACACS+ accounting process keeps a log of activities performed by the user. As with the authorization process, the network device sends a REQUEST packet that contains the START RECORD or STOP RECORD response to the TACACS+ Server. The TACACS+ Server returns a RESPONSE packet to acknowledge the request. The START RECORD accounting notice indicates the beginning of the process, while the STOP RECORD response indicates the end of the process.

RADIUS

The RADIUS protocol was originally developed by Livingston Enterprises Inc. and is now part of the IETF-based standard described by RFC 2138 and 2139. Cisco introduced support for RADIUS in Cisco IOS Release 11.1. Similar to TACACS+, a RADIUS Server provides authentication and accounting services to one or more network devices that are acting as RADIUS Clients. A RADIUS Server runs as a service over an OS such as

Windows or Linux. The RADIUS Client sends authentication requests to a central RADIUS Server that contains all user authentication and network service access information. Typically, a RADIUS Server is deployed as a dedicated machine that is connected to the network. You can have multiple RADIUS Servers for redundancy.

RADIUS offers the following features:

- **Centralized access control**—Provides a centralized management of access control services across the network.
- **Encryption**—Unlike TACACS+, RADIUS only encrypts the password. The RADIUS client uses Message Digest 5 (MD5) algorithm to send password to the RADIUS server. The MD5 algorithm produces a *message digest* or *hash* of the password. Instead of the password, the hash is sent to ensure that no one can learn the password by eavesdropping on the line.
- **UDP-based protocol**—Uses User Datagram Protocol (UDP) ports 1812 and 1645 for authentication and ports 1813 and 1646 for accounting. The use of UDP provides faster performance because the RADIUS protocol includes a built-in mechanism for handling retransmission and timeout issues, thus eliminating the need for TCP.
- **Cisco support**—Is supported on all Cisco platforms, but some RADIUS-supported features run only on specific platforms.
- **Industrywide standard**—Support by various vendors for AAA implementation make it ideal for networks with multiple-vendor access servers. Because it is a fully open protocol and is distributed in source code format, RADIUS can be modified to work with any security system that is currently on the market.
- **Vendor-specific attributes (VSA)**—Allows customization by letting vendors support extended attributes that are unique to their designs.

TIP For a list of Cisco-specific RADIUS VSAs, refer to the article "RADIUS Attributes" on Cisco.com. The URL is as follows:

http://www.cisco.com/en/US/products/sw/secursw/ps5338/products_user_guide_chapter09186a008023360b.html#wp242440

The operation of RADIUS is similar to that of the TACACS+ protocol. However, during the authentication process, the RADIUS Server responds with one of the following messages to the RADIUS Client:

- **ACCEPT**—The user authentication is successful.
- **REJECT**—The user authentication has failed. The user is prompted to re-enter a username and password; otherwise, access is denied.
- **CHALLENGE**—The RADIUS Server prompts the user for more information.

- **CHANGE PASSWORD**—The RADIUS Server requests the user to change the existing password.

The ACCEPT or REJECT response can contain additional data required for authorization.

RADIUS and TACACS+ Comparison

This chapter focuses on the basic functionality of AAA, using RADIUS and TACACS+ protocols, to secure access to the network devices.

While both RADIUS and TACACS+ provide AAA functionality, their industrywide usage pattern is different. TACACS+ is often used for securing access to networking devices such as routers and switches. RADIUS is widely used for controlling access to network resources such as http, ftp, e-mail, and file and print sharing through dial-up or Virtual Private Networks (VPN). In such scenarios, the access devices (called network access servers, or NAS) are configured to query the RADIUS Servers to verify the user's request to a particular resource. Examples of devices that use RADIUS are as follows:

- Access routers with a modem pool for remote dial-up
- Routers with a per-user access list
- Switches with port security
- Firewalls with authentication proxies
- VPN concentrators for remote users
- WLANs with 802.1X user authentication
- Wireless application protocol (WAP) devices

Table 3-1 summarizes the main differences between the two popular choices of AAA protocols.

Table 3-1 *TACACS+ and RADIUS Comparison*

	TACACS+	RADIUS
Developer	Cisco.	Livingston; it is now an open-protocol standard.
Deployment	Cisco.	Multiple vendors including Cisco.
Ports	TCP 49.	UDP 1812, 1813, 1645, 1646.
RFC	IETF draft-grant-TACACS.	RFC 2865.
Encryption	Entire packet is encrypted, except the header.	Only password is encrypted; packet is in clear text.
Modularity	Separates authentication, authorization, and accounting, providing greater control.	Authentication and authorization are combined.

Table 3-1 *TACACS+ and RADIUS Comparison (Continued)*

	TACACS+	RADIUS
Protocol Support	Multiprotocol support.	No support for the following: AppleTalk Remote Access (ARA) Protocol, NetBIOS Frame Protocol Control Protocol, Novell Asynchronous Services Interface (NASI), and X.25 PAD connection.
Router Commands	Provides granular control over each router command that can be executed on a per-user or per-group basis.	No support for controlling each router command.

Using TACACS+ for AAA

Most Cisco devices, including IOS routers and switches, CatOS-based switches, PIX Firewalls, and VPN concentrators, have a built-in TACACS+ Client. To implement TACACS+-based AAA functionality, Netadmins must do the following:

- Deploy a TACACS+ Server in the network
- Configure the built-in TACACS+ Client in each Cisco device

The sections that follow provide details about the following items:

- Deploying a Linux-based TACACS+ Server
- Configuring a Cisco router for TACACS+
- Configuring a Cisco switch for TACACS+
- Configuring a Cisco PIX Firewall for TACACS+
- Configuring a Cisco VPN concentrator for TACACS+

Deploying a Linux-Based TACACS+ Server

To deploy a Linux-based TACACS+ Server, you must first have a Linux machine preconfigured with basic network settings. The examples depicted in this discussion were created in Debian Linux, which was installed on an Intel Pentium III–based workstation with 256 MB RAM and an Ethernet network interface card (NIC).

Following is the partial list of UNIX/Linux–based TACACS+ Servers:

- TACACS+ freeware from http://www.cisco.com
- Jffnms from http://www.jffnms.org/
- TACPPD from http://tacppd.org/

Of these three servers, this discussion covers TACACS+ freeware from Cisco for the following reasons:

- Ease of configuration.
- Wide array of sample configurations on the Cisco website.
- Tested stability and scalability, with a proven capacity to support 75,000 user entries.
- The configuration and properties of the TACACS+ freeware are controlled through an arbitrary text file. The deployment process for the TACACS+ freeware involves installing the software, editing the configuration file, and starting the service. The following discussion covers these steps, including details of the TACACS+ configuration file.

Downloading the Installation Files

The TACACS+ freeware for UNIX/Linux was developed by Cisco and is available under the open source license. Download and save the TACACS+ freeware installable files through FTP at ftp://anonymous@ftp-eng.cisco.com/pub/tacacs/. If you are prompted by the Cisco ftp site for a password, you can enter your e-mail address as the password. The name of the file is tac_plus.F4.0.4.alpha.tar.z. The tar.z extension indicates that the file is a compressed archive file in tar format. The tar file contains the TACACS+ Daemon. In this example, the TACACS+ Daemon is assumed to be saved in the /home directory.

NOTE Throughout this chapter, the TACACS+ Daemon is referred to as the TACACS+ Server or simply as TACACS+. Likewise, the RADIUS Server and RADIUS Daemon are one and same. Professionals from the UNIX world use the term *daemon,* whereas those from Windows use *server.*

Installing the TACACS+ Daemon

After downloading the tar files, follow these steps to install the TACACS+ Daemon:

Step 1 Open a command prompt, use the **cd /home** command to change to the /home directory, and extract the tar file using the **tar zxvf tac_plus.F4.0.4.alpha.tar.Z** command. This command extracts the uncompressed content in the /home/tac_plus.F4.0.4.alpha subdirectory.

Step 2 The extracted subdirectory (/home/tac_plus.F4.0.4.alpha) contains a file called Makefile. Edit Makefile using your favorite text editor, such as vi, to specify the OS. For the Linux environment, Makefile should reflect the following changes:

```
# For Solaris (SUNOS 5.3, 5.4, 5.5, 5.6) uncomment the following two
  lines
#OS=-DSOLARIS
```

```
#OSLIBS=-lsocket -lnsl
...
# output suppresses for clarity
...
# On REDHAT 5.0 systems, or systems that use the new glibc,
# you might instead need the following:
OS=-DLINUX -DGLIBC
OSLIBS=-lcrypt
...
```

Step 3 Within the extracted subdirectory (tac_plus.F4.0.4.alpha, in this example), run the install script by entering the **make tac_plus** command followed by the **make install** command.

Step 4 Using your favorite text editor, edit the /etc/services file to enable the TACACS+ Server to listen on the TCP 49 port. The /etc/services file must contain the following entry:

```
tacacs      tcp/49
```

The TACACS+ Server is now ready for configuration.

TIP **Timesaver:** For Debian Linux, avoid the four-step installation routine by using the single command **apt-get install tac-plus**.

Configuring the Text File

The TACACS+ Daemon is configured through a single configuration file in text format. Users can create a configuration file from scratch or customize the sample file created by the install script in the /usr/local/bin directory. Information regarding the configuration file is explained in the users_guide file. This file, included with the source tar file, can be found in the directory from which all the other install files were extracted. If you used the **apt-get install tac-plus** command to install the TACACS+ Daemon on a Debian system, the users_guide file is located in the /usr/share/doc/tac-plus/ directory.

The configuration file controls the generic properties of the TACACS+ Daemon, including the TACACS+ encryption key, the default authentication mechanism, and the location of the accounting log file. The username, passwords, account expiry, exec shell authorization, and command authorization are also controlled through the configuration file. This file allows you to group multiple users under common groups for efficient management. Line entries beginning with # (the pound sign) are treated as comments. Example 3-1 shows the content of the sample file /etc/tac-plus/tacacs.conf after suitable edits. This file illustrates a typical configuration needed to run the TACACS+ Daemon.

Example 3-1 */etc/tac-plus/tacacs.conf File*

```
#######################
# CONFIGURE  ENCYPTION KEY
key = VerYs3cr3taqskey
#######################
# CONFIGURE DEFAULT AUTHENTICATION
# Query the /etc/passwd file for default authentication
default authentication = file /etc/passwd
# Location of text file to log Accounting records
#######################
# CONFIGURE  ACCOUNTING LOG FILE
accounting file = /var/log/tac.log
######################
# CONFIGURE GROUP
######################
# Network administrator group
group = netadmin {
# netadmin group for supervisor access
default service = permit
service = exec {
priv-lvl = 15
}
}
# Regular user group
group = regularusers {
# regular users will be added to this group
default service = deny
service = exec {
priv-lvl = 1
}
}
######################
# CONFIGURE USERS
######################
# Netadmin users
# note that there is no password entry
# tacacs+ daemon will query the /etc/passwd file for this user
user = spope {
member = netadmin
}
# Users with limited privileges
user = jkeith {
member = regularusers
login = cleartext "securepassword123"
cmd = show {
permit .*
}
cmd = exit {
permit .*
}
```

Example 3-1 */etc/tac-plus/tacacs.conf File (Continued)*

```
cmd = telnet {
permit 192\.168\.1\.[0-9]+
deny .*
}
}
# Temp user account for consultant
user = consultant1 {
expires = "Dec 15 2005"
login = des egCv7fX.G5FgQ
service = exec {
# When an exec is started, autocmd starts
autocmd = "show ip interface brief"
}
}
# End  file
```

The general format for specifying the parameters in the configuration file is **attribute = value**. The value might have additional subparameters. In such cases, the subparameters are enclosed in braces ({}).

CAUTION You can use the **chmod** command to limit access to the configuration file because it contains sensitive information. The following example code shows that the file permissions are changed to allow read and write access for the root user only:

```
linuxbox:~# chmod 600 /etc/tac-plus/tacacs.conf
linuxbox:~# ls -l  /etc/tac-plus/tacacs.conf
-rw-------  1 root root   1855 Mar 20 22:27 tacacs.conf
```

The following sections describe the significance of each component of the configuration file. The discussion also covers the syntax and sample code for each component.

Configuring the Encryption Key

TACACS+ uses an encryption key to encrypt the packets. The same key is specified on both the client and the server. The syntax is **key =** *tacacs-encryption-key*.

Configuring Default Authentication

For every user listed in the TACACS+ Daemon file, you must specify a password (discussed in the section "Configuring the Password (User Authentication)," later in this chapter. Manually maintaining the passwords for a large number of users can be cumbersome and inefficient. To circumvent this limitation, the TACACS+ Daemon can use the passwords listed in the /etc/passwd file on the local Linux servers to authenticate users. Before using the /etc/passwd file for authentication, you must define the users on the local Linux machine. For example, before adding user spope in the configuration file, you must create the user spope using the **adduser** command on the local Linux machine.

Using the /etc/passwd file eliminates the need to specify a password for every user within the configuration file. The command syntax is **default authentication = file** *location-of-password-file*. Configuring the TACACS+ Daemon to use the /etc/passwd file enables users to change their passwords without accessing the configuration file. This feature frees the Netadmin from having to maintain individual passwords.

NOTE The authentication mechanism of using the local passwords listed in the /etc/passwd file fails for secure Linux versions that use shadow passwords. In such cases, Debian Linux users can turn off the shadow password feature by using the **shadowconfig off** command. However, you should not turn off this feature for security reasons. For more information on shadow passwords, visit the following URL:

http://www.tldp.org/HOWTO/Shadow-Password-HOWTO.html

Configuring Groups

Groups provide an easy way to group similar users. Instead of modifying the properties of each user, you can simply modify the properties of the group to which the users belong. Apart from saving time, groups also provide ease and efficiency in managing a large number of users. The syntax for configuring groups is as follows:

```
group = group-name {
# comments for describing the group
attribute-1 = value {
attribute-2 = value
}
. . .
attribute-n = value
}
```

The **attribute** and **value** are used to specify authentication and authorization information (discussed in the following sections) for the group.

Example 3-1 shows two groups—netadmin and regularusers. The following excerpt shows just the group and description from the configuration file:

```
group = netadmin {
    # netadmin group for supervisor access
}
group = regularusers {
    # regular users will be added to this group
}
```

Configuring Users

The most important element of the configuration file, and, in turn, the TACACS+ Daemon, is the username. Without a username, authentication cannot occur. Moreover, without authentication, neither authorization nor accounting can occur. Although, there is no documented limit to the number of users you can create, the TACACS+ Daemon has been tested successfully with 75,000 usernames. You can optionally assign each user to any group; however, the TACACS+ user can only belong to a single TACACS+ group. You can define parameters such as the group membership and authentication and authorization properties for each user under the user's profile. The syntax is as follows:

```
user = username {
# comment for describing the user
member = groupname
attribute-1 = value {
attribute-2 = value
}
. . .
attribute-n = value
}
```

If the user also belongs to a group, the properties defined for the user take precedence over those defined for his group. Consider a case of user joe being defined as a member of the sysadmin group. If the expiration date (discussed in the section "Configuring Expiration Dates," later in this chapter) for user joe is defined as January 2, 2006, but that for the sysadmin group is March 3, 2006, Joe's account will expire after January.

The following is an excerpt from Example 3-1, showing just three users and their group membership:

```
user = spope {
              # user spope is a member of netadmin group
              member = netadmin
}
user = jkeith {
    # jkeith is a member of regularusers group
    member = regularusers
}
user = consultant1 {
    # consultant1 is a not member of any  group
}
```

While spope and jkeith are defined as members of the netadmin and regularusers groups, respectively, consultant1 is not a member of any group. The netadmin group has administrative privileges that allow unrestricted access, while regularusers has limited privileges. A typical case of limited privilege is help-desk or remote-admin staff, who can only view device status but cannot change any configuration. In other cases, such as a temporary consultant, you should provide that person with extremely limited access.

Configuring the Password (User Authentication)

Despite defining the default authentication at the top level, per-user authentication can be defined under each user profile. The user authentication password can be specified as clear text or DES encrypted, or from the /etc/passwd file. The syntax for the three possible values is as follows:

```
user = username1 {
login = cleartext password-in-clear-text
}
user = username2 {
login = des DES-encryptedin-password
}
user = username3 {
login = file path-to-local-file
}
```

Note that the clear-text password is accessible to anyone who can access the configuration file. To overcome this security limitation, you can use encrypted passwords. The TACACS+ Daemon includes a utility, called generate_passwd, that allows you to create DES-encrypted passwords from clear-text passwords. You can manually copy and paste the encrypted password into the configuration file, but manually copying each password can be cumbersome for a large number of users. In such cases, you can instruct the TACACS+ Daemon to use the local passwords that are contained in the /etc/passwd file for the user. Note that the username and password should be defined on the local Linux machine; passwords should be defined using the Linux command **passwd** *username*. Also, as noted earlier, you cannot use a local password file (such as /etc/passwd) for Linux systems that use shadow passwords.

NOTE The following is sample output for the generate passwd utility that demonstrates the encryption of the clear-text password cisco123:

```
linuxbox:~# generate_passwd
Password to be encrypted: cisco123
egCv7fX.G5FgQ
linuxbox:~#
```

The following excerpt from Example 3-1 shows the password configuration for the three users—spope, jkeith, and consultant1:

```
user = spope {
member = netadmin
}
    user = jkeith {
        login = cleartext "securepassword123"
        }
    user = consultant1 {
        # this is encrypted DES password, manually generated by
    # program "generate_passwd" which is included with source tar
    password = des egCv7fX.G5FgQ
    }
```

This example does not specify a password mechanism for the user spope. Hence, the TACACS+ Daemon uses the default authentication mechanism (using the /etc/passwd file) for user spope. For user jkeith, the password securepassword123 is specified in clear text, while for user consultant1, the DES-encrypted password is egCv7fX.G5FgQ. To set the password for local users in Linux, you can use the **passwd** *username* command. The following code shows the procedure for setting the password longpassword for user spope on a Linux machine:

```
linuxbox:~# passwd spope
Enter new UNIX password: longpassword
Retype new UNIX password: longpassword
passwd: password updated successfully
```

Configuring Expiration Dates

To limit the age of a user account, specify the expiration date in the MMM DD YYYY format. Expiration applies to all password types except file passwords. The syntax is as follows:

```
user = username {
    expires = "MMM DD YYYY"
}
```

The following excerpt from Example 3-1 shows the expiration date for user consultant1:

```
user = consultant1 {
    expires = "Dec 15 2005"
}
```

In the absence of an expiration date for the user (or the group the user belongs to), the account will never expire.

Configuring Service Authorization

Authorization allows the TACACS+ Daemon to permit or deny commands and services on a global or per-user basis. Authorization also provides the ability to modify commands and services on a per-user (or per-group) basis.

By default, the TACACS+ Daemon denies authorization for all services, including the exec service. You must explicitly authorize each service for every user (or group).

The default service authorization is specified at the group level and is applied to all members of the group. However, to provide tighter control for a single user, you can also declare a service authorization for each user under the user profile.

For groups, the syntax is as follows:

```
group = group-name {
default service = permit
attribute-1 = value {
atribute-2 = value
. . .
}
}
```

For users, the syntax is as follows:

```
user = user-name {
default service = permit
attribute-1 = value {
atribute-2 = value
. . .
}
}
```

The **default service = permit** command must always be the first entry within the list of attributes.

The following excerpt from Example 3-1 shows the commands that configure default authorization for the netadmin and regularusers groups:

```
group = netadmin {
default service = permit
service = exec {
priv-lvl = 15
}
}
group = regularusers {
default service = deny
service = exec {
priv-lvl = 1
}
}
```

The **service = exec** command adds an exec prompt (better known as the command shell) as the authorized service that is available to the group. The **priv-lvl =** *n* command sets the privilege level for the command shell. Note that *n* can be any integer between 0 and 15. Setting the privilege level to 15 (the highest privilege level) authorizes the group members to run all the commands. The regularusers group members can only run commands that have a privilege level of 1.

NOTE The commands available within the enable mode of Cisco IOS, CatOS, and PIX CLI are at privilege level 15. For more information on privilege levels, visit the "Understanding Privilege Level" page at the following URL:

http://www.cisco.com/en/US/products/sw/iosswrel/ps1839/products_feature_guide09186a0080112495.html

Configuring Command Authorization

The commands entered at the exec prompt of a Cisco device can be authorized on a per-user or per-group basis. This is done by specifying a list of egrep-style regular expressions to match command arguments along with the deny or permit option on the TACACS+ Daemon. By default, the TACACS+ Daemon denies authorization for any command. The syntax for configuring command authorization is as follows:

```
cmd = command {
permit arguments
deny arguments
}
```

The following excerpt from Example 3-1 shows the command authorization for user jkeith. The user is authorized to run the **show** commands. The **permit .*** entry authorizes all the arguments of the **show** command. The **exit** command allows the user to exit the session. Also, note the entry authorizing the **telnet** command. The **permit 192\.168\.1\.[0-9]+** statement authorizes the user to Telnet to any address starting with 192.168.1. The subsequent **deny .*** statement prevents the user from Telnetting to any other address. The excerpt is as follows:

```
user = jkeith {
#... output suppressed for clarity
cmd = show {
permit .*
}
cmd = exit {
permit .*
}
cmd = telnet {
permit 192\.168\.1\.[0-9]+
deny .*
}
}
```

The TACACS+ Daemon also provides the autocommand feature. This feature automatically instructs the IOS to execute a command after successful user authentication and prevents the user (or the group) from running any other command. After the **autocmd** command is executed, the user session automatically terminates. You must define autocommand after configuring the service authorization. The syntax is as follows:

```
service = exec {
autocmd = "command with argument"
}
```

The following excerpt from Example 3-1 shows the autocommand configuration for user consultant1. Before declaring the autocommand, the user must be authorized for the exec shell. The autocommand arguments are specified within the quotation marks. After user consultant1 successfully logs in to a router (preconfigured to use the TACACS+ Daemon for AAA), the **show ip interface brief** command runs automatically and ends the user session. This particular example is handy for selectively allowing remote users to log in to routers and determine the status of the LAN/WAN interfaces. The excerpt is as follows:

```
user = consultant1 {
# output suppressed for clarity
service = exec {
autocmd = "show ip interface brief"
}
}
```

Note the absence of service authorization parameters, such as the exec service and privilege levels, for consultant1. You do not need to define service authorization when configuring autocommand.

Configuring Accounting

You can enable accounting on the TACACS+ Daemon through the **accounting file =** *log-file-on-the-linux-machine* command. By specifying the accounting file, the TACACS+ Daemon records all the accounting file logins, using plain-text format. The command is configured at the top level of the configuration file.

The following excerpt from Example 3-1 shows the location of the accounting log file:

```
accounting file = /var/log/tac.log
```

The TACACS+ Daemon records all the accounting logins in the /var/log/tac.log file. You can view the contents of the log file using any text editor (such as vi) or using built-in Linux commands (such as **cat**, **tail**, **head**, **grep**, and so on).

Verifying the Configuration File

Now that the file has been created, it should be verified for syntax errors. The tac_plus executable file provides the verification functionality through the **-P** flag. The configuration file is specified using the **-C** flag. The command syntax is **tac_plus -P -C** *config_file*. Use the following syntax to verify the tacacs.conf file created in Example 3-1:

```
linuxbox:/usr/local/bin# tac_plus -P -C /etc/tac-plus/tacacs.conf
```

Edit the tacacs_config.txt file to remove errors that were encountered during the verification process.

Starting the TACACS+ Daemon

Following the successful verification of the configuration file, the TACACS+ Daemon is ready to be started. The command syntax is **tac_plus -C *config_file* –d 248**. The following syntax is used to start the daemon with the configuration file tacacs_config.txt:

```
linuxbox:/usr/local/bin#tac_plus -C /etc/tac-plus/tacacs.conf  -d 248
```

The **-d 248** flag generates debugging output in the var/tmp/tac_plus.log file. For debug messages with more details, specify a higher value in the **–d** flag. The possible values are listed in Table 3-2.

Table 3-2 *TACACS+ Debug Levels*

Value	Debug Level
8	Authorization
16	Authentication
32	Processing of password file
64	Accounting
128	Configuration file parsing

Table 3-2 *TACACS+ Debug Levels (Continued)*

Value	Debug Level
256	Packet transmission and reception
512	Encryption and decryption
1024	MD5 hash algorithm
2048	Detailed encryption/decryption

You can add each value for the desired level of debugging. For example, to view authorization and authentication messages together, you should specify the **-d 24** flag (that is, 8 + 16 = 24).

To verify that the TACACS+ Daemon has started, use the **ps -f -C tac_plus** command. The output of the **ps** command shows details such as the USERID, process identification (PID), time, and command used to start the process. Note that **ps** is a Linux system command that displays a snapshot of the current processes. The **-f** flag shows the full (detailed) output, whereas the **-C tac_plus** flag shows the processes started by the **tac_plus** command. The PID is useful for stopping the TACACS+ Daemon, using the **kill -9** *PID* command, as follows:

```
linuxbox:~# ps -f -C tac_plus
UID        PID  PPID  C STIME TTY          TIME CMD
tacacs   22840     1  0 01:07 ttyp0    00:00:00 /usr/sbin/tac_plus -C /etc/tac-
   plus/tacacs.conf -d 248
linuxbox:~# kill -9 22840
```

Note that you must stop and restart the daemon after making changes to the configuration file; otherwise, the changes do not take effect.

TIP In Debian Linux, you can also use the **/etc/init.d/tac-plus restart** command to restart the TACACS+ Daemon**.**

You can also use the **netstat -a | grep tacacs** command to verify that the Linux machine is listening on the TACACS+ port, as follows:

```
linuxbox:~# netstat  -a ¦ grep tacacs
tcp        0      0 *:tacacs                *:*                     LISTEN
```

Viewing Debug Messages

The debug messages generated by the TACACS+ Daemon are logged in the /var/tmp/tac_plus.log file. These messages can be viewed by using the **tail** command. The debug messages provide information regarding authentication, authorization, and accounting activities between the TACACS+ Daemon and the TACACS+ Client. The debug logs are not only useful for troubleshooting but are also helpful in creating various reports.

As mentioned in the previous section, the TACACS+ Daemon, running at the debug level of 248, logs every authentication and authorization attempt. A successful login attempt is reported as **login query for user ... accepted**, whereas a failed attempt is reported as **login query for user ... rejected**. By using the Linux **grep** command, you can parse the TACACS+ Daemon log file to create reports of successful and failed login attempts.

To view successful login attempts, use the Linux **cat** command in conjunction with the **grep** command to capture line entries that contain the word *accepted,* as shown in Example 3-2.

Example 3-2 *Report of Successful Login Attempts*

```
linuxbox:~# cat /var/tmp/tac_plus.log | grep accepted
Sun Mar 20 22:49:28 2005 [2774]: login query for 'spope' tty1 from 192.168.0.10
accepted
Sun Mar 20 22:50:02 2005 [2804]: login query for 'spope' tty1 from 192.168.0.10
accepted
Sun Mar 20 23:20:49 2005 [3200]: login query for 'spope' tty2 from 192.168.0.10
accepted
Sun Mar 20 23:21:02 2005 [3214]: login query for 'consultant1' tty2 from 192.168.0.10
accepted
Sun Mar 20 23:21:17 2005 [3222]: login query for 'jkeith' tty2 from 192.168.0.10
accepted
Sun Mar 20 23:22:08 2005 [3232]: login query for 'spope' tty2 from 192.168.0.10
accepted
Sun Mar 20 23:34:13 2005 [3412]: login query for 'jkeith' tty1 from 192.168.0.10
accepted
Sun Mar 20 23:36:22 2005 [3463]: login query for 'jkeith' tty2 from 192.168.0.10
accepted
```

To limit the output of the report shown in Example 3-2, you can use the **tail** command. The syntax is **cat /var/tmp/tac_plus.log | grep accepted | tail -n 5**. The **-n 5** option displays the last five entries. Similarly, to view failed attempts, parse the log file for the word *rejected.* The command is **cat /var/tmp/tac_plus.log | grep rejected**.

Additional Configuration Templates

The following sections describe two additional sample templates for the TACACS+ Daemon configuration file.

Configuring Unknown Users

In the case of a large number of users, it is not practical to list every user within the configuration file. Moreover, Netadmins might prefer to use the usernames that are already defined on the local Linux machine. In such cases, you can use the template listed in Example 3-3. The **user = DEFAULT** entry instructs the TACACS+ Daemon to include all the users that are already defined on the local Linux machine. You must also configure the

TACACS+ Daemon to use the /etc/passwd file to authenticate unknown users. The authorization for all the unknown users is controlled by the contents of the **user = DEFAULT** entry. In Example 3-3, the default authorization permits all the local users to use the exec shell with privilege level 15.

Example 3-3 *Configuring Unlisted Users*

```
# Specify the default authentication
default authentication = file /etc/passwd
# Users not listed in the file
user = DEFAULT {
      default service = permit
      service = exec {
      priv-lvl = 15
      }
}
```

Configuring Session Timeout

The TACACS+ Daemon provides the ability to configure idle timeout and absolute timeout on a per-session basis. The timeout parameters are part of the service authorization parameters. Therefore, you must declare the timeout parameters within the service authorization configuration. You can configure the timeout parameters on a per-group or per-user basis. An idle timeout terminates a session that is idle after a period of no activity. The absolute timeout terminates the session irrespective of the activity status. If any of the timers are not specified, the TACACS+ Daemon uses the default value of 0, causing the session not to expire. In Example 3-4, the user ciscouser is configured with an idletime of 3 minutes and an absolute timeout of 30 minutes. The netadmin group is configured with an idletime of 25 minutes and an absolute timeout of 45 minutes.

Example 3-4 *Configuring the Session Timeout*

```
user =  ciscouser {
    login = cleartext cisco123
    service = exec {
# disconnect, if user idle for 3 minutes
idletime = 3
# disconnect, the user after 30 minutes
        timeout = 30
}
group =  netadmin {
    service = exec {
# disconnect the group-members, if idle for 25 minutes
idletime = 25
# disconnect the group-members, after 45 minutes
        timeout = 45
}
```

TIP

The Cisco website provides a good example of controlling access to IOS devices by using privilege levels and the TACACS+ Daemon. You can find the document "How to Assign Privilege Levels with TACACS+ and RADIUS" at the following URL:

http://www.cisco.com/en/US/tech/tk59/technologies_tech_note 09186a008009465c.shtml

Configuring Cisco Routers for TACACS+

Cisco IOS devices (routers and switches) conform to the TACACS+ protocol and provide built-in TACACS+ Client functionality within the IOS code. However, by default, TACACS+ features are not enabled on IOS devices. To control access to IOS devices, you must not only configure the devices for TACACS+ but also deploy a TACACS+ Server. While previous sections cover the topic of deploying a TACACS+ Server, the following sections discuss details regarding TACACS+ Client functionality on Cisco IOS–based devices such as routers and Catalyst switches.

TACACS+ configuration on an IOS-based device can be categorized into the following steps:

Step 1 Preparing the IOS device for AAA

Step 2 Configuring authentication

Step 3 Configuring authorization

Step 4 Configuring accounting

Step 1: Preparing the IOS Device for AAA

To prepare an IOS device for AAA, you must use the commands shown in Table 3-3. The global configuration mode commands listed in Table 3-3 create a local user, enable AAA, and configure the TACACS+ Client on the IOS device. These commands are mandatory for configuring authentication, authorization, and accounting on the IOS devices.

NOTE

IOS CLI Modes: You use the command-line interface (CLI) to access Cisco IOS Software. When you log in to the CLI, you are in user EXEC mode. User EXEC mode contains only a limited subset of commands. To have access to all commands, you must enter privileged EXEC mode, normally by using a password. From privileged EXEC mode, you can enter global configuration mode by using the **configure terminal** command. Global configuration mode allows you to make changes to the running configuration. From global configuration mode, you can enter interface configuration mode and a variety of other modes, such as protocol-specific modes. The router prompt **Router(config)#** indicates that you are in global configuration mode.

Table 3-3 *IOS Commands for TACACS+*

Command	Purpose
Router(config)#**username** *username* **password** *secret*	Creates a local user on the IOS device. Although not needed for the operation of TACACS+, this command provides a back door for the Netadmin to securely access the router if the TACACS+ Server is down.
Router(config)#**username** *username* **privilege** *level*	Specifies the privilege level for the user; *level* can be any number between 0 and 15.
Router(config)# **aaa new-model**	Enables the use of AAA using TACACS+.
Router(config)# **tacacs-server host** *host* [**port** *integer*]	Specifies the TACACS+ server by IP address or name. Optionally, you can also specify the TCP port number, if it is different from the standard TCP 49 used by TACACS+.
Router(config)# **tacacs-server key** *key*	Specifies an encryption key that encrypts all exchanges between the IOS device and the TACACS+ Daemon. The same key must also be configured on the TACACS+ Daemon.

Example 3-5 shows the IOS device configuration session for enabling AAA.

Example 3-5 *Preparing the IOS Device for AAA*

```
c:\windows\system32> telnet 192.168.0.10
User Access Verification
Password:
Dallas-Router>enable
Password:
Dallas-Router#
Dallas-Router#config terminal
Enter configuration commands, one per line.  End with CNTL/Z.
Dallas-Router(config)#username admin password s3curepassword
Dallas-Router(config)#username admin privilege 15
Dallas-Router(config)#aaa new-model
Dallas-Router(config)#tacacs-server host 192.168.0.30
Dallas-Router(config)#tacacs-server key VerYs3cr3taqskey
Dallas-Router(config)#exit
Dallas-Router#
```

Step 2: Configuring Authentication

After defining the TACACS+ Server and encryption key in Step 1, you must configure the login authentication. The login authentication is configured by creating a list of authentication methods. The list contains various authentication mechanisms, such as TACACS+ Server, local username database, and enable password. To configure the login authentication, use the commands shown in Table 3-4.

Table 3-4 *IOS Commands for Login Authentication*

Command*	Purpose
Router(config)#**aaa authentication login** {**default** | *list-name*} *method1* [*method2...*]	Creates a list of methods used by the IOS device for login authentication. Authentication can be configured on a per-line or per-interface basis. The default keyword uses the listed authentication methods that follow this argument as the default list of methods when a user logs in. The possible values for *method* are enable, line, local, none, radius, and tacacs+.

*These commands are global-configuration-mode commands.

Based on the commands listed in Table 3-4, the syntax to configure login authentication is as follows:

```
aaa authentication login default group tacacs+ local enable
```

This command creates a default authentication list for all login authentications if no other list is specified. When a user tries to log in, the list first contacts a TACACS+ Server to validate the username and password. If no server is found or the TACACS+ Server returns an error, the list will then use the local username and password. If the local username is not defined, the list prompts for enable password.

Step 3: Configuring Authorization

AAA authorization enables you to set parameters that restrict a user's access to the network. TACACS+ authorization can be configured for commands, network connections, and EXEC sessions. Table 3-5 provides the command for configuring authorization on IOS devices.

Table 3-5 *IOS Commands for Authorization*

Command*	Purpose
Router(config)#**aaa authorization** {**network** | **exec** | **commands** *level* | **reverse-access**} {**default** | *list-name*} [*method1* [*method2...*]]	Configures authorization for exec shell, commands, and network access. The **exec** keyword runs authorization to determine whether the user is allowed to run an EXEC shell. The **commands** keyword runs authorization for all commands at the specified privilege level.

*These commands are global-configuration-mode commands.

Authorization is now configured for the exec shell and commands at privilege level 0, 1, and 15. Also, the default list first looks for the TACACS+ Server. If no server is found, TACACS+ returns an error and AAA tries to use the local list. If the local list is not defined, no authorization is performed. The list is shown in Example 3-6.

Example 3-6 *Configuring the IOS Device for Authorization*

```
aaa authorization exec default group tacacs+ local none
aaa authorization commands 0 default group tacacs+ local none
aaa authorization commands 1 default group tacacs+ local none
aaa authorization commands 15 default group tacacs+ local none
```

Step 4: Configuring Accounting

AAA accounting enables you to track the services that users are accessing as well as the amount of network resources they are consuming. The accounting can be configured using the commands shown in Table 3-6.

Table 3-6 *IOS Commands for Accounting*

Command*	Purpose
Router(config)# **aaa accounting** {**system** | **network** | **exec** | **connection** | **commands level**} {**default** | **list-name**} {**start-stop** | **wait-start** | **stop-only** | **none**} [method1 [method2...]	Enables accounting for TACACS+ connections. The **start-stop** option sends a start accounting notice at the beginning of a process and a stop accounting notice at the end of a process. The **stop-only** option sends a stop record accounting notice at the end of the process. However, if you use the **wait-start** keyword, the requested service does not begin until the start accounting record is acknowledged by the AAA server.

*These commands are global-configuration-mode commands.

Accounting is now configured on the IOS device, as shown in Example 3-7, for logging all the commands entered by the authenticated user. Three separate entries are created for the three privilege levels specified during authorization.

Example 3-7 *Configuring the IOS Device for Accounting*

```
aaa accounting exec default start-stop group tacacs+
aaa accounting commands 0 default start-stop group tacacs+
aaa accounting commands 1 default start-stop group tacacs+
aaa accounting commands 15 default start-stop group tacacs+
```

The Cisco IOS device is now ready to be accessed using the username and password defined in the TACACS+ Server.

Example 3-8 shows the complete configuration of an IOS device according to the discussion in preceding sections.

Example 3-8 *IOS Device with AAA Configuration*

```
Dallas-Router# show running-config
! ---Output truncated---

! Enable AAA
aaa new-model
! Configure default login authentication using
! TACACS+,local database and enable password
aaa authentication login default group tacacs+ local enable
! Configure service authorization for exec shell
aaa authorization exec default group tacacs+ local none
! Configure command authorization for commands with privilege level 0
aaa authorization commands 0 default group tacacs+ local none
! Configure command authorization for commands with privilege level 1
aaa authorization commands 1 default group tacacs+ local none
! Configure command authorization for commands with privilege level 15
aaa authorization commands 15 default group tacacs+ local none
! Configure service accounting for exec shell
aaa accounting exec default start-stop group tacacs+
! Configure command accounting for commands with privilege level 0
aaa accounting commands 0 default start-stop group tacacs+
! Configure command accounting for commands with privilege level 1
aaa accounting commands 1 default start-stop group tacacs+
! Configure command accounting for commands with privilege level 15
aaa accounting commands 15 default start-stop group tacacs+

!
enable password 7 03075218050070
! Configure local username
username admin privilege 15 password 0 s3curepassword
!
interface Ethernet0
 ip address 192.168.0.10 255.255.255.0
!
interface Serial0
 ip address 192.168.1.1 255.255.255.252

!
ip classless
ip route 0.0.0.0 0.0.0.0 192.168.0.1
ip route 192.168.2.0 255.255.255.0 192.168.1.2
!
! Define the TACACS+ server
tacacs-server host 192.168.0.30
! Define the TACACS+ key
tacacs-server key VerYs3cr3taqskey
!
line con 0
line vty 0 2
 password 7 030752180500
```

Example 3-8 *IOS Device with AAA Configuration (Continued)*

```
line vty 3 4
 password 7 13061E010803
!
end
```

Configuring a Cisco Switch for TACACS+

Similar to IOS, Cisco CatOS (the Cisco Catalyst operating system) also conforms to the TACACS+ protocol and provides built-in TACACS+ Client functionality within the CatOS code. Also, by default, TACACS+ features are not enabled on CatOS switches. To control access to CatOS switches, you must not only configure the switches for TACACS+ but also deploy a TACACS+ Server. While the TACACS+ Server is discussed in the section "Deploying a Linux-Based TACACS+ Server," earlier in this chapter, the following sections discuss TACACS+ Client functionality on Cisco CatOS switches.

Note that Cisco switches use both the IOS and CatOS. Switches with IOS (also called *native OS*) can be configured as explained in the section "Configuring Cisco Routers for TACACS+," earlier in this chapter.

The steps involved in configuring a Cisco switch for TACACS+ are as follows:

Step 1 Preparing the switch for AAA

Step 2 Configuring authentication

Step 3 Configuring authorization

Step 4 Configuring accounting

Step 1: Preparing the Switch for AAA

To prepare the switch to use AAA, use the privileged-mode commands shown in Table 3-7.

Table 3-7 *CatOS AAA Commands*

Command	Purpose
set password	Sets the login password for access. Enter your old password (press **Return** on a switch with no password configured), enter your new password, and re-enter your new password.
set enablepass	Sets the password for privileged mode. Enter your old password (press **Return** on a switch with no password configured), enter your new password, and re-enter your new password.
set tacacs server *ip_addr* **[primary]**	Specifies the IP address of one or more TACACS+ Servers.
set tacacs key *key*	Specifies the key that encrypts packets.

Although not needed for AAA, it is good practice to configure the login and enable password on the switch for added security. Additionally, the enable password provides a last-resort option for the Netadmin to access the switch if the AAA server is down.

Based on the commands discussed in Table 3-7, the AAA configuration for a CatOS switch is shown in Example 3-9.

Example 3-9 *Preparing a CatOS Switch for AAA*

```
Console> (enable) set password
Enter old password:cisco
Enter new password:longsecret
Retype new password: longsecret
Password changed.
USF-LM-MC2b> (enable)Console> (enable) set enablepass
Enter old password: cisco123
Enter new password: s3curepassword
Retype new password: s3curepassword
Password changed.
Console> (enable) set tacacs server 192.168.0.30
192.168.0.30 added to TACACS server table as primary server.
Console> (enable) set tacacs key VerYs3cr3taqskey
The tacacs key has been set to VerYs3cr3taqskey.
```

Step 2: Configuring Authentication

The switches to use TACACS+ for authentication are configured in privileged mode, as listed in Table 3-8.

Table 3-8 *CatOS Commands for Authentication*

Command	Purpose
set authentication login tacacs enable [**all** | **console** | **http** | **telnet**] [**primary**]	Enables TACACS+ authentication for normal login mode. Enter the **console** or **telnet** keyword to enable TACACS+ only for console port or Telnet connection attempts.
set authentication enable tacacs enable [**all** | **console** | **http** | **telnet**] [**primary**]	Enables TACACS+ authentication for enable mode. Enter the **console** or **telnet** keyword to enable TACACS+ only for console port or Telnet connection attempts.

Based on the commands listed in Table 3-8, Example 3-10 shows configuring the switch for TACACS+ authentication.

Example 3-10 *Configuring a Switch for TACACS+ Authentication*

```
Console> (enable) set authentication login tacacs enable
tacacs login authentication set to enable for console and telnet session.
Console> (enable) set authentication enable tacacs enable
tacacs enable authentication set to enable for console and telnet session.
```

Step 3: Configuring Authorization

TACACS+ authorization is enabled on a switch in privileged mode using the commands shown in Table 3-9.

Table 3-9 *CatOS Commands for Authorization*

Command	Purpose
set authorization exec enable {*option*}{*fallbackoption*} [**console** | **telnet** | **both**]	Enables exec shell authorization on the switch using the method specified through *option*. You can specify additional method using *fallbackoption*. The possible values for *option* are **tacacs+**, **if-authenticated**, and **none**; for *fallbackoption*, the possible values are **tacacs+**, **deny**, **if-authenticated**, and **none**. Following is the significance of each keyword: • **tacacs+**—Specifies the TACACS+ authorization method. • **deny**—Authorization is denied regardless of condition. • **if-authenticated**—Authorization is allowed if authentication is successful. • **none**—Authorization is allowed if TACACS+ Server does not respond. • **console**—Enables authorization for console port connections. • **telnet**—Enables authorization for Telnet connections. • **both**—Enables authorization for both console port and Telnet connections.
set authorization enable enable {*option*} {*fallbackoption*} [**console** | **telnet** | **both**]	Enables authorization for enable mode.
set authorization commands enable {**config** | **all**} {*option*}{*fallbackoption*} [**console** | **telnet** | **both**]	Enables authorization of configuration commands.

To control access to a switch, you must enable TACACS+ authorization for the exec shell, enable mode, and the commands entered by the authenticated users. Moreover, you must apply authorization on both console and Telnet connection attempts. Example 3-11 shows the configuration procedure for enabling authorization on a CatOS switch.

Example 3-11 *Configuring a Switch for TACACS+ Authorization*

```
Console> (enable) set authorization exec enable tacacs+ if-authenticated both
Successfully enabled enable authorization.
Console> (enable) set authorization enable enable tacacs+ if-authenticated both
Successfully enabled enable authorization.
Console> (enable) set authorization commands enable config tacacs+ if-authenticated
both
Successfully enabled commands authorization.
```

The configuration in Example 3-11 specifies TACACS+ as the primary authorization option. If the TACACS+ Server is unavailable, the fallback option **(if-authenticated)** authorizes all authenticated users. Without the fallback option, access to the switch is denied during TACACS+ Server outage.

Step 4: Configuring Accounting

Accounting is enabled on a switch in privileged mode using the commands shown in Table 3-10.

Table 3-10 *CatOS Commands for Accounting*

Command	Purpose
set accounting connect enable {**start-stop** | **stop-only**} {**tacacs+** | **radius**}	Enables accounting for connection events
set accounting exec enable {**start-stop** | **stop-only**} {**tacacs+** | **radius**}	Enables accounting for exec mode
set accounting system enable {**start-stop** | **stop-only**} {**tacacs+** | **radius**}	Enables accounting for system events
set accounting commands enable {**config** | **all**} {**stop-only**} **tacacs+**	Enables accounting of configuration commands

Based on the commands listed in Table 3-10, Example 3-12 shows the switch configuration for accounting. The configuration specifies the switch to log all the exec events and to log all the commands run by authenticated users.

Example 3-12 *Configuring a Switch for TACACS+ Accounting*

```
Console> (enable) set accounting exec enable start-stop tacacs+
Accounting set to enable for exec events in start-stop mode.
Console> (enable) set accounting commands enable all start-stop tacacs+
Accounting set to enable for commands-all events in start-stop mode.
```

The Cisco switch (with CatOS) is now ready to be accessed using the username and password defined in the TACACS+ Server. Example 3-13 lists the TACACS+-based AAA configuration for a CatOS-based switch.

Example 3-13 *Switch Configuration for a TACACS+-Based AAA*

```
set tacacs server 192.168.0.30
set tacacs key VerYs3cr3taqskey
set authentication login tacacs enable
set authentication enable tacacs enable
set authorization exec enable tacacs+ if-authenticated both
set authorization enable enable tacacs+ if-authenticated both
set authorization commands enable config tacacs+ if-authenticated both
set accounting exec enable start-stop tacacs+
set accounting commands enable all start-stop tacacs+
```

Configuring Cisco PIX Firewalls for TACACS+

Firewalls provide network security and are an integrated part of modern networks. Cisco offers a range of firewall appliances called PIX Firewalls, which use a proprietary operating system. Similar to Cisco routers and switches, you can also implement AAA functionality on a PIX Firewall.

The PIX operating system can act as a AAA Client using both TACACS+ and RADIUS protocols. In addition, PIX can also use AAA to authenticate users who are trying to access network resources through the firewall. But, in comparison with the AAA implementation on IOS devices, PIX offers limited AAA functionality for controlling console (or Telnet) access to the firewall itself. This discussion is limited to securing console and Telnet access to the firewall.

To control access to the PIX Firewall using the TACACS+ protocol, you must not only configure the firewall for TACACS+ but also deploy a TACACS+ Server. While the TACACS+ server is discussed in the section "Deploying a Linux-Based TACACS+ Server," earlier in this chapter, this section discusses TACACS+ Client functionality on Cisco PIX Firewalls.

Table 3-11 lists the commands for configuring a TACACS+ Client over a PIX Firewall.

Table 3-11 *PIX AAA Commands*

Command	Purpose
aaa-server *tag* **protocol tacacs+ | radius**	Creates a server group on the PIX Firewall to use the TACACS+ or RADIUS protocol. The arbitrary text string used as the *tag* will represent this server group
aaa-server *tag* **[(*if_name*)] host** *ip-address* [*key*] **[timeout** *seconds*]	Specifies the IP address and encryption key for the TACACS+ Server.
aaa authentication serial | telnet | ssh | http | enable console *tag*	Specifies the authentication to be used for console access through serial, Telnet, or SSH.

Based on the commands listed in Table 3-11, Example 3-14 shows the PIX Firewall configuration for authentication. The TACACS+ Server details are grouped under the tag MYAAA and are then applied to authenticate access to the firewall console through Telnet and the SSH console. You can choose any arbitrary text instead of the string MYAAA for grouping the AAA commands on the PIX Firewall.

Example 3-14 *Configuring the PIX Firewall for Authentication*

```
c:\windows\system32>telnet 192.168.0.20
User Access Verification
Password:
Type help or '?' for a list of available commands.
Dallas-Firewall> enable
Password:
```

continues

Example 3-14 *Configuring the PIX Firewall for Authentication (Continued)*

```
Dallas-Firewall# config terminal
Dallas-Firewall(config)# aaa-server MYAAA protocol tacacs+
Dallas-Firewall(config)# aaa-server MYAAA (inside) host 192.168.0.30
VerYs3cr3taqskey
Dallas-Firewall(config)# aaa authentication ssh console MYAAA
Dallas-Firewall(config)# aaa authentication telnet console MYAAA
Dallas-Firewall(config)# exit
```

The PIX Firewall is now ready to be accessed using the username and password defined in the TACACS+ Server. Recalling from the TACACS+ configuration in Example 3-1, the following username and password combinations should be able to log in into the PIX:

- Username spope, password longpassword
- Username jkeith, password securepassword123
- Username consultant1, password cisco123

TIP The PIX Firewall provides back-door access to prevent a lockout if the TACACS+ Server is down. In such cases, use the following combination to access the PIX:

Username: pix

Password: <*Enable password*>

CAUTION Unlike the IOS AAA feature set, the PIX does not offer local authentication as a fallback feature. Hence, it is good administrative practice to configure the serial console of the PIX for local authentication. This avoids denial to the serial console because of problems with the AAA server or wrong configurations. The suggested configuration on the PIX is as follows:

```
username admin password somepassword privilege 15
username helpdesk password someothepassword privilege 1
aaa-server LOCAL protocol local
aaa authentication serial console LOCAL
```

Configuring a Cisco VPN Concentrator for TACACS+

A VPN, or virtual private network, consists of remote private networks connected through the Internet. In comparison with traditional leased lines, VPNs are cheaper because VPNs use the public network (Internet). A VPN concentrator, such as the Cisco VPN 3000 appliance, is the device used to connect remote users or networks through the Internet. Cisco VPN 3000 concentrators use proprietary operating systems with a web-based GUI for configuration and administration. The administrative console of a VPN 3000 concentrator provides the GUI for configuring and monitoring the concentrator and is accessible through any Internet browser. Beginning with VPN 3000 Concentrator Release 3.0, you can implement a TACACS+-based AAA to control access to the administrative console. However, unlike the IOS devices, the VPN 3000 concentrator only supports basic authentication services and does not support authorization and accounting.

To control access to VPN 3000 concentrators using the TACACS+ protocol, you must not only configure the concentrator for TACACS+ but also deploy a TACACS+ Server. While the TACACS+ Server is discussed in the section "Deploying a Linux-Based TACACS+ Server," earlier in this chapter, this section discusses TACACS+ Client functionality on Cisco VPN 3000 concentrators.

To configure authentication on a concentrator, follow these steps:

Step 1 Log in to the concentrator using a web browser.

Step 2 Navigate to the AAA authentication server page using the following commands:

Administration > **Access Rights** > **AAA Servers** > **Authentication** > **Add**

Step 3 Enter the IP address and the encryption key for the TACACS+ Server, as shown in Figure 3-2. The values entered are as follows:

Authentication server: 192.168.0.30

Server secret: VerYs3cr3taqskey

Step 4 Navigate to the **Administration properties** page and choose the following commands:

Administration > **Access Rights** > **Administrators**

Step 5 Select the username **admin** and click the **Modify** button.

Step 6 On the Modify properties page for the user admin, change the **AAA Access Level** to **15** and click the **Apply** button. This action sets the privilege level for user admin to 15.

The VPN concentrator is now ready to be accessed using the username and password defined in the TACACS+ Server. Based on the TACACS+ configuration file in Example 3-1, the username spope should be able to log in to the concentrator using the password longpassword.

Figure 3-2 *VPN Concentrator—Authentication Configuration*

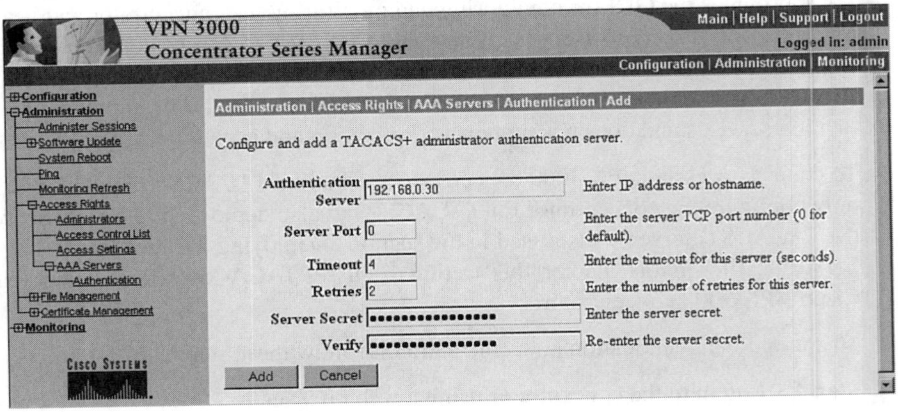

CAUTION After you configure TACACS+, make sure that you test authentication before you log out. An improper configuration of TACACS+ can lock you out. If you are locked out, a serial port login (using the locally defined username and password) is required to disable TACACS+ and rectify the problem. Note that regardless of the TACACS+ configuration, the concentrator always uses the locally defined username and password for the serial port connection. If you change the default username and password combination, (admin and admin, respectively), be sure to test the new combination before configuring the TACACS+-based authentication.

Using RADIUS for AAA

The RADIUS protocol is the de facto standard for implementing centralized authentication, authorization, and accounting by multiple vendors. RADIUS is widely popular across the industry because it is a fully open protocol. A RADIUS server is distributed in source code format and can be modified to work with any security system that is currently on the market. Similar to the TACACS+-based AAA deployment covered in previous sections, the following sections discuss RADIUS deployment. Specifically, the discussion covers deploying a RADIUS Server and configuring RADIUS-based AAA on various Cisco devices.

Deploying a Linux-Based RADIUS Server

RADIUS, originally developed by Livingston, was later enhanced by various open source projects. Several of the open source RADIUS products were enterprise grade and are still used by Internet service providers (ISP) around the world. The following is a partial list of the most popular enterprise-grade RADIUS Server products that run in Linux (and other UNIX variants):

- **Cistron**—This is the most widely used RADIUS Server in the free-software community. Although it is no longer in active development, maintenance release 1.6.7 is still supported. The home page is http://www.radius.cistron.nl.
- **XtRADIUS**—This Cistron variant offers extensions that run external programs for accounting or authentication. It is included with Debian as the default RADIUS package. The home page is http://xtradius.sourceforge.net/.
- **OpenRADIUS**—This RADIUS flavor offers pluggable modules for all the functionalities, providing better control for the Netadmin. The home page is http://www.openradius.org.
- **GNU-RADIUS**—This revamped variant of Cistron has been rewritten with newer configuration files. The home page is http://www.gnu.org/software/radius/radius.html.
- **FreeRADIUS**—This forked variant of Cistron is currently under development, providing the latest enhancements. The home page is http://www.freeradius.org/.

Of all these RADIUS Servers, this discussion covers FreeRADIUS because it offers the following advantages:

- Uses the stable and tested Cistron code
- Is one of the most widely deployed RADIUS Servers
- Is under active development
- Supports newer features such as Cisco LEAP

You must have a Linux machine, with network connectivity, to install the FreeRADIUS server software. After installation, you must edit the configuration text files that control the FreeRADIUS server properties. Following configuration, you can start the server for use within the network.

Installing the FreeRADIUS Server

Download the FreeRADIUS installation files, in compressed tar file format, from the FreeRADIUS home page at http://www.freeradius.org. This discussion is based on the stable release file freeradius-1.0.0.tar.gz. The compressed tar file (represented by the tar.gz extension) contains the installation files for the FreeRADIUS server.

To uncompress and install the server, follow these steps:

Step 1 Extract the installable files from the downloaded tar file as follows:

```
[root@Linuxbox root]# ls
freeradius-1.0.0.tar.gz
[root@Linuxbox root]$ tar zxvf freeradius-1.0.0.tar.gz
```

Step 2 Change the directory to the extracted location using the following command:

```
[root@Linuxbox root]# cd freeradius-1.0.0
```

Step 3 Run the configuration process by using the following commands:

```
[root@Linuxbox freeradius-1.0.0]# ./configure
[root@Linuxbox freeradius-1.0.0]# make
[root@Linuxbox freeradius-1.0.0]# make install
```

NOTE Debian users can use the **apt-get install freeradius** command to quickly install the FreeRADIUS server.

Configuring the FreeRADIUS Server

The text files located in the default directory (/etc/raddb) control the properties of the FreeRADIUS server. These files are automatically created during the installation process and must be edited before starting the FreeRADIUS server. However, unless specified otherwise, do not delete or remove the default content of these files. Instead, add the newer configuration at the bottom of the existing file. Within each of these text files, every line starting with a hash sign (#) is treated as a comment. Table 3-12 provides a list of relevant files that must be tweaked before deploying the FreeRADIUS server in a Cisco network.

Table 3-12 *FreeRADIUS Configuration Files*

Filename	Purpose
/etc/raddb/clients.conf	Specifies the list of clients that will be accessing the FreeRADIUS server; the list includes the IP addresses and the secret key for each client.
/etc/raddb/users	Specifies the list of users; the list includes the authentication and authorization parameters for each user.
/etc/raddb/radiusd.conf	Specifies the global configuration for the FreeRADIUS server; exercise caution while editing this file.
/etc/raddb/dictionary	Specifies the list of dictionary files for each supported vendor; the server has separate dictionary files for each supported vendor that contain RADIUS attributes and values.
/etc/raddb/acct_users	Specifies the parameters for logging accounting messages.

NOTE In Debian Linux, if the FreeRADIUS server is installed using the **apt-get install freeradius** command, the default directory of the text files is /etc/freeradius instead of /etc/raddb. However, there is no other impact on the properties of the FreeRADIUS server.

The following sections provide more information for each of the files listed in Table 3-12.

/etc/raddb/clients.conf File

The /etc/raddb/client.conf file contains a list of all the RADIUS clients that can query the FreeRADIUS server for AAA requests. The format for adding each RADIUS client is as follows:

```
# CLIENT CONFIG BEGINS
client hostname-or-IP-address {
        secret          = encryption-key
        shortname       = hostname
        nastype         = type-of-RADIUS-client
}
# CLIENT CONFIG ENDS
```

You can specify the client either by host name or IP address. The encryption key for specifying the value of **secret** should be exactly similar to that specified for the RADIUS Client. The **shortname** parameter is used to specify an alias for the host, while the nastype is always **cisco** for Cisco devices. The default /etc/raddb/clients.conf file only contains one entry for the localhost. Each additional client should be appended to the default file. Optionally, you can also specify a network address (for example, 192.168.5.0/24) instead of a single client. The following sample snippet can be appended to the default /etc/raddb/clients.conf file:

```
# ADD A SINGLE CLIENT
client 192.168.0.10 {
        secret          = testing123
        shortname       = CiscoRouter
        nastype         = cisco
}
# ADD A NETWORK SUBNET
client 192.168.5.0/24 {
        secret          = testing123567
        shortname       = Brach-office
        nastype         = cisco
}
# CONFIG ENDS
```

The first entry adds a single client with IP address 192.168.0.10, while the second entry adds all the clients in the 192.168.5.0/24 subnet.

/etc/raddb/users File

The /etc/raddb/users file contains a list of users and their credential information. The format for adding a user in the /etc/raddb/users file is as follows:

```
user            Auth-Type := "local-or-system-authentication"
                 Service-Type = Shell-User,
                 Cisco-AVPair = " protocol:attribute sep value"
```

Table 3-13 provides an explanation of each field used to define user credentials in the /etc/raddb/users file.

Table 3-13 *Fields in the /etc/raddb/users File*

Field	Description
user	Specifies the username.
Auth-type	Specifies the type of authentication for the user. Possible values are **System**, for using the password defined on Linux machines, and **Local**, for using a clear-text password. Additionally, for Local authentication, specify the password in the same line using the syntax **User-password ==** "***password***".
Service-Type	Defines the service type for the user; the value for authenticating the exec shell is **Shell-User**.
Cisco-AVPair = " *protocol*:*attribute sep value*"	Specifies a full set of TACACS+ authorization features to be used for an authenticated user by RADIUS. The keyword *protocol* is a value of the Cisco protocol attribute for a particular type of authorization. The pair, of keywords *attribute* and *value*, is an appropriate Attribute-Value (AV) pair defined in the Cisco TACACS+ specification. The keyword *sep* can be replaced by the equal sign (=) for mandatory attributes and asterisk (*) for optional attributes.

Based on the description in Table 3-13, the following code can be added to the /etc/raddb/users file. This code snippet defines two users, with username spope and jkeith, respectively:

```
spope           Auth-Type := System
                 Service-Type = Shell-User,
                 Cisco-AVPair = "shell:priv-lvl=15",
                 Cisco-AVPair = "shell:cmd*"
jkeith           Auth-Type := Local, Password == "securepassword123"
                 Service-Type = Shell-User,
                 Cisco-AVPair = "shell:priv-lvl=1",
                 Cisco-AVPair = "shell:cmd*"
```

Note that user spope is configured to use the system password, while user jkeith is using the local password securepassword123. For authentication to succeed for the user spope, you must create a user spope using the Linux command **adduser**. User spope is assigned privilege level of 15, whereas user jkeith has a limited privilege level of 1. Additionally, the statement **Cisco-AVPair = "shell:cmd*"** exclusively authorizes the use of the command shell for each user.

NOTE The default contents of the /etc/raddb/users file might conflict with the configurations for new users and can lead to unexpected results. In such cases, either insert the new configuration at the beginning of the default file, or better yet, create a fresh /etc/raddb/users file that contains the new configuration only. In the latter case, rename the original /etc/raddb/users file before creating the new one.

/etc/raddb/radiusd.conf File

The /etc/raddb/radiusd.conf file defines the global configuration for the FreeRADIUS server. The /etc/raddb/radiusd.conf file is a large file, and most of the contents do not need tweaking. However, to use the FreeRADIUS server in a Cisco environment, you must tweak the parameters listed in Table 3-14.

Table 3-14 *\/etc/raddb/radiusd.conf File Parameters*

Parameter	Description
log_auth_badpass	Controls the logging of failed authentication requests; possible values are **yes** on **no**. Useful in catching suspicious login activities.
log_auth_goodpass	Controls the logging of successful authentication requests; possible values are **yes** on **no**. Useful in catching suspicious login activities.
passwd	Specifies the location of user passwords on the Linux machine.
shadow	Specifies the location of user passwords on the Linux machine that are using shadow passwords.
group	Specifies the location of group files on the Linux machine.
with_cisco_vsa_hack	Enables the RADIUS Server to correctly interpret the response received from the Cisco devices; possible values are **yes** and **no**.

Referring to the parameters listed in Table 3-14, the contents of the /etc/raddb/radiusd.conf file should match the following output:

```
#OUTPUT SUPPRESSED
log_auth_badpass = yes
log_auth_goodpass = yes
#OUTPUT SUPPRESSED
unix {
              #OUTPUT SUPPRESSED
              passwd = /etc/passwd
              shadow = /etc/shadow
              group = /etc/group
              #OUTPUT SUPPRESSED
}
#OUTPUT SUPPRESSED
     preprocess {
               #OUTPUT SUPPRESSED
               with_cisco_vsa_hack = no
              #OUTPUT SUPPRESSED
        }
```

CAUTION Exercise caution while editing the radiusd.conf file. You should make a backup copy of this file before making changes. Except for the parameters discussed in this section, do not make changes to this file. Also, do not change the order in which the commands appear within the file.

/etc/raddb/dictionary File

A dictionary file contains a list of RADIUS attributes and values for a particular vendor. The /etc/raddb/dictionary file is a master file that references other dictionary files by using the following statement:

```
$INCLUDE /usr/share/freeradius/dictionary
```

For the FreeRADIUS server to include Cisco-specific dictionary files, the /usr/share/freeradius/dictionary file must contain the following three statements:

```
$INCLUDE dictionary.cisco
$INCLUDE dictionary.cisco.vpn3000
$INCLUDE dictionary.cisco.vpn5000
```

/etc/raddb/acct_users File

By default, the accounting feature on the FreeRADIUS server is turned off. To enable accounting, you must uncomment the two DEFAULT Acct-Status-Type statements in the /etc/raddb/acct_users file, as follows:

```
# BEFORE ENABLING ACCOUNTING
# DEFAULT Acct-Status-Type == Start
# DEFAULT Acct-Status-Type == Stop
# AFTER ENABLING ACCOUNTING
DEFAULT Acct-Status-Type == Start
DEFAULT Acct-Status-Type == Stop
# END OF CONFIGURATION
```

The RADIUS server records the accounting logs in the /var/log/radius/radacct **directory**.

Running the FreeRADIUS Server

So far, the discussion has covered the installation and configuration of the Linux-based RADIUS Server to implement access control over Cisco devices. This section prepares you to run and debug the FreeRADIUS server.

The command to run the FreeRADIUS server is **radiusd**. The **radiusd** command offers various CLI switches that can override the options specified in configuration files. A partial list of options is shown in Table 3-15.

Table 3-15 *Options for the* **radiusd** *Command*

Option	Description
-a *accounting-directory*	Specifies the directory for logging accounting messages.
-A	Logs the authentication detail.
-c	Verifies the syntax and contents of the configuration text files and the password/group/shadow files without loading into the server; useful for testing purposes without affecting the production environment.
-h	Prints this help message.
-l *logging-directory*	Specifies the directory for sending system logs; optionally uses the keyword **syslog** to send all messages to the system logger.
-p *port*	By default, the FreeRADIUS server listens on the ports specified for RADIUS authentication (radius) and RADIUS accounting (radacct) in the /etc/services file. To change the default behavior, specify the UDP port used by the FreeRADIUS server to listen to radius requests; the server uses *port*+1 to listen to radacct requests.
-v	Shows the server version information.
-X	Turns on complete debugging; this is the maximum debugging level.
-x	Turns on partial debugging; use the **-xx** option for more information.
-y	Logs authentication failures, including the password; the option is similar to the **log_auth_badpass** parameter within the radiusd.conf file.
-z	Logs authentication successes, including the password; similar to the **log_auth_goodpass** parameter within the radiusd.conf file. Use this option only for troubleshooting, because it logs all the passwords in clear text.

Before starting the FreeRADIUS server, always verify the configuration using the **radiusd** command with the **-c** option, as follows:

```
[root@Linuxbox raddb]# radiusd -c
Sat Aug 28 11:44:21 2004 : Info: Starting - reading configuration files ...
```

Follow the messages to rectify any errors.

To verify that the server is running, use the **ps** command, as follows:

```
 [root@Linuxbox raddb]# ps -ef | grep radius
root      20099     1  0 11:44 ?        00:00:00 radiusd -c
root      20106 19872  0 11:44 pts/0    00:00:00 grep radius
```

The changes made to the configuration files do not take effect until the FreeRADIUS server is restarted. In such cases, to stop the service, use the **kill** *pid* command, where *pid* is the ID of the server process as identified using the **ps –ef** command. The command example is as follows:

```
[root@Linuxbox raddb]#kill 20099
```

After verifying the configuration files, restart the FreeRADIUS server in debug mode. Based on the options listed in Table 3-15, the command for running FreeRADIUS in debug mode is **radiusd -xxyz**. Using the **radiusd -X** command produces the same result as the **radiusd -xxyz** command. After starting in debug mode, test the server by sending authentication requests from a Cisco device. (The configuration of Cisco devices, specifically IOS devices, CatOS switches, and PIX Firewalls, as RADIUS Clients is discussed in later sections of this chapter.)

The server displays the transactions to and from the clients that request authentication. The debug messages are helpful in troubleshooting both server and client issues. The output of the **radiusd -xxyz** command is shown in Example 3-15.

Example 3-15 *Output of the **radiusd** Command in Debug Mode*

```
[root@linuxbox root]# radiusd -xxyz
Starting - reading configuration files ...
Using deprecated naslist file.  Support for this will go away soon.
Module: Loaded exec
rlm_exec: Wait=yes but no output defined. Did you mean output=none?
Module: Instantiated exec (exec)
Module: Loaded expr
Module: Instantiated expr (expr)
Module: Loaded PAP
Module: Instantiated pap (pap)
Module: Loaded CHAP
Module: Instantiated chap (chap)
Module: Loaded MS-CHAP
Module: Instantiated mschap (mschap)
Module: Loaded System
Module: Instantiated unix (unix)
Module: Loaded eap
rlm_eap: Loaded and initialized type md5
rlm_eap: Loaded and initialized type leap
rlm_eap: Loaded and initialized type gtc
rlm_eap: Loaded and initialized type mschapv2
Module: Instantiated eap (eap)
Module: Loaded preprocess
Module: Instantiated preprocess (preprocess)
Module: Loaded realm
Module: Instantiated realm (suffix)
Module: Loaded files
Module: Instantiated files (files)
Module: Loaded Acct-Unique-Session-Id
Module: Instantiated acct_unique (acct_unique)
Module: Loaded detail
Module: Instantiated detail (detail)
Module: Loaded radutmp
Module: Instantiated radutmp (radutmp)
Initializing the thread pool...
Listening on authentication *:1812
Listening on accounting *:1813
```

Example 3-15 *Output of the* ***radiusd*** *Command in Debug Mode (Continued)*

```
Listening on proxy *:1814
Ready to process requests.

rad_recv: Access-Request packet from host 192.168.0.10:1645, id=102, length=78
NAS-IP-Address = 192.168.0.10
NAS-Port = 1
NAS-Port-Type = Virtual
User-Name = "spope"
Calling-Station-Id = "192.168.0.100"
User-Password = "something"
rlm_unix: [spope]: invalid password
rad_recv: Access-Request packet from host 192.168.0.10:1645, id=102, length=78
Sending Access-Reject of id 102 to 192.168.0.10:1645
Cisco-AVPair = "shell:priv-lvl=15"
rad_recv: Access-Request packet from host 192.168.0.10:1645, id=103, length=78
NAS-IP-Address = 192.168.0.10
NAS-Port = 1
NAS-Port-Type = Virtual
User-Name = "spope"
Calling-Station-Id = "192.168.0.100"
User-Password="password123"
Sending Access-Accept of id 103 to 192.168.0.10:1645
Service-Type = Administrative-User
Cisco-AVPair = "shell:priv-lvl=15"
rad_recv: Accounting-Request packet from host 192.168.0.10:1646, id=104, length=94
NAS-IP-Address = 192.168.0.10
NAS-Port = 1
NAS-Port-Type = Virtual
User-Name = "spope"
Calling-Station-Id = "192.168.0.100"
Acct-Status-Type = Start
Acct-Authentic = RADIUS
Service-Type = NAS-Prompt-User
Acct-Session-Id = "0000006D"
Acct-Delay-Time = 0
Sending Accounting-Response of id 104 to 192.168.0.10:1646
rad_recv: Accounting-Request packet from host 192.168.0.10:1646, id=105, length=106
NAS-IP-Address = 192.168.0.10
NAS-Port = 1
NAS-Port-Type = Virtual
User-Name = "spope"
Calling-Station-Id = "192.168.0.100"
Acct-Status-Type = Stop
Acct-Authentic = RADIUS
Service-Type = NAS-Prompt-User
Acct-Session-Id = "0000006D"
Acct-Terminate-Cause = User-Request
Acct-Session-Time = 32
Acct-Delay-Time = 0
Sending Accounting-Response of id 105 to 192.168.0.10:1646
```

TIP If you do not have a Cisco device configured as a RADIUS Client, you can use the **radtest** command to test authentication on the FreeRADIUS server. The syntax is as follows:

> **radtest** *user password radius-server*[**:***port*] ***nas-port-number*** *secret*

Output from the **radtest** command is as follows:

```
root@linuxbox:~# radtest spope password123 127.0.0.1 10 testing123
Sending Access-Request of id 84 to 127.0.0.1:1812
        User-Name = "spope"
        User-Password = "password123"
        NAS-IP-Address = linuxbox
        NAS-Port = 10
rad_recv: Access-Accept packet from host 127.0.0.1:1812, id=84, length=20
```

After verifying the configuration and running the server in debug mode, start the FreeRADIUS server by using the **radiusd** command, as follows:

```
[root@Linuxbox raddb]# radiusd
Sat Aug 28 12:25:21 2004 : Info: Starting - reading configuration files ...
```

The server is now ready for deployment.

Configuring a Microsoft IAS Server as a RADIUS Server

Within the realm of access control using a RADIUS Server in a Cisco network, this discussion focuses on the use of a Windows-based Internet Authentication Service (IAS) server. IAS is a built-in RADIUS server within a Windows server.

Microsoft Windows 2000 IAS is the Microsoft implementation of a RADIUS Server. IAS is fully compliant with RFC 2138 and RFC 2139. To provide backward-compatibility, IAS uses UDP ports 1812 and 1645 for authentication and UDP ports 1813 and 1646 for accounting. Although an earlier version of IAS was included in the NT 4.0 option pack, a newer version is shipped as part of the Windows 2000 and 2003 servers. Windows 2000 IAS server for RADIUS provides the following advantages to the Netadmin:

- Integration with Windows 2000 Active Directory services. This provides a single centralized authentication database across the enterprise for all clients, including non-LDAP devices.
- No additional licensing or software requirements, because the product is part of Windows 2000 and 2003 servers and can be installed through the **Add/Remove Programs** icon.
- Easy administration through the Microsoft Management Console (MMC).
- Authorized users can access Cisco devices using their Windows username and password.

The first step in deploying an IAS server is installing it over a Windows server. Next, you must add RADIUS Clients and configure policies and accounting parameters in the IAS server.

Installing the Microsoft IAS-Based RADIUS Server

The IAS service can be added to any existing Microsoft Windows 2000 or 2003 server as long as enough resources are available to support the installed applications. Follow these steps to install a Microsoft IAS-based RADIUS Server:

Step 1 Choose **Start > Settings > Control Panel > Add/Remove Programs**.

Step 2 In the **Add/Remove Programs** window, click the **Add/Remove Windows Components** button to open the **Windows components** window.

Step 3 In the **Windows components** window, select **Networking Services** and click the **Details** button.

Step 4 In the **Networking Services** window, select the **Internet Authentication Service** check box (as shown in Figure 3-3) and click the **OK** button to return to the **Windows components** window.

Figure 3-3 *Installing IAS*

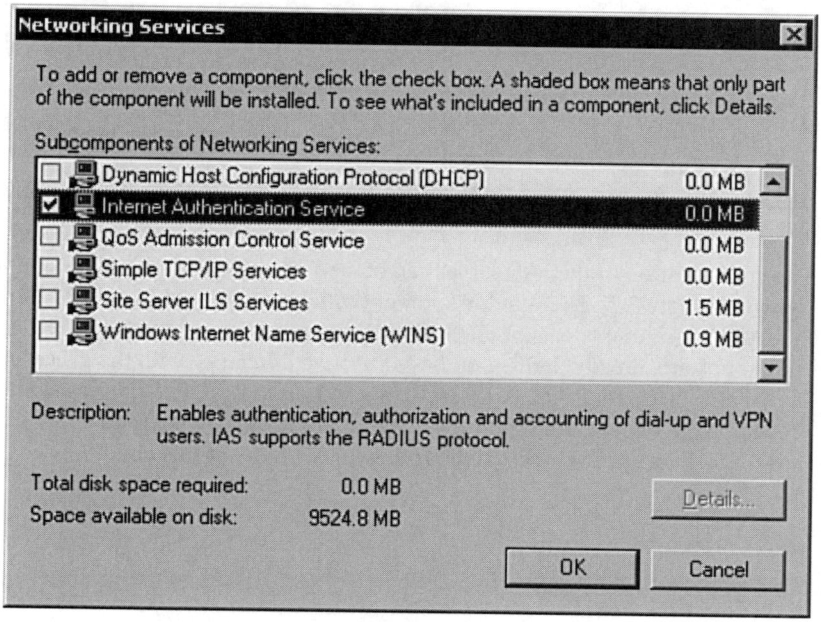

Step 5 In the **Windows components** window, click the **Next** button to begin the installation, and then click the **Finish** button.

The IAS server is now added.

Note that after installing a new server, it is good practice to update the server with the latest security patches and service packs from the Microsoft website.

Configuring the Microsoft IAS-Based RADIUS Server

After IAS has been added to your Microsoft server, you must configure it. The IAS MMC, as shown in Figure 3-4, is the graphical user interface (GUI) for administration and configuration of IAS services. To open the IAS MMC, choose **Start > Programs > Administrative Tools > Internet Authentication Service**.

Figure 3-4 *IAS MMC*

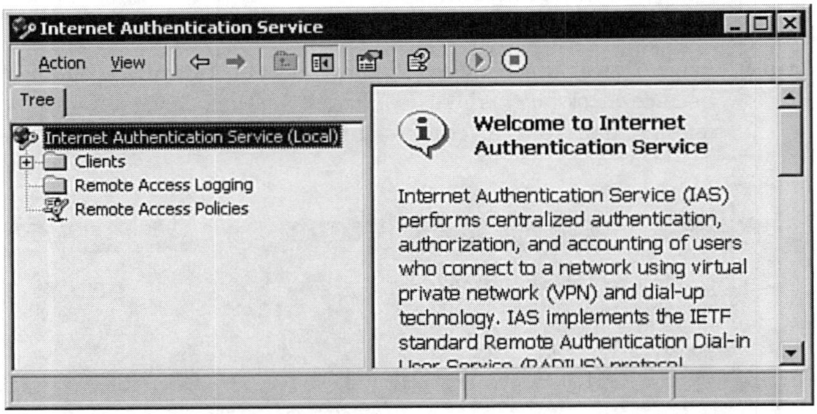

The configuration of the IAS server can be best described by using the sample scenario shown in Figure 3-5. The Windows server (with host name DALLAS-RADIUS) is running the IAS service and is part of the Active Directory domain IASTEST. The network users and groups are already defined in the MS Active Directory with the group memberships shown in Table 3-16. DALLAS-RADIUS responds to RADIUS queries from the router and firewall. Note that the configuration of Cisco routers, switches, and PIX Firewalls as RADIUS clients is discussed in the following sections of this chapter.

Figure 3-5 *Network with IAS Server*

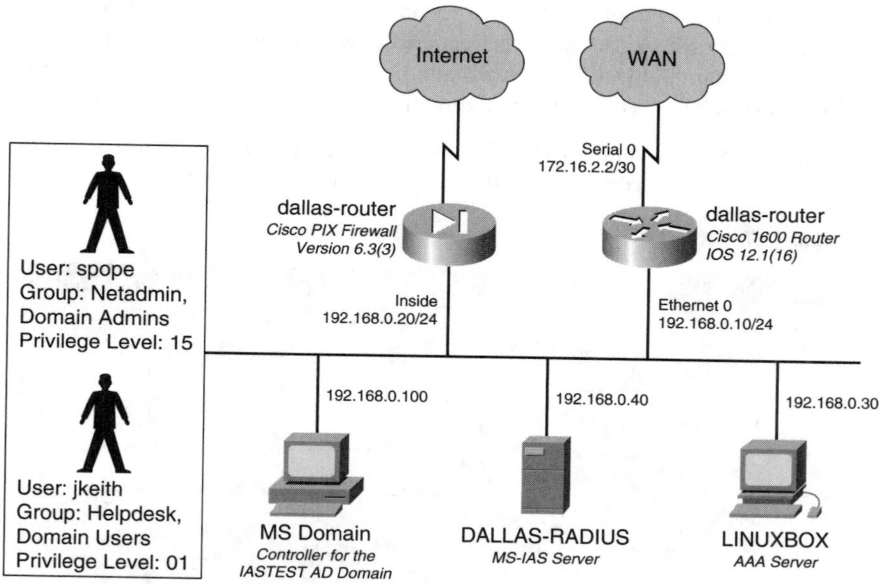

Table 3-16 *User Group Membership*

User	Username	Windows Group Membership
1	spope	Netadmin, Domain Admins
2	jkeith	Helpdesk, Domain Users

NOTE Domain Admins and Domain Users are the default groups created within the MS Active Directory. The groups (Netadmin and Helpdesk) and users (spope and jkeith) were created using the Active Directory Users and Computers MMC snap-in. To open this snap-in in the MMC, choose **Start > Programs > Active Directory Users and Computers**.

The steps involved in configuring the IAS server are as follows:

- Adding the clients
- Configuring remote access policies
- Configuring accounting parameters

Adding the Clients

The first task in configuring the IAS server is to add the RADIUS Clients to the IAS server using the IAS MMC. Based on the scenario shown in Figure 3-5, the Cisco network devices (Dallas-Router and Dallas-Firewall) are the clients that would be querying the IAS server for authentication. The steps for adding these RADIUS Clients are as follows:

Step 1 From within the IAS MMC window, choose **Clients > New > Client** to open the **Add Client** window, as shown in Figure 3-6.

Figure 3-6 *Adding Clients in IAS*

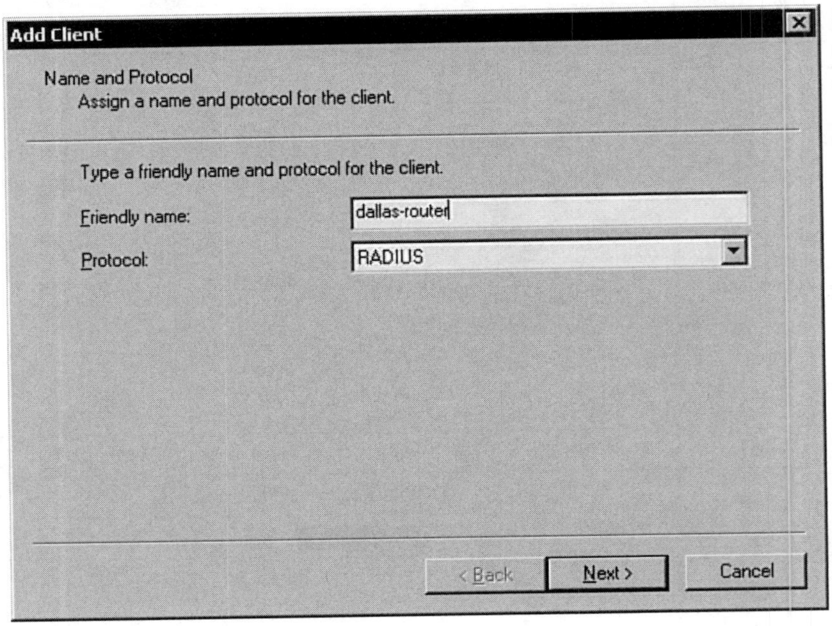

Step 2 In the **Add Client** window, specify **dallas-router** as the name of the client and click the **Next** button.

Step 3 In the **Add RADIUS Client** window, as shown in Figure 3-7, specify the IP address used by dallas-router. In the **Shared secret** field, enter the same encryption key that is defined in the AAA configuration of dallas-router. For this example, the key is **testing123**.

Figure 3-7 *Client Parameters in IAS*

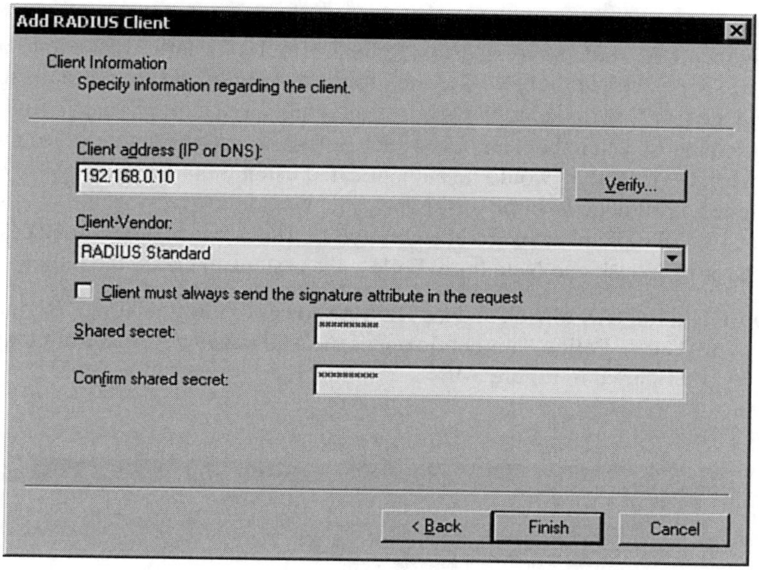

Step 4 Repeat Steps 1 to 3 to add Firewall-Dallas to the IAS server.

Step 5 Figure 3-8 shows the IAS MMC with two clients, dallas-router and dallas-firewall.

Figure 3-8 *IAS MMC Clients*

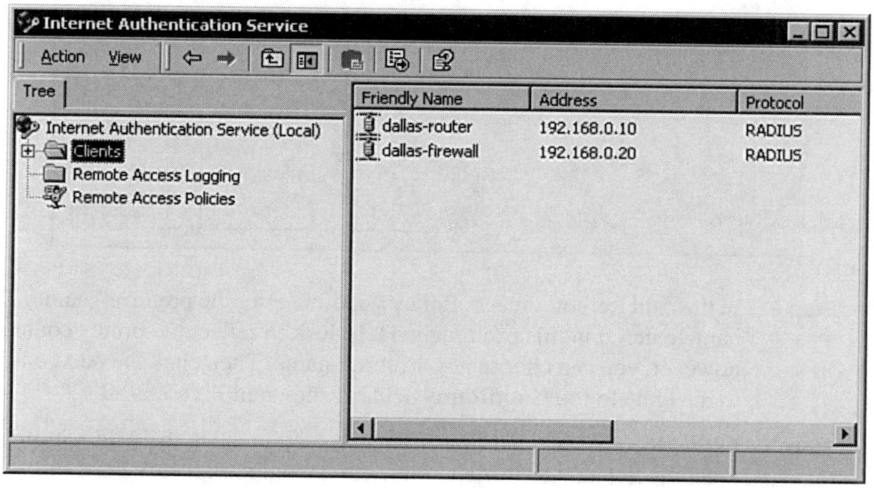

Configuring Remote-Access Policies

Remote-access policies determine the authentication and authorization permissions to be assigned to the authenticating users. Referring to the scenario shown in Figure 3-5, the two users, spope and jkeith, belong to the groups Netadmin and Helpdesk, respectively. The privilege levels assigned to the groups Netadmin and Helpdesk are 15 and 1, respectively. Consequently, when the members of the Helpdesk Active Directory group log in to the network devices, they would be authenticated using their Active Directory passwords and assigned a privilege level of 1. Similarly, the Netadmin group would be assigned privilege level 15. To implement such a scenario, you must create two remote-access policies, one each for Helpdesk and Netadmin. Follow these steps to create the policies:

Step 1 In the IAS MMC, choose **Remote Access Policy > New > Remote Access Policy**. This action opens the Add Remote Access Policy window, as shown in Figure 3-9.

Figure 3-9 *Add Remote Access Policy*

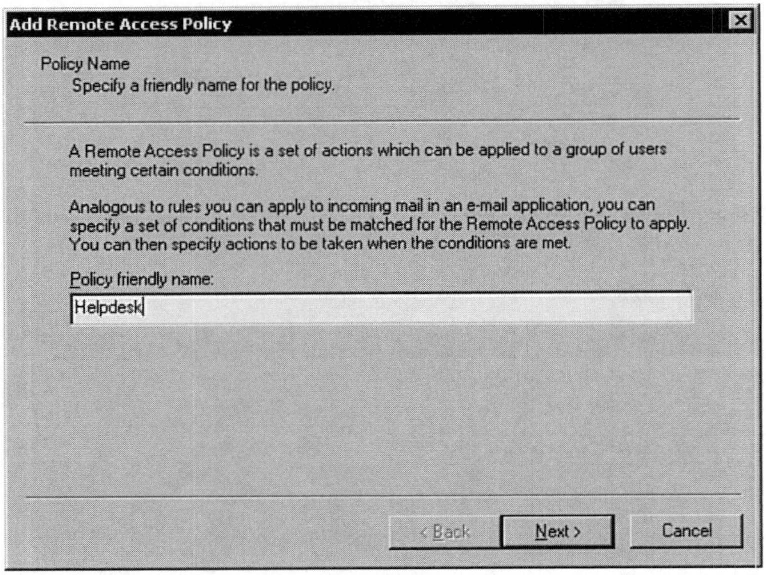

Step 2 In the Add Remote Access Policy window, enter the preferred name. The name entered in this example is **Helpdesk** to reflect the policy content; however, you can choose any arbitrary name. Then click the **Next** button to navigate to the **Conditions** field, as shown in Figure 3-10.

Step 3 In the Specify the conditions to match section, click the **Add** button to open the **Select Attribute** window, as shown in Figure 3-11.

Figure 3-10 *Add Remote Access Policy—Conditions*

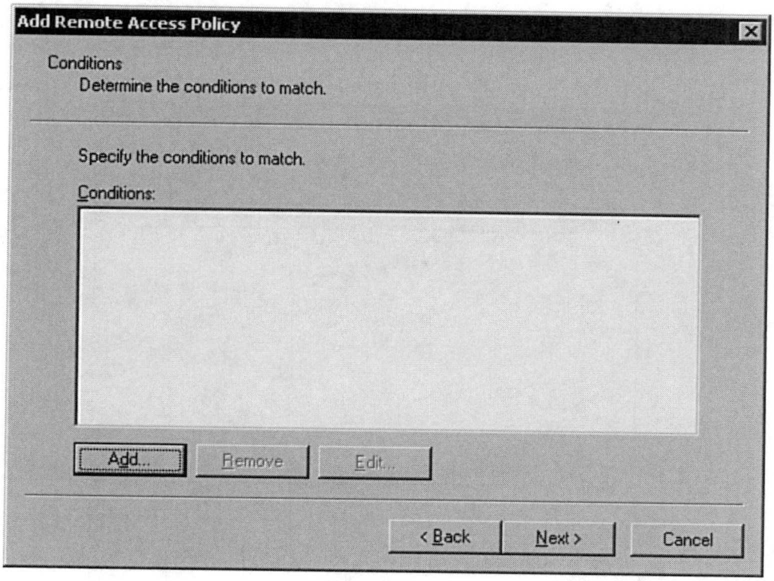

Figure 3-11 *Select Attribute*

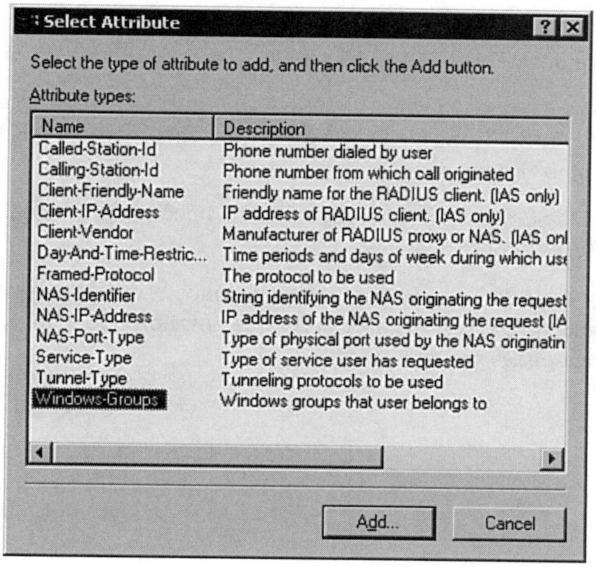

Step 4 In the Select Attribute window, select **Windows-Groups** and click the **Add** button to open the Groups window, as shown in Figure 3-12.

Figure 3-12 *Groups*

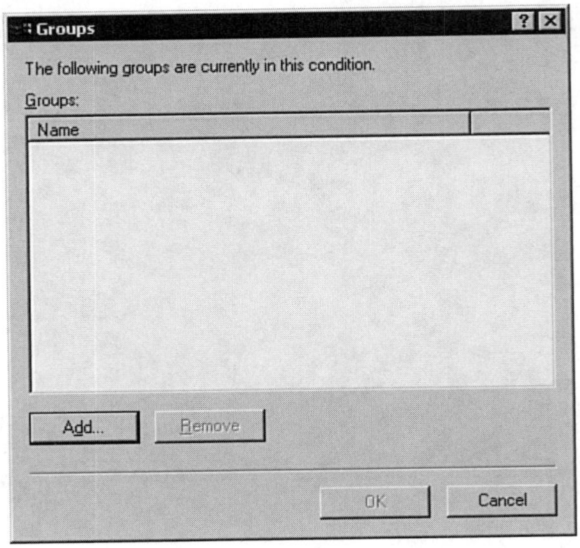

Step 5 Click the **Add** button in the Groups window to open the Select Groups window. This window lists all the Active Directory users and groups.

Step 6 Scroll down to locate the Helpdesk Active Directory group, as shown in Figure 3-13, and click the **Add** button. Then click the **OK** button to return to the Groups window.

Step 7 In the Groups window, click the **OK** button to return to the Add Remote Access Policy window.

Step 8 In the Add Remote Access Policy window, click the **Next** button and select the **Grant remote access permission** option in the Permissions section, as shown in Figure 3-14.

Figure 3-13 *Active Directory Groups*

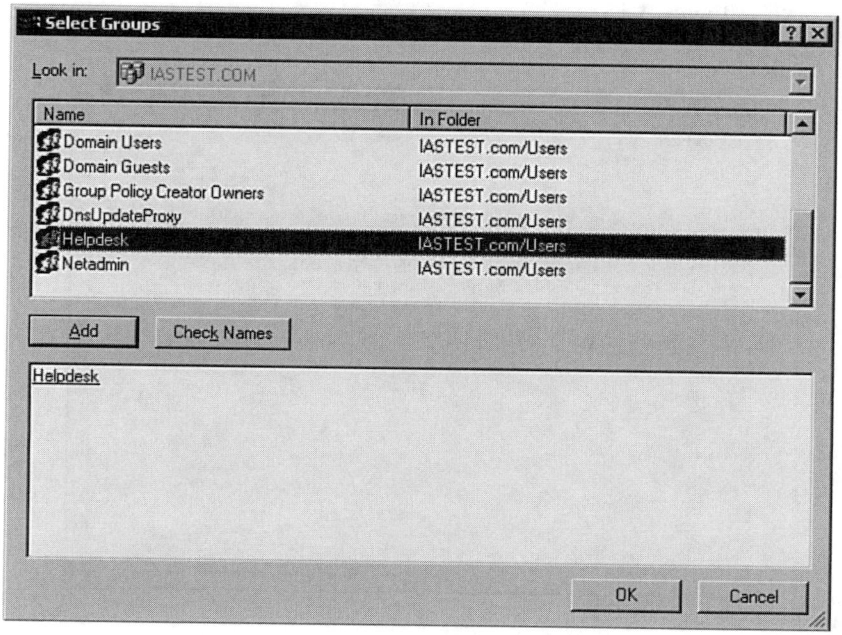

Figure 3-14 *Permissions*

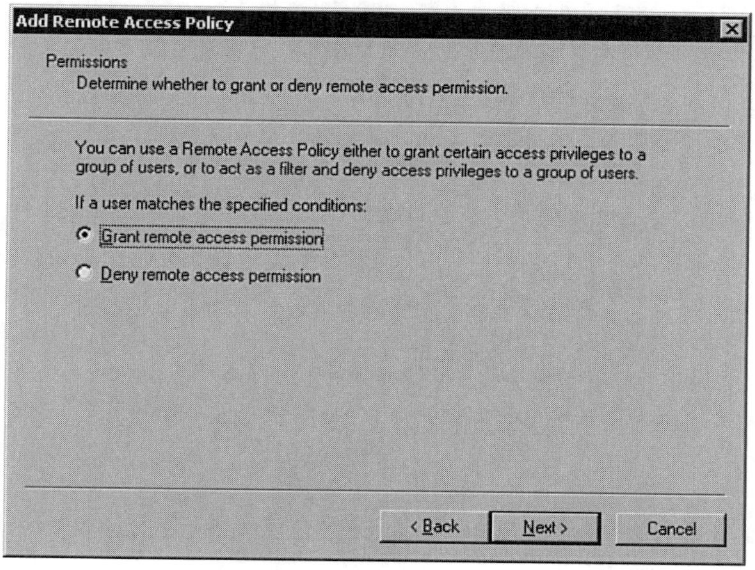

Step 9 Click the **Next** button again to enter the User Profile section, as shown in Figure 3-15.

Figure 3-15 *User Profile*

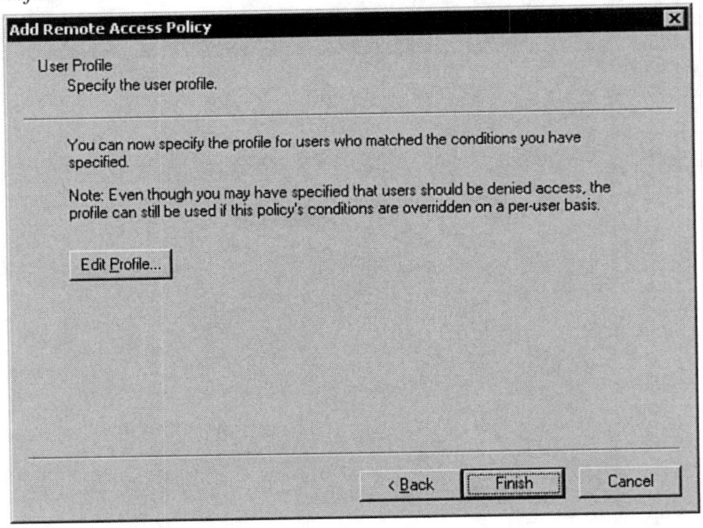

Figure 3-16 *Edit Dial-In Profile*

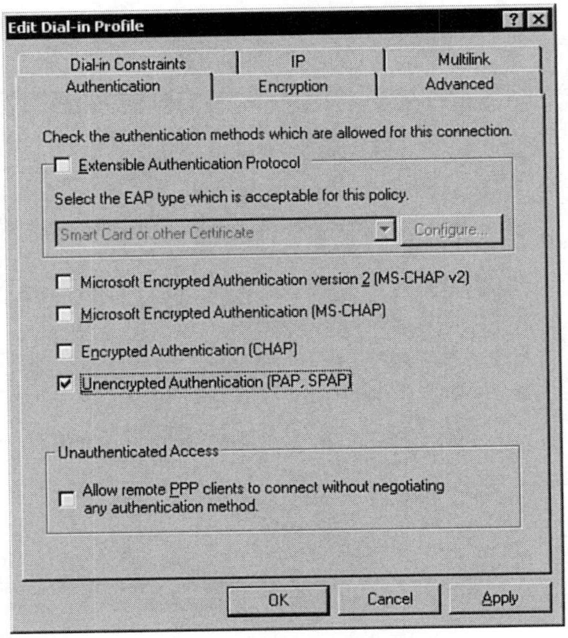

Step 10 In the User Profile section, click the **Edit Profile** button to open the Edit Dial-in Profile window.

Step 11 In the Edit Dial-in Profile window, select the **Authentication** tab and select the **Unencrypted Authentication** check box, as shown in Figure 3-16.

Step 12 Click the **Advanced** tab and remove all the entries in the Parameters section, as shown in Figure 3-17. Then click the **Add** button to open the Add Attributes window, as shown in Figure 3-18.

Figure 3-17 *Advanced Tab*

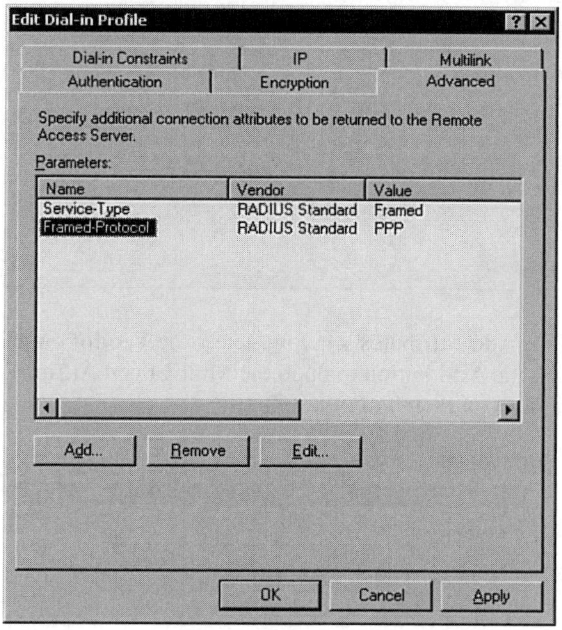

Figure 3-18 *Add Attributes*

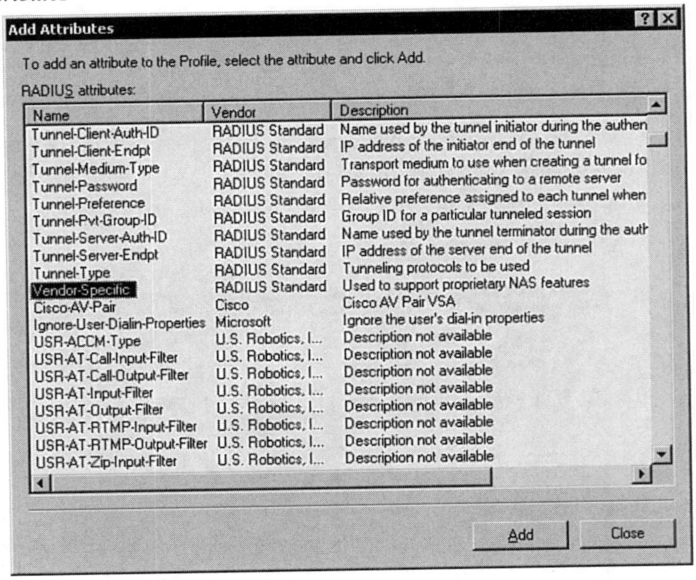

Step 13 In the Add Attributes window, select the **Vendor-Specific** attribute and click the **Add** button to open the Multivalued Attribute Information window, as shown in Figure 3-19.

Figure 3-19 *Multivalued Attribute Information*

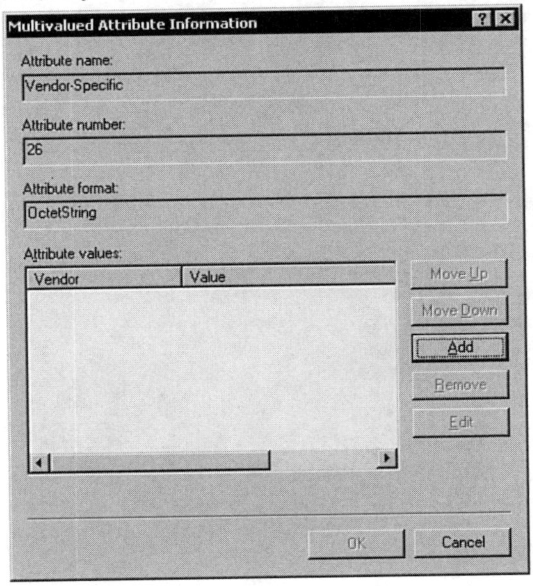

Step 14 In the Multivalued Attribute Information window, click the **Add** button to open the Vendor-Specific Attribute Information window.

NOTE The vendor-specific attributes, or VSAs, are RADIUS attributes defined by vendors to customize how RADIUS works on their servers.

Step 15 In the Vendor-Specific Attribute Information window, select the options that are shown in Figure 3-20. Then click the **Configure Attribute** button to open the Configure VSA (RFC compliant) window.

Figure 3-20 *Vendor-Specific Attribute*

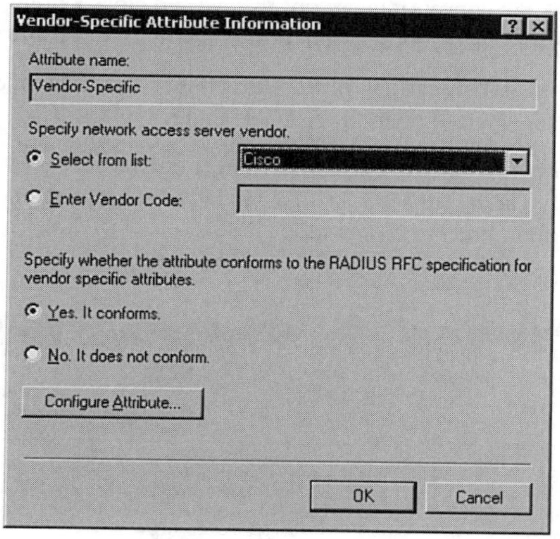

Step 16 Change the fields in the Configure VSA (RFC compliant) window to match those shown in Figure 3-21. Note the string **shell:priv-lvl=1**. This string assigns the privilege level of 1 to the authenticated users.

Figure 3-21 *Configure VSA (RFC Compliant)*

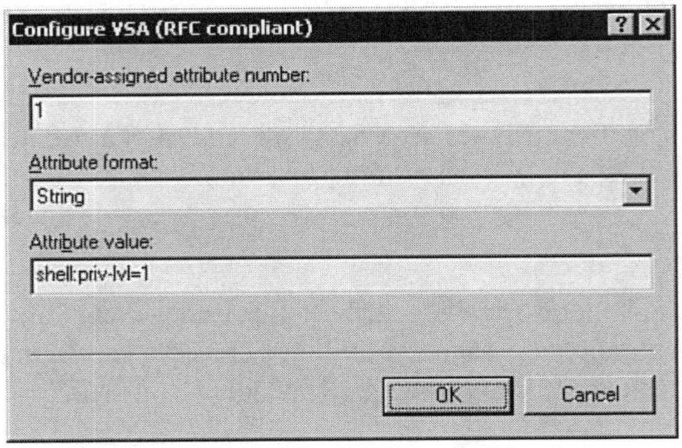

Step 17 Click the appropriate buttons to save and close all the open windows and return to the **Advanced** tab of the Edit Dial-in Profile window.

Step 18 On the **Advanced** tab of the Edit Dial-in Profile window, click the **Add** button again to open the Add Attributes window.

Step 19 In the Add Attributes window, select the **Service-Type** attribute, as shown in Figure 3-22. Then click the **Add** button to open the Enumerable Attribute Information window.

Figure 3-22 *Add Attribute*

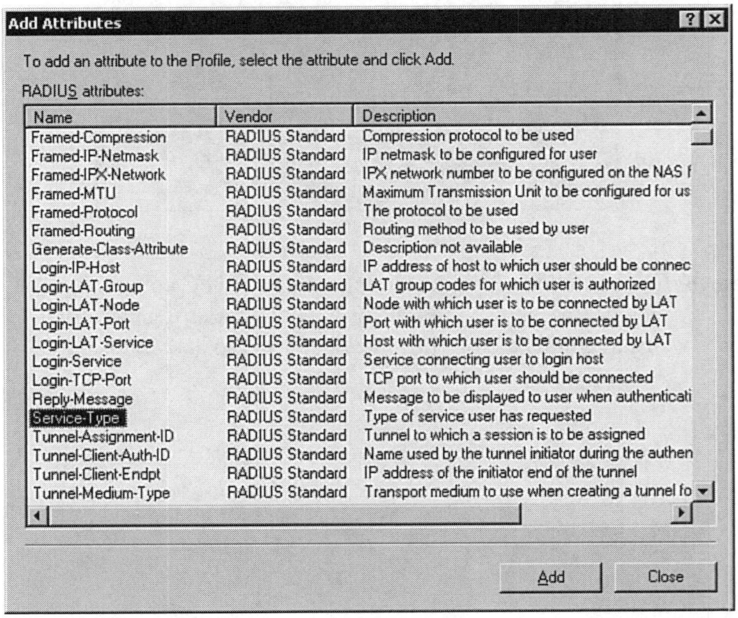

Step 20 In the Enumerable Attribute Information window, change the Attribute value field to **Login**, as shown in Figure 3-23.

Figure 3-23 *Enumerable Attribute Information*

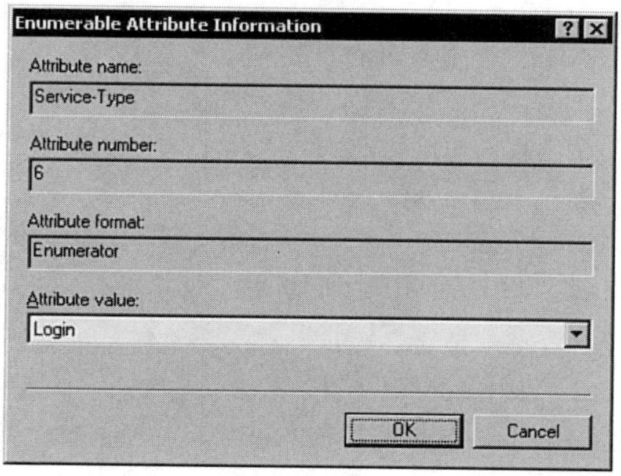

Step 21 Click the appropriate buttons to save and close the open windows and return to the Add Remote Access Policy window. Click the **Finish** button to return to the IAS MMC.

Step 22 Repeat Steps 1 through 21 to create the Netadmin policy with a privilege level of 15.

Configuring Accounting Parameters

The accounting parameters are configured through the Remote Access Logging window. The default location of the logs is the %WINDOWS%/system32/Logfiles directory. To view or change the default accounting parameters through the IAS MMC, select the **Remote Access Logging** option and choose **Local File > Properties** to open the Local File Properties window, as shown in Figure 3-24.

As shown in Figure 3-24, by default, the New log time period section is set to the **Unlimited file size** option. This results in a single log file that can grow considerably. For ease of administration, you should limit the log file either by size or by frequency. For example, choosing the **Monthly** option creates a new log file every month.

Figure 3-24 *Local File Properties*

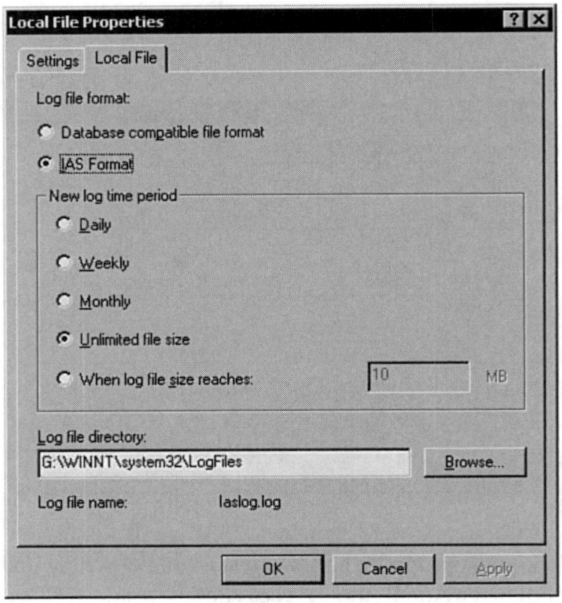

Always restart the IAS server after making any changes. To restart, choose **Start > Run**. Enter **services.msc** and click the **OK** button. Right-click the **Internet Authentication Service** option and choose **Restart**.

The Systems section of the Windows Event Viewer provides helpful information for troubleshooting an IAS server. For authentication issues related to a particular user, verify the user's membership.

NOTE In the MS Active Directory, the Remote Access Permission option for a new user is, by default, set to **Deny access**. This setting prevents the user from logging in to a networking device. You must manually change this setting to **Allow access**. To make this change, right-click the user in the **Active Directory User and Computers** snap-in and choose **Properties**. In the **Properties** window, select the **Dial-in** tab and choose **Allow access** in the Remote Access Permission (Dial-in or VPN) section. Click the **OK** button to save the settings.

The Microsoft IAS RADIUS server is now ready to provide AAA services to Cisco clients.

Configuring a Cisco Router for RADIUS

The steps involved in configuring a Cisco IOS–based routers for RADIUS-based AAA are almost identical to those of TACACS+-based AAA. However, RADIUS-based AAA requires an additional step of defining the UDP ports numbers to be used by the IOS devices to communicate with the RADIUS Server. This step is required to avoid incompatibility issues arising because of differences in the versions of RADIUS. Some RADIUS vendors are using the old UDP ports of 1812 and 1813 for authentication and accounting, respectively, while others are using UDP 1645 and 1646.

The global-configuration-mode command for specifying a RADIUS Server, UDP ports, and the encryption key on an IOS device is as follows:

> Router(config)# **radius-server host** {*hostname* | *ip-address*} [**auth-port** *port-number*] [**acct-port** *port-number*] [**timeout** *seconds*] [**retransmit** *retries*] [**key** *string]* [**alias** {*hostname* | *ip address*}]

Use the auth-port and acct-port options, respectively, to specify the UDP port for authentication and accounting.

Example 3-16 shows the configuration of an IOS device configured as a AAA Client using RADIUS. The RADIUS Server is configured with following parameters:

- MS IAS RADIUS Server IP address 192.168.0.40
- Linux FreeRADIUS Server IP address 192.168.0.30
- Encryption key testing123
- Authentication port UDP 1812
- Accounting port UDP 1813

Example 3-16 *IOS Device with RADIUS-Based AAA Configuration*

```
Dallas-Router# show running-config
Building configuration...
!
version 12.1
hostname Dallas-Router
!
aaa new-model
aaa authentication login default group radius local enable
aaa authorization exec default group radius local none
aaa authorization commands 0 default group radius local none
aaa authorization commands 1 default group radius local none
aaa authorization commands 15 default group radius local none
aaa accounting exec default start-stop group radius
aaa accounting commands 0 default start-stop group radius
aaa accounting commands 1 default start-stop group radius
aaa accounting commands 15 default start-stop group radius
enable password 7 03075218050070
!
username admin privilege 15 password 0 s3curepassword
```

continues

Example 3-16 *IOS Device with RADIUS-Based AAA Configuration (Continued)*

```
!
interface Ethernet0
 ip address 192.168.0.10 255.255.255.0
!
interface Serial0
 ip address 172.16.2.2 255.255.255.252

!
ip classless
ip route 0.0.0.0 0.0.0.0 192.168.0.20
!This entry is for using Linux FreeRADIUS server
radius-server host 192.168.0.30 auth-port 1812 acct-port 1813 key testing123
! This entry is for using MS-IAS based RADIUS server
radius-server host 192.168.0.40 auth-port 1812 acct-port 1813 key testing123
radius-server retransmit 3
!
line con 0
line vty 0 2
 password 7 030752180500
line vty 3 4
 password 7 13061E010803
!
end
```

Configuring a Cisco Switch for RADIUS

The configuration steps involved in enabling RADIUS on CatOS-based switches are similar to those for TACACS+. However, RADIUS lacks authorization on CatOS. No command exists to enable RADIUS exec authorization. The workaround is to set the **Service-Type** (RADIUS attribute 6) to **Administrative** (a value of 6) in the RADIUS Server to place the user in enable mode. If the **Service-type** is set for anything other than **Administrative** (for example, 1-login, 7-shell, or 2-framed), the user arrives at the switch exec prompt, not the enable prompt.

Example 3-17 shows the configuration of the switch as a AAA Client using RADIUS.

Example 3-17 *Cisco Switch Configuration for RADIUS-Based AAA*

```
set radius server 192.168.0.30
set radius key testing123
set authentication login radius enable
set authentication enable radius enable
set accounting exec enable start-stop radius
```

Configuring Cisco PIX Firewalls for RADIUS

Just as in IOS and CatOS, the commands used to configure RADIUS-based AAA on PIX Firewalls are similar to those used for TACACS+. However, an additional step is involved, that is, to specify the port numbers used by RADIUS.

Table 3-17 lists the commands involved in configuring RADIUS-based authentication on PIX.

Table 3-17 *Configuring RADIUS on PIX*

<table>
<tr><th>Command</th><th>Purpose</th></tr>
<tr><td>aaa-server <tag> protocol tacacs+|radius</td><td>Creates a server group on the PIX to use the RADIUS protocol</td></tr>
<tr><td><b>aaa-server</b> <i><tag></i> [<<b>(if_name)</b>>] <b>host</b> <i><ip_address></i> [<i><key></i>] [<b>timeout</b> <i><seconds></i>]</td><td>Specifies the IP address and encryption key for the RADIUS Server</td></tr>
<tr><td>aaa authentication serial | telnet | ssh | http | enable console <tag></td><td>Specifies the authentication to be used for console access through serial, Telnet, or SSH</td></tr>
<tr><td>aaa-server radius-authport <auth_port></td><td>Specifies the UDP port used by the RADIUS Server for exchanging authentication packets</td></tr>
<tr><td>aaa-server radius-acctport <acct_port></td><td>Specifies the UDP port used by the RADIUS Server for exchanging accounting packets</td></tr>
</table>

Based on these commands, Example 3-18 shows the configuration of the PIX Firewall for authentication. The RADIUS Server details are grouped under the tag MYAAA and are then applied to authenticate access to the firewall console through Telnet and the serial interface.

Example 3-18 *Configuring PIX for Authentication*

```
c:\windows\system32>telnet 192.168.0.20
User Access Verification
Password:
Type help or '?' for a list of available commands.
Firewall-Dallas> enable
Password:
Dallas-Firewall# conf t
Dallas-Firewall(config)# aaa-server MYAAA protocol radius
Dallas-Firewall(config)# aaa-server MYAAA (inside) host 192.168.0.30 testing123
Dallas-Firewall(config)# aaa-server radius-authport 1812
Dallas-Firewall(config)# aaa-server radius-acctport 1813
Dallas-Firewall(config)# aaa authentication telnet console MYAAA
Dallas-Firewall(config)# aaa authentication ssh console MYAAA
Dallas-Firewall(config)# exit
```

The PIX Firewall is now ready to be accessed using the username and password defined in the RADIUS Server.

CAUTION Unlike the IOS AAA feature set, PIX does not offer local authentication as a fallback feature in the same **aaa authentication** statement. Hence, it is good administrative practice to configure the serial console of the PIX for local authentication. This avoids denial to the serial console because of problems with the AAA server or misconfigurations. The suggested configuration to enable local authentication on the PIX serial console is as follows:

```
username admin password somepassword privilege 15
username helpdesk password someothepassword privilege 1
aaa-server LOCAL protocol local
aaa authentication serial console LOCAL
```

Commercial Products

While this chapter is based on products that are freely available (or can be obtained at no extra cost), it would be unfair to neglect one of the excellent commercial tools. Cisco Secure Access Control Server (CSACS) is the Cisco AAA server that provides almost all the features that are provided by the tools mentioned in this chapter. Additionally, CSACS provides the following functionality:

- Runs on both Windows and Solaris
- Supports both RADIUS and TACACS+ protocols
- Is fully administered through a user-friendly and intuitive web browser–based GUI
- Provides native support for most Cisco devices

A 90-day trial version of CSACS is available for download from Cisco.com in the **Products and Solution > Security and VPN** section.

Summary

The topics covered in this chapter prepare the Netadmin for securing access to all the networking devices. The Netadmins should be able to perform the following tasks within the AAA framework:

- Deploy a Linux-based TACACS+ Server to support Cisco devices
- Deploy a Microsoft Windows 2000 Server–based RADIUS Server using an Active Directory database for authentication
- Secure administrative access to Cisco IOS–based routers and switches using the TACACS+ and RADIUS protocols

- Secure administrative access to CatOS-based Cisco switches using the TACACS+ and RADIUS protocols
- Secure administrative access to Cisco PIX Firewalls using the TACACS+ and RADIUS protocols
- Secure administrative access to Cisco VPN concentrators using the TACACS+ protocol

Table 3-18 summarizes all the tools, including the source of the installation files, that are discussed in this chapter.

Table 3-18 *Tools Used in Chapter 3*

Tool	Function	Supported OS	Installation Files
TACACS+ freeware	TACACS+-based authentication, authorization, and accounting	Linux and major UNIX flavors	ftp://anonymous@ftp-eng.cisco.com/pub/tacacs/
FreeRADIUS	RADIUS-based authentication, authorization, and accounting	Linux, FreeBSD, OpenBSD, OSF/UNIX, Solaris	http://freeradius.org
Microsoft IAS	RADIUS-based authentication, authorization, and accounting	Windows 2000 Server, Windows 2003 Server	Included with the MS 2000/2003 Server software

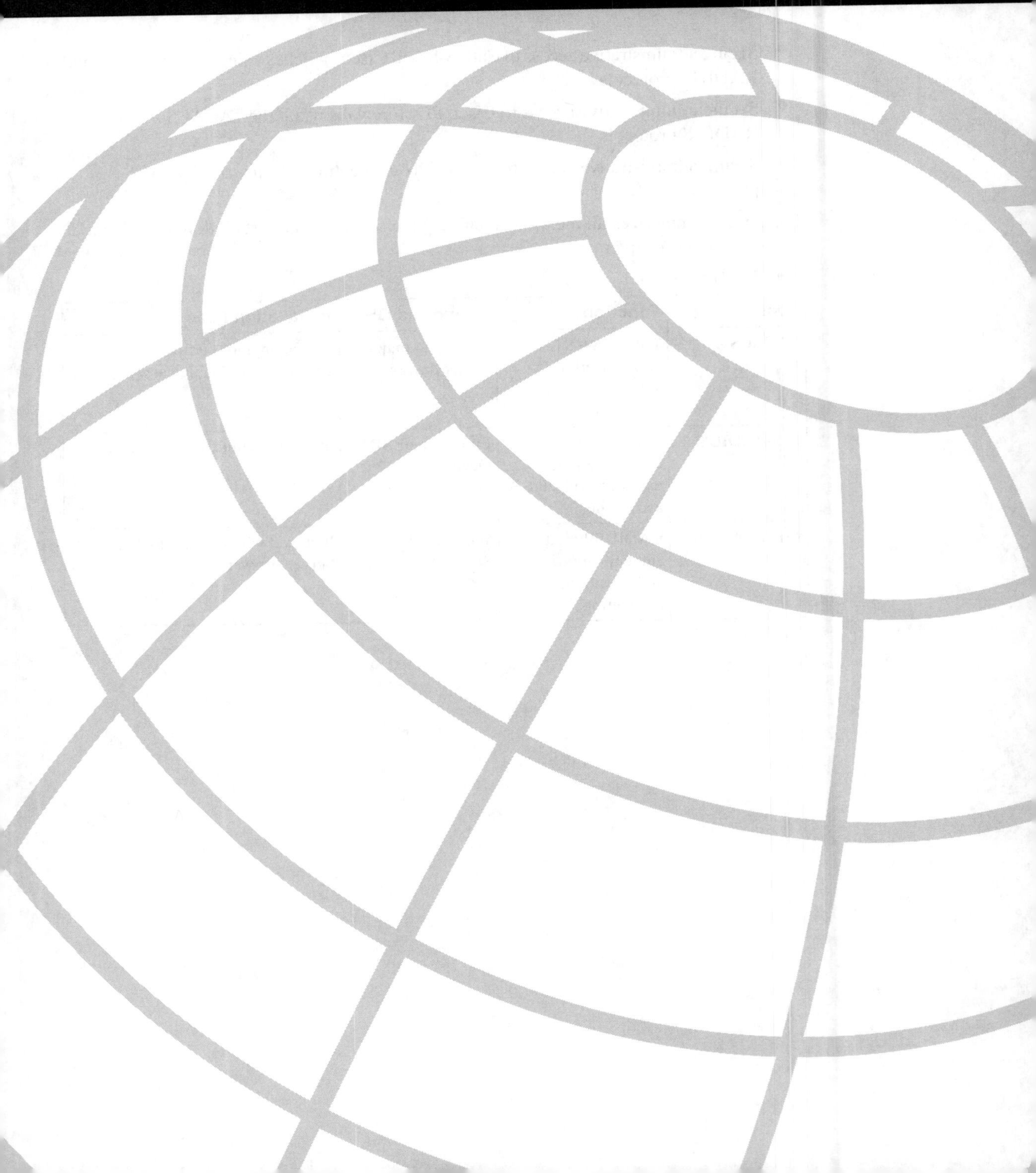

CHAPTER 4

Using Syslog

This chapter presents an overview of the syslog protocol and shows you how to deploy an end-to-end syslog system. The chapter includes a discussion about the syslog architecture and discusses deploying syslog servers in Linux and Windows OSs with a focus on their relevance in a Cisco environment. Also included are the steps involved in configuring Cisco devices for syslog.

Overview of Syslog

The syslog protocol, defined in RFC 3164, was originally written by Eric Allman. This protocol provides a transport to allow a device to send event notification messages across IP networks to event message collectors, also known as syslog servers. The protocol is simply designed to transport these event messages from the generating device to the collector. The collector doesn't send back an acknowledgment of the receipt of the messages.

In a UNIX operating system, the kernel and other internal components generate messages and alerts. These messages are typically stored in a file system or relayed to another device in the form of syslog messages. The internal daemon, called Syslogd, handles the syslog process. This daemon is an integral part of most UNIX/Linux distributions and does not need to be downloaded or installed. Syslog provides a central point for collecting and processing system logs. These system logs are useful later for troubleshooting and auditing. For example, when a hacker breaks into a system, the trail left behind by the hacker's activity is logged in the syslog messages. These messages can then be used to understand the attack, assess the damage, and patch the system.

Various Cisco devices, including routers, switches, PIX Firewalls, VPN concentrators, and so on, generate syslog messages for system information and alerts. For example, a Cisco router can generate a syslog message when an interface goes down or the configuration is changed. Similarly, a Cisco PIX Firewall can generate a syslog message when it blocks a TCP connection. Cisco devices can be configured to send the syslog messages to an external machine that acts as a central syslog server. However, if the connectivity between the Cisco device and the syslog server is down, no syslog messages would be captured by the server. In such cases, the syslog messages stored locally by the Cisco devices are the only source of information to determine the root cause of the issue.

Syslog uses the User Datagram Protocol (UDP), port 514, for communication. Being a connectionless protocol, UDP does not provide acknowledgments. Additionally, at the application layer, syslog servers do not send acknowledgments back to the sender for receipt of syslog messages. Consequently, the sending device generates syslog messages without knowing whether the syslog server has received the messages. In fact, the sending devices send messages even if the syslog server does not exist.

The syslog packet size is limited to 1024 bytes and carries the following information:

- Facility
- Severity
- Hostname
- Timestamp
- Message

A clear understanding of each of the syslog packet parameters can help you easily deploy syslog systems across your network. Note that the first two parameters, facility and severity, are often misunderstood.

Facility

Syslog messages are broadly categorized on the basis of the sources that generate them. These sources can be the operating system, the process, or an application. These categories, called facility, are represented by integers, as shown in Table 4-1. The local use facilities are not reserved and are available for general use. Hence, the processes and applications that do not have pre-assigned facility values can choose any of the eight local use facilities. As such, Cisco devices use one of the local use facilities for sending syslog messages.

Table 4-1 *Facility Values*

Integer	Facility
0	Kernel messages
1	User-level messages
2	Mail system
3	System daemons
4	Security/authorization messages
5	Messages generated internally by Syslogd
6	Line printer subsystem
7	Network news subsystem
8	UUCP subsystem
9	Clock daemon

Table 4-1 *Facility Values (Continued)*

Integer	Facility
10	Security/authorization messages
11	FTP daemon
12	NTP subsystem
13	Log audit
14	Log alert
15	Clock daemon
16	Local use 0 **(local0)**
17	Local use 1 **(local1)**
18	Local use 2 **(local2)**
19	Local use 3 **(local3)**
20	Local use 4 **(local4)**
21	Local use 5 **(local5)**
22	Local use 6 **(local6)**
23	Local use 7 **(local7)**

By default, Cisco IOS devices, CatOS switches, and VPN 3000 Concentrators use facility local7 while Cisco PIX Firewalls use local4 to send syslog messages. Moreover, most Cisco devices provide options to change the facility level from their default value.

Severity

The source or facility that generates the syslog message also specifies the severity of the message using a single-digit integer, as shown in Table 4-2.

Table 4-2 *Severity Values*

Integer	Severity
0	Emergency: System is unusable.
1	Alert: Action must be taken immediately.
2	Critical: Critical conditions.
3	Error: Error conditions.
4	Warning: Warning conditions.
5	Notice: Normal but significant condition.
6	Informational: Informational messages.
7	Debug: Debug-level messages.

Cisco devices use severity levels of Emergency to Warning to report software or hardware issues. A system restart or interface up/down messages are sent through the Notice level. A system reload is reported through the Informational level. The output of debug commands is expressed through the Debug level.

Hostname

The hostname field consists of the host name (as configured on the host itself) or the IP address. In devices such as routers or firewalls, which use multiple interfaces, syslog uses the IP address of the interface from which the message is transmitted.

Timestamp

The timestamp is the local time, in MMM DD HH:MM:SS format, of the device when the message was generated. Although RFC 3164 does not specify the use of a time zone, Cisco IOS allows configuring the devices to send the time-zone information in the message part of the syslog packet. Such timestamps are generally prefixed with a special character, such as an asterisk (*) or colon (:), to prevent the syslog server from misinterpreting the message. The timestamp format, including the time-zone information, is MMM DD HH:MM:SS Timezone *.

NOTE For the timestamp information to be accurate, it is good administrative practice to configure all the devices to use the Network Time Protocol (NTP). The NTP configuration on each Cisco device is beyond the scope of this discussion. Refer to the product documentation at Cisco.com for specific information on NTP configuration.

Message

This is the text of the syslog message, along with some additional information about the process that generated the message. The syslog messages generated by Cisco IOS devices begin with a percent sign (%) and use the following format:

```
%FACILITY-SEVERITY-MNEMONIC: Message-text
```

Following is a description of each field:

- **FACILITY**—Refers to the source of the message, such as a hardware device, a protocol, or a module of the system software. Note that this FACILITY is Cisco specific and is only relevant within the message string. It is different from the facility defined in RFC 3164 for the syslog protocol.
- **SEVERITY**—This is similar to the severity defined in Table 4-2.
- **MNEMONIC**—This is a device-specific code that uniquely identifies the message.
- **Message-text**—This is a text string that describes the message and can contain details such as port numbers and network addresses.

Following is a sample syslog message generated by a Cisco IOS device:

```
*Mar  6 22:48:34.452 UTC: %LINEPROTO-5-UPDOWN: Line protocol on Interface Loopback0,
  changed state to up
```

Note that the message begins with a special character (*) and that the timestamp includes the time-zone information. The message was generated by the LINEPROTO facility at severity 5 (Notice). The MNEMONIC UPDOWN along with the message-text describe the event.

The format of the syslog message generated by CatOS is slightly different from that generated by the IOS devices. Following is the format of the message generated by CatOS switches:

```
mm/dd/yyy:hh/mm/ss:facility-severity-MNEMONIC:Message-text
```

The syslog messages generated by a Cisco PIX Firewall begin with a percent sign (%) and are slightly different than the IOS syslog messages. Following is the format of syslog messages generated by a Cisco PIX Firewall:

```
%PIX-Level-Message_number: Message_text
```

For a complete list of the *Message_number* and *Message_text* and associated details , refer to the Cisco PIX Firewall System Log Messages section on the Cisco product documentation website (http://www.cisco.com/univercd/home/home.htm).

The syslog messages generated by Cisco VPN 3000 Concentrators follow the format of the IOS syslog messages, as discussed earlier in this section.

Deploying Syslog Servers

Consider a typical campus network of an organization consisting of routers, firewalls, VPN concentrators, and switches to interconnect the application servers to the users' workstations. Figure 4-1 shows a scaled-down version of the campus network of one such organization, ABC Investments.

To enable a centralized location to collect all the messages and alerts generated by various Cisco devices, the Netadmin has installed a syslog server. This server should be configured to accept, filter, and store syslog messages generated by the Cisco devices. Figure 4-2 illustrates LAN devices sending syslog messages to a central syslog server (with IP address 192.168.0.30). The following sections cover the step-by-step process of deploying the syslog server based on the choice of operating system.

Figure 4-1 *Campus Network of ABC Investments*

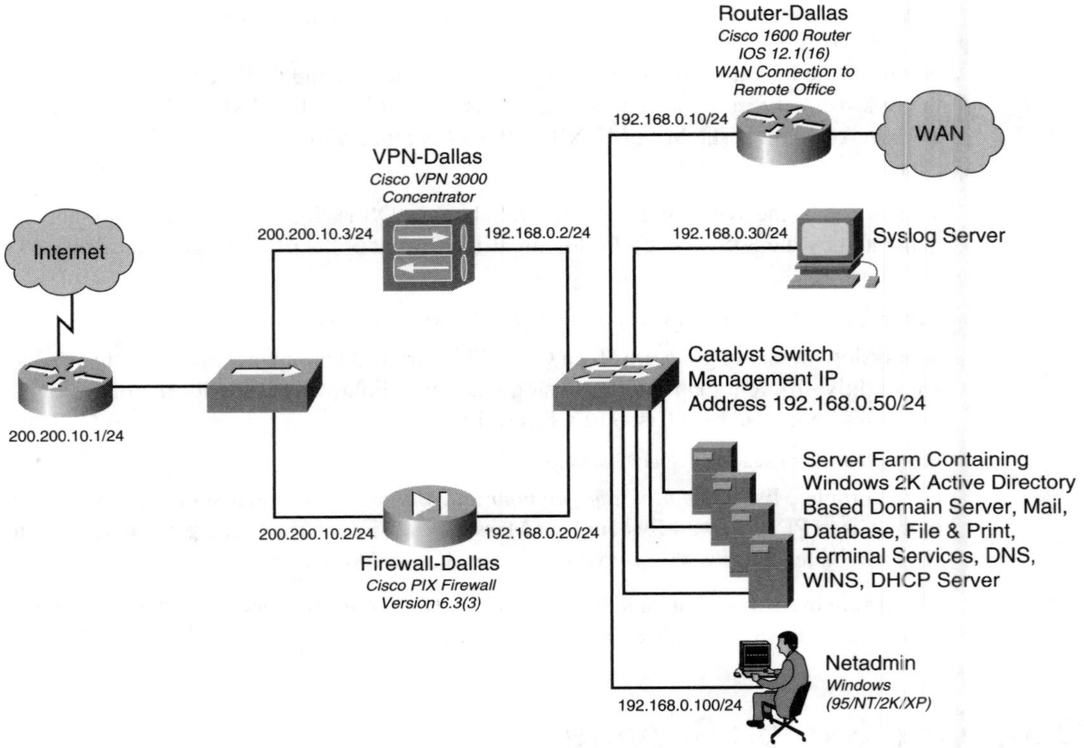

Deploying the Default Syslog Daemon

To collect syslog messages generated by Cisco devices, many Netadmins might prefer to use the default syslog daemon that is included with the Linux operating system. Although it is well integrated with the operating system, the internal syslog server is not enabled for use as a network-based syslog server. To use the syslog daemon as a network-based syslog server, you must configure it through the /etc/syslog.conf file. Additionally, you must enable the syslog daemon to receive syslog messages from the network.

Figure 4-2 *Network Devices Sending Syslog Messages*

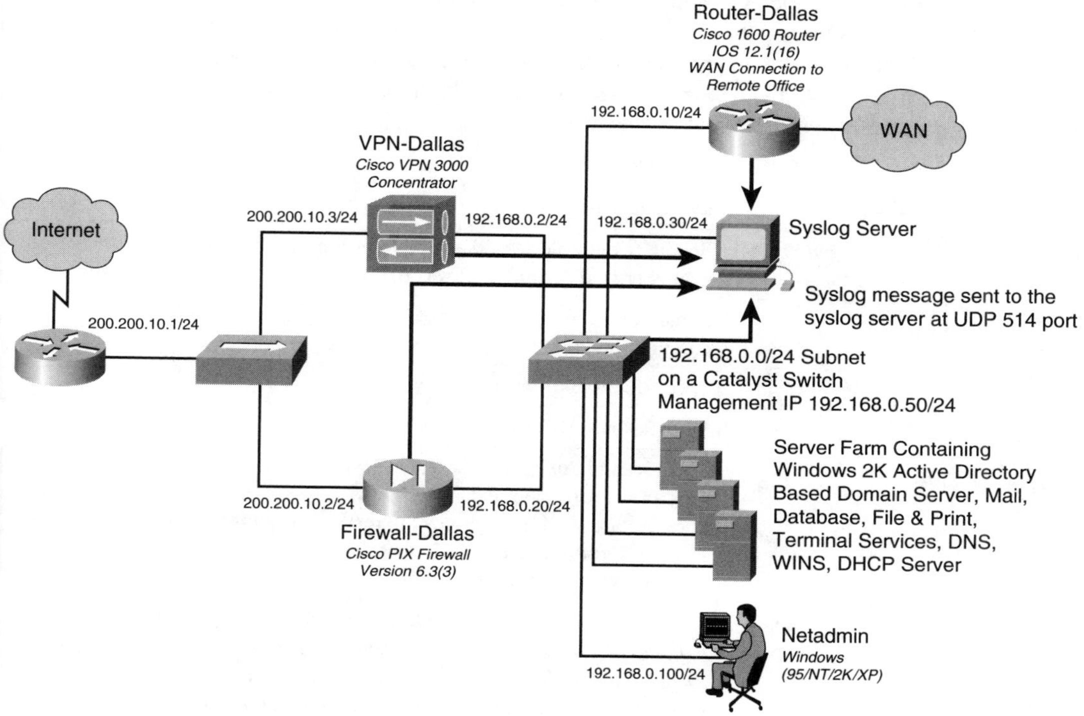

Configuring the Syslog Daemon

The /etc/syslog.conf file controls the configuration of the syslog daemon. This file contains the rules for sorting syslog messages. The rules specify the criteria by which to sort syslog messages on the basis of facility and severity levels, and to send them to destination log files. The default contents of the /etc/syslog.conf file are used to log the OS messages and should not be altered. To log messages from Cisco devices, simply append the new rules to the /etc/syslog.conf file. The syntax for specifying a rule is as follows:

```
facility.severity<Tab>destination-file-path
```

To log messages from Cisco devices, the possible values for facility are **local0** through **local7** and those for severity are **debug**, **info**, **notice**, **warning**, **err**, **crit**, **alert**, **emerg**, and **none**. The keyword **none** indicates no severity for the given facility. Although abbreviated, the keywords correspond to the severity levels listed in Table 4-2.

In addition, recall from Table 4-2 that debug is the highest level of severity. Specifying **debug** in the /etc/syslog.conf file results in all the messages (from severity debug to emergency) being logged. The use of **crit** results in logging all messages with a severity of critical, alert, and emergency, thereby excluding the higher levels (error, warning, notice, informational, and debug). To override this default behavior, you can use the special characters described in Table 4-3.

Table 4-3 *Special Characters in /etc/syslog.conf File**

Option	Description
,	Specifies multiple facilities with the same severity in one statement. The syntax is *facility1,facility2.severity*. Example: **local1,local5.debug**
;	Separates multiple pairs of *facility.severity* in the same line. Useful in conjunction with the **!** option.
*	Specifies all facilities or all severities.
none	Specifies no severity for the given facility.
=	Specifies only using the indicated severity level. The syntax is *facility.=severity*. For example, **local7.=debug** only logs level7 messages at the debug level and ignores the rest, such as info, notice, warning, and so on. Useful in overriding the default behavior of the syslog daemon to include lower severity messages.
!	Ignores the specified severity level, including the lower levels. The syntax is *facility.!severity*. Useful in conjunction with the **;** option. For example, **local7.*;local7.!err** logs all local7 messages but ignores messages with severity levels of error, critical, alert, and emergency.
destination-file-path	Specifies the location of the log file for storing the sorted messages. Instead of using the local file, you can also specify remote hosts using the @ option.
@	Specifies the host name or IP address of the remote syslog server. The syntax is *facility.severity***<Tab>**@*hostname*. If you use the host name, make sure that the host name is added in the /etc/hosts file.

*The contents of this table are derived from the syslog, sysklogd, and syslog.conf manual pages. Use the Linux **man** *command-name* for accessing the manual pages of any command. For example **man syslog** command will display the information about the syslog command.

You can create customized rules for sorting and storing various syslog messages based on the options listed in Table 4-3. For example, the following entry sends all the local7 messages to the file /var/log/router.log:

```
local7.debug   /var/log/router.log
```

By using the debug severity level, all the messages (from severity debug to emergency) are included. You can add multiple rules to the /etc/syslog.conf file. Depending on the configuration, a message can match multiple rules and hence can be sent to multiple log files.

NOTE Always use the Tab character instead of a space between the severity and destination fields of the /etc/syslog.conf file. Many Linux systems do not work with spaces in the /etc/syslog.conf file.

Example 4-1 contains several sample rules to be added to the /etc/syslog.conf file.

Example 4-1 *Sample Entries for the /etc/syslog.conf File*

```
# all message from all facilities will be sent to /var/log/allmessages.log file
*.debug                                          /var/log/allmessages.log
#
# Send all local4 messages to the /var/log/pix.log file
# By default Cisco PIX firewall uses local4 facility
local4.debug                                     /var/log/pix.log
#
# Send messages with facility local5 and severity level notice through emergency,
# to the /var/log/notice.log file
local5.notice                                    /var/log/notice.log
#
# Only send messages with facility local4 and severity level of info
local4.=info                                     /var/log/onlyinfo.log
#
# Send all messages with facility local4 to the /var/log/errorandbelow.log file, but
# exclude messages with severity error, critical, alert and emergency
local4.*;local4.!err                             /var/log/errorandbelow.log
#
# Send all messages with facility local6 to the /var/log/allexcepterror.log file,
  and
# only exclude messages with severity level err
local6.*;local6.!=err                            /var/log/allexcepterror.log
```

By default, the syslog daemon only accepts local syslog messages. To enable the daemon to accept remote syslog messages, you must run the **syslogd** process in conjunction with the **-r** option. In Debian systems, the syslogd process is run through the /etc/init.d/sysklogd file. Using a text editor such as **vi**, you can edit the contents of the /etc/init.d/sysklogd file, as shown in Example 4-2.

Example 4-2 *Partial Contents of the /etc/init.d/sysklogd File*

```
#! /bin/sh
# /etc/init.d/sysklogd: start the system log daemon.
PATH=/bin:/usr/bin:/sbin:/usr/sbin
pidfile=/var/run/syslogd.pid
binpath=/sbin/syslogd
test -x $binpath || exit 0
# Options for start/restart the daemons
#   For remote UDP logging use SYSLOGD="-r"
#
#SYSLOGD=""
SYSLOGD="-r"
# ---OUTPUT SUPPRESSED---
```

Running the Syslog Daemon

After editing the configuration files, you must restart the syslog daemon. On Debian Linux machines, you can use the **init** script, as follows:

```
root@linuxbox:~# /etc/init.d/sysklogd restart
Restarting system log daemon: syslogd.
```

The syslog daemon is now ready for use as a network syslog server. To verify the operation of the syslog daemon, use the **ps** command, in conjunction with **grep**, as follows:

```
root@linuxbox:~# ps -ef | grep syslog
root      5750     1  0 19:45 ?        00:00:00 /sbin/syslogd -r
```

To verify that the syslog daemon is listening for remote syslog messages on the default UDP port of 514, use the **netstat** command, as follows:

```
root@linuxbox:~# netstat -na | grep 514
udp        0      0 0.0.0.0:514             0.0.0.0:*
```

The line entry beginning with udp indicates that the system is listening at UDP port 514.

If you make changes in the /etc/syslog.conf file, you can instruct the syslog daemon to reload the file, without restarting the entire syslog daemon, using the **kill** command, as follows:

```
root@linuxbox:~# kill -HUP `cat /var/run/syslogd.pid`
```

You can also use the **kill -1 `cat /var/run/syslog.pid`** command to get the same results.

To view the syslog messages, you can use the Linux system commands such as **cat**, **tail**, and **head**. For example, to view the last five syslog messages in the /var/log/pix.log file, use the **tail -n 5 /var/log/pix.log** command, as shown in Example 4-3.

Example 4-3 *Viewing Syslog Messages Using the* **tail** *Command*

```
root@linuxbox:~# tail -n 5 /var/log/pix.log
Apr 16 16:03:01 192.168.0.20 Apr 16 2005 15:37:27: %PIX-7-710002: TCP access
  permitted
from 192.168.0.150/20184 to inside:192.168.0.20/telnet
Apr 16 16:03:03 192.168.0.20 Apr 16 2005 15:37:29: %PIX-6-605005: Login permitted
  from
192.168.0.150/20184 to inside:192.168.0.20/telnet for user ""
Apr 16 16:03:07 192.168.0.20 Apr 16 2005 15:37:33: %PIX-7-111009: User 'enable_15'
executed cmd: show logging
Apr 16 16:04:37 192.168.0.20 Apr 16 2005 15:39:03: %PIX-7-111009: User 'enable_15'
   executed cmd: show running-config | inc logg
Apr 16 16:04:43 192.168.0.20 Apr 16 2005 15:39:09: %PIX-6-302010: 0 in use, 0 most
  used
root@linuxbox:~#
```

To view the messages in real time, use the **tail** command with **-f** option. In this case, the command would be **tail -f /var/log/pix.log**.

Deploying a Linux-Based Syslog-ng Server

As discussed earlier, Linux has a preinstalled syslog server, called Syslogd, that is an integral part of the operating system. However, the Syslogd daemon is older and suffers from the following limitations:

- **Facility**—The facilities labels (local0 to local7) are too general and are used by many programs. Such generic labels do not reflect the real facility that is generating the messages. For example, while the facility code 0 clearly indicates kernel messages, the facility code 20 (local4) does not indicate a particular facility and can be potentially used by any Cisco device.
- **Filtering**—Because all external programs are crowded together in the eight available local use facilities, many of the messages would end up using the same facility code. In such cases, selecting or filtering the messages from different devices becomes difficult. This makes it difficult to find the necessary information in the large number of log messages.

Several open source and commercial projects have tried to develop alternatives to the original syslog daemon. Some of them are Syslog-ng, SDSC Syslog, and Secure Syslog. Of these three, Syslog-ng, by Balazs Scheidler, is the next generation of syslog and offers the following advantages:

- **Filtering**—Syslog-ng can filter messages based on the contents of messages in addition to the priority/facility pair. This enables the Netadmin to log messages that are generated by each Cisco device to its own log file.
- **Ports**—Syslog-ng can use both Transmission Control Protocol (TCP) and UDP. This feature is useful for logging messages from devices, such as Cisco PIX Firewalls, that provide options to use syslog over TCP. Using syslog over TCP provides reliability because TCP is a connection-oriented protocol.
- **Long host name format**—The relay function offered by Syslog-ng allows syslog messages to traverse multiple Syslog-ng servers. In such cases, the long host name format, which records every intermediate Syslog-ng server, makes it easy to find the originating host and chain of forwarding hosts, even if a log message traverses several computers.
- **Active development and support**—Syslog-ng's development is ongoing, and it enjoys communitywide popularity and support.

Because Syslog-ng offers more options and flexibility to the Netadmin, the following sections discuss the details of deploying a Syslog-ng server.

Installing the Syslog-ng Daemon

The steps involved in installing a Syslog-ng daemon on a Linux server are as follows:

Step 1 Log in to the Linux machine using suitable login credentials.

Step 2 Open a web browser and download the Syslog-ng source file from http://www.balabit.com. The source file is in a compressed tar file (for example, syslog-ng-1.6.5.tar.gz). Additionally, download the source files for libol, which is the support library for Syslog-ng. (An example is libol-0.3.14.tar.gz.)

Step 3 Unpack the libol distribution by using the **tar xvfz libol-*x.x.xx*.tar.gz** command, where ***x.x.xx*** indicates the version number. This creates a directory named libol-x.xx, where the source for libol is unpacked. For the example shown in Step 2, the directory name is libol-0.3.14.

Step 4 Enter the libol-*x.x.xx* directory using the **cd libol-*x.x.xx*** command.

Step 5 Enter the following three commands to compile the source code:

```
./configure
make
make install
```

Step 6 After installing the libol package, change the working directory back to the one that contains the Syslog-ng source files. Unpack the distribution by using the **tar xvfz syslog-ng-*x.xx*.tar.gz** command, where ***x.xx*** stands for the version number. This creates a directory named syslog-ng-x.xx, where the source files for Syslog-ng are unpacked. For the example shown in Step 2, the directory name is syslog-ng-1.6.5.

Step 7 Enter the syslog-ng-*x.xx* directory using the **cd syslogng-*x.xx*** command.

Step 8 Enter the following three commands to compile the source code:

```
./configure
make
make install
```

The Syslog-ng daemon is now ready for configuration. Example 4-4 shows the commands that are used in the installation process.

Example 4-4 *Syslog-ng Installation*

```
[root@linuxbox]# tar zxvf libol-0.3.14.tar.gz
[root@linuxbox]# cd libol-0.3.14/
[root@linuxbox libol-0.3.14]# ./configure
[root@linuxbox libol-0.3.14]# make
[root@linuxbox libol-0.3.14]# make install
[root@linuxbox libol-0.3.14]# cd ..
[root@linuxbox]# tar xvfz syslog-ng-1.6.5.tar.gz
[root@linuxbox  root]# cd  syslog-ng-1.6.5
[root@linuxbox syslog-ng-1.6.5]# ./configure
[root@linuxbox syslog-ng-1.6.5]# make
[root@linuxbox syslog-ng-1.6.5]# make install
```

NOTE Debian users can avoid all the steps listed in this section and install Syslog-ng by using the **apt-get install syslog-ng** command.

Configuring the Syslog-ng Daemon

The Syslog-ng daemon is configured through the /etc/syslog-ng file. The following five components are used to configure the syslog-ng.conf file:

- options
- source
- destination
- filter
- log

Options

Syslog-ng.conf uses the **options** parameter to define global options for the Syslog-ng daemon. The command syntax is as follows:

```
options { option1(value); option2(value); ... };
```

Table 4-4 provides a partial list of options.

Table 4-4 *Partial List of Global Options in Syslog-ng*

Option Name	Accepted Values	Description
sync()	Number	The number of lines buffered before being written to the file.
create_dirs()	**yes** or **no**	Enables or disables directory creation; helpful when using macros in the file destination drivers.
chain_hostnames()	**yes** or **no**	Enables or disables the chained host name format.
long_hostnames()	**yes** or **no**	Alias for **chain_hostnames**.
keep_hostname()	**yes** or **no**	Replaces the host name in the message with its DNS name. If **keep_hostname** is **yes** and **chain_hostnames** is **yes**, the sender's name is appended to the DNS host name; otherwise the name is replaced.
use_dns()	**yes** or **no**	Enables or disables DNS usage. Syslog-ng blocks on DNS queries, so enabling DNS can lead to a denial of service (DoS) attack. To prevent DoS attacks, protect your Syslog-ng network endpoint with firewall rules, and make sure that all hosts that can get to Syslog-ng are resolvable.
use_fqdn()	**yes** or **no**	Adds a fully qualified domain name (FQDN) instead of a short host name.

Example 4-5 shows a sample snippet for the options components of the /etc/syslog-ng.conf file. This code prepares the Syslog-ng daemon to be used as a central syslog server for Cisco devices.

Example 4-5 *Syslog-ng.conf—Options Components*

```
options {
        chain_hostnames(yes);
        keep_hostname(yes);
        use_fqdn(yes);
use_dns(no)
        sync(0);
};
```

Source

The **source** statement defines one or more source categories used by the Syslog-ng daemon to collect messages. The /etc/syslog-ng.conf file refers to these sources as source-drivers. The command syntax for declaring all the sources is as follows:

```
source identifier { source-driver(params); source-driver(params); ... };
```

The *identifier* is a text string that uniquely identifies the source. Table 4-5 provides a partial list of source-drivers.

Table 4-5 *Partial List of Source-Drivers in Syslog-ng*

Source-Driver Name	Description
internal	Indicates messages that are generated internally in Syslog-ng
unix-stream	Opens the specified UNIX socket in SOCK_STREAM mode and listens for messages
unix-dgram	Opens the specified UNIX socket in SOCK_DGRAM mode and listens for messages
udp	Listens on the specified UDP port for messages
tcp	Listens on the specified TCP port for messages

Note the last two entries in Table 4-5. The UDP and TCP source-drivers enable the Syslog-ng daemon to act as a central syslog server. These source-drivers instruct the daemon to accept messages through the network.

Example 4-6 shows a sample snippet for the source components of the syslog-ng.conf file. The code (with identifier **s_cisconetwork**) prepares the Syslog-ng daemon to get syslogs sent by Cisco devices through the network at the default UDP port of 514.

Example 4-6 *Syslog-ng.conf—Source Components*

```
# source s_cisconetwork will listen on default UDP514
source s_cisconetwork {
     udp();
};
```

destination

The **destination** statement is used by the daemon to direct the syslog messages after filtering. Similar to sources, destinations use one or more destination-drivers to define message handling.

The command syntax for declaring the all the sources is as follows:

```
destination identifier { destination-driver(params); destination-driver(params);
... };
```

The identifier is a text string that uniquely identifies the destination list. Table 4-6 provides a partial list of destination-drivers.

Table 4-6 *Partial List of Destination-Drivers in Syslog-ng*

Destination-Driver Name	Description
file	Writes messages to the given file; this is the most commonly used option.
udp	Sends messages to the specified host and UDP port; this enables the syslog server to act as a relay server.
tcp	Sends messages to the specified host and TCP port; this enables the syslog server to act as a relay server.
program	Launches the specified program in the background and sends messages to its standard input; useful for incorporating **syslog-ng** with external scripts.

The first entry in Table 4-6, the file driver, is one of the most important destination-drivers in Syslog-ng. It allows you to include macros to automatically create new files based on the syslog message content. Note that this functionality requires the use of the **create_dirs(yes)** option in the destination-driver statement. The macros are included by prefixing the macro name with a dollar sign ($) (such as $HOSTS and $LEVEL).

For example, the following statement uses the $HOST macro in the file destination-driver:

```
destination hosts { file("/var/log/host/$HOST" create_dirs(yes)); };
```

This creates a new log file for each of the hosts that sends a network message to this Syslog-ng daemon. The syslog messages sent by the host Router-Dallas are stored in the log file /var/log/host/router-dallas. If the router-dallas file does not exist, it is automatically created. Table 4-7 provides a complete list of macros that are available for the file destination-driver. As shown in this example, these macros provide highly flexible methods of handling syslog messages. A Netadmin can control the logging of syslog based on the host name, facility, severity, date, and timestamp of the syslog messages generated by Cisco devices.

Table 4-7 *Available Macros in the File Destination-Driver*

Name	Description
FACILITY	The name of the facility that the message is tagged as coming from.
PRIORITY or LEVEL	The priority or the severity level of the message.
TAG	The priority and facility encoded as a 2-digit hexadecimal number.
DATE	Date of the transaction.
FULLDATE	Long form of the date of the transaction.
ISODATE	Date in ISO format.
YEAR	The year the message was sent. Time expansion macros can either use the time specified in the log message (for example, the time the log message is sent) or the time the message was received by the log server. This is controlled by the **use_time_recvd()** option.
MONTH	The month the message was sent.
DAY	The day of the month the message was sent.
WEEKDAY	The three-letter name of the day of the week the message was sent (for example, **Thu**).
HOUR	The hour of the day the message was sent.
MIN	The minute the message was sent.
SEC	The second the message was sent.
FULLHOST	The full host name of the system that sent the log.
HOST	The name of the source host where the message originated. If the message traverses several hosts, and **chain_hostnames()** is set to **yes**, the name of the first host is used.
PROGRAM	The name of the program that the message was sent by.
MSG or MESSAGE	Message contents.

TIP Instead of grouping by host name, you can also group files by time, such as day, date, or weekday. For example by using the DATE macro, messages are sorted by their date of creation. Consequently, by the end of the year, you will have 365 different files. Additionally, each file will contain messages generated by all the devices on the given day. This chronological grouping of all the messages helps Netadmins to correlate events across multiple devices. The command syntax is as follows:

```
destination hosts { file("/var/log/host/$DATE" create_dirs(yes)); };
```

Along with using the macros listed in Table 4-7, the file destination-driver also allows the use of local options that override the global options listed in the beginning of the syslog-ng.conf file. Table 4-8 shows a partial list of these options.

Table 4-8 *Partial List of Options for File Destination-Driver*

Name	Type	Description
owner()	String	Sets the owner of the created filename to the one specified. The default is **root**.
group()	String	Sets the group of the created filename to the one specified. The default is **root**.
perm()	Number	Indicates the permission mask of the file if it is created by Syslog-ng. The default is **0600**.
dir_perm()	Number	Indicates the permission mask of directories created by Syslog-ng. Log directories are only created if a file, after macro expansion, refers to a nonexisting directory, and dir creation is enabled using **create_dirs()**. The default is **0600**.
create_dirs()	**yes** or **no**	Enables the creation of nonexisting directories. The default is **no**.

Example 4-7 shows a sample snippet for the destination components of the /etc/syslog-ng.conf file. This code instructs the Syslog-ng daemon to create separate log files for each host that sends syslog messages. The second part of the code (with the **d_cisco_facility** identifier) instructs the Syslog-ng daemon to create separate files for each message based on the facility code. The third part of the code (with the **d_cisco_severity** identifier) instructs the Syslog-ng daemon to create separate files for each message based on the severity code.

Example 4-7 *Syslog-ng.conf—Destination Components*

```
destination d_hosts {
    file("/var/log/HOSTS/$HOST.log"
    create_dirs(yes));
};
destination d_cisco_facility {
    file("/var/log/FACILITY/$FACILITY.log"
    create_dirs(yes));
};
destination d_cisco_severity {
    file("/var/log/LEVEL/$LEVEL.log"
    create_dirs(yes));
};
```

filter

The **filter** statement is used by Syslog-ng to route the syslog messages. You can use a Boolean expression to allow a message to pass through the filter. The syntax is as follows:

```
filter identifier { expression; };
```

The identifier is a text string that uniquely identifies the filters in the log statements. An expression can contain parentheses; the Boolean operators AND, OR, and NOT; and any of the functions listed in Table 4-9.

Table 4-9 *Available Filter Functions in Syslog-ng*

Filter Function Name	Description
facility(*facility*[*,facility*])	Matches messages having one of the listed facility codes.
level(*pri*[*,pri1..pri2*[*,pri3*]])	Matches messages based on priority or severity level. Multiple priorities are separated by commas, and range of priorities is specified by listing the upper and lower priorities separated by two periods.
program(*regexp*)	Matches messages by using a regular expression against the program name field of log messages.
host(*regexp*)	Matches messages by using a regular expression against the host name field of log messages.
match()	Tries to match a regular expression to the message itself. This feature is useful for customized filtering based on a specific text string in a message.
filter()	Calls another filter rule and evaluates its value.

Example 4-8 shows a sample snippet for the filter components of the /etc/syslog-ng.conf file. The first four filter statements sort the messages based on their facility code. For this filter to work as intended, the Netadmin must configure all the routers to use facility at local2, switches at local3, firewall at local4, and VPN concentrators at local5. If the Netadmin needs to catch all messages with severity level error and above, he can use the last filter (with identifier **f_errandabove**).

Example 4-8 *Syslog-ng.conf—Filter Components*

```
filter      f_router       { facility(local2); };
filter      f_switch       { facility(local3); };
filter      f_firewall     { facility(local4); };
filter      f_vpnbox       { facility(local5); };
filter      f_errandabove  { level(err..emerg);};
```

log

The **log** statement is used to combine the source, filter, and destination components. The syntax is as follows:

```
log { source(s1); source(s2); ...
      filter(f1); filter(f2); ...
      destination(d1); destination(d2); ...
      flags(flag1[, flag2...]); };
```

Messages coming from any of the listed sources that match the listed filters are sent to all listed destinations. Because log statements are processed in the order they appear in the config file, a single log message might be sent to the same destination several times. This default behavior can be changed by using the **flag** parameters listed in Table 4-10.

Table 4-10 *Log Statement Flags*

Flag	Description
final	This flag means that the processing of log statements ends here. Note that this doesn't necessarily mean that matching messages will be stored once because they can be matching log statements processed prior to the current one.
fallback	This flag makes a log statement "fall back." A fallback statement means that only messages not matching any nonfallback log statements are dispatched.
catchall	This flag means that the source of the message is ignored; only the filters are taken into account when matching messages.

Example 4-9 shows a sample snippet for the log components of the /etc/syslog-ng.conf file.

Example 4-9 *Syslog-ng.conf—Log Components*

```
log { source(s_cisconetwork); filter(f_errandabove); destination(d_cisco_severity);
 };
log { source(s_cisconetwork); filter(f_router); destination(d_cisco_facility); };
log { source(s_cisconetwork); destination(d_hosts); };
```

The first log statement does the following:

1. Listens for all network messages at UDP port 514.
2. Filters to only select messages with a severity level between error and emergency.
3. Sends the filtered messages to the respective log files. The name of destination file matches the severity level of the message. For example, the messages with severity level "*error*" will be sent to the "/var/log/LEVEL/*err.log*" file.

The second log statement does the following:

1. Listens for all network messages at UDP port 514.
2. Filters to only select messages with a facility of local2.
3. Sends these filtered messages to respective log files. The name of the destination file matches the facility level of the message. For example messages from facility level "*Local 2*" will be sent to the "*/var/log/FACILITY/local2.log*" file.

The third log statement does the following:

1. Listens for all network messages at UDP port 514.

2 Sends these messages to the respective log files. The name of destination file matches the name of the host who generated the message. For example, messages from the host "*router-dallas*" will be sent to "*/var/log/HOSTS/router-dallas.log*" file.

CAUTION Deleting the default statements in the original /etc/syslog-ng.conf is not recommended. To prepare the Syslog-ng daemon as a central syslog server, just add the relevant code snippets in the respective sections of the syslog-ng.conf file. Also, it is good administrative practice to save the original /etc/syslog-ng/syslog-ng.conf file using the following command:

```
linuxbox:~# mv /etc/syslog-ng/syslog-ng.conf  /etc/syslog-ng/syslog-
  ng.conf.orig
```

Example 4-10 shows the working copy of the /etc/syslog-ng.conf file after editing. The new configuration is highlighted throughout the file. Note that this is the default /etc/syslog-ng.conf file that is installed with the **apt-get install syslog-ng** command on a Debian 3.0 stable release.

Example 4-10 *Edited Copy of the /etc/syslog-ng/syslog-ng.conf File*

```
# Syslog-ng configuration file, compatible with default Debian syslogd
# installation. Originally written by anonymous (I can't find his name)
# Revised, and rewrited by me (SZALAY Attila <sasa@debian.org>)
# First, set some global options.
#options { long_hostnames(off); sync(0); };
# NOTE THE NEW OPTIONS LIST
options {
chain_hostnames(yes); keep_hostname(yes);
use_fqdn(yes);
use_dns(no);
sync(0);
};
#
# This is the default behavior of sysklogd package
# Logs may come from unix stream, but not from another machine.
#
source src { unix-dgram("/dev/log"); internal(); };
#
# If you wish to get logs from remote machine you should uncomment
# this and comment the above source line.
#
# source src { unix-dgram("/dev/log"); internal(); udp(); };
# the following source driver will enable listening for network mssg on udp514
source s_cisconetwork {udp(); };
# After that set destinations.
# First some standard logfile
#
destination authlog { file("/var/log/auth.log" owner("root") group("adm")
  perm(0640)); };
destination syslog { file("/var/log/syslog" owner("root") group("adm") perm(0640)); };
```

Example 4-10 *Edited Copy of the /etc/syslog-ng/syslog-ng.conf File (Continued)*

```
destination cron { file("/var/log/cron.log" owner("root") group("adm") perm(0640)); };
destination daemon { file("/var/log/daemon.log" owner("root") group("adm")
 perm(0640)); };
destination kern { file("/var/log/kern.log" owner("root") group("adm") perm(0640)); };
destination lpr { file("/var/log/lpr.log" owner("root") group("adm") perm(0640)); };
destination mail { file("/var/log/mail.log" owner("root") group("adm") perm(0640)); };
destination user { file("/var/log/user.log" owner("root") group("adm") perm(0640)); };
destination uucp { file("/var/log/uucp.log" owner("root") group("adm") perm(0640)); };

# This files are the log come from the mail subsystem.
#
destination mailinfo { file("/var/log/mail.info" owner("root") group("adm")
 perm(0640)); };
destination mailwarn { file("/var/log/mail.warn" owner("root") group("adm")
 perm(0640)); };
destination mailerr { file("/var/log/mail.err" owner("root") group("adm")
 perm(0640)); };
# Logging for INN news system
#
destination newscrit { file("/var/log/news/news.crit" owner("root") group("adm")
 perm(0640)); };
destination newserr { file("/var/log/news/news.err" owner("root") group("adm")
 perm(0640)); };
destination newsnotice { file("/var/log/news/news.notice" owner("root")
 group("adm") perm(0640)); };
# Some `catch-all' logfiles.
#
destination debug { file("/var/log/debug" owner("root") group("adm") perm(0640));
 };
destination messages { file("/var/log/messages" owner("root") group("adm")
 perm(0640)); };
# The root's console.
#
destination console { usertty("root"); };
# Virtual console.
#
destination console_all { file("/dev/tty8"); };
# The named pipe /dev/xconsole is for the nsole' utility.  To use it,
# you must invoke nsole' with the -file' option:
#
#    $ xconsole -file /dev/xconsole [...]
#
destination xconsole { pipe("/dev/xconsole"); };
destination ppp { file("/var/log/ppp.log" owner("root") group("adm") perm(0640)); };
# following destination drivers were added for cisco devices
destination d_hosts {
    file("/var/log/HOSTS/$HOST.log"
        create_dirs(yes));
        };
destination d_cisco_facility {
    file("/var/log/FACILITY/$FACILITY.log"
    create_dirs(yes));
};
```

continues

Example 4-10 *Edited Copy of the /etc/syslog-ng/syslog-ng.conf File (Continued)*

```
destination d_cisco_severity {
    file("/var/log/LEVEL/$LEVEL.log"
    create_dirs(yes));
};

# Here's come the filter options. With this rules, we can set which
# message go where.
filter f_authpriv { facility(auth, authpriv); };
filter f_syslog { not facility(auth, authpriv); };
filter f_cron { facility(cron); };
filter f_daemon { facility(daemon); };
filter f_kern { facility(kern); };
filter f_lpr { facility(lpr); };
filter f_mail { facility(mail); };
filter f_user { facility(user); };
filter f_uucp { facility(uucp); };
filter f_news { facility(news); };
filter f_debug { not facility(auth, authpriv, news, mail); };
filter f_messages { level(info .. warn)
    and not facility(auth, authpriv, cron, daemon, mail, news); };
filter f_emergency { level(emerg); };
filter f_info { level(info); };
filter f_notice { level(notice); };
filter f_warn { level(warn); };
filter f_crit { level(crit); };
filter f_err { level(err); };
filter f_cnews { level(notice, err, crit) and facility(news); };
filter f_cother { level(debug, info, notice, warn) or facility(daemon, mail); };
filter ppp { facility(local2); };
# following filters were added for cisco devices
filter      f_router       { facility(local2); };
filter      f_switch        { facility(local3); };
filter      f_firewall        { facility(local4); };
filter      f_vpnbox       { facility(local5); };
filter      f_errandabove  { level(err..emerg); };

log { source(src); filter(f_authpriv); destination(authlog); };
log { source(src); filter(f_syslog); destination(syslog); };
#log { source(src); filter(f_cron); destination(cron); };
log { source(src); filter(f_daemon); destination(daemon); };
log { source(src); filter(f_kern); destination(kern); };
log { source(src); filter(f_lpr); destination(lpr); };
log { source(src); filter(f_mail); destination(mail); };
log { source(src); filter(f_user); destination(user); };
log { source(src); filter(f_uucp); destination(uucp); };
log { source(src); filter(f_mail); filter(f_info); destination(mailinfo); };
log { source(src); filter(f_mail); filter(f_warn); destination(mailwarn); };
log { source(src); filter(f_mail); filter(f_err); destination(mailerr); };
log { source(src); filter(f_news); filter(f_crit); destination(newscrit); };
log { source(src); filter(f_news); filter(f_err); destination(newserr); };
log { source(src); filter(f_news); filter(f_notice); destination(newsnotice); };
log { source(src); filter(f_debug); destination(debug); };
```

Example 4-10 *Edited Copy of the /etc/syslog-ng/syslog-ng.conf File (Continued)*

```
log { source(src); filter(f_messages); destination(messages); };
log { source(src); filter(f_emergency); destination(console); };
#log { source(src); filter(f_cnews); destination(console_all); };
#log { source(src); filter(f_cother); destination(console_all); };

log { source(src); filter(f_cnews); destination(xconsole); };
log { source(src); filter(f_cother); destination(xconsole); };
log { source(src); filter(ppp); destination(ppp); };
# following logs were added for cisco devices
log { source(s_cisconetwork); filter(f_errandabove); destination(d_cisco_severity);
 };
log { source(s_cisconetwork); filter(f_router); destination(d_cisco_facility); };
log { source(s_cisconetwork); destination(d_hosts); };
# config ends here
```

Starting the Syslog-ng Daemon

After configuring the syslog-ng.conf file to deploy a Linux-based central syslog server, you must restart the daemon. The Syslog-ng daemon can be started or stopped using the init script, as follows:

```
/etc/init.d/syslog-ng {start | stop | restart | reload | force-reload}
```

The following example shows the command that restarts the daemon:

```
linuxbox:~# /etc/init.d/syslog-ng restart
```

Viewing the Logs

All the logs are stored in the location defined by the file destination-driver. Use the **tail** command to view the latest messages added to a particular log file. Examples are as follows:

```
Linuxbox:~# tail /var/log/HOSTS/router-dallas.log
Linuxbox:~# tail /var/log/LEVEL/err.log
Linuxbox:~# tail /var/log/FACILITY/local2.log
```

Configuring a Windows-Based Syslog Server

The MS-Windows–based servers have a syslog-like feature called the Event Viewer. However, the message format used by the Event Viewer is proprietary to Microsoft and is not compatible with the UNIX syslog. To run a syslog server on MS-Windows machines, you need to install a third-party utility. One of the most popular syslog servers for Windows is Kiwi Syslogd Server. Some of the outstanding features of Kiwi Syslogd Server are as follows:

- It is available as freeware, allowing users to run it indefinitely.
- It runs as a service in the background.

- It offers a GUI for easy management.
- It uses both TCP and UDP ports, thus enabling the server to accept PIX TCP syslogs.
- Its built-in syslog viewer displays messages in real time.
- It features automatic log-file archiving based on a custom schedule.
- It shows syslog statistics with a graph of syslog trends (last 24 hours/last 60 minutes).
- It features a messages-per-hour alarm with sound or e-mail notification.
- It has an alarm with sound or e-mail notification if the log file size exceeds a threshold.
- It can send daily e-mails of syslog traffic statistics.

Deploying a Kiwi Syslog Server consists of following steps:

- Installing the syslog server
- Configuring the syslog server
- Starting the syslog server
- Viewing the syslog messages from the clients

Installing the Syslog Server

Download and save the service version of the Kiwi Syslog Daemon from http://www.kiwisyslog.com. The service version runs syslog as a service in the background instead of as an application on the desktop. At the time of this writing, the current stable version is 7.14, and the installation filename is Kiwi_Syslogd_Service.exe.

Begin the installation process by double-clicking the downloaded file and following the default values when prompted.

Configuring the Syslog Server

After the installation is complete, follow these steps to configure the Kiwi Syslog Server:

Step 1 Choose **Start > Programs > Kiwi Enterprises > Kiwi Syslog Daemon > Kiwi Syslog Daemon** to open the Kiwi Syslog Service Manager window (see Figure 4-3).

Step 2 Choose **Manage > Install the Syslogd service** to install the syslog service.

Step 3 After the syslog service is installed, the syslog server should be configured for archiving, e-mails, alarms, and TCP ports. To begin configuration, choose **File > Setup** to open the Kiwi Syslog Daemon Setup window, as shown in Figure 4-4.

Figure 4-3 *Kiwi Syslog Manager*

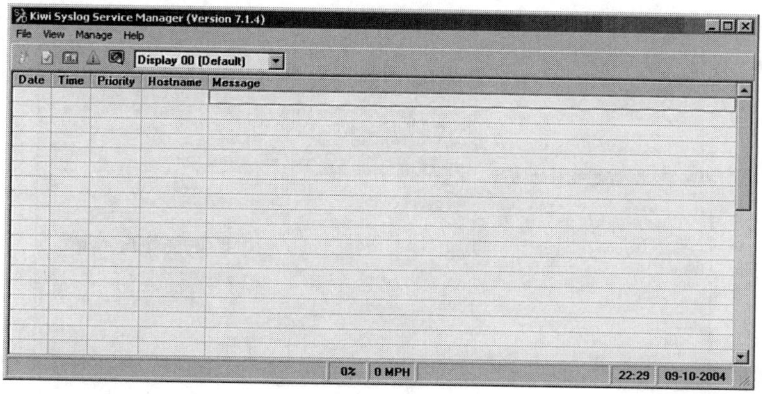

Figure 4-4 *Kiwi Syslog Setup*

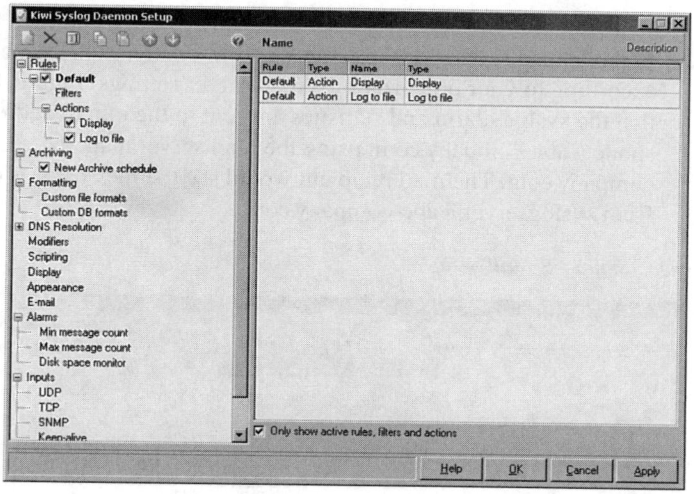

Step 4 In the left pane of the setup window, click **Archiving** and select the **New Archive schedule** check box. Netadmins can choose archive frequencies ranging from hourly to yearly (or customized). Your choice should be based on the network environment, frequency of system backups, and amount of logs generated. Figure 4-5 shows daily archiving. Also, note that the Destination folder field indicates the network drive z:\logs. Archiving to a network drive helps to avoid loss of data because of local device failures.

Figure 4-5 *Kiwi Syslog Setup—Archiving*

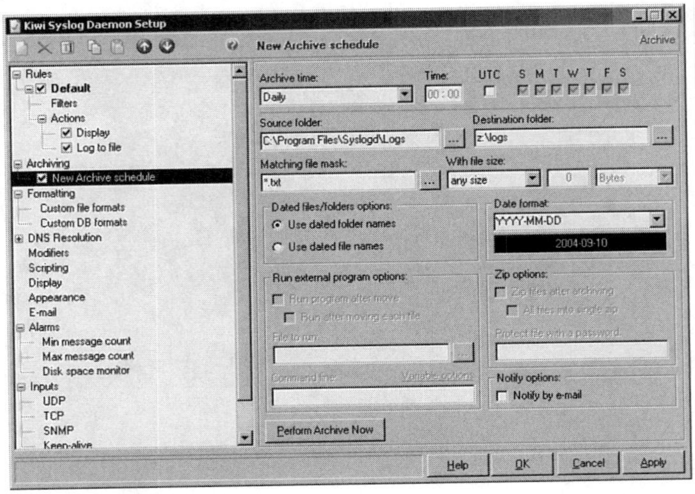

Step 5 In the E-mail section of the setup window, configure the e-mail settings according to your organization's mail server settings. Figure 4-6 shows that the syslog alarm and statistics are sent to the e-mail address spope@abc-company.com, using the mail server mail.abc-company.com. The mail recipient would see the messages as coming from syslogserver@abc-company.com.

Figure 4-6 *Kiwi Syslog Setup—E-Mail Setup*

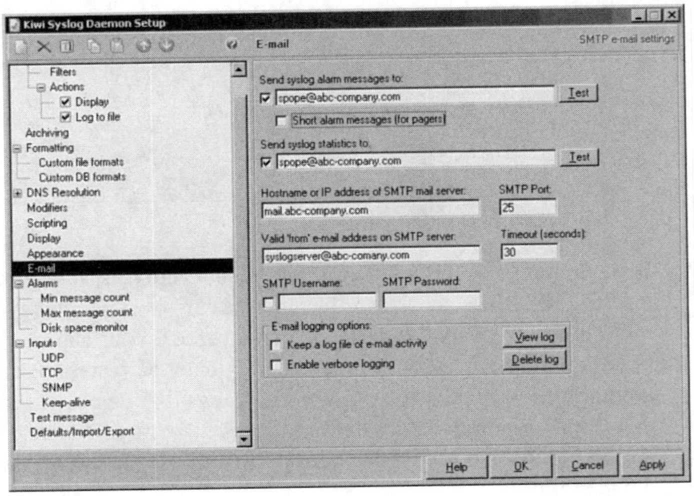

Step 6 In the Alarms section of the setup window, enter the settings shown in Figure 4-7. You should set a limit for the number of messages received in an hour because an unusually high number can indicate a problem. However, the exact number depends on your network environment. Also, setting up the alarms for disk space (see Figure 4-8) notifies the Netadmin before the server stops working because of insufficient disk space. This option is useful for Cisco PIX Firewalls that use TCP syslogs. Cisco PIX Firewalls, using the TCP syslog feature, stop processing traffic if the hard drive on the syslog server is full. This is a security feature, but it can effectively cause a denial of service for legitimate users.

Figure 4-7 *Kiwi Syslog Setup—Message Count*

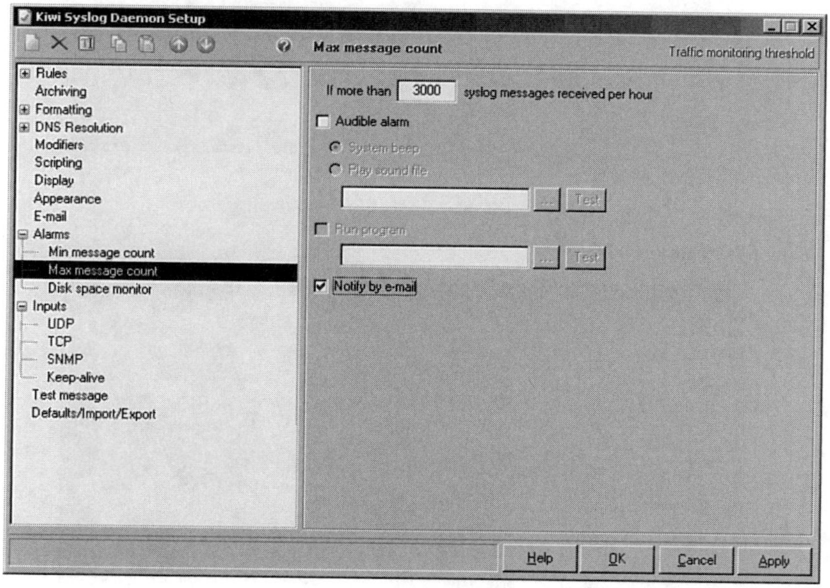

Step 7 To configure the syslog server to listen over TCP ports, click **Inputs > TCP** in the setup window and enter the settings shown in Figure 4-9. Note that the TCP port 1468 is the default port used by PIX for TCP syslogs.

Figure 4-8 *Kiwi Syslog Setup—Disk Space*

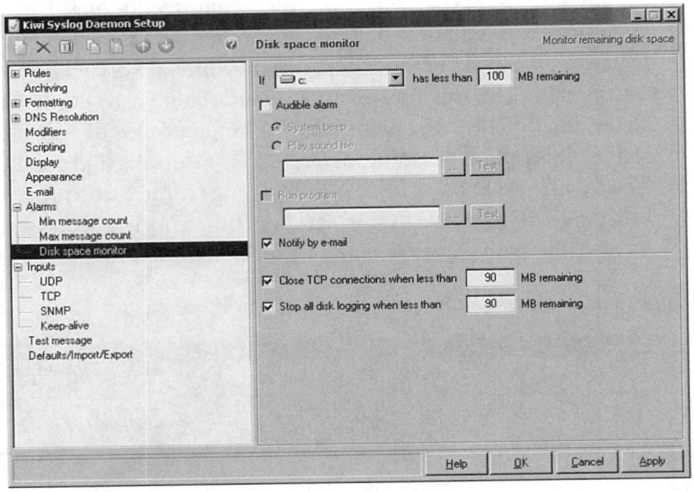

Figure 4-9 *Kiwi Syslog Setup—TCP*

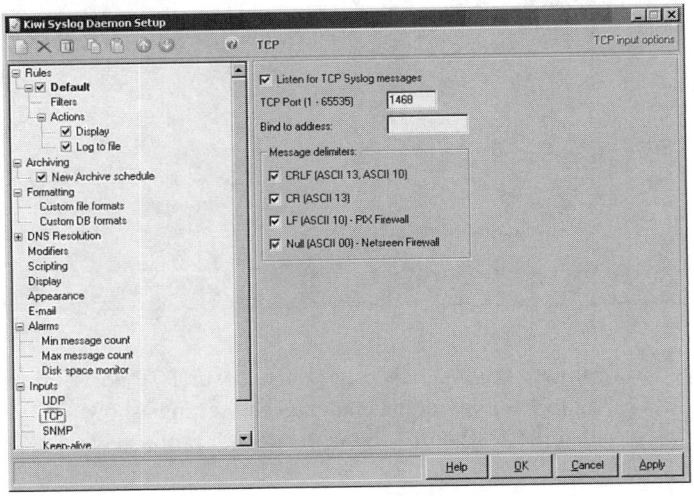

Step 8 Now that the syslog server is configured, save the settings and close the setup window by clicking the **OK** button.

Starting the Syslog Server

Start the Syslog service by choosing **Manage > Start the Syslogd service**. The status bar briefly displays the message **The syslog server has been started**.

The server is now ready to accept the syslog messages.

Viewing Messages on the Syslog Server

To test the operation of the syslog server, choose **File > Send test message to localhost** in the Service Manager window.

The Service Manager window displays the message shown in Figure 4-10.

Figure 4-10 *Kiwi Syslog Manager*

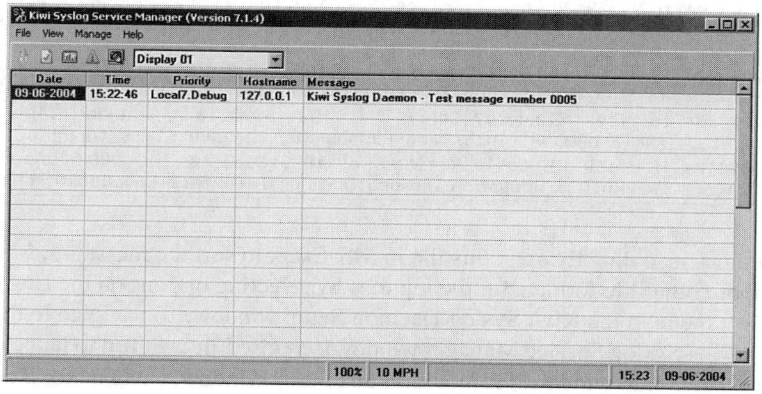

By default, the syslog server saves all logs to the following text file: C:\Program Files\Syslogd\Logs\SyslogCatchAll.txt.

To view the logs, open the SyslogCatchAll.txt file in a text editor. Example 4-11 shows the sample content of the SyslogCatchAll.txt file as viewed using Windows Notepad.

Example 4-11 *Contents of the SyslogCatchAll.txt File*

```
2005-04-16 21:50:56 Local7.Notice      192.168.0.10      9071: Apr 16 20:50:57.852
  PST: %SYS-5-CONFIG_I: Configured from console by vty0 (192.168.0.150)
2005-04-16 21:50:56 Local7.Notice      192.168.0.10      9072: Apr 16 20:50:58.388
  PST: %LINK-5-CHANGED: Interface Loopback0, changed state to administratively down
2005-04-16 21:50:58 Local7.Notice      192.168.0.10      9073: Apr 16 20:50:59.380
  PST: %LINEPROTO-5-UPDOWN: Line protocol on Interface Loopback0, changed state to
  down
2005-04-16 21:51:13 Local4.Debug      192.168.0.20      %PIX-7-710005: UDP request
  discarded from 192.168.0.151/33375 to inside:192.168.0.255/sunrpc
2005-04-16 21:51:17 Local4.Debug      192.168.0.20      %PIX-7-710005: UDP request
  discarded from 192.168.0.151/33375 to inside:192.168.0.255/sunrpc
2005-04-16 21:51:22 Local7.Notice      192.168.0.10      9074: Apr 16 20:51:23.588
  PST: %SYS-5-CONFIG_I: Configured from console by vty0 (192.168.0.150)
```

continues

Example 4-11 *Contents of the SyslogCatchAll.txt File (Continued)*

```
2005-04-16 21:51:23 Local7.Error        192.168.0.10       9075: Apr 16 20:51:24.771
 PST: %LINK-3-UPDOWN: Interface Loopback0, changed state to up
2005-04-16 21:51:23 Local7.Notice       192.168.0.10       9076: Apr 16 20:51:25.763
 PST: %LINEPROTO-5-UPDOWN: Line protocol on Interface Loopback0, changed state to up
2005-04-16 21:58:12 Local7.Notice       192.168.0.10       9077: .Apr 16 20:58:12.142
 PST: %SYS-5-CONFIG_I: Configured from console by vty0 (192.168.0.150)
2005-04-16 21:58:45 Local7.Notice       192.168.0.10       9078: .Apr 17 04:58:45.596
 UTC: %SYS-5-CONFIG_I: Configured from console by vty0 (192.168.0.150)
2005-04-16 21:58:49 Local4.Debug        192.168.0.20       %PIX-7-710005: UDP request
 discarded from 192.168.0.151/33382 to inside:192.168.0.255/sunrpc
2005-04-16 21:58:57 Local4.Debug        192.168.0.20       %PIX-7-710005: UDP request
 discarded from 192.168.0.151/33382 to inside:192.168.0.255/sunrpc
2005-04-16 21:59:07 Local4.Debug        192.168.0.20       %PIX-7-710005: UDP request
 discarded from 192.168.0.151/33382 to inside:192.168.0.255/sunrpc
2005-04-16 21:59:09 Local7.Notice       192.168.0.10       9079: .Apr 17 04:59:08.748
 UTC: %LINK-5-CHANGED: Interface Loopback0, changed state to administratively down
2005-04-16 21:59:09 Local7.Notice       192.168.0.10       9080: .Apr 17 04:59:09.740
 UTC: %LINEPROTO-5-UPDOWN: Line protocol on Interface Loopback0, changed state to
 down
2005-04-16 21:59:11 Local7.Notice       192.168.0.10       9081: .Apr 17 04:59:11.324
 UTC: %SYS-5-CONFIG_I: Configured from console by vty0 (192.168.0.150)
2005-04-16 21:59:13 Local7.Error        192.168.0.10       9082: .Apr 17 04:59:12.998
 UTC: %LINK-3-UPDOWN: Interface Loopback0, changed state to up
2005-04-16 21:59:13 Local7.Notice       192.168.0.10       9083: .Apr 17 04:59:13.990
 UTC: %LINEPROTO-5-UPDOWN: Line protocol on Interface Loopback0, changed state to up
```

You can also directly open this file in MS-Excel to sort the messages. Moreover, you can choose other file formats for the log files by selecting options on the **Log file format** drop-down menu in the Kiwi Syslog Daemon Setup window. To navigate to the choices (from the Kiwi Syslog Service Manager window), choose **File > Setup** to launch the Kiwi Syslog Daemon Setup window. From within this Setup window, navigate to **Rules > Default > Actions > Log to file > Log File Format**.

To view a graphical summary of syslog statistics, choose **View > View Syslog Statistics** in the Service Manager window**.** Fig 4-11 shows the 1-hour history report for syslog statistics. Each bar represents the number of messages received during each 1-minute interval. The chart scrolls from right to left, and the rightmost bar (0) indicates the current traffic.

Apart from the 1-hour history report, the Syslog Statistics windows also features four other tabs, as shown in Figure 4-11. These tabs are History (24hr), Severity, Top 20 Hosts, and Counters. The History (24hr) tab shows a bar chart of the last 24 hours of traffic and is similar to the 1-hour history window.

The Severity tab lists a summary of messages by priority level. The Top 20 Hosts tab comes in handy for quickly identifying chatty hosts. A large number of messages from a particular host indicates a problem on that device.

Figure 4-11 *Syslog Statistics*

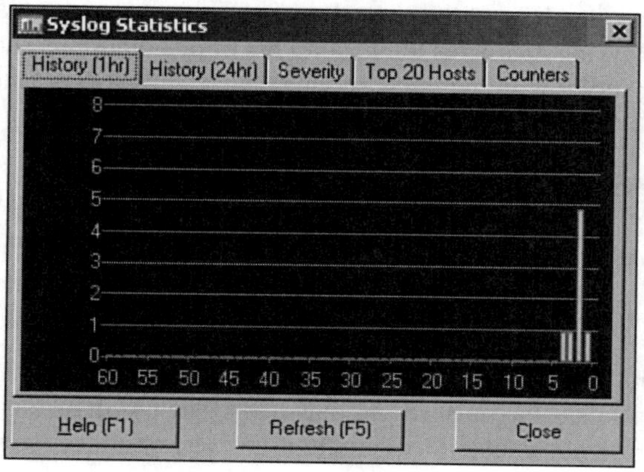

The Counters tab reports the traffic and error statistics for the syslog server. The **Messages - Average** counter is handy for setting maximum thresholds for alarm notification.

NOTE Cisco offers the PIX Firewall Syslog Server (PFSS), an MS-Windows–based syslog server for Cisco PIX Firewalls. It runs as a service, has no GUI, listens on either UDP or TCP ports, and is controlled through the Windows Services management console. It can also be used as a syslog server for other devices. The syslog messages are stored in the following text file: C:\Program Files\Cisco\PIX Firewall Syslog Server\pfss.log. The PFSS can be downloaded by registered users from the Cisco website.

Securing Syslog Servers

So far, you have learned about deploying Linux- and Windows-based syslog servers to collect syslog messages from Cisco devices in a network. However, regardless of the type of operating system or the type of the syslog server, the biggest drawback of the syslog protocol is security. The syslog protocol inherently lacks security for the following reasons:

- **Clear text**—Because a syslog sends its information in clear text, a sniffer on the network can easily capture the messages. To avoid this, syslog messages should be sent on a separate network using a second network interface, if possible. You can also use IP Security (IPSec) tunnels to encrypt the traffic flowing to the syslog server.
- **UDP**—Because syslog uses UDP, an attacker can spoof the source address and send spurious messages to the syslog server. Users should use syslog over TCP, if possible, to mitigate this threat.

- **Centralized location**—While centralized logging is good for Netadmins, it is equally good for attackers. If the central syslog server is compromised, the attacker can delete all the syslog messages to clean up his trail. Netadmins should regularly update the syslog server with the latest service packs and security patches.

Configuring Cisco Devices to Use a Syslog Server

Most Cisco devices use the syslog protocol to manage system logs and alerts. But unlike their PC and server counterparts, Cisco devices lack large internal storage space for storing these logs. To overcome this limitation, Cisco devices offer the following two options:

- **Internal buffer**—The device's operating system allocates a small part of memory buffers to log the most recent messages. The buffer size is limited to few kilobytes. This option is enabled by default. However, when the device reboots, these syslog messages are lost.
- **Syslog**—Use a UNIX-style SYSLOG protocol to send messages to an external device for storing. The storage size does not depend on the router's resources and is limited only by the available disk space on the external syslog server. This option is not enabled by default.

TIP Before configuring a Cisco device to send syslog messages, make sure that it is configured with the right date, time, and time zone. Syslog data would be useless for troubleshooting if it shows the wrong date and time. You should configure all network devices to use NTP. Using NTP ensures a correct and synchronized system clock on all devices within the network. Setting the devices with the accurate time is helpful for event correlation.

To enable syslog functionality in a Cisco network, you must configure the built-in syslog client within the Cisco devices.

Cisco devices use a severity level of warnings through emergencies to generate error messages about software or hardware malfunctions. The debugging level displays the output of debug commands. The Notice level displays interface up or down transitions and system restart messages. The informational level reloads requests and low-process stack messages.

Configuring Cisco Routers for Syslog

To configure a Cisco IOS-based router for sending syslog messages to an external syslog server, follow the steps in Table 4-11 using privileged EXEC mode.

Table 4-11 *Configuring Cisco Routers for Syslog*

Step	Command	Purpose
1	Router# **configure terminal**	Enters global configuration mode.
2	Router(config)# **service timestamps** *type* **datetime** [*msec*] [*localtime*] [*show-timezone*]	Instructs the system to timestamp syslog messages; the options for the *type* keyword are **debug** and **log**.
3	Router(config)#**logging** *host*	Specifies the syslog server by IP address or host name; you can specify multiple servers.
4	Router(config)# **logging trap** *level*	Specifies the kind of messages, by severity level, to be sent to the syslog server. The default is informational and lower. The possible values for *level* are as follows: Emergency: **0** Alert: **1** Critical: **2** Error: **3** Warning: **4** Notice: **5** Informational: **6** Debug: **7** Use the debug level with caution, because it can generate a large amount of syslog traffic in a busy network.
5	Router(config)# **logging facility** *facility-type*	Specifies the facility level used by the syslog messages; the default is **local7**. Possible values are **local0**, **local1**, **local2**, **local3**, **local4**, **local5**, **local6**, and **local7**.
6	Router(config)# **End**	Returns to privileged EXEC mode.
7	Router# **show logging**	Displays logging configuration.

NOTE When a level is specified in the **logging trap** *level* command, the router is configured to send messages with lower severity levels as well. For example, the **logging trap** warning command configures the router to send all messages with the severity warning, error, critical, and emergency. Similarly, the **logging trap** *debug* command causes the router to send all messages to the syslog server. Exercise caution while enabling the debug level. Because the debug process is assigned a high CPU priority, using it in a busy network can cause the router to crash.

Example 4-12 prepares a Cisco router to send syslog messages at facility local3. Also, the router will only send messages with a severity of warning or higher. The syslog server is on a machine with an IP address of 192.168.0.30.

Example 4-12 *Router Configuration for Syslog*

```
Router-Dallas#
Router-Dallas#config terminal
Enter configuration commands, one per line.  End with CNTL/Z.
Router-Dallas(config)#logging 192.168.0.30
Router-Dallas(config)#service timestamps debug datetime localtime show-timezone
 msec
Router-Dallas(config)#service timestamps log datetime localtime show-timezone msec
Router-Dallas(config)#logging facility local3
Router-Dallas(config)#logging trap warning
Router-Dallas(config)#end
Router-Dallas#show logging
Syslog logging: enabled (0 messages dropped, 0 flushes, 0 overruns)
    Console logging: level debugging, 79 messages logged
    Monitor logging: level debugging, 0 messages logged
    Buffer logging: disabled
    Trap logging: level warnings, 80 message lines logged
        Logging to 192.168.0.30, 57 message lines logged
```

Configuring a Cisco Switch for Syslog

To configure a Cisco CatOS-based switch for sending syslog messages to an external syslog server, use the privileged EXEC mode commands shown in Table 4-12.

Table 4-12 *Configuring a Cisco Switch for Syslog*

Step	Command	Purpose
1	Switch>(enable) **set logging timestamp** {**enable** | **disable**}	Configures the system to timestamp messages.
2	Switch>(enable)**set logging server** *ip-address*	Specifies the IP address of the syslog server; a maximum of three servers can be specified.
3	Switch>(enable) **set logging server severity** *server_severity_level*	Limits messages that are logged to the syslog servers by severity level.

Table 4-12 *Configuring a Cisco Switch for Syslog (Continued)*

Step	Command	Purpose
4	Switch>(enable) **set logging server facility** *server_facility_parameter*	Specifies the facility level that would be used in the message. The default is **local7**. Apart from the standard facility names listed in Table 4-1, Cisco Catalyst switches use facility names that are specific to the switch. The following facility levels generate syslog messages with fixed severity levels: **5**: System, Dynamic-Trunking-Protocol, Port-Aggregation-Protocol, Management, Multilayer Switching **4**: CDP, UDLD **2**: Other facilities
5	Switch>(enable) **set logging server enable**	Enables the switch to send syslog messages to the syslog servers.
6	Switch>(enable) **Show logging**	Displays the logging configuration.

Example 4-13 prepares a CatOS-based switch to send syslog messages at facility local4. Also, the switch will only send messages with a severity of warning or higher. The syslog server is on a machine with an IP address of 192.168.0.30.

Example 4-13 *CatOS-Based Switch Configuration for Syslog*

```
Console> (enable) set logging timestamp enable
System logging messages timestamp will be enabled.
Console> (enable) set logging server 192.168.0.30
192.168.0.30 added to System logging server table.
Console> (enable) set logging server facility local4
System logging server facility set to <local4>
Console> (enable) set logging server severity 4
System logging server severity set to <4>
Console> (enable) set logging server enable
System logging messages will be sent to the configured syslog servers.
Console> (enable) show logging
Logging buffered size: 500
timestamp option: enabled
Logging history size: 1
Logging console: enabled
Logging server: enabled
{192.168.0.30}
server facility: LOCAL4
server severity: warnings(4
Current Logging Session: enabled

Facility            Default Severity        Current Session Severity
------------        ---------------------   ----------------------
```

continues

Example 4-13 *CatOS-Based Switch Configuration for Syslog (Continued)*

```
cdp                3                        4
drip               2                        4
dtp                5                        4
dvlan              2                        4
earl               2                        4
fddi               2                        4
filesys            2                        4
gvrp               2                        4
ip                 2                        4
kernel             2                        4
mcast              2                        4
mgmt               5                        4
mls                5                        4
pagp               5                        4
protfilt           2                        4
pruning            2                        4
radius             2                        4
security           2                        4
snmp               2                        4
spantree           2                        4
sys                5                        4
tac                2                        4
tcp                2                        4
telnet             2                        4
tftp               2                        4
udld               4                        4
vmps               2                        4
vtp                2                        4

0(emergencies)        1(alerts)             2(critical)
3(errors)             4(warnings)           5(notifications)
6(information)        7(debugging)
Console> (enable)
```

Configuring a Cisco PIX Firewall for Syslog

Proactive monitoring of firewall logs is an integral part of a Netadmin's duties. The firewall syslogs are useful for forensics, network troubleshooting, security evaluation, worm and virus attack mitigation, and so on. The configuration steps for enabling syslog messaging on a PIX are conceptually similar to those for IOS- or CatOS-based devices. To configure a Cisco PIX Firewall with PIX OS 4.4 and above, perform the steps shown in Table 4-13 in privileged EXEC mode.

Table 4-13 *PIX Configuration for Syslog*

Step	Command	Purpose
1	Pixfirewall# **config terminal**	Enters global configuration mode.
2	Pixfirewall(config)#**logging timestamp**	Specifies that each syslog message should have a timestamp value.
3	Pixfirewall(config)#**logging host** [*interface connected to syslog server*] *ip_address* [*protocol/port*]	Specifies a syslog server that is to receive the messages sent from the Cisco PIX Firewall. You can use multiple **logging host** commands to specify additional servers that would all receive the syslog messages. The *protocol* is UDP or TCP. However, a server can only be specified to receive either UDP or TCP, not both. A Cisco PIX Firewall only sends TCP syslog messages to the Cisco PIX Firewall syslog server.
4	Pixfirewall(config)#**logging facility** *facility*	Specifies the syslog facility number. Instead of specifying the name, the PIX uses a 2-digit number, as follows: local0 - **16** local1 - **17** local2 - **18** local3 - **19** local4 - **20** local5 - **21** local6 - **22** local7 - **23** The default is **20**.

continues

Table 4-13 *PIX Configuration for Syslog (Continued)*

Step	Command	Purpose
5	pixfirewall(config)#**logging trap** *level*	Specifies the syslog message level as a number or string. The *level* that you specify means that you want that *level* and those values less than that *level*. For example, if *level* is **3**, syslog displays **0**, **1**, **2**, and **3** messages. Possible number and string *level* values are as follows: **0**: Emergency; System-unusable messages **1**: Alert; Take immediate action **2**: Critical; critical condition **3**: Error; error message **4**: Warning; warning message **5**: Notice; normal but significant condition **6**: Informational: information message **7**: Debug; debug messages and log FTP commands and WWW URLs
6	pixfirewall(config)#**logging on**	Starts sending syslog messages to all output locations.
7	pixfirewall(config)#**no logging message** *<message id>*	Specifies a message to be suppressed.
8	pixfirewall(config)#**exit**	Exits global configuration mode.

Example 4-14 prepares the Cisco PIX Firewall to send syslog messages at facility local5 and severity debug and below to the syslog server. The Netadmin does not want the PIX to log message 111005. The syslog server has an IP address of 192.168.0.30.

Example 4-14 *Configuring a Cisco PIX Firewall for Syslog*

```
Firewall-Dallas#
Firewall-Dallas# config terminal
Firewall-Dallas(config)# loggin time
Firewall-Dallas(config)# logging host 192.168.0.30
Firewall-Dallas(config)# logging facility 21
Firewall-Dallas(config)# logging trap 7
Firewall-Dallas(config)# logging on
Firewall-Dallas(config)# no logging message 111005
rewall-Dallas(config)# exit
Firewall-Dallas# show logging
Syslog logging: enabled
    Facility: 21
    Timestamp logging: enabled
    Standby logging: disabled
```

Example 4-14 *Configuring a Cisco PIX Firewall for Syslog (Continued)*

```
    Console logging: disabled
    Monitor logging: disabled
    Buffer logging: disabled
    Trap logging: level debugging, 6 messages logged
        Logging to inside 192.168.0.30
    History logging: disabled
    Device ID: disabled
```

For added reliability, the Cisco PIX Firewall can be configured to send syslog messages through TCP. Please note that if the syslog server disk is full, it can close the TCP connection. This will cause a denial of service because the Cisco PIX Firewall will stop all traffic until the syslog server disk space is freed. Both Kiwi Syslogd Server and PFSS offer this feature. Kiwi Syslogd has an alert mechanism to warn the Netadmin through e-mail or pager when the disk is nearing its capacity. The setting can be established from the Syslog Daemon Setup window, as shown in Figure 4-9, for Kiwi syslog configuration.

If the PIX stops because of a disk-full condition, you must first free some disk space. Then disable syslog messaging on the PIX by using the **no logging host** *host* command, followed by reenabling syslog messaging using the **logging host** *host* command.

CAUTION The change in facility level for a particular message in the previous example is for illustration purposes only. Changing the facility level from its default value is an advanced Netadmin function and is strongly discouraged.

Example 4-15 shows the configuration steps for a Cisco PIX Firewall to send syslog messages at TCP port 1468.

Example 4-15 *PIX Configuration for TCP Syslog*

```
Firewall-Dallas# config terminal
Firewall-Dallas(config)# logging host inside 192.168.0.30  tcp/1468
Firewall-Dallas(config)# exit
Firewall-Dallas# show logging
Syslog logging: enabled
    Facility: 21
    Timestamp logging: enabled
    Standby logging: disabled
    Console logging: disabled
    Monitor logging: disabled
    Buffer logging: disabled
    Trap logging: level debugging, 12 messages logged
        Logging to inside 192.168.0.30 tcp/1468
    History logging: disabled
    Device ID: disabled
Firewall-Dallas#
```

CAUTION A Cisco PIX Firewall facing the Internet is subjected to a large amount of unsolicited traffic in the form of ping scans, port scans, and probes. This can cause the log file to become large within days. It will be filled with data, making it difficult to search for useful information. You should fine-tune your firewall to suppress certain common messages using the **no logging message** *message-id-number* command. Additionally, use the IOS firewall features on the edge router to filter unwanted traffic before it hits the Cisco PIX Firewall.

Configuring a Cisco VPN Concentrator for Syslog

The Cisco VPN 3000 Series Concentrator provides an appliance-based solution for deploying VPN functionality across remote networks. VPN concentrators are often connected parallel to the firewalls, as shown earlier in Figure 4-1. The design simplifies the management of the network but creates security concerns. After a user has been authenticated through VPN concentrators, the user has complete access to the network. This makes a strong case for logging the messages from the VPN concentrator. To configure the Cisco VPN 3000 Series Concentrator for sending syslog messages, follow these steps:

Step 1 Log in to the VPN concentrator using a web browser.

Step 2 Navigate to the syslog server page by choosing **Configuration** > **System** > **Events** > **Syslog Servers**, as shown in Figure 4-12.

Figure 4-12 *VPN Concentrator—Syslog Server*

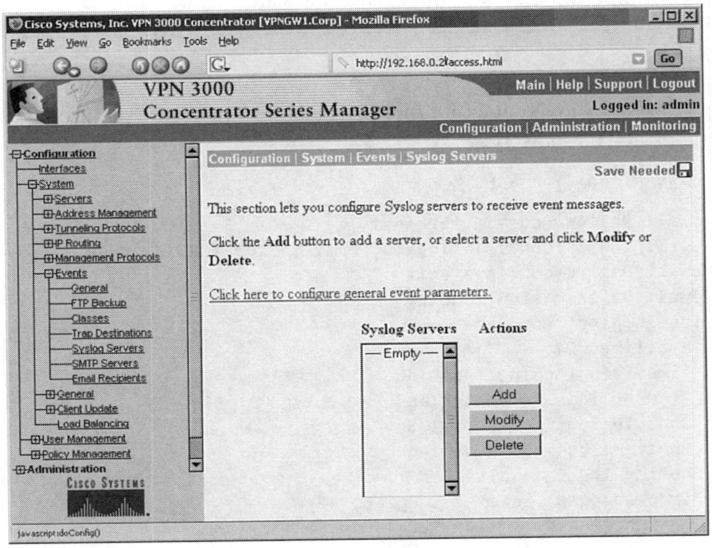

Step 3 On the Syslog Servers page, click the **Add** button (see Figure 4-12).

Step 4 Enter the IP address of the syslog server and select the facility level from the Facility drop-down menu, as shown in Figure 4-13. Save these settings and return to the Syslog Servers page by clicking the **Add** button.

Figure 4-13 *VPN Concentrator—Add Syslog Server*

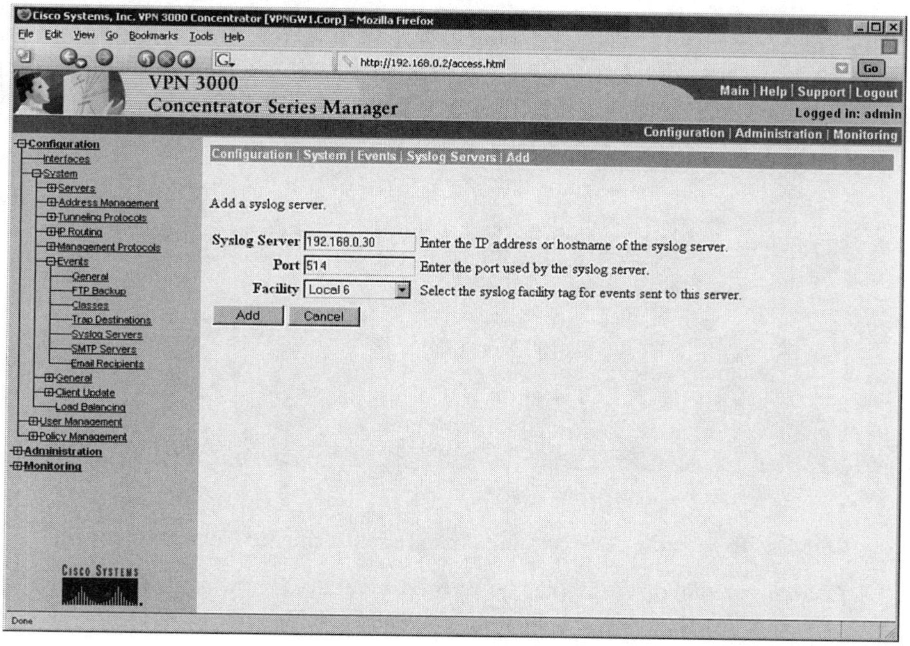

Step 5 To select the kind of messages that are to be sent to the syslog server, navigate to the General page by choosing **Configuration > System > Events > General**.

Step 6 On the General page, select an option from the Severity to Syslog drop-down menu, as shown in Figure 4-14, and click the **Apply** button.

Figure 4-14 *VPN Concentrator—General Configuration*

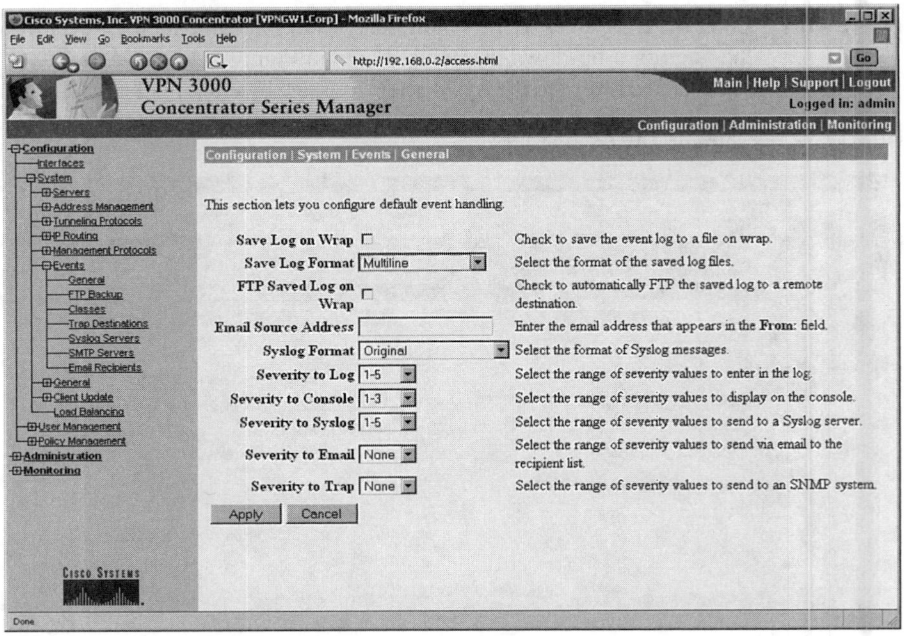

Step 7 To save the configuration changes, click the **Save Needed** icon.

As configured in this example, the VPN concentrator is now ready to send syslog messages at facility local6, severity 1–5 to server 192.168.0.30.

Commercial Cisco Products

In addition to the free PFSS, Cisco also offers a syslog server that is integrated into the CiscoWorks suite of network-management products. The syslog server with an advanced reporting engine is part of the Resource Manager Essentials (RME) module of CiscoWorks. The RME offers the following features:

- Provides web-based applications
- Maintains a database of current network information
- Generates a variety of reports that can be used for troubleshooting and capacity planning
- Periodically retrieves and updates device information, such as hardware, software, and configuration files

- Automatically records changes made to network devices, making it easy to identify when changes are made and by whom
- Deploys Cisco software images and views configurations of Cisco routers and switches
- Links to Cisco.com service and support for Terminal Access Controller (TAC) case management

Because RME has advanced features integrated with the syslog server, it can correlate the syslog events with other functions and provide enhanced reporting.

Summary

The topics covered in this chapter prepare the Netadmin for deploying a centralized logging facility to collect syslog messages from all the network devices. The Netadmins should be able to perform the following syslog-related tasks:

- Deploy a Linux-based syslog server to support Cisco devices
- Deploy a Microsoft Windows–based syslog server
- Centrally log events and alarms generated by Cisco IOS–based routers and switches
- Centrally log events and alarms generated by Cisco CatOS–based switches
- Centrally log events and alarms generated by Cisco PIX Firewalls
- Centrally log events and alarms generated by Cisco VPN 3000 Series Concentrators.

Table 4-14 provides a list of all the tools discussed in this chapter. The table also provides the source of documentation for each tool.

Table 4-14 *Tools Discussed in Chapter 4*

Tool	Function	Supported OS	Installable Files	Documentation Sources
Syslogd	UNIX-style syslog	Part of the standard Linux/UNIX OS for handling system and kernel logs	Part of the standard OS; installation not required	man syslogd
Syslog-ng	UNIX-style syslog with advanced filtering capabilities	Linux/UNIX	http://www.balabit.com	http://www.campin.net/var/docs/syslog-ng/html http://www.campin.net/usr/share/doc/syslog-ng/html/book1.html INSTALL and README docs included in the source code

continues

Table 4-14 *Tools Discussed in Chapter 4 (Continued)*

Tool	Function	Supported OS	Installable Files	Documentation Sources
Kiwi Syslogd Server	UNIX-style syslog with e-mails and alerts; also works for Cisco PIX Firewall syslogging	Windows 95, 98, Me, NT 4, 2000, 2003, XP	http:// www.kiwisyslog.com	Help file with system management window
PIX Firewall syslog server	UNIX-style syslog; has no GUI; works for Cisco PIX Firewalls as well as other devices	Windows NT4 with SP6, 2000, XP	http://www.cisco.com (user needs cisco.com login)	Documentation file readme.rtf installed with the server
3Com syslog server	UNIX-style syslog	Windows 95/98/NT	http:// support.3com.com/ software/ utilities_for_windows _32_bit.htm	Help file with the GUI

PART II

Network Management Systems (NMS)

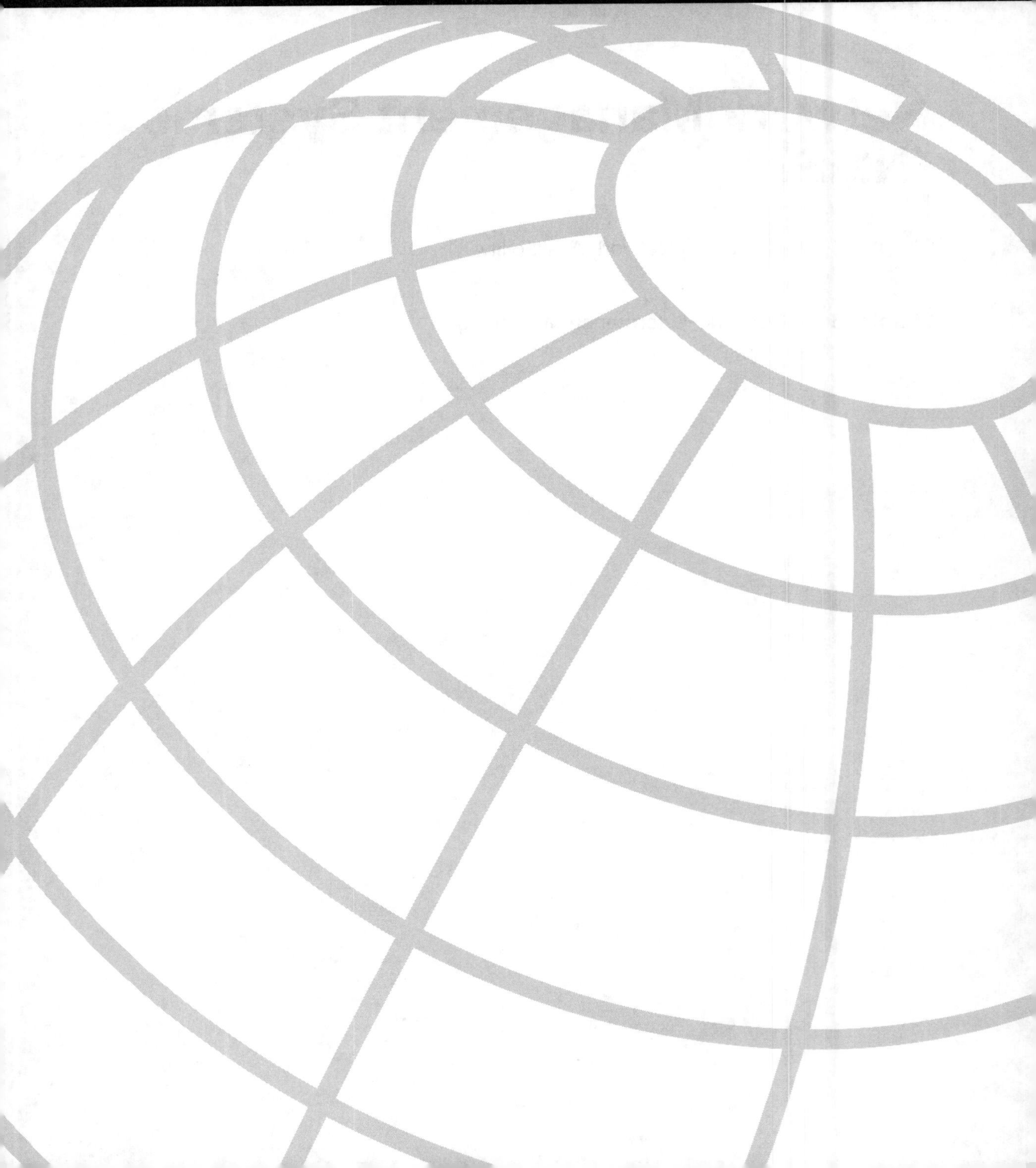

CHAPTER 5

Monitoring Network Availability

Network monitoring is the concept of observing, measuring, and comparing the performance of a computer network using both technology and personnel. The purpose of network monitoring is to detect faults within a network and ensure steady network operations. Monitoring network devices is a proactive approach to troubleshooting potential performance issues. Typically, a network-monitoring system is comprised of Windows- or UNIX-based network-ready computers loaded with network-monitoring software. The network-monitoring system polls the monitored nodes at regular intervals to determine the overall health of the network and its components. Based on the polled results, the network-monitoring system generates alerts. These alerts can be e-mailed, sent through pager messages, or relayed through a web page. The network-monitoring system also stores the historical data for reporting and trending. A properly functioning network-monitoring system helps the Netadmin to do the following:

- Get a bird's-eye view of the entire network
- Determine the availability of network resources to the users
- Create trending reports for availability and outages
- Identify and respond to network issues in real time

This chapter prepares the Netadmin to understand the terminology and techniques used for network monitoring. Further discussion focuses on deploying Linux- and Windows-based network-monitoring systems using tools that are freely available in the public Internet domain.

Network-Monitoring Fundamentals

Network monitoring is a vast field comprised of a wide array of techniques and protocols. Additionally, various commercial or regulatory bodies create terminologies that become part of the industry jargon. A basic awareness of the common terms and techniques used for network monitoring helps the Netadmin to better understand and deploy network-monitoring systems.

Network-Monitoring Terms

Network monitoring has been overhyped by the use of marketing jargon such as SLA, MTTR, five nines, and others. The precise definitions of these terms are subject to interpretation by different organizations. The following sections describe some of the most common terms with reference to their accepted use within the industry.

Service-Level Agreement

A service-level agreement (SLA) is the description of the services that would be provided by the telco (or ISP) to the consumer. This agreement or contract typically specifies the following details:

- Responsibilities and expectations of the parties involved
- Network metrics, such as latency, jitter, and packet loss
- Durations of scheduled or unscheduled downtimes and the minimum notice period before scheduling maintenance downtimes
- Time to respond to and resolve help desk calls

To set expectations, organizations also define SLAs for the services offered by their IT departments to other internal departments and employees.

Mean Time to Repair

The mean time to repair (MTTR) is the average downtime for a device or service over a predefined time period. The downtime is measured from the instant the device fails to the moment when it is brought back to a fully functional state.

Mean Time to Respond

The time to respond is measured from the instant a user reports a failure to the moment a service representative responds. The mean time to respond is the average of all the instances of time to respond.

Mean Time Between Failure

The mean time between failure (MTBF) is the average uptime for a device or service over a predefined time period. The uptime is measured from the instant the device is fully functional to the moment it fails.

Availability

For a given period, availability is the percentage of time that the device is up or available. If a device is up for 90 days (MTBF = 90 days) and down for 10 days (MTTR = 10 days), over a 100-day period, its availability is 90 percent. This can be written as any of the following equations:

Availability = 100 * [Uptime / (Total time)]
Availability = 100 * [Uptime / (Uptime + Downtime)]
Availability = 100 * [MTBF / (MTTR + MTBF)]

Five Nines

A system with an availability of 99.999 percent is called a *five nines* system. This is perhaps one of the most popular terms among executives and managers when discussing the performance of a network. A system with an availability of five nines over one calendar year can be expressed as follows:

99.999% = 100 * [Uptime / (1 year)]
Uptime = 0.99999 year

Because, Downtime = Total time – Uptime, the following equations apply:

Downtime = 1 year – 0.99999 year = 0.00001 year
Downtime = 0.00001 year * (365 * 24 * 60) minutes/year
Downtime = 5.256 minutes

To maintain a network so that it is down for only 5.256 minutes in an entire year is quite impressive; hence the hype attached to five nines.

Network-Monitoring Techniques

Network monitoring, in its simplest form, involves probing a network device by sending a ping (Internet Control Message Protocol [ICMP] Echo Request) packet to a destination machine. The successful receipt of the ping packet (the ICMP Echo Reply) is a confirmation of network reachability. Also, it is a reasonable indication that the Transmission Control Protocol/Internet Protocol (TCP/IP) stack is working properly.

Most network-monitoring systems (both open source and proprietary) use this technique as their primary means of monitoring network availability. This technique is also called agentless monitoring because it eliminates the installation of a software agent on the monitored node. The round-trip time (RTT) delay of the packet provides information regarding the network conditions. Comparing the new RTT value with historic values can help the Netadmin to identify bottlenecks and performance issues or alert the Netadmin to communication failures.

Advantages of network monitoring using ICMP are as follows:

- Allows agentless monitoring, which requires no installation or configuration on the monitored devices
- Provides the ability to monitor any network device irrespective of operating system, vendor, or device type
- Provides a quick bird's-eye view of the entire network
- Is simple to implement

Some disadvantages are as follows:

- Is limited to monitoring device status at the network layer only
- Cannot monitor services such as HTTP, FTP, and SMTP
- Can fail because many networks block ICMP traffic
- Can choke links when monitoring traffic on networks with slower WAN links by consuming excessive bandwidth
- Can produce false results in redundant networks by reporting standby interfaces as being down

CAUTION ICMP traffic is often assigned a lower priority. If the router CPU utilization is high, the router might not respond to ICMP messages but still process the network traffic. Additionally, many ISPs block ICMP packets. These factors can result in high round-trip times or timeouts. This can lead to inaccurate results when monitoring networks.

Deploying a Network-Monitoring System

The open source community offers many network-monitoring tools. Some started off as simple ping scripts and evolved into stable and commercial-quality network-monitoring products. Some of the popular tools are as follows:

- Big Brother
- BigSister
- NMIS (Network Management Information System)
- OpenNMS
- Nagios/Netsaint
- Spong

Whereas the overall goal of each tool is to monitor a network, each tool is unique in terms of installation, configuration, and architecture. Many of these tools have a widely satisfied user base. In the following sections, you learn about deploying Nagios and Big Brother.

These tools are selected because of their communitywide popularity and support. Additionally, each of these tools offers plug-in features for customizing or enhancing monitoring capabilities.

Deploying a Linux-Based Big Brother Network-Monitoring System

Big Brother offers the following advantages:

- Works on both Linux and Windows machines
- Has been in development since 1997
- Is relatively simple to install
- Provides a web-based graphical user interface (GUI) for monitoring and reporting
- Is robust and scalable and can monitor up to 1000 nodes
- Uses ICMP to monitor network nodes
- Provides built-in plug-ins to monitor services such as Hypertext Transfer Protocol (HTTP), Domain Name System (DNS), File Transfer Protocol (FTP), Simple Mail Transfer Protocol (SMTP), Post Office Protocol 3 (POP3), disk space, and CPU utilization on servers
- Boasts a wide user base and support community on the web

To deploy the Linux version of Big Brother, the first step is to install the Big Brother Server on the Linux computer. Configuration is next, followed by running the Big Brother Server in the network.

Installing Big Brother in Linux

A Big Brother Server on Linux requires the following features to work correctly:

- A C compiler (for example, GCC)
- A web server (for example, Apache)

Installation of these programs is beyond the scope of this discussion. For installation details, refer to the documentation for your Linux distribution.

Additionally, before installing Big Brother on the target Linux computer, you must create a new user and a group (for example, username **bb** and group name **bb**) using the **adduser** system command. This username and group name are used for running the Big Brother daemon, because for security reasons, Big Brother does not run as a root user. For the benefit of new Linux users, Example 5-1 shows the commands used in Debian-Linux to create a user bb and a group bb with the home directory /home/bb.

Example 5-1 *Creating a User and Group in Debian-Linux*

```
linuxbox:~# adduser bb
Adding user bb...
Adding new group bb (1003).
Adding new user bb (1003) with group bb.
Creating home directory /home/bb.
Copying files from /etc/skel
Enter new UNIX password:
Retype new UNIX password:
passwd: password updated successfully
Changing the user information for nn
Enter the new value, or press return for the default
        Full Name []: Big Brother User
        Room Number []:
        Work Phone []:
        Home Phone []:
        Other []:
Is the information correct? [y/n] y
linuxbox:~#
```

After defining the new user and group, you can install Big Brother using the source code files. The source code is available as a zipped tar file at http://www.bb4.org. Download the latest source code and unpack the zipped tar file using the **tar xzvf** *bigbrother-source-file-name* command. At the time of this writing, the Big Brother source code (in zipped tar format) contained both the Big Brother Server and the Big Brother Client. The Big Brother Client monitors local resources, such as CPU and disk activity, on a remote Windows or Linux computer and is beyond the scope of this discussion. After uncompressing the original source file, you might need to further extract the server files using the **tar xvf BBSVRxxx.tar** command. The unpacked server source files contain the bbconfig script in the install directory. The purpose of the bbconfig script is to automate the installation process. Run the bbconfig script and follow the prompts to complete the installation of Big Brother Server.

A sample installation is provided in the command-line interface (CLI) session shown in Example 5-2. Refer to the highlighted comments for explanations of each step.

Example 5-2 *Installing Big Brother in Debian-Linux*

```
# The Big Brother zipped tar file is in the home directory
linuxbox:/home/bb# ls
bb-1.9e.tar.gz
# uncompress the zipped tar file
linuxbox:/home/bb# tar xzvf bb1 -1.9e.tar.gz
BB.README.FIRST
BBSVR-bb1.9e-btf.tar
BBCLT-bbc1.9e-btf.tar
# extract Big Brother Server files from the tar file archive
```

Example 5-2 *Installing Big Brother in Debian-Linux*

```
linuxbox:/home/bb# tar xvf BBSVR-bb1.9e-btf.tar
# verify the contents of the directory
linuxbox:/home/bb# ls -l
total 1984
-rw-r--r--   1  200 daemon     305 Jan  2  2004 BB.README.FIRST
-rw-r--r--   1  200 daemon  406528 Jan  2  2004 BBCLT-bbc1.9e-btf.tar
-rw-r--r--   1  200 daemon 1147392 Jan  2  2004 BBSVR-bb1.9e-btf.tar
-rw-r--r--   1 root staff   447216 Apr 30  2004 bb-1.9e.tar.gz
drwxr-sr-x  10 root staff     4096 Apr 30  2004 bb1.9e-btf
# Create a link /home/bb/bb to the new directory "bb1.9e-btf"
# per instruction in the accompanied README.INSTALL file
linuxbox:/home/bb# ln -s /home/bb/bb1.9e-btf /home/bb/bb
# Run the bbconfig scipt to begin installation routine
linuxbox:/home/bb/# /home/bb/bb/install/bbconfig
```

Configuring Big Brother Using the Text Files

Big Brother is mainly configured through the bb-hosts file, a text file that is located in the $BBHOME/etc directory. ($BBHOME stands for the home directory of Big Brother; in this example, it is /home/bb/bb/etc/.) The bb-hosts file contains the list of hosts to be monitored. The format for adding a host entry in the bb-hosts file is as follows:

```
IP-ADDR      HOSTNAME        # DIRECTIVES
```

For example, to test the availability of the host Dallas-router by pinging its IP address 192.168.0.10, the entry in the bb-hosts file is as follows:

```
192.168.0.10     Dallas-router  # testip
```

Table 5-1 provides a partial list of directives and their details.

Table 5-1 *Bb-host Service Directives*

	Directive	Explanation
1	**testip**	This is the most useful directive; it instructs Big Brother to ping the IP address to test the node. It also instructs Big Brother not to use the host name.
2	**BBDISPLAY***	This host displays the HTML results; can be more than one for redundancy.
3	**BBPAGER***	This host acts as the notification server to inform Netadmins and processes; can be more than one for redundancy.
4	**BBNET***	This host monitors the network services; can be more than one for redundancy.
5	**ftp**	Tests FTP service.
6	**Smtp**	Tests SMTP service.
7	**telnet**	Tests Telnet service.

continues

Table 5-1 *Bb-host Service Directives (Continued)*

	Directive	Explanation
8	**ssh**	Tests SSH service.
9	**noping**	Specifies no ping test for this host and displays a clear dot.
10	**noconn**	Specifies no ping test for this host and not to generate a colored dot.
11	**!**	Tests to see whether this service is not running. For example, the **!telnet** directive tests to determine whether Telnet is not running; very useful for monitoring unauthorized activities on a host.

*A single server is typically configured to perform the three roles of BBDISPALY, BBPAGER, and BBNET.

To control the HTML tables in the Big Brother output pages, use the directives defined in Table 5-2.

Table 5-2 *Bb-host HTML Table Directives*

	Directive	Explanation
1	**group**	Defines a block of hosts to be grouped in the same HTML table.
2	**group-compress**	Is identical to the **group** directive, except it only displays services (columns) that contain data for that group.
3	**group-only**	Creates a table with only the columns defined in the directive. The columns are delimited with the pipe symbol (|).

Based on the discussion of the various directives for the bb-host file, Example 5-3 shows a sample file. Note the first line, where multiple directives are defined for the Linux server with the host name linuxbox. The server is acting as BBPAGER, BBNET, and BBDISPLAY. This file instructs Big Brother to monitor the four nodes by pinging their IP addresses. The availability status is displayed in a single table on the HTML page.

Example 5-3 *Sample bb-host File*

```
192.168.0.30 linuxbox # BBPAGER BBNET BBDISPLAY http://linuxbox/
group-compress <H3><I>Network Devices</I></H3>
192.168.0.10   Dallas-router # testip
192.168.0.20   Dallas-Firewall # testip
192.168.0.50   Dallas-Switch # testip
192.168.0.100  FileServer # testip
```

To verify the configuration of the bb-hosts, use the bbchkhost.sh script, which is located in the $BBHOME/etc directory, as follows:

```
bb@linuxbox:~/bb/etc$ ./bbchkhosts.sh
If any comments are displayed, please fix the entries in your configuration
Note that some error messages may be for tags of external scripts
```

Running the Big Brother Server

After verifying the bb-host file for errors, change your user ID to user bb through the **su** *username* command. Remember, you cannot run bb as a root user. Next, start the Big Brother Server by using the bbrun.sh script located in the $BBHOME directory. The bbrun.sh script is also used to stop or restart the Big Brother Server. The bbrun.sh script is as follows:

```
linuxbox:/home/bb/bb# su bb
bb@linuxbox:~/bb$ ./runbb.sh start
Starting Big Brother
        Starting Big Brother Daemon (bbd)...
        Starting Network tests (bb-network)...
        Starting Display process (bb-display)...
Big Brother 1.9e started
bb@linuxbox:~/bb/etc$
```

After starting the Big Brother Server, you can view the network status by pointing your web browser to the URL http://*bigbrother-server-ip-address*/bb/bb.html, as shown in Figure 5-1.

Figure 5-1 *Big Brother Output Web Page*

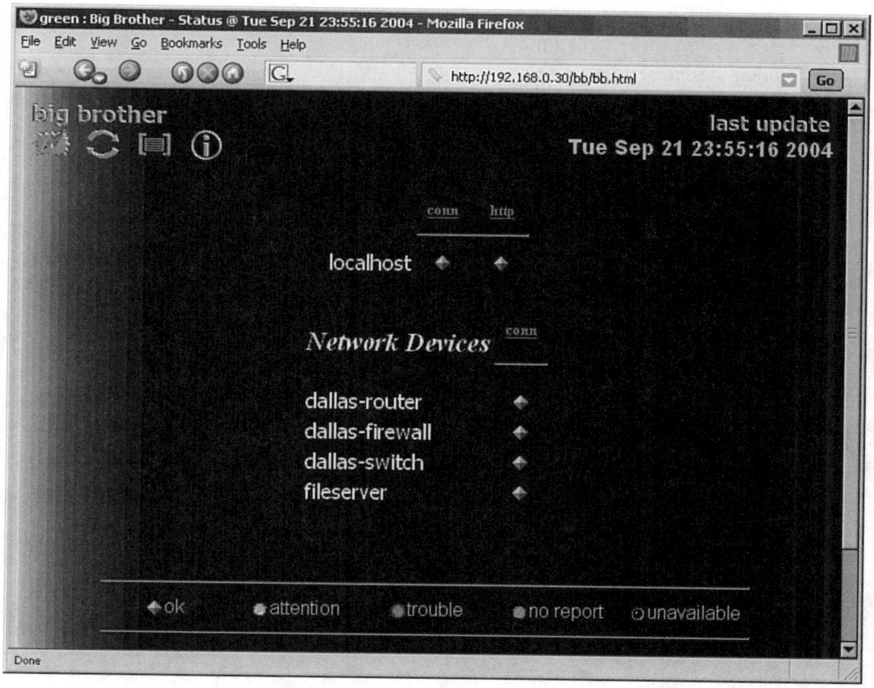

NOTE The Big Brother screen captures shown in this chapter are in grayscale and do not indicate the true color of the web page output.

The dots next to each host name indicate the status of that host. Green indicates normal operation, red indicates trouble, and yellow indicates critical but not yet down or unreachable. Additionally, the color of the background also indicates the overall health of the network. A green background indicates that all the monitored services are working. A red background indicates a network issue. If Big Brother is monitoring a large number of nodes and services, the main page (bb.html) becomes large and difficult to navigate. In that case, Netadmins can use the bb2.html page, which provides a summarized view. The summarized view only shows the hosts whose status is currently other than green. If all the hosts are up, the summary page shows the message **All Monitored Systems OK**. The summary page also provides a list of all events in the last 240 minutes. Figure 5-2 shows the summary page and the list of events in the last 240 minutes. This view allows Netadmins to quickly assess the network status and the recent history.

Figure 5-2 *Big Brother—Summary Page*

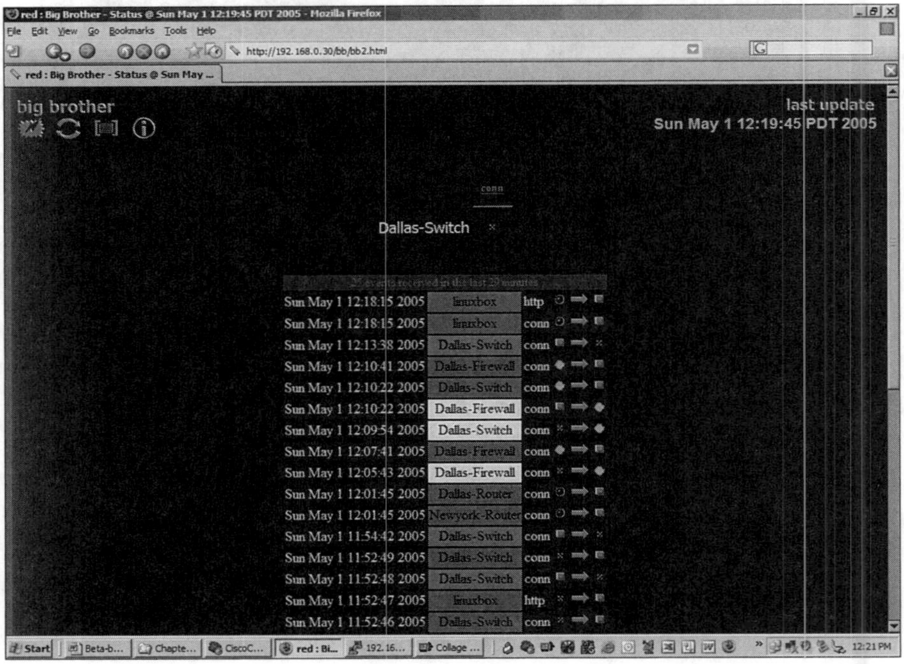

To view a historic availability report for the network, use the reporting function through the following URL:

http://*bigbrother-server-ip-address*/bb/help/bb-rep.html

Choose the starting and ending dates and click the **Generate Report** button. The availability of each host is indicated in terms of percentage. A solid green dot next to the host name indicates 100 percent availability.

Tips for Advanced Users

The following sections provide some tips that are helpful in fine-tuning a Big Brother Server.

Change Notification Interval

By default, Big Brother runs the tests and sends notifications every 300 seconds. To change this, edit all the occurrences of the BBSLEEP timers in the $BBHOME/runbb.sh script to the desired value. Note that **BBSLEEP=300** is found in four places in the runbb.sh script. Changing the BBSLEEP timers also changes the rate at which the web pages are generated.

NOTE In some case, the default BBSLEEP value of 300 seconds (5 minutes) is slightly higher, and outages lasting for less than 300 seconds can go unnoticed. On the other hand, reducing this parameter to a low value (such as 5 seconds) causes high CPU utilization and traffic on the Big Brother Server, often resulting in incomplete tests and false results. The exact value depends on various factors and should be left to the discretion of the Netadmin.

Sending E-Mail Notifications

Big Brother has the built-in capability to send alerts to the Netadmin through e-mails. The e-mail address of the recipient is specified in the $BBHOME/etc/bbwarnrules.cfg file. The format is as follows:

```
hosts;exhosts;services;exservices;day;time;recipients-email-address
```

The bbwarnrules.cfg file also provides information regarding the details of the format. As highlighted in Example 5-4, spope@abcinvestment.com is the recipient of e-mail alerts. Additionally, the statement ***;;*;;*;*;spope@abcinvestment.com** causes Big Brother to send e-mails regarding all hosts and all services during all 7 days of the week and any time of the day. The keyword **unmatched-** ensures that at least one recipient is sent the alerts for hosts that do not match any of the previous rules.

Example 5-4 *Sample bbwarnrules.cfg File*

```
# Rules are written in the following format:
# hosts;exhosts;services;exservices;day;time;recipients
# hosts: match on these hosts (* is a wildcard for all hosts)
# exhosts: exclude these hosts
# services: match on these services (* is wildcard for all hosts)
# exservices: exclude these services
# day: 0-6 (sunday-saturday)
# time: 0000-2359
# recipients: email address, numeric pager, sms number
#
*;;*;;*;*;spope@abcinvestment.com
unmatched-*;;*;;*;*;spope@abcinvestment.com
```

The bbwarnrules.cfg file is a good location for customizing your notifications. For example, the following configuration instructs Big Brother to send notifications for all hosts to jkeith@abcinvestment.com from 8:30 a.m. to 5:30 p.m. on weekdays:

```
*;;*;;1-5;00830-1730;jkeith@abcinvestment.com
```

Increasing Performance

By default, Big Brother only runs a single thread to run all the tests. If you have a large number of hosts and services, you can increase the number of concurrent threads for the tests executed by the Big Brother Server. By running concurrent tests, Big Brother reduces the time required to check all the hosts and services. The number of concurrent threads is increased by modifying the value of BBNETTHREADS in the $BBHOME/etc/bbdef-server.sh file. You can set the value to 5 for a reasonable boost in performance without an adverse effect on CPU utilization. Use the following code:

```
#
BBNETTHREADS=5
export BBNETTHREADS
```

However, if you set BBNETTHREADS higher than 5, the boost in Big Brother performance comes at the expense of CPU utilization. The underlying hardware (CPU and RAM) should be robust enough to support Big Brother for running multiple threads.

Monitoring Additional Services

Netadmins often need to monitor additional services on network devices or servers. This monitoring functionality can be incorporated into Big Brother to provide a centralized monitoring system. Any text-based TCP/UDP service can be checked by taking the following actions:

1. Using the service name as the directive in the bb-host file. The name should match what appears in the /etc/services file on the Linux machine that is hosting the Big Brother Server.

2 Adding the service name in the list of services in the BBNETSVCS variable of the $BBHOME/etc/bbdef-server.sh file.

A common case of network services is the network administrator running a Terminal Access Controller Access Control System Plus (TACACS+) or Remote Authentication Dial-In User Service (RADIUS) Server to support the AAA feature on Cisco routers and switches. Sample lines, shown in Examples 5-5 and 5-6, depict the configuration needed to monitor the TACACS+ service running on the TACACS+ server.

Example 5-5 *Sample Line in bb-host File*

```
192.168.0.55  AAASERVER # testip tacacs
```

Example 5-6 *Sample Line in bbdef-server.sh File*

```
#
BBNETSVCS="smtp telnet ftp pop pop3 pop-3 ssh imap ssh1 ssh2 imap2 imap3 imap4 pop2
pop-2 nntp tacacs"
export BBNETSVCS
```

Improving Scalability

The original code for Big Brother (Linux version) faces performance issues because it does not scale well when monitoring more that 50 nodes. The BBGen patch, created by Henrik Storner, provides high-performance replacements and enhancements to several Big Brother components. Big Brother, in conjunction with BBGen, has been reported to successfully monitor 1000 nodes simultaneously. The installation of BBGen is straightforward, and the process is documented in the INSTALL file that is included with the source code. To install BBGen, download and unpack the tar file from http://www.deadcat.net.

Creating Hyperlinks for Node Information

Using hyperlinks to view information about specific nodes is an excellent feature that can help the Netadmin to centrally locate needed information at critical times. You can set up hyperlinks for a host in the bb.html or bb2.html pages to point to an information page. This is achieved by creating files in the $BBHOME/bb/www/notes directory. The filenames should match the system names that are specified in the $BBHOME/bb/etc/bb-hosts file.

For each monitored node, create a text or HTML file with information such as the serial number, location, warranty information, circuit ID, and vendor or service-provider contact information for the specific device. When the node goes down, the Netadmin can click the hyperlink to get the necessary information to solve the problem.

Deploying a Windows-Based Big Brother Network-Monitoring System

Netadmins searching for a Windows-based network monitoring system have limited choices. The following three are the good options:

- Big Brother
- BigSister
- JFFNMS

Again, because of ease of installation and configuration compared to other tools, Big Brother is the preferred tool and is discussed in this section. The Windows version of Big Brother runs on Windows NT 4.0, 2000, and 2003. Although the overall process of deploying Big Brother in Windows is similar to that in Linux, a few differences exist. One of the most distinct difference is that unlike its Linux counterpart, you do not need to create a separate user in Windows to run the Big Brother Server. The following sections cover the installation and configuration of Big Brother in Windows. However, details regarding the usage of Big Brother are covered in the section "Deploying a Linux-Based Big Brother Network-Monitoring System," earlier in this chapter.

Installing Big Brother in Windows

The target Windows machine for hosting the Big Brother Server must have a preconfigured and functional Internet Information Services (IIS) web server. The IIS web server is part of the Windows NT/2000/2003/XP operating system. IIS is installed through the **Add/Remove Programs** icon in the Windows Control Panel. Refer to the Windows documentation for more details on installing and configuring IIS.

After installing the IIS web server, download and save the Big Brother executable file for Windows from http://www.bb4.org. Double-click the downloaded .exe file to begin the installation process. During the installation process, Big Brother prompts you for OS-specific information; the default values should work in most cases. Follow the prompts to finish the installation process.

Configuring Big Brother

Big Brother on Windows is configured through the .cfg files located in the default directory \Program Files\Quest Software\Big Brother BTF*xx*\etc (where *xx* is the version number). Before proceeding with the configuration, Netadmins should understand the function of each of these cfg files. The seven cfg files are as follows:

- bb-hosts.cfg
- bbdef.cfg
- bbskin-eng.cfg

- bbskin-fra.cfg
- bbwarnrules.cfg
- bbwarnsetup.cfg
- security.cfg

bb-hosts.cfg File

The bb-hosts.cfg file is used to list all the nodes that are to be monitored by Big Brother. The format is similar to the Linux version, as shown in Example 5-7. Note the similarity between the files in Examples 5-3 and 5-7.

Example 5-7 *Sample bb-host.cfg file*

```
192.168.0.30 localhost # BBPAGER BBNET BBDISPLAY http://localhost/
group-compress <H3><I>Network Devices</I></H3>
192.168.0.10   Dallas-router # testip
192.168.0.20   Dallas-Firewall # testip
192.168.0.50   Dallas-Switch # testip
192.168.0.100  FileServer # testip
```

bb-def.cfg File

The bb-def.cfg file controls the behavior of Big Brother. The parameters are similar to those in the Linux version. The default configuration should work for most situations. BBNETSLEEP controls the frequency at which Big Brother performs the monitoring tests. The interval between successive generations of the bb.html (or bb2.html) page is controlled by BBSLEEP. The default value is 300 seconds for both. Netadmins can increase the monitoring frequency by decreasing these parameters, as shown in the sample bb-def.cfg file in Example 5-8. However, excessively decreasing these values (for example, to 5 seconds) leads to higher traffic and CPU utilization. Moreover, Big Brother might not complete the testing of all hosts or services within the specified interval, thus causing false results.

Example 5-8 *Sample bb-def.cfg File*

```
# -- output suppressed --
# INTERVAL TO WAIT IN SECONDS TO REGENERATE THE bb.html/bb2.html files
BBSLEEP="30"
# -- output suppressed --
# INTERVAL BETWEEN NETWORK TESTS (IN SECONDS)
BBNETSLEEP="30"
# -- output suppressed --
```

bbskin-eng.cfg File

The bbskin-eng.cfg file controls the display properties, such as the size or color of fonts, for the bb.html and bb2.html pages. This file is for the English version of the HTML pages. While the default content works well in most cases, you can edit the font properties or the text labels to seamlessly integrate Big Brother pages with your web portals.

bbskin-fra.cfg File

This file is same as the bbskin-eng.cfg file, except it controls the French version of the bb.html and bb2.html pages.

bbwarnrules.cfg File

The bbwarnrules.cfg file contains rules for sending alerts and notifications to suitable e-mail recipients. The format is as follows:

```
hosts;exhosts;services;exservices;day;time;recipients
```

In this code, *hosts* and *services* are the list of host names and services, respectively, as specified in the bb-hosts.cfg file. Additionally, *exhosts* is the list of hosts to be excluded, *exservices* is the list of services to be excluded, *day* specifies the day of the week (Sunday is expressed as 0, Monday as 1, Saturday as 6, and so on), and *time* is the range of time specified in HHMM (0000–2359) format. You can use the asterisk (*) as a wildcard to match all values. The first entry in Example 5-9 causes Big Brother to send e-mail alerts to spope@abcinvestment.com and pager alerts at the phone number 333-4444 for all hosts and all services, for all 7 days of the week, and finally during all 24 hours of the day. You can specify multiple recipients using separate line entries. The second entry in Example 5-9 sends e-mail alerts to ksmith@abcinvestment.com only on weekdays (Monday through Friday) between 8:00 a.m. and 5:00 p.m. The last entry in Example 5-9 is a catchall entry. The **unmatched-** keyword ensures that at least one recipient is sent the alerts for hosts that do not match any of the previous rules. The original bbwarnrules.cfg file contains templates for further customizing the Big Brother alerts and notifications.

Example 5-9 *Sample bbwarnrules.cfg File*

```
*;;*;;*;*;spope@abcinvestment.com 333-4444
*;;*;;1-5;0800-1700*;ksmith@abcinvestment.com
unmatched-*;;*;;*;*;spope@abcinvestment.com
```

TIP Many cell-phone service providers now allow e-mail messages to be sent directly to the phones. The e-mail address is of the format *xxx-xxx-xxxx@providerdomain.com*, where *xxx-xxx-xxxx* is the 10-digit cell-phone number. Netadmins can use this feature to their advantage and avoid carrying pagers. On the other hand, if an outage interrupts the Internet or mail server connection, the e-mail alerts are not received. You should implement fallback options, such as connecting a modem with a public switched telephone network (PSTN) line to the network-monitoring system to send pager alerts. Or you can use a separate digital subscriber line (DSL) as an alternate path to send e-mail or cell-phone alerts.

bbwarnsetup.cfg File

The bbwarnsetup.cfg file is used to modify the overall settings for the notification feature of Big Brother. The default content of the file should work fine for most environments and should not be modified by beginner-level users. Advanced users can refer to the embedded comments within the original bbwarnsetup.cfg file that comes with the installation.

security.cfg File

You should not edit this file, because it is irrelevant to the regular operation of the Big Brother Server. This file is only relevant in scenarios that feature Big Brother monitoring clients talking to the Big Brother Server. By default, the Big Brother Server listens for messages from any Big Brother Client. You can restrict the Big Brother Server to listen for messages only from Big Brother Clients with IP addresses listed in the security.cfg file. Note that this file has no impact on accessing Big Brother web pages (bb.html and bb2.html).

Running the Big Brother Server

After configuring the .cfg files, you can start the Big Brother Server to monitor the network. Big Brother runs as a Windows service and can be controlled through the Windows Services Microsoft Management Console (MMC) snap-in.

Follow these steps to start the Big Brother service:

Step 1 Choose **Start > Run**, enter **Services.msc**, and click the **OK** button to launch the Services MMC snap-in.

Step 2 In the **Services** window, right-click **Big Brother SNM Server** to access the Properties menu. On the Properties menu, choose **Start** to start the Big Brother service.

You can use the Services MMC snap-in to stop or restart the Big Brother service. You can find the messages generated by the Big Brother service in the Application section of the Windows Event Viewer. To access the Windows Event Viewer, choose **Start > Run**, enter **eventvwr.exe**, and click the **OK** button.

Step 3 To view the current status of the network, access the Big Brother web page at the following URL:

http://*ipaddress_of_bigbrotherserver*/bb/bb.html

Alternately, to view the summary results of the network status, visit the following URL:

http://*ipaddress_of_bigbrotherserver*/bb/bb2.html

Big Brother displays the results of network monitoring through the bb.html and bb2.html web pages. These pages are identical to those generated by the Linux version of Big Brother. For more information on using Big Brother web pages in Linux, see the section "Running the Big Brother Server," earlier in this chapter.

Deploying Nagios for Linux-Based Network Monitoring

Nagios is another Linux-based system and network-monitoring application that is popular in the open source community. Nagios provides the following:

- A web-based GUI for viewing current network status, notification and problem history, log files, and host configurations
- The ability to monitor services (such as HTTP, SSH, FTP) that are running on a host
- The ability to send e-mail or pager-alert notifications
- The ability to display hierarchical network configuration for defining parent and child hosts
- Active development and support from the open source community
- A customizable network map

Of the listed features, the ability to create network hierarchy is useful in minimizing the number of alerts during network outages. For example, consider a WAN router connected to four remote routers. When the WAN router is down, the connectivity to the remote routers is also affected. Without network hierarchy, the monitoring system generates alerts for all five devices. However, with the network hierarchy defined, the monitoring system generates alerts only for the parent device (the WAN router, in this example).

Nagios also allows you to use MySQL or PostgreSQL databases to store data instead of using flat files. Despite its versatility and features, Nagios is comparatively intensive in terms of deployment time and effort. This discussion is aimed at helping Netadmins to quickly understand and deploy a functional Nagios system using text files to store data. Such a system should suffice when monitoring a medium-size network with 50 to 500 nodes. The following sections provide details regarding Nagios installation, configuration, and usage.

Nagios Installation

Before installing Nagios, the TCP/IP stack on the target Linux machine should be preconfigured and the Linux machine should be connected to the network. The Nagios source code is available from the Nagios home page at http://www.nagios.org. To compile Nagios using the source code, the target Linux machine requires the following features:

- C compiler (for example, GCC)
- Web server (for example, Apache)

Additionally, for advanced use of Nagios for database support, you must also install and configure the MySQL or PostgreSQL database on the Linux machine. Installation of these programs is beyond the scope of this book. Refer to the documentation for your Linux distribution.

However, Debian-Linux users can benefit from the simplified routine for installing Nagios by using the **apt-get install nagios-text** command. The entire discussion about Nagios in this chapter is based on deploying Nagios on a Debian-Linux system. The choice of Nagios on Debian is credited to the extreme convenience and stability provided by Debian-Linux.

NOTE Your Debian system might give you the following error:

```
E: Couldn't find package nagios-txt
```

In this case, you should edit the /etc/apt/sources.list file to add the following statement:

```
deb http://ftp.debian.org/debian unstable main non-free contrib
```

The **apt-get install nagios-text** command automatically installs Nagios and takes care of other system dependencies. By default, the Debian installation process defines nagiosadmin as the default user for administering Nagios. You must configure the password for the nagiosadmin user when prompted during the installation process.

You can verify the installation by pointing your web browser to the Nagios machine using the URL http://*Nagios-server-IP-address*/nagios/. The default home page consists of the navigation pane at the left, as shown in Figure 5-3.

Figure 5-3 *Nagios Home Page*

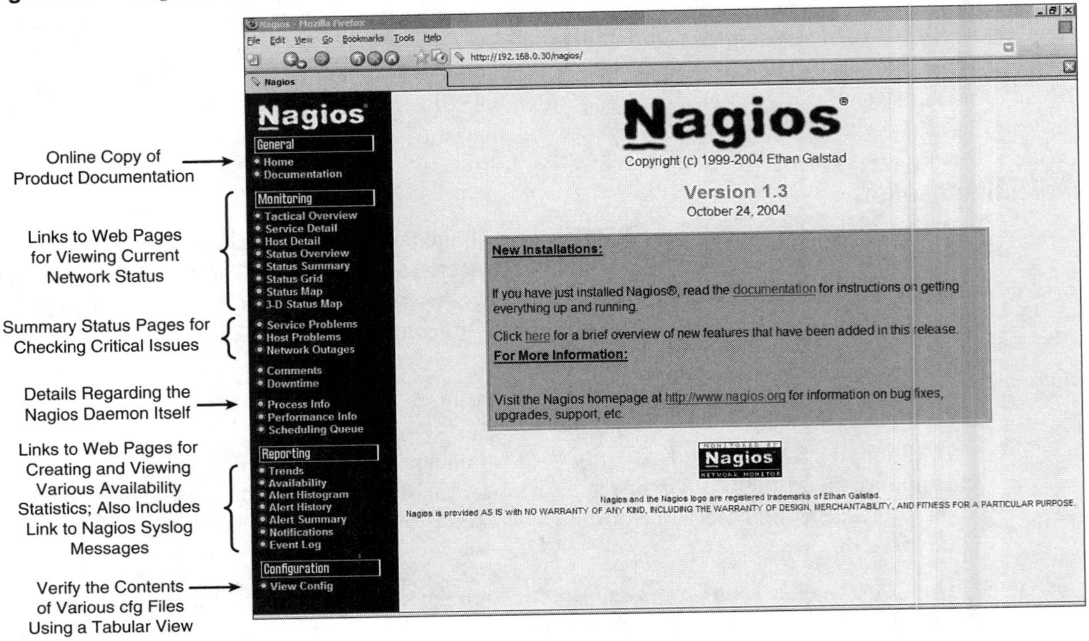

The navigation pane provides links to documentation, monitoring, and reporting pages. The default navigation pane is organized into four subsections for easy usage. The username for accessing the Nagios web GUI is nagiosadmin; the password is the one that you set during the Nagios installation process. The default installation also includes detailed product documentation. Beginners are strongly encouraged to read this online manual.

Nagios Configuration

Nagios is configured through the .cfg files located in the default directory /etc/nagios. The main configuration file (/etc/nagios/nagios.cfg) controls the Nagios daemon and contains the location of other .cfg files. Nagios monitors the services (listed in the service.cfg file) running on the hosts listed in the hosts.cfg file. For ease of administration and notification, hosts can be grouped in the hostgroups.cfg file. This file defines the contact groups for each host group. The contactgroups.cfg file groups various contacts. The e-mail or pager information for each contact (individual recipient) is listed in the contacts.cfg file.

To deploy a basic Nagios monitoring system, you must configure each of the following five files:

- /etc/nagios/hosts.cfg
- /etc/nagios/hostgroups.cfg

- /etc/nagios/services.cfg
- /etc/nagios/contactgroups.cfg
- /etc/nagios/contacts.cfg

These configuration files are created automatically during the installation process. Each file contains sample templates for ease of configuration. Lines beginning with a hash (#) are treated as comments. Similarly, any text following a semicolon (;) is ignored. A detailed explanation of each of these files, as well as all the parameters included within these files, is provided in the online product documentation.

For a better understanding of each of the .cfg files, consider the network scenario shown in Figure 5-4. The configuration of each of the subsequent .cfg files discussed in this chapter is based on this network scenario.

Figure 5-4 *Sample Network Scenario*

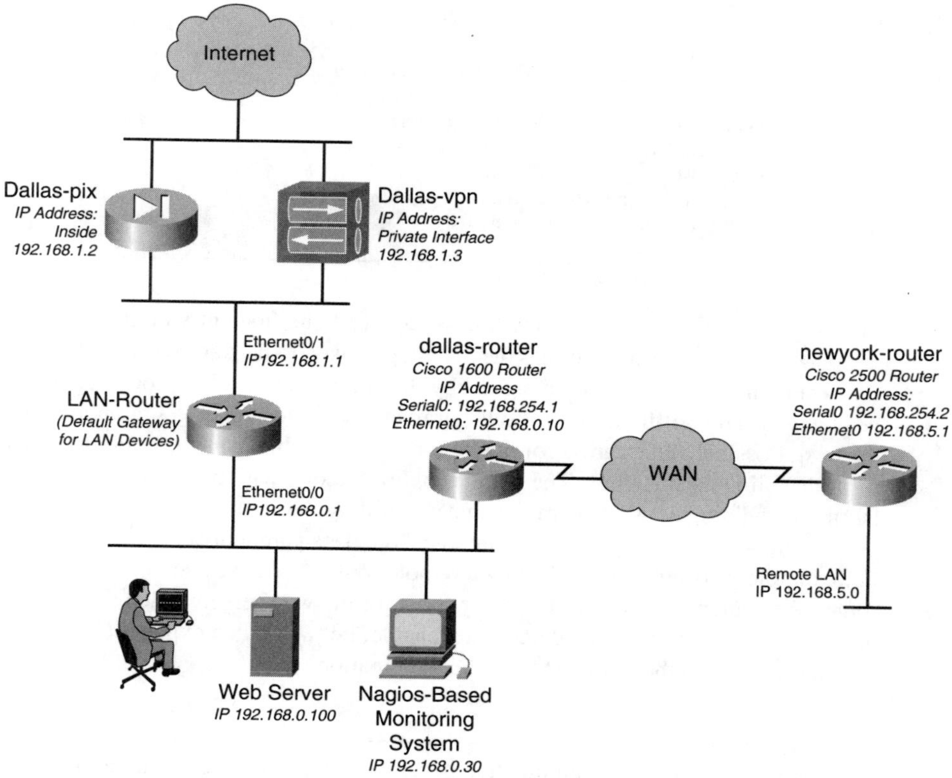

Editing the /etc/nagios/hosts.cfg File

The /etc/nagios/hosts.cfg file contains a list of every host to be monitored by Nagios. Example 5-10 provides the default contents of the /etc/nagios/hosts.cfg file.

Example 5-10 *Default Contents of the /etc/nagios/hosts.cfg File*

```
define host{
name generic-host
        notifications_enabled          1
        event_handler_enabled          0
        flap_detection_enabled         0
        process_perf_data              1
        retain_status_information      1
        retain_nonstatus_information   1
        register                       0
        }

define host{
        use                     generic-host ; Name of host template to use
        host_name               gw
        alias                   Default Gateway
        address                 192.168.0.1
        check_command           check-host-alive
        max_check_attempts      20
        notification_interval   60
        notification_period     24x7
        notification_options    d,u,r
        }
```

Each host definition is contained within braces ({}). The first entry defines a generic host template. The second entry defines the default gateway of the Nagios server itself. Note that the host name gw is internally assigned by the Nagios installation process and should not be changed. The **notification_options** parameter specifies when to send notifications for the host. Possible values are **d** for down, **u** for unreachable, **r** for recovery to up state, and **n** for disabling notifications. The **u** and **d** options, along with the **parents** parameter, are helpful in defining network hierarchy and controlling the alert notifications (as shown in the next example). A host is considered unreachable if its parent host is down or unreachable. For example, if Nagios is monitoring a remote router and a web server located behind the router, the router is defined as the parent host for the web server. When the router goes down, the web server is considered unreachable. For a detailed explanation of each parameter, refer to the online product documentation.

NOTE The configuration for gw is automatically created only during the installation and is static. If you move the Nagios server to a different subnet, you must manually change the IP address for gw to match the new network.

To add new hosts, you can use the configuration of the host gw as a template. Simply edit and append the configuration for each host to the existing /etc/nagios/hosts.cfg file. Example 5-11 shows the configuration snippet for the hosts depicted in the network scenario of Figure 5-4. Note that host dallas-router is connected to a remote host newyork-router through a WAN link. So the host dallas-router is defined as the parent for newyork-router, as highlighted in Example 5-11. This helps when creating network hierarchy. Additionally, only the down (**d**) and recovery (**r**) notification options are enabled for host newyork-router. Consequently, when newyork-router or the WAN link is not functional, Nagios generates alerts for newyork-router. On the other hand, when the parent device dallas-router is down, newyork-router is unreachable. Nevertheless, Nagios only generates alerts for dallas-router and not for newyork-router. Similar logic applies to host dallas-pix, dallas-vpn and their parent host gw (LAN-router) in Figure 5-4.

NOTE While network hierarchy is a useful feature, it requires the appropriate personnel to have a thorough understanding of the network topology. If you need to generate unreachable alerts for a device irrespective of the status of its parent device, simply add **u** to the **notification_options** parameter in the host definition.

Example 5-11 *Contents of the hosts.cfg File*

```
# -- default entries for generic-host and gw should be included here --
#
# 'dallas-router' host definition
define host{
        use                     generic-host        ; Name of host template to use
        host_name               dallas-router
        alias                   Router-Dallas Cisco 1600
        address                 192.168.0.10
        check_command           check-host-alive
        max_check_attempts      20
        notification_interval   60
        notification_period     24x7
        notification_options    d,u,r
        }
# 'newyork-router' host definition
define host{
        use                     generic-host
        host_name               newyork-router
        alias                   Cisco 2600 router
        address                 192.168.254.2
        parents                 dallas-router
        check_command           check-host-alive
        max_check_attempts      5
        notification_interval   60
        notification_period     24x7
        notification_options    d,r
```

continues

Example 5-11 *Contents of the hosts.cfg File (Continued)*

```
    }
# 'dallas-pix' host definition
define host{
        use                     generic-host
        host_name               dallas-pix
        alias                   Firewall pix535
        address                 192.168.1.2
        parents                 gw
        check_command           check-host-alive
        max_check_attempts      5
        notification_interval   60
        notification_period     24x7
        notification_options    d,r
    }
# 'dallas-vpn' host definition
define host{
        use                     generic-host
        host_name               dallas-vpn
        alias                   VPN3030 Concentrator
        address                 192.168.1.3
        parents                 gw
        check_command           check-host-alive
        max_check_attempts      5
        notification_interval   60
        notification_period     24x7
        notification_options    d,r
    }
# 'web-server' host definition
define host{
        use                     generic-host
        host_name               web-server
        alias                   Intranet web server
        address                 192.168.0.100
        check_command           check-host-alive
        max_check_attempts      5
        notification_interval   60
        notification_period     24x7
        notification_options    d,u,r
    }
#
```

Editing the /etc/nagios/services.cfg File

After defining each host monitored by Nagios, you must specify the services to be monitored on each of these hosts. The services are defined in the /etc/nagios/services.cfg file. Example 5-12 provides the contents of a sample /etc/nagios/services.cfg file. The first two definitions are default entries created by the Nagios installation process. The first definition creates a generic service and is a placeholder for a system-specific configuration that can be applied to all the services. The second entry is added by the Nagios installation process to monitor the availability of the default gateway through the ICMP **ping** command. Do not delete any of these entries. However, when monitoring other hosts through ICMP ping, you can simply append host names within the default entry for the host gw. The exact configuration is provided in Example 5-12. The third definition monitors web services running over the host web-server. The **notification_options** parameter determines when to send notifications for the service; possible values are **w** for warning, **u** for unknown, **c** for critical, **r** for recovery, and **n** for disabling notifications. The **service_description** parameter refers to the predefined name of the service within Nagios. The **contact_groups** parameter defines the group of administrators responsible for the maintenance of the monitored host or service. The /etc/nagios/services.cfg file also contains built-in templates for monitoring other common services that are predefined by Nagios, such as SMTP, SSH, FTP, and POP3.

Example 5-12 *Contents of the /etc/nagios/services.cfg File*

```
define service{
    ; The 'name' of this service template, referenced in other service definitions
   name             generic-service
   active_checks_enabled     1  ; Active service checks are enabled
   passive_checks_enabled    0  ; Passive service checks are enabled/disabled
   parallelize_check         1  ; Active service checks should be parallelized
                       ; (disabling this can lead to major performance problems)
    obsess_over_service       1 ; We should obsess over this service (if necessary)
   check_freshness            0 ; Default is to NOT check service 'freshness'
   notifications_enabled      0 ; Service notifications are disabled
   event_handler_enabled      0 ; Service event handler is disabled
   flap_detection_enabled     0 ; Flap detection is disabled
   process_perf_data          1 ; Process performance data
   retain_status_information  1 ; Retain status information across program restarts
   retain_nonstatus_information 1 ; Retain non-status information across program restarts
    register          0       ; DONT REGISTER THIS DEFINITION - ITS NOT A REAL SERVICE, JUST
A TEMPLATE!
   }
#
# the PING service for 'gw' is created by the Nagios installation process
# additional hosts can be added in the same line as "gw"
define service{
        use                           generic-service       ; Name of service template to use
        host_name                     gw, dallas-router, newyork-router, dallas-pix, dallas-
vpn, web-server
        service_description           PING
        is_volatile                   0
        check_period                  24x7
        max_check_attempts            3
        normal_check_interval         1
        retry_check_interval          1
        contact_groups                router-admins, web-admins
        notification_interval         240
        notification_period           24x7
        notification_options          c,r
        check_command                 check_ping!100.0,20%!500.0,60%
        }
```

continues

Example 5-12 *Contents of the /etc/nagios/services.cfg File*

```
#
# 'web-server' service for monitoring http
#
define service{
        use                         generic-service
        host_name                   web-server
        service_description         HTTP
        is_volatile                 0
        check_period                24x7
        max_check_attempts          3
        normal_check_interval       5
        retry_check_interval        1
        contact_groups              web-admins
        notification_interval       120
        notification_period         24x7
        notification_options        w,u,c,r
        check_command               check_http
        }
```

TIP Here is a timesaving tip for configuring the service.cfg file: Instead of individually adding each host to a service definition, you can specify the **hostgroup** definition. So instead of using the following:

```
host_name        HOST1,HOST2,HOST3,...,HOSTN
```

you can use the following:

```
hostgroup_name        HOSTGROUP1,HOSTGROUP2,...,HOSTGROUPN
```

Alternatively, you can include all the hosts by using the * character, as shown here:

```
host_name        *
```

Editing the /etc/nagios/hostgroups.cfg File

The /etc/nagios/hostgroups.cfg file groups similar hosts on the basis of features or functionality. The idea behind the hostgroups.cfg file is to identify a similar set of hosts and tie them to a group of administrators who should receive alerts related to those hosts. The host group definitions are also used in the status map pages that are created by Nagios. Each host group definition contains a list of hosts separated by a comma (,). A host can belong to multiple groups, but it must belong to at least one group. Each host group definition also contains the **contact_groups** parameter, which specifies the group of Netadmins responsible for maintaining the hosts. When the status of a host changes, Nagios sends notifications to the contact groups of each host group to which the host belongs. Example 5-13 shows two host group definitions, each with a different group of contacts.

Example 5-13 *Contents of the /etc/nagios/hostgroups.cfg File*

```
define hostgroup{
        hostgroup_name  gateways
        alias           Network devices
        contact_groups  router-admins
        members         gw, dallas-router, newyork-router, dallas-pix, dallas-vpn
        }
#
define hostgroup{
        hostgroup_name  webserver
        alias           Web servers
        contact_groups  web-admins
        members         web-server
}
```

Editing the /etc/nagios/contactgroups.cfg File

The /etc/nagios/contactgroups.cfg file defines the contact groups that are used within the host group and service definitions. The contact groups definition also contains the individual members for each of the contact groups. Each group definition must contain the list of members assigned to the group. Multiple member names must be separated by a comma (,). Example 5-14 shows the contents of the /etc/nagios/contactgroups.cfg file for two contact groups, router-admins and web-admins.

Example 5-14 *Contents of the contactgroups.cfg File*

```
# 'router-admins' contact group definition
define contactgroup{
        contactgroup_name       router-admins
        alias                   Router and Network admins
        members                 spope
        }
# 'web-admins' contact group definition
define contactgroup{
        contactgroup_name       web-admins
        alias                   Web admins
        members                 jkeith, spope
        }
```

Editing the /etc/nagios/contacts.cfg File

After defining the contact group, the next step is to define the information for each contact (or member). The contact information, such as e-mail address or pager number, is specified through the /etc/nagios/contacts.cfg file. The value for the **contact_name** parameter in the /etc/nagios/contacts.cfg file must match that specified for the value of the **members** parameter in the /etc/nagios/contactgroups.cfg file. Example 5-15 provides the configuration of the /etc/nagios/contacts.cfg file for two contacts, spope and jkeith.

Example 5-15 *Contents of the /etc/nagios/contacts.cfg File*

```
# 'spope' contact definition
define contact{
        contact_name                    spope
        alias                           Network Admin
        service_notification_period     24x7
        host_notification_period        24x7
        service_notification_options    w,u,c,r
        host_notification_options       d,u,r
        service_notification_commands   notify-by-email,notify-by-epager
        host_notification_commands      host-notify-by-email,host-notify-by-epager
        email                           spope@abcinvestment.com
        pager                           111-222-3333@pagingcompany.net
        }
# 'jkieth' contact definition
define contact{
        contact_name                    jkeith
        alias                           web Admin
        service_notification_period     24x7
        host_notification_period        24x7
        service_notification_options    w,u,c,r
        host_notification_options       d,u,r
        service_notification_commands   notify-by-email,notify-by-epager
        host_notification_commands      host-notify-by-email,host-notify-by-epager
        email                           jkeith@abcinvestment.com
        pager                           111-222-4444@pagingcompany.net
        }
```

For details regarding other parameters included in the /etc/nagios/contact.cfg file, refer to the Nagios product documentation.

Running Nagios

After editing the .cfg files, Nagios is ready to be started. But before running Nagios, you should verify the configuration using the **nagios -v** *main-config-file* command. The **-v** option forces Nagios to parse each of the .cfg files and look for errors without loading the files for production use. Example 5-16 shows the output of the **nagios -v** command.

Example 5-16 *Verifying the Nagios Configuration*

```
root@linuxbox:# nagios -v /etc/nagios/nagios.cfg

Nagios 1.3
Copyright  1999-2004 Ethan Galstad (nagios@nagios.org)
Last Modified: 10-24-2004
License: GPL

Reading configuration data...

Running pre-flight check on configuration data...
```

Example 5-16 *Verifying the Nagios Configuration (Continued)*

```
Checking services...
        Checked 7 services.
Checking hosts...
        Checked 6 hosts.
Checking host groups...
        Checked 2 host groups.
Checking contacts...
        Checked 2 contacts.
Checking contact groups...
        Checked 2 contact groups.
Checking service escalations...
        Checked 1 service escalations.
Checking host group escalations...
        Checked 0 host group escalations.
Checking service dependencies...
        Checked 0 service dependencies.
Checking host escalations...
        Checked 0 host escalations.
Checking host dependencies...
        Checked 0 host dependencies.
Checking commands...
        Checked 90 commands.
Checking time periods...
        Checked 4 time periods.
Checking for circular paths between hosts...
Checking for circular service execution dependencies...
Checking global event handlers...
Checking obsessive compulsive service processor command...
Checking misc settings...

Total Warnings: 0
Total Errors:   0

Things look okay - No serious problems were detected during the pre-flight check
root@linuxbox:/etc/nagios#
```

Issues encountered during the parsing process are reported by Nagios and must be rectified. After verifying the configuration, you can start the Nagios daemon using the **nagios** *main-config-file* command. Debian users can also use the init script to start, stop, or restart Nagios, as shown here:

```
root@linuxbox:~# /etc/init.d/nagios restart
Stopping nagios: nagios.
Starting nagios: nagios.
```

After the Nagios daemon is started, you can access the Nagios page for network monitoring, using the following URL:

http://*ip-address-of-Nagios-machine*/nagios/

The Nagios web GUI provides an HTML version of the product documentation. To view the Nagios product documentation, click the **Documentation** link in the navigation pane. Figure 5-5 shows the table of contents of the Nagios documentation web page.

Figure 5-5 *Nagios Documentation Page*

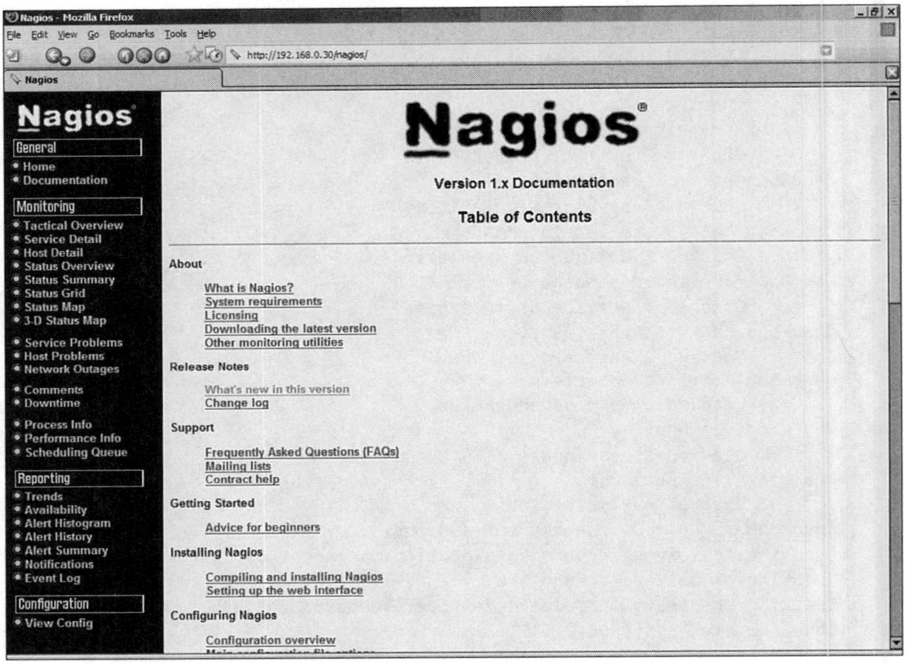

To view the current network status, click the **Status Map** link in the navigation pane. By default, the Status Map layout is circular, as shown in Figure 5-6. You can customize the layout by choosing the Layout Method drop-down menu in the upper-right corner of the Status Map page.

You can click each of the nodes displayed on the **Status Map** page for more details on each of the hosts and associated services. Alternatively, you can click the **Service Detail** link in the navigation pane to view the service details for all the listed hosts, as shown in Figure 5-7.

The navigation pane in the Nagios web GUI also provides links for viewing host details, status summary, and status overview. When monitoring larger network with Nagios, these status pages can get crowded. For such cases, the Nagios navigation pane provides two links—Service Problems and Host Problems. The Service Problems page only displays a list of hosts that are experiencing service issues. Figure 5-8 illustrates the Service Problems page, showing two service issues. The status of the PING service (on host dallas-vpn) and the HTTP service (on host web-server) is critical.

Figure 5-6 *Nagios Status Map Page*

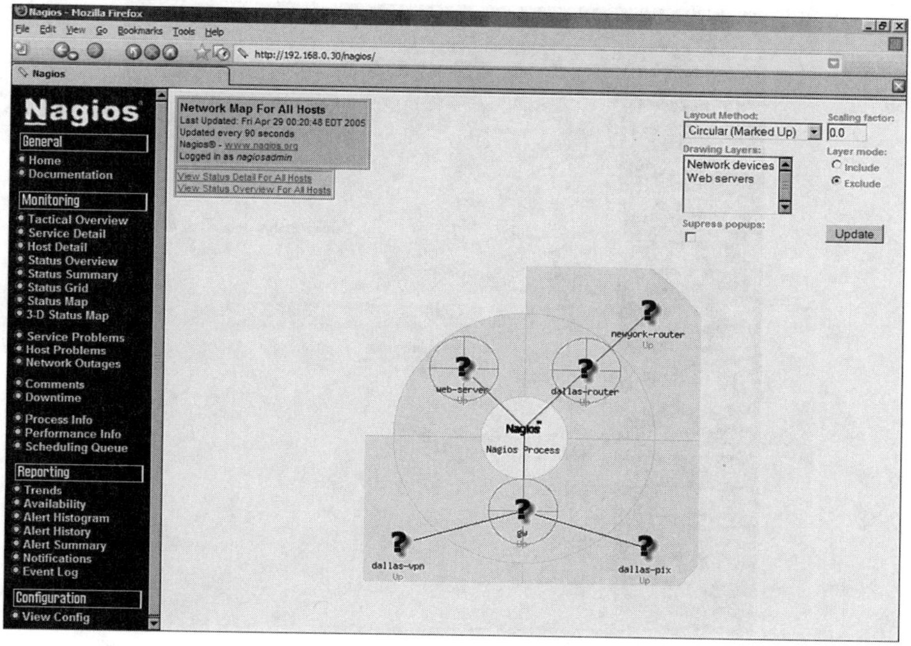

Figure 5-7 *Nagios Service Detail Page*

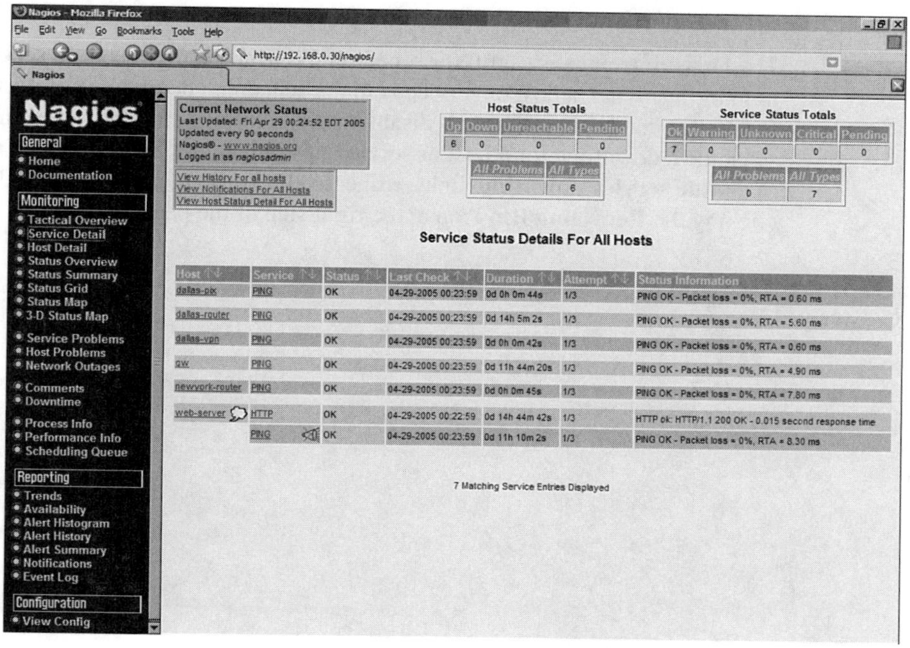

Figure 5-8 *Nagios Service Problems Page*

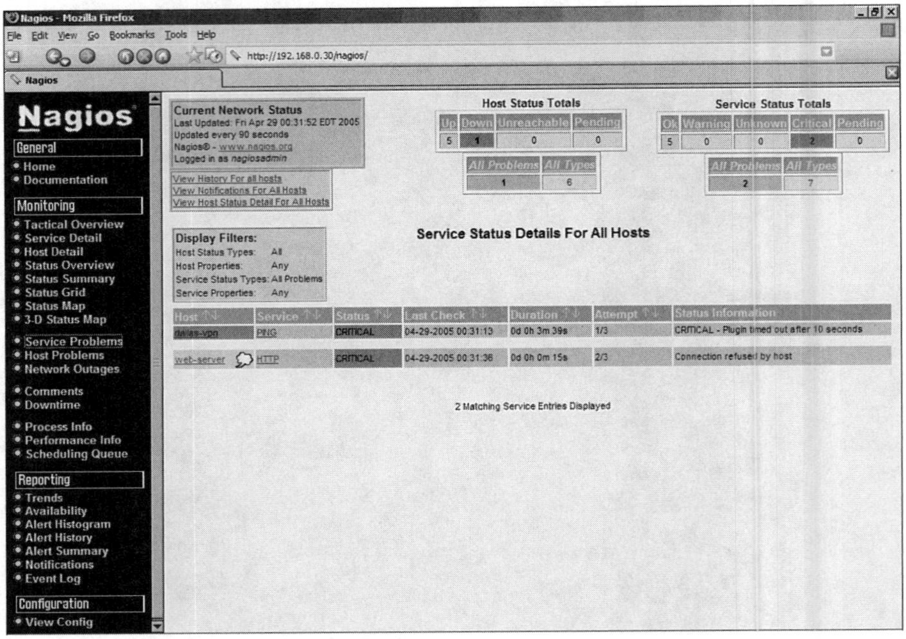

Similarly, the **Host Problems** page, shown in Figure 5-9, provides a list of all hosts that are currently down.

The Downtime page is useful for scheduling downtime for hosts and services that you are monitoring. When a host or service is in the scheduled downtime period, the notification feature for that host or service is disabled. Figure 5-10 shows the Downtime page. You can schedule a downtime for a host or service by clicking the **Schedule host downtime** and **Schedule service downtime** links, respectively. You can cancel a scheduled downtime by clicking the **Recycling Bin** icon at the right side of the particular entry.

Figure 5-9 *Nagios Hosts Problems Page*

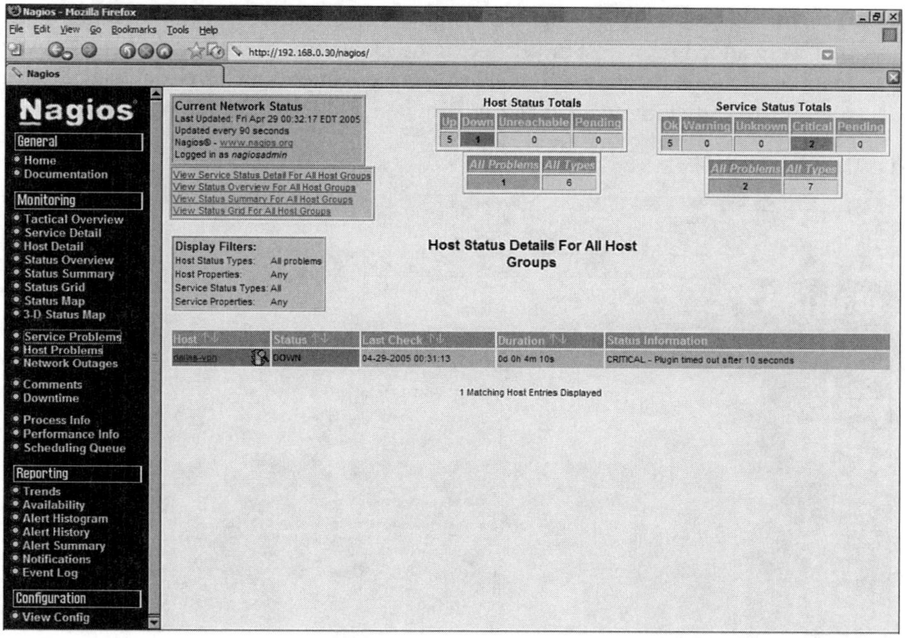

Figure 5-10 *Nagios Downtime Page*

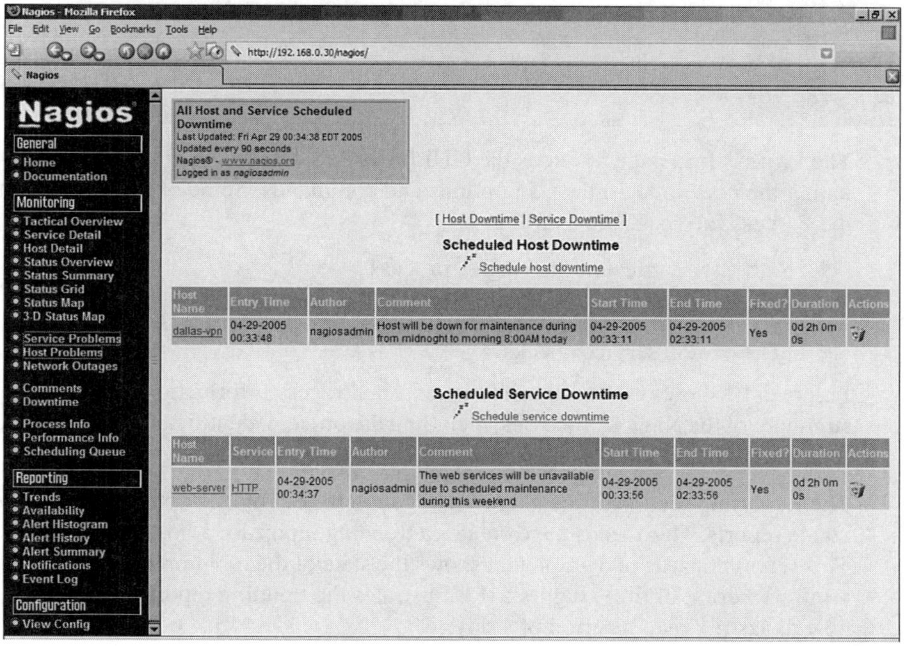

The Comment links in the navigation pane enables you to add arbitrary text as a comment for a host or service. Note that the Comments page automatically includes the comments that were added for a host or service in the Downtime page. Figure 5-11 shows the Comments page. As expected, the downtime comments are also included. You can delete a comment by clicking the **Recycling Bin** icon at the right of the particular comment.

Figure 5-11 *Nagios Comments Page*

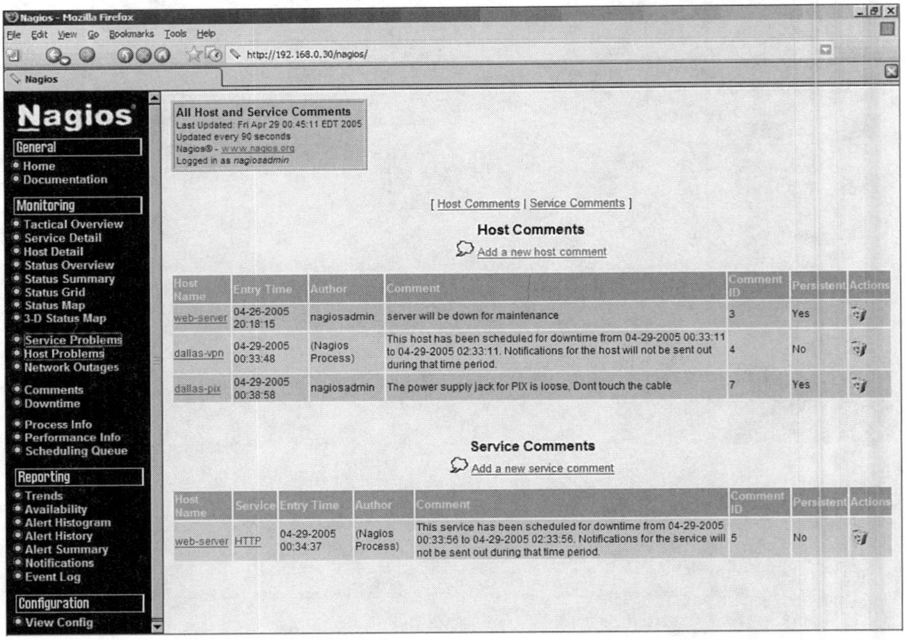

The Process Info page provides the GUI for controlling the Nagios process, thus eliminating the need to learn the CLI options and commands. Some of the options provided by the Process Info page are as follows:

- Start, stop, or restart the Nagios process
- Disable or enable notifications
- Start or stop service checks

Figure 5-12 shows the Process Info page. The Process Information section provides a summary of the Nagios processes, including the process identification (PID), start time, and total running time.

The Reporting section of the Nagios navigation pane provides options for creating customizable reports. The Trends page creates a trending report for a host or a monitored service. This report consists of a graph that shows the state of the monitored host or service over an arbitrary period of time. Figure 5-13 illustrates the trending report graph for the state of host dallas-pix over a period of 1 day.

Figure 5-12 *Nagios Process Info Page*

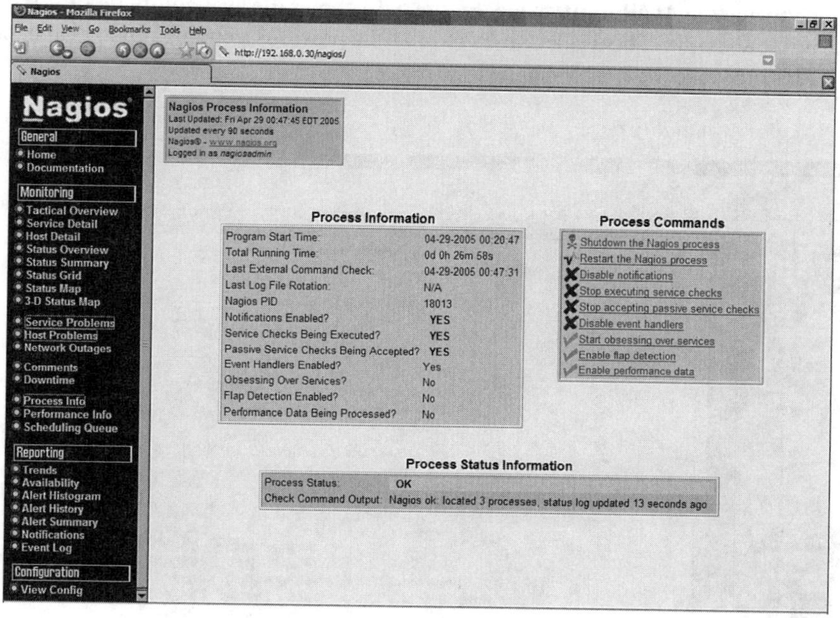

Figure 5-13 *Nagios Trends Page*

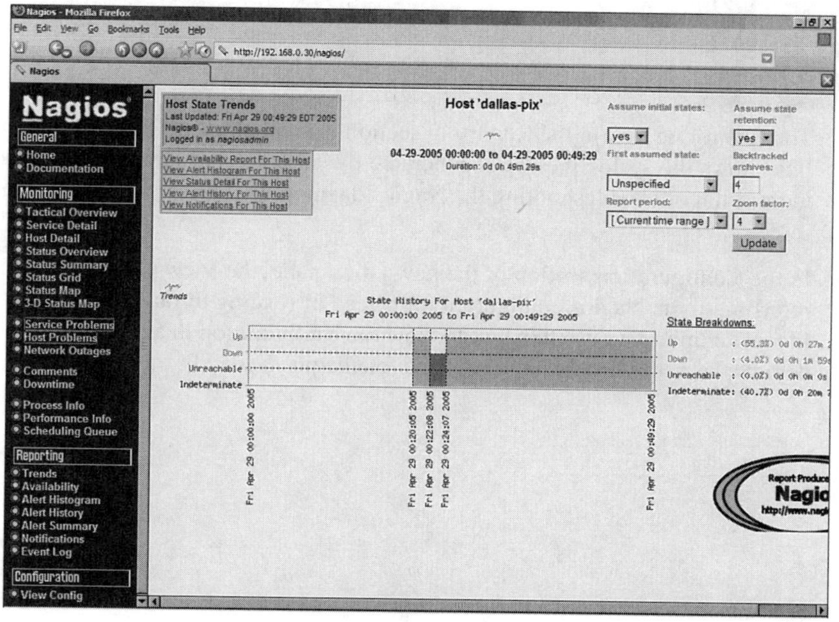

Instead of a graphic illustration, you can also view the same report in numeric format by choosing the **Availability** page. Figure 5-14 shows the availability report for the state of the host dallas-pix. This is the same report as the previous trending report graph, but in numeric format.

Figure 5-14 *Nagios Availability Page*

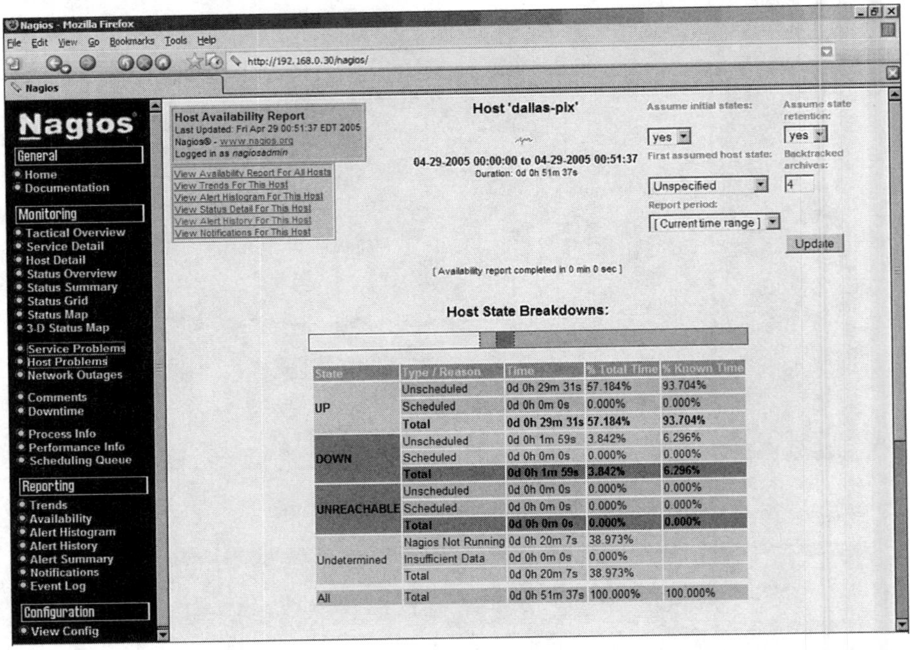

The Event Log link in the Reporting section is another useful feature for Netadmins. This link shows the syslog messages generated by Nagios. These messages are useful for monitoring or troubleshooting the Nagios daemon. Figure 5-15 shows a sample event log screen.

In the Configuration section of the navigation pane, the View Config link is handy for referring to the Nagios configuration. Instead of reading through the contents of each .cfg file, Netadmins can use this link to view the configuration in a tabular format. Figure 5-16 depicts the configuration details of the /etc/nagios/hosts.cfg file.

Figure 5-15 *Nagios Event Log Page*

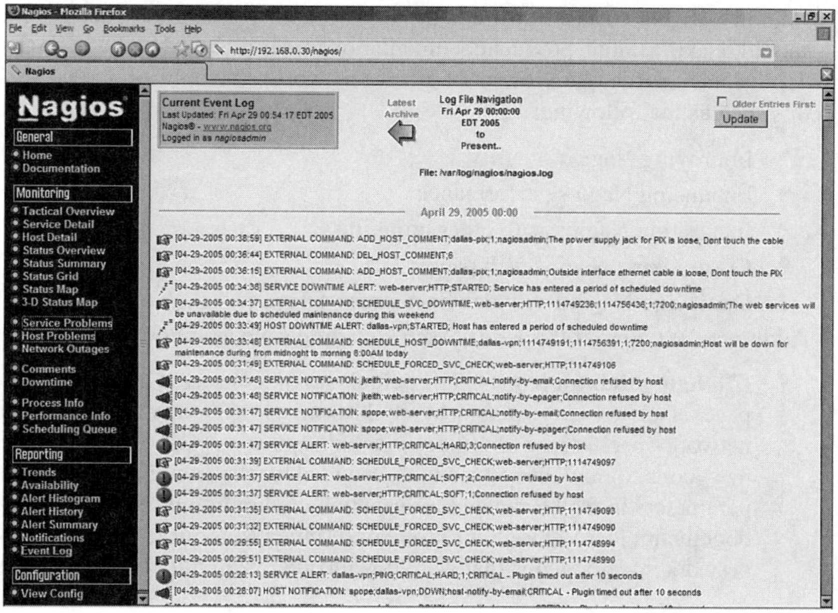

Figure 5-16 *Nagios View Config Page: Hosts*

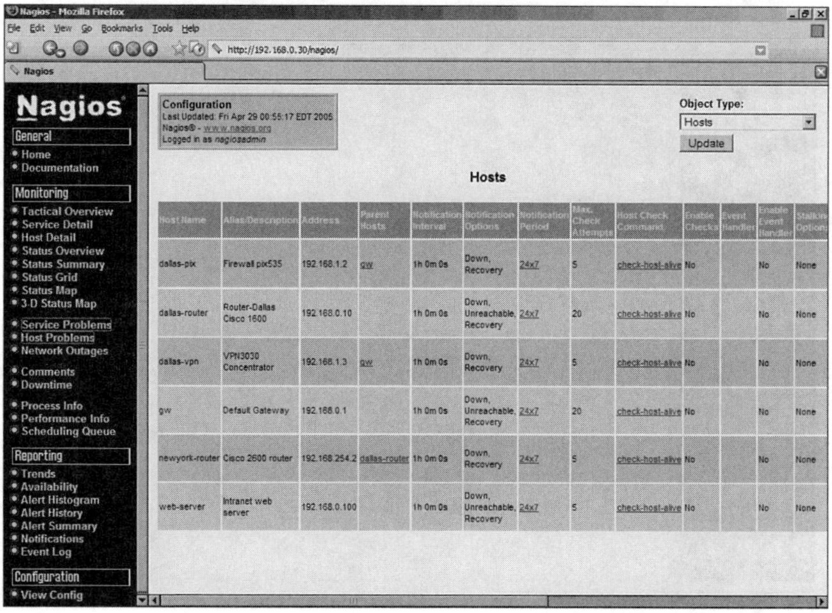

Notes for Advanced Nagios Use

Nagios is highly customizable and provides a variety of features for advanced users. You should read the online product documentation that is included with the installation files. To deploy Nagios in larger (enterprise-grade) networks, the online documentation includes tips such as the following:

- Improving Nagios security
- Enhancing Nagios performance
- Integrating Nagios with other programs
- Customizing Nagios web pages
- Deploying Nagios with database support

Additionally, two useful tips for Cisco Netadmins are as follows:

- **Changing default icons**—The default set of icons used by Nagios, to create web pages, lack network-specific symbols, such as router and firewall. You can download network-specific icons for Nagios from http://www.nagiosexchange.org. To use the new icons, follow the instructions provided for the icon_image and statusmap_image parameters in the "Extended information configuration" section of the product documentation. Figure 5-17 provides a screen shot of the Nagios status map using network-specific icons that were downloaded from http://www.nagiosexchange.com.

Figure 5-17 *Nagios Status Map with New Icons*

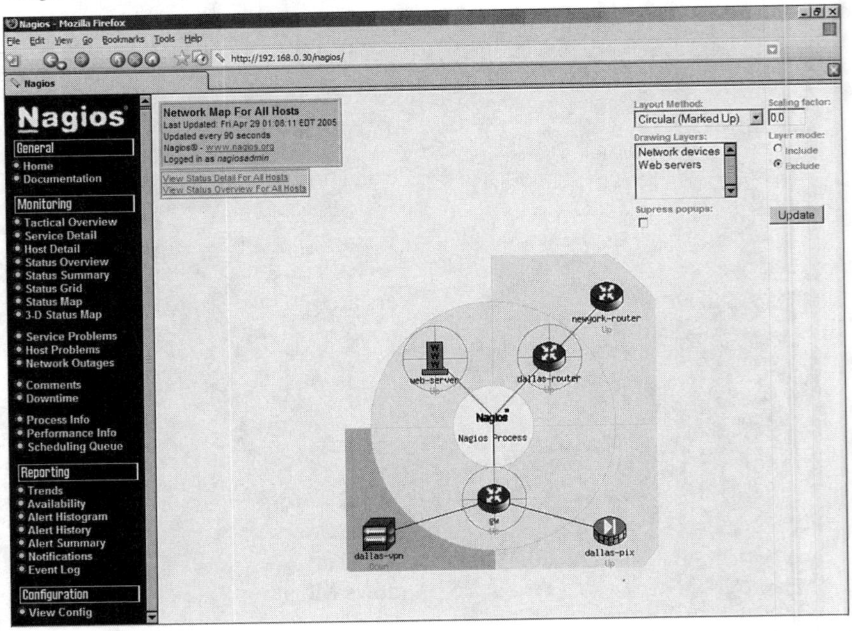

- **Inserting additional information**—While troubleshooting network issues, additional logistic information, such as circuit ID, serial number, and support contract details, is often required. You can insert such details for each host on a separate web page. To include the link to these web pages, use the **notes_url** parameter. Details regarding the use of the **notes_url** parameter are also provided in the product documentation in the "Extended information configuration" section.

Adding Redundancy and Security to Network-Monitoring Systems

Network-monitoring systems are deployed to monitor the network for potential problems. Unfortunately, the network-monitoring system itself is equally prone to hardware or software failure. This can leave the entire system susceptible to unnoticed failures while the Netadmin has let his guard down. It is good practice for Netadmins to add a second network-monitoring system in conjunction with the primary server. Big Brother allows multiple instances of BBDISPLAY, BBPAGER, and BBNET server. The only requirement is that the bb-hosts files must be identical on all the servers. Note that multiple BBPAGER servers can result in multiple notifications for the same event. Similarly, Nagios allows you to run dual servers in redundancy or failover mode. In redundancy mode, two Nagios servers monitor the network concurrently, but the one designated as slave sends notification only when the other Nagios server is down. In the failover mode, the slave Nagios server sits idle and neither runs tests nor sends notifications. The slave starts monitoring and sending notifications only when the master is down.

Also, ensure that the secondary monitoring system is connected to a different switch and uninterrupted power supply (UPS) than the primary one, to avoid a single point of failure.

When monitoring systems on both public and private sides of the firewall, you should place the network-monitoring systems on the inside network. The Netadmin should ensure that the operating system on the network-monitoring server has been patched with the latest security updates. Network-monitoring servers are often left unsecured and with weak passwords, whereas the production servers are given special attention. Netadmins should be aware that the unprotected network-monitoring server can act as a back door for attackers.

NOTE To secure your Linux system, use the Bastille Linux hardening script from http://www.bastille-linux.org/. Another URL for hardening Debian-Linux is http://www.debian-hardened.org/. A Windows server must be updated regularly with the latest service packs and security patches. In addition, turn off all services and features that are not required, including default programs such as Windows Media Player and Outlook Express.

Commercial Cisco Products

Resource Manager Essentials (RME) is part of the powerful CiscoWorks suite of network-management products from Cisco. The RME module includes an advanced network-monitoring tool called the Availability Manager.

The Availability Manager displays the following items:

- The up or down status of the monitored devices
- A drill-down option that reveals the status of individual ports
- Device reload history
- RME can also display protocols that the devices are responding to, such as UDP, TCP, HTTP, TFTP, Telnet, and Simple Network Management Protocol (SNMP). RME has a browser-based interface that is integrated with other network-management tasks offered by the CiscoWorks Suite.

Summary

The topics covered in this chapter prepare the Netadmin for deploying network-monitoring systems to examine individual network devices and overall network availability. The Netadmins should be able to perform the following network-monitoring tasks:

- Deploy a Linux-based unified network-monitoring system to monitor network nodes, including Cisco devices, network servers, and related services such as HTTP, FTP, and SMTP
- Deploy a Windows-based unified network-monitoring system to monitor network nodes, including Cisco devices, network servers, and related services such as HTTP, FTP, and SMTP
- Use the notification feature of the network-monitoring systems to alert on-call technicians about network issues
- Use the reporting feature of network-monitoring systems to maintain SLAs

Table 5-3 provides a summary of the network-monitoring tools that this chapter covers.

Table 5-3 *List of Network-Monitoring Tools*

Tool	Function	Supported OS	Documentation Sources/Notes
Big Brother	Network monitoring through ICMP and TCP messages	Windows and Linux	• Home page: http://www.bb4.org • Help files in html file included with the installation (http://*BigBrother_ip*/bb/skins/eng/help/bb-help.html) • README and INSTALL files included with the tar file • Additional plug-ins and documentation at http://www.deadcat.net
BigSister	Network monitoring through ICMP and TCP messages (Big Brother clone)	Windows and Linux	• Home page: http://bigsister.graeff.com/ • Additional documentation: http://www.joerg.cc/html/bigsis/index.html
NMIS	Network monitoring using ICMP and SNMP	Linux	• Home page: http://www.sins.com.au/default.html • Comparatively complex setup procedure
Nagios/ NetSaint	Network monitoring using ICMP and SNMP	Linux	• Home page: http://www.nagios.org/ • Additional plug-ins: http://www.nagiosexchange.org • Comparatively complex setup procedure
OpenNMS	Network monitoring using ICMP and SNMP	Linux	• Home page: http://www.opennms.org/ • Comparatively complex setup procedure, Java-based client needs more resources
JFFNMS	Network monitoring through ICMP and TCP messages	Windows and Linux	Home page: http://www.jffnms.org/
SPONG	Network monitoring through ICMP and TCP messages	Linux	Home page: http://spong.sourceforge.net/

CHAPTER 6

Network Performance Monitoring

This chapter discusses performance monitoring and its importance for Netadmins. Based on the tasks involved in deploying a performance-monitoring system, this chapter is divided into the following parts:

- Performance-monitoring overview
- Deploying network performance-monitoring tools
- Configuring Cisco devices for performance monitoring

Performance-Monitoring Overview

Network performance monitoring is the process of collecting, storing, and analyzing network statistics. The most common parameters for monitoring network performance are as follows:

- **Throughput**, or network traffic accounting, is the amount of data flowing through an interface in a given amount of time. Throughput is typically expressed in units of kilobits per second (kbps), megabits per second (Mbps), and gigabits per second (Gbps). The value of throughput depends on various factors and is always changing. For example, the throughput of a Fast Ethernet interface can range from 0 to 100 Mbps.
- **Latency**, or delay, is the amount of time it takes a packet to traverse from source to destination. Latency is often expressed in milliseconds (ms). Round-trip time (RTT) is also referred to as latency.
- **Jitter** is the variation in latency and is important for real-time applications such as Voice over IP (VoIP).
- **Packet loss** is the number of packets lost during a measured time period.
- **CPU and memory utilization** of a network device are affected by the internal processes that are handling the data. A network denial of service (DoS) attack often causes CPU and memory utilization to increase. On the other hand, low or no CPU utilization can indicate that the device is not receiving data.
- **Hard drive space** on network servers gets filled quickly. Additionally, a lack of free space can affect the performance of operating systems.

Typically, performance-monitoring systems use the Simple Network Management Protocol (SNMP) to communicate with the monitored hosts. Using SNMP, the performance-monitoring system regularly polls the monitored hosts and collects performance-parameter samples. The samples are then stored in a central database for analysis and reporting, such as historical trending. The Netadmin can use these trending reports to do the following:

- Create a network performance baseline
- Predict or identify network performance issues
- Perform capacity planning for future needs
- Troubleshoot network issues and identify the source of outages

---

SNMP, defined in RFC 1157, is an application-layer protocol used for monitoring and managing network devices. SNMP, which works on the client/server model, uses UDP ports 161 and 162 for communications. Essentially, the SNMP framework defines the following four components:

- **SNMP manager**—A central control and monitoring system that uses SNMP commands to control SNMP clients. The SNMP manager, often called a network management system (NMS), can be a workstation or a server running the SNMP-capable network management application. The SNMP manager polls the SNMP clients to gather information.
- **SNMP agent**—An SNMP-capable client that can be managed by the SNMP manager. Network devices generally have embedded SNMP agents in the operating system. In addition to responding to polling by the SNMP manager, the client can arbitrarily send SNMP messages, called *SNMP traps.*
- **Management Information Base (MIB)**—A collection of parameters that can be managed by the SNMP manager. MIBs are ASCII text files that are defined in structured and standard format.
- **Object identifiers (OID)**—The objects in an MIB are organized and uniquely identified by OIDs that are defined by the Internet Engineering Task Force (IETF) and other organizations. Objects can refer to a physical device (such as a chassis or motherboard), software parameter (such as an IP address), or operational statistics (such as the number of packets passed or the temperature). OIDs can be expressed as numbers or names or can be mixed. Cisco Systems was assigned the OID of 9, so most OIDs for items that are specific to Cisco platforms start with 1.3.6.1.4.1.9.

Figure 6-1 illustrates the various components of SNMP and their operation.

Figure 6-1 *SNMP Operation*

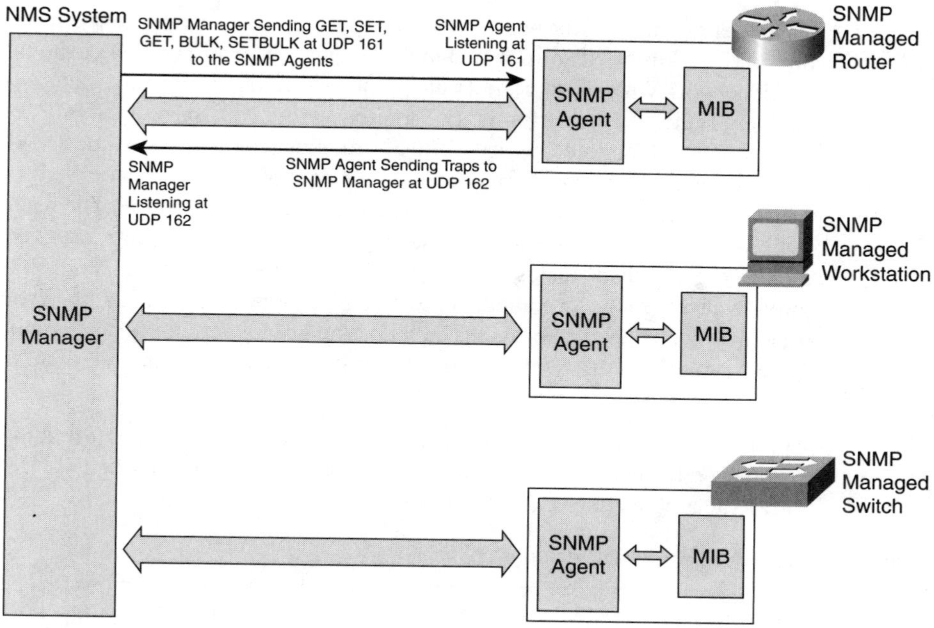

SNMP has three different versions. SNMPv1 is defined in RFC 1157, whereas SNMPv2c is defined in RFCs 1901, 1905, and 1906. SNMPv3, defined in RFCs 2273–2275, provides better security than previous versions because it features authentication and encryption. Both SNMPv1 and SNMPv2c use a text string for security. This text string, which should be defined on both the agent and the manager, is called *community*. Although SNMPv3 is more secure, SNMPv2C is the most widely used version.

The snmpwalk tool, available from http://www.net-snmp.org, is an excellent utility for querying the SNMP agent through the Windows or Linux command line.

Deploying Network Performance–Monitoring Tools

When deploying a performance-monitoring system, you can install performance-monitoring tools on a Linux or Windows computer. The host computer should be connected to the network with appropriate Transmission Control Protocol/Internet Protocol (TCP/IP) settings. Typically, the performance-monitoring tool consists of an SNMP-manager engine for polling the monitored devices. The SNMP manager also listens for SNMP traps sent by the monitored devices. Performance-monitoring tools also use custom scripts or plug-ins to collect other information that cannot be measured through SNMP. The results of SNMP polls, SNMP traps, and custom scripts are stored in an internal database. The performance-monitoring tool then creates trending reports from the database and publishes these reports through a web server. In comparison with the network-monitoring system (discussed in the previous chapter), which provides only host-up or -down status, a performance-monitoring system provides far more details, such as traffic flowing into and out of an interface or the CPU utilization on the router.

Although SNMP-based network-management systems are often referred to as NMSs, network performance–monitoring tools can also be loosely classified as NMSs. Figure 6-2 shows the architecture of a network performance–monitoring system.

Figure 6-2 *Network Performance–Monitoring System*

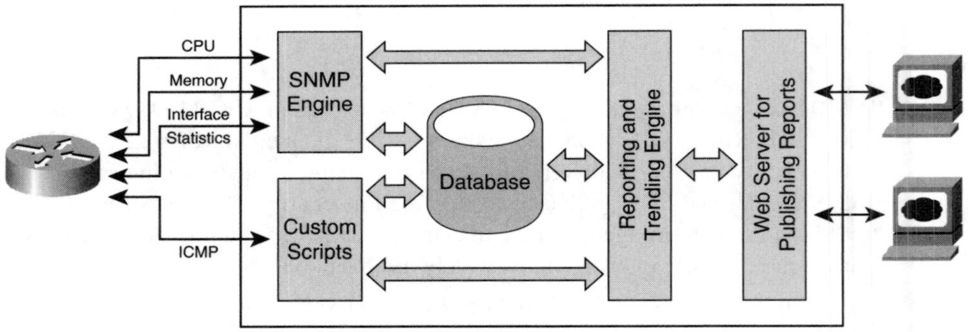

The following sections discuss deploying Linux- and Windows-based performance-monitoring tools based on the operating system used.

Deploying a Linux-Based Performance-Monitoring System—MRTG

The Multi-Router Traffic Grapher (MRTG), by Tobias Oetiker, is arguably one of the most popular open source tools used by the Cisco community. MRTG is an excellent tool for performance monitoring of network devices. Although the name suggests that MRTG is for routers, it can also monitor other network devices, including switches, firewalls, VPN concentrators, web servers, and so on. MRTG was originally developed as a Perl script to monitor the traffic load on router interfaces and provide a visual representation. Since then, the product has matured into a fully functional SNMP-based tool capable of monitoring any SNMP parameters in network devices. The internal architecture of MRTG consists of a collection of Perl scripts that query target SNMP agents. The results of the queries are logged in a database that generates graphic and HTML files that can be published by Apache or other web servers. Note that the MRTG reports only contain histogram graphs that depict the monitoring results over time intervals ranging from hourly to yearly periods. The MRTG reports do not provide other formats such as text, spreadsheets, or pie charts. Following are some features of MRTG:

- **Display**—Displays daily, weekly, monthly, and yearly histogram graphs through web pages. These web pages can be viewed in any web browser.
- **Database**—Stores all the data in a circular database that does not grow over time but still holds all the relevant information for the last two years. When the circular database is full, the oldest data is overwritten, thus keeping the size constant.
- **SNMP**—Uses SNMP to monitor device variables, including interface traffic through routers and switches, CPU utilization, and memory utilization. MRTG also provides plug-ins for monitoring non-SNMP variables such as network latency.
- **Configuration**—Features built-in configuration tools for quick-and-easy deployment. MRTG can also be easily customized for different network environments.
- **Support**—Enjoys the support of the worldwide user community and is under active development.

Figure 6-3 provides a sample of MRTG. The figure shows the Daily Graph for traffic flowing into and out of the Ethernet0 interface of Router-Dallas. The graph is created by MRTG using samples collected from the router at regular intervals. Although not included in the screenshot, by default, MRTG creates four separate histogram graphs for each monitored parameter.

Figure 6-3 *MRTG Sample Page*

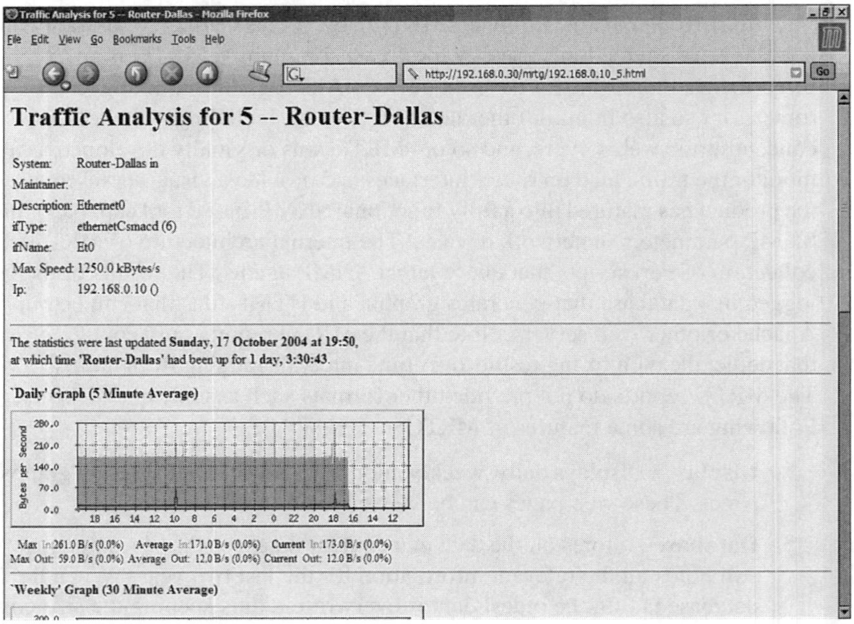

The histogram for the daily view is created by using samples collected every 5 minutes. The weekly graph is created by calculating a 30-minute average from the collected samples, while the monthly and yearly graphs use 2-hour averages and 1-day averages, respectively. Additional information at the bottom of each graph provides a snapshot of the maximum, average, and current value in absolute and percentage terms. For example, the daily graph in Figure 6-3 shows that the maximum traffic flowing in is 261 bytes per second. The 0.0% in parentheses indicates the value relative to the maximum speed of 1250.0 kilobytes per second (kBps) of the Ethernet interface, according to the following equation:

$$100 * (261/1{,}250{,}000) = 0.02088\%$$

Although not apparent in this text, different colors indicate different parameters within the graph. This particular graph shows the bytes per second flowing into and out of the Ethernet interface. The darker line (closer to the *x* axis of the graph) indicates the bytes per second flowing out of the interface, while the lighter shaded region (covering the middle part of the graph) indicates the bytes per second flowing into the interface.

Such views provide a quick snapshot of the overall performance of that particular interface (or the device on the associated network) and help to identify potential bottlenecks.

For deployment in a Linux environment, you must first install and configure MRTG according to your needs. You can then start running MRTG to monitor various devices. The following sections cover several of these tasks in detail. Additionally, for clarity, the configuration section is based on a sample Cisco network.

Installing MRTG

MRTG is available in source code for download at http://www.mrtg.org. For MRTG to function correctly, it requires the precompiled libraries listed in Table 6-1.

Table 6-1 *MRTG Prerequisites*

Package	Explanation	Home Page
Apache	Needed to display the graphical web pages generated by MRTG; comes precompiled with most Linux distributions.	http://www.apache.org
GCC	The GNU C compiler comes preinstalled in most Linux distributions.	http://gcc.gnu.org/
Perl	The MRTG needs version 5.005 or higher of Perl.	http://www.perl.com/
gd	The basic graph-drawing library for generating PNG images by the MRTG.	http://www.boutell.com/gd/
libpng	Required by gd to create PNG graphics.	http://www.libpng.org/pub/png/libpng.html
zlib	Required by libpng to compress the graphics files.	http://www.gzip.org/zlib

To install MRTG, follow these steps:

Step 1 Compile all the required libraries, as listed in Table 6-1.

Step 2 Download MRTG source code tar file from http://www.mrtg.org. This example uses MRTG version 2.10.15.

Step 3 Extract the source code using the following **tar** command:

```
linuxbox:~# tar -zxvf mrtg-2.10.15
```

Step 4 Change the directory to the uncompressed MRTG folder using the following command:

```
linuxbox:~# cd mrtg-2.10.15
```

Step 5 Launch the installation script using the **configure** command. You can optionally use the --**prefix** option to specify the destination directory. You should also specify the location of the libraries that MRTG depends on. The following code assumes that gd, zlib, and libpng are installed in the /usr/local/bin directory:

```
linuxbox:~/mrtg-2.10.15#./configure --prefix=/usr/local/bin \
          --with-gd=/usr/local/bin/gd       \
```

```
--with-z=/usr/local/bin/zlib     \
--with-png=/usr/local/bin/libpng
```

These installation steps are generic and should work for most Linux distributions. MRTG is also available as a precompiled package with many Linux distributions. Debian users can avoid the previous installation steps by using the **apt-get** command, as follows:

```
linuxbox:~# apt-get install mrtg
```

This command is a timesaver and provides a hassle-free method of deploying MRTG.

NOTE Linux users often spend too much time troubleshooting dependency issues when installing multiple libraries. Try to use the precompiled version of MRTG. The precompiled MRTG Debian packages are stable and suitable for use in Cisco environments.

Configuring the MRTG

MRTG is configured through the mrtg.cfg text file. This file contains the details of the network devices and their interfaces that are to be monitored by MRTG. Based on the contents of the mrtg.cfg file, MRTG generates graphs that illustrate the traffic pattern for each monitored interface. Although you can manually edit the mrtg.cfg file, MRTG includes a handy utility called cfgmaker. The cfgmaker tool provides a quick-and-easy way of populating the mrtg.cfg file with details of the monitored devices. However, cfgmaker can only help monitor the interface statistics. To monitor other parameters, such as CPU utilization, VPN sessions, or firewall connections, you must manually edit the mrtg.cfg file.

To simplify the learning and deployment process, the following sections first discuss the cfgmaker tool and demonstrate its use for creating a sample mrtg.cfg file. Next are the details regarding the mrtg.cfg file itself. Finally, you learn about the indexmaker utility.

Understanding the cfgmaker Tool

As previously mentioned, the purpose of cfgmaker is to create mrtg.cfg files on-the-fly. The cfgmaker tool queries each monitored host through SNMP, collects interface-related details, and generates the configuration for monitoring each discovered interface. The output of cfgmaker is ready for use within the mrtg.cfg file.

The default location of this tool is the /usr/bin/cfgmaker directory. The command syntax is as follows:

```
cfgmaker [options] [snmpstring@]router > destination_file
```

In this syntax, *router* can be the IP address or host name of the any SNMP-capable device, including routers or switches; *snmpstring* is the SNMP community configured on the monitored device. The SNMP community is used as a password by cfgmaker to poll the target hosts and collect information through SNMP. Multiple devices can be specified in a single instance. For a large number of devices, separate each entry using the backslash (\) character. By default, the output of cfgmaker is stdout, meaning that the output is displayed onscreen. The output should be redirected to a file for MRTG to use, as indicated by the > *destination_file* option within the syntax.

Figure 6-4 shows the network of ABC Investments. The Netadmin is using the Linux machine to monitor the performance of Cisco devices using SNMP.

Figure 6-4 *ABC Investments—Network Monitoring*

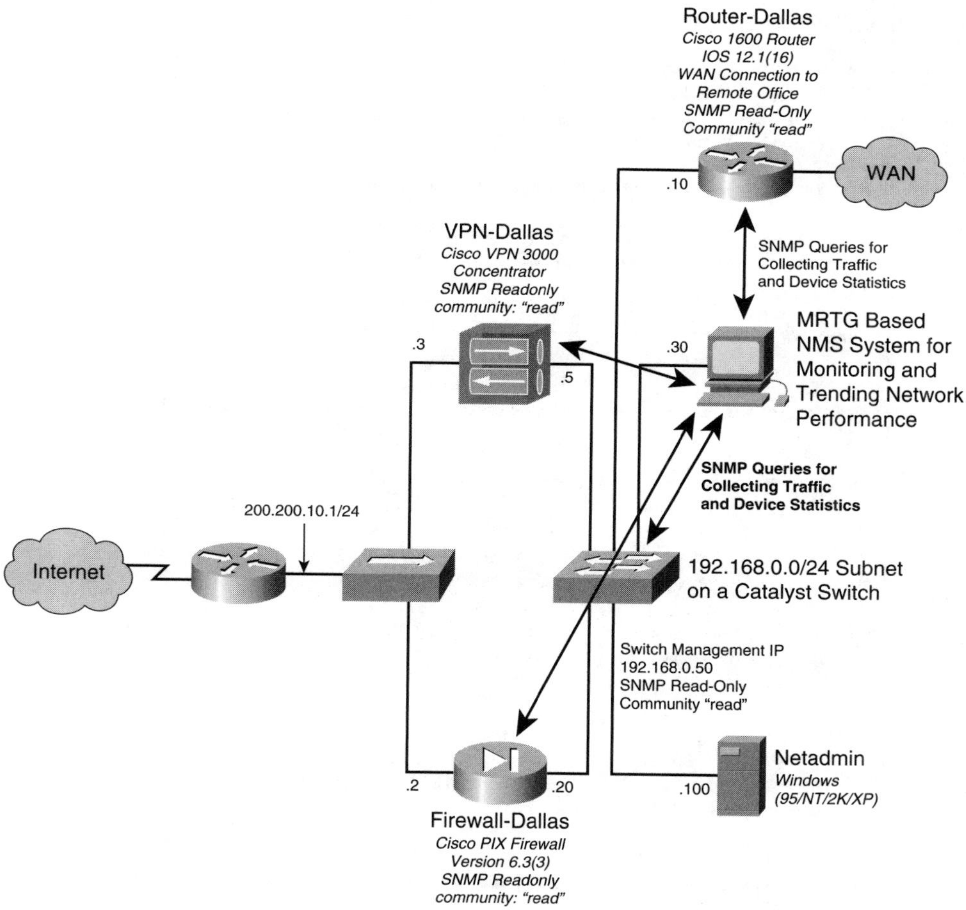

Example 6-1 shows the use of cfgmaker to create the /etc/mrtg.cfg file for the LAN devices of ABC Investments. The example uses the IP address of the monitored device. You can also specify the host name if the MRTG server can resolve the host name through the Domain Name System (DNS). The example also shows the contents of the resultant file. Note that lines starting with a hash mark or pound sign (#) are treated as comments.

Example 6-1 *Sample mrtg.cfg File*

```
linuxbox~# cfgmaker read@192.168.0.5 read@192.168.0.10 read@192.168.0.20  > /etc/
mrtg.cfg
linuxbox~# cat /etc/mrtg.cfg
# Created by
# /usr/bin/cfgmaker read@192.168.0.5 read@192.168.0.10 read@192.168.0.20

### Global Config Options
#  for Debian
WorkDir: /var/www/mrtg
#  or for NT
# WorkDir: c:\mrtgdata
### Global Defaults
#  to get bits instead of bytes and graphs growing to the right
# Options[_]: growright, bits

######################################################################
# System: 1
# Description: Cisco Systems, Inc./VPN 3000 Concentrator Version 4.1.3.Rel built by
vmurphy on Apr 12 2004 01:57:36
# Contact:
# Location:
######################################################################


### Interface 1 >> Descr: '' ¦ Name: '' ¦ Ip: '192.168.0.5' ¦ Eth: '00-90-a4-00-4c-
5c' ###

Target[192.168.0.5_1]: 1:read@192.168.0.5:
SetEnv[192.168.0.5_1]: MRTG_INT_IP="192.168.0.5" MRTG_INT_DESCR=""
MaxBytes[192.168.0.5_1]: 12500000
Title[192.168.0.5_1]: Traffic Analysis for 1 -- 1
PageTop[192.168.0.5_1]: <H1>Traffic Analysis for 1 -- 1</H1>
 <TABLE>
   <TR><TD>System:</TD>     <TD>1 in </TD></TR>
   <TR><TD>Maintainer:</TD> <TD></TD></TR>
   <TR><TD>Description:</TD><TD>  </TD></TR>
   <TR><TD>ifType:</TD>     <TD>ethernetCsmacd (6)</TD></TR>
   <TR><TD>ifName:</TD>     <TD></TD></TR>
   <TR><TD>Max Speed:</TD>  <TD>12.5 MBytes/s</TD></TR>
   <TR><TD>Ip:</TD>         <TD>192.168.0.5 ()</TD></TR>
 </TABLE>


######################################################################
# System: Router-Dallas
# Description: Cisco Internetwork Operating System Software
#        IOS (tm) 1600 Software (C1600-OSY56I-L), Version 12.1(16), RELEASE SOFTWARE
(fc1)
#        Copyright  1986-2002 by cisco Systems, Inc.
#        Compiled Mon 08-Jul-02 18:51 by kellythw
# Contact:
# Location:
######################################################################
```

Example 6-1 *Sample mrtg.cfg File (Continued)*

```
### Interface 5 >> Descr: 'Ethernet0' | Name: 'Et0' | Ip: '192.168.0.10' | Eth: '00-
50-73-21-d0-67' ###

Target[192.168.0.10_5]: 5:read@192.168.0.10:
SetEnv[192.168.0.10_5]: MRTG_INT_IP="192.168.0.10" MRTG_INT_DESCR="Ethernet0"
MaxBytes[192.168.0.10_5]: 1250000
Title[192.168.0.10_5]: Traffic Analysis for 5 -- Router-Dallas
PageTop[192.168.0.10_5]: <H1>Traffic Analysis for 5 -- Router-Dallas</H1>
 <TABLE>
   <TR><TD>System:</TD>     <TD>Router-Dallas in </TD></TR>
   <TR><TD>Maintainer:</TD> <TD></TD></TR>
   <TR><TD>Description:</TD><TD>Ethernet0  </TD></TR>
   <TR><TD>ifType:</TD>     <TD>ethernetCsmacd (6)</TD></TR>
   <TR><TD>ifName:</TD>     <TD>Et0</TD></TR>
   <TR><TD>Max Speed:</TD>  <TD>1250.0 kBytes/s</TD></TR>
   <TR><TD>Ip:</TD>         <TD>192.168.0.10 ()</TD></TR>
 </TABLE>


######################################################################
# System: Firewall-Dallas
# Description: Cisco PIX Firewall Version 6.3(3)
#
# Contact: SPOPE
# Location: DALLAS
######################################################################



### Interface 2 >> Descr: 'PIX Firewall 'inside' interface' | Name: '' | Ip:
'192.168.0.20' | Eth: '00-07-50-57-e2-69' ###

Target[192.168.0.20_2]: 2:read@192.168.0.20:
SetEnv[192.168.0.20_2]: MRTG_INT_IP="192.168.0.20" MRTG_INT_DESCR="PIX Firewall
'inside' interface"
MaxBytes[192.168.0.20_2]: 12500000
Title[192.168.0.20_2]: Traffic Analysis for 2 -- Firewall-Dallas
PageTop[192.168.0.20_2]: <H1>Traffic Analysis for 2 -- Firewall-Dallas</H1>
 <TABLE>
   <TR><TD>System:</TD>     <TD>Firewall-Dallas in DALLAS</TD></TR>
   <TR><TD>Maintainer:</TD> <TD>SPOPE</TD></TR>
   <TR><TD>Description:</TD><TD>PIX Firewall 'inside' interface  </TD></TR>
   <TR><TD>ifType:</TD>     <TD>ethernetCsmacd (6)</TD></TR>
   <TR><TD>ifName:</TD>     <TD></TD></TR>
   <TR><TD>Max Speed:</TD>  <TD>12.5 MBytes/s</TD></TR>
   <TR><TD>Ip:</TD>         <TD>192.168.0.20 ()</TD></TR>
 </TABLE>
```

TIP By default, cfgmaker generates the configuration for all the interfaces but comments out the configurations for inactive (or administratively down) interfaces. Use the **--no-down** option with cfgmaker to override this behavior. Additionally, cfgmaker selects the interfaces by their number, which can change because of the addition or removal of modules. This change can cause MRTG to misinterpret the contents of the mrtg.cfg file. In such cases, cfgmaker provides the **--ifref descr** option, to select the interfaces by their description, or the **--ifref ip** option, to select interfaces by IP addresses.

The cfgmaker utility is great for setting up a basic MRTG system that can monitor traffic flowing into and out of interfaces. Readers interested in only setting up such a basic MRTG system can skip the next section, which covers the details of the mrtg.cfg file.

Understanding the mrtg.cfg File

As previously discussed, cfgmaker has a major limitation in that it can only create mrtg.cfg files to monitor interface traffic. To monitor other SNMP variables, such as CPU and memory utilization, router uptime, and chassis environments, Netadmins should manually edit the mrtg.cfg file. However, before editing, you must have a thorough understanding of the various options that are used within the mrtg.cfg file. The default location of the mrtg.cfg file for the precompiled Debian package is /etc/mrtg.cfg. The mrtg.cfg file uses predefined keywords to specify various monitoring options. The keywords must be specified at the beginning of the line. Also, lines starting with a hash mark or pound sign (#) are treated as comments. Table 6-2 provides a partial list of global keywords that affect the default behavior of MRTG.

Table 6-2 *Mrtg.cfg Global Keywords*

Keyword	Explanation	Example
Workdir	Specifies the target location for creating log files and the web pages. For the Debian package, the default location is /var/www/mrtg.	`workdir: /var/www/mrtg`
Refresh	Instructs the browser to reload the page; the default is **300** seconds (5 minutes).	`Refresh: 600`
Interval	Indicates the frequency at which the MRTG is run; the minimum and default are **300** seconds (5 minutes).	`Interval: 600`

Table 6-2 *Mrtg.cfg Global Keywords (Continued)*

Keyword	Explanation	Example

RunAsDaemon	Enables the MRTG to run as a daemon; improves performance because configuration files are loaded only once. When using this option, set the interval to a suitable value and run the MRTG as a nonroot user.	`RunAsDaemon: Yes`
		`Interval:`
		`mrtg --user=muser --group=muser mrtg.cfg`

As mentioned in the introduction to the MRTG, all the reports generated by the MRTG are histogram graphs. The generation and display of these graphs can be customized by using various keywords in the mrtg.cfg file. Additional keywords within the mrtg.cfg file control the MRTG properties, such as the web-page formats, SNMP variables, and even external scripts for pulling non-SNMP statistics. Table 6-3 provides a partial list of these keywords that are helpful in customizing monitoring properties and graphs generated by the MRTG.

Table 6-3 *mrtg.cfg Per-Node Keywords*

Keyword	Explanation	Example

Name	Each node that is monitored by MRTG must be identified by a unique name. This name must be appended to each parameter that belongs to the same target. The name is also used to identify the generated web pages, log files, and images for this target. The format is as follows:
	Keyword [*node-name*]: *values*
		`Target[RTR-DALLAS]: 5:read@192.168.0.10:`
		`SetEnv[RTR-DALLAS]: MRTG_INT_IP="192.168.0.10" MRTG_INT_DESCR="Ethernet0"`
		`MaxBytes[RTR-DALLAS]: 1250000`

Target	Specifies the target node to be monitored by the MRTG. The basic format is as follows: **Target**[*interface*]:*snmp-string@router* Advanced formats allow you to specify explicit OIDs, MIB variables, interfaces by IP, names, types, or descriptions and even run an external script for non-SNMP parameters.	`Target[192.168.0.20_2]: 2:read@192.168.0.20:`
MaxBytes	Specifies the maximum allowed value for the monitored variables; also used in calculating the Y range for unscaled graphs. Calculated by dividing the interface bandwidth (in bits per second) by 8 to generate a value in bytes per second. For example, for a T1 line, the bandwidth is 1.544 MBps, or 1,544,000 / 8 = 193,000 bytes per second. If a number greater than MaxBytes is returned, it is ignored.	`MaxBytes[RTR-DALLAS-T1]:9600`

continues

Table 6-3 *mrtg.cfg Per-Node Keywords (Continued)*

Keyword	Explanation	Example
AbsMax	Used to monitor links, such as Frame Relay, that can handle more traffic than specified by the MaxBytes value; without AbsMax, MRTG ignores values greater than MaxBytes.	AbsMax[192.168.0.10]: 19200
Unscaled	Suppresses the default behavior of vertically scaling each graph to display actual data, even if it is very small compared to MaxBytes.	Unscaled[192.168.0.10]: ym
Title	Adds a title to the generated HTML page.	Title[192.168.0.10]: Traffic Accounting for Ethernet page
PageTop	Adds text at the top of the generated HTML page.	PageTop[r1]: <H1>Stats for our ISDN Line</H1>
RouterUptime	Displays the uptime of the monitored router.	RouterUptime[RTR-DALLAS]: public@192.168.0.10
WithPeak	Instructs the MRTG to display the peak 5-minute values in the weekly, monthly, and yearly graphs.	WithPeak[myrouter]: ym
Suppress	Suppresses any of the four graphs that are generated by default.	Suppress[myrouter]: y
XSize and **YSize**	Specifies the size of the MRTG graph; the default is XSize 400 by YSize 100 pixels wide. XSize must be between 20 and 600; YSize must be greater than 20.	XSize[myrouter]: 300 YSize[myrouter]: 300
Colours	Overrides the default color scheme; requires all four colors to be specified. Note the spelling of the keyword Colour because the MRTG originated in Europe.	Colours[myrouter]: GREEN#00eb0c,BLUE#1000ff,DARK GREEN#006600,VIOLET#ff00ff
YLegend	The *y*-axis label of the graph.	YLegend[myrouter]: Bits per Second
ShortLegend	The units string (used for Max, Average, and Current); the default is b/s (bits per second).	ShortLegend[myrouter]: b/s
Legend[1234IO]	The strings for the colour legend.	Legend1[myrouter]: Incoming Traffic in Bits per Second Legend2[myrouter]: Outgoing Traffic in Bits per Second Legend3[myrouter]: Maximal 5 Minute Incoming Traffic Legend4[myrouter]: Maximal 5 Minute Outgoing Traffic LegendI[myrouter]: In: LegendO[myrouter]: Out:

Table 6-3 *mrtg.cfg Per-Node Keywords (Continued)*

Keyword	Explanation	Example
Options	• The Options keyword allows you to set the following additional switches: • **growright**—Instructs the graph to grow to the right side instead of the default left side. • **bits**—Displays the values in bits (by multiplying by 8), instead of the default bytes. • **perminute**—Displays the values in per minute (by multiplying by 60) instead of the default per second. • **perhour**—Displays the values in per hour (by multiplying by 3600) instead of the default in per second. • **gauge**—Monitors variables such as CPU load, memory, and temperature, where the values are absolute integers rather than incrementing counters. • **nopercent**—Specifies to not print usage percentages. • **unknaszero**—Logs unknown data as 0s instead of the default of repeating the last value seen.	• Options[myrouter]: growright, bits, gauge

In Table 6-3, the Target keyword is the most important local directive of the mrtg.cfg file. Table 6-4 provides a list of commonly used Target options.

Table 6-4 *Target Keyword—Options*

Option	Explanation	Example
Basic	The basic format is *port:community@router* Replace *port* by the interface-number, *community* by the router SNMP read-only string, and *router* by IP address of the router.	`Target[myrouter]: 2:public@192.168.0.10`
Reversing	To swap incoming traffic as outgoing and vice versa, use the minus sign (-) in front of the **Target** description.	`Target[myrouter]: -1:public@192.168.0.10`

continues

Table 6-4 *Target Keyword—Options (Continued)*

Option	Explanation	Example
Explicit OIDs	Used to pull specific SNMP variables from monitored devices; the syntax is as follows: *OID1&OID2:community@router*	To monitor the two pools of free memory (proc and io) on a Cisco router, use the following format: Target[myrouter]: 1.3.6.1.4.1.9.9.48.1.1.1.6.1&1.3.6.1.4.1.9.9.48.1.1.1.6.2:public@192.168.0.10
MIB variables	Instead of using OIDs, MRTG also allows you to specify the MIB variable names that are already known to the MRTG through the /usr/shar/doc/mrtg/mibhelp.txt file.	To use the **ifInErrors** and **ifOutErrors** variables, the format is as follows: Target[myrouter]: ifInErrors.1&ifOutErrors.1:public@192.168.0.10
External monitoring scripts	To monitor non-SNMP variables such as latency, specify the path of the external script enclosed in backticks (`).	Target[myrouter]: `/usr/local/bin/myping 192.168.0.10` Note the use of the backticks (`), not apostrophes ('), around the command.

Now that you have a better understanding of the various components of the mrtg.cfg file, this section provides several templates that can be added to this file. These templates help Netadmins to monitor some of the common parameters, such as memory and CPU utilization, of Cisco IOS–based routers and switches, VPN 3000 Series concentrators, and PIX Firewalls. Note that these templates do not come preinstalled with MRTG installation files, but they are included here for Netadmins. You can use each of these templates by replacing *community* by the read-only SNMP community string and *host* by the IP address of your device. Additionally, some of the templates include embedded comments for specific information.

You can add the following templates to the mrtg.cfg file:

- Router CPU utilization

```
# Router CPU load
# Replace community@host by information specific to your IOS device
Target[cpu.1]:1.3.6.1.4.1.9.2.1.58.0&1.3.6.1.4.1.9.2.1.58.0:community@host
 RouterUptime[cpu.1]: community@host
 MaxBytes[cpu.1]: 100
 Title[cpu.1]: CPU LOAD
 PageTop[cpu.1]: <H1>CPU Load %</H1>
 Unscaled[cpu.1]: ymwd
 ShortLegend[cpu.1]: %
 XSize[cpu.1]: 380
 YSize[cpu.1]: 100
 YLegend[cpu.1]: CPU Utilization
 Legend1[cpu.1]: CPU Utilization in % (Load)
 Legend2[cpu.1]: CPU Utilization in % (Load)
 Legend3[cpu.1]:
 Legend4[cpu.1]:
 LegendI[cpu.1]:
 LegendO[cpu.1]:  Usage
 Options[cpu.1]: gauge
#End ####################################
```

- Router memory utilization

```
#Router Memory utilization
# Replace community@host by information specific to your IOS device
Target[rtr-mem]: 1.3.6.1.4.1.9.2.1.8.0&1.3.6.1.4.1.9.2.1.8.0:community@router
Directory[rtr-mem]: memory
WithPeak[rtr-mem]: wmy
YLegend[rtr-mem]: Memory Utilization
ShortLegend[rtr-mem]: Used
# replace 16384 by  the value of your Router RAM,  below
# use "show version" to determine the RAM
MaxBytes[rtr-mem]: 16384
Options[rtr-mem]: gauge, growright
Unscaled[rtr-mem]: dwmy
# replace 16384 by  the value of your Router RAM,  below
AbsMax[rtr-mem]: 16384
Title[rtr-mem]: Router
Colours[rtr-mem]: GREEN#00eb0c,BLUE#1000ff,BLUE#1000ff,VIOLET#ff00ff
Legend1[rtr-mem]: Memory Utilized
Legend2[rtr-mem]:
Legend3[rtr-mem]: " "
Legend4[rtr-mem]:
LegendI[rtr-mem]:  Memory:
LegendO[rtr-mem]:
PageTop[rtr-mem]: <H1> Memory Utilization </H1>
#End ####################################
```

- PIX Firewall CPU utilization

```
#PIX CPU Utilization
# Replace community@host by information specific to your PIX
Target[pix-cpu]:
 1.3.6.1.4.1.9.9.109.1.1.1.1.8.1&1.3.6.1.4.1.9.9.109.1.1.1.1.6.1:community@pix_
 IP
MaxBytes[pix-cpu]: 100
Title[pix-cpu]: CPU Utilization
PageTop[pix-cpu]: <H1>PIX CPU Utilization</H1>
Options[pix-cpu]: gauge
Unscaled[pix-cpu]: dwmy
YLegend[pix-cpu]: % CPU
ShortLegend[pix-cpu]: % CPU
Legend1[pix-cpu]: Five Minute CPU Utilization
Legend2[pix-cpu]: Five Second CPU Utilization
Legend3[pix-cpu]: Peak CPU Util, Min
Legend4[pix-cpu]: Peak CPU Util, Sec
LegendI[pix-cpu]: Min
LegendO[pix-cpu]: Sec
#End ####################################
```

- PIX Firewall memory utilization

```
#PIX Memory utilization
# Replace community@host by information specific to your PIX
Target[PIX_mem]:
 1.3.6.1.4.1.9.9.48.1.1.1.5.1&1.3.6.1.4.1.9.9.48.1.1.1.6.1.1:community@pix_IP
YLegend[pix_mem]: Used and Free
ShortLegend[pix_mem]: Bytes
#Specify the RAM in the PIX below
# If not sure use the "show memory" command
Maxbytes[pix_mem]: 16777216
Options[pix_mem]: gauge
Unscaled[pix_mem]: dwmy
Title[pix_mem]: Memory
Legend1[pix_mem]: Free memory
Legend2[pix_mem]: Used memory
```

```
Legend3[pix_mem]: Peak Free memory
Legend4[pix_mem]: Peak Used memory
LegendI[pix_mem]: Free
LegendO[pix_mem]: Used
PageTop[pix_mem]: <H1>PIX Memory</H1>
#End ##################################
```

- PIX Firewall active connections

```
# PIX Connections
# Replace community@host by information specific to your PIX
Target[pix_conn]:
 1.3.6.1.4.1.9.9.147.1.2.2.2.1.5.40.6&1.3.6.1.4.1.9.9.147.1.2.2.2.1.5.40.7:comm
 unity@pix_IP
# Specify the maximum connection supported by PIX license
MaxBytes[pix_conn]: 1000
Title[pix_cpS]: Connections in Use
PageTop[pix_conn]: <H1>Current PIX Connections</H1>
Options[pix_conn]: gauge
Unscaled[pix_conn]: dwmy
YLegend[pix_conn]: # Connections in Use
ShortLegend[pix_conn]: # Conn in Use
Legend1[pix_conn]: Conn in Use
Legend2[pix_conn]: Max Conn
Legend3[pix_conn]: Peak Conn in Use
Legend4[pix_conn]: Peak Max Conn
LegendI[pix_conn]: In Use
LegendO[pix_conn]: Max
#End ##################################
```

- VPN concentrator CPU utilization and sessions

```
# VPN 3000 - CPU & Session
# Replace community@host by information specific to your VPN concentrator
Target[VPN.cpu]:
 1.3.6.1.4.1.3076.2.1.2.25.1.2.0&1.3.6.1.4.1.3076.2.1.2.17.1.9.0:community@VPNB
 OX_IP
MaxBytes[VPN.cpu]: 100
Title[VPN.cpu]: CPU and Sessions -- VPN 3005
PageTop[VPN.cpu]: <H1>CPU and Sessions - VPN 3000</H1>
Options[VPN.cpu]: gauge, nopercent
XSize[VPN.cpu]: 380
YSize[VPN.cpu]: 100
YLegend[VPN.cpu]: CPU / Sessions
ShortLegend[VPN.cpu]:  
Legend1[VPN.cpu]: CPU Usage gauge 
Legend2[VPN.cpu]: Active sessions 
LegendI[VPN.cpu]: CPU Usage (%)  
LegendO[VPN.cpu]: Active sessions 
#End ##################################
```

Understanding the indexmaker Tool

When monitoring multiple interfaces and variables, the number of HTML pages can get very large. Fortunately, MRTG provides a tool, called indexmaker, that parses the mrtg.cfg file and generates a summary page in HTML format. The single-page summary provides the daily view of the histogram graph that depicts the current status of all the monitored parameters. Moreover, each graph contains embedded hyperlinks that, when clicked, take you to the page that contains the daily, weekly, monthly, and yearly views of the histogram graphs. The command syntax is **indexmaker** [*options*] **mrtg.cfg**. Similar to cfgmaker, indexmaker also outputs the result to the screen. You should redirect the output to a file using the **>** option. Example 6-2 shows the command that creates the summary page index.html from the /etc/mrtg.cfg file.

Example 6-2 *Indexmaker Tool*

```
linuxbox:~# indexmaker /etc/mrtg.cfg > /var/www/mrtg/index.html
linuxbox:~# cat /var/www/mrtg/index.html
<!DOCTYPE html PUBLIC "-//W3C//DTD HTML 4.0 Transitional//EN">
<HTML>
<HEAD>
    <TITLE>MRTG Index Page</TITLE>
    <META HTTP-EQUIV="Refresh" CONTENT="300">
    <META HTTP-EQUIV="Cache-Control" content="no-cache">
    <META HTTP-EQUIV="Pragma" CONTENT="no-cache">
    <META HTTP-EQUIV="Expires" CONTENT="Sat, 16 Oct 2004 07:56:58 GMT">
</HEAD>
# --- output truncated ---
```

The resulting web page from the index.html code (generated in the previous example) is illustrated in Figure 6-5.

Figure 6-5 *Output of index.html*

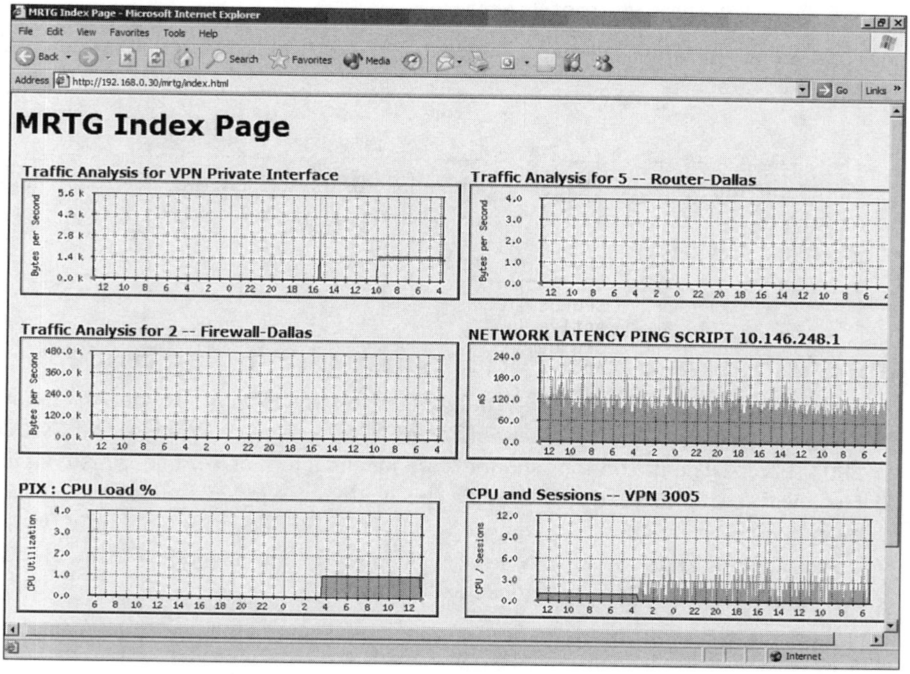

Running MRTG

Before running MRTG, test the mrtg.cfg file by using the following mrtg script:

```
linuxbox:~#/usr/bin/mrtg /etc/mrtg.cfg
```

Note that the first two instances of running MRTG will generate error messages regarding the missing log files.

After successfully testing the mrtg.cfg file, you can automate MRTG process using cron, which is a Linux utility that periodically runs specified tasks in the background. Crontab is a file that contains the schedule of cron entries to be run and the specified times. The steps for running MRTG through cron are as follows:

Step 1 Create a text file called mrtgcron that contains the command to run MRTG at an interval of 5 minutes. The command syntax is as follows:

```
0-55/5 * * * * /usr/bin/mrtg /etc/mrtg/cfg --logging /var/log/mrtg
```

This command is based on the assumption that the MRTG executable script is located in the /usr/bin directory and that the mrtg.cfg file is located in the /etc directory.

Step 2 Use the **crontab** *<filename>* command to update the system cron with new job, as follows:

```
linuxbox:~# crontab mrtgcron
```

These steps run MRTG every 5 minutes, poll the devices listed in the mrtg.cfg file, and update the graphs.

NOTE By default, the MRTG package for Debian installs the script in the /etc/cron.d/ directory for running the MRTG program daily every 5 minutes. MRTG Debian package users can ignore the previous steps.

Deploying a Windows-Based Performance-Monitoring System—MRTG

Because MRTG also comes in a Windows version, the Netadmin can easily deploy it on a Windows machine. The Windows version of MRTG supports Windows NT, XP, 2000, and 2003 servers. The file options and tools are identical to those of the Linux counterpart. However, several minor differences are specific to the Windows environment. These differences are covered in the following steps. MRTG in Windows requires fully functional installations of Perl and web servers to work correctly. The general guidelines for deploying a Windows-based MRTG system are as follows:

Step 1 Install Perl for Windows from http://www.activeperl.com/.

Step 2 Install the IIS web server using the **Add/Remove Programs** icon in the Windows Control Panel.

Step 3 Create a folder for MRTG in the home directory of the IIS web server. For example, if the home directory points to d:\inetpub\wwwroot, the new folder would be d:\inetpub\wwwroot\mrtg.

Step 4 Download and unzip the Windows version of MRTG files from http://www.mrtg.org. Copy the unzipped archives to a folder such as d:\mrtg. By default, MRTG stores the Perl scripts, such as mrtg, cfgmaker, and indexmaker, in the \mrtg\bin directory.

Step 5 Use the cfgmaker Perl script to create the mrtg.cfg file. The command syntax is as follows:

```
perl cfgmaker [options] [community@]router1 [[options]
[community@]router2 ... ]
```

Note the use of the keyword **perl**. In this example, cfgmaker is used to create the mrtg.cfg file for host 192.168.0.10. The host is preconfigured to use the text string **read** as the SNMP community string for replying to SNMP queries, as follows:

```
d:\mrtg\bin>perl cfgmaker  read@192.168.0.10  > mrtg.cfg
```

Step 6 After creating the mrtg.cfg file, edit the file to add Windows-specific parameters. These parameters help MRTG to determine the location of the working directory, log files, HTML pages, and so on. Edit the file using the following code:

```
# the webserver home directory is "d:\inetpub\wwwroot\"
Workdir: d:\inetpub\wwwroot\mrtg\
Htmldir: d:\inetpub\wwwroot\mrtg\
Imagedir: d:\inetpub\wwwroot\mrtg\
Logdir: d:\inetpub\wwwroot\mrtg\
# specify the location of mrtg icons
# default location is under "\mrtg\images"
Icondir: d:\mrtg\images
# MRTG should be run as daemon after every 5 minutes
RunAsDaemon: Yes
Interval: 5
```

Step 7 Use the indexmaker script to create index files for all the monitored nodes. The syntax is as follows:

```
perl indexmaker [options] [.cfg file]
```

Note the use of the keyword **perl**. This example creates the index.html file in the d:\inetpub\wwwroot\mrtg directory using the d:\mrtg\bin\mrtg.cfg file. The syntax is as follows:

```
C:\mrtg\bin>perl indexmaker mrtg.cfg >
d:\inetpub\wwwroot\mrtg\index.html
```

Step 8 Use the following syntax to run MRTG from the command line:

```
perl mrtg [config file]
```

Based on this syntax, the following command illustrates MRTG being executed from the command line using the mrtg.cfg file:

```
d:\mrtg\bin> perl mrtg mrtg.cfg
```

TIP To run MRTG in the background, use the following command, as suggested by MRTG website:

```
d:\mrtg\bin> start /Dc:\mrtg\bin wperl mrtg --logging=eventlog mrtg.cfg
```

You can also use Microsoft's RunsAsService tool to run MRTG as a background service.

Performance and Scalability Enhancements

MRTG uses flat-file databases to store its results. Also, every time the database is updated, new HTML and graphic pages are generated, creating high CPU utilization and disk activity. These factors contribute to the performance and scalability limitations of MRTG; the most notable limitations are as follows:

- **Number of monitored notes**—A maximum of 50 to 200 nodes, depending on the hardware and the number of interfaces monitored per node
- **Interval of data collection**—A minimum of 5 minutes between successive data collections

Additionally, MRTG can only display two variables in a single graph.

When monitoring a large number of nodes, you can use one of the following two options:

- Integrate MRTG with RRDTool
- Replace MRTG with other applications, such as Cricket or Cacti

RRDTool

RRDTool, an acronym for Round Robin Database Tool, is a fixed-size database tool with the capability to generate graphs. It was created by Tobias Oetiker, the author of MRTG. RRDTool acts as a database and graphing back end. RRDTool can be integrated into MRTG for improved performance, reduced data-collection intervals, and better graphs. However, after adding RRDTool, MRTG (version 2.*x*) also needs an external script to generate HTML pages. According to the author, RRDTool will be fully integrated in MRTG version 3.

Cricket

Cricket, according to its author, Jeff Allen, is the MRTG on steroids. Cricket can easily monitor more than 50 nodes, providing a significant performance improvement over MRTG. Cricket also uses RRDTool as its back-end component. Although Cricket is similar to MRTG, the configuration files are not compatible. Cricket provides the **config-tree** command to apply configuration parameters in a hierarchical manner to the child objects. This makes it comparatively easy to manage a large number of monitored devices. Cricket enjoys community-wide support and can be downloaded from http://cricket.sourceforge.net.

Figure 6-6 shows a sample screen shot of traffic flow through the Fast Ethernet interface of the host Router-NewYork. Notice the similarity of the graphs to those generated by MRTG. Also, in the upper-right corner, Cricket includes a link for generating various views, such as daily, weekly, monthly, and yearly.

Figure 6-6 *Cricket Sample Page*

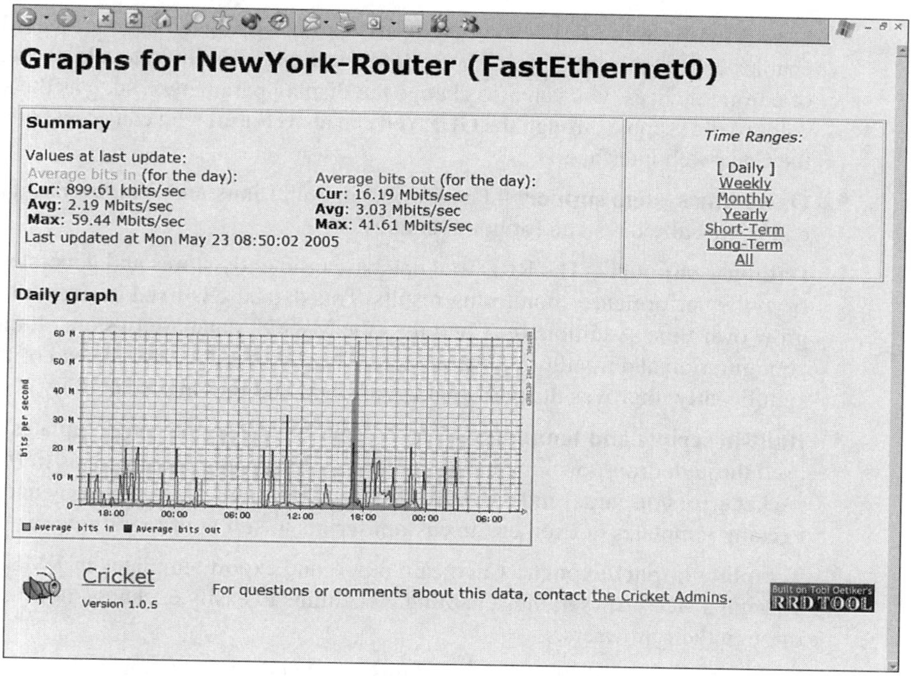

Cricket has been further enhanced into another product called Percival, which can be downloaded from http://percival.sourceforge.net. According to the developers of Percival, it can monitor 22,000 interfaces within a polling interval of 300 seconds.

Deploying a Windows-Based Performance-Monitoring System—Cacti

Cacti, available at http://www.cacti.net, is another performance-monitoring tool that is based on the original work of MRTG. Similar to MRTG, Cacti creates HTML reports that contain histogram graphs. Unlike its predecessor, Cacti graphs can be customized on-the-fly by using drop-down menus.

Cacti periodically polls and collects performance-monitoring data from network devices through built-in SNMP scripts. The Cacti architecture consists of the RRDTool and MySQL database back ends for storing the monitoring data and creating graphs. However, the biggest advantage of using Cacti rather than other tools is its web-based graphical user interface (GUI). This allows complete administration of Cacti with no knowledge of its internal configuration files. After the initial installation and some manual tweaking, routine administration of Cacti can be done by IT staff with basic Windows and web-browser skills. This feature is important in environments that need better monitoring tools but have IT personnel with only basic skills and little (or no) Linux knowledge. Some other useful features of Cacti are as follows:

- **User-friendly web GUI**—The easy-to-use and intuitive web browser–based GUI enables complete configuration and administration. In addition to adding, removing, or editing devices, you can also change the display parameters, such as the size and color of the graphs, through the GUI. You can also control who can access and modify the Cacti web interface.
- **Operating system support**—Cacti works in both Linux and Windows, and the front end is virtually the same for both versions.
- **Database support**—The RRDTool database efficiently stores and generates graphs from the performance-monitoring results. This database is fixed in size and does not grow over time. Additionally, Cacti uses the MySQL database to store all the configuration and monitoring parameters. The use of a database instead of text files significantly improves the performance of Cacti and provides scalability.
- **Built-in scripts and templates**—The built-in SNMP scripts and templates can be used through drop-down menus to monitor various parameters such as traffic flow, packet errors/discards, and CPU utilization. Furthermore, you can copy and modify existing templates or even create custom scripts to suit your requirements.
- **Template import/export**—Cacti can import and export templates in XML format through a web browser, thus enabling Netadmins to easily exchange new templates through their browsers.
- **Support**—The product website contains detailed documentation and includes a user forum. The user forum is a good source of community support, and most common issues can be resolved by referring to the forum.

The following sections cover the details of deploying Cacti on a Windows machine. Note that with the exception of the installation procedure and location of the system files, the discussion is equally applicable to deploying Cacti on Linux machines.

Installing Cacti

Cacti is ideally suited for deployment in Windows-based (read click-n-run) environments but requires significant installation efforts. Cacti needs the Windows version of the following third-party applications or tools to run correctly:

- **IIS web server**, to publish the graphic reports in HTML format and provide the Cacti GUI console; or **Apache web server**, available at http://www.apache.org
- **MySQL database** to store the configuration tables; available at http://www.mysql.com
- **PHP** for scripting; available at http://www.php.net
- **RRDTool** to efficiently store the performance-monitoring results in a compact database; available at http://www.rrdtool.org
- **Net-snmp** for querying the devices through SNMP; available at http://www.net-snmp.org

Cacti can have incompatibility issues with various versions of these tools because they are under constant development. Check the Cacti documentation at http://www.cacti.net for more up-to-date details on using the correct version of each tool and to obtain the associated installation steps. After installing each of these tools, you can download and install the Windows version of Cacti from http://www.cacti.net.

Configuring Cacti

After installing Cacti and the prerequisite tools (or applications), you can configure Cacti through the web-based GUI. The GUI provides an interface for configuring as well as viewing the performance-monitoring graphs. To access the Cacti GUI, point your web browser to the URL http://*cacti-server-ip-address*/cacti and enter the following default authentication information:

- Username: **admin**
- Password: **admin**

After logging in, Cacti might prompt you to change the default password of admin. After changing the default password, you see the Cacti console screen, as shown in Figure 6-7. The navigation bar on the left side of the console page provides links for adding devices and graphs. Figure 6-7 provides details regarding some of the useful links.

Figure 6-7 *Cacti Console*

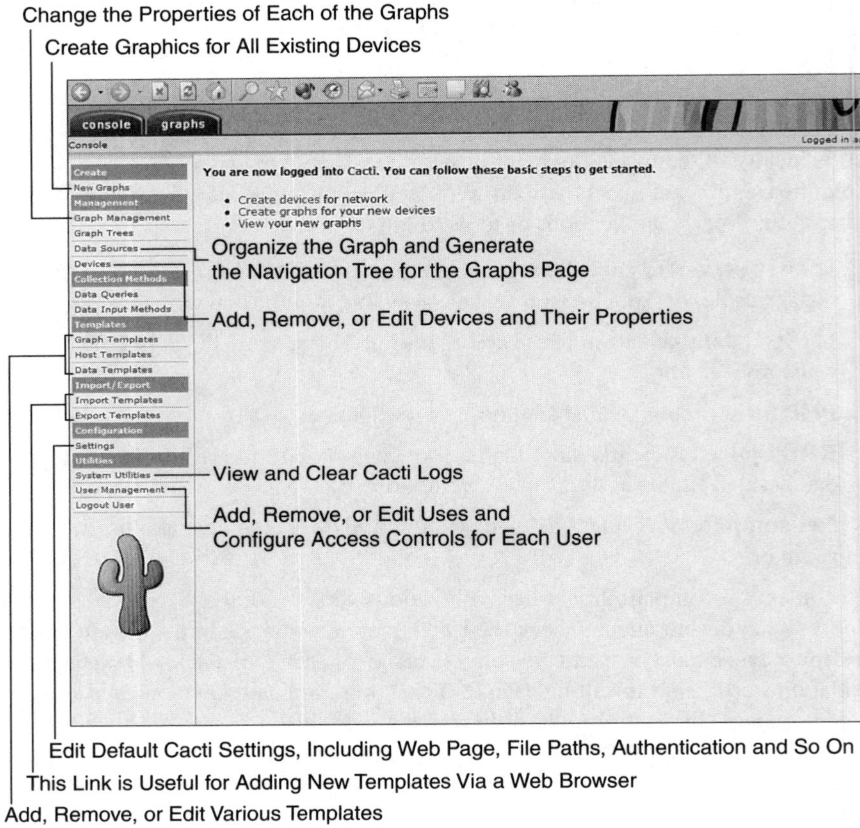

Next, navigate to the **Paths** page by clicking **Configuration > Settings > Paths** in the navigation bar at the left of the default console screen. Enter the destination path for each tool according to your installation. Correct configuration of this screen is important and any misconfiguration can render Cacti inoperable. The entries shown in Figure 6-8 are based on the working copy of Cacti on the author's Cacti server. Note that the installation was done according to the Cacti installation manual provided at the Cacti website (http://www.cacti.net).

Figure 6-8 *Cacti Settings—Paths Page*

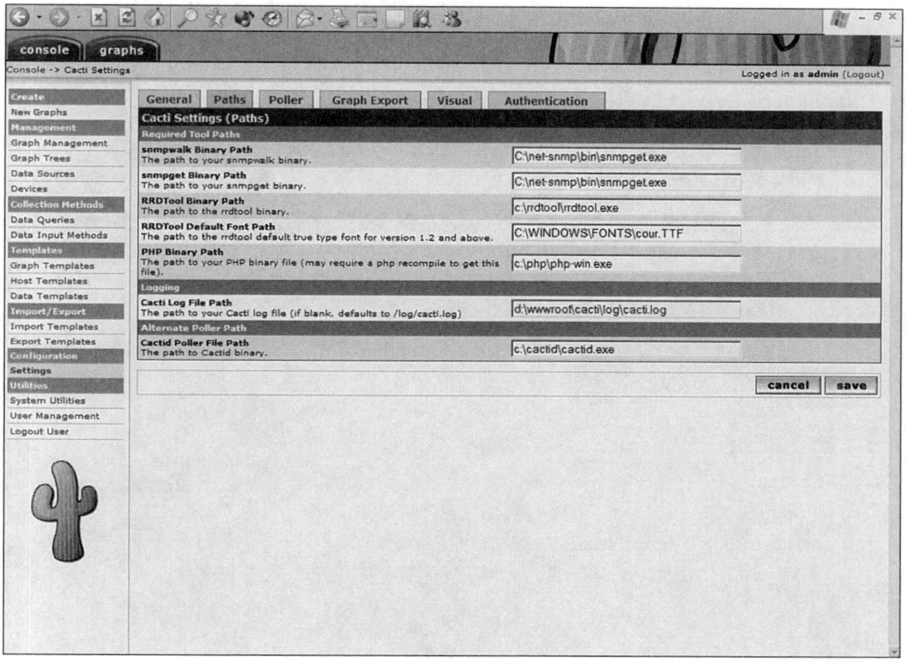

Out of the box, Cacti contains the entry for monitoring the host machine itself (the **Localhost** entry). Additionally, Cacti contains built-in templates for monitoring CPU usage and interface statistics on Cisco routers. To configure Cacti to monitor a Cisco device, follow these steps:

Step 1 **Add the device**—To add a device, use the new devices page, which is accessible through the Cacti console. To open the new devices page, navigate to the **Management** section in the navigation bar and click **Devices > Add**. Enter the details for the device in the new devices page, as shown in Figure 6-9. In the Hostname field, enter the IP address, and make sure that the SNMP community string matches the read-only SNMP community string on your router. Additionally, in the **Host** Template field**,** select **Cisco Router** using the drop-down menu.

Figure 6-9 shows the host **Dallas-Router**, with IP address **192.168.0.10** and **read** as the **SNMP Community** string. Next, click the **create** button to add the device to the Cacti database. If Cacti can successfully query the new host, you will see the same screen with the message **Save Successful** and the system information (including uptime and host name) gathered through SNMP. If the SNMP string is incorrect or the device cannot communicate with the Cacti server, the page will show an SNMP error message.

Figure 6-9 *Adding Devices*

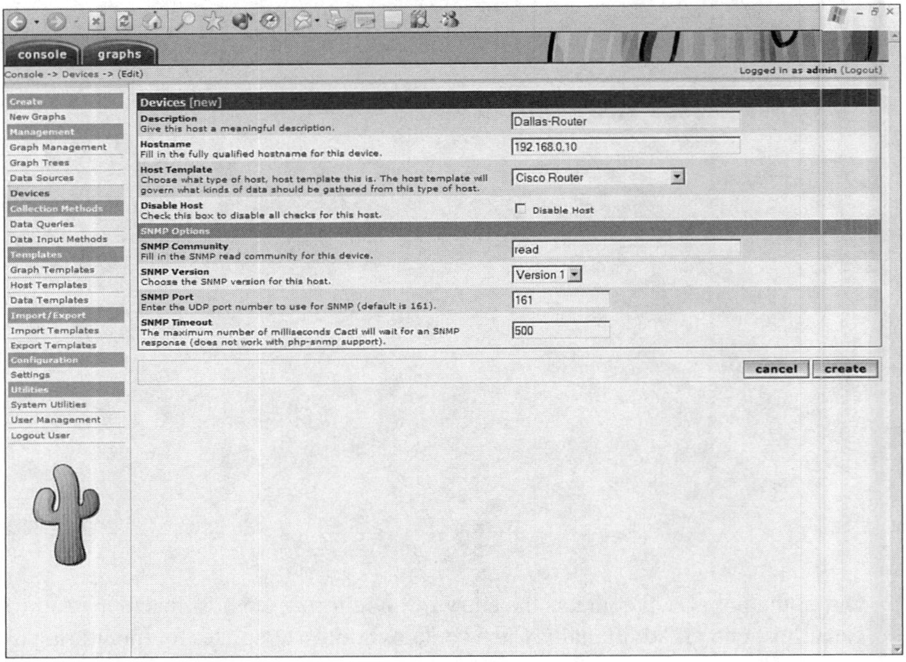

Step 2 **Create graphs**—After adding the router, you must create the graphs for monitoring CPU usage and interface statistics on the router. First, click **New Graphs** in the Create section of the navigation bar. In the resulting screen, use the drop-down menu to select the recently added router (Dallas-Router in this case). The page will update with two subsections, as shown in Figure 6-10. The first section contains the CPU usage template for graphing the CPU utilization of Cisco routers. The next section, Data Query, provides a list of all the interfaces of the router. Cacti automatically creates this list by sending SNMP queries to the router. You can select the check box (at the end of each row) to choose any of these interfaces or the CPU usage graphs, according to your requirements.

Additionally, the bottom of the page contains a drop-down list for choosing the type of graph, such as In/Out Bytes, In/Out Bits, and so on. After making the desired selections of graphs, click the **create** button.

Cacti might prompt you for additional information needed for the selected graphs, such as the color of the legend. After entering the desired information, click the **create** button to create the graph.

Figure 6-10 *Creating Graphs*

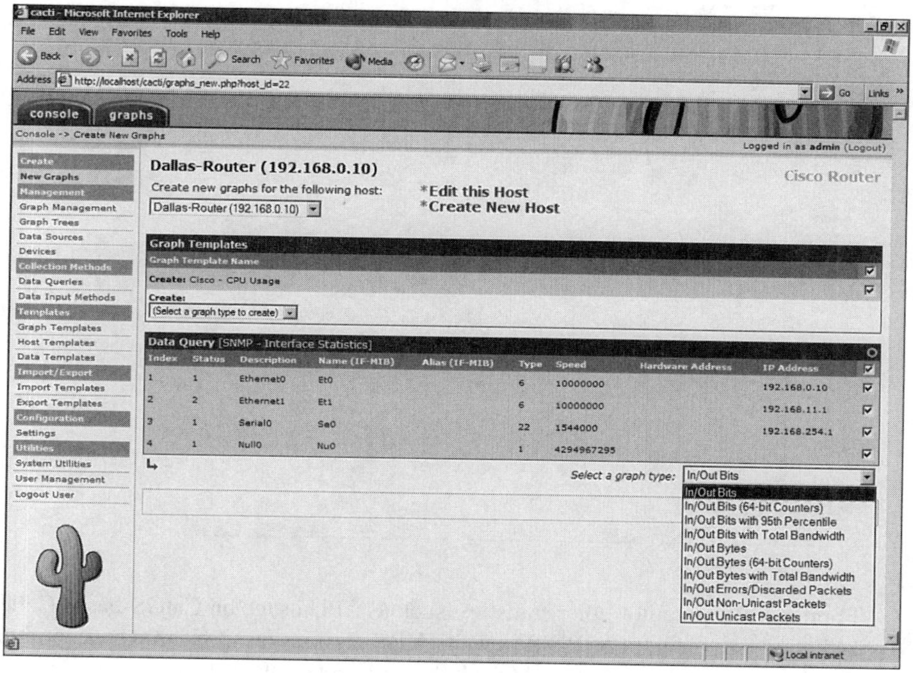

Step 3 **Modify the Graph Tree**—After the graphs are created, you must assign them to the Graph Tree. Graph Tree is a means of organizing various graphs and devices in a hierarchical manner. The structure of the Graph Tree is used by Cacti to create the navigation bar in the Graphs output page for viewing the performance-monitoring data. To add the newly created graphs to the Graph Tree from within the Cacti console page, click **Graph Trees > Default Tree**. In the resulting page in the **Tree Items** section, click the **Add** button to launch the Graph Tree Items edit page. On this page, through the Tree Item Type drop-down menu, you can choose from adding the entire host, adding just a particular graph, or creating a new heading. Figure 6-11 illustrates adding the host Dallas-Router in the default Parent Item-root. After making the desired selections, click the **create** button to return to the Graph Trees page. In the Tree Items section of this page, all the items are listed, and they can be moved by clicking the up- or down-arrow icons next to each item.

Figure 6-11 *Creating a Graph Tree*

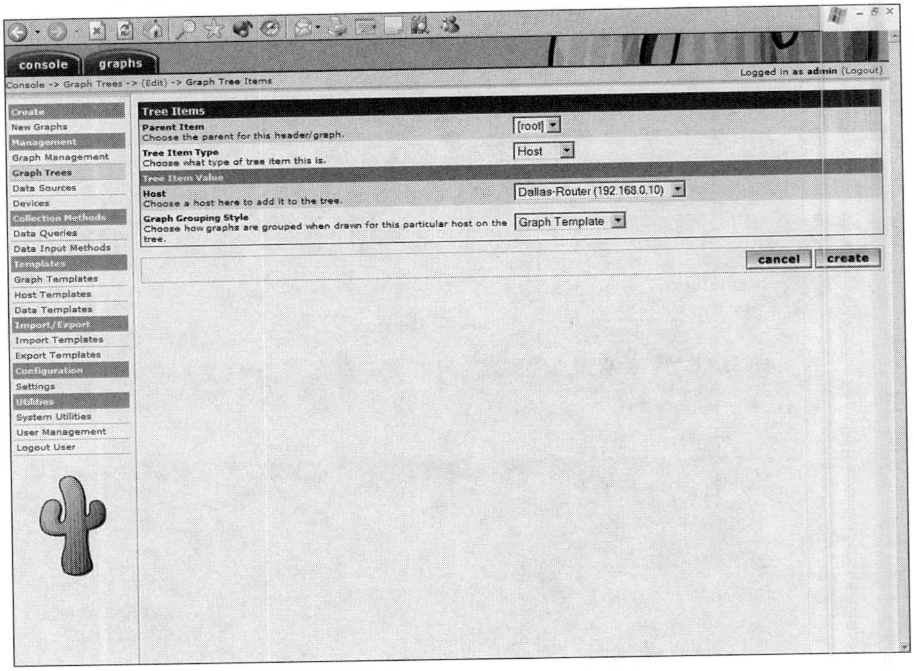

Cacti can also monitor other statistics, such as CPU usage on CatOS-based Catalyst switches, free memory on PIX Firewalls, VPN sessions on VPN 3000 concentrators, and so on. You can manually copy and tweak the built-in templates to suit your needs. However, the user forum on the Cacti website has a section dedicated to such add-on scripts. Moreover, these additional templates are available in XML format that can be easily imported into your existing Cacti server. You can find many such useful templates in the Scripts and Other Addons for Cacti section of the Cacti user forum at http://www.cacti.net.

Download the desired templates and save them on your local computer. To import these templates into Cacti, follow these steps:

Step 1 From the Import/Export section of the navigation bar, click **Import Templates > Browse**.

Step 2 Locate the downloaded template and click the **save** button to import the template into Cacti.

After you import the template, it is ready for use. Figure 6-12 illustrates the use of the new host template **Cisco - VPN 3000**. This template adds a Cisco VPN 3000 concentrator with host name VPN-Dallas and IP address 192.168.0.5. Note the four graph template entries in the Associated Graph Templates section. These entries were automatically added by Cacti as result of selecting the Cisco - VPN 3000 template.

Figure 6-12 *Adding a Device Using the Cisco-VPN 3000 Template*

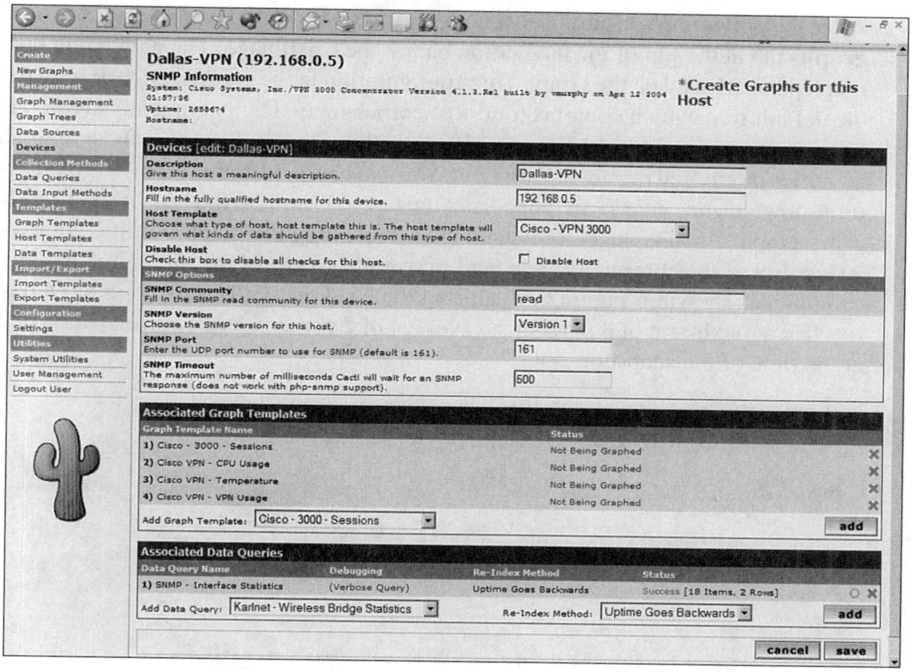

Running the Cacti Server

Cacti uses poller.php script for polling all the devices to collect the monitoring data. To test the configuration and operation of Cacti, you must first run the poller.php script from the Windows CLI as follows:

```
C:\php>PHP.EXE d:\wwwroot\cacti\poller.php
OK u:0.01 s:0.00 r:0.96
OK u:0.01 s:0.00 r:1.06
OK u:0.01 s:0.00 r:1.07
OK u:0.01 s:0.01 r:1.98
05/22/2005 12:47:42 AM - SYSTEM STATS: Time: 2.0913 s, Method: cmd.php, Processes: 1,
 Threads: N/A, Hosts: 2, Hosts/Process: 2
```

This command also shows the total time taken by the poller.php script to poll all the devices. As highlighted in the command output, poller.php took 2.0913 seconds. You can use this command to diagnose performance issues caused by monitoring a larger number of devices or parameters. For Cacti to work properly, the total time should not exceed 300 seconds. The 300-second limitation is discussed in the following paragraphs.

After manually testing the poller.php script, you can automate the polling process by using the Windows Scheduler service. The poller.php script must run every 5 minutes using the suitable PHP executable file. For details regarding setting up the Windows Scheduler, along with other details such as filenames and paths, refer to the Cacti installation manual.

After the poller.php script runs a couple of times, you can view the graphs by clicking the **graphs** tab at the top of the navigation bar on the Cacti page. The navigation bar on the graph page is based on the Graph Tree configuration in the console page. Figure 6-13 shows the default tree, which contains four host entries in the navigation bar. Additionally, the page shows various graphs associated with Dallas-Router. Note that the graphs show the activities monitored during the last hour. You can choose different views through the Presets drop-down menu; views can range from the last half-hour to the last 2 years. The bottom of every graph contains the color legend used in creating the graph. Additional text provides a snapshot of the current, average, and maximum values of the monitored parameters. For example, as shown in Figure 6-13, during the last hour, CPU utilization of Dallas-Router reached a maximum of 3 percent, an average of 2 percent, and a current value of 2 percent at the time of the snapshot.

Figure 6-13 *Cacti Graphs—Host View*

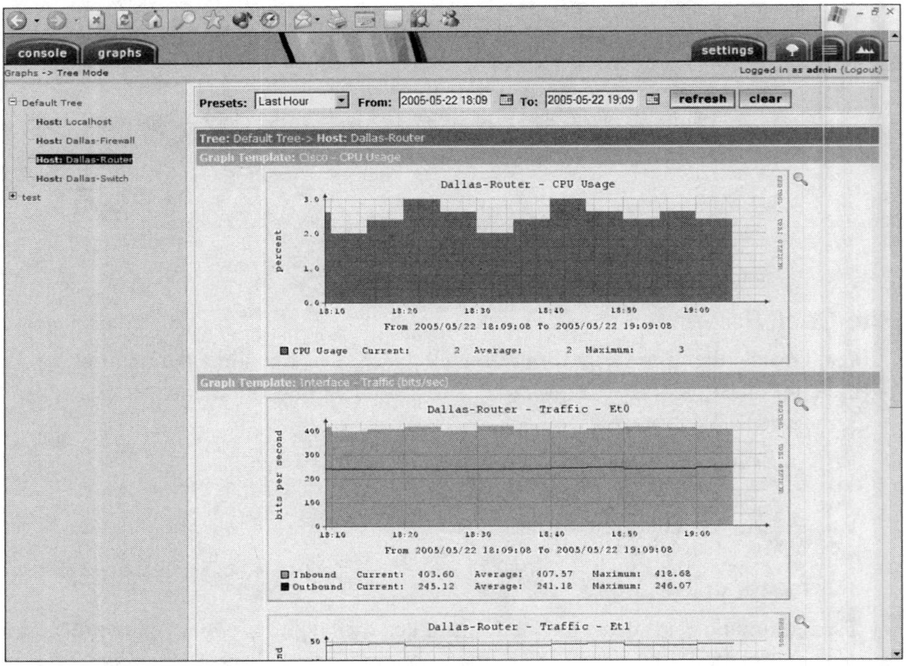

You can click each of the hosts to view the graphs associated with the hosts. Furthermore, you can click each graph to check the daily, weekly, monthly, and yearly views. Figure 6-14 shows the weekly, monthly, and yearly views for the CPU usage of Dallas-Router. Such reports are useful for providing a quick snapshot of the overall status of the device (or the associated network) and to help avoid potential bottlenecks; they are also handy for capacity planning for your future needs.

Figure 6-14 *Cacti Graphs—Detailed View*

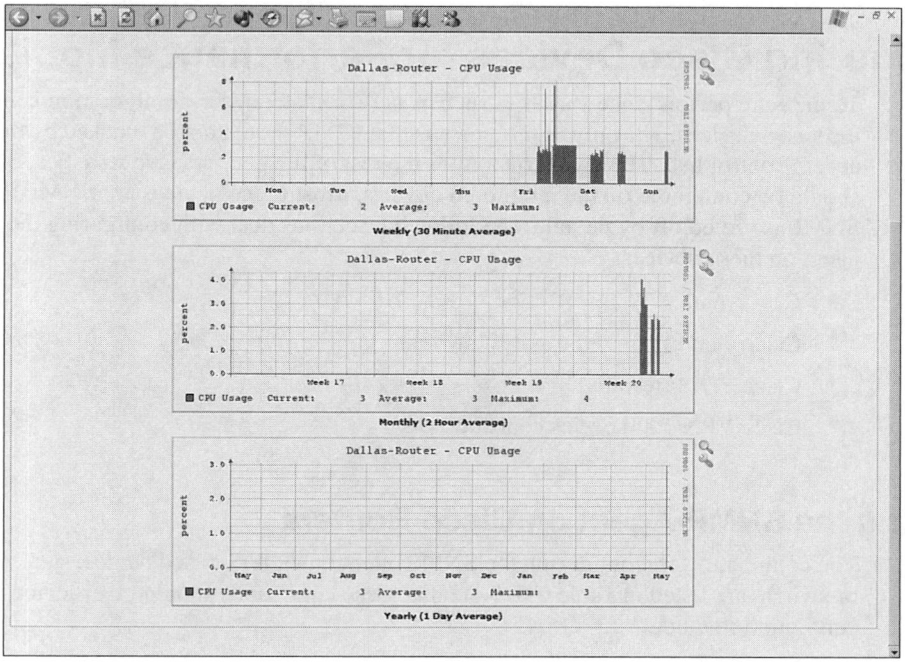

After it is configured, Cacti is easy to maintain and administer. You can control access to the Cacti web pages through the **User Management** link in the **Utilities** section of the navigation bar. Moreover, you can also use the following URL to provide guest access to the Cacti pages:

http://*cacti-ip-address*/cacti/graph_view.php?action=tree

This URL lacks a tab for the console section, does not require authentication, and is handy for providing view-only access to help desk personnel. You can also use the URL to integrate network performance–monitoring graphs into company intranets.

The poller.php script runs every 5 minutes and uses the cmd.php script. Consequently, Cacti has 300 seconds to poll all the devices, collect the information, and update the RRDTool database. This can lead to performance bottlenecks when monitoring a large number of hosts or graphs. To circumvent this potential problem, Cacti offers Cactid as a replacement for the slower cmd.php. To use Cactid, first install it on the same machine that is hosting the Cacti server. Next, choose **Console > Configuration > Settings > Poller**, and in the Poller Type section, choose **Cactid** from the drop-down menu. Click the **save** button to save the settings. Cacti now uses Cactid instead of cmd.php every time the Windows Scheduler runs the poller.php script.

Configuring Cisco Devices for Performance Monitoring

To measure performance variables such as network latency, no configuration is needed on the Cisco devices. The only requirement is that ICMP should not be blocked by firewalls or access control lists. However, to monitor the rest of the performance statistics, SNMP should be configured on the monitored devices. Most Cisco devices are SNMP aware, but SNMP is turned off by default. The following sections deal with configuring the SNMP agent on these devices:

- Cisco routers
- Cisco CatOS—based Catalyst switches
- Cisco PIX Firewalls
- Cisco VPN 3000 Series concentrators

Enabling the SNMP Agent on Cisco Routers

The commands for configuring the SNMP agent on an IOS-based device, such as a router or switch, are listed in Table 6-5. Note that these commands should be executed in global configuration mode.

Table 6-5 *IOS SNMP Configuration*

Command	Purpose
snmp-server contact *text*	Sets the system contact string
snmp-server location *text*	Sets the system location string
snmp-server chassis-id *number*	Sets the system serial number
access-list *access-list-number* {**deny** | **permit**} *source* [*source-wildcard*] [**log**]	Creates an access list to limit the SNMP managers who can access the SNMP agent
snmp-server community ***community_string*** [**ro** | **rw**] [*number*]	Specifies the community string for the IOS SNMP agent and the access list for limiting access to SNMP managers

Based on the commands discussed, Example 6-3 shows a sample configuration for enabling the SNMP agent on an IOS device. Within the example, note the highlighted comments that explain some of the relevant configurations.

Example 6-3 *Configuring the IOS-Based SNMP Agent*

```
Router-Dallas#config terminal
Enter configuration commands, one per line.  End with CNTL/Z.
Router-Dallas(config)#access-list 10 permit 192.168.0.30
Router-Dallas(config)#access-list 10 permit 192.168.0.35
Router-Dallas(config)#snmp-server contact spope@abcinvestment.com
Router-Dallas(config)#snmp-server location Dallas office 4th floor
Router-Dallas(config)#snmp-server chassis-id 123456
Router-Dallas(config)#snmp-server community read ro 10
Router-Dallas(config)#exit
Router-Dallas# show running
! Access-list will restrict SNMP agent to
! respond to queries from the following 2 hosts only
access-list 10 permit 192.168.0.30
access-list 10 permit 192.168.0.35
! the snmp community is set to "read"
! snmp agnet will only respond to manager
! permitted by Access-list 10
snmp-server community readw RW
snmp-server community read RO 10
snmp-server location Dallas office 4th floor
snmp-server contact spope@abcinvestment.com
snmp-server chassis-id 123456
!
end
Router-Dallas#show snmp
Chassis: 123456
Contact: spope@abcinvestment.com
Location: Dallas office 4th floor
16527 SNMP packets input
    0 Bad SNMP version errors
    15 Unknown community name
    0 Illegal operation for community name supplied
    0 Encoding errors
    33534 Number of requested variables
    0 Number of altered variables
    6981 Get-request PDUs
    9531 Get-next PDUs
    0 Set-request PDUs
16512 SNMP packets output
    0 Too big errors (Maximum packet size 1500)
    66 No such name errors
    0 Bad values errors
    0 General errors
    16512 Response PDUs
    0 Trap PDUs

SNMP logging: disabled
Router-Dallas#
```

NOTE Routers often use access lists (also called access control lists, or ACLs) to block SNMP requests from the rest of the network. If your SNMP server cannot communicate with the router despite a correct configuration, use the **show access-list** or **show running-configuration** command on the router to verify the access lists. Additionally, the firewall between the SNMP server and the router might be blocking SNMP traffic.

Enabling the SNMP Agent on Cisco Switches

To configure the SNMP agent on a CatOS-based Catalyst switch, use the privileged-mode commands listed in Table 6-6.

Table 6-6 *CatOS SNMP Configuration*

Command	Task
set snmp community read-only *community-string*	Defines read-only SNMP community strings
set snmp community read-write *community-string*	Defines read/write SNMP community strings
show snmp	Verifies SNMP configurations

Example 6-4 shows the commands for configuring the SNMP agent on the Catalyst switch.

Example 6-4 *Configuring the CatOS SNMP Agent*

```
Console> (enable) set snmp community read-only read
SNMP read-only community string set to 'read'.
Console> (enable) show snmp
RMON: Disabled
Extended RMON: Extended RMON module is not present
Traps Enabled:
Port,Module,Chassis,Bridge,Repeater,Vtp,Auth,ippermit,Vmps,config,entity,stpx
Port Traps Enabled: 1/1-2,4/1-48,5/1
Community-Access Community-String
---------------- --------------------
read-only read
----------------------------------------
```

Enabling the SNMP Agent on a Cisco PIX Firewall

To configure the SNMP agent on a Cisco PIX Firewall version 5.3 and higher, use the privileged-mode commands listed in Table 6-7. Note that unlike routers and switches, the PIX Firewall does not provide read/write access through SNMP. For the sake of security, the PIX Firewall only provides read-only access through SNMP.

Table 6-7 *PIX SNMP Configuration*

Command	Purpose
snmp-server contact *text*	Sets the system contact string.
snmp-server location *text*	Sets the system location string.
snmp-server host [*if_name*] ***ip_addr*** [**trap** | **poll**]	Specifies the IP addresses of the SNMP management station to which traps should be sent and/or from which the SNMP requests come. Use the *if_name* keyword to specify the interface name that connects the SNMP manager.
snmp-server community *community_string*	Specifies the community string for the IOS SNMP agent.
show snmp-server	Verifies the SNMP configuration.

Example 6-5 shows the commands for configuring the SNMP agent on a PIX Firewall.

Example 6-5 *Configuring the PIX SNMP Agent*

```
Firewall-Dallas# config terminal
Firewall-Dallas(config)# snmp-server host inside 192.168.0.30
Firewall-Dallas(config)# snmp-server location DALLAS
Firewall-Dallas(config)# snmp-server contact SPOPE
Firewall-Dallas(config)# snmp-server community read
Firewall-Dallas(config)# exit
Firewall-Dallas# show snmp
snmp-server host inside 192.168.0.30
snmp-server location DALLAS
snmp-server contact SPOPE
snmp-server community read
no snmp-server enable traps
```

Enabling the SNMP Agent on Cisco VPN 3000 Concentrators

Cisco VPN 3000 Series concentrators contain a built-in SNMP agent with read-only capabilities. As a security measure, this feature only allows viewing the statistics of the concentrator but does not facilitate configuring through SNMP. To configure the SNMP agent on a VPN 3000 Series concentrator, follow these steps:

Step 1 Log in to the VPN concentrator using a web browser.

Step 2 Navigate to the SNMP server page by choosing **Configuration > System > Management Protocols > SNMP**.

Step 3 On the SNMP server page, match the settings as shown in Figure 6-15 and enable SNMP by clicking the **Apply** button.

Figure 6-15 *VPN Concentrator—Enable SNMP*

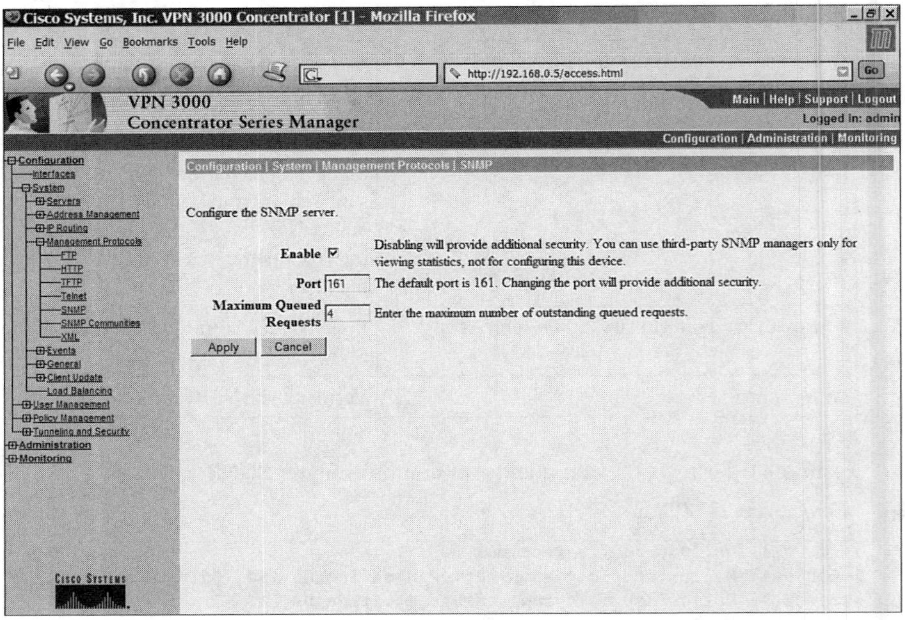

Step 4 Navigate to the SNMP communities page and click the **Add** button.

Step 5 Add the SNMP read-only community (as shown in Figure 6-16) and click the **Add** button to return to SNMP communities page.

Step 6 On the SNMP Communities page, save the configuration by clicking the **Save Needed** button in the upper-right corner.

Figure 6-16 *VPN Concentrator—SNMP Community*

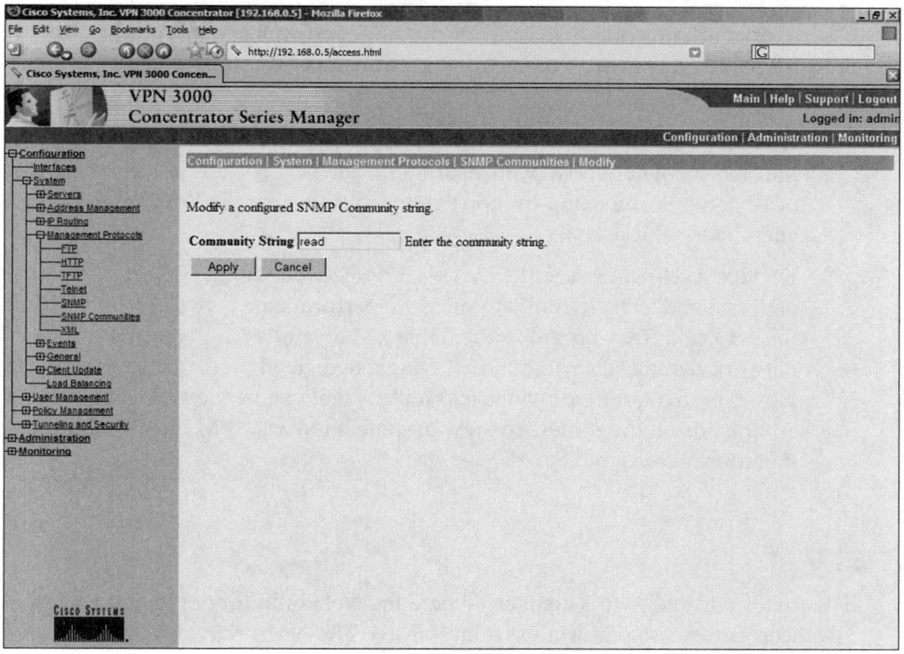

Securing SNMP

SNMP was originally designed as a quick-and-easy way to monitor devices. Earlier versions lacked security features such as encryption and authentication. Additionally, the SNMP stack suffers from a series of security vulnerabilities. To enhance the security of their networks, Netadmins should take the following actions:

- Minimize the use of SNMP in the network.
- Turn off SNMP on devices that are not monitored.
- Block UDP/TCP ports 161 and 162 at the firewall and edge routers.
- Block UDP/TCP ports 161 and 162 from user VLANs because regular users do not need SNMP.
- Use SNMP version 3 if possible, although MRTG and Cacti do not support it yet.
- Always use longer and stronger community strings.
- Limit the number of SNMP managers (network management systems that can poll the SNMP agents) using the SNMP access-list features in IOS. Also, exercise caution while allowing SNMP managers read/write access.

Commercial Cisco Offerings

CiscoWorks offers a range of tools for probing, performance monitoring, and trending network parameters. The two main components that offer traffic analysis and trending are as follows:

- **Internet Performance Monitor (IPM)**—Can monitor the performance of multiprotocol networks by measuring the latency, packet loss, errors, and availability of IP networks on a hop-by-hop (router-to-router) basis. IPM provides both real-time and historical reports.
- **Service Assurance Agent (SAA)**—Is embedded within IOS devices, and can generate and analyze traffic to measure performance between Cisco IOS devices and the network. SAA provides a scalable and cost-effective solution for monitoring network parameters without deploying a dedicated performance-monitoring server. However, SAA only provides text reports that can be viewed using various show commands on the router. To view graphical reports, IPM must be configured to pull the information from SAA.

Summary

The topics covered in this chapter prepare the Netadmin for deploying an SNMP-based advanced network-monitoring system (NMS). The NMS provides trending for network parameters including, but not limited to, interface traffic, CPU and memory utilization, and VPN and firewall connections. Netadmins should be able to perform the following performance-monitoring tasks:

- Deploy a Linux-based network-monitoring system to monitor interface traffic through Cisco devices, including routers, switches, VPN concentrators, and PIX Firewalls
- Deploy a Windows-based network-monitoring system to monitor interface traffic through Cisco devices, including routers, switches, VPN concentrators, and PIX Firewalls
- Use the trending feature of a network-monitoring system for long-term network analysis and capacity planning

Table 6-8 provides details of the tools discussed in this chapter.

Table 6-8 *Performance-Monitoring Tools Discussed in This Chapter*

Tool	Function	Supported OS	Installable Files Source	Additional Documentation Sources/Notes
MRTG	Trending of network traffic and other parameters through SNMP	Windows and Linux	http://www.mrtg.org	• Documentation in HTML format included with the installation (../doc/mrtg/html/) • README and other text files located in ../doc/mrtg • Collection of mrtg.cfg templates at http://www.somix.com/
RRDTool	Back-end database and graphing tool	Windows and Linux	http://www.rrdtool.org	• Documentation in HTML format included with the installation (../doc/rrdtool/html/) • README and other text files located in ../doc/rrdtool
Cricket	Improved version of MRTG	Windows and Linux	http://cricket.sourceforge.net	http://cricket.sourceforge.net
Cacti	RRDTool-based trending tool	Linux	http://www.cacti.net/	http://www.cacti.net/
Percival	High-performance version of Cricket	Linux	http://percival.sourceforge.net	http://percival.sourceforge.net
Snmpwalk	Command-line tool for querying SNMP-enabled devices	Windows and Linux	http://www.net-snmp.org	—
Cisco MIB Locator	Web-based tool for browsing MIBs and OIDs for Cisco devices	—	—	http://www.cisco.com/go/mibs

PART III

Security

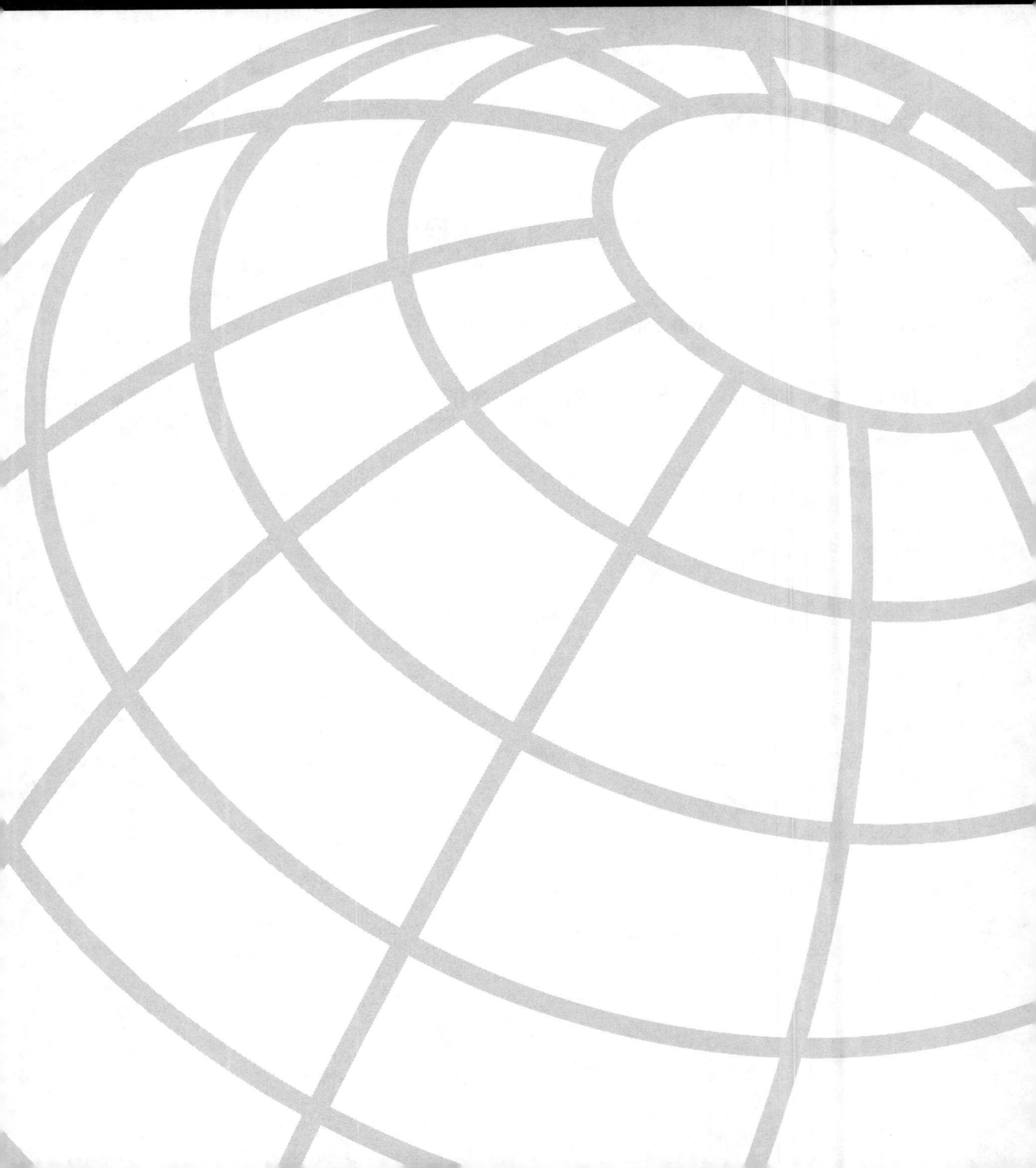

CHAPTER 7

Network Security Testing

Netadmins perform network security testing to assess and verify the threats and vulnerabilities of their network. This chapter introduces you to the following tools and methodologies of security testing:

- Linux-based live CD
- Network scanners
- Vulnerability scanners
- Packet analyzers

The topics covered in this chapter require you to be familiar with the mechanics of the Transmission Control Protocol/Internet Protocol (TCP/IP) model, with reference to the seven layers of the Open System Interconnection (OSI) reference model.

Network Security Testing Overview

Network security is an ongoing process that is best described by the Cisco security wheel. The security wheel, as shown in Figure 7-1, consists of the following four items:

- Secure
- Monitor
- Test
- Improve

Figure 7-1 *Cisco Security Wheel*

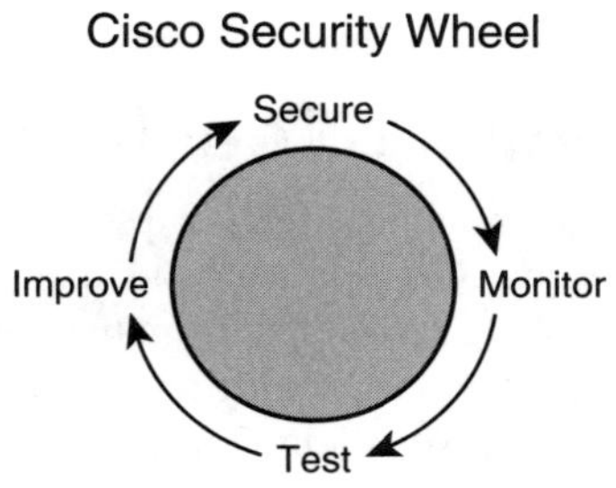

The third item, Test, or network security testing, helps the Netadmin to verify the security design and to discover vulnerabilities within the network.

The process of testing network security is also known as any of the following:

- Security audit
- Penetration testing
- Posture assessment
- Ethical hacking
- Vulnerability assessment

All these terms essentially mean the same thing—a legitimate process of attacking, discovering, and reporting security holes in a network. A security-testing process uses tools and methods that are similar to those of the underground hacking community.

The tools used for security auditing can be loosely classified into the following two categories:

- **Scanners**—Active tools that send out probe packets to the target host or network to attack or gather information.
- **Packet analyzers**—Passive in their operation because they do not send probe packets. Instead, packet analyzers work by capturing and analyzing the data that is flowing across the network.

NOTE **Active Versus Passive—**Active tools work by sending out probe packets to the target and then analyzing the response received from the target. In contrast, passive tools work by analyzing the traffic flowing across the wire. As an analogy, active tools are like police interrogators, while passive packet analyzers are like surveillance police officers.

This chapter discusses some of the popular network security scanners and packet analyzers that Netadmins can use. These tools are widely available as ready-to-use packages in the form of Linux-based bootable CD-ROMs. The following section covers some of these bootable CD-ROM–based tool kits that Cisco Netadmins can use.

Bootable CD-ROM–Based Tool Kits

The easy-to-install commercial products for testing network security are feature rich, but many of them are expensive. On the other hand, many of the comparable open source alternatives are freely available for download from the Internet. However, the installation and configuration process (for the open source tools) often demands significant time and resources of the overworked Netadmin. Fortunately, the Linux-based live CD-ROM provides a preinstalled security tool kit that can be deployed in less than five minutes. The live CD-ROM consists of a fully functional Linux operating system with built-in hardware detection for Intel (or similar architecture) computers.

The live CD-ROM (also referred to as a bootable CD-ROM) requires no installation. Deployment is as easy as inserting the CD-ROM into a bootable CD-ROM drive and rebooting the computer. The tools are ready to use because they are precompiled and, in most cases, preconfigured. The live CD-ROM does not write to the existing hard drives and uses only system memory. Thus, after removing the CD-ROM, the original operating system is left untouched. Moreover, despite issues with a preinstalled OS or with hard drive malfunctions, you can still boot your computer using a live CD-ROM. In addition, you can connect to the network resource through SSH, Telnet, a browser, or a mail client and administer your network. This is a major advantage offered by live CD-ROM as a backup option for Netadmins. Another advantage is the availability of a fully installed Linux system with preloaded security tools that can be used on any laptop/computer without installation on the hard drive.

Table 7-1 provides a list of the feature-rich Linux live CD-ROMs that are relevant to Cisco Netadmins. Most of the tools discussed in this chapter are available on the CD-ROMs listed in Table 7-1.

Table 7-1 *Linux Live CD-ROMs*

Name	Features	URL
Knoppix	Although Knoppix is not a security-specific tool, it is one of the best Debian-based live CD-ROMs, with the largest collection of applications. It has excellent hardware-detection capabilities and is under active development with frequently updated releases.	http://www.knoppix.net
Knoppix-STD (Security Tools Distribution)	Customized distribution of the Knoppix live Linux CD-ROM; focuses on information security and network-management tools.	http://www.knoppix-std.org/
Network Security Toolkit (NST)	A Redhat/Fedora-based live CD-ROM that contains a majority of the "Top 75 Security Tools" surveyed at http://www.insecure.org.	http://www.networksecuritytoolkit.org/
Trinux	Slackware-based live CD-ROM; is small enough to run on a floppy disk; has older and limited collection of tools; has no GUI.	http://trinux.sourceforge.net/
F.I.R.E.	Good collection of tools; older and limited hardware detection compared to Knoppix and NST.	http://fire.dmzs.com

To use the tools included with the live CD-ROM, you must first create the live CD-ROM. Live CD-ROMs are created by transferring the ISO image file of the CD-ROM to a recordable CD-ROM. (An ISO image file is an image of a CD-ROM that is saved in ISO 9660 format and is commonly used to create bootable CDs.) The ISO images of each CD-ROM listed in previous table are available at the respective websites.

Follow these steps to create a live CD-ROM:

Step 1 Download the ISO image file for the latest stable release of the live CD-ROM distribution. The ISO files can be as large as 700 MB, and download times can be long depending on your Internet connection.

Step 2 Using a CD-ROM-burning application (such as Roxio for MS-Windows or K3b for Linux), create a bootable CD-ROM from the downloaded ISO image file. Most CD-burning software has a "record from image" option for creating bootable CD-ROMs.

CAUTION Do not simply copy the ISO image to a blank CD-ROM because this process does not create a bootable CD-ROM; instead, it renders the CD-ROM useless. This is a common mistake of new users.

The Knoppix CD-ROM provides an easy-to-use graphical user interface (GUI) with basic security-testing tools, including Nmap, Nessus, Ethereal, and Tcpdump. Knoppix also includes the following tools and services:

- **SSH server and SSH client**—Provides SSH connectivity to and from the local machine that is running Knoppix.
- **SAMBA server**—Creates Windows-style network shares on the local machine; allows other Windows machines to access the local drive.
- **Lin Neighborhood**—Similar to the Windows Network Neighborhood; used to connect to Windows machines in the network.
- **Mozilla web browser**—Similar to the Netscape browser.
- **RDP client**—Used to connect to Windows machines through Windows terminal services.
- **Mail clients**—Provide connectivity to a mail server.
- **FAT/NTFS support**—Permits automatic detection and mounting of local hard drives with FAT and NT File System (NTFS) partitions; this enables you to access the local drives and share them with the network through a SAMBA server.
- **OpenOffice**—Used to view and compose word processor, spreadsheet, and presentation documents; supports most of the commonly used formats, including .doc, .xls, .ppt, and .wpd.

These features allow the Netadmin to use the Knoppix CD-ROM and easily export results and reports to external data stores.

Similar to Knoppix, the NST and Knoppix-STD CDs also provide a command-line interface (CLI) and a GUI. These CD-ROMs provide a pre-installed copy of the Firefox browser, VNC server, SSH server and SSH client, PDF viewers, and minicom.

Both Knoppix and Knoppix-STD contain pre-installed Java-enabled web browsers, which can be used by Cisco Netadmins to run Pix Device Manager (PDM) and Cisco Router and Security Device Manager (SDM). Additionally, Cisco is developing similar tools for many other products to enable browser administration for new users. Most of these tools only work with Java-enabled browsers. While Java-enabled web browsers work well in the Windows environment, Linux users often need to manually tweak the Java installation. In such cases, the Knoppix CD-ROM comes in handy for using Java-enabled web browsers from within the Linux OS.

Network Scanners

Network scanners are software tools that probe a network to determine the hosts present on the network. Network scanners also probe the discovered hosts to determine the TCP and UDP ports that are open. Furthermore, based on the response of the probes, scanners can identify the OS, the services that are running, and the associated security vulnerabilities present on the discovered hosts. Some scanners can also display the results in the form of graphical reports. Some of the most popular open source network scanners are as follows:

- **Nmap**—Known as the Swiss army knife of network scanners; a popular and versatile tool.
- **Netcat**—A port scanner with the additional capability to read and write data across a network through TCP and UDP ports.
- **Nessus**—The most popular vulnerability scanner with the ability to regularly update the vulnerability database; comes preinstalled with many Linux live CD-ROMs; good reporting capability.
- **SARA/SATAN**— Security Auditor's Research Assistant (SARA) is a vulnerability scanner that is based on the now-defunct Security Administrator's Tool for Analyzing Networks (SATAN) project; the vulnerability database is updated less frequently than that of Nessus.

This chapter covers Nmap and Nessus because both are feature rich and under active development. Furthermore, both of these tools come pre-installed with the live CD-ROM–based tool kits.

Nmap Scanner

Nmap is highly versatile tool for scanning and enumerating networks. Nmap also looks for services that are running on hosts by scanning TCP and UDP ports. Often referred to as the Swiss army knife of security tools, Nmap is an integral part of every network security professional's tool kit. Nmap is pre-installed in all the live CD-ROM distributions listed in Table 7-1. The MS-Windows version is also available at the Nmap home page (http://www.Nmap.org).

Some of the routine (and cumbersome) Netadmin tasks that Nmap can do are as follows:

- Verify unused IP addresses in a network
- Verify available hosts in a network
- Verify services running on a host in a network
- Verify the firewall security configurations
- Verify the OS running on a remote host

In addition to using Internet Control Message Protocol (ICMP) ping scans for network discovery, Nmap can use other scanning techniques using TCP and UDP packets. These techniques enable network scanning even if ICMP traffic is blocked in a network.

CAUTION The Nmap scans can trigger security alarms by intrusion detection systems (IDS). Additionally, Nmap scans can potentially crash certain TCP/IP stacks (or certain applications) of poorly designed systems. Many organizations have security policies that ban the use of network scanners such as Nmap. Always verify with the network operations and network security departments of the organization before using Nmap (or other security-related tools mentioned in this chapter).

Nmap is a command-line tool and can be invoked through the command shell. The syntax is as follows:

nmap [**options**] *target hostname or ip address*

Example 7-1 shows Nmap scanning host 192.168.0.1.

Example 7-1 *Using Nmap*

```
root@0[knoppix]# nmap  192.168.0.1
Starting Nmap 3.48 ( http://www.insecure.org/Nmap/ ) at 2004-11-04 00:26 CET
Interesting ports on 192.168.0.1:
(The 1656 ports scanned but not shown below are in state: closed)
PORT   STATE SERVICE
80/tcp open  http

Nmap run completed -- 1 IP address (1 host up) scanned in 3.900 seconds
```

As highlighted in Example 7-1, Nmap scanned 1656 ports and reported an open port on the scanned target. Nmap also reported that the target is up.

NOTE Some of the advanced Nmap options use special packets that do not conform to the TCP/IP standards. These nonstandard packets can only be created by using the raw socket capabilities of the OS. Hence, Nmap needs root privilege access to use the advanced scanning options.

Nmap also provides a fast and efficient means of scanning the entire network. To specify a target network based on the length of the network mask, use the slash (/) option. For example, the **nmap 192.168.10.0/24** command scans the entire class C network ranging from 192.168.10.0 to 192.168.10.255.

You can also use the wildcard character asterisk (*) to specify matches. For example, the **nmap 192.168.*.*** command is similar to **nmap 192.168.0.0/16**.

To scan only specific subnets or hosts in a larger network, Nmap allows the use of the hyphen (-) to specify ranges. For example, the **nmap 192.168.35-79.0-255** command scans all the class C subnets that range from 192.168.35.0/24 to 192.168.79.0/24. Similarly, the **nmap 192.168.35-79.99** command scans all the nodes with **99** as the host address in the subnet range of 192.168.35.0/24 to 192.168.79.0/24 (such as IP addresses 192.168.35.99, 192.168.36.99, 192.168.37.99 and all the way up to 192.168.79.99).

Finally, you can use the comma (,) to specify individual hosts or networks. For example, the **nmap 192.168.35,38,56.5,31** command scans the following hosts: 192.168.35.5, 192.168.35.31, 192.168.38.5, 192.168.38.31, 192.168.56.5, and 192.168.56.31.

For more control and flexibility in scanning various network environments, Nmap provides several options. Some of these options are listed in Table 7-2.

Table 7-2 *Nmap Options*

Option	Explanation
-sT	TCP regular port scan (default for unprivileged users); connects to target port with a three-way TCP handshake.
-sS	TCP SYN* stealth port scan (also called a half-open scan); sends a SYN packet and waits for SYN+ACK signals for open ports and RST+ACK signals for closed ports.
-sF	TCP FIN* stealth port scan; sends a FIN packet and expects an RST packet for all closed ports.
-sU	UDP port scan.
-sP	ICMP ping scan.
-sV	Version scan probes open ports to determine service and application names/versions.
-O	TCP/IP fingerprinting that guesses the remote operating system.

continues

Table 7-2 *Nmap Options (Continued)*

Option	Explanation
-p *<range>*	Specifies the ports to scan.
-F	Scans only ports listed in the nmap-services file; useful for quickly scanning common services or ports. The nmap-services file is installed with Nmap and contains a list of common TCP/UDP ports and the associated services.
-v	Verbose or detailed output; can be used in conjunction with any other option.
-p0	Do not use ping for scanning hosts.
-n	Do not use Domain Name System (DNS) resolution.
-R	Use DNS resolution.
-oN *<logfile>*	Send the output to the specified log file in normal format.
-iL *<inputfile>*	Use the input file for the list of targets to be scanned.
-S *<ipaddress>*	Specifies the source IP address.
-e *<interface-name>*	Specifies the network interface as the source.

*SYN, ACK, RST and FIN are the flags in the TCP packet.

The examples in the sections that follow highlight the utility of nmap as a versatile network scanner. These example are based on the options listed in Table 7-2 and explain nmap usage for routine Netadmin tasks.

Scanning a Network

To scan a range of networks, you can use special characters, as discussed in the previous section. Consider the following three commands:

```
nmap -v -sP 192.168.*.*
nmap -v -sP 192.168.0-255.0-255
nmap -v -sP 192.168.0.0/16
```

All three commands scan the entire class B range of 192.168.0.0 to 192.168.255.255 and produce the output shown in Example 7-2. The output displays the result of the ping scan sent to each host address within the specified range. By using the –**v** option (for verbose output), the display also reports the hosts that are down. Without using the **-v** switch, nmap displays only the hosts that are up. The **-v** option can be used in conjunction with any other nmap option to get more information from the **nmap** command output. Additionally, without the **-v** option, nmap displays the summary results after the scan is complete. With the use of the **-v** option, nmap starts displaying the scan results as they appear, instead of waiting until the end of the scan. You can use the **-vv** option for even more details. Also, note the **-sP** option, which specifies using an ICMP ping scan. Without this switch, nmap uses the default method of a TCP connect scan. In Example 7-2, the output is suppressed for the sake of clarity.

Example 7-2 **nmap** *Scanning a Class B Network*

```
root@0[knoppix]# nmap -v -sP 192.168.0.0/16
Starting Nmap 3.48 ( http://www.insecure.org/Nmap/ ) at 2004-11-04 00:26 PST
Host 192.168.0.0 appears to be up.
Host 192.168.0.1 appears to be up.
Host 192.168.0.2 appears to be up.
Host 192.168.0.3 appears to be up.
Host 192.168.0.4 appears to be up.
Host 192.168.0.5 appears to be up.
...
Host 192.168.0.34 appears to be down.
Host 192.168.0.35 appears to be down.
Host 192.168.0.36 appears to be down.
...
Host 192.168.2.233 appears to be up.
Host 192.168.2.234 appears to be down.
...
Host 192.168.12.5 appears to be up.
...
Host 192.168.90.236 appears to be up.
...
Host 192.168.135.237 appears to be up.
...
Host 192.168.220.23 appears to be up.
...
Host 192.168.224.139 appears to be up.
Host 192.168.224.140 appears to be down.
...
Host 192.168.255.1 appears to be up.
...
Host 192.168.255.253 appears to be up.
Host 192.168.255.254 appears to be up.
```

Note that the version of Nmap in Example 7-2 is 3.48. Higher versions of Nmap also display the message authentication code (MAC) address and the vendor name (based on the MAC address). The remainder of this chapter is based on Nmap version 3.55, which is included with the Knoppix CD.

Scanning TCP Ports

The network services running on host machines use TCP or UDP ports to communicate with other machines. For example, web services use TCP port 80 to listen for HTTP requests. The Netadmin can estimate the services running on the target hosts by scanning for open ports. Port scans are useful in discovering unneeded services that are running on the target host and verifying firewall configurations. Armed with the port scan results, the Netadmin can enhance network security through the following methods:

- Hardening the host by shutting down unneeded services that are running over it
- Tightening network access by denying access to these ports or hosts through firewall access control lists (ACL)

To scan the TCP ports on the hosts or the network, use the –**sT** option, as shown in Example 7-3. You can also use the **-sS**, **-sA**, **-sF**, and **-sX** options for stealth scanning or when scanning through firewalls.

Example 7-3 **nmap** *Scanning TCP Ports*

```
root@0[knoppix]# nmap -sT 192.168.0.10
Starting nmap 3.55 ( http://www.insecure.org/nmap/ ) at 2004-11-06 11:19 EST
Interesting ports on 192.168.0.10:
(The 1657 ports scanned but not shown below are in state: closed)
PORT   STATE SERVICE
23/tcp open  telnet
79/tcp open  finger
80/tcp open  http
MAC Address: 00:50:73:21:D0:67 (Cisco SYSTEMS)

Nmap run completed -- 1 IP address (1 host up) scanned in 6.068 seconds
```

NOTE Unlike regular TCP scans, stealth scanning techniques only send a single TCP datagram to the target and do not establish the three-way TCP handshake. As a result, stealth scans can pass through some firewalls and often do not show up in the IDS logs.

Scanning UDP Ports

Several network services, such as Simple Network Management Protocol (SNMP), Remote Authentication Dial-In User Service (RADIUS), Windows file sharing, and so on, use UDP. But, unlike TCP, UDP is connectionless and does not use the three-way handshake. Therefore, **nmap** provides limited options for UDP scanning. Nonetheless, UDP scanning using the **-sU** option provides a list of UDP port numbers in the listening state on the target host. UDP scans also list the name of the services associated with the UDP ports. Similar to the TCP port scan, UDP port scan reports can help Netadmins to enhance network security. Example 7-4 shows a UDP scan on a target with IP address 192.168.0.100.

Example 7-4 **nmap** *Scanning UDP Ports*

```
root@0[knoppix]# nmap -sU 192.168.0.100
Starting nmap 3.55 ( http://www.insecure.org/nmap/ ) at 2004-11-06 11:13 EST
Interesting ports on 192.168.0.100:
(The 1475 ports scanned but not shown below are in state: closed)
PORT    STATE SERVICE
137/udp open  netbios-ns
138/udp open  netbios-dgm
445/udp open  microsoft-ds
MAC Address: 00:0D:56:DF:86:A6 (Dell PCBA Test)
Nmap run completed -- 1 IP address (1 host up) scanned in 3.065 seconds
```

Scanning a Port Range

By default, Nmap scans all the ports from 1 through 1024. Nmap also scans ports that are listed in the nmap-services file. Therefore, scanning a large number of ports, especially for a larger subnet, is a time-consuming process. Moreover, the Netadmin might prefer to avoid scans on certain ports to prevent application malfunctions. (Nmap scans are known to crash certain applications and OSs.) Fortunately, similar to the options for scanning a range of IP addresses, Nmap also provides a method to specify port ranges, through the **-p** *range* option. You can specify the range using the starting and ending port numbers. Multiple ports or ranges can be separated by a comma. Example 7-5 shows **nmap** performing a TCP and UDP port scan. The ports to be scanned range from 25 to 50 and 51 to 120.

Example 7-5 **nmap** *Scanning a Range of Ports*

```
root@0[knoppix]# nmap -sT -sU -p 20-25,51-120 192.168.0.30
Starting nmap 3.55 ( http://www.insecure.org/nmap/ ) at 2004-11-06 11:17 EST
Interesting ports on 192.168.0.30:
(The 141 ports scanned but not shown below are in state: closed)
PORT     STATE SERVICE
21/tcp   open  ftp
22/tcp   open  ssh
23/tcp   open  telnet
25/tcp   open  smtp
53/tcp   open  domain
53/udp   open  domain
79/tcp   open  finger
80/tcp   open  http
110/tcp  open  pop3
111/tcp  open  rpcbind
111/udp  open  rpcbind
MAC Address: 00:D0:59:17:77:46 (Ambit Microsystems)

Nmap run completed -- 1 IP address (1 host up) scanned in 76.177 seconds
```

Scanning Common Ports

As seen in the previous example, Nmap provides the option to scan a range of ports. However, it is difficult to efficiently summarize the port range through the CLI options. To address this issue, Nmap includes the nmap-services file, which contains a list of commonly used TCP and UDP port numbers along with the names of the associated services. Note that the nmap-services file is part of the Nmap installation and needs no user input.

To perform a quick scan on common TCP ports listed in the nmap-services file, use the **nmap** command in conjunction with the **-F** option, as demonstrated in Example 7-6.

Example 7-6 **nmap** *Scanning Common Ports*

```
knoppix@ttyp0[knoppix]# nmap -F 192.168.0.100
Starting Nmap 3.55 ( http://www.insecure.org/Nmap/ ) at 2004-11-06 10:40 EST
Interesting ports on 192.168.0.100:
(The 1213 ports scanned but not shown below are in state: closed)
```

continues

Example 7-6 **nmap** *Scanning Common Ports (Continued)*

```
PORT     STATE SERVICE
135/tcp  open  msrpc
139/tcp  open  netbios-ssn
445/tcp  open  microsoft-ds
1025/tcp open  NFS-or-IIS
3389/tcp open  ms-term-serv
MAC Address: 00:0D:56:DF:86:A6 (Dell PCBA Test)

Nmap run completed -- 1 IP address (1 host up) scanned in 1.003 seconds
```

By default, nmap always uses TCP scans. To scan common UDP ports, add the **-sU** option, as shown in Example 7-7.

Example 7-7 **nmap** *Scanning Common UDP Ports*

```
knoppix@ttyp0[knoppix]# nmap -sU -F 192.168.0.100

Starting Nmap 3.55 ( http://www.insecure.org/Nmap/ ) at 2004-11-06 10:40 EST
Interesting ports on 192.168.0.100:
(The 1005 ports scanned but not shown below are in state: closed)
PORT    STATE SERVICE
137/udp open  netbios-ns
138/udp open  netbios-dgm
445/udp open  microsoft-ds
MAC Address: 00:0D:56:DF:86:A6 (Dell PCBA Test)

Nmap run completed -- 1 IP address (1 host up) scanned in 3.875 seconds
```

Remote OS Detection

When probed by network scans, the TCP/IP stack of every OS replies with a signature response unique to that OS. The process of comparing the response against the known signature to determine the OS of the target device is called *OS fingerprinting.* nmap sends prebuilt probe packets to the target host and analyzes the signature to estimate the OS. To invoke the OS fingerprinting function, use the **-O** option. (Note: This is the letter *O* and not the number zero.) Example 7-8 shows nmap scanning a target with IP address 192.168.0.20 and correctly diagnosing it as a Cisco PIX Firewall running PIX OS 6.2 or higher.

Example 7-8 *OS Fingerprinting Using* **nmap**

```
root@0[knoppix]# nmap -O 192.168.0.20

Starting nmap 3.55 ( http://www.insecure.org/nmap/ ) at 2004-11-06 11:44 EST
Interesting ports on 192.168.0.20:
(The 1656 ports scanned but not shown below are in state: closed)
PORT     STATE SERVICE
22/tcp   open  ssh
23/tcp   open  telnet
443/tcp  open  https
1467/tcp open  csdmbase
```

Example 7-8 *OS Fingerprinting Using* **nmap (Continued)**

```
MAC Address: 00:07:50:57:E2:69 (Cisco Systems)
Device type: firewall
Running: Cisco PIX 6.X
OS details: Cisco PIX Firewall running PIX 6.2 - 6.3.3

Nmap run completed -- 1 IP address (1 host up) scanned in 5.389 seconds
```

Detailed Outputs

By default, Nmap shows the output onscreen after completing the scanning process. If the scan takes a long time, there might be no output for a while. By using the **-v** (verbose) option, Nmap shows the output on-screen as soon as the scanning begins. Also, the use of the **-v** option provides more details in the output. Users can specify the option more than once (**-vv**) to obtain even more details for the accompanying option. Like the other options, the verbose option can be used in conjunction with all other options. Example 7-9 shows the detailed output of guessing the OS of target 192.168.0.20. When compared to Example 7-8, the output provides more information.

Example 7-9 *Detailed* **nmap** *Output*

```
root@0[knoppix]# nmap -vv -O 192.168.0.20

Starting nmap 3.55 ( http://www.insecure.org/nmap/ ) at 2004-11-06 11:49 EST
Host 192.168.0.20 appears to be up ... good.
Initiating SYN Stealth Scan against 192.168.0.20 at 11:49
Adding open port 23/tcp
Adding open port 1467/tcp
Adding open port 443/tcp
Adding open port 22/tcp
The SYN Stealth Scan took 0 seconds to scan 1660 ports.
For OSScan assuming that port 22 is open and port 1 is closed and neither are
  firewalled
Interesting ports on 192.168.0.20:
(The 1656 ports scanned but not shown below are in state: closed)
PORT     STATE SERVICE
22/tcp   open  ssh
23/tcp   open  telnet
443/tcp  open  https
1467/tcp open  csdmbase
MAC Address: 00:07:50:57:E2:69 (Cisco Systems)
Device type: firewall
Running: Cisco PIX 6.X
OS details: Cisco PIX Firewall running PIX 6.2 - 6.3.3
OS Fingerprint:
TSeq(Class=TR%IPID=I%TS=U)
T1(Resp=Y%DF=N%W=1000%ACK=S++%Flags=AS%Ops=M)
T2(Resp=Y%DF=N%W=800%ACK=S%Flags=AR%Ops=WNMETL)
T3(Resp=Y%DF=N%W=1000%ACK=S++%Flags=AS%Ops=M)
T4(Resp=N)
T5(Resp=Y%DF=N%W=800%ACK=S++%Flags=AR%Ops=WNMETL)
```

continues

Example 7-9 *Detailed* **nmap** *Output (Continued)*

```
T6(Resp=Y%DF=N%W=400%ACK=S%Flags=AR%Ops=WNMETL)
T7(Resp=Y%DF=N%W=C00%ACK=S++%Flags=UAPR%Ops=WNMETL)
PU(Resp=N)

TCP Sequence Prediction: Class=truly random
                         Difficulty=9999999 (Good luck!)
TCP ISN Seq. Numbers: DBDE7435 91F6251F DDED40C8 EAFD9725 5F5B10D8 94B552C6
IPID Sequence Generation: Incremental

Nmap run completed -- 1 IP address (1 host up) scanned in 5.363 seconds
```

TIP **nmap** commands can be difficult for new users to remember. Knoppix-STD also includes a graphical front end for **nmap** called **nmapfe**. This front end is found in the Vulnerability Assessment menu.

Nessus Scanner

Nessus is an open source network scanner with the additional capability of scanning known vulnerabilities present on the target hosts. Vulnerabilities are the weaknesses in an operating system or software that can potentially be exploited by malicious users with an intent to cause system damage. Network vulnerability scanners such as Nessus provide security vulnerability detection and reporting for networks and host systems. The Nessus operation can be summarized in the following four steps:

1. Perform network scans to discover available targets.
2. Based on the scanning results, enumerate the available OS and services.
3. Based on the enumerated list of OS and services, probe the target hosts using the internal database of known vulnerabilities.
4. Based on the results of the probes, create a report for future reference.

Nessus uses a client/server architecture with the server (nessusd) listening for incoming connections from the clients. The clients instruct the server to perform security tests.

The following features have led to the popularity of Nessus:

- Provides a scalable and modular client/server architecture.
- Plug-ins provide a modular means for easily adding new tests to the core engine.
- Plug-ins database is updated on a daily basis.
- Uses intelligent scanning to accurately detect services, even if they are running on a nonstandard port.
- Is stable and has been under active development since 1998.
- Has a large user and support base.

Nessus comes preinstalled on all the live CD-ROMs listed in Table 7-1. This discussion is based on Nessus that is included with the Knoppix CD-ROM, but it should be applicable to the Knoppix-STD and NST CDs as well. The steps involved in assessing the vulnerability of a network using Nessus are as follows:

- Running the Nessus server and client
- Generating Nessus reports

Running the Nessus Server and Client

The Knoppix CD-ROM provides a single-click option to start the Nessus server and client. To launch Nessus, click **K menu > System > Security > Nessus Security Tool**.

While the server, nessusd, launches in the background, the Nessus Setup page appears on-screen, as shown in Figure 7-2. For ease of configuration and usage, the setup page is organized into several tabs. This page is used for configuring the client to specify the target and scanning options. The server is listening on TCP port 1241 for an active connection from the Nessus client.

Figure 7-2 *Nessus Setup*

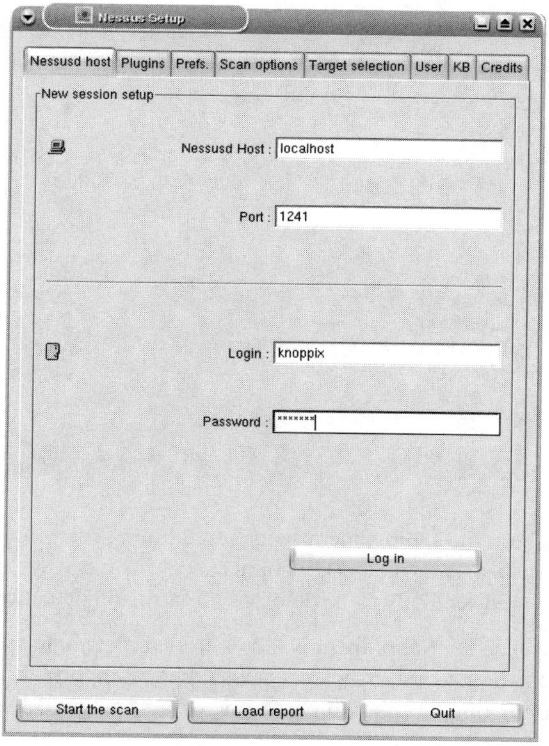

On the **Nessusd host** tab of the Nessus Setup page, enter the username **knoppix** and the password **knoppix**; then click the **Log in** button.

The **Plugins** tab, as shown in Figure 7-3, provides a range of security checks, grouped by vendor and services. The **Enable all** option includes the dangerous tests that can crash the target host or create a DoS situation in a network. For nondestructive testing in a production network, always click the **Enable all but dangerous plugins** button.

Figure 7-3 *Nessus Setup*

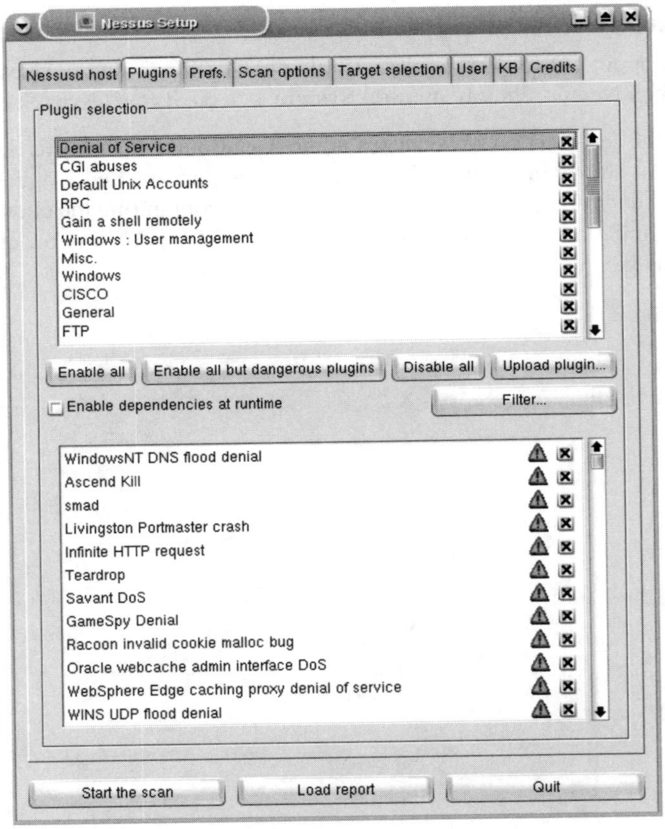

The **Prefs.** tab on the setup page provides fine-tuning for your scanning preference. By default, Nessus uses an Nmap TCP connect scan. You can specify a SYN or a FIN scan because they are less likely to be detected by intrusion detection systems.

Next, you can use the **Scan options** tab on the setup page to specify the port range to be scanned on the target host. Specifying this range is important for Nessus to recognize services running on nonstandard ports. The default range of **1-8000** works well for most situations. You should also select the **Safe checks** check box when testing in a production environment. Selecting this check box forces Nessus to use less intrusive scans. The reports can be less accurate, but the chances of disrupting services are minimized. The **Port scanner** section provides the port scan options to be used by Nessus. The **Ping the remote host** check box should be deselected when scanning hosts behind a firewall, if ICMP is blocked. Figure 7-4 shows the **Scan options** tab with the settings discussed in this paragraph.

Figure 7-4 *Nessus Setup*

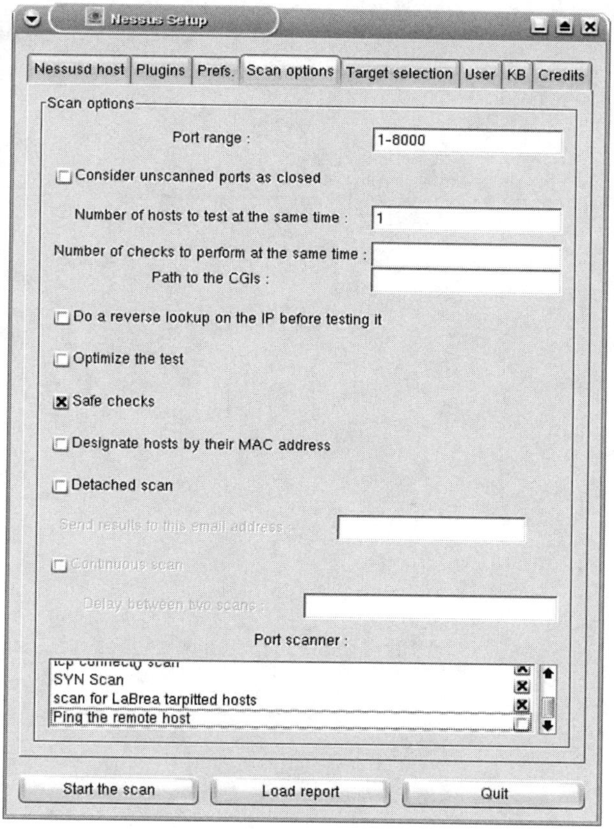

NOTE For more information on any option on the setup page, hover your mouse pointer over that option to reveal a popup box with the embedded comments.

The **Target selection** tab allows you to specify the target to be tested. You can specify a host name or IP address. Multiple hosts can be specified by separating them with commas, as shown in Figure 7-5. You can also specify a range of IP addresses separated by a hyphen, such as **192.168.10.10-25**. To start the scanning, click the **Start the scan** button.

Figure 7-5 *Nessus Setup*

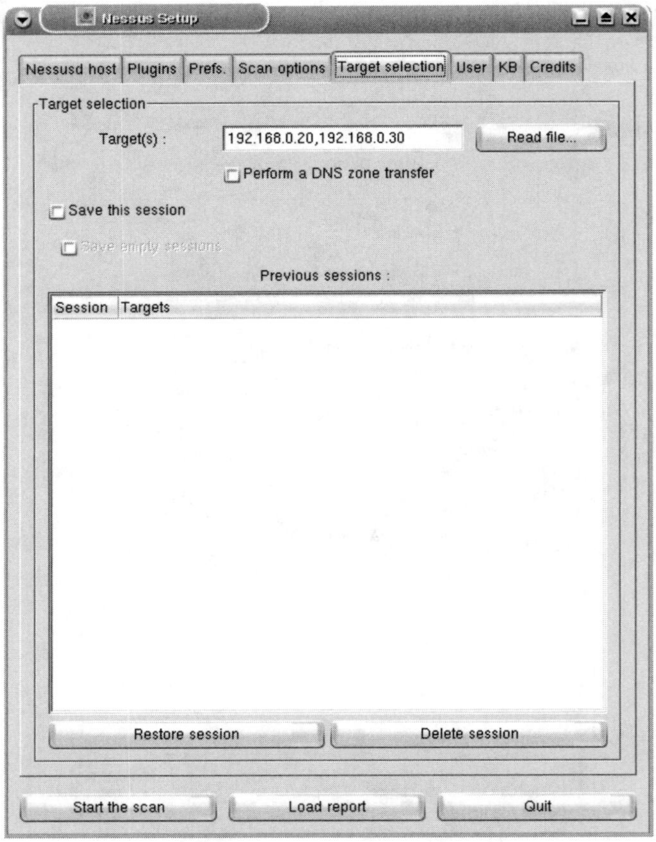

Generating Nessus Reports

After finishing the scan, Nessus generates reports with a list of vulnerabilities. Details for each reported vulnerability are presented as security warnings and security notes, as shown in Figure 7-6.

Figure 7-6 *Nessus Report*

The reports are not saved and are lost after closing the program. To save the reports for future use, click the **Save report** button. In the **Report file format** drop-down list, choose **HTML with Pies and Graphs** to save the reports in HTML format with pie charts and graphs, as shown in Figure 7-7. Additionally, you can specify the location of the destination folder to store the HTML reports.

The HTML reports are saved in web-server-ready format and can be viewed using a standard web browser, as shown in Figure 7-8.

Figure 7-7 *Saving Nessus Reports*

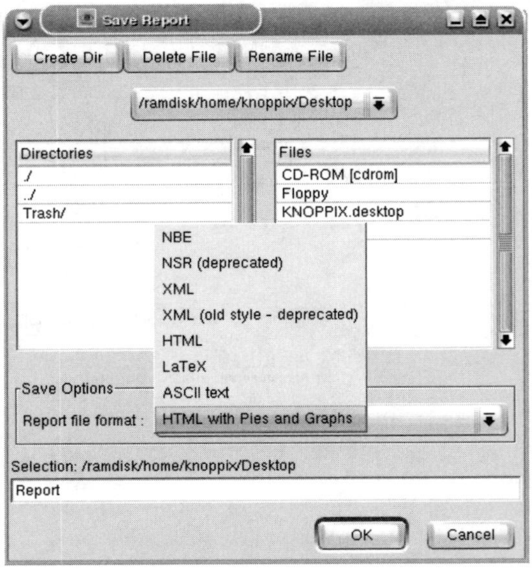

Figure 7-8 *Nessus HTML Report*

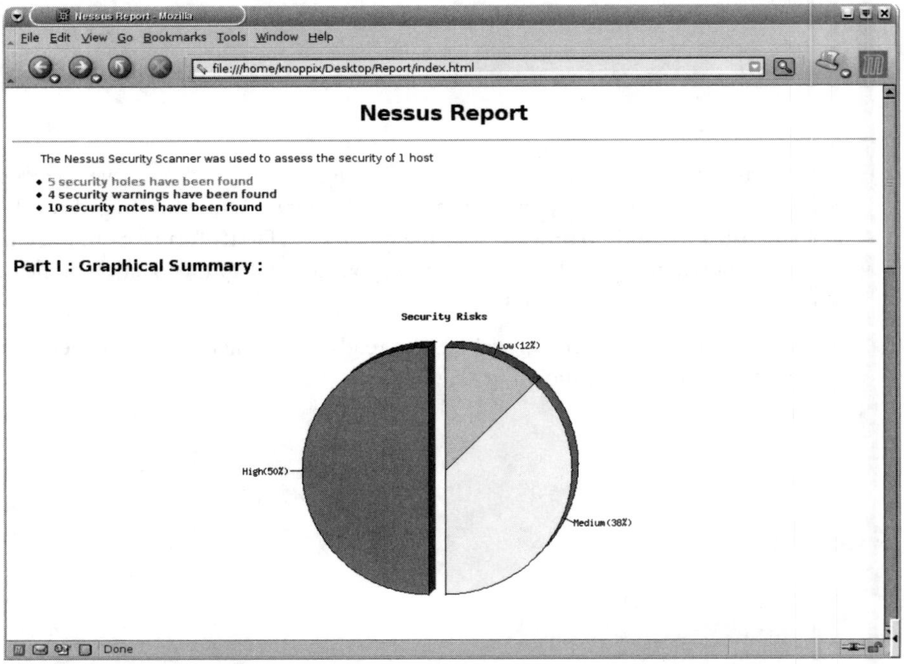

NOTE Live CD-ROMs such as Knoppix automatically detect and mount the local hard drives present on the host computer. Newer versions of Knoppix allow writing on the NTFS partition of the local drives. You can benefit from this feature to save the Nessus reports directly to the hard drive. You can also start the SAMBA server on Knoppix or use the Lin Neighborhood tool in Knoppix to transfer reports to a Windows machine.

A Word of Caution about Nessus

Nessus users should be careful about the following items:

- **Dangerous plug-ins**—As previously mentioned, Nessus plug-ins can crash systems and lead to DoS attacks. Netadmins should exercise caution while using Nessus in a production environment.
- **False positives**—Nessus reports are not a silver bullet for securing your network. The reports can contain false positives and should be verified.
- **Nessus-update plug-ins**—Because new vulnerabilities are constantly discovered, Nessus plug-ins should be updated frequently. Nessus provides an automated script called nessus-update-plugins for maintaining an up-to-date list of plug-ins from the Nessus website. However, because of the read-only nature of live CD-ROMs, the script will not work. Refer to the support section of each live CD-ROM for possible workarounds.

Finally, good Netadmin practices suggest the following:

- Running complete Nessus tests on network devices before deploying them in a production environment
- Running safe scans at least once every quarter on regular production networks
- Informing the concerned departments and authorities before running full scans in production environments
- Using the newer version of Nessus, updated with the latest vulnerabilities database to ensure accurate results

The suggested good practices are equally applicable to Nmap scans. On the other hand, various security mechanisms, such as firewall access lists, rate limiting, private VLANs, and so on, can adversely affect the capability of both Nmap and Nessus.

Packet Analyzers

Packet analyzers are software or hardware devices that capture and analyze the data flowing through the network. Packet analyzers are also called *sniffers, protocol analyzers,* and *network analyzers.* The term *sniffer* became popular after the release of the commercial product Sniffer Pro. Many packet analyzers provide capabilities to filter, store, and analyze the captured data. In fact, most network intrusion detection systems (NIDS) are packet analyzers that watch for peculiar traffic patterns that are unique to network attacks. Packet analyzers work at Layers 1 and 2 of the OSI model but can also decode data at higher layers. This feature enables networking professionals to have a cross-sectional view of the data flowing through the network in real time. The ability to slice and view the raw data flowing through the wires is important when troubleshooting. Such views also help networking professionals to learn and understand the functioning of various protocols and applications. The views also provide clear proof that the network and its components are operational.

Network auditing using packet analyzers is a two-step process, as follows:

Step 1 Preparing the network for using packet analyzers

Step 2 Using packet analyzers for network auditing

Preparing the Network

Packet analyzers function by capturing and analyzing all the data flowing through the wire. Packet analyzers can capture the data through one of the following techniques:

- **Using a hardware wiretap**—Hardware-based wiretaps are expensive and require rewiring of the network segment to accommodate the wiretap.
- **Using port mirroring**—Software-based wiretaps are implemented using the port-mirroring functionality. Port mirroring is built into Ethernet switches and, as such, does not require physical rewiring of the network segment. Consequently, this method is less expensive, more flexible, and preferred over the hardware wiretaps.

Cisco Catalyst switches offer the port-mirroring function, which allows all the traffic flowing through a source port to be broadcast to a mirrored port. The process is transparent to the devices that are connected to the source port. However, the mirrored port receives an exact copy of the data flowing through the source port. By connecting the packet analyzer to the mirrored port, all packets flowing through the source port are available for sniffing.

Port mirroring, also called port monitoring, is referred to as Switched Port Analyzer (SPAN) by Cisco. In addition to the ability to mirror a single source port, Cisco SPAN also allows mirroring of groups of ports or even an entire VLAN. For more information on the limitations and additional SPAN features available on a particular model of Catalyst switch, refer to the product documentation section of the Cisco website (cisco.com).

To configure SPAN on a Cisco Catalyst switch, you should specify the source port, the destination port, and the direction of the traffic through the source that you want to mirror to the destination port. Moreover, you need to physically connect the packet analyzer to the destination SPAN port to enable the packet analyzer to receive the traffic.

The following two sections cover the details involved in configuring SPAN ports on both CatOS- and IOS-based Cisco Catalyst switches.

SPAN for CatOS Switches

To configure a SPAN port on CatOS-based switches, perform the privileged-mode-command specified in Table 7-3.

Table 7-3 *SPAN Configuration—CatOS*

Task	Command
Configure the SPAN source and destination ports.	**set span** {*src_mod/src_ports* | *src_vlans* | **sc0**} {*dest_mod/dest_port*} [**rx** | **tx** | **both**] [**inpkts** {**enable** | **disable**}] [**learning** {**enable** | **disable**}] [**multicast** {**enable** | **disable**}] [**filter** *vlans...*] [**create**]
Verify the SPAN configuration.	**show span**
Disable SPAN.	**set span disable** [*dest_mod/dest_port* | **all**]

Example 7-10 shows how to configure SPAN so that both transmit traffic and receive traffic from port 1/1 (the SPAN source) are mirrored on port 2/1 (the SPAN destination).

Example 7-10 *SPAN Configuration—CatOS*

```
Console> (enable) set span 1/1 2/1

Destination       : Port 2/1
Admin Source      : Port 1/1
Oper Source       : Port 1/1
Direction         : transmit/receive
Incoming Packets: disabled
Learning          : enabled
Multicast         : enabled
Filter            : -
```

SPAN for IOS Switches

To configure a local SPAN session for IOS-based Catalyst switches, use the global-configuration-mode commands listed in Table 7-4.

Table 7-4 *SPAN Configuration—IOS*

Task	Command
Associate the local SPAN source session number with the source.	Router(config)# **monitor session** *local_span_session_number* **source** {{*single_interface* | *interface_list* | *interface_range* | *mixed_interface_list* | *single_vlan* | *vlan_list* | *vlan_range* | *mixed_vlan_list*} [**rx** | **tx** | **both**]}}
Associate the local SPAN session number and the destination ports.	Router(config)# **monitor session** *local_span_session_number* **destination** {*single_interface* | *interface_list* | *interface_range* | *mixed_interface_list*}
Disable the SPAN configuration.	Router(config)# **no monitor session** {*session_number* | **all** | **local** | **range** ***session_range***[[,*session_range*],...]}
Display the SPAN information.	Router# **show monitor** [**session** *session_number*]

Example 7-11 shows how to configure SPAN session 1 so that both transmit traffic and receive traffic from port 5/1 (the SPAN source) are mirrored on port 5/48 (the SPAN destination).

Example 7-11 *SPAN Configuration—IOS*

```
Router(config)# monitor session 1 source interface fastethernet 5/1
Router(config)# monitor session 1 destination interface fastethernet 5/48
```

Using Packet Analyzers

The open source community enjoys a rich choice of versatile packet analyzers that range from general-purpose network analyzers, such as Tcpdump, to specialized password sniffers, like Dsniff. Table 7-5 provides a list of popular packet analyzers and their functions.

Table 7-5 *Popular Packet Analyzers*

Name	Features	Included with Live CD
Tcpdump	Command-line based; provides an array of options for customizing filters and displays.	Knoppix, Knoppix-STD, NST, F.I.R.E., Trinux
Ethereal	GUI based; excellent array of filters for protocols; more than 680 protocols supported.	Knoppix, Knoppix-STD, NST, F.I.R.E., Trinux
EtherApe	Graphical network monitoring tool with visual display of network nodes and traffic.	Knoppix-STD, NST, F.I.R.E.
Ntop	Web-based display of current list of hosts and network usage based on protocols including TCP, UDP, ICMP, ARP, FTP, HTTP, DNS, Telnet, SMTP, POP, IMAP, and SNMP; excellent tool for creating web-based network reports complete with pie charts. Although Ntop is beyond the scope of this chapter, Netadmins are encouraged to try this tool.	Knoppix-STD, NST, Trinux

Both Tcpdump and Ethereal are powerful tools capable of sniffing and analyzing network traffic. Both packet analyzers are under active development and enjoy communitywide support. The following sections cover these tools in more detail.

Tcpdump

Tcpdump is a general-purpose network analyzer capable of capturing and displaying network packets. Tcpdump prints the headers of packets on a network interface, provided that the packet matches the filtering criteria. Tcpdump requires root privileges to run in promiscuous mode and to function correctly. In promiscuous mode, the network interface card (NIC) captures every packet flowing through the wire, even if the packet is destined for other addresses. The syntax for running Tcpdump is as follows:

```
tcpdump [options] [filter]
```

Tcpdump is command-line based, making it ideal for remote use. Netadmins can quickly analyze network anomalies by looking at the raw data captured and filtered by Tcpdump. Tcpdump's greatest strength, its powerful command-line interface, also makes it difficult to work with. The online manual (which can be opened by using the **man tcpdump** command in Linux) is well written, but it can be overwhelming for new users. However, when mastered, Tcpdump is a great asset in a Netadmin's tool kit. Tcpdump options can be classified into the following three categories:

- Input options
- Display options
- Filters

Table 7-6 provides a list of common options for controlling the input behavior of Tcpdump.

Table 7-6 *Tcpdump Input Options*

Option	Explanation
-c *packet-count*	Stop after counting specified packets.
-F *filename*	Specify a text file for filters.
-i *interface*	Listen on interface. If unspecified, Tcpdump searches for the lowest-numbered working interface.
-r *filename*	Read packets from the file created by the **-w** option.
-w *filename*	Write the raw packets to a file and use the –**r** option to read the file.
-n	Don't resolve IP addresses to host names.

By default, Tcpdump output is displayed on the console. Even in a small network, the output can be large and, thus difficult to read on the screen. Table 7-7 provides a list of options for controlling Tcpdump output.

Table 7-7 *Tcpdump Display Options*

Option	Explanation
-e	Display the Layer 2 header information on each output line.
-S	Display absolute TCP sequence numbers.
-s *packet-length*	Specify the length of packet to be captured. The default length of 68 bytes is adequate for IP, ICMP, TCP, and UDP but not for DNS or NFS packets.
-t	Don't display a timestamp on each dump line.
-tttt	Add the date to the timestamp.
-q	Display less information.
-v	Display detailed information; specify **–vv** or **–vvv** for more details.
-x	Display the packet in hexadecimal (HEX) format.
-X	Display the packet in hexadecimal and ASCII formats; useful for analyzing new protocols.

The real strength of Tcpdump lies in its highly flexible filters. These filters can be applied through the command line or using a text file. The text file should include each filter as a separate line. Table 7-8 lists common keywords for Tcpdump filters.

Table 7-8 *Tcpdump Filter Keywords*

Keyword	Explanation
host *hostname-or-ip-address*	Only display the packet from or to the specified host.
net *address/length* or **net** *address* **mask** *mask*	Only display the packet from or to the specified network.
port *port number*	Only display the packet if the source or destination port number matches the specified number.
from	Specify the source host, network, or port.
to	Specify the destination host, network, or port.
src	Specify the source host, network, or port.
dst	Specify the destination host, network, or port.
ether	Specify the Ethernet address.
lp	Specify choosing IP packets.
arp	Specify choosing ARP packets.

Table 7-8 *Tcpdump Filter Keywords (Continued)*

Keyword	Explanation
rarp	Specify choosing RARP packets.
tcp	Specify choosing TCP packets.
udp	Specify choosing UDP packets.
not *parameter*	Negation; can also be expressed by **!**.
and *parameter*	Concatenation; can also be expressed as **&&**.
or *parameter*	Alteration; can also be expressed as ||.

Understanding Tcpdump Output

Because it is a CLI-based tool, Tcpdump lacks the advantage of easy-to-read GUI-based output. Nonetheless, Tcpdump developers have done a great job simplifying the display output. Example 7-12 shows the Tcpdump output. Without the **–c** option, Tcpdump continues to capture packets until the user presses **Ctrl-C**. After stopping, Tcpdump displays a summary of the packets captured, filtered, and dropped by the kernel.

Example 7-12 **tcpdump** *Output*

```
root@ttyp1[knoppix]# tcpdump
tcpdump: verbose output suppressed, use -v or -vv for full protocol decode
listening on eth0, link-type EN10MB (Ethernet), capture size 96 bytes
. . . # output suppressed for clarity
09:40:31.114308 IP 192.168.0.10.www > 192.168.0.101.55411: S
  2675891891:2675891891(0)
  ack 1652868034 win 4128 <mss 1460>
09:40:31.114362 IP 192.168.0.101.55411 > 192.168.0.10.www: . ack 1 win 5840
09:40:31.114464 IP 192.168.0.101.55411 > 192.168.0.10.www: P 1:426(425) ack 1 win
  5840
09:40:31.221797 IP 192.168.0.10.www > 192.168.0.101.55411: . 1:561(560) ack 426 win
  3703

55 packets captured
55 packets received by filter
0 packets dropped by kernel
```

Consider the first packet captured in Example 7-12. Figure 7-9 provides an explanation of each field. While comparing the first line of the output in Example 7-12 to the subsequent line, notice an interesting property of Tcpdump. During the initial TCP handshake, Tcpdump displays the entire sequence number. After the TCP connection is established, Tcpdump converts the absolute sequence numbers to relative sequence numbers for ease in tracking the TCP conversation.

Figure 7-9 *Explanation of Tcpdump Output Fields*

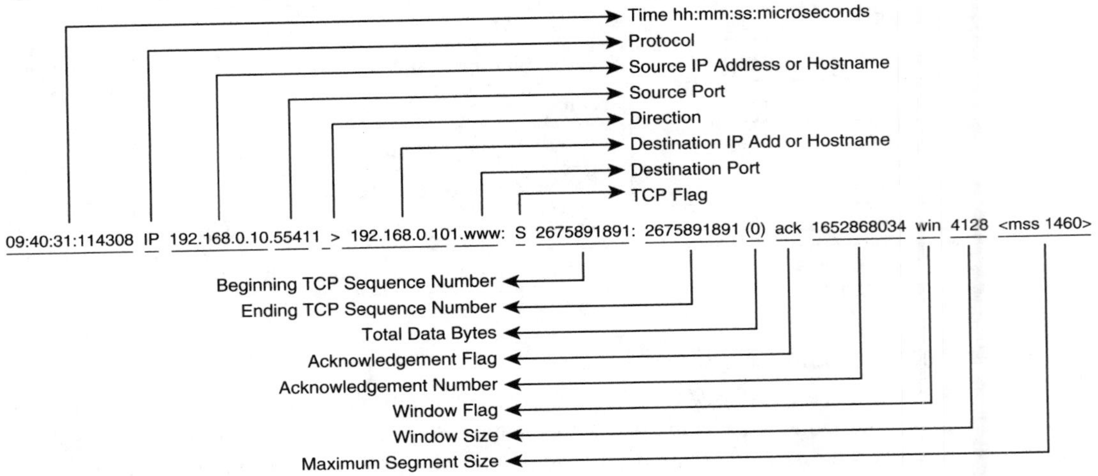

Tcpdump Examples

Table 7-9 shows a list of common examples that illustrate the use of Tcpdump.

Table 7-9 *Common* **tcpdump** *Examples*

Example	Explanation
tcpdump host 192.168.0.10	Display all packets with a source or destination IP address of 192.168.0.10.
tcpdump –i eth0	Display all packets captured through the eth0 interface.
tcpdump not host 192.168.0.20	Display all traffic except that with a source or destination address of 192.168.0.20.
tcpdump ip host 192.168.0.20 and not 192.168.0.1	Display all IP packets between 192.168.0.20 and any host except 192.168.0.1.
tcpdump not port ssh	Display all traffic except SSH traffic; useful when connected to the remote machine through SSH for monitoring.
tcpdump udp	Display UDP packets only.
tcpdump –c 5	Display and capture the first 5 packets only.
tcpdump icmp	Display all ICMP traffic.
tcpdump –w datacapture.txt	Capture all the traffic and save it in raw format in the file capture.txt; useful for saving the output for later analysis.

Table 7-9 *Common* **tcpdump** *Examples (Continued)*

Example	Explanation
tcpdump –r datacapture.txt	Display the traffic from the datacapture.txt file. You can add filters or options to control the output, for example, **tcpdump –r datacapture.txt not host 192.168.0.10**.
tcpdump ether src host 00:50:73:21:d0:67	Display all the traffic with a source MAC address of 00:50:73:21:D0:67.
tcpdump -e net 192.168.22.0 mask 255.255.255.0 a	Display the Layer 2 information for all packets in the 192.168.22.0/24 network.
tcpdump –n –q –c 25 –i eth0 port 80	Display the IP addresses instead of host names; do not show details; capture first 25 packets through interface eth0 with source or destination port 80.
tcpdump –q –i eth0 arp	Display all ARP requests captured through eth0; the **-q** option produces less details.

Tcpdump can be used for the following tasks:

- Scanning network activity caused by Trojan horses, viruses, and worms
- Troubleshooting firewall, routing, and switching issues
- Analyzing the existing network for capacity-planning purposes

TIP Cisco PIX Firewall version 6.2 and higher offers a packet capture feature similar to Tcpdump. Although limited in functionality, this feature can be handy when troubleshooting firewall issues.

Ethereal

Ethereal is a commercial-grade network analyzer with built-in support for more than 680 protocols. Ethereal is similar to Tcpdump but provides the following advantages:

- Has an intuitive and user-friendly graphical user interface that eliminates the need for users to learn command-line options.
- Can read and save capture files from formats supported by other packet analyzers, including Tcpdump, NA-SnifferPro, MS-NetworkMonitor, and Novell LaNalyzer.
- Features an easy-to-read output format with split windows that offer drill-down options to slice through packet headers at various layers of the OSI model.
- Has a GUI for easily creating filters with the ability to mark and color-code certain packets.

- Offers a TCP stream feature that enables re-creating the higher-layer data from raw packets by following the entire TCP conversation. This feature provides the ability to reassemble data in ASCII format from unencrypted sessions such as FTP, SMTP, WWW, and Telnet.
- Provides the ability to view captured packets and the traffic I/O graphical reports in real time.
- Offers multiple options to analyze the captured traffic and create statistical reports; these reports can be generated on the basis of protocols or hosts.
- Also available for Windows OS

Ethereal should be started with root privileges to enable the network interface in promiscuous mode. To start Ethereal with root privileges in Knoppix CD, click **K Menu > Internet > Ethereal (as root)**.

As shown in Figure 7-10, the Ethereal window is split into three panes. The top pane lists all the packets, and the middle pane provides the details of the packet selected in the upper pane. The bottom pane displays the byte-level data contained in the selected packet.

Figure 7-10 *Ethereal Window*

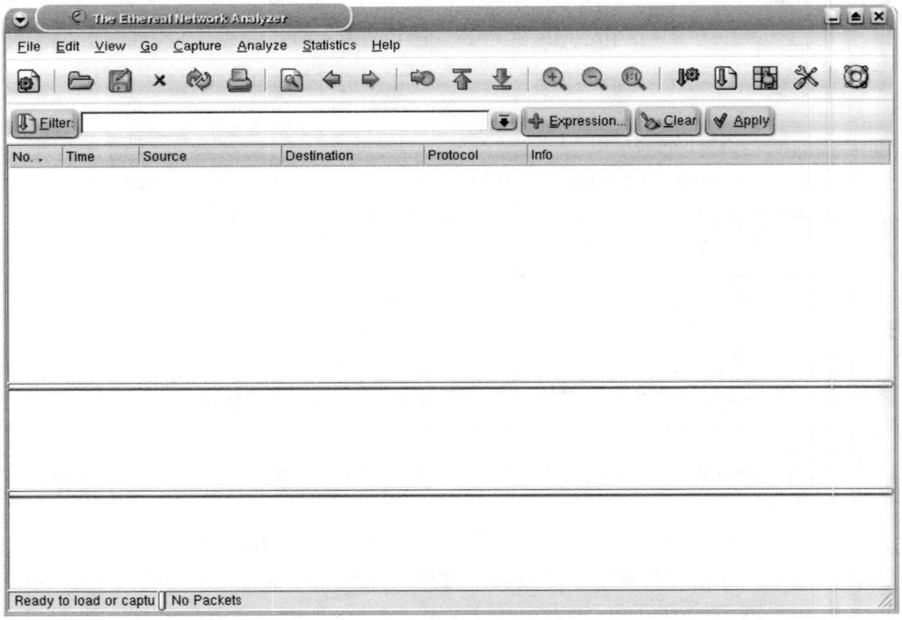

NOTE When starting some applications, including Ethereal, the Knoppix CD might prompt you for a root password. As a security measure, Knoppix does not distribute the preset password for root and instead provides a manual way to reset the password. To set the root password in Knoppix, follow these steps:

1. Open the root shell by clicking **K-menu > KNOPPIX > Root Shell**.
2. In the root shell, set the root password using the following command:

```
root@ttyp0[knoppix] passwd
```

The steps involved in using Ethereal are as follows:

1 Starting a capture session to collect packets
2 Viewing the captured packets
3 Filtering the output
4 Saving the captured files

Starting a Capture Session to Collect Packets

To start capturing packets, choose **Capture > Start** from the Ethereal toolbar.

The Capture Options window (see Figure 7-11) provides various options that are self-explanatory. The Capture Filter options can be used to specify the filters before adding data to the buffer. The Stop Capture section provides a means to limit the amount of packets captured by count, size, or time. To begin capturing data, click the **OK** button in the Capture Options window. The Capture window, which shows a summary of captured packets, is displayed.

Viewing the Captured Packets

Unless an option is selected in the Stop Capture section, Ethereal continues to capture packets while displaying a summary through the Capture window (see Figure 7-12). To view the captured packets, you must stop the capturing process by clicking the **Stop** button in the Capture window. After stopping the capturing process, Ethereal automatically displays all the captured packets.

Figure 7-11 *Ethereal—Capture Options Window*

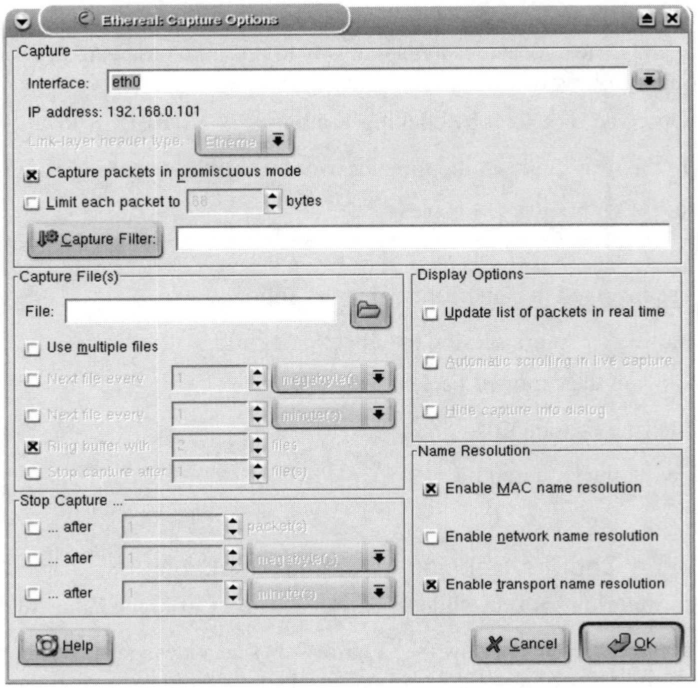

Figure 7-12 *Ethereal—Capture Window*

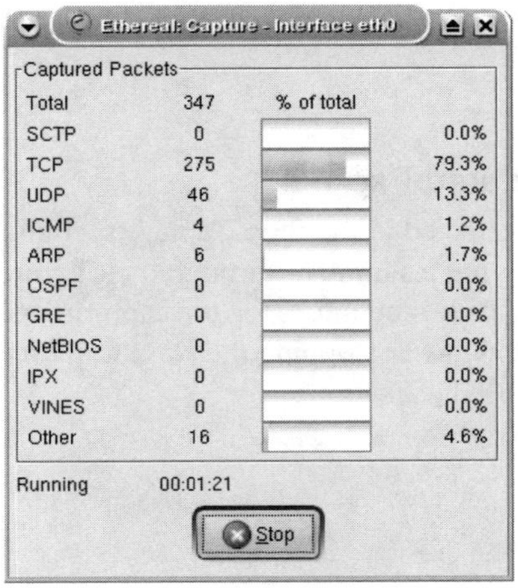

NOTE Ethereal can display the packets in real time, as they are captured. To view packets in real time, you must choose the **Update list of packets in real time** option along with the **Automatic scrolling in live capture** option. Both of these options can be selected in the **Display Options** section of the **Capture Options** window.

Filtering the Output

As shown in Figure 7-13, Ethereal captures a large number of packets. In the upper pane, packet number 265 is highlighted. Ethereal has correctly identified the packet as a CDP packet. The middle pane shows the drilled-down packet details, such as the Device ID string that is contained in the CDP packet. The third pane shows the HEX and ASCII details. The string Router-Dallas is highlighted in both HEX and ASCII formats.

Figure 7-13 *Ethereal—Packet Details*

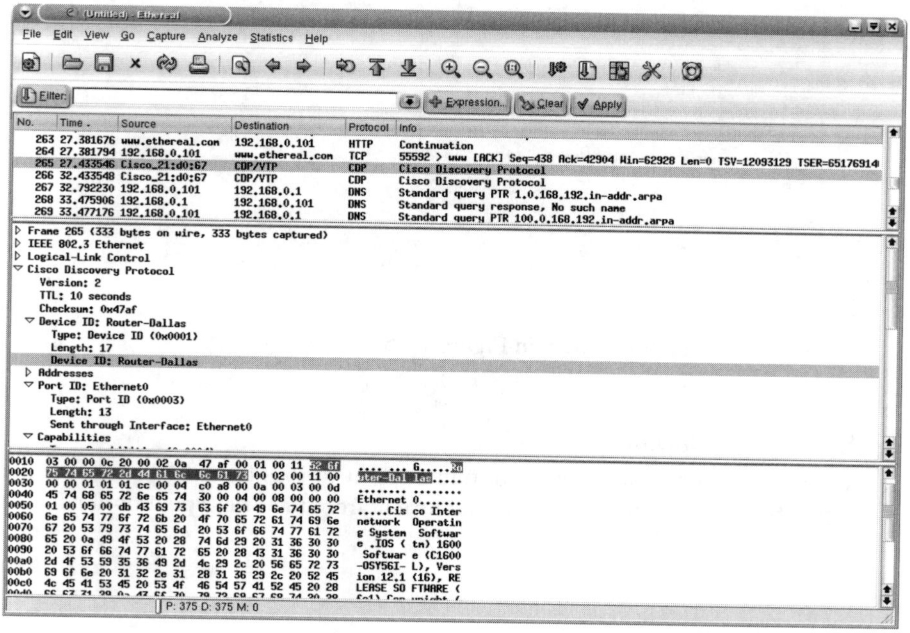

Ethereal also provides a GUI based filter tool for viewing selective packets. To launch the filter GUI, click on the **Expression** button on the toolbar. Figure 7-14 shows the Filter GUI. This example illustrates a filter for selecting packets destined for IP address 192.168.0.20.

Figure 7-14 *Ethereal—Filter Expression*

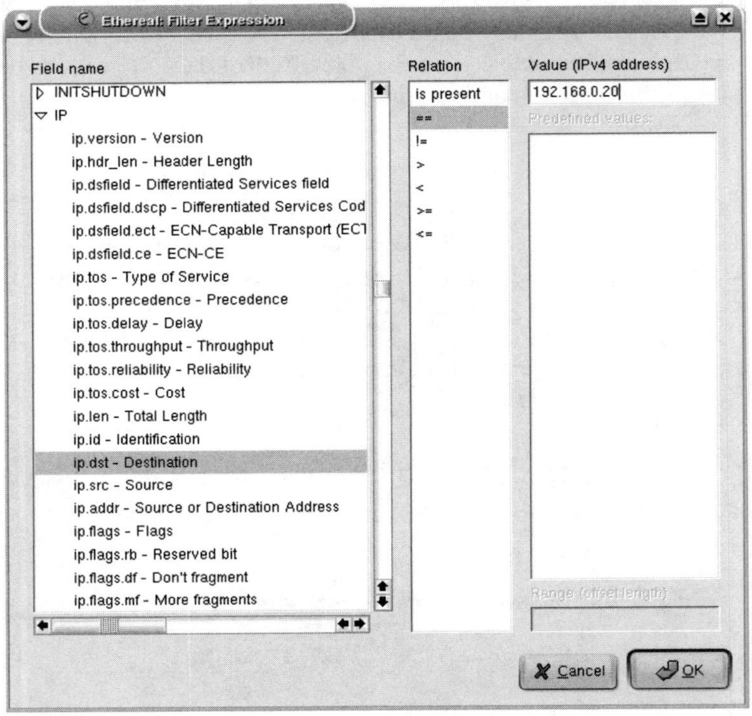

The resulting output is shown in Figure 7-15.

Saving the Captured Files

The captured files can be saved for future use in various formats. To save the files, choose **File > Save As** and choose the desired format from the **File type** drop-down menu.

Figure 7-15 *Ethereal—Filtered Output*

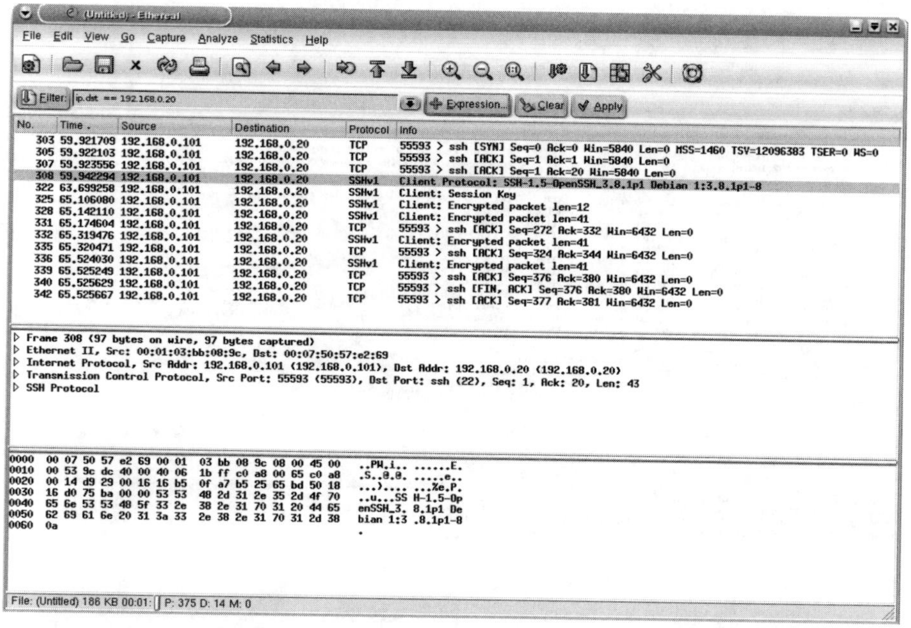

Reassembling TCP Packets

TCP-based applications transfer data by breaking it into smaller pieces. The receiving host reassembles the pieces in the correct order to create the original data. Ethereal can watch a TCP conversation and reassemble the data for display in ASCII format. This feature is useful for troubleshooting mail, web, or Telnet applications.

To re-create the TCP conversation, select and right-click one of the TCP packets in the upper pane. Select the **Follow TCP Stream** option (see Figure 7-16) to view the complete reassembled packet. Figure 7-17 shows the reassembled Telnet session to the host 192.168.0.20.

Figure 7-16 *Ethereal—Follow TCP Stream*

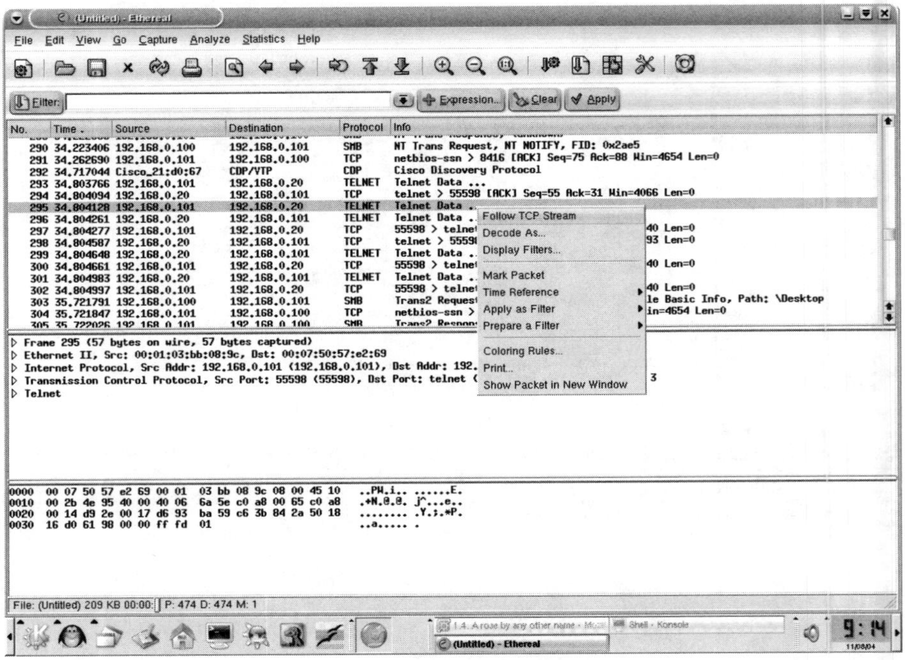

NOTE Nmap, Ethereal, and Tcpdump are also available for the MS-Windows OS; the Windows version is known as Windump. The URL for downloading each of the tools is listed in Table 7-10. The installation procedure is simple, and the usage is similar to the Linux counterpart, thus facilitating Netadmins with these versatile tools without having to leave the familiarity of the Windows environment.

Figure 7-17 *Ethereal—Reassembled Packet*

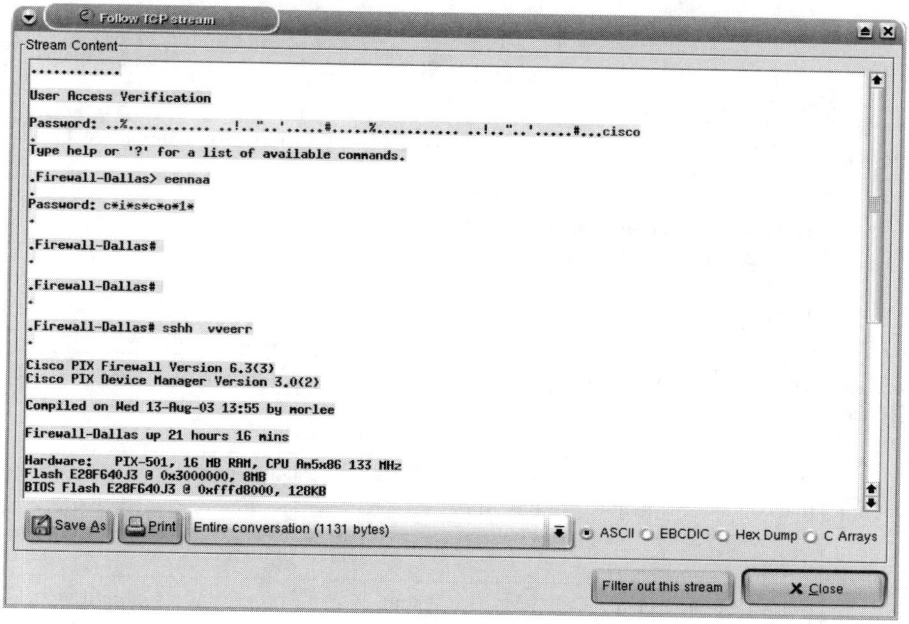

Summary

This chapter introduces Netadmins to bootable CD-ROM–based security tool kits. The bootable CD-ROMs contain fully functional OSs with pre-installed tools that can immediately be used with no installation or configuration requirements. The chapter prepares the Netadmin to use bootable live CD-ROMs for the following tasks:

- Network scanning
- Port scanning
- Remote OS detection
- Vulnerability scanning
- Using CLI-based packet analyzers for network and security analysis
- Using GUI-based packet analyzers for network and security analysis
- Using GUI-based packet analyzers to reassemble a TCP data stream

Table 7-10 lists all the tools discussed in this chapter.

Table 7-10 *Network Security Tools*

Tool	Function	Supported OS	Home Page
Knoppix	Although it is not a security-specific tool, Knoppix is one of the best Debian-based live CD-ROMs with the largest collection of applications; it has excellent hardware-detection capabilities; it is under active development with frequently updated releases.	Linux	http://www.knoppix.net
Knoppix-STD (Security Tools Distribution)	Customized Knoppix CD-ROM with security and network-management tools.	Linux	http://www.knoppix-std.org/
Network Security Toolkit (NST)	Redhat/Fedora-based live CD-ROM that contains the majority of the "Top 75 Security Tools" surveyed at http://www.insecure.org.	Linux	http://www.networksecuritytoolkit.org/
Trinux	Slackware-based live CD-ROM; small enough to run through a floppy disk; older and limited collection of tools; no GUI.	Linux	http://trinux.sourceforge.net/
F.I.R.E.	Good collection of tools; older and limited hardware detection compared to Knoppix and NST.	Linux	http://fire.dmzs.com
Nmap	Network scanner.	Linux, Windows	http://www.nmap.org
Netcat	Port scanner with the additional capability to read and write data across the network using any TCP/UDP port.	Linux	http://netcat.sourceforge.net/
Nessus	Powerful and popular vulnerability scanner.	Linux	http://www.nessus.org/
SARA	Vulnerability scanner based on the SATAN project.	Linux, Windows	http://www-arc.com/sara/

Table 7-10 *Network Security Tools (Continued)*

Tool	Function	Supported OS	Home Page
Tcpdump	CLI-based packet analyzer.	Linux, Windows (Windows version is called Windump)	http://www.tcpdump.org/ http://windump.polito.it/
Ethereal	GUI-based packet analyzer.	Linux, Windows	http://www.ethereal.com/
EtherApe	Graphical network-monitoring tool with a visual display of network nodes and traffic; included with Knoppix-STD, NST, and F.I.R.E. live Linux CD-ROMs.	Linux	http://etherape.sourceforge.net/
Ntop	Web-based tool for displaying current list of hosts and network usage based on protocol; included with Knoppix-STD, NST, and Trinux live Linux CD-ROMs; excellent set of built-in reports for detailed statistical analysis of network traffic.	Linux, Windows	http://www.ntop.org

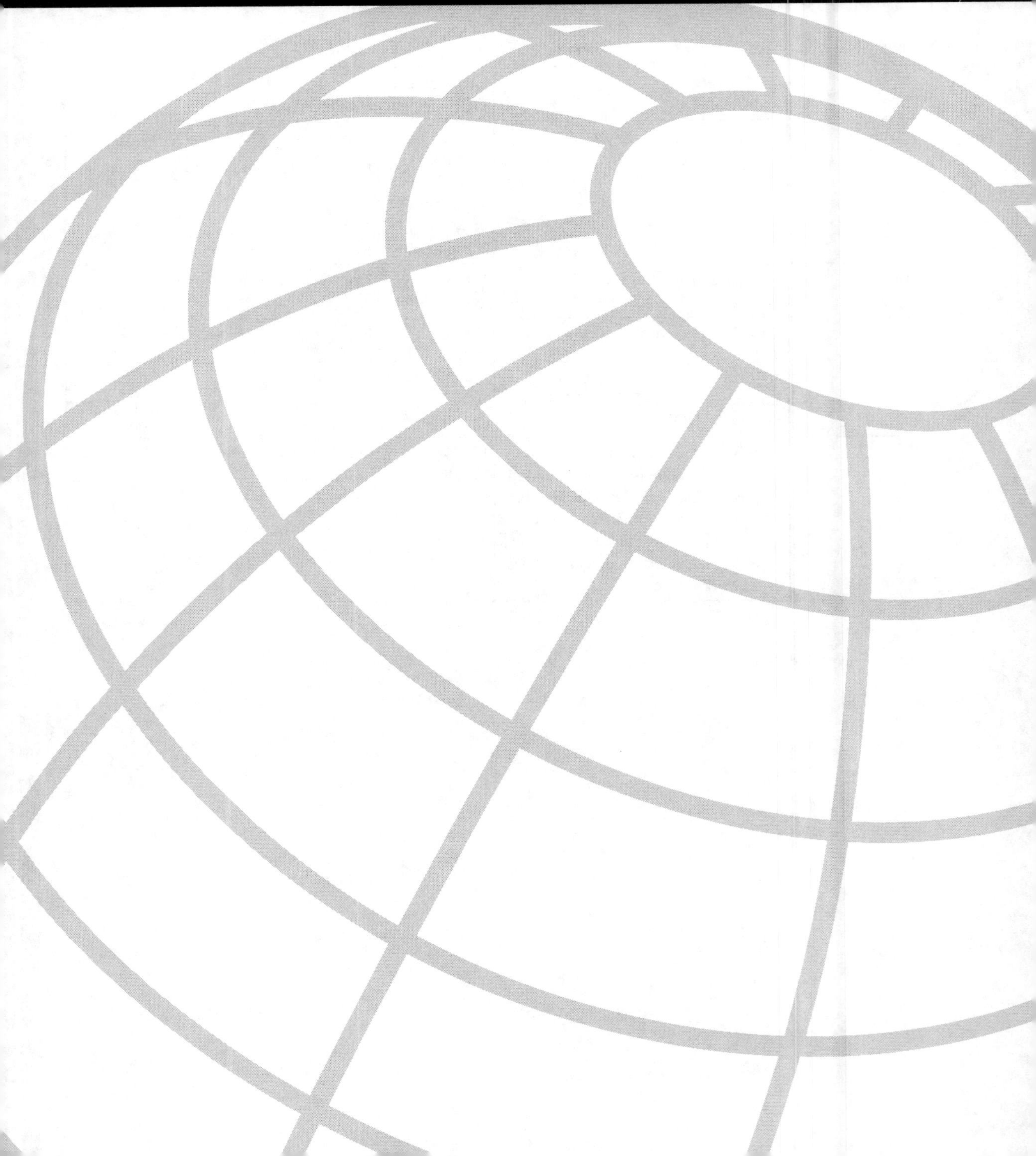

CHAPTER 8

Router and Switch Security

Routers and switches are an integral part of present-day networks. Hardening the routers and switches against potential attacks is an essential part of a Netadmin's duties. This chapter covers the tools used for the following tasks:

- Securing Cisco routers
- Securing Cisco switches

This chapter includes references to many of the security features offered by Cisco routers and switches; however, the primary goal of this chapter is to introduce some of the commonly available tools for testing and implementing security on Cisco routers and switches.

Router and Switch Security Overview

"You are only as secure as your weakest link." Network security professionals often encounter this adage. Present-day networks deploy security measures such as firewalls, intrusion detection systems (IDS), virtual private networks (VPN), and antivirus software to fortify the network. Unfortunately, the most basic network elements—routers and switches—are often ignored as security devices because routers and switches were originally created to enhance network connectivity rather than to provide network security. Consequently, routers and switches are conceptually less secure than dedicated security devices such as firewalls and IDSs.

While an attack on a web server can just render it unoperational, an attack on the edge router can cut off the entire network from its users. Consequently, an attacker can exploit vulnerabilities in the routers or switches to compromise the security of the entire network. Netadmins should make additional efforts to secure the routers and, in turn, the entire the network. Hence, contrary to popular belief, an edge router, rather than a firewall, is the first line of network defense against outside attacks.

Throughout this chapter, the term *router* refers to Cisco IOS-based devices. Because Cisco IOS also supports Catalyst switches, many of the tools and technologies discussed in this chapter are applicable for switches as well.

Securing Cisco Routers

The most common causes of security breaches in routers are as follows:

- **Weak passwords**—This is the most common cause of security breaches; even encrypted passwords are not secure because IOS uses a simpler and reversible encryption algorithm.
- **Unneeded services**—Unnecessary services or features can introduce related vulnerabilities or provide platforms for launching attacks. Some of the services run by default, while others are inadvertently left on after testing or troubleshooting.
- **Protocol and OS vulnerabilities**—Vulnerabilities in the implementation of protocols such as Hypertext Transfer Protocol (HTTP), H.323, or Simple Network Management Protocol (SNMP) can be exploited to crash the router.
- **IOS configuration errors**—A seemingly harmless mistake in router configuration can allow a virus or worm to create a denial of service (DoS) attack, or allow unauthorized access to the router or switch by an attacker.

The following sections cover the tools that a Netadmin can use to discover weaknesses and secure IOS devices.

Cisco Router Passwords

Cisco IOS configuration files offer the following three options for encrypting passwords:

- **Plain text**—Displays the configured passwords with no encryption; it is the least secure method and is not recommended.
- **Type 7 encryption**—Encrypts passwords using a proprietary encryption algorithm; it is better than plain text but still not recommended.
- **Type 5 encryption**—Encrypts passwords using the Message Digest 5 (MD5) hash mechanism. Although it is the most secure option, Type 5 passwords can be cracked with some effort.

By default, IOS configuration files display passwords and other authentication strings in plain text. The **service password-encryption** command can conceal the password by showing it in encrypted form. However, the IOS passwords and other authentication strings are encrypted using the Cisco proprietary Vigenere-based cipher. The Vigenere algorithm, better known as the Type 7 algorithm, is reversible and simpler compared to other current encryption techniques. According to Cisco, "the encryption scheme was designed to avoid password theft via simple snooping or sniffing. It was never intended to protect against someone conducting a password-cracking effort on the configuration file."

The **enable secret** command encrypts the password using the one-way MD5 hash mechanism. To determine which scheme has been used to encrypt a specific password, check the digit that precedes the encrypted string in the configuration file. If that digit is a 7, the password has been encrypted using the Type 7 algorithm. If the digit is a 5, the password has been hashed using the stronger MD5 algorithm. The sample IOS configuration snippet in Example 8-1 depicts encrypted passwords. The Type 5 MD5 algorithm encrypts the **enable secret** password only. The remaining passwords are Type 7.

Example 8-1 *Sample Router Configuration—Router-Dallas.txt*

```
hostname Router-Dallas
service password-encryption
! enable password is encrypted using MD5 algorithm
enable secret 5 $1$rQrR$1j1XTXMbCt/1RGh7Y3BlU1
! user password is encrypted using the weaker algorithm
username user1 password 7 030752180500701E1D
!
key chain MYKEY
 key 1
  key-string 7 141C17125D5679
!
line vty 0 4
 password 7 1511021F0725
 login
!
end
```

Many tools are available for decrypting Cisco IOS passwords from the configuration files. Among the choices, Cain & Abel, available at http://www.oxid.it, is the most versatile and user-friendly tool for decrypting passwords. Cain & Abel can decrypt both Type 7 and Type 5 passwords. The following sections cover the steps used to recover both of these types of passwords from IOS devices.

This tool is compatible with MS-Windows NT/2000/2003/XP, and the installation process is simple. Download the .exe file from the home page and save it locally. Double-click the saved file to begin the installation procedure. The tool provides a ready-to-use graphical user interface (GUI) and requires no postinstallation configuration. The only information required is the configuration file from the target router that contains the encrypted passwords.

NOTE The router configuration file can be captured by using the **show running-configuration** command on the router. You can also download the configuration file from the router to a Trivial File Transfer Protocol (TFTP) server using the **copy runn tftp** command on the router.

Decrypting Type 7 Passwords

Follow these steps to decrypt a Cisco IOS Type 7 password:

Step 1 Start the Cain & Abel tool kit by choosing **Start > Programs > Cain > Cain**.

Figure 8-1 shows the main window for Cain & Abel.

Figure 8-1 *Cain & Abel*

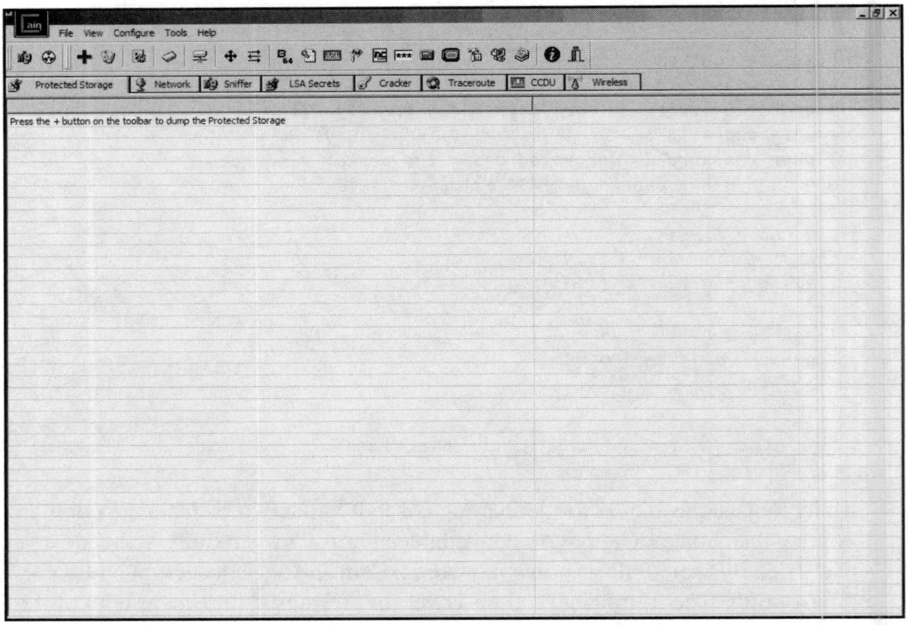

Step 2 From the Cain & Abel main window, launch the Cisco Type 7 Password Decoder by choosing **Tools > Cisco Type-7 Password Decoder**.

Step 3 Paste the Type 7–encrypted password (from the router configuration file) in the Password Decoder window. The decrypted password is instantly displayed in the Decrypted password field.

Figure 8-2 shows the encrypted password string 030752180500701E1D being decrypted as cisco123. Note that the encrypted password was copied from the **username user1 password** 7 030752180500701E1D command in Example 8-1.

Figure 8-2 *Decrypting a Type 7 Password*

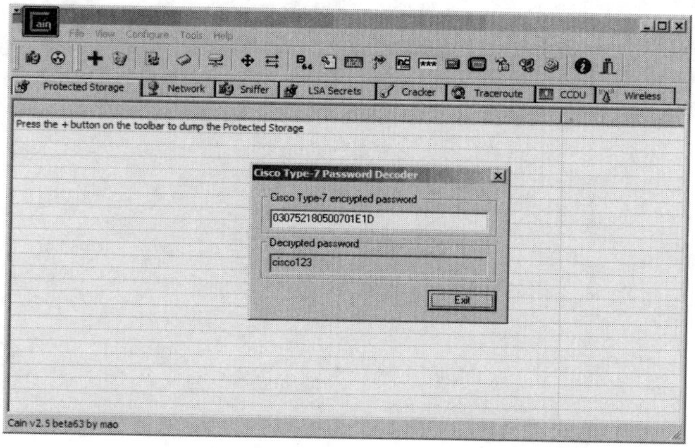

TIP The GetPass utility, from Boson Software Inc. (http://www.boson.com), provides a similar functionality for decrypting Type 7 passwords. But unlike Cain & Abel, GetPass does not offer any other feature.

Decrypting Type 5 Passwords

The Cain & Abel tool, discussed in the previous section of this chapter, can also recover type 5 passwords. Unlike Type 7 passwords, which are encrypted using a reversible algorithm, Type 5 passwords are encrypted using a one-way nonreversible algorithm. The encrypted password string is an MD5 hash that is created from the original password. The Type 5 password-recovery mechanism, used by tools like Cain & Abel, compares the original MD5 hash of the password with the MD5 hash of a known text string. If both the hashes are the same, the password is the same as the known text string. The password-recovery tools work by trying various combinations and lengths of characters. Depending on the length of the original password, decrypting the password can take a large amount of time.

Using Cain & Abel, the Type 5 password-recovery steps are as follows:

Step 1 Start the Cain & Abel tool kit by choosing **Start > Programs > Cain > Cain**.

Step 2 From the Cain & Abel main window, click the **Cracker** tab and then click the **Cisco IOS-MD5 Hashes** option in the left pane, as shown in Figure 8-3.

Figure 8-3 *Cisco IOS-MD5 Hashes Window*

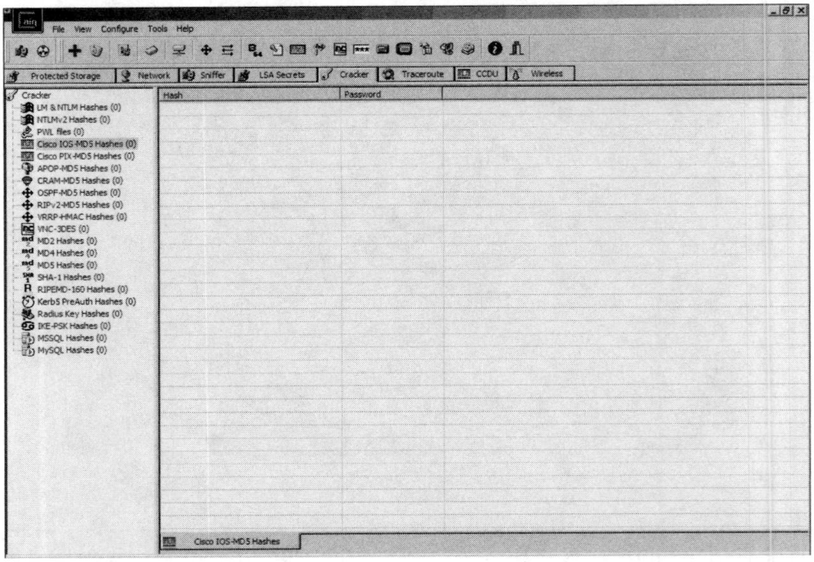

Step 3 As shown in Figure 8-4, right-click in the right pane and select **Add to list** from the menu that appears. Follow the prompts to provide the location of the IOS configuration file that contains the MD5 hashes. This example uses the Router-Dallas.txt file from Example 8-1.

The program parses the configuration file and lists all the MD5 hashes in the **Hash** column.

Step 4 Right-click the hash and select **Brute-Force Attack** to launch the Brute-Force Attack window, as shown in Figure 8-5. Accept the default values and click the **Start** button to begin the process. Depending on the length of the password and the CPU utilization, the process can take a large amount of time.

The process automatically stops after cracking the hash. As shown in Figure 8-6, the process recovered the original password **pal** that was specified on the router using the **-enable secret pal** command.

TIP The short password used in this section is for illustration purposes only. Actual passwords should always be more than eight characters long, with a combination of uppercase and lowercase letters, numbers, and special characters (such as #, %, and &). An eight-character-long password composed only of numbers and uppercase and lowercase alphabetic characters can have 62^8 (218 trillion) possible combinations.

Simply by making that password nine characters long, the possible combinations increase to 13 quadrillion. On the other hand, an eight-character-long password that also uses special characters (such as #, %, and &) can have 6 quadrillion combinations. Using the same set of characters, a nine-character-long password increases to 572 quadrillion combinations.

Figure 8-4 *Cain & Abel—IOS Configuration File*

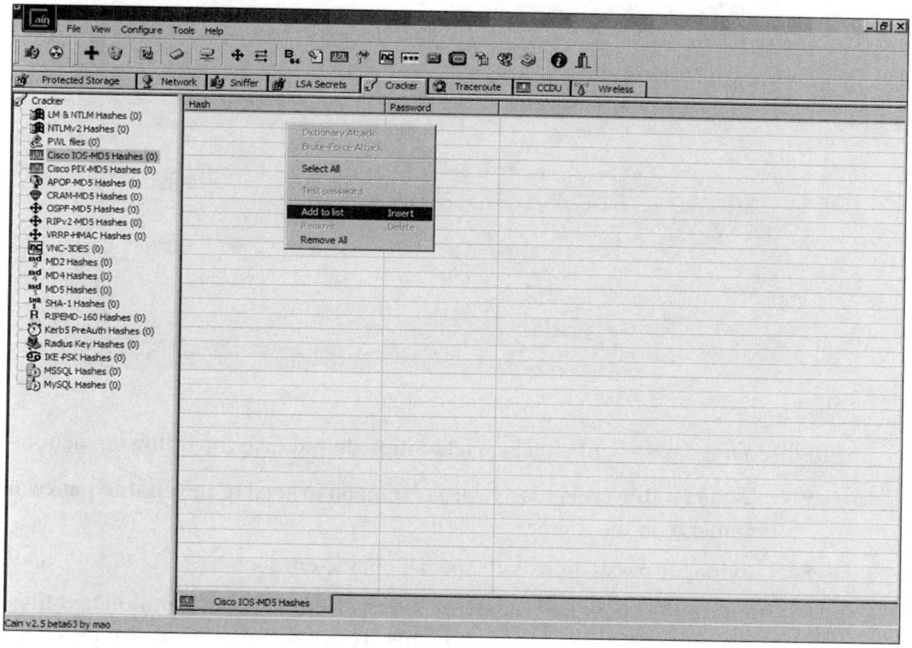

Figure 8-5 *Cain & Abel—Brute-Force Attack Window*

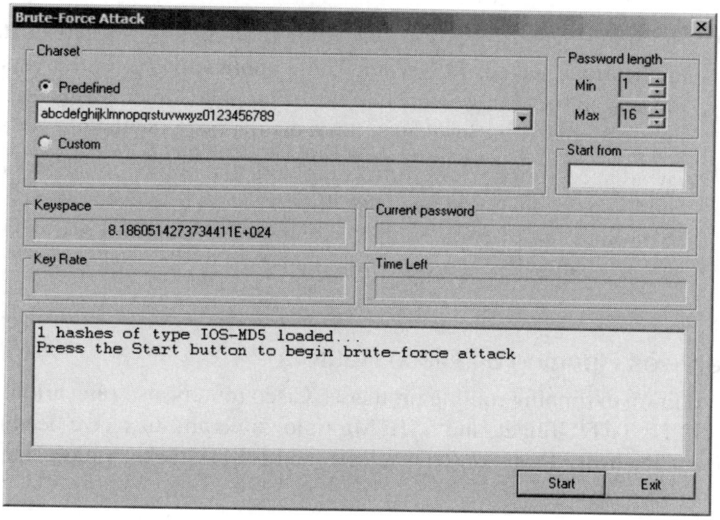

Figure 8-6 *Cain & Abel—Brute-Force Attack Result*

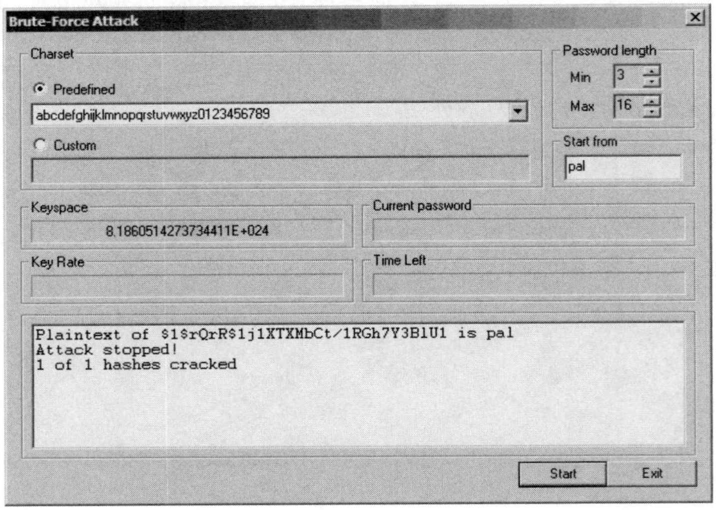

To discourage password attacks, Netadmins should take the following actions:

- Use the **enable secret** *password* command instead of the **enable password** *password* command on the router.
- Use longer passwords, with special characters such as *, %, #, $, ~, and!.
- Remove the encrypted password strings from the configuration text files before e-mailing or making offline backups. To remove password strings, open the configuration file in a text editor (such as Notepad or WordPad), delete the encrypted text, and save the file.
- Be careful when directly saving configuration files in sophisticated word processing applications such as MS-Word. These applications offer the Version feature, which records all the changes made to the original document. This feature can unintentionally disclose deleted passwords from the document.
- Avoid accessing devices from computers that belong to others because a keystroke-capture program might be in use. If you access a device in front of unauthorized users or through a third-party computer, change the password as quickly as possible, but be sure to change it in a secure environment.

Unneeded Services Running on Cisco Routers

In addition to running routing protocols, Cisco routers also run various other services, such as HTTP, TFTP, Telnet, and SSH. Multiple vulnerabilities have been reported in SNMP, Cisco Discovery Protocol (CDP), SSH, and HTTP stacks implemented in IOS. These vulnerabilities can crash the router or help an attacker to gain access to the router. Netadmins often start a service or protocol for testing and troubleshooting. Later, the Netadmin might forget about it and unintentionally leave these services running. By conducting a port scan, an attcker can learn about these ports that are in listening state on this router. Armed with this information, the attacker can make an educated guess regarding the services that are running on the router.

Nmap, discussed in Chapter 7, "Network Security Testing," is the ideal tool for port-scanning the router. The command syntax to perform a Transmission Control Protocol (TCP) and User Datagram Protocol (UDP) scan on a router is as follows:

nmap -sT -sU *hostname-or-IP-address*

Example 8-2 shows a TCP and UDP port scan performed on a router with an IP address of 192.168.0.10.

Example 8-2 *Port Scanning Using Nmap*

```
linuxbox:~# nmap -sT -sU 192.168.0.10
Starting nmap 3.75 ( http://www.insecure.org/nmap/ ) at 2004-11-20 12:33 PST
Interesting ports on 192.168.0.10:
(The 3136 ports scanned but not shown below are in state: closed)
PORT     STATE          SERVICE
23/tcp   open           telnet
67/udp   open|filtered  dhcpserver
79/tcp   open           finger
80/tcp   open           http
520/udp  open|filtered  route
MAC Address: 00:10:7B:CC:57:EB (Cisco Systems)
Nmap run completed -- 1 IP address (1 host up) scanned in 1242.591 seconds
linuxbox:~#
```

The port scan results, highlighted in Example 8-2, indicate that the router is running the Routing Information Protocol (RIP) because it is listening on port UDP 520. The other services running on the router are as follows:

- Telnet on TCP 23
- DHCP Server (Bootp) on UDP 67
- Finger on TCP 79
- HTTP on TCP 80

To secure the router, these services should be manually turned off or configured for restricted access. The global-configuration-mode commands for securing the router in this case are listed in Example 8-3.

Example 8-3 *Securing the Router*

```
! access-list to restrict  Telnet and http access to the router
access-list 10 permit host 192.168.0.100
access-list 10 permit host 192.168.0.101
! limit Telnet to the router from host listed in acess-list 10
line vty 0 4
 access-class 10 in
```

continues

Example 8-3 *Securing the Router (Continued)*

```
! disable Dhcp/Bootp service
no ip bootp server
! disable finger service
no ip finger
! limit http access to the router from host listed in acess-list 10
ip http access-class 10
```

Protocol and OS Vulnerabilities

The information provided by the port scanner is limited to the ports and services that are running on the router. Nessus, discussed in Chapter 7, provides detailed discovery of the vulnerabilities associated with the services running on the router. Nessus reports include possible solutions for each discovered vulnerability. To scan the router for vulnerabilities, follow these steps:

Step 1 Start Nessus using the Knoppix live CD.

Step 2 Log in to the Nessus client using the username **knoppix** and the password **knoppix** on the **Nessusd host** tab.

Step 3 Choose the appropriate plug-ins from the **Plugins** tab, as shown in Figure 8-7. Nessus includes a Cisco-specific plug-in that scans for vulnerabilities in Cisco hardware. Along with the Cisco plug-in, you should also include the following plug-ins for a thorough scan:

- Denial of Service
- Misc.
- General
- Useless Services

Step 4 Specify the IP address of the target router on the **Target selection** tab, and click the **Start the scan** button to begin the scanning process.

Step 5 After the scan is complete, save the results in the desired format.

Example 8-4 provides a partial report of the vulnerability scan performed on Router 192.168.0.10. As indicated by the highlighted section, Nessus can detect more information than the port scans. Nessus reports the lists of security holes, warnings, and notes associated with each of the ports that were discovered in listening state. In this example, Nessus discovered that the target router is running Telnet, Finger, WWW, RIP, and Open Shortest Path First (OSPF). The router is also responding to Internet Control Message Protocol (ICMP) traffic. Additional highlighted text shows why Nessus thinks that running RIP is a security risk. The report also provides security holes, warnings, notes, and solutions to the discovered vulnerabilities.

Figure 8-7 *Nessus Plug-In Selections*

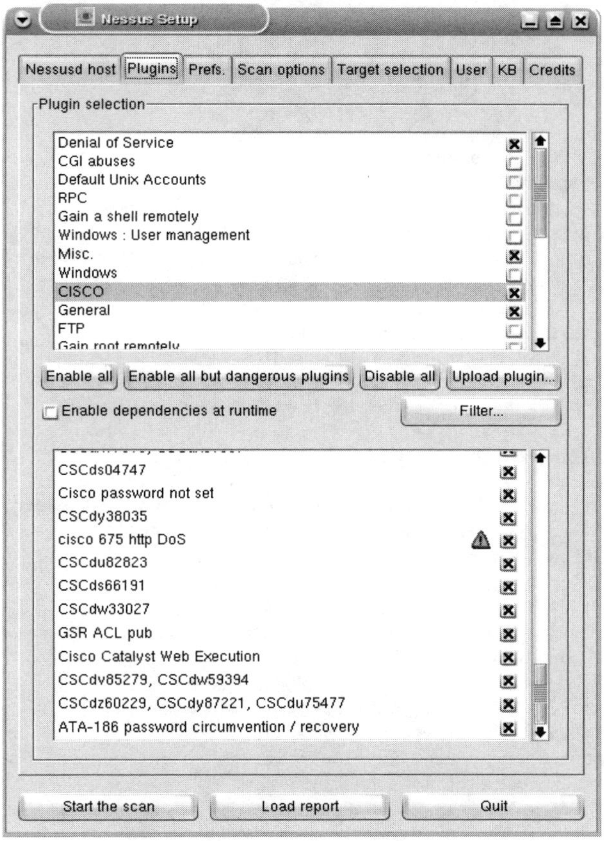

Example 8-4 *Nessus Scan Report in Text Format*

```
Nessus Scan Report
------------------
SUMMARY
 - Number of hosts which were alive during the test : 1
 - Number of security holes found : 1
 - Number of security warnings found : 2
 - Number of security notes found : 9
TESTED HOSTS
 192.168.0.10 (Security holes found)
DETAILS
+ 192.168.0.10 :
 . List of open ports :
   o telnet (23/tcp) (Security notes found)
   o finger (79/tcp) (Security notes found)
   o www (80/tcp) (Security notes found)
```

continues

Example 8-4 *Nessus Scan Report in Text Format (Continued)*

```
    o general/tcp (Security warnings found)
    o general/udp (Security notes found)
    o route (520/udp) (Security hole found)
    o general/ospf (Security notes found)
    o general/icmp (Security warnings found)
  . Information found on port telnet (23/tcp)
     Remote telnet banner :
     User Access Verification
         Password:
  . Information found on port telnet (23/tcp)
     This port was detected as being open by a port scanner but is now closed.
     This service might have been crashed by a port scanner or by a plugin
!. . . .
!. . . . text suppressed for clarity
! . . . .
  . Warning found on port general/tcp
     The remote host does not discard TCP SYN packets which
     have the FIN flag set.
     Depending on the kind of firewall you are using, an
     attacker may use this flaw to bypass its rules.
     See also : http://archives.neohapsis.com/archives/bugtraq/2002-10/0266.html
                http://www.kb.cert.org/vuls/id/464113
     Solution : Contact your vendor for a patch
     Risk factor : Medium
     BID : 7487
  . Information found on port general/tcp
     Nmap found that this host is running Cisco IOS 12.0(5)WC3 - 12.0(16a)
. . . .
. Vulnerability found on port route (520/udp) :
     RIP-1 does not implement authentication.
     An attacker may feed your machine with bogus routes and
     hijack network connections.
     Solution : disable the RIP agent if you don't use it, or use
                RIP-2 and implement authentication
     Risk factor : Medium
. . . .
  . Information found on port general/ospf
     An OSPF v2 agent is running on this host.
     The netmask is 255.255.255.0
     The Designated Router is 192.168.0.10
     Risk factor : Low
  . Warning found on port general/icmp
     The remote host answers to an ICMP timestamp request. This allows an
      attacker to know the date which is set on your machine.
      This may help him to defeat all your time based authentication protocols.

     Solution : filter out the ICMP timestamp requests (13), and the outgoing
      ICMP timestamp replies (14).
     Risk factor : Low
     CVE : CAN-1999-0524
  . . . .
------------------------------------------------------
This file was generated by the Nessus Security Scanner
```

The report shown in Example 8-4 was saved in text format. Nessus also provides options to save the report in colorful Hypertext Markup Language (HTML) format, with embedded hyperlinks, graphs, and pie charts. Figure 8-8 shows the graphical version of the same report. The report shows a pie chart and bar graph that summarize the results. Although not shown in the figure, the report also contains a summary of the scan in text format, complete with hyperlinks for detailed explanations of each item.

Figure 8-8 *Nessus Graphical Report*

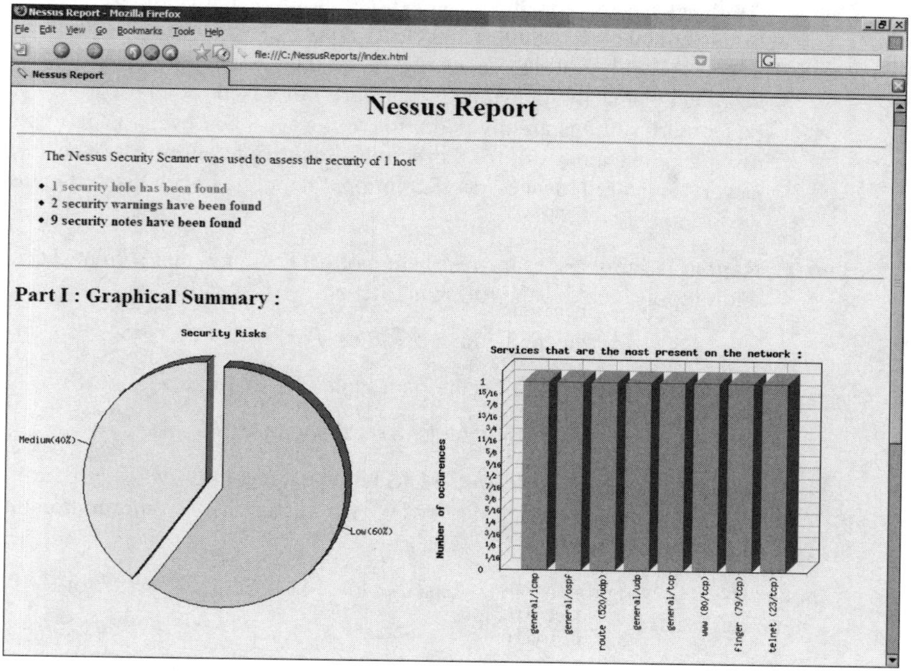

IOS Configuration Errors: Audit Using RAT

Router Audit Tool (RAT), distributed by the Center for Internet Security (CIS), is a benchmark and audit tool for Cisco IOS routers and switches. Unlike the generic security tools, such as Nmap or Nessus, RAT focuses on Cisco routers. RAT reports are detailed and include specific IOS commands for fixing the discovered weaknesses. RAT is supported in both Windows and Linux OSs. The Linux version of RAT is similar to the MS-Windows version, including the command-line interface (CLI) options. Overall, RAT is an excellent tool that Netadmins can use to secure Cisco routers and switches. RAT works for both routers and switches, because many of the router-hardening commands also apply to IOS-based switches. RAT is under development to keep pace with the latest Cisco IOS features.

However, RAT is not a silver bullet for network security or router configuration. Netadmins should exercise caution and common sense while using RAT.

RAT functions as a three-step process:

Step 1 **Acquire**—Specify the configuration for the target router. RAT can either use a configuration file in text format or Telnet into the destination router to pull the running configuration.

Step 2 **Audit**—Checks and compares the configuration against the benchmark rules defined by the National Security Agency (NSA) Cisco Router Security Configuration Guide. The predefined benchmark rules are designed primarily to enhance the security of Cisco routers. The benchmark settings are divided into two levels. The Level 1 benchmark provides the framework for a minimum-security requirement, whereas Level 2 is geared toward specific optional features. Level 2 is still under development.

Step 3 **Report**—Summarizes the results in both HTML and text format. The audit report includes the following items:

- Each rule checked with a pass/fail score
- A weighted overall score on a scale of 1 to 10
- Suggested IOS commands to fix the vulnerabilities

RAT is available for download from the CIS home page at http://www.cisecurity.org/. The installation files include the pdf version of the Router Security Configuration Guide from the National Security Agency.

Although the following discussion is based on the MS-Windows version of RAT, the usage is similar to that of the Linux version.

Installing RAT

The RAT installation steps for the MS-Windows version are as follows:

Step 1 Download the installer file in .exe format from http://www.cisecurity.org.

Step 2 Save the file to your local hard drive.

Step 3 Double-click the saved .exe file and follow the prompts to begin the installation process. The default location for the program files is C:\CIS\RAT. If you install RAT in a nondefault location, avoid using filenames or folder names that contain spaces.

Configuring RAT

RAT is shipped with predefined default rules. These rules are generic and require customization for site-specific information, such as the IP addresses of the syslog server, NTP server, or internal network. RAT documents refer to the customizing process as *localizing.* RAT provides ncat_config, a CLI-based interactive tool for localizing.

To configure RAT, run the ncat_config.exe file from the command line. Ncat_config prompts you for information specific to the local network, as shown in Example 8-5. The highlighted text indicates data that is input by the user in response to the ncat_config queries. The example is for illustration purposes only; the exact response depends on your network environment.

Example 8-5 *Configuring RAT Using ncat_config*

```
C:\CIS\RAT\bin>ncat_config.exe
ncat_config: Select configuration type [cisco-ios] ?
ncat_config: Applying rules from:
ncat_config:   C:\CIS\RAT/etc/configs/cisco-ios/common.conf
ncat_config:   C:\CIS\RAT/etc/configs/cisco-ios/cis-level-1.conf
ncat_config:   C:\CIS\RAT/etc/configs/cisco-ios/cis-level-2.conf
ncat_config: Apply some or all of the rules that are selectable [Yes] !
ncat_config:   Apply some or all of CIS level 1 rules [Yes] ?
ncat_config:     Check rules and data related to system management [Yes] !
ncat_config:       Use local authentication [Yes] ?
ncat_config:         Create new AAA model using local usernames and passwords [y
es] !
ncat_config:         Create local usernames [yes] !
ncat_config:           Username of user for local authentication [username1] ?
  spope

ncat_config:       Apply standard SNMP checks [Yes] !
ncat_config:         Disable SNMP server [yes] ? no
ncat_config:         Forbid SNMP read-write [yes] ?
ncat_config:         Forbid SNMP community string 'public' [yes] !
ncat_config:         Forbid SNMP community string 'private' [yes] !
ncat_config:         Require an ACL to be applied for all SNMP access [no] ? yes
ncat_config:        Specify ACL number to be used for filtering SNMP requests [99] ?
ncat_config:         Define SNMP ACL [no] ? yes
ncat_config:        Address block and mask for SNMP access [192.168.1.0 0.0.0.255] ?
  192.168.0.0 0.0.0.255
ncat_config:       Apply standard checks to control access to the router [Yes] ?
ncat_config:         Allow Telnet access for remote administration? [Yes] ?
ncat_config:           Allow only telnet access for remote login [yes] !
ncat_config:         Specify maximum allowed exec timeout [yes] !
ncat_config:           Exec timeout value [10 0] ?
ncat_config:         Disable the aux port [yes] ?
ncat_config:         Use default AAA login authentication on each line [Yes] ?
Info: skipping IOS - login named list because it conflicts with IOS - login defa
  ult which is already selected
ncat_config:         require line passwords [yes] ?
ncat_config:         Require an enable secret [yes] !
ncat_config:         Check line password quality [yes] ?
```

continues

Example 8-5 *Configuring RAT Using ncat_config (Continued)*

```
ncat_config:        Check user password quality [yes] ?
ncat_config:        Require VTY  ACL to be applied [yes] !
ncat_config:          Specify ACL number to be used for telnet or ssh [182] ?
ncat_config:        Define simple (one netblock + one host) VTY ACL [yes] ?
ncat_config:          Address block and mask for administrative hosts [192.168.
  1.0 0.0.0.255] ? 192.168.0.0 0.0.0.255
ncat_config:          Address for administrative host [192.168.1.254] ? 192.168
  .0.100
ncat_config:      Disable unneeded management services [Yes] ?
ncat_config:        Forbid finger service (on IOS 11) [yes] !
ncat_config:        Forbid identd service (on IOS 11) [yes] !
ncat_config:        Forbid finger service (on IOS 12) [yes] !
ncat_config:        Forbid finger service (on IOS 12) [yes] !
ncat_config:        Forbid http service [yes] !
ncat_config:        Encrypt passwords in the configuration [yes] !
ncat_config:    Check rules and data related to system control [Yes] !
ncat_config:      Synchronize router time via NTP [Yes] ?
ncat_config:        Designate an NTP time server [yes] !
ncat_config:          Address of first NTP server [1.2.3.4] ? 192.168.0.30
ncat_config:        Designate a second NTP time server [yes] ?
ncat_config:          Address of second NTP server [5.6.7.8] ? 192.168.0.35
ncat_config:        Designate a third NTP time server [yes] ? no
ncat_config:      Apply standard logging rules [Yes] ?
ncat_config:        Use GMT for logging instead of localtime [Yes] ? no
ncat_config:        Timestamp log messages [yes] !
ncat_config:        Timestamp debug messages [yes] !
ncat_config:        enable logging [yes] !
ncat_config:        Designate syslog server [yes] !
ncat_config:          Address of syslog server [13.14.15.16] ? 192.168.0.30
ncat_config:        Designate local logging buffer size [yes] !
ncat_config:          Local log buffer size [16000] ?
ncat_config:        Require console logging of critical messages [yes] !
ncat_config:        Require remote logging of level info or higher [yes] !
ncat_config:      Disable unneeded control services [Yes] ?
ncat_config:        Forbid small TCP services (on IOS 11) [yes] !
ncat_config:        Forbid small UDP services (on IOS 11) [yes] !
ncat_config:        Forbid small TCP services (on IOS 12) [yes] !
ncat_config:        Forbid small UDP services (on IOS 12) [yes] !
ncat_config:        Forbid bootp service [yes] !
ncat_config:        Disable CDP service [yes] ?
ncat_config:        Forbid config service [yes] ?
ncat_config:        Use tcp-keepalive-in service to kill stale connections [yes
  ] !
ncat_config:        Forbid tftp service [Yes] ?
ncat_config:    Check rules and data related to data flow [Yes] !
ncat_config:      Apply standard routing protections [Yes] ?
ncat_config:        Forbid directed broadcasts (on IOS 11) [yes] !
ncat_config:        Forbid directed broadcasts (on IOS 12) [yes] !
ncat_config:        Forbid IP source routing [yes] !
ncat_config:  Apply some or all of CIS Level 2 rules [No] ?
Saving selections to C:\CIS\RAT/etc/configs/cisco-ios/local.conf
C:\CIS\RAT\bin>
```

Most of the rules work well with their default values. However, Example 8-5 shows customizing information, such as usernames and SNMP access control lists (ACL). A complete list of the ncat_config questions is also included in the cisco-ios-router-questionnaire.pdf document, located at the default location of C:\CIS\RAT.

Running RAT

RAT is currently only available as a CLI-based tool. The command syntax for running RAT to audit a router configuration text file is as follows:

```
rat router-config-file
```

In this syntax, *router-config-file* is the name and location of the text file that contains the router configuration. Example 8-6 shows RAT auditing the configuration from the text file router-dallas.cfg, located in the C:\CIS\RAT\bin directory.

Example 8-6 *RAT Auditing Configuration from Text File*

```
C:\CIS\RAT\bin>rat router-dallas.cfg
auditing router-dallas.cfg...
Parsing: /C:\CIS\RAT/etc/configs/cisco-ios/common.conf/
Parsing: /C:\CIS\RAT/etc/configs/cisco-ios/cis-level-1.conf/
Parsing: /C:\CIS\RAT/etc/configs/cisco-ios/cis-level-2.conf/
Parsing: /C:\CIS\RAT/etc/configs/cisco-ios/local.conf/
Checking: router-dallas.cfg
done checking router-dallas.cfg.
Parsing: /C:\CIS\RAT/etc/configs/cisco-ios/common.conf/
Parsing: /C:\CIS\RAT/etc/configs/cisco-ios/cis-level-1.conf/
Parsing: /C:\CIS\RAT/etc/configs/cisco-ios/cis-level-2.conf/
Parsing: /C:\CIS\RAT/etc/configs/cisco-ios/local.conf/
ncat_report: writing router-dallas.cfg.ncat_fix.txt.
ncat_report: writing router-dallas.cfg.ncat_report.txt.
ncat_report: writing router-dallas.cfg.html.
ncat_report: writing rules.html (cisco-ios-benchmark.html).
ncat_report: writing all.ncat_fix.txt.
ncat_report: writing all.ncat_report.txt.
ncat_report: writing all.html.
C:\CIS\RAT\bin>
```

As highlighted in Example 8-6, RAT creates various report files in text and HTML format. Table 8-1 provides details of some of the files created by RAT.

Table 8-1 *Report Files Generated by RAT*

Filename/Extension*	Details
index.html	HTML index of reports; suitable for publishing directly to a web server.
all.html	HTML report listing pass/fail status for all rules checked on all devices.
rules.html	HTML version of the benchmark data that was used by RAT to create the audit report.
router-config-filename.html	Audit report in HTML format; this is the most useful report for Netadmins because it contains the pass/fail results, weighted score, and cut-and-paste commands for fixing the problems.
router-config-filename.txt.ncat_report.txt	Audit report in text format.
router-config-filename.txt.ncat_fix.txt	List of cut-and-paste commands that fix problems discovered by RAT.

The device-specific HTML report is split into three sections, as follows:

- **First section**—Lists the pass/fail results for each rule applied
- **Second section**—Provides a summary of the results with their score
- **Third section**—Provides IOS commands for fixing the configurations that were reported as failed in Section 1

The ability to provide ready-to-use IOS commands is a significant advantage offered by RAT over other tools such as Nmap or Nessus.

Figure 8-9 shows the first section of the router-dallas.cfg.html report. Each rule is hyper-linked to the details section in the rules.html file. Also, the rules that failed the benchmark test are color-coded red (shaded gray in this figure) for easy viewing.

Figure 8-10 depicts the remaining two sections of the router-dallas.cfg.html report. The summary section provides scoring results for the audit checks. The results are expressed as both a percentage and a weighted score. Weighted scores are based on the importance of each rule, as listed in the first column of Section 1.

Figure 8-9 *RAT Audit Report: Rules Test Results*

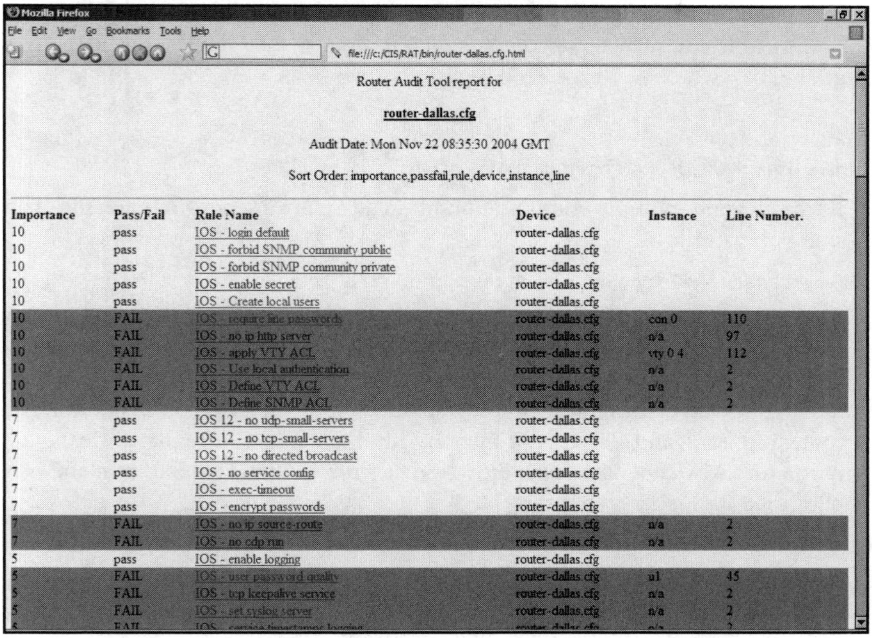

Mozilla Firefox

File Edit View Go Bookmarks Tools Help

file:///c:/CIS/RAT/bin/router-dallas.cfg.html

Router Audit Tool report for

router-dallas.cfg

Audit Date: Mon Nov 22 08:35:30 2004 GMT

Sort Order: importance,passfail,rule,device,instance,line

Importance	Pass/Fail	Rule Name	Device	Instance	Line Number.
10	pass	IOS - login default	router-dallas.cfg		
10	pass	IOS - forbid SNMP community public	router-dallas.cfg		
10	pass	IOS - forbid SNMP community private	router-dallas.cfg		
10	pass	IOS - enable secret	router-dallas.cfg		
10	pass	IOS - Create local users	router-dallas.cfg		
10	FAIL	IOS - require line passwords	router-dallas.cfg	con 0	110
10	FAIL	IOS - no ip http server	router-dallas.cfg	n/a	97
10	FAIL	IOS - apply VTY ACL	router-dallas.cfg	vty 0 4	112
10	FAIL	IOS - Use local authentication	router-dallas.cfg	n/a	2
10	FAIL	IOS - Define VTY ACL	router-dallas.cfg	n/a	2
10	FAIL	IOS - Define SNMP ACL	router-dallas.cfg	n/a	2
7	pass	IOS 12 - no udp-small-servers	router-dallas.cfg		
7	pass	IOS 12 - no tcp-small-servers	router-dallas.cfg		
7	pass	IOS 12 - no directed broadcast	router-dallas.cfg		
7	pass	IOS - no service config	router-dallas.cfg		
7	pass	IOS - exec-timeout	router-dallas.cfg		
7	pass	IOS - encrypt passwords	router-dallas.cfg		
7	FAIL	IOS - no ip source-route	router-dallas.cfg	n/a	2
7	FAIL	IOS - no cdp run	router-dallas.cfg	n/a	2
5	pass	IOS - enable logging	router-dallas.cfg		
5	FAIL	IOS - user password quality	router-dallas.cfg	u1	45
5	FAIL	IOS - tcp keepalive service	router-dallas.cfg	n/a	2
5	FAIL	IOS - set syslog server	router-dallas.cfg	n/a	2

Figure 8-10 *RAT Audit Report: Summary and Fixes*

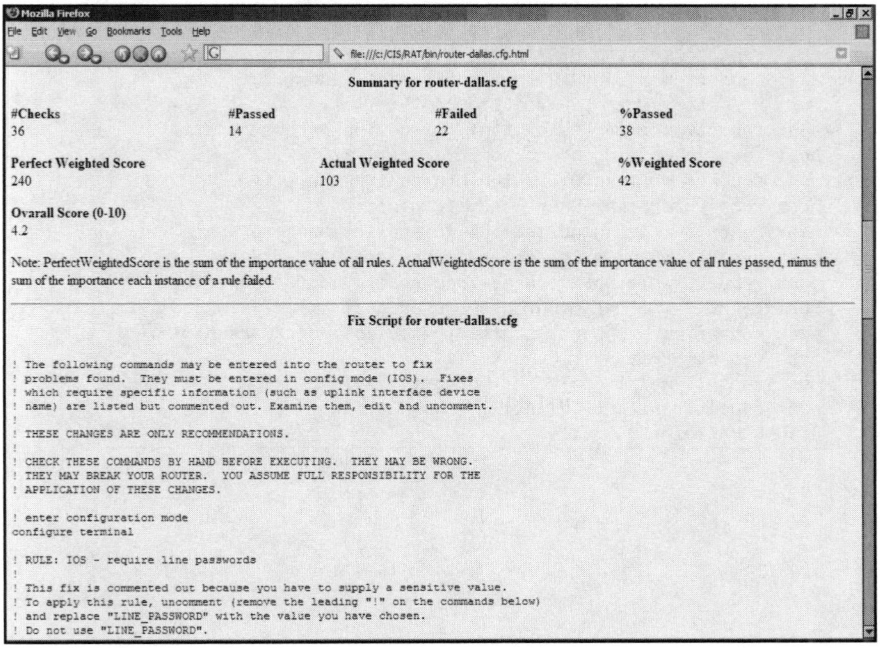

Mozilla Firefox

File Edit View Go Bookmarks Tools Help

file:///c:/CIS/RAT/bin/router-dallas.cfg.html

Summary for router-dallas.cfg

#Checks	#Passed	#Failed	%Passed
36	14	22	38

Perfect Weighted Score	Actual Weighted Score	%Weighted Score
240	103	42

Ovarall Score (0-10)
4.2

Note: PerfectWeightedScore is the sum of the importance value of all rules. ActualWeightedScore is the sum of the importance value of all rules passed, minus the sum of the importance each instance of a rule failed.

Fix Script for router-dallas.cfg

```
! The following commands may be entered into the router to fix
! problems found.  They must be entered in config mode (IOS).  Fixes
! which require specific information (such as uplink interface device
! name) are listed but commented out. Examine them, edit and uncomment.
!
! THESE CHANGES ARE ONLY RECOMMENDATIONS.
!
! CHECK THESE COMMANDS BY HAND BEFORE EXECUTING.  THEY MAY BE WRONG.
! THEY MAY BREAK YOUR ROUTER.  YOU ASSUME FULL RESPONSIBILITY FOR THE
! APPLICATION OF THESE CHANGES.

! enter configuration mode
configure terminal

! RULE: IOS - require line passwords
!
! This fix is commented out because you have to supply a sensitive value.
! To apply this rule, uncomment (remove the leading "!" on the commands below)
! and replace "LINE_PASSWORD" with the value you have chosen.
! Do not use "LINE_PASSWORD".
```

The last section of the report in Figure 8-10, "Fix Script for router-dallas.cfg," provides IOS commands that can be directly pasted into the global configuration mode of Cisco routers. Some of the commands are commented out because they require further editing, such as adding passwords or customized security strings.

Auditing Multiple Configurations

RAT can audit multiple configuration files and create a report for each file. The command syntax is as follows:

rat *router-config-file1 router-config-file2 . . .*

Example 8-7 shows the command used to audit the configuration files SFO-router.cfg, NY-router.cfg, and Corporate-router.cfg. RAT firsts parses all the configuration files for auditing. Next, it creates individual reports for each router configuration file. As shown by the highlighted text in this example, the three reports (SFO-router.cfg.html, NY-router.cfg.html, and Corporate-router.cfg.html) are named after the corresponding configuration file. Also, note that each file is directly created in HTML format and is ready to be published through a web server.

Example 8-7 *RAT Auditing Multiple Configuration Files*

```
C:\CIS\RAT\bin>rat SFO-router.cfg NY-router.cfg Corporate-router.cfg
auditing SFO-router.cfg...
Parsing: /C:\CIS\RAT/etc/configs/cisco-ios/common.conf/
. . .
. . .! IRRELEVENT TEXT REMOVED FOR CLARITY
. . .
Parsing: /C:\CIS\RAT/etc/configs/cisco-ios/local.conf/
ncat_report: writing SFO-router.cfg.ncat_fix.txt.
ncat_report: writing SFO-router.cfg.ncat_report.txt.
ncat_report: writing SFO-router.cfg.html.
ncat_report: writing rules.html (cisco-ios-benchmark.html).
ncat_report: writing NY-router.cfg.ncat_fix.txt.
ncat_report: writing NY-router.cfg.ncat_report.txt.
ncat_report: writing NY-router.cfg.html.
ncat_report: writing rules.html (cisco-ios-benchmark.html).
ncat_report: writing Corporate-router.cfg.ncat_fix.txt.
ncat_report: writing Corporate-router.cfg.ncat_report.txt.
ncat_report: writing Corporate-router.cfg.html.
ncat_report: writing rules.html (cisco-ios-benchmark.html).
ncat_report: writing all.ncat_fix.txt.
ncat_report: writing all.ncat_report.txt.
ncat_report: writing all.html.
C:\CIS\RAT\bin>
```

Auditing Live Routers

As shown in the previous example, RAT audits a router by reading the configuration text files. RAT can also directly Telnet into the target router, pull the configuration file, and then perform auditing. The command syntax is as follows:

```
rat --snarf [options] ipaddress-of-target-router
```

The **--snarf** switch instructs RAT to download the configuration file through Telnet. You can supply Telnet authentication parameters, such as a username and password, through CLI options. Table 8-2 provides a list of CLI options used by RAT.

Table 8-2 *RAT Options*

Option	Details
--snarf	Instructs RAT to Telnet into the target router and download the running configuration file
--user	Specifies the name to be used to log in to the router
--userpw	Specifies the Telnet password or the password associated with the username specified by the **-- user** option
--enablepw	Specifies the enable password for entering the router's privileged mode
--noenable	Instructs RAT not to enter enable mode before downloading the running configuration file

If you use the **--snarf** option with no other option, RAT prompts you for various passwords. Note that as each of the passwords is entered, RAT echoes them on-screen in clear text.

Example 8-8 illustrates RAT using the –**-snarf** option, with no other options, to audit the router. As shown in the highlighted text, RAT prompts for the login (Telnet) password and enable password. RAT also warns about displaying the password in clear text. RAT downloads, saves, and parses the configuration file to create the audit report. Also note that RAT prompts for a TACACS or SecureID passcode. You can press **Enter** to skip the prompt because most Cisco routers do not use passcodes.

Example 8-8 *RAT Audit Through Telnet*

```
C:\CIS\RAT\bin>rat --snarf 192.168.0.10
snarfing 192.168.0.10...WARNING: Password will be echo'd to screen.
Password: cisco
WARNING: Password will be echo'd to screen.
Hit Enter unless using TACACS or SecureID.
Passcode:
WARNING: Password will be echo'd to screen.
Enable password: ciscopal123
C:\CIS\RAT/bin/snarf: Saved ./192.168.0.10
done.
auditing 192.168.0.10...
Parsing: /C:\CIS\RAT/etc/configs/cisco-ios/common.conf/
Parsing: /C:\CIS\RAT/etc/configs/cisco-ios/cis-level-1.conf/
```

continues

Example 8-8 *RAT Audit Through Telnet (Continued)*

```
Parsing: /C:\CIS\RAT/etc/configs/cisco-ios/cis-level-2.conf/
Parsing: /C:\CIS\RAT/etc/configs/cisco-ios/local.conf/
Checking: 192.168.0.10
done checking 192.168.0.10.
Parsing: /C:\CIS\RAT/etc/configs/cisco-ios/common.conf/
Parsing: /C:\CIS\RAT/etc/configs/cisco-ios/cis-level-1.conf/
Parsing: /C:\CIS\RAT/etc/configs/cisco-ios/cis-level-2.conf/
Parsing: /C:\CIS\RAT/etc/configs/cisco-ios/local.conf/
ncat_report: writing 192.168.0.10.ncat_fix.txt.
ncat_report: writing 192.168.0.10.ncat_report.txt.
ncat_report: writing 192.168.0.10.html.
ncat_report: writing rules.html (cisco-ios-benchmark.html).
ncat_report: writing all.ncat_fix.txt.
ncat_report: writing all.ncat_report.txt.
ncat_report: writing all.html.
C:\CIS\RAT\bin>
```

CAUTION The passwords shown in this example (Telnet password cisco and enable password ciscopal123) are for illustration purposes only. Always use passwords that are at least eight characters long and contain special characters such as #, %, and &.

You can also specify the Telnet and enable passwords through the CLI. To get the same results as shown in Example 8-8, the command is as follows:

```
rat --snarf --userpw=cisco --enablepw=ciscopal123 192.168.0.10
```

For routers that need a username and password combination for Telnet login, you can use the - -**username** option. For example, to audit Router 192.168.0.5 with username spope, use the following RAT command:

```
rat --snarf --username=spope --userpw=cisco --enablepass=cisco123 192.168.0.5
```

The password associated with username spope is cisco, and the enable password is cisco123.

IOS Configuration Errors: Audit Using SDM

Cisco Router and Security Device Manager (SDM) is a web-based device-management tool for configuring routing, switching, security, and quality of service (QoS) services on Cisco routers. The SDM wizards enable users to deploy, configure, and monitor a Cisco router without requiring knowledge of the CLI. Cisco Netadmins can use the Cisco SDM for faster and easier deployment of Cisco routers for both network security features and WAN access. Cisco SDM is supported on Cisco 830S, 1700, 1800, 2600XM, 2800, 3600, 3700, 3800, 7200, and 7301 Series routers. Cisco SDM also provides monitoring, fault management, and troubleshooting for Cisco routers. Unlike RAT, SDM supports only IOS routers.

CAUTION The configurations generated by SDM are approved by the Cisco Technical Assistance Center (TAC), and the checks that are built into Cisco SDM reduce configuration errors. Despite these facts, Netadmins should exercise caution and common sense while pushing configurations through SDM.

From a router security perspective, SDM provides the following security audit tools:

- **Security Audit Wizard**—Tests your router configuration to discover potential security problems and then presents you with a screen that lets you determine which problems you want to fix. After you have made this determination, the wizard makes the necessary changes to the router configuration to fix those problems. The wizard is based on security best practices recommended by the International Computer Security Association (ICSA) and the Cisco TAC.
- **One-Step Lockdown**—Automatically makes the necessary configuration changes to correct potential security problems without going through the wizard.

To use the security audit tool, you must first install and configure SDM on the router. After SDM is installed, you can connect to the router through your browser to launch SDM. From within the SDM window, you can use the built-in utilities such as the Security Audit Wizard or the One-Step Lockdown. The following sections cover each of these tasks.

Deploying SDM on Cisco Routers

SDM comes preinstalled on new router models. You can also download the latest SDM files from the Cisco website and copy them to the router using the following command:

```
Router# copy tftp://tftp-server-IP-address/sdm.tar flash:
```

A complete list of router models and IOS versions supported by SDM is available at the Cisco SDM home page:

http://www.cisco.com/go/sdm

NOTE At the time of publication, Cisco released a newer version of SDM that can also be installed locally on a PC rather than running it off of a router.

Configuring SDM

To configure the router for SDM, enable the HTTP server on the router and define a local username and password. Example 8-9 provides a list of commands that enable the HTTP server with local authentication using the username **user1** and the password **cisco123**. The **ip http secure-server** command enables an HTTPS server on the router. HTTPS is more secure and is supported on every IOS version that supports the Crypto/IPSec feature set, starting with Cisco IOS Release 12.2.5(T).

Example 8-9 *Configuring IOS to Enable SDM*

```
Router#configure terminal
Enter configuration commands, one per line. End with CNTL/Z.
Router(config)#ip http server
! --you can also enable https server if supported by the IOS image--
Router(config)#ip http secure-server
Router(config)#ip http authentication local
Router(config)#username user1 privilege 15 password 0 cisco123
```

NOTE If you enable an HTTPS server, disable the HTTP server using the **no ip http server** command to prevent unencrypted access.

Launching SDM to Use the Security Audit Tools

Follow these steps to launch SDM:

Step 1 Open a Java-enabled web browser on the PC and use the URL https://*router-IP-address*. If the IOS version does not support HTTPS, use the URL http://*router-IP-address*.

Step 2 Enter the username and password in the username/password dialog box and follow the prompts to launch the IOS home page, as shown in Figure 8-11. Based on Example 8-9, the username is user1 and the password is cisco123.

Step 3 In the left pane of the IOS home page, click **Cisco Router and Security Device Manager** to launch the SDM Java applet. SDM is a signed Java applet. This can cause your browser to display a security warning or reprompt you for login credentials. Accept the certificate and supply the same login credentials as you did in Step 2.

The SDM home page provides hardware and software summaries and a configuration overview of the router, as shown in Figure 8-12. The home page is also the starting point for configuring and monitoring the router.

Figure 8-11 *IOS Home Page*

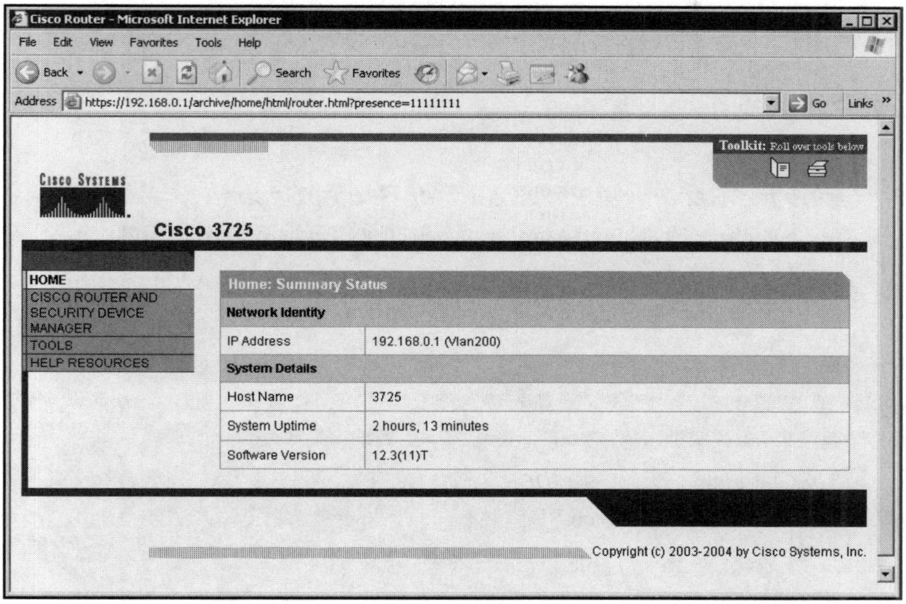

Figure 8-12 *SDM Home Page*

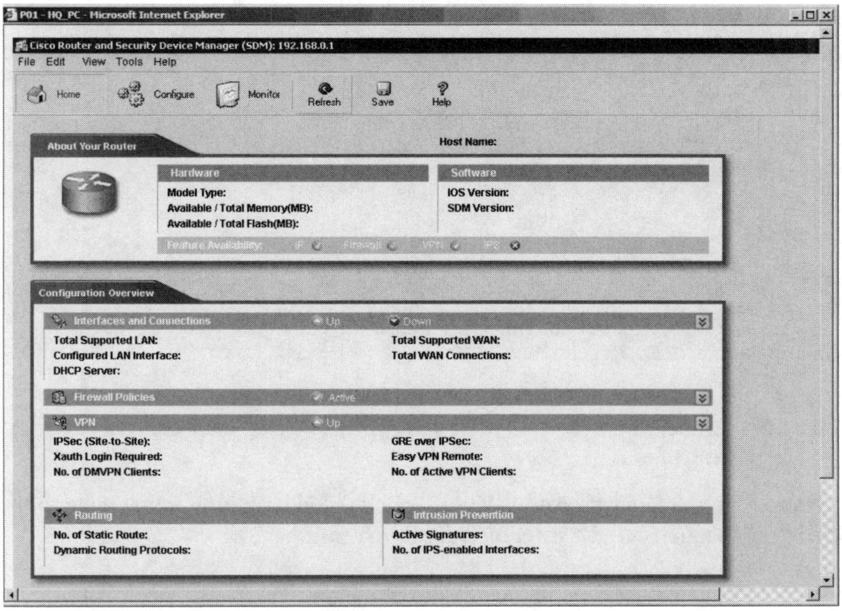

Using the SDM-Based Security Audit Tools

As previously discussed, the following security audit tools allow you to secure the router:

- Security Audit Wizard
- One-Step Lockdown

Using the Security Audit Wizard for Router Security

After launching SDM, you can start the Security Audit Wizard by following these steps:

Step 1 From the SDM home page, navigate to the Security Audit page by clicking **Configure > Security Audit**, as shown in Figure 8-13.

Figure 8-13 *SDM—Security Audit Home Page*

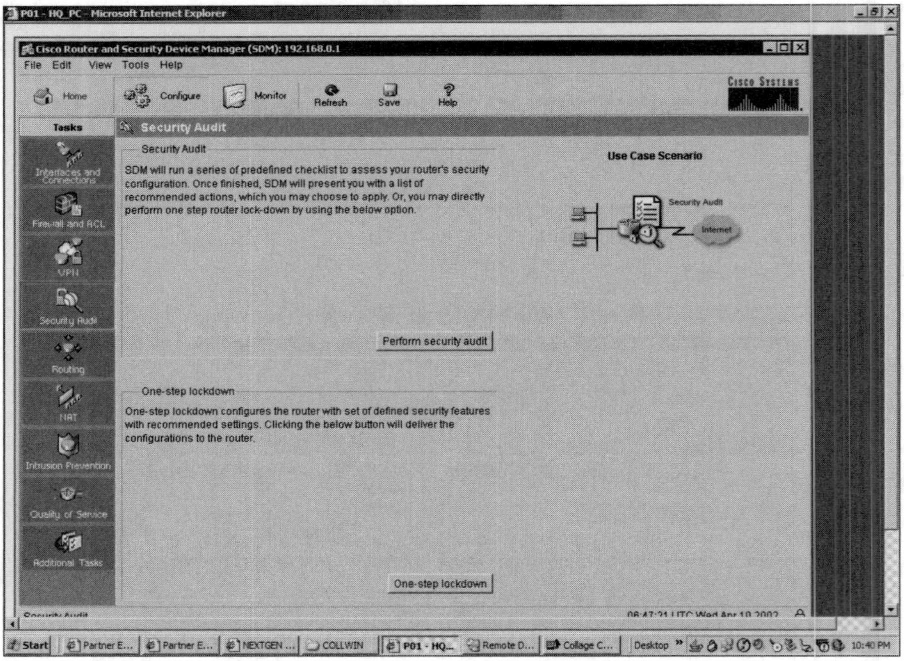

Step 2 Launch the Security Audit Wizard by clicking the **Perform security audit** button.

Step 3 In the Security Audit Wizard, click the **Next** button to navigate to the **Security audit interface configuration** page.

Step 4 Choose the inside (trusted) and outside (untrusted) interface on the Security audit interface configuration page and click the **Next** button.

SDM tests the configuration and provides a status report of each test, as shown in Figure 8-14. To save a local copy of the report in HTML format, click the **Save Report** button. Click the **Close** button to return to the wizard.

Figure 8-14 *SDM—Security Audit Status Report*

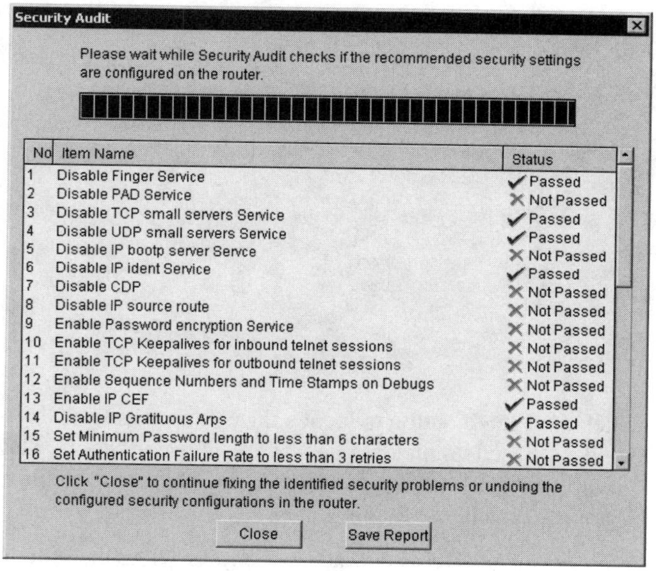

Based on the report, the wizard provides a list of security problems identified in the configuration, as shown in Figure 8-15.

Step 5 In the Select an option field, choose **Fix the Security problems**. The **Fix it** check box next to each problem allows you to selectively apply the fixes. You can also click the **Fix All** button to fix all the listed problems. Click the **Next** button to launch the Summary page. The Summary page lists all the fixes that SDM will apply to the router.

Figure 8-15 *Security Audit—List of Problems*

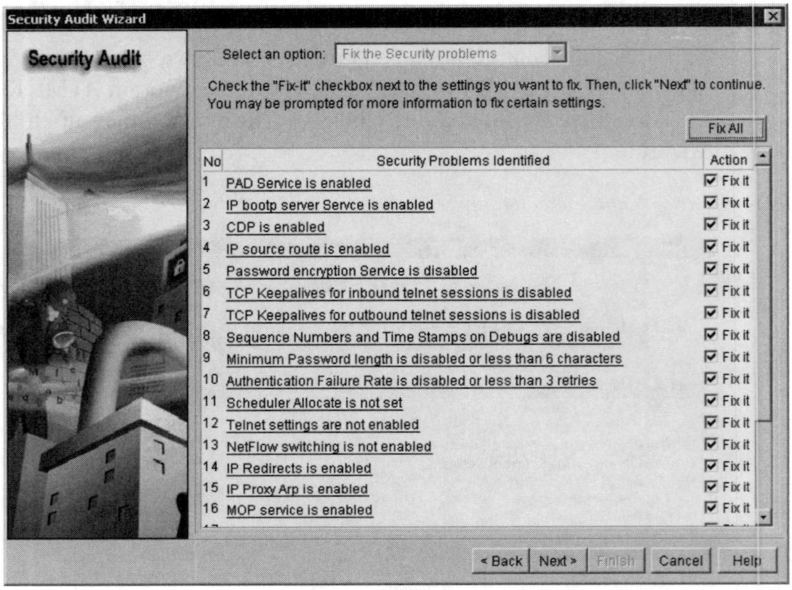

Step 6 Click the **Finish** button to launch the Commands Delivery Status window. Based on the options that you chose in Step 5, SDM might prompt you for fixes on advanced settings before launching the Commands Delivery Status window.

The Commands Delivery Status window provides the status of delivering the commands to the router. After the commands are delivered to the router, click the **OK** button to return to the Security Audit page.

The router is now secured in accordance with the security best practices recommended by the ICSA and Cisco TAC. To view the new configuration, choose **Tools > Running Config** on the SDM toolbar.

Using One-Step Lockdown for Router Security

The **One-step lockdown** button on the Security Audit page configures the router with predefined security settings. Unlike the security wizard**,** One-Step Lockdown directly applies the settings to the router without prompting the user for customization.

To secure the router using the One-Step Lockdown feature, click the **One-step lockdown** button on the Security Audit page, as shown in Figure 8-12. To roll back the commands applied by One-Step Lockdown, run the Security Audit Wizard again. On the Security Audit Wizard page, select **Undo Security configurations**, as shown in Figure 8-16. The

Undo check boxes allow you to restore the router to a usable state, especially if problems occur due to One-Step Lockdown.

Figure 8-16 *Security Audit—Undo Security Configurations*

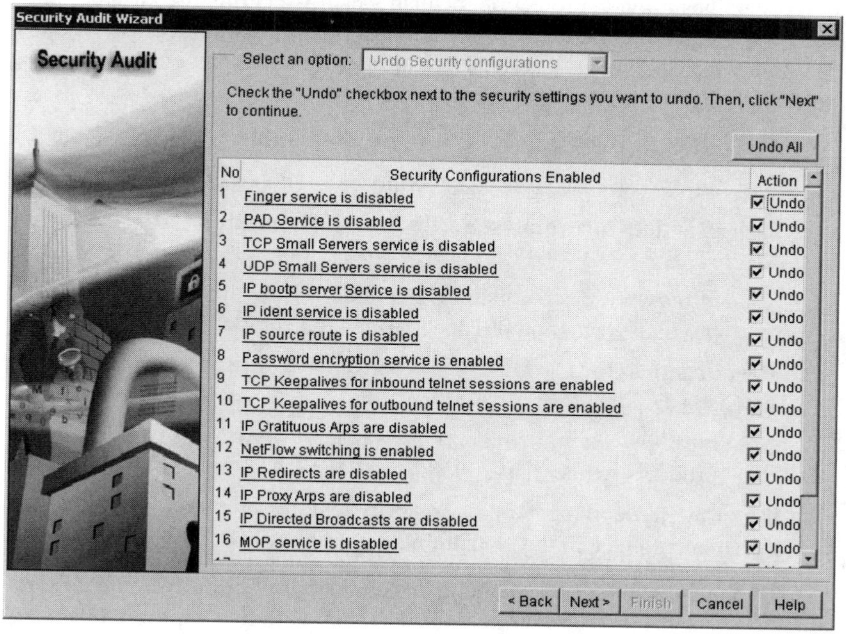

CAUTION One-Step Lockdown can cause a service disruption. Always verify the changes in a test environment before deploying the tool in a production environment.

Best Practice Recommendations

In addition to the tools discussed in this chapter, following are two good documents for hardening Cisco routers. Both documents provide good insight into the nuances of hardening Cisco routers and the services running over them. Although the second document appears to be for Internet service providers (ISP), the information is useful for anyone who deals with IOS devices. The URL for each of these documents is as follows:

- **Cisco Router Security Configuration Guide**—Issued by the National Security Agency (NSA):
  - http://www.nsa.gov/snac/downloads_cisco.cfm?MenuID=scg10.3.1

- **Cisco ISP Essentials—IOS Features Every ISP Should Consider**—Issued by Cisco TAC:
  - http://www.cisco.com/public/cons/isp/documents/IOSEssentialsPDF.zip

Cisco switches provide protection mechanisms for securing the switches and the network against network attacks. Many of the features provide immunity against Layer 2 attacks. The following documents provide Netadmins with a comprehensive checklist for protecting their networks against Layer 2 attacks:

- **Cisco IOS Switch Security Configuration Guide**—Issued by the NSA:
  - http://www.nsa.gov/snac/downloads_switches.cfm?MenuID=scg10.3.1
- **Best Practices for Catalyst Series Switches Running CatOS Software**—Issued by Cisco TAC:
  - http://www.cisco.com/en/US/products/hw/switches/ps663/products_tech_note09186a0080094713.shtml
- **Best Practices for Catalyst Series Switches Running Cisco IOS Software**—Issued by Cisco TAC:
  - http://www.cisco.com/en/US/products/hw/switches/ps700/products_white_paper09186a00801b49a4.shtml

Because of the in-depth coverage of security features provided, these documents should find a permanent place in the Netadmin's security tool kit.

Finally, none of the tools discussed in this chapter provide a silver bullet for router security. Each tool has its merits and limitations. Netadmins should appropriately weigh these tools against their network environment and business needs. A configuration change might be in accordance with security best practices but can result in cutting off your corporate network from the rest of the world. Remember, the most secure computer on the Internet is the one with no network connection. Unfortunately, that same computer is of little value.

Summary

This chapter covers the concept of securing the most common elements of today's networks—IOS-based routers and switches. The chapter prepares the Netadmins for the following tasks:

- Improving password security for IOS devices
- Detecting and turning off unneeded services and features on IOS devices
- Discovering vulnerabilities and configuration errors in IOS devices
- Configuring IOS devices in accordance with industry best practices
- Configuring CatOS switches in accordance with industry best practices

Table 8-3 lists the tools that are relevant to securing Cisco routers and switches.

[illegible] *List of Device Security Tools*

[illegible]	Function	Supported OS	URL/Notes
[illegible]	IOS password recovery	MS-Windows NT, 2000, XP	http://www.oxid.it
[illegible]	IOS password recovery (Type 7 only)	MS-Windows NT, 2000, XP	http://www.boson.com
[illegible]	Port scanning and OS detection	Linux, MS-Windows	http://www.nmap.org
[illegible]	Vulnerability scanning	Linux, MS-Windows	http://www.nessus.org
RAT	Securing IOS devices	Linux, MS-Windows	http://www.cisecurity.org
SDM	Securing IOS devices	MS-Windows (Java-enabled web browser)	http://www.cisco.com/go/sdm
Cisco ISP Essentials	IOS security features and configuration tips based on Cisco TAC's experience; a good source of information	—	http://www.cisco.com
Cisco IOS Switch/ Router Security Configuration Guides	Step-by-step guidelines for securing Cisco routers and switches	—	http://www.nsa.gov
Best Practices for Catalyst Series Switches Running Cisco IOS Software	Cisco TAC–recommended best practices for Cisco Catalyst switches	—	http://www.cisco.com

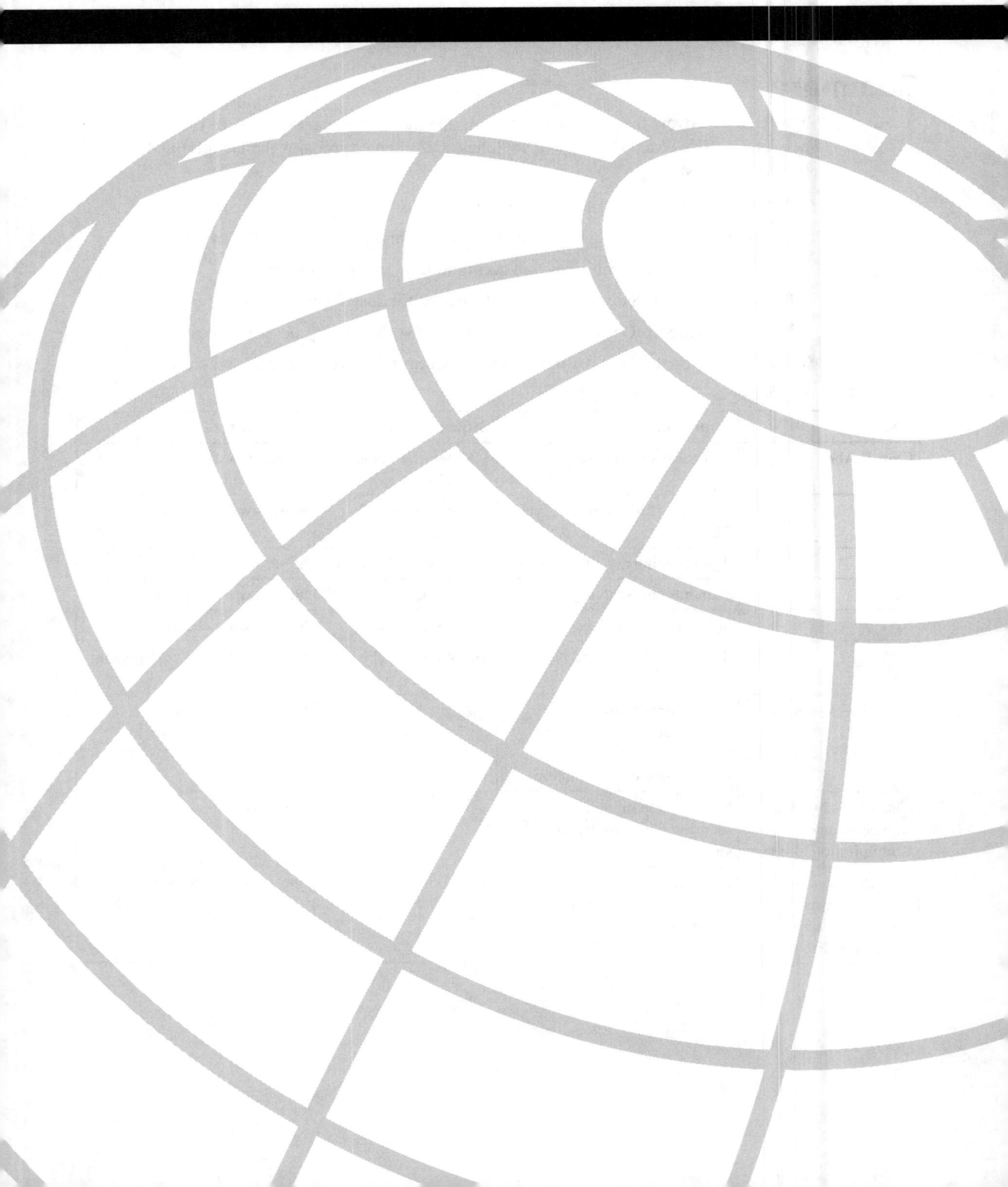

CHAPTER 9

Intrusion Detection System (IDS)

This chapter covers deploying an intrusion detection system (IDS) in a Cisco network. The chapter is comprised of the following three sections:

- IDS introduction
- Deploying open source IDS tools
- Deploying IDS sensors embedded within Cisco devices

IDS Overview

An IDS monitors traffic within a network to detect unauthorized network activity. After detecting malicious activity, the IDS sends an alert message to a central monitoring console so that action can be taken by the Netadmin. The alerts are sent in the form of syslog messages or pager/e-mail alerts. IDSs are available as appliances (hardware-based devices) as well as software-based agents. The hardware systems are ready to be deployed within the network, whereas the software-based systems can be installed on servers and desktops running various operating systems. IDS performance is often evaluated in terms of the accuracy of the generated alerts. An IDS provides the following advantages for a Netadmin:

- Exposes the security vulnerabilities present in the network
- Provides 24/7 monitoring and alerting, thus freeing a Netadmin's time and resources
- Provides logs for forensic analysis of attacks and intrusions

The next-generation IDSs boast an intrusion-prevention mechanism, thus further enhancing network security. The intrusion-prevention mechanism thwarts attacks in real time, using techniques such as modifying access control on the firewall or resetting the Transmission Control Protocol (TCP) connection.

The following section describes the various types of IDSs on the basis of their detection mechanism as well as their location within a network.

IDS Classification

An IDS constantly monitors the target system and compares its results against a set of rules to detect an act of intrusion. Depending on the way these rules are defined as well as the comparison mechanism, the IDSs can be classified as follows:

- **Anomaly-based IDS**—Watches for data patterns that deviate from a pre-established baseline. Any deviation from the normal behavior generates alerts. The biggest advantage of such systems is the protection from day-zero, or unknown, attacks. Anomaly-based systems require an initial learning phase to create a baseline profile. However, any change in this baseline can lead to a high number of false positives.
- **Signature-based IDS**—Also called a misuse-based IDS, this IDS monitors the traffic and identifies patterns that match a network attack. Such systems are easy to deploy and are extremely effective in protecting the network against known attacks. The lack of a constantly updated signature database can lead to a high number of false negatives, and hence this is the biggest drawback of a signature-based IDS.

To leverage the advantages offered by each detection mechanism, many IDSs use a hybrid model that incorporates both of these techniques.

NOTE **False Positives Versus False Negatives—***False positives* are the alarms generated by an IDS after incorrectly identifying legitimate traffic as an attack. In other words, the IDS is "crying wolf." *False negatives* are situations where the IDS does not detect an attack or other malicious activity, giving a false sense of security to the Netadmin. Fine-tuning the system to reduce false negatives can often lead to increased instances of false positives, and vice versa. On the other hand, responding to false positives can cause significant drains on time and resources.

IDS Placement

The design and operation of an IDS largely depends on the location of deployment in the network. Based on the location of deployment, IDSs are categorized as follows:

- **Host-Based IDS (HIDS)**—Host-based IDS software runs on individual devices, such as servers, to monitor the operating system or applications. An HIDS analyzes local data such as system log files, processes, and system calls on a particular machine. The HIDS can detect successful network attacks that reach the target host. HIDSs can be difficult to deploy and manage because they are specific to operating systems. Additionally, HIDSs cannot detect network attacks outside of the specific monitored device.
- **Network-Based IDS (NIDS)**—NIDSs are placed within network segments to monitor the network traffic on that segment. NIDSs are network sniffers with added intelligence to match the traffic pattern against the unique signatures of known attacks. An NIDS is easier to deploy and is not OS-specific. NIDSs have higher visibility of the monitored network. However, higher network bandwidth limits NIDS performance. An NIDS can also have difficulty with encrypted or fragmented network traffic.

To function correctly, the NIDS must be able to see all the traffic passing through the network segments. The preferred method of allowing the NIDS to see all the traffic flowing through a network segment is to use the port-mirroring feature of LAN switches. Alternatively, you can use a hardware-based Ethernet tap to capture all the traffic flowing through a network segment. However, hardware-based taps are expensive and require the network segment to be recabled.

NOTE You can find more details about the port-mirroring feature in the "Packet Analyzer" section of Chapter 7, "Network Security Testing."

For a better understanding of the location and operation of HIDSs and NIDSs, consider the sample network shown in Figure 9-1. The network diagram illustrates a scaled-down version of a typical corporate network, complete with routers, switches, a VPN concentrator, servers, and users in their respective VLANs.

NOTE Because an IDS acts as a probe that senses intrusion activities, IDSs are also loosely referred to as *IDS sensors,* or simply *sensors.*

The NIDS sensor A, which is located outside the firewall, can detect the largest number of reconnaissance and attack activities. Most of the alert information would be due to the viruses and automated scripts that are present on the Internet. Although the alerts are not false positives, they are large in number, and hence the IDS requires further fine-tuning. Additionally, these alerts are a good source of information for tightening holes in the firewall.

The NIDS sensors B and D would detect attacks that were able to bypass the firewall. As such, the alerts are useful in verifying the operation of the firewall and further tightening the holes. Alerts created by NIDS sensors B and D contain less noise and hence provide better efficiency. Also, NIDS sensor B can detect attacks aimed at inside hosts or LANs.

The HIDS sensor C can detect attacks on the workstation, including the ones that evaded NIDS sensors A and B. However, HIDS sensor C has no information about attacks in the rest of the network. Likewise, HIDS sensor E can only detect an attack on the database server. HIDSs are generally deployed on servers that contain sensitive information, such as payroll or customer billing databases.

Figure 9-1 *IDS Placement in a Network*

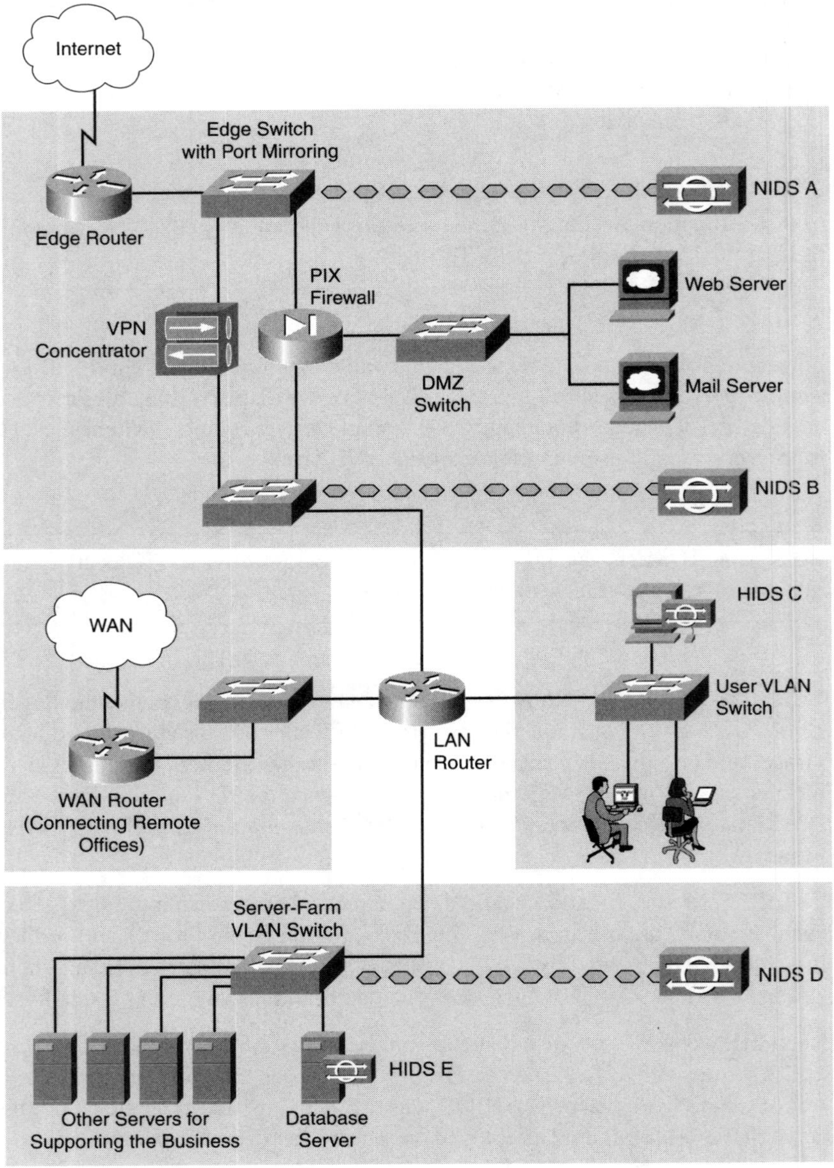

IDS Tools

The following sections cover tools that can be used to protect a Cisco-based network infrastructure. The focus is on deploying an easily available IDS that can provide adequate protection against network intrusion. These sections also cover tools that monitor Cisco devices and, on detecting a change in the configuration, send out alerts to Netadmins. The popular IDS tools discussed in this section are as follows:

- **Snort**—A signature-based NIDS
- **Rancid**—An HIDS for detecting IOS configuration changes

Snort

Snort, created by Martin Roesch, is inarguably one of the most popular IDSs. Snort is primarily a signature-based NIDS with alerting capabilities. Snort can detect a wide range of network attacks and probes, including port scans, OS fingerprinting, and buffer overflows. Snort uses a modular architecture to apply the signature database for intrusion detection. Snort refers to the signatures as *rules.* Snort uses a flexible and powerful rules language to define the inspection engine. In fact, some of the commercially available IDS appliances are based on Snort.

Snort is available for both the Linux and MS-Windows platforms at http://www.snort.org/. While the exact hardware requirements depend on the version of Snort and the network traffic, Snort performs better with a larger amount of RAM and faster processors. As a reference point, when monitoring a T-1 link to the Internet, the following combination worked well:

- Snort v2.1
- Debian-Linux
- 1-GHz Pentium III
- 512 MB RAM
- 40-GB hard disk
- Dual 100-MB network interface cards (NIC)

Snort is a command-line interface (CLI)–based tool but can be managed and configured through a number of third-party graphical user interface (GUI) tools such as ACID, IDSCenter, and BASE.

Deploying Linux-Based Snort

The steps involved in deploying a simple Snort system on a Debian-Linux system are as follows:

1 Installation
2 Configuration
3 Running Snort
4 Viewing Snort alerts

Installing Snort

To install Snort in Debian-Linux, use the **apt-get install** command as follows:

```
apt-get install snort
```

The system prompts you for information regarding the local environment, such as the network address and the interface used to run Snort. Based on the information that you enter, the installation script automatically creates the snort.debian.conf file for customizing Snort in your network.

Configuring Snort

Snort uses the /etc/snort/snort.conf file for configuring. The default file should work for most environments. However, you can customize the file as necessary.

The default /etc/snort/snort.conf file is divided into the following four sections:

- **Setting the network variables**—Defines the local network environment.
- **Configuring the preprocessors**—Defines the plug-ins for scanning the packets before sending them to the scanning engine.
- **Configuring the output plug-ins**—Defines the format, such as Syslog or MySQL, used by Snort to output the logs and alerts.
- **Customizing your rule set**—Selects the rules to be applied to the detection engine. The rules are grouped according to the category of attacks.

Running Snort

To start Snort from the command line, enter the following syntax:

snort [-options] *option-parameters*

Table 9-1 provides a list of common options for running Snort.

Table 9-1 *Snort Options*

Option	Details
-A	Sets alert mode; possible values are fast, full, console, and none
-c *config-file*	Uses the specified configuration file
-d	Dumps the Application layer
-D	Runs Snort in background mode
-e	Displays the Layer 2 (ethernet)header information
-h *network-address*	Specifies the home network in classless interdomain routing (CIDR) block format, such as 192.168.1.0/24; useful for logging and traffic analysis
-i *interface*	Listens on the specified interface
-s	Logs alert messages to the syslog
-v	Specifies verbose mode to provide detailed output

You should test the configuration first by starting Snort in the verbose mode using the **–v** option, as follows:

```
snort -v -c /etc/snort/snort.conf
```

Snort should start displaying the captured packets onscreen. Snort also displays errors that it encounters during the startup. To stop Snort, press **Ctrl-C**.

After testing the configuration and eliminating any errors, you can start using Snort. To run Snort in a production environment, use the -D option. This option forces Snort to run in background (daemon) mode. The command syntax is as follows:

```
snort -c /etc/snort/snort.conf -D
```

Viewing Snort Alerts

All the alerts are stored in text format in the /var/log/snort/alert file. You can check the alerts by using the **tail** command, as shown in Example 9-1.

Example 9-1 *Snort Alerts*

```
root@linuxbox2:~# tail -f /var/log/snort/alert
[**] [1:469:3] ICMP PING NMAP [**]
[Classification: Attempted Information Leak] [Priority: 2]
12/05-14:51:39.637594 192.168.0.100 -> 192.168.0.103
ICMP TTL:54 TOS:0x0 ID:19283 IpLen:20 DgmLen:28
Type:8  Code:0  ID:47944   Seq:19719  ECHO
[Xref => http://www.whitehats.com/info/IDS162]
[**] [1:1418:11] SNMP request tcp [**]
[Classification: Attempted Information Leak] [Priority: 2]
12/05-14:51:45.734136 192.168.0.100:50173 -> 192.168.0.103:161
```

continues

Example 9-1 *Snort Alerts (Continued)*

```
TCP TTL:59 TOS:0x0 ID:29955 IpLen:20 DgmLen:40
******S* Seq: 0x7344580C  Ack: 0x0  Win: 0x1000  TcpLen: 20
[Xref => http://cve.mitre.org/cgi-bin/cvename.cgi?name=2002-0013][Xref => http://
 cve.mitre.org/cgi-bin/cvename.cgi?name=2002-0012][Xref => http://
 www.securityfocus.com/bid/4132][Xref => http://www.securityfocus.com/bid/
 4089][Xref => http://www.securityfocus.com/bid/4088]
```

As highlighted in Example 9-1, Snort identifies the Internet Control Message Protocol (ICMP) ping scan traffic generated by the Nmap scan. The alerts also include hyperlinks that provide more information about the particular attack.

WARNING Depending on various factors, such as the location of Snort in the network and the network traffic, the log file can grow quickly. To efficiently manage log files, you can use the Linux logrotate utility. You can also consult the frequently asked questions (FAQs) section at the Snort website for more information on managing Snort logs.

Deploying MS-Windows–Based Snort

The steps involved in deploying a simple Snort system on a Windows system are the same as those for a Linux system. These steps are as follows:

1. Installation
2. Configuration
3. Running Snort
4. Viewing Snort alerts

Installing Snort

Snort is supported by Windows NT, 2000, 2003, and XP. Installing Snort in MS-Windows is a two-step process, as follows:

1. Installing Snort
2. Installing the WinPcap driver

Installing Snort

The installation files are available at http://www.snort.org. Download the Snort binary files for MS-Windows, save them, and double-click the executable file to begin installation. By default, the files are installed in the C:\snort directory. Other important file locations are as follows:

- **Snort executable file**—C:\snort\bin\snort.exe
- **Snort configuration file**—C:\snort\etc\snort.conf
- **Snort log files**—C:\snort\log\

Although the sample installation discussed in this chapter is based on these defaults, you should install Snort on a separate partition (and preferably a separate drive) for better performance and security.

Installing the WinPcap Driver

A packet-capture driver such as WinPcap allows applications to directly access raw packets that are flowing through the wire. WinPcap also provides packet filtering prior to passing on the captured packets to upper-level programs. The MS-Windows version of Snort requires the WinPcap driver to capture packets. However, not all versions of WinPcap are compatible with Snort. For example, Snort 2.3 for Windows runs with WinPcap 3.0. Download and save the installation files from http://winpcap.polito.it/ and double-click the executable file to begin installation. Reboot your machine after the installation is complete.

Configuring Snort

Snort uses the C:\snort\etc\snort.conf file for configuring. Edit the default snort.conf file according to your network environment. The three variables that should be changed are as follows:

- HOME_NET
- EXTERNAL_NET
- RULE_PATH

Example 9-2 depicts the partial configuration of the snort.conf file.

Example 9-2 *Snort.conf—Partial Configuration*

```
# specify local network to be monitored
var HOME_NET 192.168.0.0/24
#define external networks
var EXTERNAL_NET !$HOME_NET
# specify the location of rules
var RULE_PATH c:\snort\rules
```

Running Snort

The command syntax to start Snort from the MS-Windows CLI is as follows:

C:\snort\bin\snort.exe [*-options*] *option-parameters*

Table 9-2 provides a list of common options for running Snort.

Table 9-2 *Snort Options*

Option	Details
-A	Sets alert mode; the options are fast, full, console, and none (alert file alerts only)
-d	Dumps the Application Layer
-E	Logs alert messages to NT Eventlog
-I *interface*	Listens on the specified interface
-c *rules*	Uses the specified rules file
-e	Displays the second-layer header information
-I	Adds the interface name to the alert output
-l *log-directory*	Logs to the directory
-N	Turns off logging (alerts still work)
-s	Logs alert messages to the syslog
-T *snort-config-file*	Tests and reports on the Snort configuration file
-W	Lists the available interfaces (MS-Windows only)

However, before running Snort, you should test the various configuration parameters. The steps for testing Snort are as follows:

Step 1 **Test the packet-capture driver**—Test the installation of WinPcap by running Snort with the **-W** option. This option lists all the available interfaces that Snort can sniff using the WinPcap driver. As shown in the following code, Snort lists two interfaces on the host machine:

```
C:\Snort\bin>snort -W
    ,,_      -*> Snort! <*-
   o"  )~    Version 2.3.0RC1-ODBC-MySQL-FlexRESP-WIN32 (Build 8)
    ''''     By Martin Roesch & The Snort Team: http://www.snort.org/
team.html
              Copyright 1998-2004 Sourcefire Inc, et al.

Interface       Device          Description
-------------------------------------------
1  \Device\NPF_{42B5C9C3-7D46-47DD-BE22-E83B88F6B68C} (Broadcom
NetXtreme Gigabi
  t Ethernet Driver (Microsoft's Packet Scheduler) )
2 \Device\NPF_{C83CF2E5-993D-4BF8-9008-49C51908ECE4} (Intel(R) PRO/
Wireless LAN
  2100 3A Mini PCI Adapter (Microsoft's Packet Scheduler) )
```

Step 2 **Verify the Snort configuration**—Test the snort.conf file for configuration errors by starting Snort using the **–T** option. Snort parses the snort.conf file and reports the test results, as shown in the following code:

```
C:\Snort\bin> snort -T -l "c:\snort\log" -c "c:\snort\etc\snort.conf"
Running in IDS mode
Log directory = c:\snort\log
#output suppressed for clarity.
Snort successfully loaded all rules and checked all rule chains!
Final Flow Statistics
,----[ FLOWCACHE STATS ]----------
Memcap: 10485760 Overhead Bytes 16400 used(%0.156403)/blocks (16400/1)
Overhead
blocks: 1 Could Hold: (0)
IPV4 count: 0 frees: 0 low_time: 0, high_time: 0, diff: 0h:00:00s
    finds: 0 reversed: 0(%0.000000)
   find_success: 0 find_fail: 0 percent_success: (%0.000000) new_flows:
0
Snort exiting
C:\Snort\bin>
```

Step 3 **Run Snort with the Windows Event Viewer**—To run Snort in a production environment and send alerts to the Windows Event Viewer, use the **–E** option, as shown in the following code:

```
C:\Snort\bin> snort -c "C:\snort\etc\snort.conf" -l "C:\snort\Log" -i 1
-E
Running in IDS mode
Log directory = C:\SNORT\LOG
Initializing Network Interface \Device\NPF_{42B5C9C3-7D46-47DD-BE22-
E83B88F6B68C
}
        --== Initializing Snort ==--
# output suppressed for clarity
Rule application order: ->activation->dynamic->alert->pass->log
        --== Initialization Complete ==--
   ,,_     -*> Snort! <*-
  o"  )~   Version 2.3.0RC1-ODBC-MySQL-FlexRESP-WIN32 (Build 8)
   ''''    By Martin Roesch & The Snort Team: http://www.snort.org/
team.html
            Copyright 1998-2004 Sourcefire Inc, et al.
```

Viewing Snort Alerts

To check the alerts generated by Snort, open the Windows Event Viewer by choosing **Start > Settings > Control Panel > Administrative Tools > Event Viewer**.

Select the **Application** tab to view all the events. You can sort the events generated by Snort by clicking the Source field, as shown in Figure 9-2.

Figure 9-2 *Windows Event Viewer*

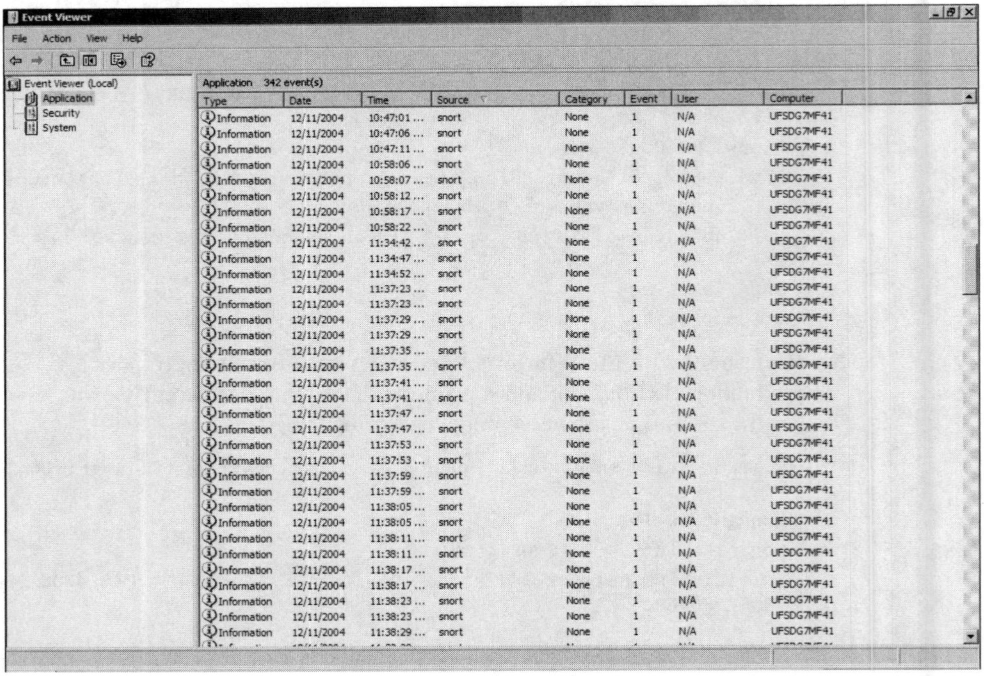

Double-click any alert to view more details, as shown in Figure 9-3.

Snort identifies the TCP port scan traffic originating from the source address 172.16.1.2.

NOTE For more information on deploying Snort in Windows, visit http://www.winsnort.com. This website provides a great deal of resources, including step-by-step guides, forums, and tips for deploying Snort in Windows.

Figure 9-3 *Windows Event Viewer—Details*

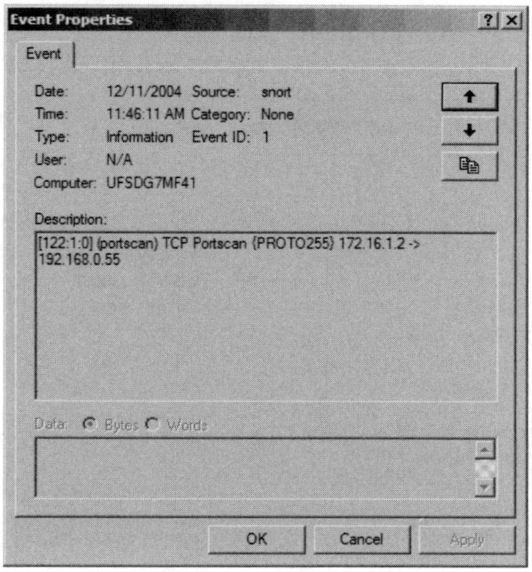

Snort for Advanced Users

The CLI-based Snort deployment, with alerts stored in a text file, provides a simple and efficient IDS for smaller networks with lower traffic. By default, the packet captures are stored in Tcpdump format.

However, in larger and busier networks, a text-based Snort system can generate a large number of alerts. Managing and searching through the alerts can be a daunting task. In such cases, you can configure Snort to send alerts and logs to an SQL database. SQL databases can store the data efficiently and hence boost the performance and scalability of Snort. Snort can interface with both open source databases (such as MySQL and PostgreSQL) as well as commercial databases (such as MSSQL and Oracle). However, the SQL database only provides a better back end for Snort. To search and view the alerts stored in the SQL database, you can use Analysis Console for Intrusion Databases (ACID), which is a web-based GUI tool specifically developed to search and process alerts generated by IDSs and firewalls. ACID, an open source tool, is available at http://acidlab.sourceforge.net/.

Figure 9-4 shows the internal architecture of a scalable IDS using Snort, an SQL database, ACID, and a web server.

Figure 9-4 *Advanced Snort Architecture*

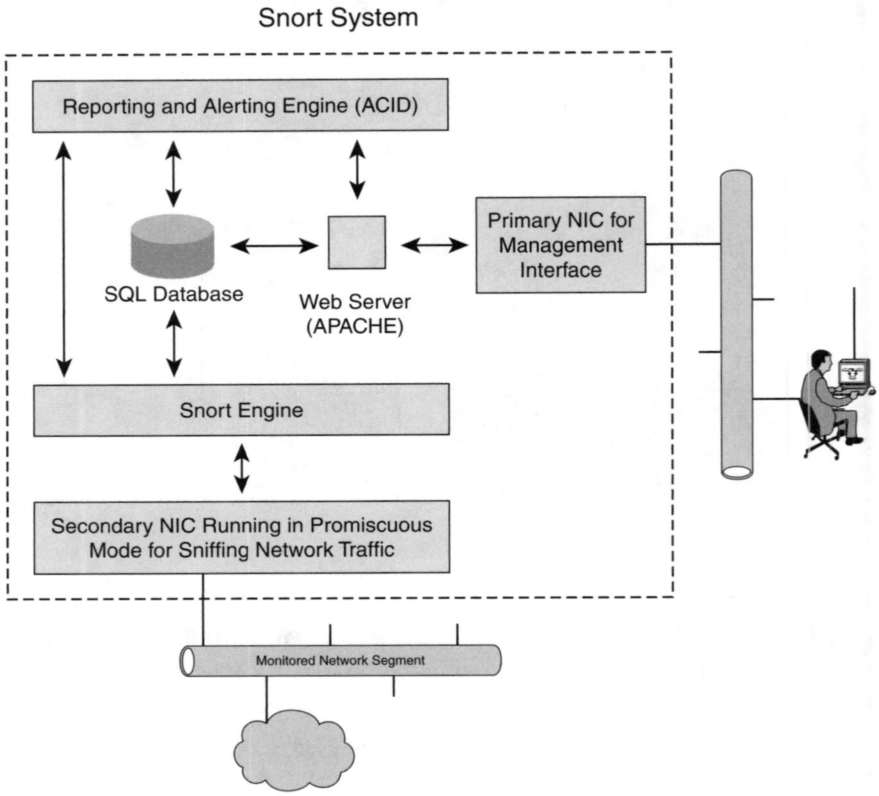

Deploying SQL- and ACID-based Snort systems is a project by itself and is beyond the scope of this discussion. Nonetheless, the Snort website provides detailed documentation for deploying Snort with MySQL and ACID.

Netadmins who are interested in evaluating the MySQL+ACID version of Snort can use the Knoppix-STD or Network Security Toolkit–based live CD-ROM. (For more information on live CD-ROM, refer to Chapter 7.) The live CD-ROM–based Snort offers following advantages:

- Quick and easy deployment of an IDS in the network
- SQL-based database for recording and managing the alerts
- Easy-to-use browser-based GUI
- Ability to create customized reports containing bar, line, and pie charts. These reports provide tangible tools for the IT department to justify the need and budget for network security.

Figure 9-5 shows a sample report generated by the ACID console on the NST live CD-ROM. The pie chart reports indicate the signature classification over a number of alerts. The live CD version of Snort is especially handy if you need a functional copy of Snort for a couple of days but do not want to install it on a dedicated computer.

Figure 9-5 *Snort Reports Using the ACID Console*

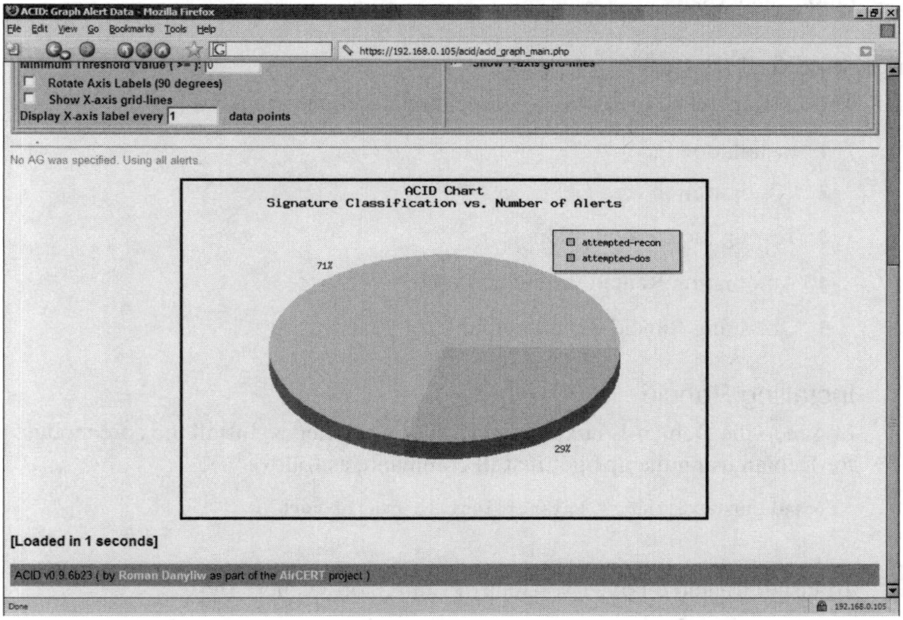

Rancid

Rancid, an acronym for Really Awesome New Cisco confIg Differ, is a tool that can detect changes in the configuration of network devices. Rancid maintains and compares recent copies of device configurations. Rancid functionality can be summarized in the following three steps:

1. Periodically Telnets into the target devices or uses SSH to download the running configurations
2. Compares the configurations with the last record to detect changes
3. Notifies the Netadmin of all the changes in the configuration through an e-mail

Rancid runs in Linux and other flavors of UNIX. However, at the time of this writing, the Windows version of Rancid was not available. Rancid works for IOS-based devices,

CatOS-based switches, and PIX Firewalls. In addition to its role as an IDS tool for detecting configuration changes, Rancid also helps track changes. The trails of changes are helpful when troubleshooting network issues.

Please note that RANCID is not a true IDS tool as it does not detect configuration changes in real time. Nonetheless, RANCID provides periodic monitoring and alerts for configuration changes.

Deploying Rancid

The steps involved in deploying Rancid on a Debian-Linux system are as follows:

1. Installation
2. Configuration
3. Testing the configuration
4. Automating Rancid through crontab
5. Obtaining Rancid e-mail output

Installing Rancid

Log in to the Debian-Linux system with root privileges. Install the core module of Rancid for Debian using the **apt-get install** command, as follows:

```
root@linuxbox2:/home# apt-get install rancid-core
```

NOTE To install Rancid on other versions of Linux, follow these steps:

1. Download the latest copy of the Rancid source files from http://www.shrubbery.net/rancid/.
2. Unzip the downloaded file.
3. Change the directory to the unzipped folder.
4. Execute the following code:

```
run ./configure
make install
```

Configuring Rancid

Follow these steps to configure Rancid:

Step 1 Edit the /etc/rancid/rancid.conf file to define a group, as shown in the highlighted section of the following code:

```
TERM=network;export TERM
umask 027
```

```
TMPDIR=/tmp; export TMPDIR
BASEDIR=/usr//../var/lib/rancid; export BASEDIR
PATH=/usr//lib/rancid/bin:/usr/bin:/usr/sbin:/bin:/usr/local/bin:/usr/
bin; export PATH
CVSROOT=$BASEDIR/CVS; export CVSROOT
LOGDIR=$BASEDIR/logs; export LOGDIR
OLDTIME=4; export OLDTIME
# Define a group
LIST_OF_GROUPS="ciscoadmin"
#end
```

Step 2 Create a user and group for running Rancid using the **adduser** command. The following code illustrates using the **adduser** command to create a user named ciscoadmin:

```
root@linuxbox2:/home# adduser ciscoadmin
Adding user `ciscoadmin'...
Creating home directory `/home/ciscoadmin'.
Copying files from `/etc/skel'
Enter new UNIX password:
Retype new UNIX password:
passwd: password updated successfully
Changing the user information for ciscoadmin
Enter the new value, or press ENTER for the default
# THIS NAME WILL SHOW UP AS EMAIL SENDER
        Full Name []: cisco admin
Is the information correct? [y/N] y
root@linuxbox2:/home#
```

Step 3 Create a file **.cloginrc** in the home directory of the user that was created in the previous step. This file is used to supply the login credentials for each router. The following code shows the contents of the .cloginrc file:

```
# add password <telnet-password> <enable-password>
add password 192.168.0.6 cisco123 cisco456
add password 192.168.0.10 secure123 secure456
add password 192.168.0.15 secret123 secret456
```

A sample .cloginrc file that provides more details is included with the install files in the /usr/share/doc/rancid-core/examples/ directory.

Step 4 Change the owner of the .cloginrc file using the **chown** command, as follows:

```
chown ciscoadmin:ciscoadmin /home/ciscoadmin/.cloginrc
```

Step 5 Change the permission of the .cloginrc file to read-only for the person who is using the **chmod** command, as follows:

```
chmod 0600 /home/ciscoadmin/.cloginrc
```

You can verify the permission and ownership of the .cloginrc file using the **ls –l** command, as follows:

```
root@linuxbox2:~# ls -l /home/ciscoadmin/.cloginrc
-rw------- 1 ciscoadmin ciscoadmin 121 Dec  4 12:24 /home/ciscoadmin/
.clog
```

Step 6 Specify the e-mail address of the Netadmin by adding an alias in the /etc/aliases file. The e-mail address will receive all the e-mail alerts that detail the change in configurations. The following code depicts the partial contents of the /etc/aliases file:

```
# This is the aliases file - it says who gets mail for whom.
postmaster: root
daemon: root
bin: root
sys: root
.
.
# add the destination email address for receiving email alerts.
rancid-ciscoadmin: spope@abcinvestment.com
mailer-daemon: postmaster
webmaster: root
```

Step 7 Run the **newaliases** command to reload the aliases.

Step 8 Create all the directory trees for each of the groups listed in LIST_OF_GROUPS, and run the rancid-cvs script located in the /usr/lib/rancid/bin/ directory.

This also creates a directory, under /var/lib/rancid/, for each group listed in LIST_OF_GROUPS.

Step 9 Edit the router.db file in the group directory, as shown in the following code:

```
192.168.0.6:cisco:up
192.168.0.10:cisco:up
192.168.0.15:cat5:up
```

The router.db file defines the database of the routers that are managed by the corresponding group. The format for listing each router is *router:mfg:state*. The possible values for each parameter are listed in Table 9-3.

Table 9-3 *Router.db File*

Parameter	Values
Router	IP address or fully qualified domain name
Mfg	**cat5** for switches running CatOS; **cisco** for IOS-based routers and switches
State	up, down

Step 10 Change the permission of the files to enable the user ciscoadmin to run the Rancid program, as follows:

```
chown -R ciscoadmin:ciscoadmin /var/lib/rancid
chown -R ciscoadmin:ciscoadmin /var/log/rancid
```

Testing Rancid Configurations

Log in as the user ciscoadmin on the Linux machine and test the configuration by running the **/usr/bin/rancid-run** command. Check the /var/log/rancid file for error messages.

Automating Rancid Through **crontab**

After verifying the configurations, Rancid should be configured to run periodically. Linux provides the **crontab –e** command for scheduling the programs to run at preset intervals. Example 9-3 creates job schedules for running Rancid every hour. A sample contents of the crontab file is included in the /usr/share/doc/rancid-core/examples/cron.example file.

Example 9-3 *Scheduling Rancid Using **crontab***

```
ciscoadmin@linuxbox2:~$ crontab -e
# run rancid every hour
1 * * * * /usr/bin/rancid-run
# clean out old logs every midnight
50 23 * * * find /var/log/rancid -type f -mtime +2 -exec rm {} \;
```

Obtaining Rancid E-Mail Output

Example 9-4 shows the e-mail sent by Rancid to spope@abcinvestments.com with the changes in the router configurations. The lines beginning with a plus sign (+) denote configurations added, while the ones beginning with a minus sign or hyphen (-) indicate configurations removed from the old configuration. Also, note that Rancid includes several lines of configuration surrounding the changes, thus making it easy to understand and correlate the changes.

Example 9-4 *E-mail Output from Rancid*

```
Index: configs/192.168.0.10
===================================================================
retrieving revision 1.5
diff -u -4 -r1.5 192.168.0.10
@@ -85,9 +85,9 @@
  logging 192.168.0.100
  access-list 100 permit ip any any
  access-list 101 permit icmp host 192.168.0.10 any
  access-list 101 permit icmp any host 192.168.0.10
- access-list 102 permit udp any any
- access-list 102 permit tcp any any
+ access-list 103 permit ip any any
  access-list 125 permit ip any host 192.168.0.35
  access-list 125 permit udp any host 192.168.0.35 eq 1813
  access-list 125 permit udp any host 192.168.0.35 eq 1646
  snmp-server community read RO
Index: configs/192.168.0.6
===================================================================
retrieving revision 1.5
diff -u -4 -r1.5 192.168.0.6
@@ -164,9 +164,9 @@
  access-list 91 permit any
  access-list 92 deny   0.0.0.66 255.255.255.0
  access-list 92 permit any
  access-list 100 permit ip any any
- access-list 101 permit udp any any
- access-list 102 permit tcp any any
+ access-list 103 permit ip any any
  access-list 162 permit ospf any any
  access-list 162 permit gre host 10.2.2.2 host 11.2.2.2
  access-list 162 permit gre host 10.2.2.5 host 11.2.6.6
```

In case the Cisco devices use the username/password combination, you can add the username information in the .cloginrc file using the **add user** command. Additionally, you can use the **add method** command, to instruct RANCID to use SSH instead of telnet for connecting to the target Cisco device. Following is sample content of the .cloginrc file for defining user user1 with password cisco123, enable password cisco456 to connect to router 192.168.0.20 via SSH

```
# add password router-ip telnet-password enable-password
add password 192.168.0.20 cisco123 cisco456
# add user router-ip user-name
add user 192.168.0.20 user1
# add method router-ip ssh
add method 192.168.0.20 ssh
```

IDS Sensors Using Common Cisco Devices

Cisco IOS routers and PIX Firewalls are the most fundamental elements of a typical network. Both of these devices feature built-in IDS sensors that are easy to deploy. The embedded sensors eliminate the need for port mirroring or wire taps to capture the traffic, thus empowering Netadmins to deploy basic IDS sensors without additional hardware purchases. The inline IDS capabilities of both IOS routers and PIX Firewalls allow these devices to directly drop suspicious traffic, thus preventing an attack. However, despite the advantages offered by both the IOS- and the PIX Firewall–based IDSs, they merely complement the overall security strategy. The IOS- and PIX-based IDSs should not be considered as an option for replacing dedicated IDS devices.

Figure 9-6 shows the logical layout of a sample network with IOS- and PIX-based IDS sensors. The intrusion alerts from all the sensors are consolidated to a central syslog server to enable ease of management.

Figure 9-6 *IOS- and PIX-Based Sensors*

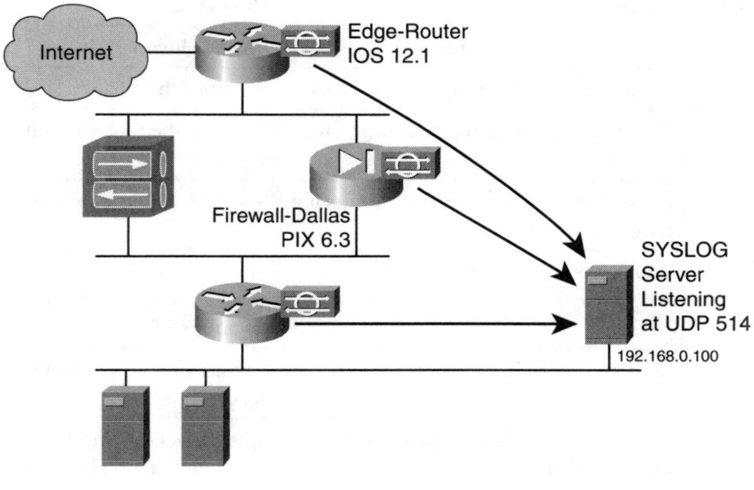

Router IDSs

Router-based embedded IDS sensor functionality was first introduced with Cisco IOS Release 12.0(5)T. The sensor supported 59 basic signatures for detecting the most common network attacks. However, the IDS feature has been renamed the Intrusion Prevention System (IPS) in Cisco IOS Release 12.3(8)T and higher. The IPS feature supports in excess of 740 signatures and is available with the following IOS software feature sets:

- Advanced enterprise services
- Advanced IP services
- Advanced security

The IDS/IPS features in the IOS allow the router to monitor the traffic, send an alert, or reset the connection when suspicious patterns are detected. Deploying an IOS-based IDS involves the following steps:

1. Configuring the sensor
2. Verifying the configuration
3. Monitoring the network

Configuring an IOS-Based IDS Sensor

Before configuring the sensor on the router, you should first enable syslog messaging with timestamps. Then configure the IDS parameters and enable the IDS on the interfaces.

Table 9-4 summarizes the steps for configuring an IOS-based IDS sensor.

Table 9-4 *IOS-Based IDS Configuration Steps*

Step	Command	Purpose
1	Router(config)# **logging on**	Enables logging.
2	Router(config)# **logging** *syslog-server*	Specifies the IP address of the syslog server.
3	Router(config)#**logging trap warning**	Instructs the router to send warning-level syslog messages.
4	Router(config)# **service timestamps log datetime msec**	Specifies to timestamp the syslog messages.
5	Router(config)# **ip audit smtp spam** *recipients*	Specifies the threshold for the maximum number of recipients in e-mail messages; the default is **250**.
6	Router(config)#**ip audit notify log**	Sends event notifications (alarms) to a syslog server.
7	Router(config)# **ip audit info** {**action** [**alarm**] [**drop**] [**reset**]}	Sets the actions for informational signatures; the default action is **alarm**.
8	Router(config)# **ip audit attack** {**action** [**alarm**] [**drop**] [**reset**]}	Sets the actions for attack signatures; the default action is **alarm**.
9	Router(config)# **ip audit name** *audit-name* {**info** | **attack**} [**list** *standard-acl*] [**action** [**alarm**] [**drop**] [**reset**]]	Creates audit rules, where *audit-name* is a user-defined name for an audit rule. You can also apply a standard ACL to an audit rule to filter out sources of false alarms.
10	Router(config)# **ip audit signature** *signature-id* {**disable** | **list** *acl-list*}	Globally disables individual signatures.
11	Router(config)# **interface** *interface-number*	Enters interface configuration mode.

Table 9-4 *IOS-Based IDS Configuration Steps (Continued)*

Step	Command	Purpose
12	Router(config-if)# **ip audit** *audit-name* {**in** | **out**}	Applies an audit rule at an interface. With this command, *audit-name* is the name of an existing audit rule and is the keyword; **in** or **out** specifies the direction in which the audit is performed.
13	Router(config-if)# **end**	Exits configuration mode.
14	Router# **copy running-config startup-config**	Saves the changes in the configuration.

TIP Beginning with the 831, 1710, 2600XM, 3700, and 7300 Series routers, you can also configure IOS-based IDSs or IPSs using the Cisco Router and Security Device Manager (SDM) GUI, without a detailed knowledge of IOS commands. SDM also allows you to add, remove, or edit signatures for the IOS IPS feature. SDM is the web browser–based GUI for configuring Cisco routers and is discussed in Chapter 8, "Router and Switch Security."

Example 9-5 shows a sample configuration of an IOS-based IDS sensor. The sensor is configured to drop all the packets that match the attack signatures. All the IDS alerts are sent to the syslog server 192.168.0.100. The highlighted text in the example provides more details regarding the relevant configuration.

Example 9-5 *IOS Configuration—IDS Sensor*

```
! enable logging before IDS setup
logging on
logging 192.168.0.100
! IOS IDS messages are sent at warning level
logging trap warnings
service timestamps log datetime msec
! default action for attack signature is set to drop the packets
ip audit attack action drop
ip audit notify log
ip audit po max-events 100
ip audit smtp spam 200
! Signature 2004 is globally disabled
ip audit signature 2004 disable
ip audit name IDS1 info action alarm
ip audit name IDS1 attack action drop
!
interface Ethernet0/0
 ip address 192.168.0.10 255.255.255.0
 ip audit IDS1 in
!
interface Serial0/0
 ip address 172.16.0.10 255.255.255.0
 ip audit IDS1 in
!end
```

Verifying the Configuration

You can verify the Cisco IOS Firewall IDS configuration using the **show ip audit configuration** command, as shown in Example 9-6.

Example 9-6 *Output of the* **show ip audit configuration** *Command*

```
Router-Dallas#show ip audit configuration
Event notification through syslog is enabled
Event notification through Net Director is disabled
Default action(s) for info signatures is alarm
Default action(s) for attack signatures is drop
Default threshold of recipients for spam signature is 200
Signature 2004 disable
PostOffice:HostID:0 OrgID:0 Msg dropped:0
          :Curr Event Buf Size:0  Configured:100
Post Office is not enabled - No connections are active
Audit Rule Configuration
 Audit name IDS1
    info actions alarm
    attack actions drop
Router-Dallas#
```

Monitoring the Network

The IDS sensor monitors the traffic flowing through it, and the alerts are sent to the syslog server. Example 9-7 shows the messages received by syslog server. Note the signature numbers denoted by the highlighted text.

Example 9-7 *Syslog Messages*

```
Dec 09 15:31:24 192.168.0.6 47: Dec  9 15:31:24.410: %IDS-4-ICMP_FRAGMENT_SIG:
  Sig:2150:Fragmented ICMP Traffic - from 192.168.0.140 to 192.168.0.6
Dec 09 15:31:37 192.168.0.6 49: Dec  9 15:31:37.097: %IDS-4-TCP_FIN_ONLY_SIG:
 Sig:3042:TCP
   - FIN bit with no ACK bit in flags - from 192.168.0.140 to 192.168.0.6
Dec 09 15:32:19 192.168.0.6 51: Dec  9 15:32:18.742: %IDS-4-TCP_FIN_ONLY_SIG:
 Sig:3042:TCP
   - FIN bit with no ACK bit in flags - from 192.168.0.140 to 192.168.0.6
Dec 09 15:33:39 192.168.0.6 53: Dec  9 15:33:38.951: %IDS-4-TCP_NO_FLAGS_SIG:
 Sig:3040:TCP
   - No bits set in flags - from 192.168.0.140 to 192.168.0.6
```

You can also monitor the network through the router CLI using the **show ip audit statistics** command, as shown in Example 9-8. The highlighted sections indicate a high number of attacks matching signatures 2150, 3040, and 3042. The information regarding these signatures matches that shown in the previous example.

Example 9-8 *Output of the* **show ip audit statistics** *Command*

```
Router-Dallas#show ip audit statistics
Signature audit statistics [process switch:fast switch]
  signature 2000 packets audited: [5:5]
```

Example 9-8 *Output of the* **show ip audit statistics** *Command (Continued)*

```
   signature 2150 packets audited: [341:481]
   signature 3040 packets audited: [3320:3332]
   signature 3041 packets audited: [0:10]
   signature 3042 packets audited: [13280:17972]
Interfaces configured for audit 2
Session creations since subsystem startup or last reset 0
Current session counts (estab/half-open/terminating) [0:0:0]
Maxever session counts (estab/half-open/terminating) [0:0:0]
Last session created never
Last statistic reset never
Post Office is not enabled - No connections are active
Router#
```

PIX IDSs

PIX-based IDS sensors are supported by PIX OS version 5.2 and higher. The sensors support 59 signatures to detect most common attacks. Deploying a PIX-based IDS involves the following steps:

1. Configuring the sensor
2. Verifying the configuration
3. Monitoring the network

Configuring a PIX-Based IDS Sensor

Similar to the IOS-based IDS, the syslog with timestamps should be enabled on the PIX Firewall before configuring the IDS sensor. The steps involved in configuring a PIX-based IDS sensor are summarized in Table 9-5.

Table 9-5 *PIX-Based IDS Configuration Steps*

Step	Command	Purpose
1	**logging on**	Starts sending syslog messages to all output locations. Stops all logging with the **no logging on** command.
2	**logging timestamp**	Specifies that syslog messages should be time stamped before being sent to the syslog server.
3	**logging trap warnings**	Sets the logging level for syslog warning messages.
4	**logging host** *interface syslog-ip-address*	Specifies the IP address of the syslog server; *interface* is the PIX interface that is connected to the syslog server.

continues

Table 9-5 *PIX-Based IDS Configuration Steps (Continued)*

Step	Command	Purpose
5	**ip audit attack** [**action** [**alarm**] [**drop**] [**reset**]]	Specifies the default actions for global policy on attack signatures; the **alarm** option instructs the PIX to send a syslog message; the **drop** option drops the offending packet; the **reset** option drops the offending packet and closes the connection.
6	**ip audit info** [**action** [**alarm**] [**drop**] [**reset**]]	Specify the default actions for global policy on informational signatures.
7	**ip audit name** *audit_name* **attack** [**action** [**alarm**] [**drop**] [**reset**]]	Creates a custom policy for attack signatures; the policy name should be different from the policy name of the information signature.
8	**ip audit name** *audit_name* ***info*** [**action** [**alarm**] [**drop**] [**reset**]]	Creates a custom policy for informational signatures; the policy name should be different from the policy name of the attack signature.
9	**ip audit interface** *if_name audit_name*	Applies a custom policy to an interface.
10 (optional)	**ip audit signature** *signature_number* ***disable***	Disables a signature from the global policy.

TIP You can also configure a PIX-based IDS using the PIX Device Manager (PDM) GUI, without a detailed knowledge of PIX commands. PDM can also create graphs to monitor IDS statistics.

Example 9-9 shows the sample configuration of a PIX-based IDS sensor. The sensor is configured to drop all the packets that match the attack signatures. All the IDS alerts are sent to the syslog server 192.168.0.100. For the sake of clarity, the example includes highlighted comments that explain the relevant details about the configuration.

Example 9-9 *PIX IDS Configuration*

```
logging on
logging timestamp
! PIX IDS messages are sent at warning level
logging trap warnings
logging host inside 192.168.0.100
!
ip audit name IDS1 attack action alarm drop reset
ip audit name IDS2 info action alarm
```

Example 9-9 *PIX IDS Configuration (Continued)*

```
!Unlike IOS IDS info and attack signatures are applied
!to the same interface using different names
ip audit interface inside IDS2
ip audit interface inside IDS1
!
ip audit interface outside IDS2
ip audit interface outside IDS1
!
ip audit info action alarm
ip audit attack action drop reset
!
ip audit signature 1000 disable
ip audit signature 2002 disable
!end
```

Verifying Sensor Configuration

To verify the sensor configuration, use the **show running** command in privileged mode.

Monitoring the Network

The sensor monitors the traffic flowing through the PIX Firewall, and the intrusion alerts are sent to the syslog server. Example 9-10 shows the messages collected by the syslog server. Note how the output contains the details of the attack signatures.

Example 9-10 *Syslog Messages*

```
Dec 09 16:16:44 192.168.0.20 Dec 09 2004 16:16:45: %PIX-4-400023: IDS:2150 ICMP
 fragment from 192.168.0.140 to 192.168.0.20 on interface inside
Dec 09 16:16:44 192.168.0.20 Dec 09 2004 16:16:45: %PIX-4-400025: IDS:2154 ICMP ping
 of death from 192.168.0.140 to 192.168.0.20 on interface inside
Dec 09 16:16:44 192.168.0.20 Dec 09 2004 16:16:45: %PIX-4-400025: IDS:2154 ICMP ping
 of death from 192.168.0.140 to 192.168.0.20 on interface inside
Dec 09 16:16:51 192.168.0.20 Dec 09 2004 16:16:51: %PIX-4-400026: IDS:3040 TCP NULL
 flags from 192.168.0.140 to 192.168.0.20 on interface inside
Dec 09 16:16:55 192.168.0.20 Dec 09 2004 16:16:56: %PIX-4-400014: IDS:2004 ICMP echo
  request from 192.168.0.140 to 192.168.0.20 on interface inside
```

The IDS statistics can also be viewed at the PIX CLI in privileged mode using the **show ip audit count** command. As highlighted in Example 9-11, the PIX has detected attacks matching the 2001, 2150, 2154, and 3040 signatures. These signature details match the output shown in the previous example.

Example 9-11 *Output of the* **show ip audit count** *Command*

```
Firewall-Dallas# show ip audit count
Signature                                inside  Global
1000 I Bad IP Options List               0       0
1001 I Record Packet Route               0       0
```

continues

Example 9-11 *Output of the* **show ip audit count** *Command (Continued)*

```
1002 I Timestamp                        0        0
1003 I Provide s,c,h,tcc                0        0
1004 I Loose Source Route               0        0
1005 I SATNET ID                        0        0
1006 I Strict Source Route              0        0
1100 A IP Fragment Attack               0        0
1102 A Impossible IP Packet             0        0
1103 A IP Teardrop                      0        0
2000 I ICMP Echo Reply                  0        0
2001 I ICMP Unreachable                 193482   193482
2002 I ICMP Source Quench               0        0
2003 I ICMP Redirect                    0        0
2004 I ICMP Echo Request                10       10
2005 I ICMP Time Exceed                 0        0
2006 I ICMP Parameter Problem           0        0
2007 I ICMP Time Request                0        0
2008 I ICMP Time Reply                  0        0
2009 I ICMP Info Request                0        0
2010 I ICMP Info Reply                  0        0
2011 I ICMP Address Mask Request        0        0
2012 I ICMP Address Mask Reply          0        0
2150 A Fragmented ICMP                  306      306
2151 A Large ICMP                       0        0
2154 A Ping of Death                    1992     1992
3040 A TCP No Flags                     3321     3321
3041 A TCP SYN & FIN Flags Only         0        0
3042 A TCP FIN Flag Only                0        0
3153 A FTP Improper Address             0        0
3154 A FTP Improper Port                0        0
4050 A Bomb                             0        0
4051 A Snork                            0        0
4052 A Chargen                          0        0
6050 I DNS Host Info                    0        0
6051 I DNS Zone Xfer                    0        0
6052 I DNS Zone Xfer High Port          0        0
6053 I DNS All Records                  0        0
6100 I RPC Port Registration            0        0
6101 I RPC Port Unregistration          0        0
6102 I RPC Dump                         0        0
6103 A Proxied RPC                      0        0
6150 I ypserv Portmap Request           0        0
6151 I ypbind Portmap Request           0        0
6152 I yppasswdd Portmap Request        0        0
6153 I ypupdated Portmap Request        0        0
6154 I ypxfrd Portmap Request           0        0
6155 I mountd Portmap Request           0        0
6175 I rexd Portmap Request             0        0
6180 I rexd Attempt                     0        0
6190 A statd Buffer Overflow            0        0
Firewall-Dallas#
```

Commercial Cisco Products

In addition to the basic IDS sensors in IOS and PIX software, Cisco also provides an extensive range of IDS products to suit most environments. Some of these products are as follows:

- **Cisco IDS 4200 Series Sensors**—Signature-based NIDS appliances.
- **IDS Network Module for Routers**—Signature-based NIDS module for space-saving and cost-effective intrusion detection using 2600, 3600, and 3700 Series routers.
- **IDS Services Module switches**—Signature-based IDS for Catalyst 6500 switches.
- **Cisco Secure Agent (CSA)**—Anomaly-based HIDS for Windows and Solaris hosts.
- **CiscoWorks RME**—Although not an IDS product, RME manages and audits the configuration of network devices. RME also sends alerts through e-mail/pagers regarding changes in configuration.

In addition to a range of IDS products, Cisco also offers various tools for centrally managing these products. Moreover, the amount of logs and alerts collected by a central logging device can be overwhelming. Cisco also offers products to efficiently manage and correlate the alerts and logs. Some of these products are as follows:

- **Cisco Threat Response**—Eliminates false alarms, quickly identifies real intrusions, and automates investigations and forensic data captures.
- **Cisco Security Monitoring, Analysis and Response System (CS-MARS)**—An appliance that collects and correlates logs and events from various network devices, including IDSs, firewalls, and routers. It provides a visual topology map of a network attack and allows the Netadmin to limit or prevent an attack in real time.
- **CiscoWorks Security Information Management Solution**—Collects, analyzes, and correlates security event data from across the enterprise using netForensics.
- **CiscoWorks VPN/Security Management Solution**—Web-based tools for configuring, monitoring, and troubleshooting network-intrusion- and host-intrusion-prevention systems (CSAs), VPNs, and firewalls; integrated with other CiscoWorks products; provides network device inventory, change audits, and software distribution features.

Summary

This chapter covers the concept of intrusion detection and the tools that are available for deploying an IDS in a network. The chapter prepares Netadmins to secure the network by the following means:

- Deploying an NIDS using Snort

- Deploying an HIDS to detect configuration changes on IOS devices and PIX Firewalls
- Deploying embedded IDS sensors using IOS routers and PIX Firewalls

Table 9-6 lists all the tools discussed in this chapter for deploying IDSs.

Table 9-6 *Device IDS Tools*

Tool	Function	Supported OS	URL/Notes
Snort	NIDS	Linux and Windows	http://www.snort.org http://www.winsnort.com
ACID	Web-based GUI front end for Snort	Linux and Windows	http://acidlab.sourceforge.net/
Knoppix-STD	Pre-installed Snort with management console	—	http://www.knoppix-std.org
Network Security Toolkit (NST)	Pre-installed Snort with management console	—	http://www.networksecuritytoolkit.org/
Rancid	HIDS for detecting changes in device configurations	Linux	http://www.shrubbery.net/rancid/
IOS-based IDSs	IOS-based NIDSs embedded in Cisco routers	—	http://www.cisco.com/go/ios
PIX-based IDSs	PIX-based NIDSs embedded in Cisco routers	—	http://www.cisco.com/go/pix

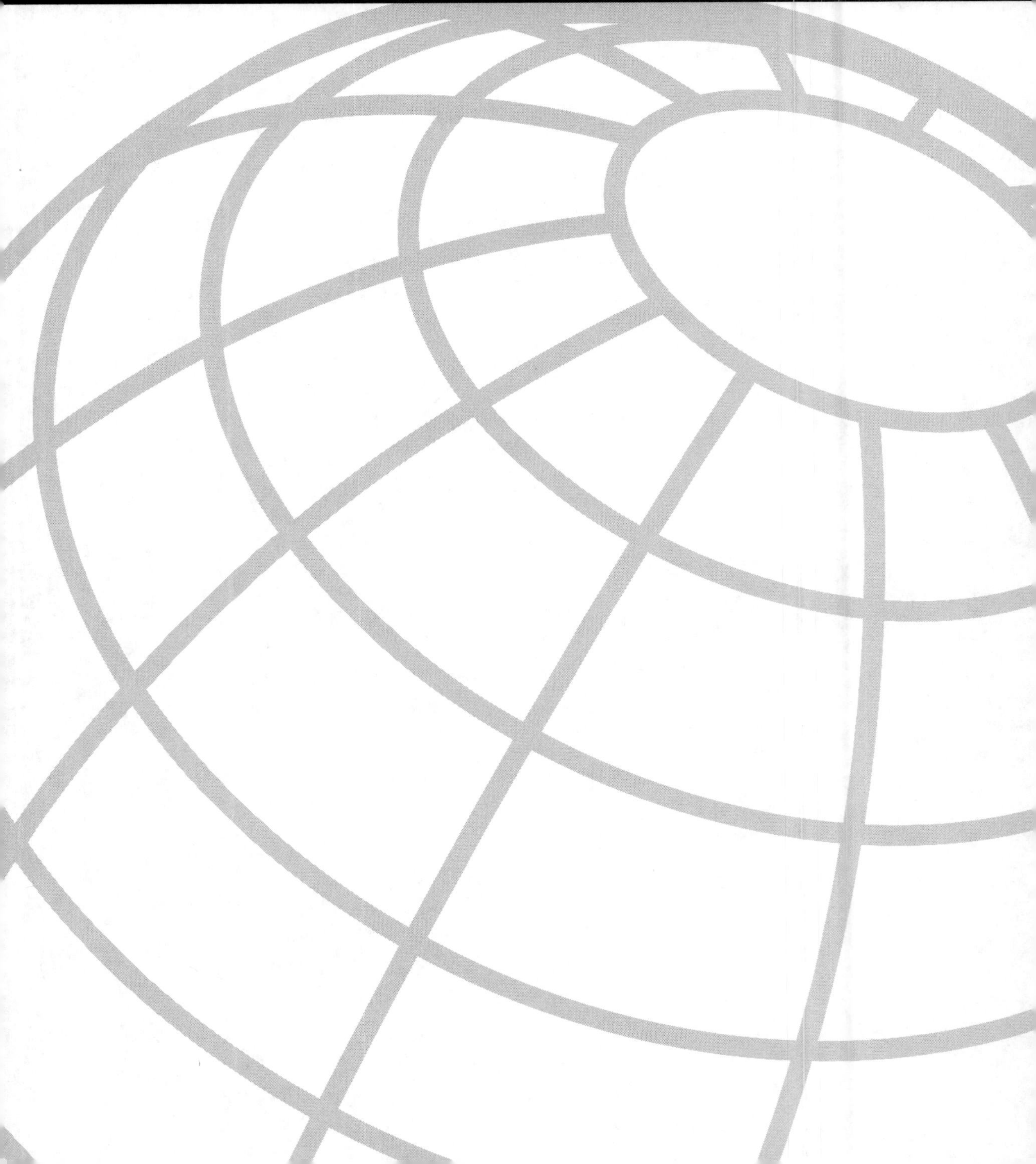

CHAPTER 10

Virtual Private Networks (VPN)

This chapter introduces the IPSec protocol and its role in providing VPN service. The focus is on implementing LAN-to-LAN VPNs using IPSec with preshared keys. The chapter also addresses interoperability issues between Cisco devices and other popular IPSec implementations.

The topics discussed in this chapter are as follows:

- VPN overview
- Linux-based VPNs
- Windows-based VPNs

VPN Overview

A virtual private network (VPN) enables private networks to communicate securely over the unsecured public network (that is, the Internet). These connections behave as a single virtual network, despite being geographically separated. VPNs provide inexpensive alternatives to expensive leased lines–WANs. VPNs also enable employees to remotely access the office network through the Internet.

A VPN works by setting up a tunnel between the two nodes. The data is then encapsulated and sent through this tunnel. Optionally, the encapsulated data can be encrypted to provide additional security. From the user's perspective, VPNs are classified into the following two categories:

- **Site-to-site**—This is a VPN between remote networks at fixed locations; it is also called a LAN-to-LAN or intranet VPN. These VPNs require a VPN gateway at each location but no changes to the end users' machines. Site-to-site VPNs provide replacement for leased lines-based WANs.
- **Remote-access**—This is a VPN that originates from a mobile user to the corporate network, through the Internet; it is also called a road-warrior or telecommuter VPN. Remote-access VPNs provide replacement for dial-up lines for access to the corporate network. Remote-access VPNs are comprised of a VPN gateway at the corporate network and a VPN client installed on each remote computer. The remote client must initiate and establish a VPN tunnel to the gateway.

Both site-to-site and remote-access VPNs can be implemented using various protocols. Some common protocols used in VPN implementations are as follows:

- **IPSec**—IPSec is the protocol of choice for implementing VPNs. IPSec works at Layer 3 of the OSI model by encrypting the Internet protocol (IP).
- **SSL (Secure Socket Layer)**—SSL-based VPNs are getting popular for deploying remote-access VPNs because they do not need the client software to be installed on the remote desktop (or laptop); the users instead use the SSL-capable browser.
- **SSH**—SSH works at Layer 4 of the OSI model by encrypting the Transmission Control Protocol (TCP) traffic.
- **GRE (generic routing encapsulation)**—GRE is a Cisco-proprietary protocol for tunneling (encapsulating) non-IP traffic. GRE does not provide encryption.
- **L2TP (Layer 2 Tunnel Protocol)**—L2TP works at Layer 2 by encapsulating Point-to-Point Protocol (PPP) traffic; it provides the benefits of MS-PPTP (Point-to-Point Tunneling Protocol) and the Cisco Layer 2 Forwarding (L2F) Protocol. L2TP provides no encryption.
- **MPLS (Multiprotocol Label Switching)**—MPLS-based VPNs are deployed at the Internet service provider (ISP) level according to the Internet Engineering Task Force (IETF) RFC 2547bis specifications for the Border Gateway Protocol (BGP).

IPSec Overview

This chapter discusses the interoperability of IPSec-based VPNs with Cisco devices. IPSec provides strong data protection and is the most popular protocol for implementing VPNs. IPSec is designed to offer access control, connectionless integrity, data origin authentication, protection against replays, and confidentiality through encryption. Because IPSec works at the IP layer (the Network layer or Layer 3 of the OSI model), all types of Internet traffic can be protected with no modifications on the upper-layer protocols or applications. IPSec can protect any traffic carried over IP, unlike other encryption-oriented protocols such as SSH and SSL, which generally protect only a particular higher-level protocol. IPSec can run on routers, firewalls, application servers, and end-user desktops and laptops. Dedicated IPSec gateway machines can protect the traffic flowing between private networks. Any two nodes that originate and terminate IPSec tunnels between each other are referred to as *IPSec peers.* Although referred to as a protocol, IPSec is a collection of various protocols that together constitute the IPSec framework, as described by RFCs 2401–2411 and 2451.

The following sections describe the IPSec protocols in detail.

Protocol and Algorithm

Before discussing IPSec in detail, you must be familiar with the following protocols and algorithms:

- **Authentication Header (AH)**—A security protocol, defined by RFC 2402, that provides data origin authentication, data integrity, and optional replay-detection services. AH does not provide data encryption but can be used either by itself or in conjunction with an Encapsulating Security Payload (ESP). It is represented as protocol 51 in the IP header.
- **Encapsulating Security Payload (ESP)**—A security protocol, defined by RFC 2406, that provides data confidentiality and protection with optional authentication and replay-detection services. ESP provides data encryption using the Data Encryption Standard (DES) and the Triple Data Encryption Standard (3DES). Data authentication is provided by Message Digest 5 (MD5) or Secure Hash Algorithm 1 (SHA-1). ESP can be used either by itself or in conjunction with AH. It is represented as protocol 50 in the IP header.
- **Data Encryption Standard (DES)**—A secret key encryption algorithm based on IBM's Lucifer algorithm. DES encrypts a 56-bit-long block of plain text into a block of ciphertext of the same size by using the secret key. In 3DES, three stages of DES are applied with a separate key for each stage, yielding an effective key length of 168 bits. The decryption process uses the same key, thus making DES/3DES a symmetric key cipher.
- **Advanced Encryption Standard (AES)**—A new cipher block chaining (CBC) mode encryption algorithm that was developed by the National Institute of Standards and Technology (NIST) as a replacement for DES. AES uses 128-, 192-, and 256-bit key lengths and is more secure than DES.
- **Message Digest 5 (MD5)**—A one-way hashing algorithm that produces a 128-bit hash digest that can be used to authenticate the data packet.
- **Secure Hash Algorithm (SHA)**—A one-way hashing algorithm, originally defined by the National Security Agency (NSA), that produces a 160-bit hash digest. SHA is stronger than MD5 but slower because of the 160-bit hash.
- **Internet Key Exchange (IKE)**—A combination of SKEME (Secure Key Exchange MEchanism), Oakley, and Internet Security Association and Key Management Protocol (ISAKMP) used to establish a shared security policy and authenticated keys for IPSec. IKE allows automated authentication and key exchange over a public network without loss of confidentiality. IKE communicates through UDP port 500. IKE uses the following two-step process:
  - Phase 1 establishes ISAKMP security associations to secure the Phase 2 IPSec negotiations.
  - Phase 2 establishes a pair of unidirectional IPSec security associations.

- **Diffie-Hellman (D-H)**—A public key cryptography mechanism used to exchange secret keys over an insecure medium with no prior knowledge of the secrets. D-H is specified in terms of groups, such as D-H group 2 or group 5. The type of group depends on the size of the prime number used in the keying algorithm. Group 5 is more secure than group 2.
- **Perfect forward secrecy (PFS)**—A security mechanism that prevents an attacker from decrypting future data, even if he knows the current encryption keys. PFS enforces the additional D-H exchange to recompute the secret key.
- **Digital certificates and certification authorities (CA)**—Contains the certificate holder's public key, expiration dates, and the digital signature of the certificate-issuing authority and other details, such as host name and serial number. Most digital certificates conform to the X.509 standard defined by the International Telecommunication Union Telecommunication Standardization Sector (ITU-T). To get a digital certificate, a client registers with a trusted entity called a certificate authority. After a CA verifies the client's credentials, a certificate is issued.

NOTE While both hashing and encryption algorithms convert the clear-text data into ciphertext, the hashing mechanism is a one-way mechanism. A hashed data packet cannot be recovered into clear text. In contrast, an encrypted data packet can be recovered to its clear-text form.

IPSec Components

IPSec architecture consists of the following four fundamental components:

- **Security protocols**—The core functionality of IPSec for encapsulating the data to be protected, using either the AH or ESP, or both.
- **Security associations (SA)**—Unidirectional logical connections, created to provide security services to the traffic. To secure mutual communication between two security gateways, two security associations (one in each direction) are required. An SA consists of a security parameter index (SPI), an IP destination address, and a security protocol (AH or ESP) identifier.
- **Key management**—IPSec relies heavily on the use of secret keys for authentication, integrity, and encryption services. The key management mechanism enables the use of the public key–based IKE protocol for handling the manual and automatic key exchanges.
- **Algorithms for authentication and encryption**—Various algorithms, such as DES, 3DES, MD5, and SHA, carry out the encryption, decryption, and message authentication to provide data integrity and protection against eavesdropping.

IPSec Operation Steps

IPSec operation can be summarized in the following five steps:

1. The peers start the IPSec process after receiving interesting traffic. The data meant to be encapsulated and sent across the VPN tunnel is called *interesting traffic.*
2. IKE phase 1 negotiates and establishes IKE SA parameters.
3. IKE phase 2 negotiates and establishes IPSec SA parameters.
4. Data is transferred between IPSec peers.
5. IPSec SAs terminate because of timeouts or deletions.

In IKE phase 1, the two ISAKMP peers negotiate and establish a secure and authenticated channel, also called the *IKE Security Association.* The primary goal of phase 1 is to protect the phase 2 message exchanges. Phase 1 can be carried out using one of two modes—Main Mode and Aggressive Mode. Main Mode involves an exchange of six messages, while Aggressive Mode involves an exchange of three messages. Although slower, Main Mode is more secure and hence preferred over Aggressive Mode. By default, the Cisco IPSec implementation uses Main Mode.

IKE phase 2 has only one mode, called Quick Mode. The goal of Quick Mode is to negotiate and establish IPSec SAs. The IPSec SAs are then used to protect the data that is flowing through the IPSec tunnel. Quick Mode also generates the keying material used by the IPSec SAs. The messages exchanged during phase 2 (Quick Mode) are protected by the IKE SAs that were established during phase 1.

Additionally, during the phase 1 negotiations, IPSec peers must authenticate each other using one of the following three authentication methods:

- **Preshared key**—The same preshared key (a text string) is manually distributed through an out-of-band mechanism to each IPSec peer. Peer A computes a hash using the preshared key and sends it to peer B. Peer B creates a hash using its own preshared key and compares the result with the hash received from peer A. If both hashes are the same, the peers are authenticated. Despite being easy to configure, preshared keys must be individually configured for each pair of the IPSec peers. For example, in a fully meshed network with ten peers, each peer must be configured with the preshared keys of the remaining nine peers. Consequently, $10 * 9 = 90$ instances of preshared key configurations exist. Hence, preshared keys do not scale well with large-scale deployments.
- **Digital signatures**—For digital signature–based authentication, peer A creates a hash of the payload, signs the hash with its own private key, and sends it to peer B. Peer B then verifies the signed hash by using the public key of peer A. The certificate that contains the public keys can be exchanged during IKE negotiations.

- **Public key encryption**—Public key encryption involves the use of a private and a public key pair to encrypt and decrypt the payload. Peer A encrypts the payload with peer B's public key and sends the encrypted data to peer B. Peer B can decrypt the payload only by using its own private key. The certificates that contain the public key must be obtained, through CAs, prior to IKE negotiations.

IPSec Modes: Tunnel Versus Transport

Based on the traffic encapsulation, IPSec operates in the following two modes:

- **Transport Mode**—Only encapsulates the upper-layer payload (data) of the original IP datagram. An IPSec header is inserted between the original IP header and the modified data payload. This mode can only be used when the peers are the endpoints of the communication because the original IP header is used to route the packet.
- **Tunnel Mode**—Completely encapsulates the original IP datagram. New IP headers and IPSec headers are added to the encapsulated datagram, as shown in Figure 10-1. Because the original IP header is encapsulated, Tunnel Mode is ideal for connecting private networks, using the RFC 1918 address, through the Internet. Tunnel Mode is widely used for site-to-site IPSec VPNs using an IPSec gateway, thus eliminating the need to modify the end systems.

Figure 10-1 *IPSec Tunnel Versus Transport Mode*

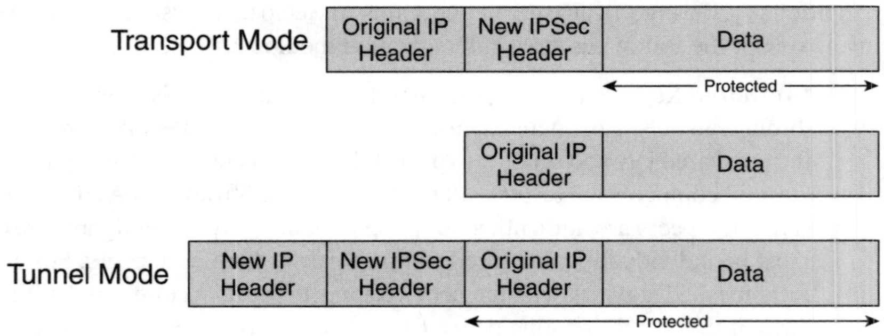

Linux-Based VPNs

Because of the pervasive nature of VPNs, Netadmins often need to support VPNs on heterogeneous platforms. Although IPSec is standards-based, the interoperability of IPSec VPNs among various vendors and OS platforms can be challenging. OpenSWAN, an IPSec-based VPN project for Linux, offers interoperability with other standards-based IPSec VPNs.

Consider the typical network scenario shown in Figure 10-2. This network consists of two remote offices connected through an IPSec VPN through the Internet. Site A uses dual-homed Linux machines with OpenSWAN as a VPN server, while site B uses a Cisco device as a VPN server. This Cisco box can be any of the three classes of devices that are capable of providing IPSec-based VPN services: an IOS-based device, a PIX Firewall, or a VPN 3000 concentrator.

Figure 10-2 *LAN-to-LAN VPN*

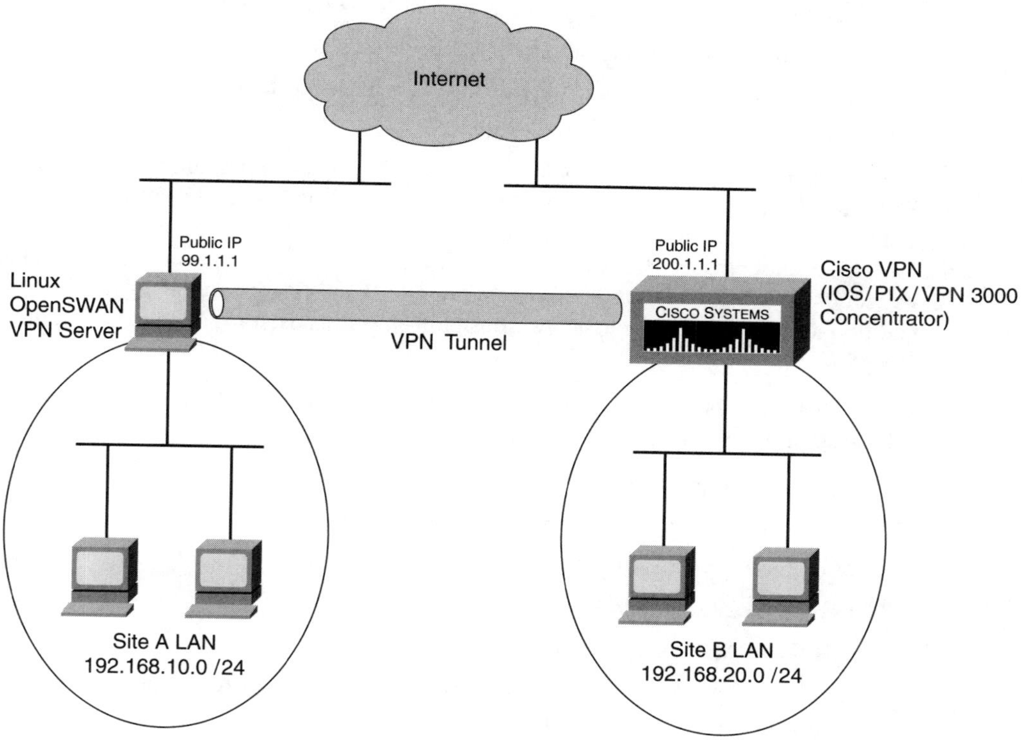

Based on this typical network scenario, the following sections discuss the IPSec-based OpenSWAN project and its interoperability with Cisco devices, such as routers, PIX Firewalls, and VPN 3000 concentrators. You will also find sample configurations for each interoperability scenario.

OpenSWAN

The OpenSWAN project (http://www.openswan.org) is by far the most successful open source project for IPSec-based VPNs running Linux. OpenSWAN is based on the now-defunct FreeSWAN project. Some features leading to the popularity of OpenSWAN (including FreeSWAN) are as follows:

- Based on IPSec standard as specified in RFC 2401
- Under active development since 1999
- Excellent interoperability with standards-compliant IPSec implementations, including Cisco IOS, PIX Firewalls, and VPN 3000 concentrators
- IKE authentication using automatic keying with shared keys
- IKE authentication using automatic keying with X.509 certificates
- Works with Linux kernel 2.0 and higher

The overall architecture of OpenSWAN consists of two main components—KLIPS and Pluto. KLIPS is the IPSec kernel module for implementing ESP and packet handling. The Linux kernel 2.6 and higher features built-in support for IPSec, thus eliminating the need for KLIPS. Note that KLIPS cannot coexist with kernel 2.6 and can cause the kernel to freeze. Pluto is the IKE daemon for negotiating IKE and IPSec parameters for ESP. In addition to these two components, various built-in scripts exist for administration of OpenSWAN.

Within its standards-compliant architectural framework, OpenSWAN supports the following protocols and algorithms:

- ESP for encryption and authentication
- IKE for negotiating SA parameters for ESP
- IKE phase 1 Main Mode
- IKE phase 2 Quick Mode
- 3DES and AES for encryption
- Preshared keys; Rivest, Shamir, and Adelman (RSA) signatures; and X.509 certificates for authentication
- PFS for added security
- D-H groups 5 and 2 for key exchange
- MD5 and SHA-1 as hashing algorithms

Deploying OpenSWAN

The steps for deploying OpenSWAN are as follows:

1. Verifying that the prerequisites are met

2 Installing the OpenSWAN files

3 Editing the configuration files

4 Running the OpenSWAN server

5 Troubleshooting the OpenSWAN server

Verifying Prerequisites

Before deploying OpenSWAN on a Linux machine, the following prerequisites should be met:

- **Hardware**—The processing of IPSec packets is CPU-intensive, and the choice of CPU and RAM depends largely on the WAN connection speed between the OpenSWAN server and its remote peer. According to the OpenSWAN website, a Pentium 133-MHz processor should suffice to support IPSec tunnels through digital subscriber line (DSL) or T1 connections. On the other hand, an OpenSWAN server running a dual Xeon 2.8-GHz CPU with 1 GB RAM can support 1000 IPSec tunnels through a 100-MB connection between the IPSec peers. These estimates do not take into account other services, such as a firewall or Domain Name System (DNS), that are running on the same machine.
- **Kernel**—OpenSWAN needs the Linux kernel 2.2 or higher. As previously noted, kernel 2.6 features native support for IPSec, thus eliminating the need for the KLIPS module. You might need to upgrade your kernel.
- **Dual homed**—The Linux machine should have two Ethernet network interface cards (NIC)—one for the public network to the Internet and the second to connect to the private network. The NIC that faces the Internet should be configured with a routable public address and a default gateway, as provided by the ISP. This step is significant, because without a publicly routable static IP address, IPSec does not work. Additionally, OpenSWAN is designed to work only with a single default gateway and does not start if multiple default gateways are specified. Hence, on the NIC that faces the inside network, do not add a default gateway.
- **Routing**—Because the Linux machine routes packets across the subnets, the routing (also called *IP forwarding*) capability should be enabled. Debian users should also disable the spoof-protection feature. Both of these tasks can be done in Debian by editing the /etc/network/options file, as shown in Example 10-1.
- **OS hardening**—Because this machine will be facing the Internet, it should be adequately secured using firewall- and OS-hardening scripts. Disable unnecessary services and ports. However, make sure that the firewall allows UDP port 500 (ISAKMP traffic) and protocol 50 (ESP) for the proper functioning of OpenSWAN.

TIP To harden Red Hat Linux, Fedora, SuSE, Mandrake, Debian, and Gentoo, visit http://www.bastille-linux.org/. Additionally, Debian users can also refer to http://www.debian-hardened.org/.

NOTE The Linux command used to assign the default gateway is **route add default gw** *next-hop-ipaddess interface-name* (for example, **route add default gw 99.1.1.2 eth0**).

Example 10-1 *Contents of the /etc/network/options File*

```
root@linuxbox:~# cat /etc/network/options
ip_forward=yes
spoofprotect=no
syncookies=no
```

Installing the OpenSWAN Files

OpenSWAN is available in both source code and packaged form for various Linux distributions. Depending on the kernel version and the distribution, the installation steps will vary. For Debian-Linux with kernel 2.6 and higher, use the following **apt-get** command:

```
apt-get install openswan
```

After the installation, you can verify the OpenSWAN environment by using the **ipsec verify** command, as shown in Example 10-2.

Example 10-2 *Output of the* **ipsec verify** *Command*

```
root@linuxbox2:~# ipsec verify
Checking your system to see if IPSec got installed and started correctly:
Version check and ipsec on-path                                   [OK]
Linux Openswan U2.2.0/K2.6.7 (native)
Checking for IPSec support in kernel                              [OK]
#This message is OK if  only using pre-shared key
Checking for RSA private key (/etc/ipsec.secrets)                 [FAILED]
ipsec showhostkey: no default key in "/etc/ipsec.secrets"
Checking that pluto is running                                    [OK]
Two or more interfaces found, checking IP forwarding              [OK]
Checking NAT and MASQUERADEing                                    [N/A]
Checking for 'ip' command                                         [OK]
Checking for 'iptables' command                                   [OK]
Checking for 'setkey' command for native IPSec stack support      [OK]
#OE is not used with Cisco interoperating, so any FAILED message for OE is ok
Opportunistic Encryption DNS checks:
   Looking for TXT in forward dns zone: linuxbox2                 [MISSING]
   Does the machine have at least one non-private address?        [OK]
   Looking for TXT in reverse dns zone: 1.1.1.99.in-addr.arpa.    [OK]
root@linuxbox2:~#
```

Editing the Configuration Files

After installation, OpenSWAN is ready for configuration. Like the configuration of most Linux-based programs, OpenSWAN configuration is controlled through text files. Netadmins must have a clear understanding of the syntax and parameters used in these text files. The two configuration files used by OpenSWAN are as follows:

- ipsec.conf
- ipsec.secrets

ipsec.conf File

The /etc/ipsec.conf file is a text file that specifies the configuration and control information for the OpenSWAN IPSec subsystem. Comments are preceded by a white space followed by the pound sign (#). The first line of the file must always specify the OpenSWAN version; an example is as follows:

```
version 2
```

The rest of the ipsec.conf file consists of two main sections: config and conn. The config section specifies general configuration information for IPSec, while the conn section specifies an IPSec connection. The syntax is as follows:

```
Section-type name
            parameter1=value
            parameter2=value
            parameter3=value
```

CAUTION Note the syntax for the ipsec.conf file. Without the white space (Tab) before the parameters, OpenSWAN will not start and it generates the following error message:

```
ipsec_setup: (/etc/ipsec.conf) section header has wrong number of fields (1)
-- 'restart' aborted
```

Config section—The first line of the config section must be **config setup**. The remaining text consists of parameters and their values. Table 10-1 lists the common parameters for the config section.

Table 10-1 *Config Section Parameters for the ipsec.conf File*

Parameter	Description
interfaces	Specifies the virtual and physical interfaces that IPSec uses. The syntax is "*virtual=physical*" (including the quotation marks). You can also use the **%defaultroute** keyword instead. The keyword instructs OpenSWAN to select the interface that points to the default gateway.

continues

Table 10-1 *Config Section Parameters for the ipsec.conf File (Continued)*

Parameter	Description
klipsdebug	Specifies the extent of the debugging output generated by KLIPS. Use the keyword **none** to suppress debugging output, and use **all** to generate full output.
plutodebug	Specifies the extent of debugging output generated by PLUTO. Use the keyword **none** to suppress debugging output, and use **all** to generate full output.

Based on the syntax discussed in Table 10-1, sample code for the config section is as follows:

```
config setup
        interfaces=%defaultroute
        klipsdebug=all
        plutodebug=all
```

Conn section—The conn section specifies the connection details. Unlike the config section, you can have multiple instances of conn in the same file. The setup for each remote VPN peer is described by its own entry using the **conn** *connection-name* syntax. The naming convention (specified by OpenSWAN developers) refers to the local peer as left and the remote peer as right. Table 10-2 lists the most common parameters for the conn section. Note that every parameter that begins with **left** has a **right** counterpart.

Table 10-2 *Conn Section Parameters for the ipsec.conf File*

Parameter	Description
type	Specifies the type of the connection. Possible values are as follows: • **tunnel**—For host-to-host, host-to-subnet, or subnet-to-subnet tunnels • **passthrough**—For disabling IPSec processing • **drop**—For discarding the packet • **reject**—Same as **drop** but includes ICMP diagnostic messaging
left	The public IP address of the local peer or fully qualified domain name (FQDN), beginning with @, can also be used.
right	The public IP address of the remote peer or FQDN, beginning with @, can also be used.
leftsubnet	Specifies the network address of the local subnet that is being protected by the VPN. The address is specified using the classless interdomain routing (CIDR) format (for example, 192.168.10.0/24).
rightsubnet	Specifies the network address of the remote subnet that is being protected by the VPN. The address is specified using the CIDR format (for example, 192.168.10.0/24).
leftnexthop	Specifies the default gateway for the local peer.

Table 10-2 *Conn Section Parameters for the ipsec.conf File (Continued)*

Parameter	Description
rightnexthop	Specifies the default gateway for the remote peer.
leftfirewall	Disables Network Address Translation (NAT) (IP masquerading) for VPN traffic flowing between the local subnet and the remote subnet. The possible values are **yes** and **no**. Only relevant if the local firewall is enabled on the local peer.
rightfirewall	Disables the NAT for remote peer.
leftid	Specifies the identity of the local peer using the IP address or an FQDN. (FQDN must be preceded by the @ sign.)
rightid	Specifies the identity of the remote peer.
leftrsasigkey	Specifies the public key of the local peer for RSA signature authentication. This should be the same for multiple connections.
rightrsasigkey	Specifies the public key of the remote peer.
auto	Specifies the automatic action to be taken during startup. The possible values are as follows: • **add**—Adds the connection details to PLUTO's internal database • **route**—Instructs PLUTO to establish a route for the specified connection • **start**—Prompts PLUTO to establish the connection and add the route to the destination subnet during startup • **ignore**—Disables automatic startup for this connection Using **auto=start** at both ends creates a permanent VPN connection, because the peers automatically renegotiate after reboots.
authby	Specifies the authentication mechanism used by the peers, as follows: • **secret**—For preshared secrets • **rsasig**—For RSA digital signatures • **secret|rsasig**—For secret or rsasig • **never**—Disables authentication
pfs	Specifies the use of perfect forward secrecy for IKE exchanges; possible values are **yes** and **no**.
keylife	Specifies the lifetime, in seconds, for connection (IPSec SA)–related encryption and authentication keys using an integer followed by *s* (for example, 3600s); the default value is 8 hours, with a maximum value of 24 hours.
rekey	Instructs PLUTO to renegotiate IPSec SAs before they expire; possible values are **yes** and **no**. Both sides should agree to the same value.
rekeymargin	Specifies the remaining time before renegotiating the IPSec SA.

continues

Table 10-2 *Conn Section Parameters for the ipsec.conf File (Continued)*

Parameter	Description
keyingtries	Specifies the maximum number of attempts to negotiate IPSec SAs; use an integer or the keyword **%forever**.
ikelifetime	Specifies the ISAKMP SA lifetime; the default value is 1 hour, with a maximum value of 8 hours.

OpenSWAN has a unique feature called Opportunistic Encryption (also referred as OE) that provides automatic encryption using public keys distributed through a DNS server. However, you should disable this feature when interoperating with a Cisco device because this feature is not supported by any major network vendor, including Cisco. The code snippet for disabling OE is as follows:

```
#Disable Opportunistic Encryption
conn block
          auto=ignore
conn private
        auto=ignore
conn private-or-clear
        auto=ignore
conn clear-or-private
        auto=ignore
conn clear
        auto=ignore
#End of config for disabling Opportunistic Encryption
```

This code snippet should be appended to the /etc/ipsec.conf file. Example 10-3 provides sample contents of the /etc/ipsec.conf file that also include the code for disabling Opportunistic Encryption.

NOTE The OpenSWAN package for Debian contains similar code for disabling OE in the text file /etc/ipsec.d/examples/no_oe.conf. To instruct OpenSWAN to read this file, simply specify the path through the **include** keyword in the ipsec.conf file, as follows:

```
include /etc/ipsec.d/examples/no_oe.conf
```

Consider the VPN scenario shown previously in Figure 10-2. The VPN tunnel is configured to allow connectivity between site A and site B LANs. Site A uses an OpenSWAN server as the VPN gateway to establish a LAN-to-LAN IPSec tunnel with preshared keys. The sample ipsec.conf file for such a setup is shown in Example 10-3.

Example 10-3 *Sample ipsec.conf File*

```
# /etc/ipsec.conf - OpenSWAN IPSec configuration file
#The version information is needed for OpenSWAN
version 2.0

# basic configuration
```

Example 10-3 *Sample ipsec.conf File (Continued)*

```
config setup
          interfaces=%defaultroute
          klipsdebug=all
          plutodebug=all

# Add connections here
conn ciscovpn
          type= tunnel
          left= 99.1.1.1
          leftnexthop= 99.1.1.2
          leftsubnet= 192.168.10.0/24
          right= 200.1.1.1
          rightnexthop= 200.1.1.2
          rightsubnet= 192.168.20.0/24
# Instruct OpenSWAN to use preshared keys
          authby=secret
          auto=add  # change this to auto=start for start at boot

# Disable Opportunistic Encryption
# essential for inertoperating with Cisco devices
conn block
          auto=ignore

conn private
        auto=ignore

conn private-or-clear
        auto=ignore

conn clear-or-private
        auto=ignore

conn clear
        auto=ignore
# End of config for disabling Opportunistic Encryption
```

NOTE When tunneling multiple subnets, you need to create an individual conn entry for each subnet. Alternatively, if possible, you can summarize multiple subnets in the same conn entry.

ipsec.secrets File

The /etc/ipsec.secrets file is the second file used to configure OpenSWAN parameters. This file contains the preshared or RSA keys to be used for authentication. The PLUTO daemon uses this file to authenticate with the remote IPSec peer. Each entry in the file contains the IP addresses of the local IPSec peers, the remote IPSec peers, and the mutual authentication key. Each entry must start as a new line. The format to specify the preshared keys is as follows:

```
Public-IP-of-local-peer Public-IP-of-remote-peer: PSK "secret-key-string"
```

To use an FQDN instead of IP addresses, precede the name with an at sign (@). The preshared key cannot contain empty spaces or quotation marks within the text string. (As an example, **mypassword123** is valid but **mypassword 123** is invalid because of the space in the string. Similarly **mypass"word"123** is invalid because of the quotation marks within the string.

Example 10-4 shows a sample configuration of the ipsec.secrets file that contains preshared keys.

Example 10-4 *Sample ipsec.secrets File*

```
# Preshared key string "cisco123" for peer 99.1.1.1 and 200.1.1.1
99.1.1.1 200.1.1.1: PSK "cisco123"
# Use the include keyword to specify additional files containing secrets
# for example
#include ipsec.test.secrets
```

WARNING The preshared key text string (**cisco123**) used in the previous example is too small and easy to use in a production network. Always use a long and complex text string as a preshared key.

Because of its sensitive contents, this file should only be accessible to those with root privileges. Access should be blocked for other users using the **chown** and **chmod** commands, as shown in Example 10-5.

Example 10-5 *Changing Permission on the ipsec.secrets File*

```
root@linuxbox2:~# chown root:root /etc/ipsec.secrets
root@linuxbox2:~# chmod 600 /etc/ipsec.secrets
root@linuxbox2:~# ls -l /etc/ipsec.secrets
-rw------- 1 root root 36 Dec 29 22:35 /etc/ipsec.secrets
```

The PLUTO daemon reads the contents of the ipsec.secrets file only during startup. To force PLUTO to read the ipsec.secrets file after the contents are changed, use the following command:

```
ipsec auto --rereadsecrets
```

Running the OpenSWAN Server

OpenSWAN is administered through the **ipsec** command.

To start, stop, or restart an IPSec subsystem, use the **ipsec setup** command, as shown in Example 10-6.

Example 10-6 *Restarting an IPSec Subsystem*

```
root@linuxbox2:~# ipsec setup
Usage: ipsec setup {--start¦--stop¦--restart¦--status}
root@linuxbox2:~# ipsec setup restart
ipsec_setup: Stopping Openswan IPSec...
ipsec_setup: Starting Openswan IPSec U2.2.0/K2.6.7...
```

To open a connection, use the **ipsec auto --up** *connection-name* command as shown in Example 10-7. The *connection-name* parameter is the name specified in the conn section of the ipsec.conf file.

Example 10-7 *Manually Starting an IPSec Connection*

```
root@linuxbox2:~# ipsec auto --up ciscovpn
104 "ciscovpn" #1: STATE_MAIN_I1: initiate
106 "ciscovpn" #1: STATE_MAIN_I2: sent MI2, expecting MR2
003 "ciscovpn" #1: ignoring Vendor ID payload [e9c9b3ac0e8f770f58170fad5a5c986b]
108 "ciscovpn" #1: STATE_MAIN_I3: sent MI3, expecting MR3
Phase 1 main mode is established
004 "ciscovpn" #1: STATE_MAIN_I4: ISAKMP SA established
112 "ciscovpn" #2: STATE_QUICK_I1: initiate
003 "ciscovpn" #2: ignoring informational payload, type IPSEC_RESPONDER_LIFETIME
Phase 2 quick mode is established
004 "ciscovpn" #2: STATE_QUICK_I2: sent QI2, IPSec SA established {ESP=>0x25b822f1
  <0x7054091b}
```

After the connection is up, the hosts in the remote subnets should be able to communicate with each other. The route to the remote host is shown in the routing table. To check the routing table, you can use the **route** or the **netstat -nr** command. Example 10-8 shows the routing table before starting the IPSec connection.

Example 10-8 *Display Routing Table*

```
root@linuxbox2:~# route
Kernel IP routing table
Destination     Gateway         Genmask         Flags Metric Ref    Use Iface
99.1.1.0        *               255.255.255.0   U     0      0        0 eth0
192.168.10.0    *               255.255.255.0   U     0      0        0 eth1
default         99.1.1.2        0.0.0.0         UG    0      0        0 eth0
```

Example 10-9 shows the routing table after the connection is established. Note the addition of the route to the remote subnet 192.168.20.0/255.255.255.0 , as shown in the highlighted text. The next hop for the 192.168.20.0/255.255.255.0 subnet is the host 99.1.1.2, which is also the default gateway.

Example 10-9 *Display Routing Table*

```
root@linuxbox2:~# route
Kernel IP routing table
Destination     Gateway         Genmask         Flags Metric Ref    Use Iface
192.168.20.0    99.1.1.2        255.255.255.0   UG    0      0        0 eth0
99.1.1.0        *               255.255.255.0   U     0      0        0 eth0
192.168.10.0    *               255.255.255.0   U     0      0        0 eth1
default         99.1.1.2        0.0.0.0         UG    0      0        0 eth0
```

To test the communication between the two subnets, you can ping to the host 192.168.10.100 from the host 192.168.20.100. A successful ping reply confirms that the IPSec VPN tunnel is working.

Troubleshooting the OpenSWAN Server

To verify the status of an IPSec subsystem, use the **ipsec setup --status** command, as shown in Example 10-10. Note that this example uses Linux kernel 2.6 with built-in IPSec support, so the KLIPS module is not running; this causes OpenSWAN to generate the KLIPS error message.

Example 10-10 *Verifying IPSec Status*

```
root@linuxbox2:~# ipsec setup --status
IPSec running
but...
KLIPS module is not loaded!
```

To verify the status of a connection subsystem, use the **ipsec auto --status** command, as shown in Example 10-11. This command displays the IPSec subsystem status report, including the list of active connections with the negotiated ISAKMP and IPSec SAs.

Example 10-11 *Verifying the OpenSWAN Connection Status*

```
root@linuxbox2:~# ipsec auto --status
000 interface lo/lo ::1
000 interface lo/lo 127.0.0.1
000 interface eth1/eth1 192.168.10.1
000 interface eth0/eth0 99.1.1.1
000 %myid = (none)
000 debug
  raw+crypt+parsing+emitting+control+lifecycle+klips+dns+oppo+controlmore+pfkey+na
  ttraversal+x509
000
# IKE Phase 1 negotiations  begin
# OpenSWAN local peer is offering encryption options
```

Example 10-11 *Verifying the OpenSWAN Connection Status (Continued)*

```
000 algorithm ESP encrypt: id=2, name=ESP_DES, ivlen=8, keysizemin=64, keysizemax=64
000 algorithm ESP encrypt: id=3, name=ESP_3DES, ivlen=8, keysizemin=192,
 keysizemax=192
000 algorithm ESP encrypt: id=7, name=ESP_BLOWFISH, ivlen=8, keysizemin=40,
 keysizemax=448
000 algorithm ESP encrypt: id=11, name=ESP_NULL, ivlen=0, keysizemin=0, keysizemax=0
000 algorithm ESP encrypt: id=12, name=ESP_AES, ivlen=8, keysizemin=128,
 keysizemax=256
000 algorithm ESP encrypt: id=252, name=ESP_SERPENT, ivlen=8, keysizemin=128,
 keysizemax=256
000 algorithm ESP encrypt: id=253, name=ESP_TWOFISH, ivlen=8, keysizemin=128,
 keysizemax=256
# OpenSWAN local peer is offering hashing options
000 algorithm ESP auth attr: id=1, name=AUTH_ALGORITHM_HMAC_MD5, keysizemin=128,
 keysizemax=128
000 algorithm ESP auth attr: id=2, name=AUTH_ALGORITHM_HMAC_SHA1, keysizemin=160,
 keysizemax=160
000 algorithm ESP auth attr: id=5, name=AUTH_ALGORITHM_HMAC_SHA2_256,
 keysizemin=256, keysizemax=256
000 algorithm ESP auth attr: id=251, name=(null), keysizemin=0, keysizemax=0
000
000 algorithm IKE encrypt: id=7, name=OAKLEY_AES_CBC, blocksize=16, keydeflen=128
000 algorithm IKE encrypt: id=5, name=OAKLEY_3DES_CBC, blocksize=8, keydeflen=192
000 algorithm IKE hash: id=2, name=OAKLEY_SHA, hashsize=20
000 algorithm IKE hash: id=1, name=OAKLEY_MD5, hashsize=16
000 algorithm IKE dh group: id=2, name=OAKLEY_GROUP_MODP1024, bits=1024
000 algorithm IKE dh group: id=5, name=OAKLEY_GROUP_MODP1536, bits=1536
000 algorithm IKE dh group: id=14, name=OAKLEY_GROUP_MODP2048, bits=2048
000 algorithm IKE dh group: id=15, name=OAKLEY_GROUP_MODP3072, bits=3072
000 algorithm IKE dh group: id=16, name=OAKLEY_GROUP_MODP4096, bits=4096
000 algorithm IKE dh group: id=17, name=OAKLEY_GROUP_MODP6144, bits=6144
000 algorithm IKE dh group: id=18, name=OAKLEY_GROUP_MODP8192, bits=8192
000
000 stats db_ops.c: {curr_cnt, total_cnt, maxsz} :context={0,6,36} trans={0,6,336}
 attrs={0,6,224}
000
000 "ciscovpn": 192.168.10.0/24===99.1.1.1---99.1.1.2...200.1.1.2---
 200.1.1.1===192.168.20.0/24; erouted; eroute owner: #7
000 "ciscovpn":   ike_life: 3600s; ipsec_life: 28800s; rekey_margin: 540s;
 rekey_fuzz: 100%; keyingtries: 0
# IKE Phase 1 (Main Mode) SA established
000 "ciscovpn":   policy: PSK+ENCRYPT+TUNNEL+PFS+UP; prio: 24,24; interface: eth0;
000 "ciscovpn":   newest ISAKMP SA: #5; newest IPSec SA: #7;
000 "ciscovpn":   IKE algorithms wanted: 5_000-1-5, 5_000-1-2, 5_000-2-5, 5_000-2-
 2, flags=-strict
000 "ciscovpn":   IKE algorithms found:  5_192-1_128-5, 5_192-1_128-2, 5_192-2_160-
 5, 5_192-2_160-2,
000 "ciscovpn":   IKE algorithm newest: 3DES_CBC_192-MD5-MODP1536
# IKE Phase 2 (Quick Mode) negotiations  begin
000 "ciscovpn":   ESP algorithms wanted: 3_000-1, 3_000-2, flags=-strict
000 "ciscovpn":   ESP algorithms loaded: 3_000-1, 3_000-2, flags=-strict
000 "ciscovpn":   ESP algorithm newest: 3DES_0-HMAC_MD5; pfsgroup=<Phase1>
000
# IPSec SA established - Phase 2 quick mode over
```

continues

Example 10-11 *Verifying the OpenSWAN Connection Status (Continued)*

```
000 #7: "ciscovpn" STATE_QUICK_I2 (sent QI2, IPSec SA established); EVENT_SA_REPLACE
 in 25566s; newest IPSEC; eroute owner
000 #7: "ciscovpn" esp.2609002f@200.1.1.1 esp.d7fdb0aa@99.1.1.1 tun.0@200.1.1.1
 tun.0@99.1.1.1
000 #5: "ciscovpn" STATE_MAIN_R3 (sent MR3, ISAKMP SA established); EVENT_SA_REPLACE
 in 860s; newest ISAKMP
000
root@linuxbox2:~#
```

For troubleshooting purposes, you can also check the OpenSWAN logs in the following locations:

- /var/log/secure
- /var/log/auth.log
- /var/log/messages

As mentioned earlier, make sure that UDP port 500 and protocol 50 are not blocked. You can also use packet sniffers like Tcpdump or Ethereal for further troubleshooting.

Table 10-3 summarizes all the IPSec commands used for operating and troubleshooting OpenSWAN.

Table 10-3 *OpenSWAN Commands*

Command	Description
ipsec verify	Checks the OpenSWAN installation
ipsec setup {**--start**|**--stop**|**--restart**|**--status**}	Starts and stops OpenSWAN's IPSec subsystem
ipsec barf [**--short**]	Debugs OpenSWAN
ipsec auto --rereadsecrets	Forces OpenSWAN to reload the secrets from the ipsec.secrets file
ipsec auto [**--verbose**] **--up** *connection-name*	Starts the specified connection
ipsec auto --{**add**|**delete**|**replace**|**down**} *connection-name*	Controls the specified connection
ipsec look	Provides a brief status of OpenSWAN
ipsec auto --status	Provides a detailed status of IPSec

NOTE To interoperate OpenSWAN and Cisco devices using an X.509 certificate, a CA server should be available. A CA server generates and distributes digitally signed X.509 certificates. The "Interoperating" section in the OpenSWAN documentation (http://wiki.openswan.org) provides a sample configuration for such advanced scenarios.

TIP The Knoppix-STD live CD provides a preinstalled and patched version of the original FreeSWAN code. The live CD provides a quick-and-easy VPN server that can be deployed in less than 5 minutes, thus making it ideally suited for test environments or troubleshooting VPN scenarios.

Interoperating OpenSWAN with Cisco IOS

Cisco routers offer IPSec capabilities with IOS Release 11.3 and higher. The IPSec security feature set is also implemented in the newer IOS-based Catalyst switches with Enhanced Multilayer Image (EMI). The Cisco implementation of IPSec enables Netadmins to deploy IPSec-based VPNs and remote access. The standards-based IPSec stack in the IOS enables interoperability with other standards-compliant IPSec products, including OpenSWAN.

IOS Configuration Tasks

To configure an IPSec-based VPN for IOS using preshared keys, follow these steps:

Step 1 Determine the following security policies:

- Phase 1 policies
- Phase 2 policies

Step 2 Configure the following IKE parameters:

- Encryption
- Hash
- Authentication
- Diffie-Hellman group
- IKE SA lifetime
- Preshared keys

Step 3 Configure the following IPSec parameters:

- IPSec SA lifetime
- Interesting traffic
- Transform sets
- Crypto maps

Step 4 Monitor and troubleshoot.

Step 1: Determine the Security Policies

To enable smoother interoperation between any two IPSec peers, the configuration must adhere to a common IPSec policy. The IPSec policies describe various parameters and their possible values. An IPSec connection only works after successful negotiation of all the IPSec parameters. Cisco IOS offers a high degree of flexibility for configuring various features and parameters that are available within the IPSec framework. Table 10-4 lists various IPSec parameters and their possible values offered by IOS.

Table 10-4 *IOS IPSec Parameters*

Parameter	Values
Phase 1 modes	Main Mode
Phase 2 modes	Quick Mode
Message encryption algorithm (phase 1)	DES, 3DES, AES128, AES192, AES256*
Hash algorithm (phase 1)	MD5, SHA-1
Authentication (phase 1)	Preshared keys, RSA encryption, RSA signature
Diffie-Hellman key exchange (phase 1)	D-H group 1, 2, 5
IKE SA lifetime (phase 1)	Seconds
Transform set (phase 2)	AH-HMAC-MD5, AH-HMAC-SHA, ESP-3DES, ESP-DES
IPSec mode (phase 2)	Tunnel, Transport
IPSec SA (phase 2)	IKE, Manual
PFS (phase 2)	Group 1, 2, 5
ID of the peer (phase 2)	IP address, FQDN
IPSec SA lifetime (phase 2)	Kilobytes, seconds

*AES is available with IOS Release 12.2(13)T and higher.

Step 2: Configure the IKE Parameters

The IPSec phase 1 (IKE parameters) configuration commands for IOS are listed in Table 10-5. Note the router prompt for each command. While the configuration starts in the global configuration mode, IKE options are mainly configured through the config-isakmp mode. The commands in Table 10-5 are specific to IKE authentication using preshared keys.

Table 10-5 *IOS—IKE Configuration Commands*

Step	Command	Description
1	Router(config)# **crypto isakmp enable**	Enables IKE on the router.
2	Router(config)# **crypto isakmp policy** *priority*	Initiates an IKE policy and assigns the priority using an integer ranging from 1 to 1000 (1 being the highest priority).
3	Router(config-isakmp)# **encryption** {**des** | **3des**}	Specifies the encryption algorithm.
4	Router(config-isakmp)# **hash** {**sha** | **md5**}	Specifies the hash algorithm.
5	Router(config-isakmp)# **authentication** {**rsa-sig** | **rsa-encr** | **pre-share**}	Specifies the authentication method.
6	Router(config-isakmp)# **group** {**1** | **2** | **5**}	Specifies the Diffie-Hellman group identifier.
7	Router(config-isakmp)# **lifetime** *seconds*	Specifies the security association's lifetime.
8	Router(config-isakmp)# **exit**	Exits the config-isakmp command mode.
9	Router(config)#**crypto isakmp key** *keystring* **address** *peer-address* or Router(config)#**crypto isakmp key** *keystring* **hostname** *peer-hostname*	Specifies the preshared key. The same key should be specified on the remote peer.
10	Router(config)# **exit**	Exits the global configuration mode.

Step 3: Configure the IPSec Parameters

The IPSec configuration on IOS is achieved by defining the IPSec SA lifetime, transform sets, crypto maps, and the interesting traffic. The SA lifetime can be specified in terms of seconds or kilobytes. The interesting traffic (the traffic that must be protected by IPSec) is defined through access lists. These access lists (also called crypto access lists) are similar in syntax to the regular IOS access-list statements. The traffic defined by the **permit** keyword is protected by IPSec, whereas the traffic defined by the **deny** statement is not selected for the VPN.

The IOS commands used to configure IPSec options are listed in Table 10-6.

Table 10-6 *OS IPSec Commands*

Step	Command	Description
1	Router(config)# **crypto ipsec security-association lifetime** {**seconds** *seconds* | **kilobytes** *kilobytes*}	Changes the global lifetime for the IPSec SA; the default is **3600** seconds and **4608000** kilobytes.
2	Router(config)# **access-list** *number* {**deny** | **permit**} *protocol source source-wildcard destination destination-wildcard* [**log**]	Defines the interesting traffic to be encrypted by IPSec. For an IOS-based remote peer, the access list on the remote peer should be a mirror image of the local access list. The access list must be granular and must not use the **any** keyword.
3	Router(config)# **crypto ipsec transform-set** *transform-set-name transform1 [transform2 [transform3]]*	Defines the name and properties for the IPSec transform set.
4	Router(cfg-crypto-trans)# **mode** [**tunnel** | **transport**]	Specifies the mode for the transform set.
5	Router(cfg-crypto-trans)# **exit**	Exits crypto transform configuration mode.
6	Router(config)# **crypto map** *map-name number* **ipsec-isakmp**	Defines the name and priority for the crypto map entry. The keyword **ipsec-isakmp** indicates that IKE is to be used to establish the IPSec SAs for protecting the traffic that is specified by this crypto map entry.
7	Router(config-crypto-map)# **match address** *access-list-id*	Specifies the crypto access list, created in Step 2, to determine the traffic to be protected by this IPSec crypto map.
8	Router(config-crypto-map)# **set peer** {*hostname* | *ip-address*}	Specifies the remote IPSec peer using the IP address or FQDN; multiple peers can be specified.
9	Router(config-crypto-map)# **set transform-set** *transform-set-name1* [*transform-set-name2...transform-set-name6*]	Specifies which transform sets are allowed for this crypto map entry. Lists multiple transform sets in the order of priority (highest priority first).
10	Router(config-crypto-map)# **set security-association lifetime** {**seconds** *seconds* | **kilobytes** *kilobytes*}	Specifies the lifetimes if different than the global lifetimes defined in Step 1.
11	Router(config-crypto-map)#**set pfs** [**group1** | **group2**]	Instructs IPSec to use perfect forward secrecy when negotiating new security associations for this crypto map entry.

Table 10-6 *OS IPSec Commands (Continued)*

Step	Command	Description
12	Router(config-crypto-map)#**exit**	Exits crypto-map configuration mode and returns to global configuration mode.
13	Router(config)# **interface** *name number*	Enters interface configuration mode.
14	Router(config-if)# **crypto map** *map-name*	Applies a crypto map set to an interface.
15	Router(config-if)# **exit**	Exits interface configuration mode and returns to global configuration mode.
16	Router(config)# **exit**	Exits global configuration mode.

CAUTION The encryption access lists must not use the **any** keyword to specify the source or destination addresses. Always use granular access lists with specific source and destination subnet addresses. The use of the **any** keyword creates various problems and prevents IPSec from functioning correctly.

Step 4: Monitor and Troubleshoot

The commands for monitoring IPSec phases 1 and 2 status and their parameters are listed in Table 10-7.

Table 10-7 *IPSec Monitoring and Troubleshooting Commands*

Command	Description
Router# **show crypto isakmp policy**	Displays the IKE policies.
Router# **show crypto isakmp key**	Displays the preshared keys configured using the **crypto isakmp key** command.
Router# **show crypto isakmp sa**	Displays existing IKE SAs.
Router# **clear crypto isakmp** [*connection-id*]	Clears the specified IKE connections.
Router# **debug crypto isakmp**	Starts debugging IKE events.
Router# **clear crypto as** [**peer** {*ip-address* | *peer-name*}] [**map** *map-name*] [**entry** *destination-address protocol spi*]	Clears IPSec security associations. Using the **clear crypto sa** command without parameters clears the full SA database and active security sessions.
Router# **show crypto ipsec transform-set**	Displays the transform set configuration.
Router# **show crypto map** [**interface** *interface* | **tag** *map-name*]	Displays the crypto map configuration.
Router# **show crypto ipsec sa** [**map** *map-name* | **address** | **identity**] [**detail**]	Displays information about IPSec security associations.

continues

Table 10-7 *IPSec Monitoring and Troubleshooting Commands (Continued)*

Command	Description
Router# **show crypto ipsec security-association lifetime**	Displays global security association lifetime values.
Router# **debug crypto ipsec**	Starts debugging IPSec events.

The output of some of these commands is shown later in Example 10-13.

Case Study—IOS and OpenSWAN VPN with Preshared Keys

Consider the network scenario, shown in Figure 10-3, for an IPSec VPN between two LANs. Site A uses a Linux OpenSWAN–based VPN server, while site B uses a Cisco IOS–based router as an IPSec-based VPN server. Also, the OpenSWAN server shown in the diagram was installed on a Debian-Linux machine with a Pentium III 1.0-GHz CPU with 512 MB RAM. (According to the OpenSWAN website, this configuration exceeds the minimum requirements for OpenSWAN for such a scenario.)

Figure 10-3 *OpenSWAN–IOS VPN*

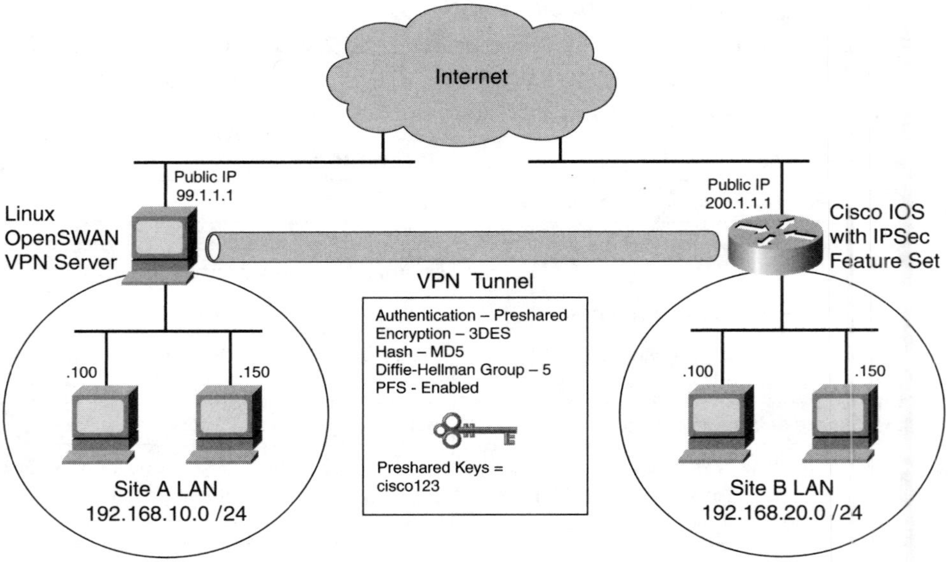

To ensure interoperability, the IPSec parameters should match on both sides. Based on the properties of OpenSWAN and IOS, following is a list of these parameters, including the suggested values. The values are based on the OpenSWAN configuration discussed in the previous sections:

- **Encryption**—3DES
- **IPSec phase 1**—Main Mode
- **Hash**—MD5
- **Authentication**—Preshared
- **Preshared key**—cisco123
- **Diffie-Hellman**—Group 5
- **Remote peer ID**—IP address
- **Data security and encapsulation**—ESP
- **IPSec key and SA negotiation**—IKE
- **PFS**—Yes

Note that the OpenSWAN IPSec SA lifetime is 8 hours by default, whereas the IOS IPSec SA lifetime is 1 hour. Although the SA lifetimes do not match, both negotiating peers propose their individual lifetimes and agree on the smaller of the two values.

IOS Configuration

The resulting configuration of the OpenSWAN server has already been shown in Examples 10-3 and 10-4. The configuration of the Cisco IOS router is shown in Example 10-12. The configuration is based on the commands discussed in the previous section.

Example 10-12 *IOS Configuration*

```
Cisco-rtr#show running-config
Building configuration...

Current configuration : 1273 bytes
!
version 12.1
no service single-slot-reload-enable
service timestamps debug uptime
service timestamps log uptime
no service password-encryption
!
hostname Cisco-rtr
!
enable password cisco
!
ip subnet-zero
no ip domain-lookup
ip domain-name test.com
!
crypto isakmp policy 3
```

continues

Example 10-12 *IOS Configuration (Continued)*

```
 encr 3des
 hash md5
 authentication pre-share
 group 5
crypto isakmp key cisco123 address 99.1.1.1
!
crypto ipsec transform-set myset esp-3des esp-md5-hmac
!
crypto map vpn 30 ipsec-isakmp
 set peer 99.1.1.1
 set transform-set myset
 set pfs group2
 match address 100
!
interface Ethernet0/0
 ip address 192.168.20.1 255.255.255.0
!
interface Serial0/0
 ip address 200.1.1.1 255.255.255.252
 crypto map vpn
!
ip classless
ip route 0.0.0.0 0.0.0.0 200.1.1.2
!
access-list 101 permit ip 192.168.20.0 0.0.0.255 192.168.10.0 0.0.0.255
!
line con 0
line aux 0
line vty 0 4
 password cisco
 login
!
end

Cisco-rtr#
```

Monitoring and Troubleshooting

To verify whether the tunnel is up, ping a host in site B from a host in site A. A successful receipt of a ping reply confirms that the VPN tunnel is up and running.

To monitor or troubleshoot, use the commands provided in Table 10-7. Example 10-13 shows the output of the various **show** commands. Also included is the output of the **debug** command during the establishment of the IPSec tunnel. Note that the highlighted text that begins with an exclamation point (!) indicates comments that are inserted within the output. These comments provide a relevant explanation for the output.

Example 10-13 *Monitoring and Troubleshooting Command Output*

```
Cisco-rtr#show crypto map
! The output shows the IPSec parameters for phase 2
Crypto Map "vpn" 30 ipsec-isakmp
        Peer = 99.1.1.1
        Extended IP access list 130
            access-list 130 permit ip 192.168.20.0 0.0.0.255 192.168.10.0 0.0.0.
255
        Current peer: 99.1.1.1
        Security association lifetime: 4608000 kilobytes/3600 seconds
        PFS (Y/N): Y
        DH group:  group2
        Transform sets={ myset, }
        Interfaces using crypto map vpn:
                Serial0/0

Cisco-rtr#show crypto isakmp sa
! The output shows the negotiated phase 1 SAs
    dst            src            state          conn-id   slot
99.1.1.1       200.1.1.1      QM_IDLE             26       0

Cisco-rtr#show crypto ipsec sa
! The output shows the negotiated phase 2 SAs
interface: Serial0/0
    Crypto map tag: vpn, local addr. 200.1.1.1

   local  ident (addr/mask/prot/port): (192.168.20.0/255.255.255.0/0/0)
   remote ident (addr/mask/prot/port): (192.168.10.0/255.255.255.0/0/0)
   current_peer: 99.1.1.1
     PERMIT, flags={origin_is_acl,}
! The increments in packet count indicates the IPSec tunnel operation
! including the operation of the access-lists
    #pkts encaps: 12041, #pkts encrypt: 12041, #pkts digest 12041
    #pkts decaps: 11677, #pkts decrypt: 11677, #pkts verify 11677
    #pkts compressed: 0, #pkts decompressed: 0
    #pkts not compressed: 0, #pkts compr. failed: 0, #pkts decompress failed: 0
    #send errors 710, #recv errors 0

     local crypto endpt.: 200.1.1.1, remote crypto endpt.: 99.1.1.1
     path mtu 1500, media mtu 1500
     current outbound spi: A1B2B3FF
! Please note that 2 separate SAs, one for inbound
! second for outbound
     inbound esp sas:
      spi: 0x151D1967(354228583)
        transform: esp-3des esp-md5-hmac ,
        in use settings ={Tunnel, }
        slot: 0, conn id: 2002, flow_id: 3, crypto map: vpn
        sa timing: remaining key lifetime (k/sec): (4607972/3335)
        IV size: 8 bytes
        replay detection support: Y

     inbound ah sas:
```

continues

Example 10-13 *Monitoring and Troubleshooting Command Output (Continued)*

```
     inbound pcp sas:

     outbound esp sas:
      spi: 0xA1B2B3FF(2712843263)
        transform: esp-3des esp-md5-hmac ,
        in use settings ={Tunnel, }
        slot: 0, conn id: 2003, flow_id: 4, crypto map: vpn
        sa timing: remaining key lifetime (k/sec): (4607972/3334)
        IV size: 8 bytes
        replay detection support: Y

     outbound ah sas:

     outbound pcp sas:


Cisco-rtr# debug crypto isakmp
Crypto ISAKMP debugging is on
Cisco-rtr# debug crypto isakmp
Crypto IPSEC debugging is on
Cisco-rtr# debug crypto engine
Crypto Engine debugging is on
Cisco-rtr#show debug
! Following debugs are currently running on the router
Cryptographic Subsystem:
  Crypto ISAKMP debugging is on
  Crypto Engine debugging is on
  Crypto IPSEC debugging is on
Cisco-rtr#
! The following debug capture was generated during the initial setup of the IPSec
  tunnel
! Phase 1 negotiations begin
05:23:05: ISAKMP (26): received packet from 99.1.1.1 (I) QM_IDLE
05:23:05: CryptoEngine0: generate hmac context for conn id 26
05:23:05: ISAKMP (0:26): processing SA payload. message ID = -118861484
05:23:05: ISAKMP (0:26): Checking IPSec proposal 0
05:23:05: ISAKMP: transform 0, ESP_3DES
05:23:05: ISAKMP:   attributes in transform:
05:23:05: ISAKMP:      group is 5
05:23:05: ISAKMP:      encaps is 1
05:23:05: ISAKMP:      SA life type in seconds
05:23:05: ISAKMP:      SA life duration (basic) of 28800
05:23:05: ISAKMP:      authenticator is HMAC-MD5
05:23:05: validate proposal 0
05:23:05: ISAKMP (0:26): atts are acceptable.
05:23:05: IPSEC(validate_proposal_request): proposal part #1,
  (key eng. msg.) dest= 99.1.1.1, src= 200.1.1.1,
    dest_proxy= 192.168.20.0/255.255.255.0/0/0 (type=4),
    src_proxy= 192.168.10.0/255.255.255.0/0/0 (type=4),
    protocol= ESP, transform= esp-3des esp-md5-hmac ,
    lifedur= 0s and 0kb,
```

Example 10-13 *Monitoring and Troubleshooting Command Output (Continued)*

```
    spi= 0x0(0), conn_id= 0, keysize= 0, flags= 0x44
05:23:05: validate proposal request 0
05:23:05: CryptoEngine0: generate alg parameter
05:23:05: CRYPTO_ENGINE: Dh phase 1 status: 0
05:23:05: CRYPTO_ENGINE: Dh phase 1 status: 0
05:23:05: ISAKMP (0:26): processing NONCE payload. message ID = -118861484
05:23:05: ISAKMP (0:26): processing KE payload. message ID = -118861484
05:23:05: CryptoEngine0: generate alg parameter
05:23:06: ISAKMP (0:26): processing ID payload. message ID = -118861484
05:23:06: ISAKMP (26): ID_IPV4_ADDR_SUBNET src 192.168.10.0/255.255.255.0 prot 0
 port 0
05:23:06: ISAKMP (0:26): processing ID payload. message ID = -118861484
05:23:06: ISAKMP (26): ID_IPV4_ADDR_SUBNET dst 192.168.20.0/255.255.255.0 prot 0
 port 0
05:23:06: ISAKMP (0:26): asking for 1 spis from ipsec
05:23:06: IPSEC(key_engine): got a queue event...
05:23:06: IPSEC(spi_response): getting spi 354228583 for SA
        from 99.1.1.1        to 200.1.1.1        for prot 3
05:23:06: ISAKMP: received ke message (2/1)
05:23:06: CryptoEngine0: generate hmac context for conn id 26
05:23:06: ISAKMP (26): sending packet to 99.1.1.1 (I) QM_IDLE
05:23:06: ISAKMP (26): received packet from 99.1.1.1 (I) QM_IDLE
05:23:06: CryptoEngine0: generate hmac context for conn id 26
05:23:06: ipsec allocate flow 0
05:23:06: ipsec allocate flow 0
05:23:06: CryptoEngine0: clear dh number for conn id 1
! Phase 2 negotiations begin
05:23:06: ISAKMP (0:26): Creating IPSec SAs
05:23:06:        inbound SA from 99.1.1.1       to 200.1.1.1      (proxy 192.168.10.0
 to 192.168.20.0    )
05:23:06:          has spi 354228583 and conn_id 2002 and flags 45
05:23:06:          lifetime of 28800 seconds
05:23:06:          outbound SA from 200.1.1.1       to 99.1.1.1        (proxy
 192.168.20.0    to 192.168.10.0    )
05:23:06:          has spi -1582124033 and conn_id 2003 and flags 45
05:23:06:          lifetime of 28800 seconds
05:23:06: ISAKMP (0:26): deleting node -118861484 error FALSE reason "quick mode
 done (await()"
05:23:06: IPSEC(key_engine): got a queue event...
05:23:06: IPSEC(initialize_sas): ,
  (key eng. msg.) dest= 200.1.1.1, src= 99.1.1.1,
    dest_proxy= 192.168.20.0/255.255.255.0/0/0 (type=4),
    src_proxy= 192.168.10.0/255.255.255.0/0/0 (type=4),
    protocol= ESP, transform= esp-3des esp-md5-hmac ,
    lifedur= 28800s and 0kb,
    spi= 0x151D1967(354228583), conn_id= 2002, keysize= 0, flags= 0x45
05:23:06: IPSEC(initialize_sas): ,
  (key eng. msg.) src= 200.1.1.1, dest= 99.1.1.1,
    src_proxy= 192.168.20.0/255.255.255.0/0/0 (type=4),
    dest_proxy= 192.168.10.0/255.255.255.0/0/0 (type=4),
    protocol= ESP, transform= esp-3des esp-md5-hmac ,
    lifedur= 28800s and 0kb,
```

continues

Example 10-13 *Monitoring and Troubleshooting Command Output (Continued)*

```
     spi= 0xA1B2B3FF(2712843263), conn_id= 2003, keysize= 0, flags= 0x45
05:23:06: IPSEC(create_sa): sa created,
  (sa) sa_dest= 200.1.1.1, sa_prot= 50,
    sa_spi= 0x151D1967(354228583),
    sa_trans= esp-3des esp-md5-hmac , sa_conn_id= 2002
05:23:06: IPSEC(create_sa): sa created,
  (sa) sa_dest= 99.1.1.1, sa_prot= 50,
    sa_spi= 0xA1B2B3FF(2712843263),
    sa_trans= esp-3des esp-md5-hmac , sa_conn_id= 2003
05:23:06: IPSEC(add_sa): peer asks for new SAs -- expire current in 120 sec.,
  (sa) sa_dest= 99.1.1.1, sa_prot= 50,
    sa_spi= 0xC11E602E(3239993390),
    sa_trans= esp-3des esp-md5-hmac , sa_conn_id= 2001,
  (identity) local= 200.1.1.1, remote= 99.1.1.1,
    local_proxy= 192.168.20.0/255.255.255.0/0/0 (type=4),
    remote_proxy= 192.168.10.0/255.255.255.0/0/0 (type=4)
```

Interoperating OpenSWAN with a Cisco PIX Firewall

The steps involved in configuring a Cisco PIX Firewall for an IPSec-based VPN using preshared keys are similar to those for IOS devices. The command syntax closely matches their IOS counterparts.

PIX Configuration Tasks

The tasks involved in enabling an IPSec-based VPN on a Cisco PIX Firewall are as follows:

Step 1 Prepare the PIX for IPSec:

— Host name and domain name

— Enable IKE

Step 2 Configure the IKE parameters:

— Encryption

— Hash

— Authentication

— Diffie-Hellman group

— IKE SA lifetime

— Preshared keys

Step 3 Configure the IPSec parameters:

— IPSec SA lifetime

— Interesting traffic

— Transform sets

— Crypto maps

Step 4 Perform the PIX-specific tasks:

— Bypass security

— Disable NAT

Step 5 Monitor and Troubleshoot.

Configuration Commands

Table 10-8 lists the global-configuration-mode commands that configure the PIX according to the tasks noted in Steps 1 through 4 in the previous section. The resulting configuration provides a preshared authentication–based IPSec VPN on a PIX Firewall version 6.0 or higher. The PIX IPSec policy parameters are similar to those offered by IOS, except for the authentication mechanism. The PIX only supports preshared and RSA signatures, while IOS also supports RSA-encrypted nonces. (*Nonces* are arbitrarily generated numbers that are created for one-time use only.) Also note that unlike the IOS configuration mode, the PIX's global configuration mode does not offer context-sensitive subconfiguration modes (such as config-if or config-isakmp).

Table 10-8 *PIX IPSec Commands*

Step	Command	Description
1	pixfirewall(config)# **hostname** *name*	Assigns a host name to the PIX Firewall.
2	pixfirewall(config)#**domain-name** *name*	Specifies the domain name to which the firewall belongs.
3	pixfirewall(config)#**isakmp enable** *interface*	Enables ISAKMP negotiation on the specified interface.
4	pixfirewall(config)#**isakmp policy** *priority encryption* {**aes** | **aes-192**| **aes-256** | **des** | **3des**}	Specifies the encryption algorithm to be used in the IKE policy.
5	pixfirewall(config)#**isakmp policy** *priority* {**hash md5** | **sha**}	Specifies the hash algorithm to be used in the IKE policy.
6	pixfirewall(config)#**isakmp policy** *priority* **authentication** {**pre-share** | **rsa-sig**}	Specifies preshared keys as the authentication method and assigns the priority using an integer ranging from 1 to 65534; priority 1 is the highest.
7	pixfirewall(config)#**isakmp policy** *priority* **group** {**1** | **2** | **5** }	Specifies the Diffie-Hellman group to be used in the IKE policy.
8	pixfirewall(config)#**isakmp policy** *priority lifetime seconds*	Specifies the lifetime of the IKE SA in seconds. The default value is **86,400** seconds; use **0** for an infinite lifetime.

continues

Table 10-8 *PIX IPSec Commands (Continued)*

Step	Command	Description
9	pixfirewall(config)#**isakmp identity** {*address* | *hostname* }	Specifies whether the PIX should use the address or the host name as the IKE identity.
10	pixfirewall(config)#**isakmp key** *keystring* **address** *peer-address* [**netmask** *mask*] or **isakmp key** *keystring* **hostname** *peer-hostname*	Specifies the preshared authentication key for the remote peer.
11	pixfirewall(config)#**crypto ipsec security-association lifetime** {**seconds** *seconds* | **kilobytes** *kilobytes*}	Specifies the IPSec SA lifetime (in kilobytes or seconds). The default is **4,608,000** kilobytes and 8 hours.
Step1 2	pixfirewall(config)#**access-list** *id* {**deny** | **permit**} **protocol** *source_addr source_mask remote_addr remote_mask*	Creates a crypto access list to define the interesting traffic for the VPN. Use the mirror image access list on the remote peer.
13	pixfirewall(config)#**crypto ipsec transform-set** *transform-set-name transform1* [*transform2* [*transform3*]]	Defines the name and properties of the IPSec transform set to create or modify. Possible transforms are ah-md5-hmac, ah-sha-hmac, esp-aes, esp-aes-192, esp-aes-256, esp-des, esp-3des, esp-null, esp-md5-hmac, and esp-sha-hmac.
14	pixfirewall(config)#**crypto ipsec transform-set** *transform-set-name* **mode transport**	Specifies that the transform set should accept transport-mode requests in addition to the default tunnel mode.
15	pixfirewall(config)#**crypto map** *map-name seq-num* {**ipsec-isakmp** | **ipsec-manual**}	Defines the name and priority for the crypto map entry. The keyword **ipsec-isakmp** indicates that IKE is to be used to establish the IPSec SAs to protect the traffic specified by this crypto map entry.
16	pixfirewall(config)#**crypto map** *map-name seq-num* **match address** *acl-id*	Specifies an access list for a crypto map entry.
17	pixfirewall(config)#**crypto map** *map-name seq-num* **set peer** {*ip_address* | *hostname*}	Specifies an IPSec peer, for the crypto map entry, using an IP address or an FQDN host name.
18	pixfirewall(config)#**crypto map** *map-name seq-num* **set pfs** [**group1** | **group2**]	Instructs IPSec to use perfect forward secrecy when negotiating new security associations for this crypto map entry.

Table 10-8 *PIX IPSec Commands (Continued)*

Step	Command	Description
19	pixfirewall(config)#**crypto map** *map-name seq-num* **set security-association lifetime** {**seconds** *seconds* | **kilobytes** *kilobytes*}	Specifies IPSec SA lifetimes in either seconds or kilobytes.
20	pixfirewall(config)#**crypto map** *map-name seq-num* **set transform-set** *transform-set-name1 ... transform-set-name6*]	Specifies the transform sets, defined in Step 12, to be used with the crypto map entry; a maximum of six transforms are allowed.
21	pixfirewall(config)#**crypto map** *map-name* **interface** *interface-name*	Applies the crypto map to the interface.
22	pixfirewall(config)#**sysopt connection permit-ipsec**	Instructs the PIX to permit IPSec traffic without checking access lists, conduits, or access group commands. An IPSec VPN does not work without this command, because the VPN traffic is subject to the firewall policies.
23	pixfirewall(config)#**nat** *interface* **0 access-list** *id*	Disables NAT for the VPN traffic defined by the access list in Step 11. Without this command, the VPN traffic gets NATed instead of getting selected by the IPSec engine.

Monitoring and Troubleshooting Commands

Table 10-9 lists the commands used to monitor and troubleshoot IPSec on a Cisco PIX Firewall.

Table 10-9 *PIX IPSec Troubleshooting Commands*

Command	Description
pixfirewall(config)#**show isakmp**	Displays the IKE configuration.
pixfirewall(config)#**show isakmp policy**	Displays the configured IKE policies; also displays the default policy.
pixfirewall(config)#**show isakmp sa**	Displays the existing IKE SA.
pixfirewall(config)#**show crypto map**	Displays the crypto map information, including the hit count on the access list.
pixfirewall(config)#**show crypto ipsec security-association lifetime**	Displays the IPSec SA lifetime.
pixfirewall(config)#**show crypto ipsec transform-set**	Displays the configured transforms.

continues

Table 10-9 *PIX IPSec Troubleshooting Commands (Continued)*

Command	Description
pixfirewall(config)#**show crypto ipsec sa**	Displays the current IPSec SAs; provides packet encryption and encapsulation statistics.
pixfirewall(config)#**clear crypto isakmp sa**	Global-configuration-mode command that resets the IKE (phase 1) SA.
pixfirewall(config)#**clear crypto ipsec sa**	Global-configuration-mode command that resets the IPSec (phase 2) SA.
pixfirewall(config)#**debug crypto isakmp**	Debugs IKE activities.
pixfirewall(config)#**debug crypto ipsec**	Debugs IPSec activities.

The output of these **show** and **debug** commands are illustrated later in Example 10-15.

Case Study: PIX Firewall and OpenSWAN VPN with Preshared Keys

Consider the network scenario, shown in Figure 10-4, for an IPSec VPN between two LANs. Site A uses a Linux OpenSWAN–based VPN server, while site B uses a Cisco PIX appliance, acting as both a firewall and an IPSec-based VPN server.

Figure 10-4 *OpenSWAN—PIX VPN*

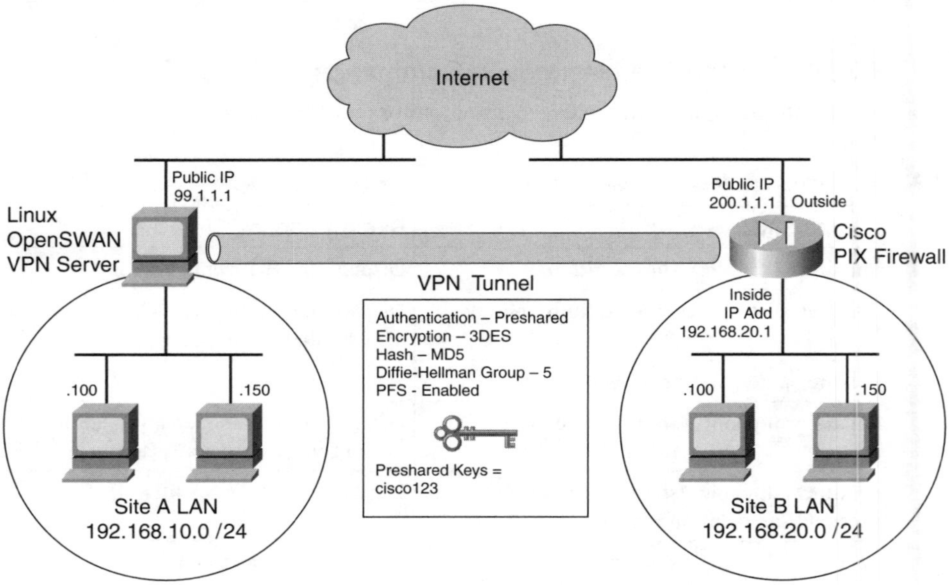

The resulting configuration of the OpenSWAN server has already been shown in Examples 10-3 and 10-4. The configuration of the Cisco PIX Firewall is shown in Example 10-14. The configuration is based on the commands discussed in Table 10-8. Note that the highlighted text that begins with an exclamation point (!) indicates comments. These comments are inserted to explain the relevant configuration.

Example 10-14 *IOS Configuration*

```
PIX-FW# show running-config
: Saved
:
PIX Version 6.3(4)
interface ethernet0 10baset
interface ethernet1 100full
nameif ethernet0 outside security0
nameif ethernet1 inside security100
enable password 8Ry2YjIyt7RRXU24 encrypted
passwd 2KFQnbNIdI.2KYOU encrypted
! Specify the Hostname for PIX firewall
hostname PIX-FW
! Specify the Domain name for PIX firewall
domain-name VPNtest.com
fixup protocol dns maximum-length 512
fixup protocol ftp 21
fixup protocol h323 h225 1720
fixup protocol h323 ras 1718-1719
fixup protocol http 80
fixup protocol icmp error
fixup protocol rsh 514
fixup protocol rtsp 554
fixup protocol sip 5060
fixup protocol sip udp 5060
fixup protocol skinny 2000
fixup protocol smtp 25
fixup protocol sqlnet 1521
fixup protocol tftp 69
names
! Define interesting traffic to be encrypted by IPSec VPN
access-list 101 permit ip 192.168.20.0 255.255.255.0 192.168.10.0 255
  .255.255.0
! Define traffic that should NOT BE NATed
access-list 102 permit ip 192.168.20.0 255.255.255.0 192.168.10.0 255
  .255.255.0
! access-list 120 is for allowing Ping traffic
! for test purpose only, should be avoided in production network
access-list 120 permit icmp any any
no pager
mtu outside 1500
mtu inside 1500
! Assign the IP address on the interfaces
ip address outside 200.1.1.1 255.255.255.0
ip address inside 192.168.20.1 255.255.255.0
ip audit info action alarm
```

continues

Example 10-14 *IOS Configuration (Continued)*

```
ip audit attack action alarm
pdm history enable
arp timeout 14400
global (outside) 1 interface
! Disable NAT for VPN traffic
nat (inside) 0 access-list 102
! NAT the non VPN traffic
nat (inside) 1 0.0.0.0 0.0.0.0 0 0
access-group 120 in interface outside
! Specify default route
route outside 0.0.0.0 0.0.0.0 200.1.1.2 1
timeout xlate 3:00:00
timeout conn 1:00:00 half-closed 0:10:00 udp 0:02:00 rpc 0:10:00 h225
   1:00:00
timeout h323 0:05:00 mgcp 0:05:00 sip 0:30:00 sip_media 0:02:00
timeout uauth 0:05:00 absolute
aaa-server TACACS+ protocol tacacs+
aaa-server TACACS+ max-failed-attempts 3
aaa-server TACACS+ deadtime 10
aaa-server RADIUS protocol radius
aaa-server RADIUS max-failed-attempts 3
aaa-server RADIUS deadtime 10
aaa-server LOCAL protocol local
http server enable
http 192.168.20.0 255.255.255.255 inside
no snmp-server location
no snmp-server contact
snmp-server community public
no snmp-server enable traps
floodguard enable
! IMPORTANT - Intruct PIX to bypass Firewall rules for IPSec traffic
! VPN will not work without sysopt command
sysopt connection permit-ipsec
! define transform set called "myset"
! "myset" use ESP with 3DES encryption and MD5 hash
crypto ipsec transform-set myset esp-3des esp-md5-hmac
!
!Define crypto map called "mymap"
! & configure  parameters for the map
crypto map mymap 10 ipsec-isakmp
crypto map mymap 10 match address 101
crypto map mymap 10 set pfs group2
crypto map mymap 10 set peer 99.1.1.1
crypto map mymap 10 set transform-set myset
crypto map mymap interface outside
!
! Define IKE parameters
!
isakmp enable outside
! the isakmp key is hidden by the "show running-config" output
! the command was "isakmp key cisco123 address 99.1.1.1 . ."
isakmp key ******** address 99.1.1.1 netmask 255.255.255.255
```

Example 10-14 *IOS Configuration (Continued)*

```
isakmp identity address
isakmp policy 10 authentication pre-share
isakmp policy 10 encryption 3des
isakmp policy 10 hash md5
isakmp policy 10 group 5
isakmp policy 10 lifetime 86400
telnet timeout 5
ssh timeout 5
console timeout 0
terminal width 80
Cryptochecksum:dbb37121c657444491a37d631b9eb82e
: end
```

Example 10-15 shows the output of the various **show** and **debug** commands that are listed in Table 10-9. The highlighted text that begins with an exclamation point indicates comments that provide more information about the command outputs.

Example 10-15 *PIX—IPSec* **show** *Commands*

```
PIX-FW# show isakmp
! Command displays the ISAKMP configuration on the Firewall
! and is useful for quickly verifying configuration
isakmp enable outside
isakmp key ******** address 99.1.1.1 netmask 255.255.255.255
isakmp identity address
isakmp policy 10 authentication pre-share
isakmp policy 10 encryption 3des
isakmp policy 10 hash md5
isakmp policy 10 group 5
isakmp policy 10 lifetime 86400
PIX-FW#
PIX-FW#  show isakmp policy

Protection suite of priority 10
        encryption algorithm:   Three key triple DES
        hash algorithm:         Message Digest 5
        authentication method:  Pre-Shared Key
        Diffie-Hellman group:   #5 (1536 bit)
        lifetime:               86400 seconds, no volume limit
Default protection suite
        encryption algorithm:   DES - Data Encryption Standard (56 bit keys).
        hash algorithm:         Secure Hash Standard
        authentication method:  Rivest-Shamir-Adelman Signature
        Diffie-Hellman group:   #1 (768 bit)
        lifetime:               86400 seconds, no volume limit
PIX-FW#
PIX-FW# show isakmp sa
! Command output provides details regarding existing phase 1 SA,
! and helps in verifying if phase 1 is working
Total     : 2
Embryonic : 0
```

continues

Example 10-15 *PIX—IPSec* **show** *Commands (Continued)*

```
        dst              src          state     pending     created
       200.1.1.1        99.1.1.1     QM_IDLE         0           0
       200.1.1.1        99.1.1.1     QM_IDLE         0           0
PIX-FW#
PIX-FW# show crypto map
! Command output displays crypto maps that are applied to the interfaces
! The hitcnt counter is useful in verifying the operation of the access-lits
! Incrementing hitcnt counter indicate the traffic is getting selected and
! encrypted by IPSec
Crypto Map: "mymap" interfaces: { outside }

Crypto Map "mymap" 10 ipsec-isakmp
        Peer = 99.1.1.1
        access-list 101; 1 elements
        access-list 101 line 1 permit ip 192.168.20.0 255.255.255.0 192.168.10.0
 255.255.255.0 (hitcnt=23695)
        Current peer: 99.1.1.1
        Security association lifetime: 4608000 kilobytes/28800 seconds
        PFS (Y/N): Y
        DH group:  group2
        Transform sets={ myset, }
PIX-FW#
PIX-FW# show crypto ipsec security-association lifetime
Security association lifetime: 4608000 kilobytes/28800 seconds
PIX-FW# show crypto ipsec transform-set

Transform set myset: { esp-3des esp-md5-hmac  }
   will negotiate = { Tunnel,  },

PIX-FW#

PIX-FW# show crypto ipsec sa
! Command output is useful in verifying the existing phase 2 SAs

interface: outside
    Crypto map tag: mymap, local addr. 200.1.1.1
! The following ouput indicates the local and remote subnets that are
! being encapsulated and encrypted by IPSec
   local  ident (addr/mask/prot/port): (192.168.20.0/255.255.255.0/0/0)
   remote ident (addr/mask/prot/port): (192.168.10.0/255.255.255.0/0/0)
   current_peer: 99.1.1.1:500
     PERMIT, flags={origin_is_acl,}
! The packet encapsulation and encryption statistics are useful in verifying the
! working of IPSec. Incrementing counters indicate the successful operation
    #pkts encaps: 7925, #pkts encrypt: 7925, #pkts digest 7925
    #pkts decaps: 7917, #pkts decrypt: 7917, #pkts verify 7917
    #pkts compressed: 0, #pkts decompressed: 0
    #pkts not compressed: 0, #pkts compr. failed: 0, #pkts decompress failed: 0
    #send errors 29, #recv errors 0

     local crypto endpt.: 200.1.1.1, remote crypto endpt.: 99.1.1.1
     path mtu 1500, ipsec overhead 56, media mtu 1500
```

Example 10-15 *PIX—IPSec* **show** *Commands (Continued)*

```
      current outbound spi: 2eff0256

      inbound esp sas:
       spi: 0x7b7cc75(129485941)
         transform: esp-3des esp-md5-hmac ,
         in use settings ={Tunnel, }
         slot: 0, conn id: 4, crypto map: mymap
         sa timing: remaining key lifetime (k/sec): (4607441/22957)
         IV size: 8 bytes
         replay detection support: Y


      inbound ah sas:


      inbound pcp sas:


      outbound esp sas:
       spi: 0x2eff0256(788464214)
         transform: esp-3des esp-md5-hmac ,
         in use settings ={Tunnel, }
         slot: 0, conn id: 3, crypto map: mymap
         sa timing: remaining key lifetime (k/sec): (4607595/22957)
         IV size: 8 bytes
         replay detection support: Y

      outbound ah sas:
      outbound pcp sas:
PIX-FW#
! Debug commands are added to capture IPSec phase 1
!  and phase 2 negotiations
PIX-FW# debug crypto isakmp
PIX-FW# debug crypto ipsec
PIX-FW# show debug
debug crypto ipsec 1
debug crypto isakmp 1
PIX-FW#
! IPSec phase 1 negotiations begin
crypto_isakmp_process_block:src:99.1.1.1, dest:200.1.1.1 spt:500 dpt:500
OAK_MM exchange
ISAKMP (0): processing SA payload. message ID = 0
! Phase 1 ISAKMP parameters are being proposed
ISAKMP (0): Checking ISAKMP transform 0 against priority 10 policy
ISAKMP:      life type in seconds
ISAKMP:      life duration (basic) of 3600
ISAKMP:      encryption 3DES-CBC
ISAKMP:      hash MD5
ISAKMP:      auth pre-share
ISAKMP:      default group 5
ISAKMP (0): atts are acceptable. Next payload is 3
ISAKMP (0): SA is doing pre-shared key authentication using id type ID_IPV4_ADDR
```

continues

Example 10-15 *PIX—IPSec* **show** *Commands (Continued)*

```
return status is IKMP_NO_ERROR
crypto_isakmp_process_block:src:99.1.1.1, dest:200.1.1.1 spt:500 dpt:500
OAK_MM exchange
ISAKMP (0): processing KE payload. message ID = 0

ISAKMP (0): processing NONCE payload. message ID = 0

return status is IKMP_NO_ERROR
crypto_isakmp_process_block:src:99.1.1.1, dest:200.1.1.1 spt:500 dpt:500
OAK_MM exchange
ISAKMP (0): processing ID payload. message ID = 0
ISAKMP (0): processing HASH payload. message ID = 0
ISAKMP (0): SA has been authenticated

ISAKMP (0): ID payload
        next-payload : 8
        type         : 1
        protocol     : 17
        port         : 500
        length       : 8
ISAKMP (0): Total payload length: 12
return status is IKMP_NO_ERROR
ISAKMP (0): sending INITIAL_CONTACT notify
ISAKMP (0): sending NOTIFY message 24578 protocol 1
VPN Peer: ISAKMP: Added new peer: ip:99.1.1.1/500 Total VPN Peers:1
VPN Peer: ISAKMP: Peer ip:99.1.1.1/500 Ref cnt incremented to:1 Total VPN Peers:1
crypto_isakmp_process_block:src:99.1.1.1, dest:200.1.1.1 spt:500 dpt:500
OAK_QM exchange
! IPSec phase 2 negotiations begins
oakley_process_quick_mode:
OAK_QM_IDLE
ISAKMP (0): processing SA payload. message ID = 545732397

ISAKMP : Checking IPSec proposal 0

ISAKMP: transform 0, ESP_3DES
ISAKMP:   attributes in transform:
ISAKMP:      group is 5
ISAKMP:      encaps is 1
ISAKMP:      SA life type in seconds
ISAKMP:      SA life duration (basic) of 28800
ISAKMP:      authenticator is HMAC-MD5
ISAKMP (0): atts are acceptable.IPSEC(validate_proposal_request): proposal part #1,
  (key eng. msg.) dest= 200.1.1.1, src= 99.1.1.1,
    dest_proxy= 192.168.20.0/255.255.255.0/0/0 (type=4),
    src_proxy= 192.168.10.0/255.255.255.0/0/0 (type=4),
    protocol= ESP, transform= esp-3des esp-md5-hmac ,
    lifedur= 0s and 0kb,
    spi= 0x0(0), conn_id= 0, keysize= 0, flags= 0x44

ISAKMP (0): processing NONCE payload. message ID = 545732397
```

Example 10-15 *PIX—IPSec* **show** *Commands (Continued)*

```
ISAKMP (0): processing KE payload. message ID = 545732397

ISAKMP (0): processing ID payload. message ID = 545732397
ISAKMP (0): ID_IPV4_ADDR_SUBNET src 192.168.10.0/255.255.255.0 prot 0 port 0
ISAKMP (0): processing ID payload. message ID = 545732397
ISAKMP (0): ID_IPV4_ADDR_SUBNET dst 192.168.20.0/255.255.255.0 prot 0 port
 0IPSEC(key_engine): got a queue event...
IPSEC(spi_response): getting spi 0xf514b0d7(4111773911) for SA
        from        99.1.1.1 to       200.1.1.1 for prot 3

return status is IKMP_NO_ERROR
crypto_isakmp_process_block:src:99.1.1.1, dest:200.1.1.1 spt:500 dpt:500
OAK_QM exchange
oakley_process_quick_mode:
OAK_QM_AUTH_AWAIT
ISAKMP (0): Creating IPSec SAs
        inbound SA from        99.1.1.1 to       200.1.1.1 (proxy    192.168.10.0
 to    192.168.20.0)
        has spi 4111773911 and conn_id 1 and flags 45
        lifetime of 28800 seconds
        outbound SA from       200.1.1.1 to        99.1.1.1 (proxy    192.168.20.0
 to    192.168.10.0)
        has spi 1483854339 and conn_id 2 and flags 45
        lifetime of 28800 secondsIPSEC(key_engine): got a queue event...
IPSEC(initialize_sas): ,
  (key eng. msg.) dest= 200.1.1.1, src= 99.1.1.1,
    dest_proxy= 192.168.20.0/255.255.255.0/0/0 (type=4),
    src_proxy= 192.168.10.0/255.255.255.0/0/0 (type=4),
    protocol= ESP, transform= esp-3des esp-md5-hmac ,
    lifedur= 28800s and 0kb,
    spi= 0xf514b0d7(4111773911), conn_id= 1, keysize= 0, flags= 0x45
IPSEC(initialize_sas): ,
  (key eng. msg.) src= 200.1.1.1, dest= 99.1.1.1,
    src_proxy= 192.168.20.0/255.255.255.0/0/0 (type=4),
    dest_proxy= 192.168.10.0/255.255.255.0/0/0 (type=4),
    protocol= ESP, transform= esp-3des esp-md5-hmac ,
    lifedur= 28800s and 0kb,
    spi= 0x5871d203(1483854339), conn_id= 2, keysize= 0, flags= 0x45
! IPSec phase 2 SA established
VPN Peer: IPSEC: Peer ip:99.1.1.1/500 Ref cnt incremented to:2 Total VPN Peers:1
VPN Peer: IPSEC: Peer ip:99.1.1.1/500 Ref cnt incremented to:3 Total VPN Peers:1
return status is IKMP_NO_ERROR
```

Interoperating OpenSWAN with a Cisco VPN Concentrator

Cisco VPN 3000 Series concentrators offer standards-compliant IPSec-based VPN services for LAN-to-LAN and remote-access VPNs. The concentrators are known to interoperate with various IPSec-compliant devices, including OpenSWAN. While Cisco routers and PIX Firewalls can also provide VPN functionality, VPN 3000 concentrators are more appropriate for networks that support a large number of remote users (more than 100).

The configuration steps for enabling site-to-site VPNs on VPN 3000 concentrators are similar to those of IOS- and PIX Firewall–based IPSec VPNs. The initial step is to prepare the concentrator for IPSec, followed by configuration of the IKE and IPSec parameters. However, unlike IOS and the PIX Firewall, the VPN 3000 concentrators provide a web-based GUI for configuration and administration. The case study presented in next section covers each of these steps with the help of screen shots of the VPN 3000 concentrator GUI.

Case Study: VPN 3000 Concentrator and OpenSWAN VPN with Preshared Keys

Consider the network scenario, shown in Figure 10-5, for an IPSec VPN between two LANs. Site A uses a Linux OpenSWAN–based VPN server, while site B uses a Cisco VPN 3000 concentrator, acting as an IPSec-based VPN server.

Figure 10-5 *OpenSWAN—PIX VPN*

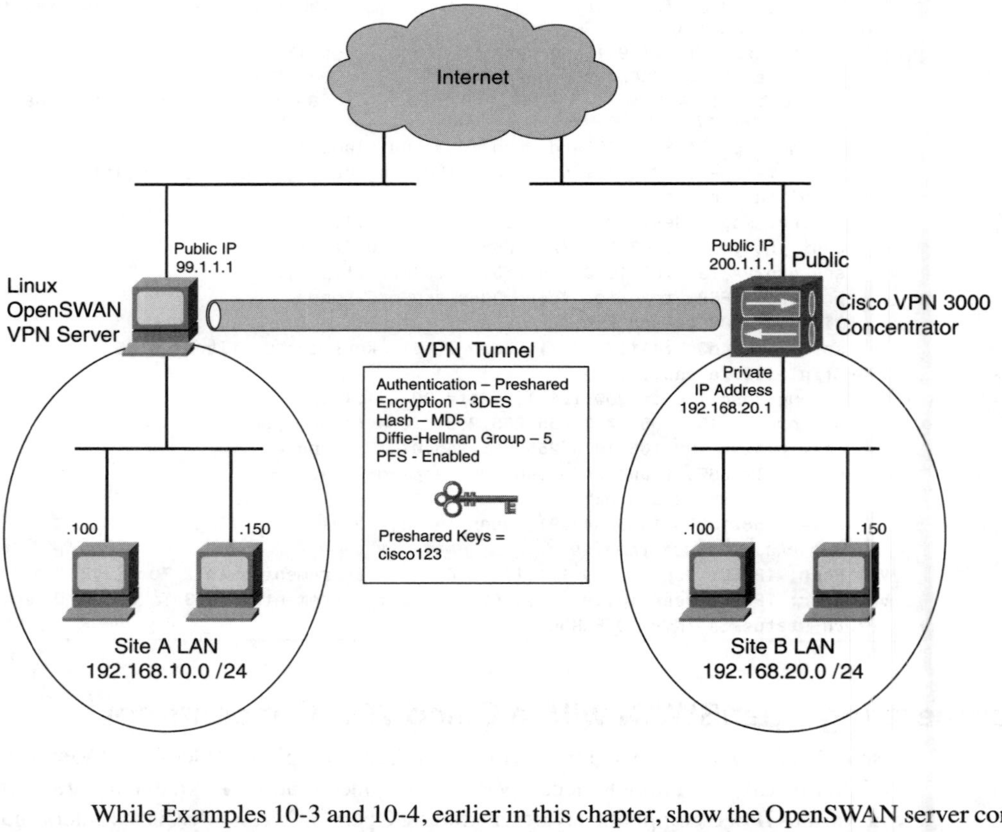

While Examples 10-3 and 10-4, earlier in this chapter, show the OpenSWAN server configuration, the following section describes the configuration of the VPN 3000 concentrator.

VPN 3000 Concentrator Configuration

This section illustrates the configuration of the VPN 3000 concentrator when enabling a site-to-site VPN using IPSec with preshared keys. The configuration steps are as follows:

Step 1 Prepare the concentrator with the IP addresses, network masks, default gateway, DNS server, and domain name, as shown in Figure 10-6.

Figure 10-6 *VPN 3000—Basic Settings*

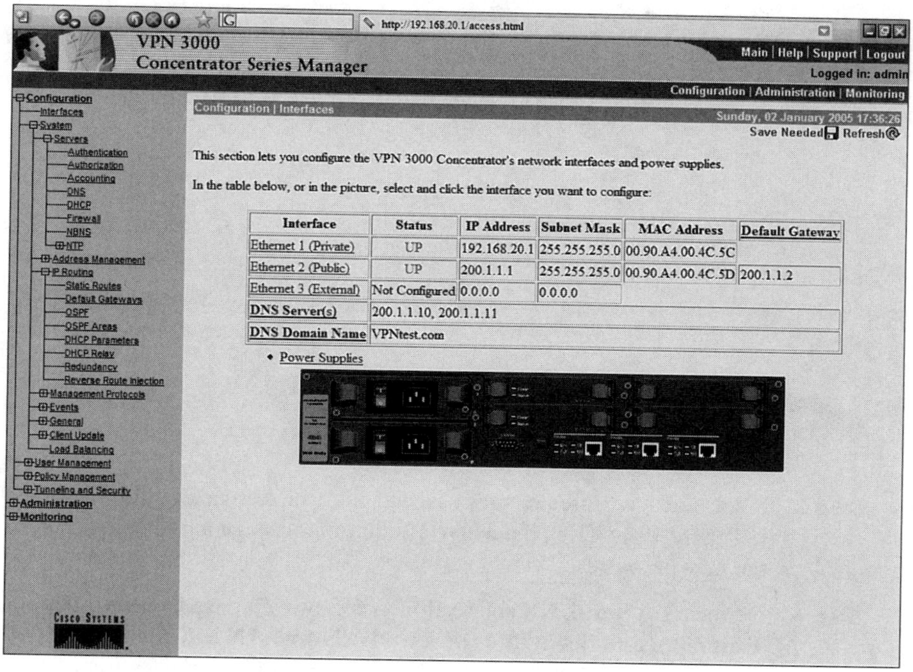

Step 2 Choose **Configuration > Tunneling and Security > IPSec > IKE Proposals** and click the **Add** button to open the Configure and add a new IKE Proposal page, as shown in Figure 10-7. The IKE parameters should match the IKE proposals offered by OpenSWAN (preshared authentication, MD5 hash, 3DES encryption, and D-H group 5). The Proposal Name field can be any arbitrary name that is to be used to identify this proposal. In this example, the name assigned is **Proposal-1**. Click the **Add** button to return to the IKE Proposal page.

Figure 10-7 *OpenSWAN—PIX VPN*

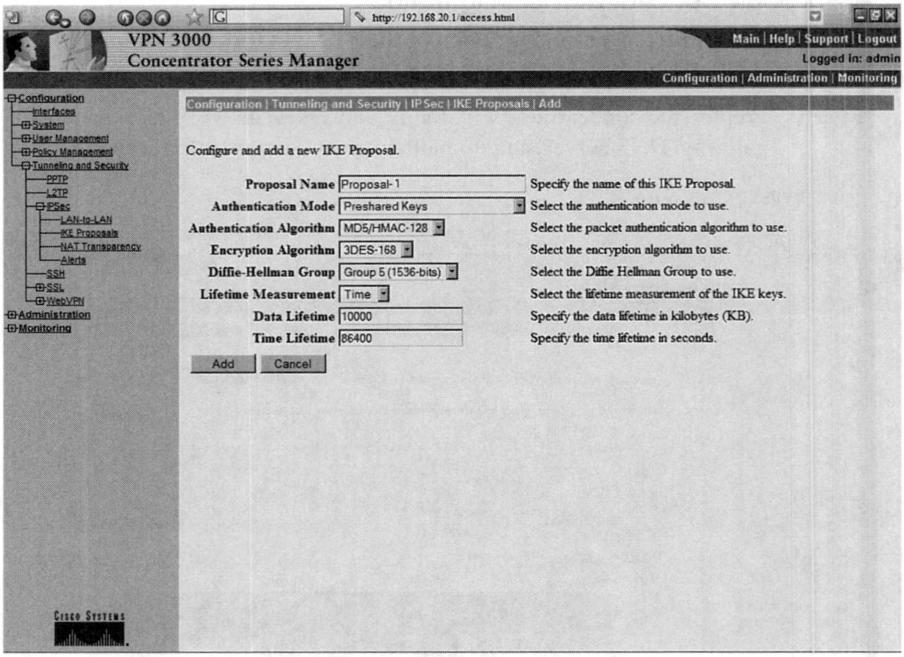

Step 3 Select the newly created proposal and click the **Activate** button, as shown in Figure 10-8. Click the **Move Up** button to assign a higher priority to the new proposal.

Step 4 Define a LAN-to-LAN connection as follows: Choose **Configuration > Tunneling and Security > IPSec > LAN-to-LAN** and click the **Add** button to launch the Add a new IPSec LAN-to-LAN connection page. Enter the name (for example, new-vpn) and other connection parameters, as shown in Figure 10-9. The Name field can contain any arbitrary name that identifies the connection. Note that the IKE Proposal field contains the IKE proposal (Proposal-1) that was created in Step 2.

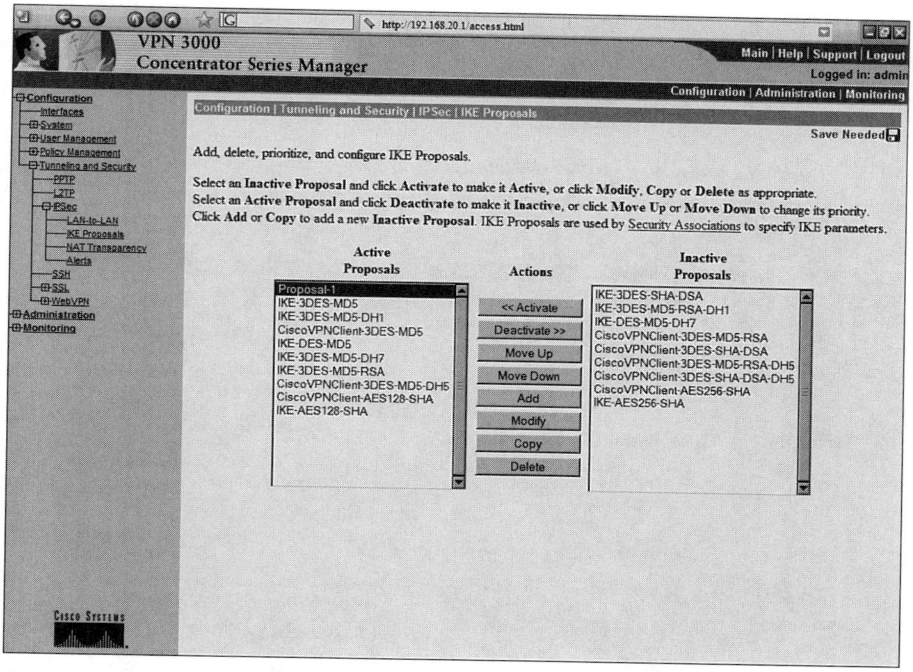

Figure 10-8 *OpenSWAN—PIX VPN*

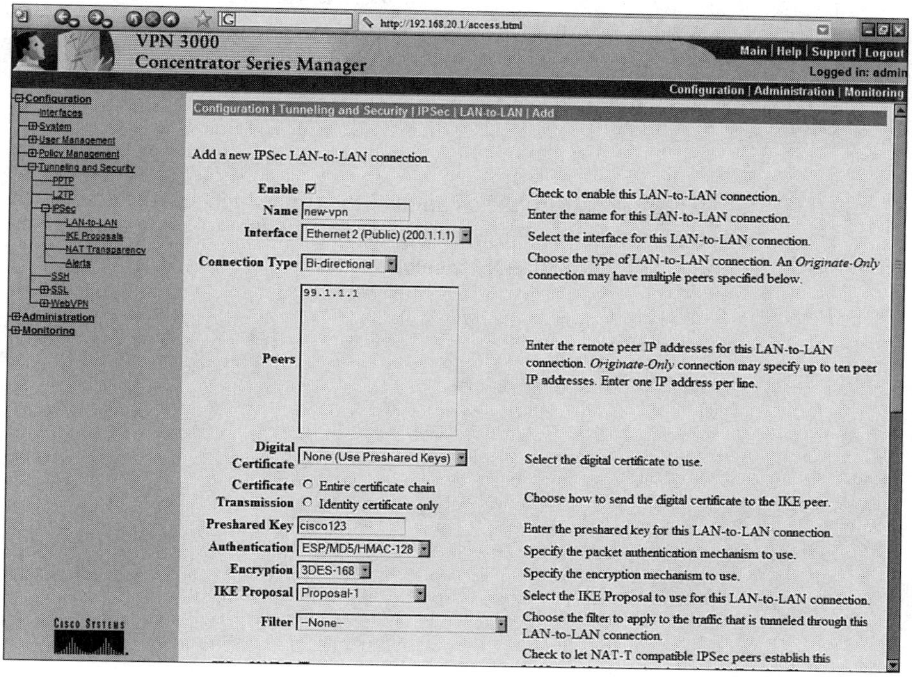

Figure 10-9 *LAN-to-LAN Connection—Parameters*

The lower section of the LAN-to-LAN connection page contains the IP address information for the local and remote networks, as shown in Figure 10-10. Click the **Add** button to save the settings and launch the confirmation page.

Figure 10-10 *LAN-to-LAN Connection—Network Details*

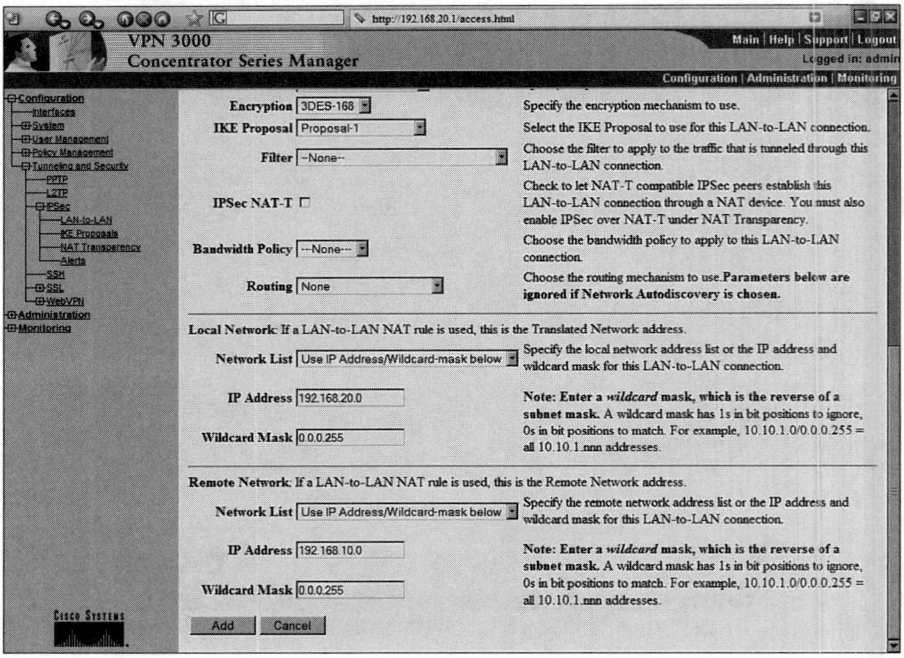

The next page confirms the creation of the connection and the associated SA and filter rules, as shown in Figure 10-11. Click the **OK** button to return to the LAN-to-LAN connection page.

Figure 10-11 *LAN-to-LAN Connection—Reports*

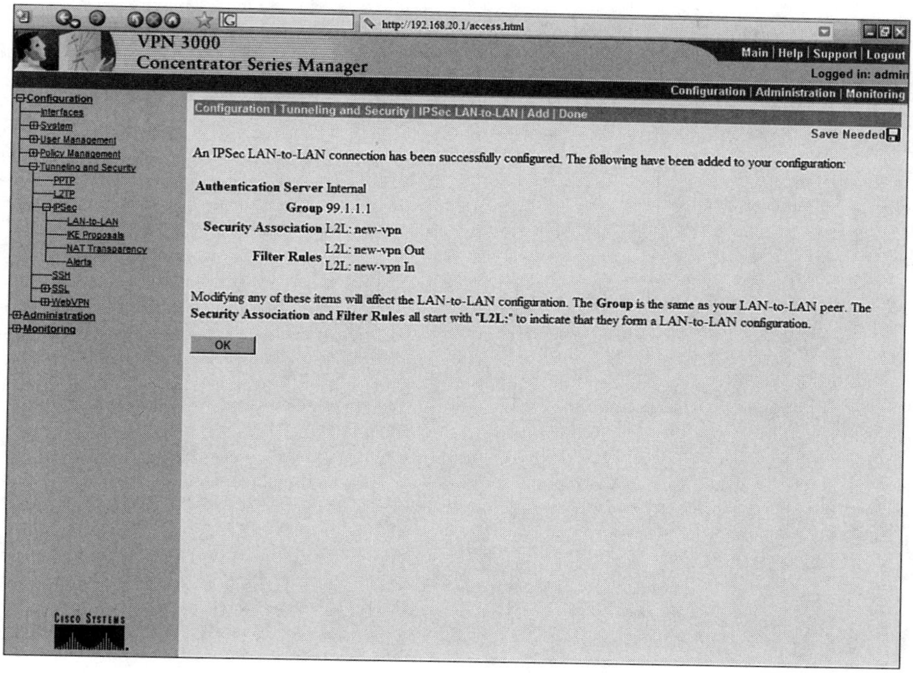

Step 5 To edit the new security association (called L2L: *connection-name*), choose **Configuration > Policy Management > Traffic Management > SAs** and select the new SA (L2L: new-vpn in this example). Click the **Modify** button to launch Modify a configured Security Association page, as shown in Figure 10-12. Make sure that the SA properties match, as shown, with the SA properties of OpenSWAN. Note the Perfect Forward Secrecy and IKE Proposal fields. Click the **Apply** button to save any changes. The concentrator is now ready for VPN traffic.

Figure 10-12 *Modify SAs*

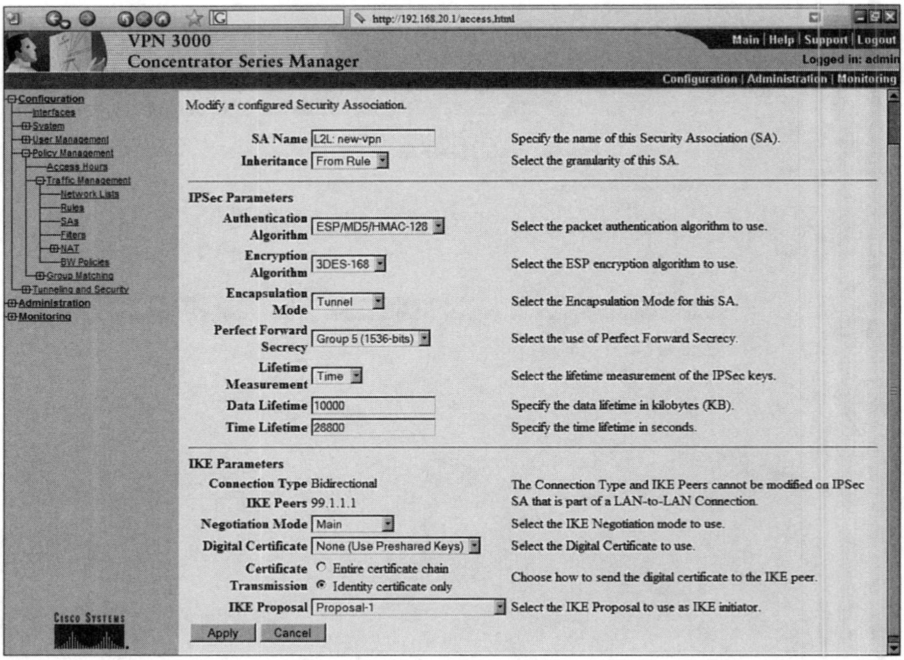

Monitoring the VPN 3000 Concentrator

The web-based GUI for the VPN 3000 concentrator provides a user-friendly interface for monitoring VPN sessions and event logs.

To monitor active sessions, choose **Monitoring > Sessions**. Click the name of the active session for more details, as shown in Figure 10-13. The details are helpful in quickly identifying the remote IPSec peers by their IP address, the encryption in use, and the duration of the IPSec session. The Bytes Tx and Bytes Rx fields provide information about traffic being encrypted and decrypted.

The system log messages generated by the concentrator are stored locally within the flash memory (of the concentrator). These messages are helpful for troubleshooting purposes and can be accessed through the navigation pane on the left side of the concentrator GUI. To view these system log messages from within the concentrator GUI, click **Monitoring > Filterable Event Log**. Example 10-16 shows the content of the event logs.

Figure 10-13 *Session Details*

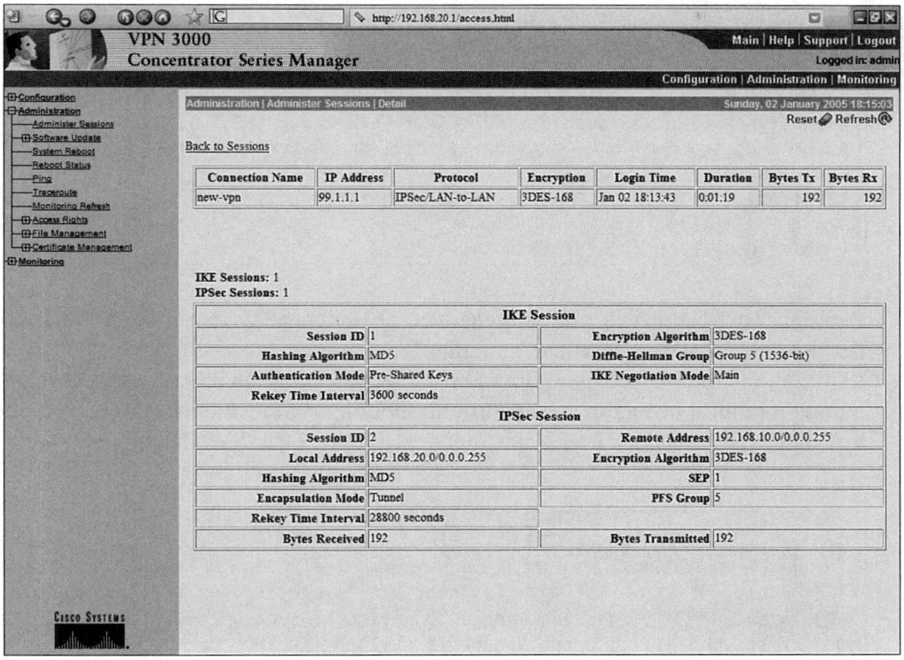

Example 10-16 *VPN 3000 Event Log*

```
2 01/02/2005 18:18:11.050 SEV=4 IKE/119 RPT=3 99.1.1.1
Group [99.1.1.1]
PHASE 1 COMPLETED

3 01/02/2005 18:18:11.050 SEV=4 AUTH/22 RPT=3
User [99.1.1.1] Group [99.1.1.1] connected, Session Type: IPSec/LAN-to-LAN

4 01/02/2005 18:18:11.050 SEV=4 AUTH/84 RPT=3
LAN-to-LAN tunnel to headend device 99.1.1.1 connected

5 01/02/2005 18:18:11.090 SEV=5 IKE/35 RPT=4 99.1.1.1
Group [99.1.1.1]
Received remote IP Proxy Subnet data in ID Payload:
 Address 192.168.10.0, Mask 255.255.255.0, Protocol 0, Port 0

8 01/02/2005 18:18:11.090 SEV=5 IKE/34 RPT=4 99.1.1.1
Group [99.1.1.1]
Received local IP Proxy Subnet data in ID Payload:
 Address 192.168.20.0, Mask 255.255.255.0, Protocol 0, Port 0

11 01/02/2005 18:18:11.090 SEV=5 IKE/66 RPT=4 99.1.1.1
```

continues

Example 10-16 *VPN 3000 Event Log (Continued)*

```
Group [99.1.1.1]
IKE Remote Peer configured for SA: L2L: new-vpn

12 01/02/2005 18:18:11.220 SEV=4 IKE/49 RPT=4 99.1.1.1
Group [99.1.1.1]
Security negotiation complete for LAN-to-LAN Group (99.1.1.1)
Responder, Inbound SPI = 0x43fbdf31, Outbound SPI = 0x6267ed2b

15 01/02/2005 18:18:11.220 SEV=4 IKE/120 RPT=4 99.1.1.1
Group [99.1.1.1]
PHASE 2 COMPLETED (msgid=cae1aa9a)
```

Example 10-17 shows the output generated on an OpenSWAN server by the **ipsec auto --up ciscovpn** command while negotiating IPSec parameters with the VPN 3000 concentrator. The output reports the status of the IPSec negotiation at various stages. Such information is helpful in diagnosing and troubleshooting IPSec session settings. The highlighted text indicates embedded comments that describe the OpenSWAN output.

Example 10-17 *OpenSWAN Debugs*

```
104 "ciscovpn" #1: STATE_MAIN_I1: initiate
003 "ciscovpn" #1: ignoring Vendor ID payload
  [4048b7d56ebce88525e7de7f00d6c2d3c0000000]
106 "ciscovpn" #1: STATE_MAIN_I2: sent MI2, expecting MR2
003 "ciscovpn" #1: ignoring Vendor ID payload [Cisco-Unity]
003 "ciscovpn" #1: ignoring Vendor ID payload [XAUTH]
003 "ciscovpn" #1: ignoring Vendor ID payload [d54e32e2f67104c8fecf02cd7237addf]
003 "ciscovpn" #1: ignoring Vendor ID payload [1f07f70eaa6514d3b0fa96542a500401]
108 "ciscovpn" #1: STATE_MAIN_I3: sent MI3, expecting MR3
003 "ciscovpn" #1: received Vendor ID payload [Dead Peer Detection]
# IPSec phase 1 is established
004 "ciscovpn" #1: STATE_MAIN_I4: ISAKMP SA established
112 "ciscovpn" #2: STATE_QUICK_I1: initiate
# IPSec phase 2 is established
004 "ciscovpn" #2: STATE_QUICK_I2: sent QI2, IPSec SA established {ESP=>0x43fbdf31
  <0x6267ed2b}
```

Windows-Based VPNs

Microsoft Windows 2000, XP, and 2003 provide built-in support for IPSec VPN connectivity. The IPSec VPN implementation within the MS-Windows OS is based on the standard architecture described by IETF RFCs 2401–2409, thus allowing easy interoperability with various vendors. Netadmins can deploy a Windows machine as a VPN gateway to establish a site-to-site VPN with remote peers. The site-to-site VPN can use either IPSec with preshared keys (for small-scale deployment) or IPSec with CA (for large-scale deployment). Furthermore, the remote peer can be a Cisco router, PIX Firewall, or VPN 3000 concentrator.

Table 10-10 lists the IPSec parameters supported by MS-Windows. Note that only Diffie-Hellman key exchange group 1 and group 2 are supported by Microsoft. An additional feature of the Windows OS is the support for MS Active Directory–based Kerberos authentication for the IPSec peer.

Table 10-10 *MS-Windows IPSec Parameters*

Parameter	Values
Phase 1 modes	Main Mode
Phase 2 modes	Quick Mode
Message encryption algorithm (phase 1)	DES, 3DES
Hash algorithm (phase 1)	MD5, SHA-1
Authentication (phase 1)	Preshared, digital certificates, Kerberos
Diffie-Hellman key exchange (phase 1)	D-H group 1, 2
IKE SA lifetime (phase 1)	Seconds, kilobytes
Transform set (phase 2)	AH-HMAC-MD5,AH-HMAC-SHA,ESP-3DES, ESP-DES
IPSec mode (phase 2)	Tunnel, Transport
IPSec SA (phase 2)	IKE
PFS (phase 2)	Group 1, 2
ID of the peer (phase 2)	IP address
IPSec SA lifetime (phase 2)	Kilobytes, seconds

Netadmins can leverage the Windows native IPSec support when deploying a site-to-site VPN, without paying for additional software. The following sections discuss VPN interoperability between MS-Windows and Cisco devices.

NOTE MS-Windows has been the target of various network attacks. Additionally, Windows offers a plethora of features and services that can introduce additional vulnerabilities. To deploy a Windows-based VPN server that faces the Internet, always follow proper security recommendations and security best practices. Ensure that you do the following:

- Apply the latest security patches and service packs.
- Apply antivirus and antispyware with latest definition updates.
- Use long and complex passwords.
- Uninstall or disable all unnecessary applications, such as Outlook Express, Internet Explorer, Media Player, and so on.
- Download and run the Microsoft Baseline Security Analyzer (MBSA) to identify potential security vulnerabilities. MBSA also provides recommendations to address the vulnerabilities.

Windows/Cisco Interoperability

Consider the network scenario shown in Figure 10-14. The two remote sites are connected to each other using an IPSec VPN tunnel through the Internet. The VPN gateway in site A is an MS-Windows (2000/XP/2003)–based IPSec peer. The gateway in site B can be a Cisco IOS, PIX Firewall, or VPN 3000 concentrator acting as the IPSec peer.

Figure 10-14 *LAN-to-LAN VPN*

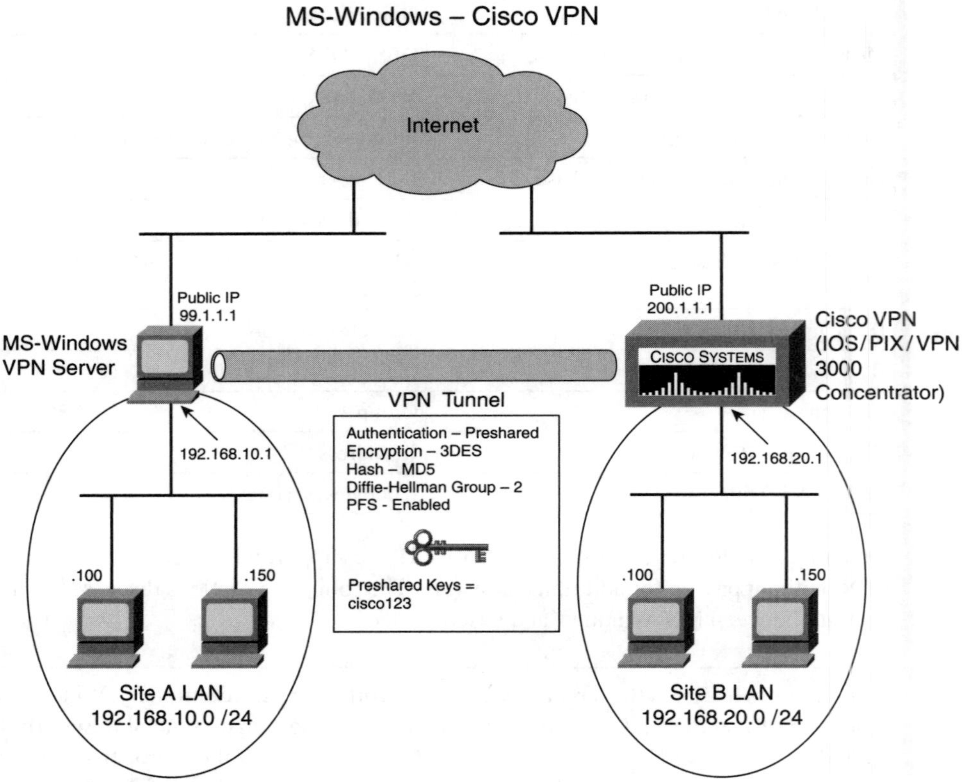

Establishing the VPN tunnel between the two remote sites uses the following two steps:

1 Deploying IPSec on Windows
2 Deploying IPSec on Cisco devices

Deploying IPSec on Windows

Deploying an IPSec-based VPN on a Windows machine is a two-stage process. You first prepare the Windows machine according to certain prerequisites for its role as an IPSec-based VPN gateway. Next is the configuration of various IPSec parameters. After the IPSec server is configured and running, you can monitor the IPSec operation using built-in tools and utilities on the Windows machine.

Prerequisites

By default, Windows machines are not ready for their role as an IPSec VPN gateway. To configure a Windows machine as an IPSec server, certain prerequisites must be met. Following is a brief list of these requirements:

- **Service packs**—Ensure that the latest service packs are installed on the IPSec server. Also note that unlike Windows XP and 2003, which are IPSec ready, Windows 2000 must be upgraded to at least Service Pack 2 to enable IPSec with 3DES.
- **Multihomed**—The Windows machine should have two NICs, one connected to the inside LAN and the other facing the Internet.
- **IP routing**—Ensure that IP routing is enabled on the Windows machine. By default, IP routing is disabled on Windows but is required to allow LAN traffic to be forwarded to the Internet. To enable IP routing, change the following Windows registry key value to 1:

  HKEY_LOCAL_MACHINE\SYSTEM\CurrentControlSet\Services\
  Tcpip\Parameters\IPEnableRouter
- **Firewall**—Host and network firewalls should allow UDP port 500 and protocol 50 to reach the Windows machine.
- **Network connectivity**—Before setting up the VPN tunnel, the LAN hosts should have Internet connectivity. Additionally, local hosts must be configured to use the Windows machine as the router to access the remote LAN.

CAUTION Although site-to-site VPNs ease the administrative burden on the Netadmin, they are a security risk, because the remote LAN users have full access to the local resources. Netadmins must always scrutinize the risks involved and ensure that the local resources are well protected through firewalls, intrusion detection systems (IDSs), and other access-control mechanisms.

Configuration

To configure a Windows IPSec VPN, follow these steps:

Step 1 Create an IPSec policy.

Step 2 Identify interesting traffic using the following filter lists:

- Traffic from the local site to the remote site
- Traffic from the remote site to the local site

Step 3 Configure phase 2 (IPSec) parameters using the following tunnel rules:

- Local-to-remote tunnel
- Remote-to-local tunnel

Step 4 Configure phase 1 (IKE) parameters.

Step 5 Assign the IPSec policy to the Windows gateway.

Note that each of these tasks must be carried out sequentially. All the steps are mandatory and must follow the order described in the following sections.

Step 1: Create an IPSec Policy

The steps used to create an IPSec policy on a Windows host are listed in Table 10-11.

Table 10-11 *Creating an IPSec Policy*

Step	Action
1	Choose **Start** > **Run** and enter **secpol.msc** to launch the IP Security Policy Management snap-in. (See Figure 10-15.)
2	Right-click **IP Security Policies on Local Computer**, and choose **Create IP Security Policy**.
3	Click the **Next** button, and enter a name for your policy (for example, windows-cisco-policy).
4	Deselect the **Activate the default response rule** check box, and then click the **Next** button.
5	Click the **Finish** button while the **Edit** check box is deselected.

Figure 10-15 *Windows IP Security Policy Management Snap-In*

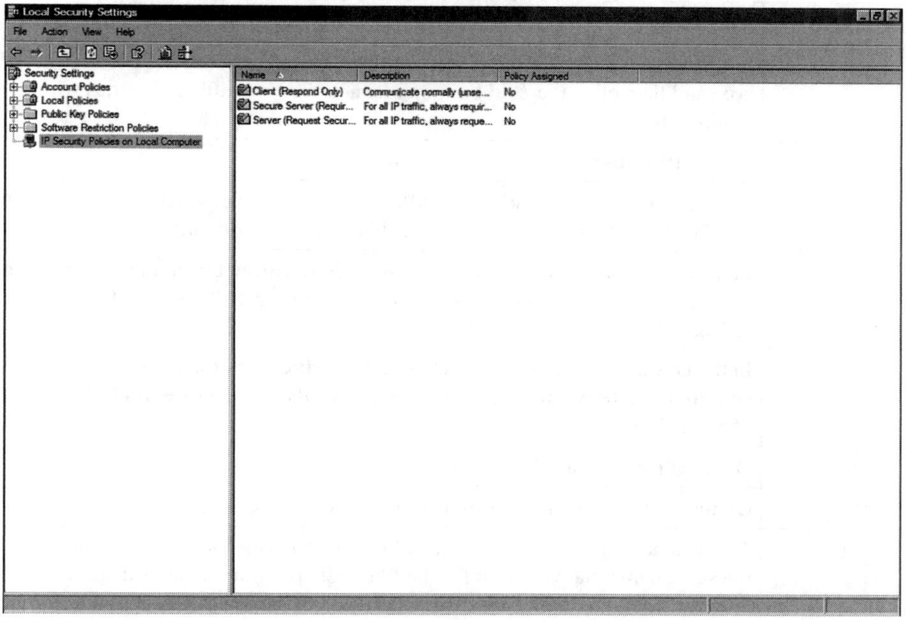

Step 2: Identify Interesting Traffic Using Filter Lists

Windows IPSec policy uses filter lists to identify traffic flowing in each direction. Hence, two filters are created for every IPSec tunnel: one for traffic destined for the remote LAN and a second for the traffic from the remote LAN. This task is similar to the mirrored access list used in IOS or PIX to define interesting traffic.

The steps used to create filter lists for traffic flowing from site A to site B are listed in Table 10-12.

Table 10-12 *Traffic Filter List—Site A to B*

Step	Action
1	In the left pane of the IP Security Policy Management snap-in window, click to select **IP Security Policies on Local Computer**. The right pane lists the policy created in the previous section (windows-cisco-policy).
2	Right-click **windows-cisco-policy** and select **Properties** to launch the Properties window.

continues

Table 10-12 *Traffic Filter List—Site A to B (Continued)*

Step	Action
3	In the windows-cisco-policy Properties window, deselect the **Use Add Wizard** check box, and then click the **Add** button to launch the New Rule Properties window. (See Figure 10-16.)
4	On the **IP Filter List** tab, click the **Add** button.
5	Type an appropriate name for the filter list (for example, windows-to-cisco), deselect the **Use Add Wizard** check box, and then click the **Add** button.
6	In the Source address area, choose **A specific IP Subnet** from the drop-down menu and fill in the IP Address and Subnet mask fields to reflect site A (192.168.10.0/ 255.255.255.0). (See Figure 10-17.)
7	In the Destination address area, choose **A specific IP Subnet** from the drop-down menu and fill in the IP Address and Subnet mask fields to reflect site B (192.168.20.0/ 255.255.255.0).
8	Deselect the **Mirrored** check box.
9	On the Protocol tab, make sure that the protocol type is set to **Any**.
10	To add a description for your filter, click the **Description** tab. You should give the filter the same name that you used for the filter list. The filter name is displayed in the IPSec monitor when the tunnel is active. Click the **OK** button to return to the IP Filter List window.
11	Click the **OK** button to return to the New Rule Properties window. Do not close this window because it is used in the next set of steps.

Figure 10-16 *New Rule Properties Window*

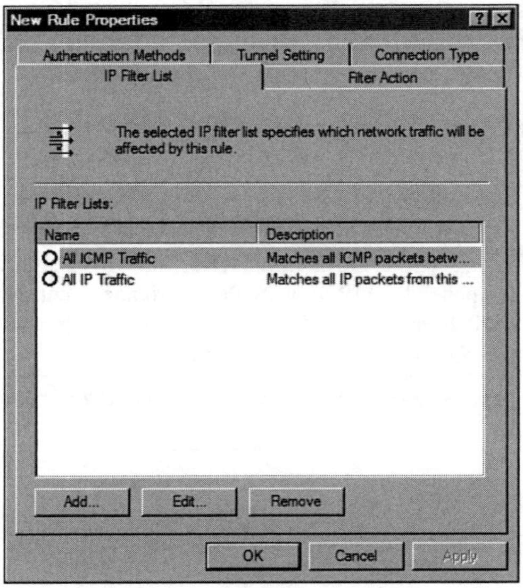

Figure 10-17 *Filter Properties Window*

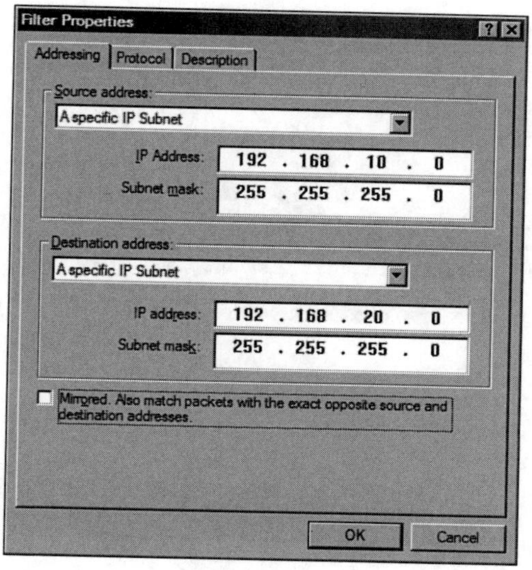

The steps used to create filter lists for traffic flowing from site B to site A are listed in Table 10-13. The steps are similar to those discussed in the previous table, with one obvious exception: The source and destination addresses are reversed.

Table 10-13 *Traffic Filter List—Site B to A*

Step	Action
1	In the New Rule Properties Window (discussed in the previous table), select the **IP Filter List** tab and click the **Add** button.
2	Type an appropriate name for the filter list (for example, cisco-to-windows), deselect the **Use Add Wizard** check box, and click the **Add** button.
3	In the Source address area, choose **A specific IP Subnet** from the drop-down menu and fill in the IP Address and Subnet mask fields to reflect site B (192.168.20.0/ 255.255.255.0).
4	In the Destination address area, choose **A specific IP Subnet** from the drop-down menu and fill in the IP Address and Subnet mask fields to reflect site A (192.168.10.0/ 255.255.255.0).
5	Deselect the **Mirrored** check box.
6	To add a description for your filter, click the **Description** tab.
7	Click the **OK** button to return to the IP Filter List window, and then click the **OK** button to return to the New Rule Properties window. The IP Filter List tab now shows both new filters. (See Figure 10-18.)

Figure 10-18 *New Rule Properties Window*

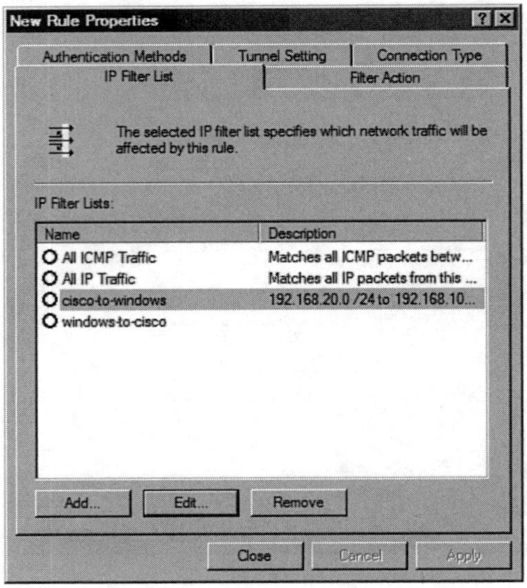

Step 3: Configure Phase 2 Parameters

Windows uses tunnel rules to define the phase 2 (IPSec SA) parameters. Because each IPSec tunnel is described by two unique one-way SAs, two rules should be configured. This task is roughly equivalent to creating crypto maps and transforms sets on Cisco devices.

The steps used to configure a rule for the site A–to–site B tunnel SA are listed in Table 10-14.

Table 10-14 *Phase 2 Rules—Site A to B*

Step	Action
1	On the IP Filter List tab, select the **windows-to-cisco** filter list you created.
2	On the **Tunnel Setting** tab, select the **The tunnel endpoint is specified by this IP Address** check box and then type the public IP address of the Cisco device (200.1.1.1).
3	On the **Connection Type** tab, select the **Local Area network (LAN)** check box.
4	On the **Filter Action** tab, deselect the **Use Add Wizard** check box and then click the **Add** button to create a new filter action.
5	Keep the **Negotiate security** option selected and click the **Add** button. Select the **Custom option** and then click the **Settings** button to launch the Custom Security Method Settings window. (See Figure 10-19.) This window is used to define specific algorithms and session key lifetimes.

Table 10-14 *Phase 2 Rules—Site A to B (Continued)*

Step	Action
6	Deselect the **Data and address integrity without encryption (AH)** check box. Select the **Data integrity and encryption (ESP)** check box, choose **MD5** as the integrity algorithm, and select **3DES** as the encryption algorithm. In the Session key settings section, only select the **Generate a new key every 3600 seconds** check box and click the **OK** button. In the Modify Security Method window, click the **OK** button to return to the New Filter Action Properties window.
7	In the New Filter Action Properties window, select the **Session key Perfect Forward Secrecy (PFS)** check box. Also click to clear the **Accept unsecured communication, but always respond using IPSec** and the **Allow unsecured communications with non-IPSec-aware computer** options. On the **General** tab, type a name for the new filter action (for example, ESP-3DES-MD5) and then click the **OK** button.
8	Select the filter action you just created (**ESP-3DES-MD5** in this example).
9	On the **Authentication Methods** tab, select **Edit** to launch the Edit Authentication Method Properties page. On the Edit Authentication Method Properties page, select the **Use this string (preshared keys)** option (radio button) and specify the preshared key (for example, cisco123); then click the **OK** button.
10	Click the **Close** button to return to the windows-cisco-policy Properties window.

Figure 10-19 *Custom Security Method Settings Window*

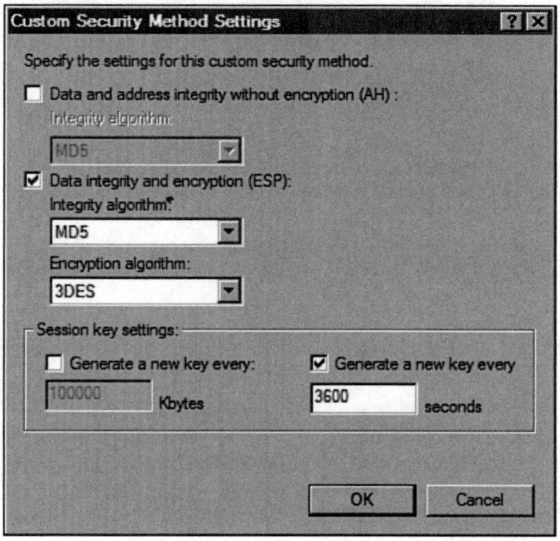

The steps used to configure a rule for the site B–to–site A tunnel SA are listed in Table 10-15.

Table 10-15 *Phase 2 Rules—Site B to A*

Step	Action
1	In the windows-cisco-policy Properties window, click the **Add** button to create a new rule. This launches the New Rule Properties window.
2	On the **IP Filter List** tab, click the filter that list you created (cisco-to-windows).
3	On the **Tunnel Setting** tab, select the **The tunnel endpoint is specified by this IP Address check** box and then enter the public IP address of the local IPSec peer (99.1.1.1).
4	On the **Connection Type** tab, select the **Local Area network (LAN)** check box.
5	On the **Filter Action** tab, click the filter action that you created (ESP-3DES-MD5).
6	On the **Authentication Methods** tab, configure the same preshared key.
7	Click the **OK** button to return to the windows-cisco-policy Properties window. This window should show both rules that were created and configured during the previous steps. Also, ensure that both of these rules are selected, as shown in Figure 10-20. Do not close the windows-cisco-policy Properties window yet, because it is required to configure the phase 1 parameters.

Figure 10-20 *Policy Properties Window*

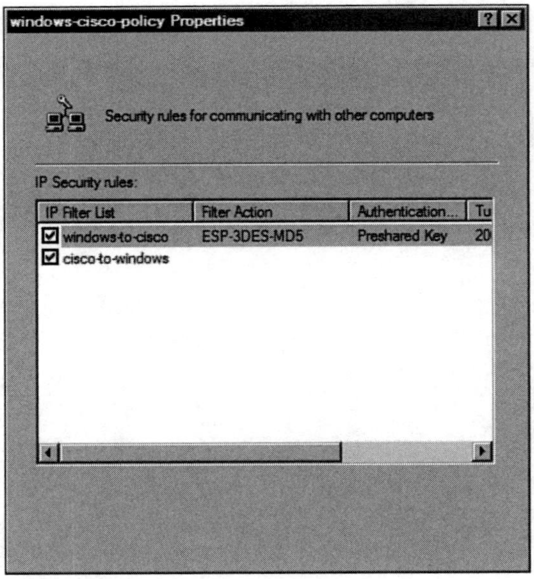

Step 4: Configure Phase 1 (IKE) Parameters

The IKE parameters for a Windows IPSec policy are configured through the **General** tab of the IPSec Policy Properties page. This task is similar to the crypto isakmp configuration for Cisco devices.

The steps used to configure the IKE parameters are listed in Table 10-16.

Table 10-16 *Phase 1 Parameters*

Step	Action
1	On the **General** tab of the windows-cisco-policy Properties window, set the Check for policy changes every field to 180 minutes.
2	Click the **Advanced** button, deselect the **Master key PFS** check box, and set the Authenticate and generate a new key after every field to **480** minutes.
3	Click **Methods** button to launch the Key Exchange security Methods window. In this window, at least one of the methods should be set to **MD5-3DES-Medium-(2)** combination and should be assigned higher preference using the **Move Up** button. Click the **OK** button to return to the Key Exchange Setting window.
4	Click the **OK** button to save your changes and return to the IPSec Policy Properties page.

Step 5: Assign the IPSec Policy to the Windows Gateway

After the IPSec policy is configured, the policy should be assigned to the Windows VPN gateway. This task is similar to applying the crypto map on the interfaces of Cisco devices.

To assign the new policy, right-click the new policy (for example, windows-cisco-policy) in the IP Security Policy Management MMC snap-in and then click the **Assign** button. A green arrow appears in the folder icon next to the policy.

After the policy is assigned, the Windows machine is ready to act as a VPN gateway. Assuming that the remote peer is configured properly, the traffic between the two LANs will be protected by IPSec. A simple ping from one of the local hosts to a host in the remote LAN can verify the operation of the IPSec tunnel.

Monitoring and Troubleshooting

To monitor and troubleshoot IPSec service in Windows, the most popular options are as follows:

- Windows Services console
- IP Security Monitor
- Windows Event Viewer

Services Console

For troubleshooting purposes, you might need to stop or restart IPSec services. Moreover, IPSec services must be restarted after making changes to the IPSec configuration. Stopping the IPSec services disables all the IPSec functionality and drops the existing IPSec sessions and tunnels. IPSec services are controlled through the Windows Services MMC snap-in console. The steps to restart IPSec services are as follows:

Step 1 Choose **Start > Run** on the Windows machine. In the Run window, enter **services.msc** and click the **OK** button. This launches the Windows Services console.

Step 2 In the Services console window, right-click **IPSEC Services** and select **Restart**. Note that in addition to the restart option, the right-click menu also provides options to start or stop IPSec services.

IP Security Monitor

Windows provides built-in utilities for monitoring IPSec sessions. These tools provide details regarding the current phase 1 and phase 2 SAs that are established on the local Windows machine. The tools also provide IPSec and ISAKMP statistics that are helpful in troubleshooting IPSec issues.

Windows 2000 provides the ipsecmon.exe utility to monitor the live IPSec activities. To launch ipsecmon.exe, choose **Start > Run**, enter **ipsecmon.exe**, and click the **OK** button.

Windows XP and 2003 provide the IP Security Monitor console to monitor the current IPSec activities. Follow these steps to launch the IP Security Monitor console:

Step 1 Start the MMC console by choosing **Start > Run**, entering **mmc**, and clicking the **OK** button.

Step 2 Choose **File > Add-remove Snap-in** to launch the Add/Remove Snap-in window. Click on the **Add** button to launch the Add Standalone Snap-in window. Select the **IP Security Monitor** and click **Add** button followed by clicking **Close** button to return to the Add/Remove Snap-in window. Click **OK** button to return to the console window. The IP security monitor snap-in is now ready for monitoring IPSec operation.

When the IP Security Monitor console is opened, you can monitor the IPSec sessions. In the left pane of the IP Security Monitor snap-in window, navigate to **IP Security Monitor > *Local-Hostname***. (*Local-Hostname* is the host name assigned to the Windows computer that is acting as the IPSec VPN gateway.) Right-click ***Local-Hostname*** and select **Statistics** to view the summarized statistics for the current IPSec sessions, as shown in Figure 10-21. Of the various parameters listed in this window, the **Bytes Sent In Tunnels** and **Bytes Received In Tunnels** parameters are useful in identifying the operation of IPSec. A constantly incrementing value of each of these parameters indicates that VPN traffic is flowing through the IPSec peers as desired.

Figure 10-21 *Windows—IPSec Statistics*

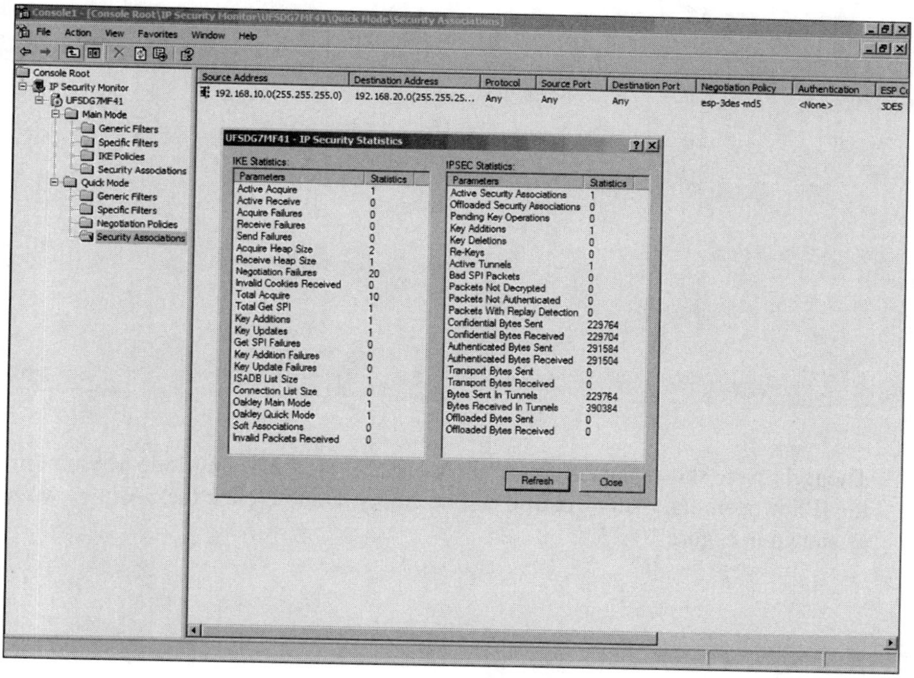

The IP Security Monitor console also displays the current Main Mode (phase 1) and Quick Mode (phase 2) details. To view the Main Mode SAs, navigate to **Main Mode > Security Associations**, as shown in Figure 10-22.

Figure 10-22 *Windows—IPSec Main Mode*

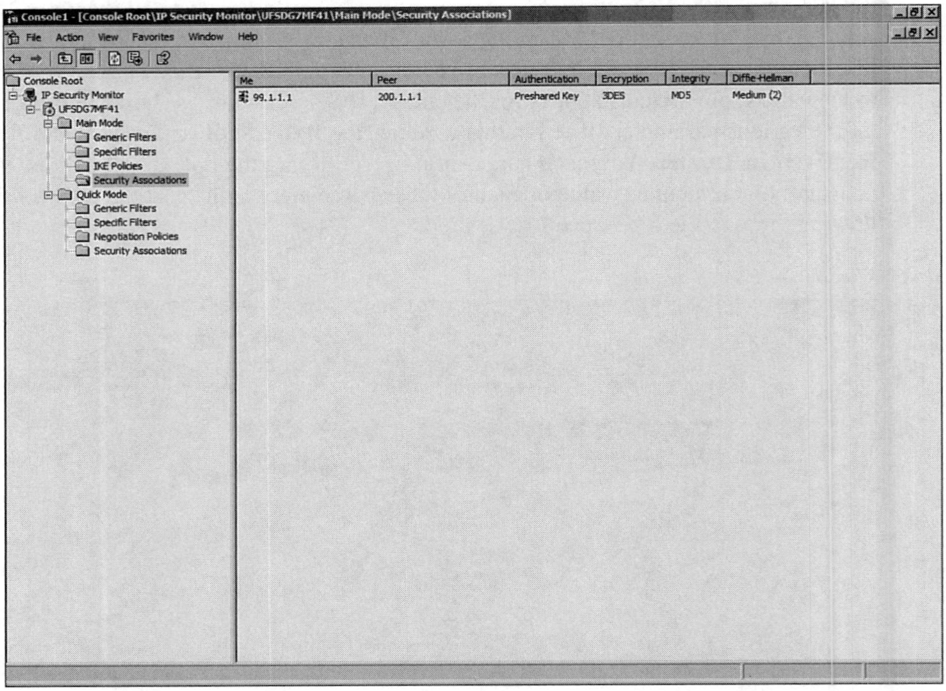

The right pane shows the current Main Mode SAs. If the Main Mode negotiation between the IPSec peers fails, this window will be empty. Double-click the SA to view the details, as shown in Figure 10-23.

Figure 10-23 *Windows—IPSec Main Mode Details*

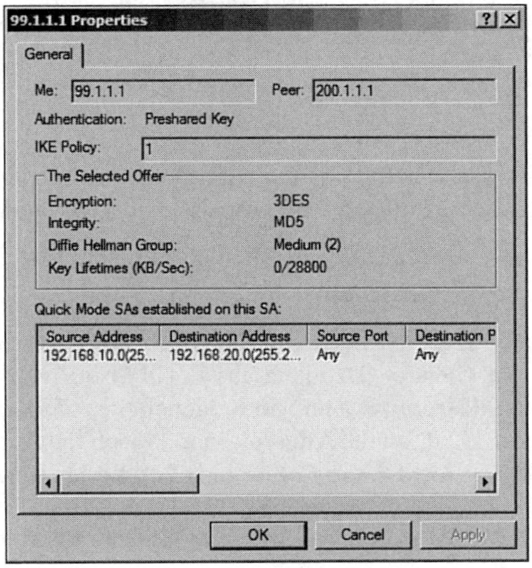

Similarly, Figure 10-24 shows the details of an SA established in Quick Mode. The Quick Mode SAs are only displayed after the peers successfully negotiate phase 2.

Figure 10-24 *Windows—IPSec Quick Mode Statistics*

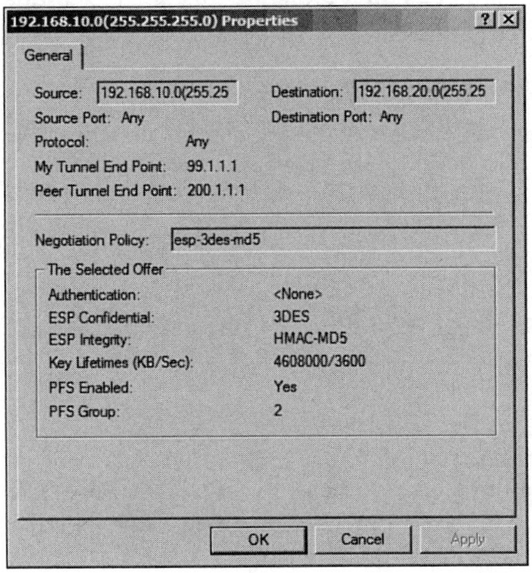

Additionally, the details of both Main and Quick Mode SAs display the IP addresses of the local (source) and remote (destination) LANs. This information can verify that IPSec is indeed tunneling the traffic as configured.

Event Viewer

To enable IPSec services logging the IKE and IPSec negotiations in the Windows Event Viewer, use the Local Policy MMC snap-in by following these steps:

Step 1 Start the MMC console by choosing **Start > Run**, entering **mmc**, and clicking the **OK** button.

Step 2 Choose **File > Add-remove Snap-in > Add > Group Policy > Add > Finish > Close > OK** to add the Local Security Policy snap-in. Choose **File > Add-remove Snap-in** to launch the Add/Remove Snap-in window. Click on the **Add** button to launch the Add Standalone Snap-in window. Select **Group Policy** and click **Add** button followed by clicking **Close** button to return to the Add/Remove Snap-in window. Click **OK** button to return to the console window.

Step 3 In the Console window, navigate to the following location:

> Local Computer Policy\Computer Configuration\Windows Settings\Security Settings\Local Policies\Audit Policy

Under the Audit Policy window, for both the **Audit logon events** and **Audit policy changes** options, enable the auditing of **Success** and **Failure** attempts.

Step 4 Restart the computer.

The IPSec logs can be viewed in the Security section of the Windows Event Viewer.

CAUTION The IKE process creates a large number of audit logs. To disable IKE logs, create the following registry key and set its value to 1:

HKEY_LOCAL_MACHINE\System\CurrentControlSet\Control\Lsa\Audit\DisableIKEAudits

---

Deploying IPSec on Cisco Devices

The configurations for Cisco PIX Firewalls, IOS, and VPN concentrators are similar to those discussed in the section "Linux-Based VPNs," earlier in this chapter; the Diffie-

Hellman group identifier is the only exception. Because MS-Windows only supports D-H groups 1 and 2, the configuration for Cisco devices should be modified to use D-H group 2 and PFS group 2.

The following are partial configurations for Cisco devices:

- **IOS-based IPSec VPN**—Refer to Example 10-18.
- **PIX-based IPSec VPN**—Refer to Example 10-19.
- **VPN 3000–based IPSec VPN**—Refer to Example 10-20.

Example 10-18 *IOS—Partial Configuration for IPSec*

```
Cisco-rtr#show running-config
! Phase 1 configuration
crypto isakmp policy 3
 encr 3des
 hash md5
 authentication pre-share
! MS-Windows only support DH group 1 & 2
 group 2
crypto isakmp key cisco123 address 99.1.1.1
!Phase 2 Configuration
crypto ipsec transform-set myset esp-3des esp-md5-hmac
!
crypto map vpn 30 ipsec-isakmp
 set peer 99.1.1.1
 set transform-set myset
! MS-Windows only support DH group 1 & 2
! set pfs group2
 match address 100
!
interface Ethernet0/0
 ip address 192.168.20.1 255.255.255.0
!
interface Serial0/0
 ip address 200.1.1.1 255.255.255.252
 crypto map vpn
!
ip route 0.0.0.0 0.0.0.0 200.1.1.2
!
access-list 101 permit ip 192.168.20.0 0.0.0.255 192.168.10.0 0.0.0.255
!
end
```

Example 10-19 *PIX—Partial Configuration for IPSec*

```
PIX-FW# show running-config
hostname PIX-FW
domain-name VPNtest.com
access-list 101 permit ip 192.168.20.0 255.255.255.0 192.168.10.0 255
  .255.255.0
access-list 102 permit ip 192.168.20.0 255.255.255.0 192.168.10.0 255
```

continues

Example 10-19 *PIX—Partial Configuration for IPSec (Continued)*

```
  .255.255.0
ip address outside 200.1.1.1 255.255.255.0
ip address inside 192.168.20.1 255.255.255.0
global (outside) 1 interface
nat (inside) 0 access-list 102
nat (inside) 1 0.0.0.0 0.0.0.0 0 0
access-group 120 in interface outside
route outside 0.0.0.0 0.0.0.0 200.1.1.2 1
sysopt connection permit-ipsec
crypto ipsec transform-set myset esp-3des esp-md5-hmac
!
crypto map mymap 10 ipsec-isakmp
crypto map mymap 10 match address 101
! MS-Windows only support DH group 1 and 2
crypto map mymap 10 set pfs group2
crypto map mymap 10 set peer 99.1.1.1
crypto map mymap 10 set transform-set myset
crypto map mymap interface outside
! Define IKE parameters
!
isakmp enable outside
isakmp key ******** address 99.1.1.1 netmask 255.255.255.255
isakmp identity address
isakmp policy 10 authentication pre-share
isakmp policy 10 encryption 3des
isakmp policy 10 hash md5
! MS-Windows only support DH group 1 and 2
isakmp policy 10 group 2
isakmp policy 10 lifetime 86400
: end
```

Example 10-20 *VPN 3000—Partial Configuration for IPSec*

```
IKE proposal: Configuration > Tunneling and Security > IPSec > IKE Proposals > Add.
Proposal Name = Proposal-1
Authentication Mode = Preshared Keys
Authentication Algorithm = MD5/HMAC-128
Encryption Algorithm = 3DES-168
!---Windows supports Diffie-Hellman group 2
Diffie Hellman Group = Group 2 (1024-bits)
Lifetime Measurement = Time
Date Lifetime = 10000
Time Lifetime = 86400

Define the LAN-to-LAN tunnel: Configuration > Tunneling and Security > IPSec > LAN-
  to-LAN > Add.:
Enabled= checked
Name = new-vpn
Interface = Ethernet 2 (Public) (200.1.1.1)
Connection Type= Bi-directional
Peer = 99.1.1.1
```

Example 10-20 *VPN 3000—Partial Configuration for IPSec (Continued)*

```
Digital Certs = none (Use Pre-shared Keys)
Pre-shared key = cisco123
Authentication = ESP/MD5/HMAC-128
Encryption = 3DES-168
IKE Proposal = Proposal-1
Filter= --None--
IPSec NAT-T= unchecked
Bandwidth Policy= --None--
Routing= --None--
!
Local Network
Network List = Use IP Address/Wildcard-mask below
IP Address= 192.168.20.0
Wildcard Mask = 0.0.0.255
!
Remote Network
Network List = Use IP Address/Wildcard-mask below
IP Address= 192.168.10.0
Wildcard Mask= 0.0.0.255

Security Association: Configuration > Policy Management > Traffic Management > SAs
 > L2L:new-vpn > Modify.
SA Name = L2L: new-vpn
Inheritance = From Rule
!
IPSec Parameters
Authentication Algorithm = ESP/MD5/HMAC-128
Encryption Algorithm = 3DES-168
Encapsulation Mode = Tunnel
!---Windows supports Diffie-Hellman group 2
PFS = Group2 (1024-bits)
Lifetime Measurement = Time
Data Lifetime = 10000
Time Lifetime = 28800
!
IKE Parameters
Connection Type= Bidirectional
IKE Peer = 99.1.1.1
Negotiation Mode = Main
Digital Certificate = None (Use Preshared Keys)
Certificate Transmission= Identity certificate only
IKE Proposal= Proposal-1
```

Summary

This chapter introduces Netadmins to IPSec-based VPNs. The initial section discusses the architecture and terminology within the IPSec framework. Successive sections cover the interoperability of Cisco-based VPN devices with Linux- and Windows-based VPN servers.

The chapter helps Netadmins do the following tasks:

- Understand the various components and functions of the IPSec protocol
- Understand IPSec-based VPNs
- Deploy Cisco IOS–based VPNs in a mixed environment using a Linux OpenSWAN VPN server
- Deploy Cisco PIX Firewall–based VPNs in a mixed environment using a Linux OpenSWAN VPN server
- Deploy Cisco VPN 3000 concentrator–based VPNs in a mixed environment using a Linux OpenSWAN VPN server
- Deploy Cisco IOS–based VPNs in a mixed environment using MS-Windows IPSec services
- Deploy Cisco PIX Firewall–based VPNs in a mixed environment using MS-Windows IPSec services
- Deploy Cisco VPN 3000 concentrator–based VPNs in a mixed environment using MS-Windows IPSec services

Table 10-17 lists the tools discussed in this chapter.

Table 10-17 *IPSec Resources*

Tool	Function	Supported OS	URL/Notes
OpenSWAN	IPSec-based VPN server	Linux	http://www.openswan.org
FreeSWAN	IPSec-based VPN server	Linux	http://www.freeswan.org
Windows IPSec Services	IPSec-based VPN server	Windows 2000/XP/2003	http://www.microsoft.com

PART **IV**

Network Documentation

CHAPTER 11

Documentation Tools: Network Diagrams

This chapter covers one of the most fundamental aspects of the networking profession—the network diagram. The chapter covers the following items:

- Network diagram overview
- Linux-based graphic design tools
- Windows-based graphic design tools

Network Diagram Overview

A network diagram is, well, worth a thousand words!

A network diagram is essentially a topological map that depicts the network elements and the connections between them. Within the diagram, network elements are illustrated by icons while connections are illustrated as links. Every networking professional should use network diagrams. An up-to-date copy of the network diagram is one of the best trouble-shooting weapons in a Netadmin's war chest.

Before creating a network diagram or deciding which software to use to create the diagram, the Netadmin must answer the following questions:

- **Topology**—Will the diagram depict the physical topology or the logical topology of the network?
- **File format**—In what file format does the Netadmin want the diagram to be?
- **Features**—What features of the diagramming software are important to the Netadmin?

Topology

Topology means the study of places. In computer network parlance, topology refers to a network diagram that shows the interconnection of various elements. Based on the network's contents, a network diagram is classified as follows:

- **Physical topology**—As the name suggests, the physical topology shows the physical connections, including the cabling layout. Physical topology often includes chassis details, such as port number, slots, and modules. Because physical topology indicates the cabling layout, logical information about communication links is not shown. For example, the physical topology of both Token Ring and Ethernet networks is a star topology. Rack layouts fall under the category of a physical topology.
- **Logical topology**—Logical topology projects the network layout in accordance with the flow of data within the network. Logical topology also includes virtual LANs (VLAN) and other Layer 2 information, such as Ethernet or Token Ring. Flow charts fall under the category of a logical topology.

File Formats

The file formats for network diagrams depend on the graphic design tools used. Most of the tools, including commercial, shareware, and freeware, use proprietary file formats. Thus, certain tools cannot edit a diagram created by another tool. However, most graphic design tools can export the diagram into common picture formats such as .bmp, .jpeg, .gif, and even .pdf file formats. The JPEG and GIF formats are highly portable and can be viewed in any web browser. On the other hand, editing JPEGs and GIFs is cumbersome at best. A common practice is to maintain the network diagram in a native format and publish JPEGs or PDFs on demand. Another common practice is to save the diagrams as web pages to an intranet web portal.

Features

Any graphic design tool with the capability to draw basic geometric shapes and sizes can be used to create network diagrams. However, certain unique features can help in simplifying the process of creating and editing network diagrams. This section discusses some of these unique requirements.

A good graphic design tool must be able to create network diagrams in a commonly supported format such as JPEG or GIF. As noted in the previous section, even if the original format is different from that of the current software, the program should at least be able to export the final diagram in a common format, such as JPEG, GIF, or PDF. Next, the design tool should be able to add or import various stencils or templates that contain new device icons. The ability to import new icons is essential for incorporating the latest genre of network devices into the diagrams.

Another desired feature is a dynamic connection for joining network icons. Generally, you can connect two icons by a line to depict a network connection. However, when one of the icons is moved, the connecting line must be adjusted accordingly. Dynamic connections overcome this limitation of static connection lines. The dynamic connection points facilitate moving the icons within the diagram by automatically adjusting the connection links. In addition to the dynamic connections, the graphic tool should also be able to resize the diagram according to the paper on which it is printed or the video monitor. This aids in viewing or printing the diagrams.

Finally, the graphic design tool must also be able to add and edit text labels. The text labels provide details such as IP addresses, circuit IDs, serial numbers, model numbers, and so on.

The subsequent sections cover several noncommercial tools that are available for creating network diagrams. Note that creating network diagrams is both an engineering skill and an art. This chapter merely introduces you to some of the tools and discusses how to use them.

Linux-Based Graphic Design Tools

The open source community has developed a wide variety of Linux-based graphic design tools for mapping networks. However, from the perspective of creating Cisco-based network diagrams, the choices are limited. On the basis of popularity and communitywide support, the following two tools are worth mentioning:

- Dia
- Kivio

Dia is an open source program for creating diagrams. Dia can be used to draw many different kinds of diagrams, including network diagrams and flow charts. The project home page for Dia is located at http://www.gnome.org/projects/dia/.

The following advantages are offered by Dia:

- The dynamic connection points on the icons facilitate resizing and relocation of objects within the diagram without the need to reconnect the point after moving the objects.
- It provides built-in Cisco stencils.
- An MS-Windows version is also available.

This chapter discusses Dia rather than Kivio because Kivio stencils are not free. Dia stencils are available at no charge and can be distributed freely.

This following sections prepare the Netadmin for understanding and using Dia:

- Deploying Dia
- Creating diagrams with Dia
- Viewing sample Dia diagrams

Deploying Dia

The steps involved in deploying Dia are as follows:

Step 1 Install Dia.

The specific installation steps can vary according to the underlying Linux distribution. To install Dia on a Debian-Linux system, use the **apt-get install** command, as follows:

```
root@linuxbox:~# apt-get install dia
```

Step 2 Run Dia.

Dia runs out of the box, and no configuration is required. To start Dia, enter **dia** at the command prompt, as follows:

```
root@linuxbox:~# dia
```

Creating Diagrams with Dia

Before creating a network diagram, you should be familiar with the toolbar and the various icons used in Dia. The main window shows the toolbar menu (as shown in Figure 11-1), which consists of three sections:

- Connectors and standard shapes
- Stencils
- Size and colors

The top section of the toolbar menu consists of connectors and standard shapes. The middle section contains a drop-down menu for stencils. The contents of the selected stencil are displayed below the menu bar. The bottom section consists of the selector for shape, size, and colors. The Diagram pane uses its own menu.

Dia refers to the stencils as *sheets.* Each sheet contains icons. Dia refers to icons as *shapes.* The six most useful sheets for network diagrams, which are preloaded in Dia, are as follows:

- Cisco - Computer
- Cisco – Hub
- Cisco - Misc
- Cisco - Network
- Cisco - Router
- Network

To start a new diagram, choose **File > New**.

Figure 11-1 *Dia Toolbar*

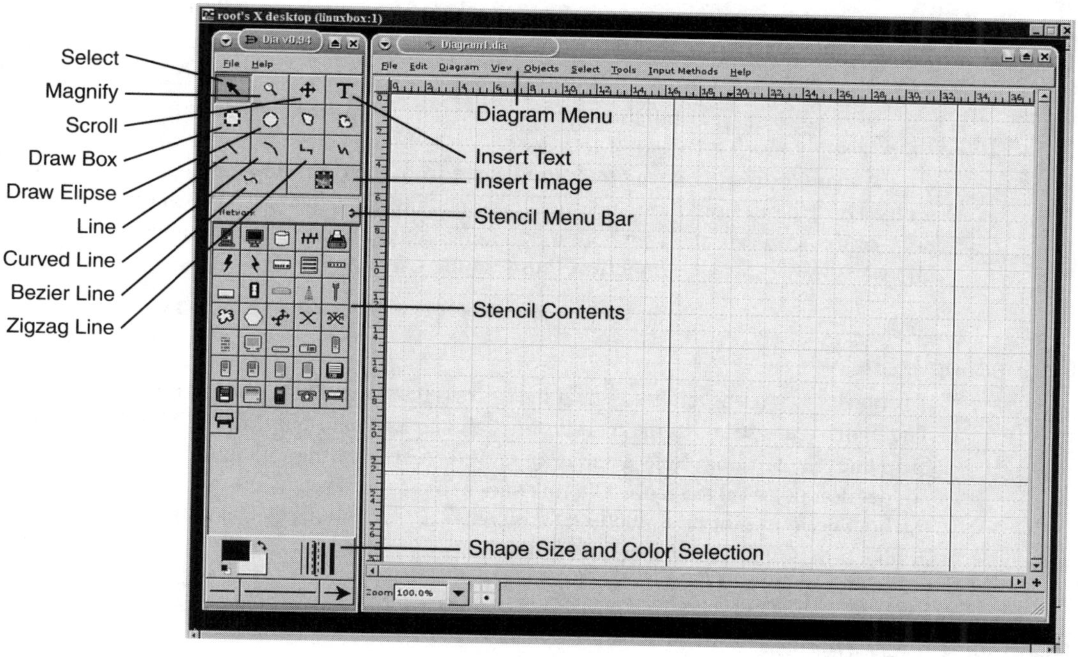

If the diagram lacks the File menu at the top, you can right-click within the blank area of the diagram to invoke the Diagram file menu.

TIP By default, the display is not antialiased, causing the icons to look fuzzy. To turn on the Antialiasing feature, choose **View > AntiAliased** on the Diagram menu.

The most common tasks involved in creating a network diagram using Dia are as follows:

- Adding icons
- Connecting icons
- Removing a connection
- Adding a text box
- Inserting an Ethernet backbone
- Exporting the diagram as a JPEG image
- Adding new icons to the stencil

These are only a few of the most common tasks available to the Netadmin. For more information, refer to the online manual that is included with the installation files. To view the manual, choose **Help > Manual** in the Diagram pane.

Adding Icons

On the main toolbar, choose the desired sheet from the drop-down menu to display the icons. Drag the desired icon and drop it on the diagram. The blue cross signs (X) on the edge of the icons are the connection points. To toggle the display of connection points, choose **View > Show Connection Point** on the Diagram menu.

Connecting Icons

To connect two icons, click to select the desired link from the upper section of main toolbar. The choices are straight line, curved line, zigzag line, and polyline. Click the drawing to drop the selected link. Select and drag the green ends of the link and drop it over the connection point on the icon. The link snaps to the icon only if the end of the link overlaps the connection point on the icon. Dia displays a red boundary around the icon when the connection point overlaps the end of the link.

Removing a Connection

To remove a connection, click the link and press **Delete**.

Adding a Text Box

To insert a text box containing information such as host name or IP address, click the **Insert Text** button on the main toolbar and then click the desired location on the diagram. Enter the desired text. Click the blank background to exit the Insert Text mode.

Inserting an Ethernet Backbone

To insert an Ethernet backbone, select the Network stencil from the stencil drop-down menu on the main toolbar. Drag and drop the Ethernet icon on the diagram. You can also insert a serial line link using the Network stencil.

Exporting the Diagram as a JPEG Image

To save the image in PNG or JPEG format, follow these steps:

Step 1 Choose **File > Export** on the Diagram menu.

Step 2 In the Determine file type field in the Export Diagram window, choose **GdkPixbuf - not antialiased (*.png, *.jpg, *.jpeg)**, enter the desired filename with the desired extension (.jpg or .png), and click the **OK** button.

Adding a New Icon to the Stencil

This feature is handy for adding new icons that are not part of the standard shapes included in Dia. To add new icons, follow these steps:

Step 1 From the Diagram menu, choose **Tools > Image** and click the desired location on the diagram.

Step 2 Double-click the **Broken Image** icon to invoke the Image properties menu.

Step 3 On the Image properties menu, use the **Browse** button to locate and insert the icon image. Click the **OK** button to close the Image properties menu.

TIP You can find a variety of Cisco icons at the home page of the Cisco *Packet* magazine: http://www.cisco.com/go/packet.

You can also use these icons with OpenOffice Draw to create simple network diagrams.

Viewing Sample Dia Diagrams

The following are three sample diagrams created by Dia.

Figure 11-2 shows Dia in action, drawing a logical topology for ABC Investments Inc.

Figure 11-2 *Dia in Action*

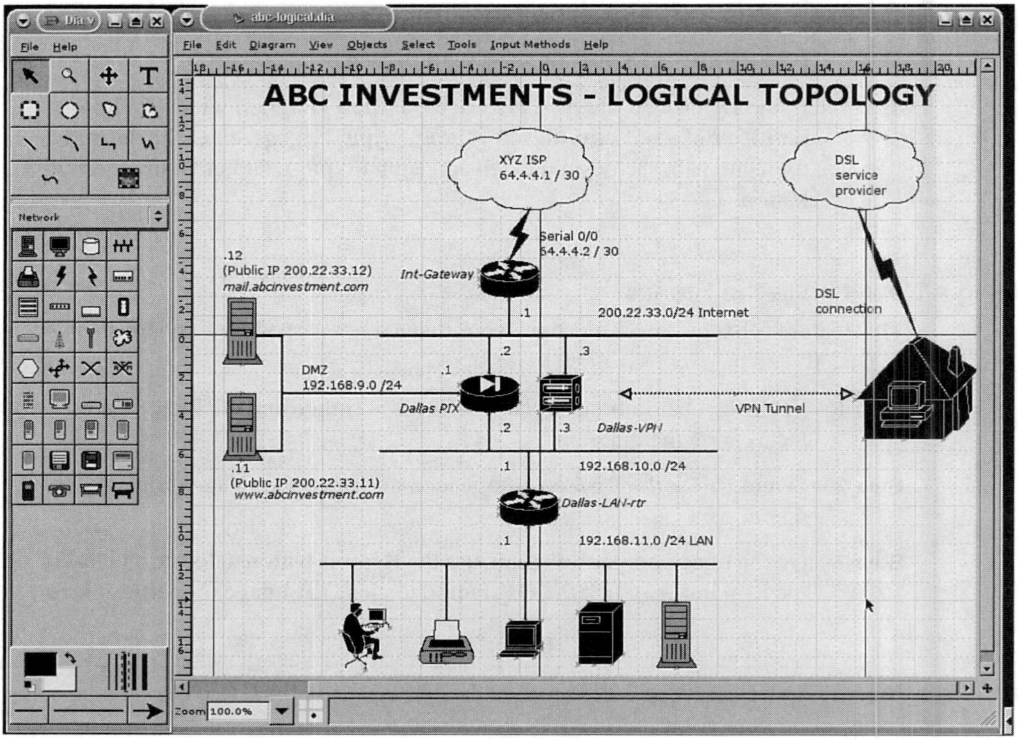

Figure 11-3 shows the final output in .jpg format.

Figure 11-3 *Dia—JPEG output*

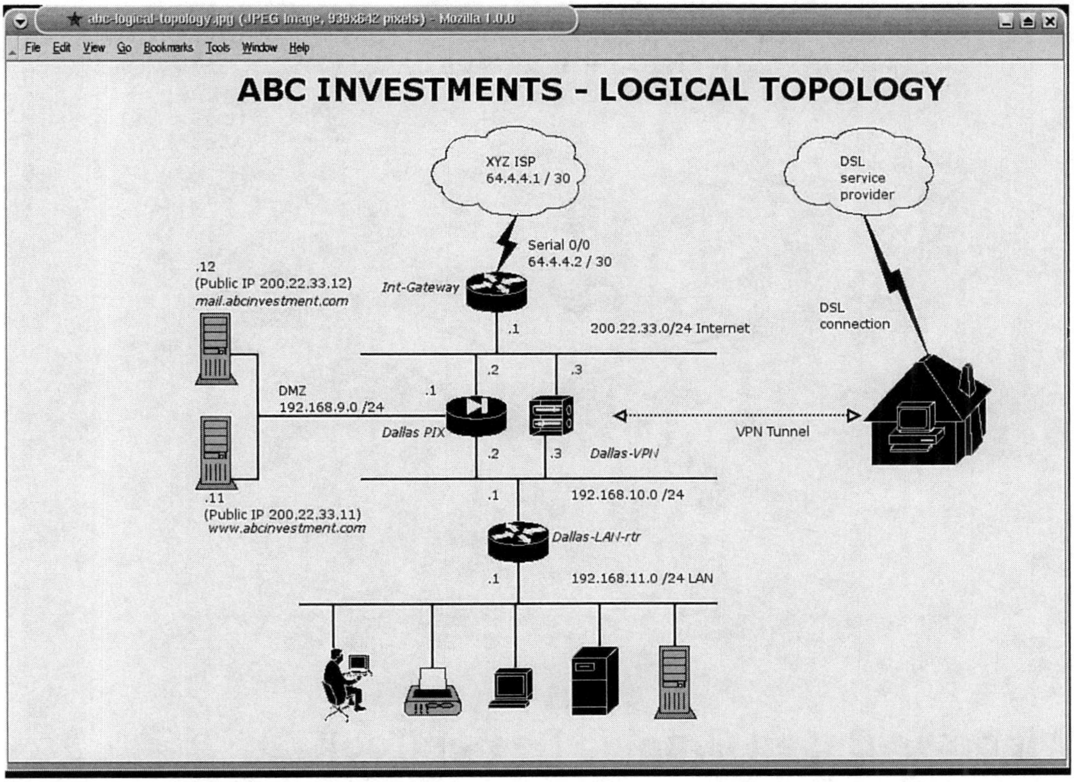

Figure 11-4 represents the physical topology of the network shown in Figure 11-3. Note the differences in physical versus logical topologies.

Figure 11-4 *Dia—Physical Topology*

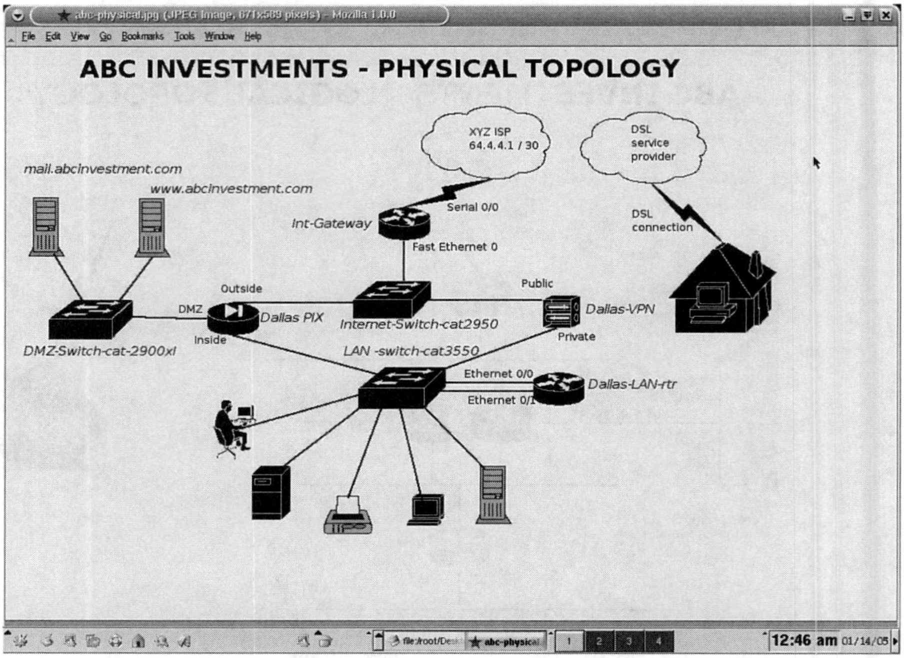

Windows-Based Graphic Design Tools

Windows-based Visio is the de facto tool for creating and editing network diagrams. However, Visio is a commercial product with strict license requirements. Windows users who are looking for noncommercial (or open source) alternatives for creating network diagrams have limited choices. Following are the two noncommercial Windows-based tools that provide adequate functionality for creating network diagrams:

- **Network Notepad**—A lightweight, easy-to-use tool for drawing Cisco network diagrams.
- **Dia**—The Windows version of Dia is similar to the Linux version. Refer to the section "Linux-Based Graphic Design Tools," earlier in this chapter, for more information.

Network Notepad (http://www.networknotepad.com) is an MS-Windows–based graphic design tool that offers the following features:

- Runs on Windows 9*x*, NT, 2000, and XP
- Is easy to install and use
- Provides drag-and-drop operation

- Allows the addition of new icons
- Exports images as .bmp files

The following sections prepare you for understanding and using Network Notepad. The discussion is organized into the following three topics:

- Deploying Network Notepad
- Creating diagrams
- Viewing sample diagrams

Deploying Network Notepad

The steps for deploying Network Notepad on an MS-Windows machine are as follows:

Step 1 **Download**—Download and save the installation file from the home page at http://www.networknotepad.com.

Step 2 **Install**—Start the installation by double-clicking the installation file. The default location is C:\program files\network notepad\.

Step 3 **Add stencils**—Stencils, referred to as *libraries* by Network Notepad, are stored in the default location C:\program files\network notepad\objects. The base package does not include extra stencils. However, you can download an additional icon library from the home page. Unzip and save the library files in the objects folder. The two available libraries are as follows:

- **Cisco Library**—The Cisco icons library is based on the network icons available in the "Network Topology Icons" section of the Cisco website (http://www.cisco.com/warp/public/503/2.html).
- **Switch Library**—The Switch library is handy for creating physical-topology (Layer 1 topology) diagrams for switched networks.

Step 4 **Run**—To run the program, choose **Start > Programs > Network Notepad**.

Creating Diagrams in Network Notepad

Before creating network diagrams, you should be familiar with the Network Notepad toolbar. Figure 11-5 illustrates some of the toolbar's functionality.

Figure 11-5 *Network Notepad Toolbar*

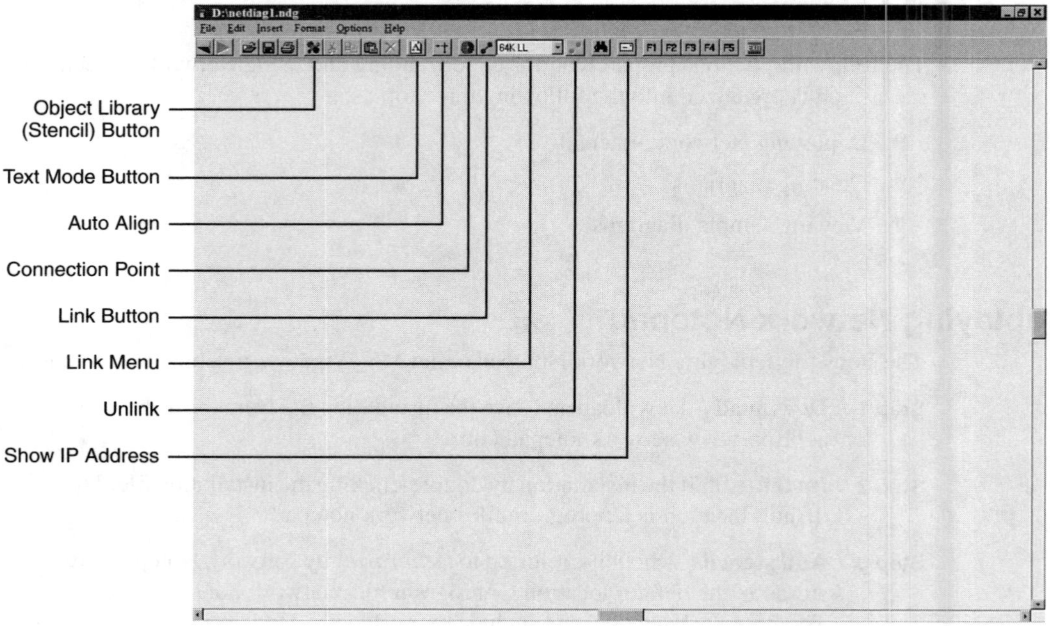

When you start Network Notepad, a blank diagram is created by default. You can create a new diagram by filling in the blank diagram. The most common tasks involved in creating a network diagram are as follows:

- Adding icons
- Connecting icons
- Removing a connection
- Adding a host name and IP information
- Adding text
- Inserting an Ethernet backbone
- Exporting the diagram as a .bmp image
- Adding new icons to the library

Adding Icons

To add icons to the diagram, follow these steps:

Step 1 Click the **Object Library** icon on the toolbar to launch the Object Library menu.

Step 2 Select the desired stencil from the drop-down menu on the toolbar.

Step 3 Drag and drop icons from the library to the diagram.

Connecting Icons

Follow these steps to connect two icons:

Step 1 Select the type of connection from the Link menu.

Step 2 Enter Connection mode by clicking the **Link** button. To link two icons, click the first icon and then click the second. You can also right-click an icon and choose **Link** from the menu that appears to enter Connection mode.

Step 3 To exit Connection mode, click the **Link** button.

TIP To create a bent connection (a connection with bends and elbows instead of one straight line), while in Link mode, click the first icon, click the background, and then click the second icon.

Removing a Connection

To remove a connection between two icons, click both icons and click the **Unlink** button.

Adding a Host Name and IP Address Information

To add a host name and IP address information, right-click an icon and select **Properties**. Enter the desired information in the Properties window and click the **OK** button to save your changes. You can also use the Properties window to edit the connection information, as shown in Figure 11-6. Note the Background feature that is found in the Properties window. When selected, this feature places the device icon behind the connection link. This is useful when indicating physical port connections.

Figure 11-6 *Object Properties Window*

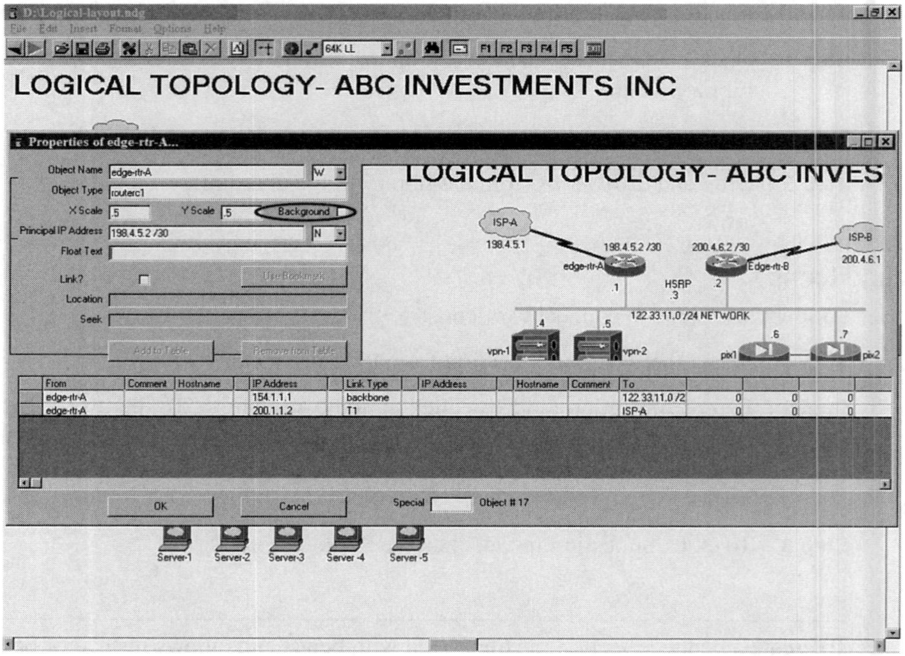

Adding Text

To add text, follow these steps:

Step 1 Click the **Text Mode** button and then click in the desired location on the diagram.

Step 2 Enter the desired text.

Step 3 To exit Insert Text mode, click the **Text Mode** button again.

Adding an Ethernet Backbone

Network Notepad also includes a built-in Ethernet backbone connection for creating LAN diagrams. Follow these steps to insert a horizontal Ethernet backbone:

Step 1 On the main menu, choose **Insert > Horizontal Backbone**.

Step 2 Click in the desired location on the diagram to paste a horizontal Ethernet backbone.

Step 3 Click the **Paste** button to exit Insert Backbone mode.

Exporting the Diagram as a .bmp Image

The default file format used by Network Notepad is a text file with the .ndg extension. To save the image in .bmp format, choose **File > Export To Bitmap Graphic File**. Windows provides tools such as Paint that can convert .bmp images into .gif and .jpg formats.

Adding New Icons to the Library

To add new icons to the library, copy the .jpg, .gif, or .bmp icons to the Clipboard from any application and paste them in the Stencil window. You can edit the name of the new icon by right-clicking the icon and selecting **Rename**.

Viewing Sample Diagrams Created by Network Notepad

Figures 11-7 and 11-8 show two sample diagrams that were created by Network Notepad. These diagrams represent the same network. However, the two versions highlight the correlation between the logical and physical topologies.

Figure 11-7 shows the logical topology for ABC Investments Inc.

Figure 11-7 *Logical Topology Diagram in Network Notepad*

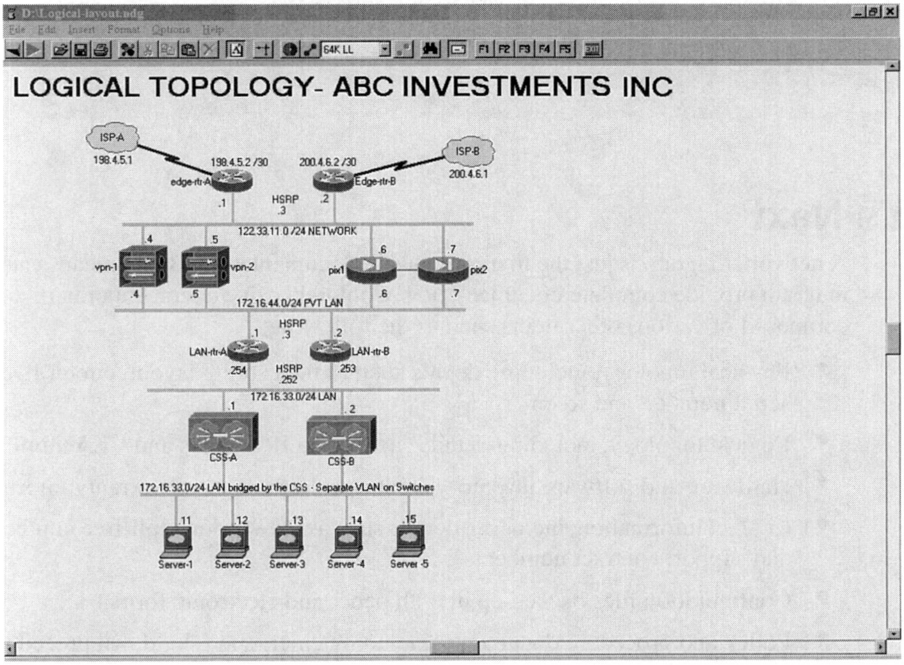

Figure 11-8 shows the physical topology of the network illustrated in Figure 11-7.

Figure 11-8 *Physical Topology Diagram in Network Notepad*

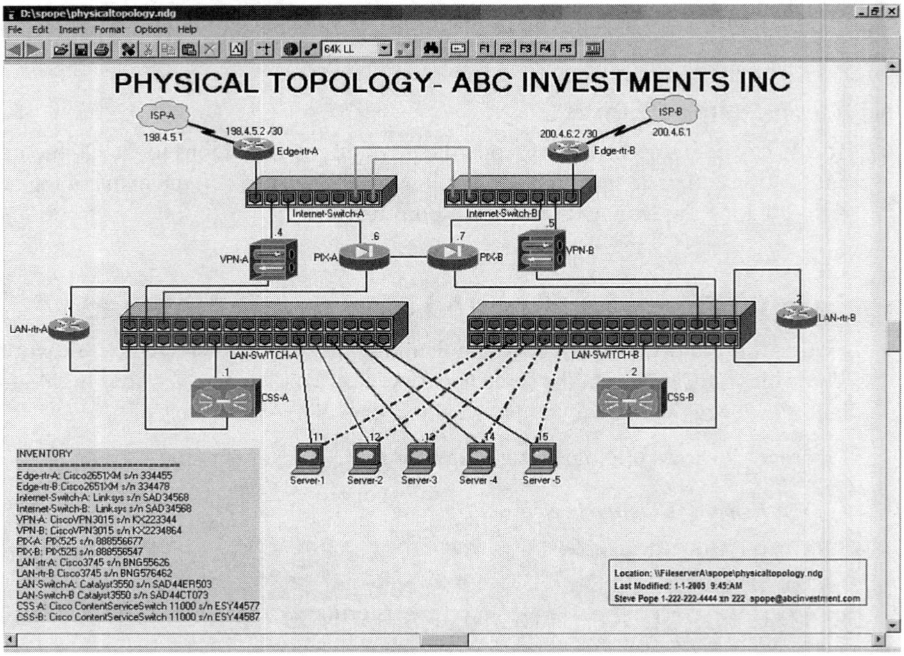

What's Next

A network diagram is just the first step toward documentation. By no means can a network diagram provide complete documentation. Comprehensive documentation of a network is composed of various other items such as the following:

- Physical topology, including details such as the cabling layout, circuit ID, chassis serial number, and so on
- Logical topology, including details such as the IP address and VLAN information
- Hardware and software inventory, including licensing and warranty information
- Contact information, including details such as the vendor's toll-free number, website, and support contract number
- Configuration files backed up in both paper and electronic format
- Policy and procedure documents, including emergency shutdown procedures and disaster-recovery plans

A common practice is to create an Internet Information Services (IIS) or Apache-based intranet web portal that contains all relevant information. Using open source programs such as OpenOffice (or any commercial program of your choice), you can save the network information as web pages. The network diagram can be inserted in the web pages as JPEG or GIF images. The content of the portal can be further enhanced by including links to the web output of various network-availability and performance-monitoring tools.

Finally, network administration (and Cisco networking in general) is a vast field composed of various tools, technologies, documentations, certifications, audits, business objectives, government regulations, and so on. This chapter—and this book—is just a humble attempt to help Cisco Netadmins with some of the technical aspects of their jobs. By efficiently supporting their networks, Netadmins can help their organization achieve its ultimate business goals and objectives. This book merely serves as a starting point and should not be treated as a complete guide for network administration. While the focus is to support Cisco networks, many tools and technologies apply to networks in general.

Although this book makes every attempt to cover suitable tools, as the network grows, the Netadmins will need additional tools. Or some of the tools might become obsolete because of a change in technology. Consequently, Netadmins need to keep abreast of the latest trends and technologies. However, even the best of tools are no replacement for the skills and experience of a seasoned Netadmin. Applications and appliances worth millions of dollars can end up on the shelf if the staff is not properly trained and skilled. As an example, the author recently encountered a customer whose data center was stacked with various commercial and open source products, including Multi-Router Traffic Grapher (MRTG), HP OpenView, CiscoWorks, and WhatsUp Gold. Despite an impressive repertoire of such tools, the IT staff was not skilled in administering the network. Consequently, the IT department ended up buying more products while the network continued to experience frequent outages. Remember, tools and machines do not make companies; people make companies.

Summary

This chapter introduced the basic concepts and tools for creating network diagrams. The discussion enables the Netadmin to do the following tasks:

- Create network diagrams using Linux-based tools
- Create network diagrams using Windows-based tools

Table 11-1 provides a summary of the tools discussed in this chapter.

Table 11-1 *Network Documentation Tools*

Tool	Function	Supported OS	URL/Notes
Dia	Network diagram	Linux and MS-Windows	http://www.gnome.org/projects/dia/
Kivio	Network diagram	Linux	http://www.koffice.org/kivio/
Network Notepad	Network diagram	MS-Windows	http://www.networknotepad.com

INDEX

Symbols

A

B

C

D

E

F

G

H

I

J-K

L

M

N

O

P

Q-R

S

T

U

V

W

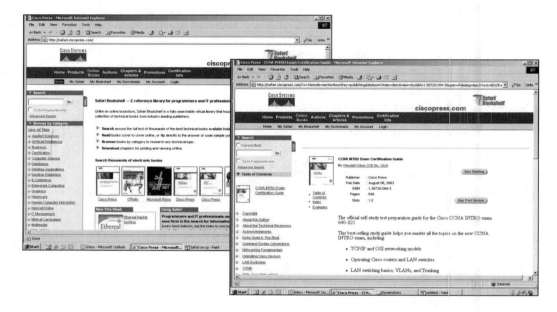